HEARTS
GROWN
BRUTAL

HEARTS
GROWN
BRUTAL

Sagas of Sarajevo

ROGER COHEN

RANDOM HOUSE
New York

Library of Congress Cataloging-in-Publication Data is available

ISBN 0-679-45243-5

Random House website address: www.randomhouse.com
Printed in the United States of America on acid-free paper
2   4   6   8   9   7   5   3
First Edition

Maps by Natasha Perkel
Book design by Deborah Kerner

For Frida,
who understood,
and for the people of Sarajevo,
who withstood

We had fed the heart on fantasies,
The heart's grown brutal from the fare.

W. B. YEATS,
"MEDITATIONS IN TIME OF CIVIL WAR"

"You know that thing in the Bible.
'The imagination of man's heart is evil from
his youth.' I used to wonder why pick on that?
Why his imagination? *But it's absolutely right."*

PAT BARKER,
REGENERATION

ACKNOWLEDGMENTS

Bosnia marked us all. It was not just the war; it was the hypocrisy and moral failure surrounding it. For Western governments, it was simply not convenient to see the horror that was visible to us.

Among the colleagues and friends whose work cut through the official veils and exposed the truths of the Bosnian war were John Burns, Chuck Sudetic, John Kifner, Mike O'Connor, Jane Perlez, and Ray Bonner of *The New York Times;* John Pomfret of *The Washington Post;* Ed Vulliamy and Ian Traynor of *The Guardian;* Christiane Amanpour of CNN; Laura Silber of *The Financial Times;* Tracy Wilkinson of the *Los Angeles Times;* Roy Gutman of *Newsday;* David Gelber, then of ABC News; Tom Gjelten of National Public Radio; Mark Heinrich and Kurt Schork of Reuters; Tom Squitieri of *USA Today;* Jean Hatzfeld of *Libération;* Robert Fox of the *Daily Telegraph;* Emma Daly of *The Independent;* Arnaut Van Lynden of Sky Television; Rémy Ourdan of *Le Monde;* David Rieff and Anna Husarska of *The New Republic;* David Rohde then of *The Christian Science Monitor;* the ubiquitous Elizabeth Rubin and Samantha Power; Charlotte Eager of *The Observer;* and Bob Simpson and Alan Little of the BBC. I learned much from the work of this exceptional corps of journalists.

I was helped, beyond measure, by Duska Anastasijević in Belgrade, Tamara Levak in Zagreb; and Sanja Mrehić and Anja Tomić in Sarajevo. In them all Yugoslavia lived and in them all the country died painfully. They were brave, braver than was reasonable, and they led me toward the mysteries of their land. To the indomitable Miriana Komarecki in Belgrade, special thanks. Her daughter, Marina Komarecki, in New York made countless excellent suggestions, for which I thank her. In Sarajevo, Amra Džaferović showed me the Bosnian soul. The journey began badly with Dragan Čičić, but he responded with a hero's humor and proceeded to educate me. I am deeply in his debt. In Zagreb, Ejup Maloku, faithful friend, helped me past countless difficulties. I am also grateful to Michael Williams, long UNPROFOR's melodious voice of despair in Zagreb, and Alexander Ivanko, a United Nations spokesman in Sarajevo, who taught me the utter folly of trying to outdrink a Russian. David Harland of the United Nations in Sarajevo cast light on several shadowy areas; the chronology owes much to him. Other UN officials helped me enormously. They know who they are and I thank them. In Zagreb and later Washington, Ron Neitzke of the State Department incarnated America's honor, an honor repeatedly betrayed in Bosnia, and always pointed me in the right direction.

I was consistently supported by the editors of *The New York Times*. I am grateful to Joe Lelyveld for believing that this project was worth a leave, Bill Keller for sharing that conviction and backing me at the crunch, and Bernie Gwertzman for sending me on my way. Kyle Crichton at the Sunday *Magazine* played a central role in shaping the story that was the germ of this book; Jack Rosenthal published it with panache. Marie Courtney was wonderful at all times. Marion Underhill in London found the books that could not be found. At the Foreign Desk, I salute one and all: greater friend hath no correspondent.

In Paris, my home through the writing of this book, the staff of *The Times* bureau were immensely helpful. I thank Mathew Lefevre-Marton, Patrick Sautin, Joshua Phillips, Natasha Leland, Sharzad Elghanayan, Alexandra Whitney, Toby Grey, Patrick Merle, Stephanie Cohn, and Bill Suon. Special thanks to Sylvie Rais. Daphne Anglès, you are an angel. Craig Whitney, the bureau chief, backed me with deft understanding and extricated me from difficulties with German. Alan Riding was the reader, editor, and friend of any author's dreams.

At Random House, Kate Medina's intelligence, patience, and sure guidance brought this book to life. She saw its rightful shape when it still lay hidden. Ruth Fecych honed the form. Meaghan Rady kept things moving with a singular grace. My agent, Amanda Urban, was an inspiration, cool in counsel and energetic in execution.

This book took longer to write, and was more painful, than I had imagined. Friends and family saw me through. I am grateful to Anna Cataldi, Richard Bernstein, Goran Tocilovac, Anne Salazar, Ed Vulliamy, Irving and Sarah Petlin, Amalia and Jose Baranek, Humberto Baranek and Leslie Rose, Bruno and Daniela Baranek, Eliezer Baranek and Robin Walden for support and hospitality. Arno J. Mayer of Princeton University made several helpful suggestions. Luc Delahaye shared the longest road and helped me see more clearly. My uncle, Bert, was a loving and most constructive critic. My sister, Jenny, coaxed me along with her winning intuition; my mother, June, and my father, Sydney, backed me with the love they have always shown. My children Jessica, Daniel, Blaise, and Adèle were the light that pointed the way; their love sustained me and was an inspiration, especially in the many moments of darkness.

To my wife, Frida, go my most heartfelt thanks. For two years we lived with a war between us, but she never wavered in her support or in her passionate belief in the pursuit of the creative life. Without her love, without her instincts, this book would not have been written.

PREFACE

I WENT TO BOSNIA IN 1992 TO COVER EUROPE'S WORST WAR since Hitler's war. Like many others, I came away wounded at the war's end in 1995. The wounds, in my own case, were not physical, but they were deep enough to prompt the writing of this book. I had watched as a Yugoslav state that was a bridge—between East and West, Christianity and Islam, the Western world and the Byzantine—was bludgeoned to death beneath the nationalist banners that unfurled as communism died. The destruction went on for four years, between 1991 and 1995, before the eyes of the modern world.

What I had seen would not leave me: the ravages of shrapnel on the body of a youth, the grimace of roofless houses, the rancid smell of suffering. But I wanted to reach beyond the war itself, for I felt that the enduring pain of Bosnia lay deeper than the blood that was shed. In those faces that kept flashing across my mind, faces bruised and unseeing, there was a wound that seemed to reach down into the gut of our age.

Yugoslavia, the state of the South Slavs, grew out of the collapse of the Habsburg and Ottoman empires during World War I. It disintegrated under attack from the Nazis, coalesced again around the dream of communism, held together under the firm hand of Tito's one-party communist rule, only to die in the resurgence of tribal fervor that accompanied the disintegration of the Soviet Union. The major destructive themes of what Isaiah Berlin called "our most terrible century" were caught in the state of Yugoslavia's seventy-three-year trajectory: the end of empire, the ravages of fascist terror based on racist ideology, the rise and fall of communism, and finally the nationalist fever of post-communist societies. Was this then the wound that I felt? Was the anguish of Yugoslavia's destruction also that of our dying century?

I believe this to be so. For what struck me was the way this twentieth-century history lived in, and divided, the individuals I met. My under-standing of the wars came through families. Each family had its own Balkan world, its own visceral sense of the past, and so the story of these scattered former Yugoslav families—now living in Europe and North America—grew to form the core of this book. Their story was the story I wanted to tell, for their lives went to the root of the matter. It seemed to me right, in the end, to consider Yugoslavia's destruction through families broken asunder, for this was a war of intimate betrayals.

I DISCOVERED in the Balkans that I had known little of the power of in-herited fear, or of how history can be transfigured into myth and legend, or of the passionate identification of stateless nations with these fables. I knew little of history as terror, tormentor, and torch. Perhaps the deepest wound of Bosnia was the discovery of the prison that bad or suppressed history can be. To go to Bosnia was to become familiar with ghosts. And not merely the ghosts of fascism. The whole lurid cast of the twentieth-century tragedy was repeatedly presented, not as historical figures, but as live actors with enduring power to inflict suffering.

As communism fell, Balkan politicians raised the specters of past vio-lence in order to inspire the fear or frenzy they needed to propel them to power, or to consolidate their hold on it. Their medium was nationalism, a nationalism that was about vengeance for past injustice—real or imag-ined, it mattered not. The poison released first by the Serbs in Belgrade, then by the Croats in Zagreb, eventually found its way into the hearts of families throughout Yugoslavia. Unions that were natural suddenly be-came questionable. Identities that had been clear were suddenly uncertain. Serbs, Croats, Muslims, and others who had lived together throughout Yu-goslavia, and most intensely in its Bosnian center, found themselves on op-posing sides of previously unimagined divisions. The more I covered the war the more I felt old scores were being settled. Not ancient Balkan tribal blood feuds, as Western politicians idly suggested; no, the issue was prin-cipally Yugoslavia itself and its failure during its strangely human seventy-three-year life span.

I concluded that I could not write about the Bosnian war without also writing the story of Yugoslavia. To try to understand the Serbs without first understanding their conception of the Yugoslav state was impossible. And so this book begins, in Book One, with the story of a boy's search for his father, a man lost and believed dead during World War II. Sead's story il-lustrates the tensions inherent in Yugoslavia's creation in 1918, the vio-lence of its midlife breakup in 1941, and the treacherous secrets of Tito's postwar communist state.

Book Two takes up the 1991–1995 wars of Yugoslavia's destruction, telling the story of the conflict largely through the eyes of three families: a Muslim-Serb family in Sarajevo and Belgrade; a Muslim family in eastern Bosnia; and a Serb-Croat family in Tuzla and Sarajevo. I have divided Book Two into three parts, reflecting major themes in the Bosnian war: the division of mixed communities into separate ethnic groups; the Serb concentration camps through which the Muslim population of Bosnia was purged; the desperately flawed international attempt to help.

Book Three is the story of the last year of the war and the completion of Bosnia's destruction, in Sarajevo, at Srebrenica, and elsewhere. America's peace came too late and only after the mass forced movement of Muslim and Serb populations in 1995. The families presented in Book Two are now scattered and broken. Their fate mirrors the fate of their country. The communities, like the families, cannot be stitched back together again. The Dayton Agreement of November 1995 had the merit of stopping the killing, but by then the united and multi-ethnic Bosnian state that still exists on paper was largely a fiction. So, too, was the state of "Yugoslavia" that emerged from the war—a truncated federation of Serbia and Montenegro that makes a mockery of the ideals that, in 1918, inspired the creation of a much larger country that would take the same name.

The original Yugoslavia straddled mental as well as physical borders. By uniting Catholic Slovenes and Croats, Muslims, and Orthodox Christian Serbs in a single state, it sought to reconcile warring archetypes of European history—"Christians" and "infidels," the "civilized" and the "barbarians," the "Latins" and the "Byzantines." Therein lay its singular beauty, the beauty of Vukovar, of Mostar, of Sarajevo. The Yugoslav idea was uplifting, but it was always vulnerable to the violence inherent in the Wilsonian recipe of creating nation-states on Europe's mottled soil after World War I. A violence that, in the 1990s, duly reduced much of Vukovar, Mostar, and Sarajevo to rubble.

AMERICA ABJURED its unique ability to lead in Bosnia. For years, the Bush and then the Clinton administrations displayed moral cowardice, tolerating a European genocide and attempting to cloak their failure in ghastly circumlocutions about supposedly intractable Balkan hatreds. The United States deferred to a Europe too fragmented to be effective, preached from afar, or took refuge in the necessity of a "multilateral approach"—a policy leading to lowest-common-denominator politics and confusion. As a result the West did not deploy an army in its European backyard, at least not for several years; instead, it dispatched that strange post–cold war beast, the humanitarian servants of the "international community." This unwieldy creature collided, naturally, with the families that are at the center of this book; and, while trying to do good, the international community, most visibly represented by the United Nations, often abetted great tragedy. The spirit of humanitarianism has an inherent preference for neutrality, for succoring the victim instead of identifying the butcher. It is a poor substitute for a foreign policy. So it was in Bosnia, where the United Nations deployed enormous resources only to find that attempts to palliate wars may prolong them.

When American forces did arrive, at the end of 1995, the war was already over. They are still there, in 1998, pursuing a mission already twice-prolonged but essentially hopeless in that it only began after the irrevocable damage had been done. Before the NATO soldiers came, through forty-two months of war, the United Nations tried to reason with the Serbs whose nationalist revolution had set in motion Yugoslavia's disintegration and who had begun the conflict—and defined it—in Bosnia with a genocidal rampage in 1992 against the Muslims. Reason! How weak and ridiculous it often seemed to use reason against the blunt Serb conviction that borders are drawn in blood.

Reason had played little role in Slobodan Milošević's rise to power in Serbia. Myth was the driving force behind Milošević—myths that had the power to see victory in defeat and to see in the largely secular Muslim population of Bosnia the Serbs' longtime enemy, the Ottoman Turks. Similarly, myths increasingly drove the Croats led by Franjo Tudjman—myths that they were a Catholic bastion facing down the Orthodox Serb or infidel Muslim hordes, myths that placed Croatia back in time and in Western Europe rather than in the dark lands of the Balkans.

Between Serbia to the east and Croatia to the west lay the Muslims of Bosnia, a place the size of Pennsylvania. Slavs like the Serbs and Croats, these Bosnian Muslims were deeply troubling to the psyche of Serb and Croat alike. Indeed, I often heard the very existence of the Muslims challenged in Zagreb or Belgrade with the argument that they were "really Croats" or "really Serbs"—that is, people somehow misled about their true identity. One Bosnian Muslim friend in Sarajevo became so exasperated by repeated questions about her origins that she adopted a radical course. When asked from whom she was descended, she would reply, "The monkey."

The Bosnian Muslims, who converted to Islam during centuries of Ottoman rule, made no claim to be defending civilization. On the whole, they viewed life with the detachment of people who have seen many armies and rulers come and go. Unlike their neighbors to the east and west, they were not, on the whole, obsessed by myth. The words closest to their soul, I found, included *"sevdah,"* a nostalgic, brooding longing associated with lost love, and *"ćeif,"* a personal pleasure taken with no regard to what anybody else thinks. These words capture the reflective pessimism and hedonistic iconoclasm of a people familiar with the passing glories of a shifting world.

But as the gale forces of violence blew through the Balkans, tolerance became rarer and rarer. A Muslim identity increasingly replaced the many-faceted Bosnian identity. Fashioned amid persecution, this nascent Muslim nationalism was often harsh; it naturally attached more importance to survival than to the merits of a multi-ethnic society.

BY THE TIME I left Bosnia in December 1995, the deed was done. Tolerance had been largely defeated, the mixed societies of Bosnia and Yugoslavia had been undone. Two destructive forces had coalesced and proved overwhelming. The first gathered its strength from the old Serb and Croatian discourse about civilization and barbarity, the Christian world and the infidel hordes. The second was formed by Tito's communist system, its distortion of the past, its cult of fear fed by repeated warning of the external enemies to the east and west, its cultivation of submissive minds. This was the realm of totalitarian mind games. Laid layer upon layer, against a background of steep economic decline, these quasi-religious and political myths made ready killers: confused and vengeful people, pliant to propaganda, poor, little educated in personal responsibility, convinced, even as they killed and mutilated, of their new place in the "Western culture" delivered to them every day, via satellite dishes, on the televisions that blare unendingly through the smoke-filled, drably furnished rooms of the Balkans.

The destruction was overwhelming: pits of bodies, crippled youths, fires amid the ruins. At Skopje airport, in the former Yugoslav republic of Macedonia, I peered through the closed doors of a warehouse to see the eerie remnants of a plane crash that had occurred more than a year earlier. There were suitcases, books, children's games, scraps of clothing, all piled helter-skelter. The abandoned wreckage was an insult to memory, but it struck me that Balkan history was like that: the tide that swept people aside was often so strong that things just lay where they fell, and people did not have the courage, the conviction, or the coherence to pick them up and place them in some kind of order. Fatalism bore down with such force that human striving seemed futile.

Still, I tried to remember. Through the Yugoslav wars I came to believe that understanding was more inextricably linked to memory here than in any place I had known. Yet memory often seemed short. As Wisława Szymborska has noted, clearing up after wars takes a long time, and

Those who knew
What this was all about

Must make way for those
Who know little.
And less than that.
And at last nothing less than nothing.

Less than nothing: it was unthinkable that we should know simply nothing, and so I have tried to present what one journalist witnessed when Yugoslavia died. If anger often drove me, understanding was my aim, for therein, it seemed, lay some slim hope of a better future. All of us who were there, and even many who were not, were devastated by the end of the Yugoslav state—the 200,000 dead, the 2.7 million refugees, the concentration camps, the destruction. Even now we tremble at the thought of it all, and even now we ask why.

I believe that part of the answer may lie in these stories of families divided by war over the course of the life of Yugoslavia, a lifetime that corresponded broadly with what has been called "the short twentieth century"—between World War I and the end of the cold war. Their pain is the pain of a century; the wounds were there; they could be exploited by politicians bent on fomenting hatred. The bereavement of these people is not just for friends or relatives killed in the wars of Yugoslavia's destruction; it is for a fluid time before the desiccation of division; it is for the lost beauty of Yugoslavia and Bosnia, places of mingling and movement.

There was a vitality to Yugoslavia, a majesty, caught for me in the countless rivers that connect the South Slavs. But each river was a mirror, and in the mirror's reflection was blood. Over the years I grew to hate the blood and yearned passionately to see the rivers run free in their beauty. Their message would then be clear, a message of connectedness, for the ties of language, culture, and history linking the South Slavs are overwhelming. These bonds are now broken, severed by war. The new nation-states of the Balkans have gone their separate ways. Yugoslavia is dead and will not be reborn. But if what amounts today to a tenuous peace in the region is to endure, then the myths that separate and kill must at last cede their place to an embracing reality. Otherwise the cycle of war, the Balkan gyre, may take another unsuspecting generation.

For the peace to be lasting this time, and the American military deployment in Bosnia to serve a purpose, people clearly need to learn to look forward. But first, it seemed to me, they had to look back and understand at last the nature of their painful Balkan memories. It is these memories that I have tried to chronicle, for the light they may shed on the destruction of a European state, and for the light they may cast on the road forward.

CONTENTS

LIST OF MAPS

NOTE ON PRONUNCIATION

The principal language of Yugoslavia was called Serbo-Croatian until the country began its disintegration in 1991. The new nation-states that have grown out of it have insisted on distinguishing their languages, sometimes by imposing new or archaic words. There are now Croatian, Serbian, and Bosnian languages. However, they are broadly the same and share a pronunciation that is regular and self-evident, with the following exceptions, given with an example in italics.

C is pronounced "ts" as in *cats. Cetinje.*
Č is pronounced "ch" as in *church. Foča.*
Ć is pronounced "tj" as in *future. Ćelo.*
Dj is pronounced like the soft "g" in *ginger. Djuradj.*
Dž is slightly harder, pronounced like the "j" in *adjunct* or *jolt. Hodžić.*
J is pronounced "y" as in *yes. Jelačić.*
Lj is pronounced like the "ll" of *medallion. Bijeljina.*
Nj is pronounced like the "ny" in *canyon. Nemanjić.*
Š is pronounced "sh" as in *ship. Milošević.*
Ž is pronounced with a "zh" sound as in *casual. Goražde.*

CAST OF CHARACTERS
IN OR LINKED TO
THE FOUR PRINCIPAL FAMILIES

MEHMEDOVIĆ-ERHAN FAMILY

Alija Mehmedović (later, in Turkish exile, **Ali Erhan**): born in Prijedor, Bosnia-Herzegovina, 1911.
Ahmed Mehmedović: Alija's father.
Gaby Kovač: Alija's first wife, born in Zagreb, Croatia, 1919.
Sead Mehmedović: son of Alija and Gaby; born in Belgrade, 1938.
Saima Kadić: Alija's second wife; born in Sarajevo.
Džemal Erhan: son of Alija and Saima, Sead's half brother; born in Sarajevo, 1942.
Osima Musanović: Saima Kadić's sister.
Ali Bilir: Alija's closest friend in Bursa.
Egon Rozenblat: Gaby Kovač's second husband.
Viktor and Kitty Starčić: Sead's guardians for two years.

ZEČEVIĆ-KARIŠIK FAMILY

Asim Zečević: born in Sarajevo, 1936.
Bisera Zečević: his late wife; born in Sarajevo, 1941; killed 1993.
Safet Zečević: Asim's father; died 1983.
Haris Zečević: the oldest son of Asim and Bisera; born in Sarajevo, 1969; refugee in Detroit.
Muris Zečević: the second son of Asim and Bisera; born in Sarajevo, 1971; killed 1992.
Vildana Zečević: Haris's wife; refugee in Detroit.
Muris Zečević: son of Haris and Vildana; born in Detroit, 1995.
Fida Karišik: Asim's sister; born and lives in Sarajevo.

Slobodan Karišik: Fida's husband; born in Rogatica, Bosnia-Herzegovina, 1941; fled Sarajevo during the war; lives in Belgrade.

Jasna Karišik: their older daughter; born in Sarajevo, 1976; lives in Belgrade.

Vesna Karišik: their second daughter; born in Sarajevo, 1978; lives in Belgrade.

ŠESTOVIĆ FAMILY

Ruzdija Šestović: born Sandzak, 1942; disappeared in Vlasenica, Bosnia-Herzegovina, 1992.

Muska Šestović: his wife; born in Milići; refugee in Sweden.

Ermin Šestović: their son; born in Milići; refugee in Sweden.

Nada Šestović: their daughter; refugee in Sweden.

Vahda Ibišević: their niece; disappeared near Vlasenica, 1992.

Rajko Dukić: once a close friend of Ruzdija Šestović; born in Milići, Bosnia-Herzegovina; founding member of Karadžić's SDS party; successful businessman in Belgrade and Milići.

Spomenka Čojnić: Rajko Dukić's sister, married to Mladen Čojnić; former neighbor of the Šestović family in Vlasenica; works in the Dukić company, Boksit Trade, in Belgrade.

ADAMOVIĆ-JELIĆ-ELAZAR FAMILY

Vojna Adamović: born in Tuzla, Bosnia-Herzegovina.

Miloš Jelić: her husband; born in Sarajevo.

Kosa Hegeduš: born in Tuzla; Vojna's aunt.

Vojna Jović: Vojna Adamović's grandmother, after whom she is named; Vojna Jović was executed by Tito's Partisans in 1943.

Mišo Adamović: Vojna's father; refugee in Bijeljina.

Milena Adamović: Mišo's wife.

Aleksandra Adamović: Vojna's sister; refugee with her young son, Filip, in Windsor, Canada.

Darko Krančević: Aleksandra's estranged husband; left Serbia for Croatia during the war, never saw Filip again.

Mladen Elazar: Vojna's cousin, born in Sarajevo; Mladen's grandparents, Jewish merchants, were killed in the Jasenovac concentration camp during World War II; refugee in Windsor, Canada.

Mira Elazar: Mladen's wife; born in Sarajevo.

CHRONOLOGY

395: Death of Roman emperor Theodosius. Division of Roman Empire into East and West at the Drina River. The Eastern empire, under the Byzantine church, is ruled from Constantinople; the Western empire, under the Roman church, from Rome.

Sixth century: Arrival of the Slavs in the Balkans after southward migration over the Danube. They encounter a mix of people including Illyrians, Greeks, Vlachs, and Romans. The Slavs include Croats and Serbs, distinct but closely related tribes. Over the centuries, the Serbs, settled east of the Drina, become Orthodox; the Croats, settled west of the Drina, Catholic.

610–1204: Byzantine Empire.

916–28: Apogee of medieval Croatia under Prince and later King Tomislav. Land embraces present-day Croatia and Bosnia.

1102: The signature of the Pacta Conventa with Hungary puts an end to the independent Croatian kingdom. For more than eight centuries, Croatia will be ruled as part of the kingdom of Hungary; under the Habsburgs from 1527. Croatia will not know independence, even then under Nazi tutelage, until 1941.

1159–95: Stefan Nemanja founds Nemanjić dynasty and lays the basis of the medieval Serbian empire. Geographical base is Raška, Kosovo, and Herzegovina. Strong identification of the dynasty and the Serbian Orthodox church, which becomes the chief repository of Serbian national sentiment.

1204: Fourth Crusade takes Constantinople.

1258: Birth of Osman, founder of Ottoman dynasty.

1180–1462: Bosnian *bans,* or leaders, and kings control varying amounts of present-day Bosnia, with degrees of autonomy from Hungary. Among most powerful are *Ban* Kulin (1180–1204) and *Ban* Stjepan Kotromanić

(1322–53), who expands his territory southward to include Herzegovina. Bosnia is distinguished by a heretical church blending the Dualist beliefs of the Bogomils with traditional Christian practices.

1331–55: Apogee of medieval Serbia under King Dušan, whose empire stretches from the Danube to the Peloponnese. Territory includes parts of eastern Bosnia, Dubrovnik, and Thessalonika.

1353–91: Apogee of medieval Bosnia under King Tvrtko. His territory reaches southward to the Dalmatian coast and embraces parts of present-day Croatia and Serbia.

1371: The Ottoman Turks, pushing westward into Europe, inflict a major defeat on the Serbs at the Marica River.

1389: The Serbs, led by Prince Lazar, are defeated by the Ottoman Turks at the Battle of Kosovo and reduced to vassal status; all Serb lands are finally overrun by the Ottomans in 1459. Serbia loses its independence until the nineteenth century. Kosovo becomes the symbol of the Serbian quest for nationhood.

OTTOMANS AND HABSBURGS

1409: Dalmatia (now Croatia's Adriatic coastline) is sold by Hungary to Venice.

1453: The Ottoman Turks conquer Constantinople.

1462: The Turks overrun most of Bosnia and annex it. Bosnia will not know an independent existence again until 1992.

1521: Turks capture Belgrade for the first time.

1526: The Turks defeat the Hungarians at the Battle of Mohacs and hold most of Hungary until 1686.

1527: The Bosnian fortress town of Jajce, held by the Hungarians since the fall of Bosnia, is captured by the Ottomans.

1529: First siege of Vienna by the Turks.

1530: The Military Frontier, or Vojna Krajina, begins to take form on the borderlands between the Ottoman and Habsburg empires, peopled partly by Serbs in flight from the Turks. Military structure of the area is codified by Habsburg emperor Ferdinand II in 1630. The Krajina eventually becomes the cradle of the Serb population of Croatia.

1557: In a gesture from the Ottomans, the Serbian church's patriarchate is reestablished in Peć (in Kosovo). In 1565, the Turkish grand vizier is Mehmed Sokollu, born Sokolović, a Bosnian Serb taken in his infancy as a tribute by the Turks and trained in Constantinople.

1583–1640: Seat of Bosnian vizier in Banja Luka.

1640–98: Seat of Bosnian vizier in Sarajevo.

1698–1850: Seat of Bosnian vizier in Travnik.

1683: Second siege of Vienna by the Turks.

1683–99: The Ottomans are defeated by the Holy League and lose Hungary and the eastern part of present-day Croatia, known as Slavonia.

1690: Under pressure from the Turks, who have rallied after defeat to the Austrians, a Serb migration takes place from Peć to the Vojvodina (now the northernmost part of Serbia), where a new patriarchate is established in Sremski Karlovci. The center of gravity of the Serbs shifts north-westward.

1699: Treaty of Sremski Karlovci (Treaty of Carlowitz). The Turks give up claims to Hungary and Croatia.

1718: Treaty of Požarevac. After further defeats by the Austrians, the Turks give up to the Habsburgs a strip of territory in northern Bosnia on the south bank of the Sava River (the Banat), and parts of northern Serbia, including Belgrade.

1739: The Ottomans force the Austrians to restore the border agreed at Sremski Karlovci. The border between the two empires remains unchanged until 1878. The V-shaped thrust of Bosnia into Croatia corresponds to the limits thus defined of the Turkish push into Europe.

1797: The Treaty of Campo Formio transfers Dalmatia from Venetian to Austrian rule.

THE STIRRING OF BALKAN NATIONS

1804: First Serbian uprising against the Turks, led by a pig farmer, Djordje Petrović (known as Karadjordje). Crushed by the Turks in 1813. Miloš Obrenović takes up the fight in 1815, has Karadjordje murdered, and in 1830 wins Turkish recognition of Serbian autonomy in the northern parts of present-day Serbia. Obrenović and Karadjordjević dynasties dispute the Serbian crown.

1805: Napoleon takes Dalmatia from the Austrians; calls the area the "Illyrian Provinces," reviving an old Roman name.

1815: Dalmatia is returned to Austro-Hungarian rule at the Congress of Vienna.

1821–32: Greek war of independence from Turks.

1842: The word *Illyrian* banned by the Austro-Hungarian government; it has become synonymous with the South Slav push for autonomy from

Vienna. The word *Yugoslav* (*"jug"* means *south* in Slavic languages) is adopted by some South Slav politicians pushing for independence.

1848: Hungarian revolution against Habsburg rule.

1849: Josip Jelačić, the Croatian *ban,* helps put down the Hungarian rebellion.

1867: The last Turkish garrisons leave Serbia.

1875–78: Revolts against the Turks in Bosnia and Bulgaria. In Bosnia, peasants, mainly Serbs, rise against the Muslim landed class. Serbia and Montenegro intervene on their behalf; the Ottomans go to war with Serbia and Montenegro; Russia intervenes on the Serbian side; the Ottomans are defeated by Russia.

1878: Congress of Berlin. Serbia and Montenegro gain new territory and are recognized as independent states. Bosnia is taken from the Ottomans and given to Austria-Hungary to administer. Exodus of many Muslims from Bosnia to Turkey and other Ottoman territories.

1881: The Vojna Krajina, or Military Frontier, is suppressed. With Austria-Hungary's occupation of Bosnia, it no longer serves a purpose.

1908: Independence of Bulgaria. Annexation of Bosnia by the Habsburgs.

1912: First Balkan War, against the Ottomans.

1913: Second Balkan War, against Bulgaria. Through these two wars, Serbia extends its territory southward, embracing present-day Macedonia. Mass movements of population—later called "ethnic cleansing"—gather pace as Turkey withdraws from Europe, leaving large Muslim minorities.

1914: Gavrilo Princip, a member of a Serb nationalist group fighting to remove Bosnia from the Austro-Hungarian empire, shoots and kills the Habsburg archduke Franz Ferdinand in Sarajevo. World War I begins.

1915: Serbia occupied by the Austro-Hungarian army. The Serbian retreat to Albania begins. Its army is decimated.

1916–18: Remains of the Serbian army fight successfully on the Allied side.

THE FIRST YUGOSLAVIA

1918: The Kingdom of Serbs, Croats, and Slovenes is formed on territory that had long been Austro-Hungarian or Ottoman and never previously joined under a single government. The name is changed to Yugoslavia in 1929. The two largest national groups in 1918 are Serbs (38.8 percent of the population) and Croats (23.77 percent). Bosnian Muslims account for 6.05 percent.

1919: The Treaty of Versailles ratifies formation of the new South Slav state.

1921: The first constitution is adopted on the anniversary of the Battle of

Kosovo, a triumph for Serbian centralism. Tensions with Croats exacerbated.

1928: Stjepan Radić, the leading Croat politician and a persistent critic of Serbian domination of the new state, is assassinated in parliament in Belgrade.

1929: Ante Pavelić, a young deputy from Zagreb, establishes the Ustasha movement with the aim of "using all means possible—including armed uprising"—to establish an independent Croatian state.

1929: Suspension of the constitution and institution of a royal dictatorship under King Aleksandar of Serbia. Political parties are abolished. The state is reorganized into nine provincial units, called *banovinas,* that cut across old borders (of Croatia, Slovenia, Bosnia, etc.) and seek to instill allegiance to central authority in Belgrade.

1934: Assassination of King Aleksandar in Marseilles by an agent in the pay of the Ustasha. Power passes to his cousin, Prince Pavle, declared regent for the duration of King Petar's childhood.

1935: Concordat signed between Yugoslavia and the Vatican. After objections from the Orthodox Serbs, the concordat is rescinded in 1937.

1939: In a last-ditch attempt to shore up relations between Serbs and Croats, the *sporazum* (agreement) is signed, creating a new Croatian *banovina,* embracing present-day Croatia plus about one third of Bosnia and a large part of the Srem region. The *ban* is granted considerable powers, but authority over foreign affairs and the army remains in Belgrade. Germany invades Poland. World War II begins.

WORLD WAR II

1940: Nazis defeat France.

1941: March 25: Yugoslavia signs a pact with the Nazis.

March 27: After protests against the signature of the pact, a coup overthrows Regent Pavle, installs King Petar II.

April 6: Nazis bombard Belgrade; Germans invade Yugoslavia; Yugoslav army crumbles; country disintegrates.

April 10: Proclamation of "Independent State of Croatia," first since 1102. It embraces all of Bosnia. Ustasha leader Ante Pavelić installed in Zagreb as *Poglavnik* (ruler) on April 15. State's real independence is scant. It is divided into German and Italian zones, and is effectively a puppet of Hitler.

May: Ustasha massacres of Serbs in Croatia and Bosnia begin. A Serbian royalist resistance movement, known as the Chetniks, takes form in Serbia, led by Draža Mihailović.

1945: Tito's Federal Yugoslavia

June: Hitler invades the Soviet Union. A communist resistance, the Partisans, led by Josip Broz, alias Tito, begins in Yugoslavia. Initially based in the Serbian town of Užice, but moves to Bosnia in November. Bosnia becomes Tito's power base for the rest of the war. The Allies eventually switch support from Mihailović to Tito (a process initiated in 1943 and completed in 1944) on the basis that he is inflicting greater damage on the Germans.

August: Milan Nedić, a former chief of the Yugoslav General Staff, is installed by the Nazis in Belgrade as a collaborationist leader. The battles between the various forces arrayed on Yugoslav soil—Ustashas, Chetniks, Nazis, Partisans, Serbian collaborators—will take over one million lives during the course of the war.

1942: Creation, in Bihać, western Bosnia, of Tito's Anti-Fascist Council of National Liberation of Yugoslavia (known by acronym AVNOJ). Begins to lay foundations for a future communist Yugoslav state.

1943: Second AVNOJ assembly in Jajce, central Bosnia, later held by communists to mark the birth of the new federal Yugoslav state.

1944: Liberation of Belgrade by Partisans and Soviet forces.

1945: Capitulation of Germany. Partisan troops enter Zagreb and pursue the forces of the crumbling Independent State of Croatia northward. Partisan massacre of Ustashas at Bleiburg, after the Allies refuse to allow them into Austria. Tito takes power, proclaiming that Yugoslavia would no longer be ruled by "a clique of the Great Serbian bourgeoisie."

TITO AND COMMUNIST YUGOSLAVIA

1946: Execution of Mihailović. Trial of Archbishop Stepinac of Zagreb. Approval of a new constitution, based largely on the 1936 constitution of the Soviet Union. Means of production and foreign trade are placed in hands of the state.

1946–48: Alija Izetbegović, later president of Bosnia, is jailed for links to a Muslim nationalist organization alleged to have collaborated with the fascists.

1948: Tito's break with Stalin. Soviet charges against Tito are announced by Cominform on June 28, the anniversary of the Battle of Kosovo.

1950: Development of a "Yugoslav way," aimed at withering of state and self-management through workers' collectives. Collectivization of the land begins to slow.

1952: Communist party of Yugoslavia changes its name to League of Communists of Yugoslavia. Change is supposed to mark the fact that Yugoslavs are embarked on a new and independent way to communism.

1954: Trial of Milovan Djilas, one of the most brilliant theoreticians of the "Yugoslav way," marks the limits of the reform process. State and party, by whatever name, will not wither away.

1955: Reconciliation with the Soviet Union.

1956: First Non-aligned Movement meeting in Brioni. Soviet intervention in Hungary. Tito's response is ambivalent.

1966: Tito ousts Aleksandar Ranković, the head of the secret police. Ranković, the highest-ranking Serb, is suspected of plotting to succeed Tito. Ranković gradually assumes status of Serbian martyr.

1968: Prague Spring. Soviet invasion of Czechoslovakia.

1971: Croatian Spring. Outpouring of Croatian national sentiment in Zagreb. Strong push for greater autonomy or independence. Crushed by Tito. Bosnian Muslims are recognized for the first time as a separate nation in the national census.

1973: Izetbegović publishes the "Islamic Declaration."

1974: Muslims are recognized as a constituent nation in the new, increasingly confederal Yugoslav constitution. Decentralization is pushed; the state frays.

1979: Economic downturn sets in and continues through the 1980s. The quest for economic self-management is bogged down in growing bureaucracy.

1980: Death of Tito. Succeeded by a rotating presidency.

1981: Riots by ethnic Albanians in Kosovo, who demand independence from Serbia and the transformation of Kosovo into a seventh Yugoslav republic.

1983: In what amounts to a show trial, Izetbegović and twelve other Muslim intellectuals are imprisoned for allegedly plotting to overthrow the state. Islamic Declaration presented as evidence. Izetbegović gets a fourteen-year sentence, but is released after five years. Ranković dies. Tens of thousands attend his funeral in Belgrade in one of the first displays of resurgent Serbian nationalism.

1985: Gorbachev becomes Soviet leader.

THE BREAKUP

1986: Publication of a Memorandum by the Serbian Academy of Arts and Sciences. It amounts to an incendiary catalog of Serbian resentments and ambitions.

1987: Slobodan Milošević, the party chief in Serbia, visits Kosovo Polje in April and speaks out in favor of the Serb minority in Kosovo. The Kosovo Serbs become the lightning rod of his rise. In December, Ivan Stambolić quits as the Serbian president, replaced by Milošević.

1988: Slovene Spring. Demonstrations in Ljubljana against the Yugoslav army. Nationalist fever rises in Serbia at "Meetings of Truth" in big towns. Government of autonomous northern Serbian province of Vojvodina dismissed; autonomy of Vojvodina quashed. Azem Vllasi, Albanian leader in Kosovo, ousted. Milan Kučan, Slovenian party leader, says Yugoslavia is turning into "Serboslavia."

1989: Montenegrin leadership ousted; the new leadership is acquiescent to Milošević. Ante Marković forms federal government in last, failed bid to reform Yugoslavia and hold it together. Serbian constitution amended in March to curtail autonomy of Kosovo and Vojvodina. Franjo Tudjman's Croatian Democratic Union (HDZ) holds its first rally; the party is legalized in December.

June 4: Solidarity party victorious in Polish elections.

June 28: One million Serbs flock to Kosovo to commemorate the six hundredth anniversary of the Battle of Kosovo. Delirious support for Milošević.

September 27: Slovenia amends its constitution; abolishes the leading role of Communist party. Tensions between Slovenia and Serbia rise sharply.

November 9: Fall of Berlin Wall.

November 27: Czechoslovakia's "Velvet Revolution."

December 21: Fall of Ceauşescu in Romania.

1990: January: Fourteenth and final congress of the Yugoslav Communist party. The Slovenes walk out. The Croats support them. Without the party, little remains to hold federal Yugoslavia together. Albanian demonstrations in Kosovo repressed.

February: Serbian Democratic Party founded in Knin, Croatia. Stirrings of Serb revolt against Croatian push for independence.

March: State of emergency in Kosovo.

April: Free elections in Slovenia; communists ousted.

May: Free elections in Croatia. Tudjman sweeps to victory. Izetbegović founds Muslim nationalist Party of Democratic Action (SDA) in Bosnia.

June: Milošević says Serbia does not accept internal republican borders as basis for division of the country.

July: Serbian Democratic Party (SDS) founded in Bosnia; Radovan Karadžić elected president of the nationalist party. Slovenia declares itself a sovereign state. Kosovo assembly dissolved and Serb crackdown on Albanians intensifies.

August: Krajina Serbs demonstrate against Tudjman. They adopt a "Declaration on the Sovereignty and Autonomy of the Serbian People," later confirmed by referendum. Tensions between Serbs and Croats fester through rest of year. Bosnian branch of Tudjman's HDZ born.

September: New Serbian constitution adopted; autonomous status of Kosovo and Vojvodina formally ended.

November: First round of free elections in Bosnia. Nationalist parties—Muslim SDA, Serb SDS, and Croat HDZ—triumph, taking 85 percent of the vote.

December: Second round of Bosnian elections; nationalist triumph confirmed. New constitution in Croatia strips Serbs of status as "constituent people." Constitution formalizes Croatian right to secede. Referendum in Slovenia shows 88.5 percent of voters support the right to secede.

1991 WAR IN CROATIA

January: Karadžić proclaims the "Parliament of Serb People in Bosnia-Herzegovina." Milošević warns that a division of Yugoslavia putting the Serb people "within separate sovereign states cannot be acceptable."

February: Izetbegović proposes holding Yugoslavia together as a "graded federation."

March: Violent incidents in Pakrac followed by first deaths in fighting between Serbs and Croats at Plitvice. End of the Gulf War. Milošević and Tudjman discuss a carving-up of Yugoslavia in meeting at Karadjordjevo.

May: Serbs kill twelve Croatian policemen at Borovo Selo. Yugoslav presidency breaks down as rotation from Borisav Jović, a Serb, to Stipe Mesić, a Croat, is aborted. Referendum in Croatia shows 93 percent of population in favor of a "sovereign and independent Croatia."

June: James Baker, the American secretary of state, makes a last-ditch attempt to save Yugoslavia during a visit to Belgrade. He warns against "preemptive unilateral actions" by Croatia and Slovenia, but is ignored. Croatia and Slovenia declare independence; the Bush administration hands the problem to the Europeans. Brief war in Slovenia, whose independence is quickly accepted by Milošević because it is Serb free.

July: Brioni Declaration establishing a three-month moratorium on the question of Slovene and Croatian independence. Mesić becomes the Yugoslav president. But the accord is quickly overtaken by events. War starts in Croatia, pitting Serbs backed by the Serb-dominated Yugoslav army against Croats.

August: Serb bombardment of Vukovar begins. Major Serb offensive in western Slavonia. Failed putsch in Moscow.

September: Serbs declare several "autonomous areas" in Bosnia-Herzegovina. UN Security Council imposes arms embargo on former Yugoslavia, locking in a massive Serb advantage in weaponry inherited from Yugoslav army.

October: Cyrus Vance becomes UN mediator. Serbs walk out of Bosnian assembly. Muslim and Croat legislators vote for the pursuit of Bosnian sovereignty. Serb bombardment of Dubrovnik. At the Hague Peace Conference, Lord Carrington proposes "a loose association or alliance of sovereign or independent states" and guarantees for minorities. Milošević rejects the proposal.

November: Vukovar, by now a latter-day Dresden, falls to Serbs. More than 250 non-Serbs disappear from Vukovar hospital and are massacred.

December: Germany says it will unilaterally recognize Croatia and Slovenia if the other European Union states refuse to do so. European Union agrees to invite all Yugoslav republics seeking recognition to present their case by December 24. A commission is established to report its findings on these applications by January 15. Carrington abandons his quest for an overall settlement.

1992 WAR IN BOSNIA

January: Cease-fire in Croatia as Vance Plan is agreed on. Plan calls for large UN deployment. An uneasy truce takes hold in Croatia. Independence of Croatia and Slovenia is recognized by states of European Union and many others, but not the United States. Milošević issues secret order transferring to Bosnia all Serb officers born in Bosnia—an evident preparation for war.

February: UNPROFOR created. Initial focus is Croatia; headquarters unhappily located in Sarajevo. Talks in Lisbon on partition of Bosnia into ethnic cantons produce a preliminary accord, later rejected by Izetbegović. United States pushes for independence of a "multi-ethnic" Bosnia; fights partition plans. Karadžić tells the Austrian paper *Der Kurier* that "two thirds of Bosnia and one third of Sarajevo should go to the Serbs."

March: Referendum on Bosnian independence, boycotted by the Serbs. Of the 64 percent of eligible voters who cast ballots, 99 percent vote for independence. A Serb is killed at a wedding in Sarajevo; Serbs erect roadblocks. Tensions explosive as armed bands of Serbs begin crossing Drina River.

Fighting in Bosanski Brod and Neretva Valley between Serbs on one side and Croats and Muslims on the other.

April: Serb rampage in Bijeljina led by Arkan. Muslims massacred. Independence of Bosnia recognized by European Union and, a day later, by the United States, which recognizes Slovene and Croatian independence at the same time. Serb shelling of Sarajevo begins. War breaks out. Serb "cleansing" of eastern, northern, and northwestern Bosnia begins in earnest. Several hundred thousand Muslims driven out or killed. Croats drive much smaller number of Serbs out of western Herzegovina.

May: Yugoslav army announces it is "withdrawing" from Bosnia; weaponry, including at least three hundred tanks and one thousand heavy guns, already in Bosnian Serb hands. Officers also in place. Ratko Mladić named commander of Bosnian Serb army, which is formally established in mid-May. Sarajevo post office destroyed with loss of forty thousand phone lines. Massacre in Tuzla as Muslim forces ambush a Yugoslav army convoy; dozens of mainly Serb cadets killed. Sixteen people killed and more than one hundred injured in Sarajevo when a Serb mortar shell lands on people in line for bread: the "bread line massacre." City of Sarajevo surrounded by Serbs and under siege. UN Security Council imposes trade sanctions on Serbia.

June: Serb concentration camps spread in the 70 percent of Bosnia now controlled by Serb forces. Western governments ignore all evidence of genocide of Bosnian Muslims that might oblige them to act. UNPROFOR takes over control of Sarajevo airport, but at Serb sufferance. Mitterrand visits Sarajevo. Airlift of food to Sarajevo begins.

July: Serb assault on Goražde. Food aid reaches Sarajevo suburb of Dobrinja after seventy-one-day isolation. Water and electricity in Sarajevo cut off. Croat community of Herceg-Bosna proclaimed.

August: Serb concentration camps revealed by journalists. Bush administration adopts panicked, contradictory, and disingenuous position. No action is taken; argument maintained that all sides are committing atrocities and that, in the Serb concentration camps, "the evidence is unpleasant conditions." Clinton, as Democratic candidate, protests. He says, "If the horrors of the Holocaust taught us anything, it is the high cost of remaining silent and paralyzed in the face of genocide." Sarajevo library destroyed in Serb bombardment. International Conference on the Former Yugoslavia in London ends with a Serb commitment to closing concentration camps and lifting the siege of Sarajevo. Promises prove empty.

September: International Conference enters permanent session in Geneva, with quest for peace led by Vance and Lord Owen of Britain. Heaviest bombardment yet of Sarajevo—925 civilian casualties in week ending September 20. Rump Yugoslavia—Serbia and Montenegro—is expelled from the General Assembly of the United Nations.

October: United Nations Security Council Resolution 780 opens inquiry into war crimes in former Yugoslavia. Resolution 781 establishes a "no-fly zone" over Bosnia. Croat forces take west Mostar from Serbs, declaring it the capital of Croatian Union of Herceg-Bosna. Clashes between nominal Croat and Muslim allies in Prozor. Jajce is captured by the Serbs.

November: Massive exodus of Muslims and Croats from Jajce. UN convoys reach Tuzla after seven-month Serb encirclement.

December: U.S. Secretary of State Lawrence Eagleburger names Milošević, Karadžić, and Mladić as potential war criminals. Changing tack at last, he acknowledges the extent of Serb crimes by declaring: "We have, on the one hand, a moral and historical obligation not to stand back a second time in this century while a people faced obliteration." But it is too late for much of Bosnia's Muslim population. Milošević reelected as president of Serbia. Boutros Boutros-Ghali, in Sarajevo, says the situation in the Bosnian capital is "better than in ten other places in the world."

1993 MUSLIM-CROAT WAR

January: Cyrus Vance and Lord Owen put forward Vance-Owen Plan, dividing Bosnia into ten provinces, with Serbs controlling provinces covering 42.3 percent of territory, Muslims 32.5 percent, and Croats 25.4 percent. Hakija Turajlić, Bosnian deputy prime minister, is killed by Serb police when traveling in a United Nations armored personnel carrier—a flagrant example of the UN's powerlessness. Clashes between Croat and Bosnian armies in Gornji Vakuf. Attacking from Srebrenica, Bosnian forces kill Serbs in Kravica. Breaking truce in Croatia, the Croatian army attacks Krajina Serbs in an attempt to take the strategic Maslenica Bridge near the Dalmatian coast.

February: A Serb soldier, Borislav Herak, is captured by Bosnian government and charged with thirty-two counts of murder. UN Security Council Resolution 808 establishes the International Criminal Tribunal for the Former Yugoslavia. But it is not until July 1994 that a chief prosecutor is named—the South African judge Richard Goldstone. Serb offensive in eastern Bosnia.

March: After Croat acceptance, the Bosnian government accepts Vance-Owen Plan. General Philippe Morillon, commander of the UN forces in Bosnia, makes a personal stand to prevent the fall of Srebrenica to the Serbs. Humanitarian aid reaches Srebrenica.

April: Thorvald Stoltenberg replaces Cyrus Vance as mediator. Karadžić says

"Serbs must militarily defeat our enemies and conquer the territories we need." Security Council Resolution 819 declares Srebrenica a "safe area." Full-scale fighting breaks out between Croats and Bosnian army; at Ahmići, more than 170 Muslim civilians massacred by Croats. Intense fighting between Croats and Muslims around Vitez. Former Yugoslav republic of Macedonia admitted to the United Nations.

May: Karadžić signs Vance-Owen Plan, after Owen has given "clarifications" to Milošević. However, the Bosnian Serb assembly rejects the plan, a rejection made definitive in a "referendum." The Vance-Owen Plan dies, ditched by the United States, to be replaced by a largely meaningless "Joint Action Plan." The Clinton administration's tough talk of "lift and strike"—lift the arms embargo and use air strikes against the Serbs—also dies, progressively replaced by muddled talk about "one-thousand-year-old Balkan rivalries" and "containment." UN Security Council Resolution 824 accords "safe area" status to Goražde, Žepa, Tuzla, Bihać, and Sarajevo, as well as Srebrenica. It is soon reinforced by UN Resolution 836 authorizing UNPROFOR, acting in self-defense, to use force, including NATO air power, "in reply to bombardments against the safe areas by any of the parties or to armed incursion into them or in the event of any deliberate obstruction in or around those areas to the freedom of movement of UNPROFOR or of protected humanitarian convoys."

June: Bosnian army takes Travnik from the Croat Council of Defense (HVO). Rasim Delić replaces Sefer Halilović as commander of Bosnian army. Milošević and Tudjman unveil a plan for the three-way division of Bosnia, known as a "union of three republics."

July: As Muslim-Croat war rages, several Croat concentration camps operate, mainly in Mostar area. Most notorious is Dretelj. Izetbegović accepts principle of a "union of three republics." Serb forces attack Mount Bjelašnica and Mount Igman near Sarajevo.

August: NATO threatens to bomb Serbs if they do not withdraw from Igman. Serb forces withdraw. Owen and Stoltenberg propose a three-way Bosnian split giving Serbs 52 percent, Muslims 30 percent, and Croats 18 percent of Bosnia.

September: Shares of land for a "union of three republics" adjusted in Bosnian government's favor during a meeting on HMS *Invincible* in September. But Izetbegović ultimately rejects the idea. Bosnian assembly demands that all territories taken by force be returned.

October: Fikret Abdić declares an Autonomous Province of Western Bosnia in the Bihać area, precipitating a Muslim-Muslim conflict between his followers and the Bosnian army. Croat massacre of Muslims at Stupni Do. In a crackdown by the Bosnian government on organized crime, Musan Topalović ("Caco") is killed.

November: Bosnian army takes Vareš from the Croats. Croat mortars destroy Mostar's Old Bridge. Runaway inflation in Serbia; a 500-billion dinar note issued. Milošević reelected president.

December: Owen and Stoltenberg report to the UN Security Council that the principle of 33.3 percent of territory for Muslims, 17.5 percent for Croats, and rest for Serbs agreed. But the plan soon dies.

1994 MUSLIM-CROAT FEDERATION

January: Cease-fire between Abdić forces and Bosnian army.

February: A mortar round explodes in the Sarajevo marketplace, killing sixty-eight people. NATO says it will bomb if Serb heavy guns are not withdrawn from around Sarajevo or put under UN control by February 21. A fudged agreement averts NATO bombing. Serb bombardment of Sarajevo stops after 676 days of shelling, only to resume in 1995. End of Muslim-Croat war.

March: Trams start to run again in Sarajevo. A semblance of normality briefly returns to the city. Bosnian and Croat leaders agree to form a federation. But the alliance never amounts to much more than a truce. Serb offensive begins around Goražde.

April: As Serb offensive against Goražde gathers pace, NATO bombs for the first time. Serbs take UN personnel hostage. Bombing brief and ineffective. A British Sea Harrier is shot down. Another NATO ultimatum obliges the Serbs to remove heavy weapons from around Goražde. But the town's plight remains desperate. The Clinton administration gives green light to Tudjman for the Iranian arms pipeline.

May: Yasushi Akashi, the senior UN envoy to the former Yugoslavia, allows Serbs to move seven battle tanks across the heavy-weapons exclusion zone around Sarajevo in return for promises to allow humanitarian aid to Goražde. The "Contact Group" takes form as foreign ministers of Russia, the United States, France, Germany, and Britain call for a settlement granting 51 percent of Bosnia to the Muslim-Croat federation, 49 percent to the Serbs.

June: One-month cease-fire signed in Geneva. Bosnian army attacks Abdić forces again.

July: A Contact Group map presented to the federation and the Serbs on a take-it-or-leave-it basis. Federation accepts the plan. Serbs reject it. Pressure mounts again on Sarajevo as Serbs tighten noose.

August: Milošević, angered by the Bosnian Serb rejection of Contact Group

Plan, says he is closing Serbian border with Bosnia to everything except food, medicine, and clothing. Abdić troops surrender to Bosnian army. A new wave of "ethnic cleansing" from Serb territories begins. By late September it is estimated that no more than fifty thousand Muslims remain on Serb-held territory (compared with about one million in 1992).

September: Pope John Paul II cancels a visit to Sarajevo for security reasons.

October: Bosnian and Serb prisoners of war exchanged on the Brotherhood and Unity Bridge in Sarajevo. In first major military victory over Serbs, Bihać-based Bosnian forces break through Serb lines on the Grabež Plateau, taking a wide swathe of territory. Serb military domination no longer absolute.

November: Bosnian Serb forces, backed by Krajina Serbs and Abdić supporters, start major counterattack against Bihać "safe area." Krajina Serb aircraft drop napalm and cluster bombs. NATO bombs Udbina airport in the Krajina, but bombing is too limited to be of any use. Serb forces enter Bihać "safe area." Amid growing rifts within NATO, the United States shifts its policy, abandoning calls for broader air strikes. Tony Lake, Clinton's national security adviser, writes in a memo, "The stick of military pressure seems no longer viable." NATO has been brought to the brink by transatlantic disagreements over Bosnian policy and is, at this stage, an alliance in need of reinvention.

December: Former American president Jimmy Carter visits Sarajevo and Pale. He announces a cease-fire. Four-month cessation of hostilities signed. But fighting continues in Bihać area.

1995 PAX AMERICANA

January: Contact Group opens direct, but fruitless, talks with the Bosnian Serbs on the map. Tudjman announces that UNPROFOR's mandate in Croatia will not be extended beyond March 31. Lieutenant General Rupert Smith takes over from General Sir Michael Rose as commander of UN troops in Bosnia.

February: Roads across Sarajevo airport for civilian traffic open after a break of more than six months.

March: Airport roads closed after Bosnian sniper kills two Serb girls in Serb-held Sarajevo district of Grbavica. Serb military and civilian leadership hold important meeting on Jahorina Mountain which concludes that a quick end to the war is essential to the Serbs. The Serbs decide that Sarajevo's isolation is to be increased, and, if necessary, eastern Muslim enclaves taken.

April: Bosnian army, shattering Carter's cessation of hostilities, takes Mount Vlašić in central Bosnia, but fails to take Mount Majevica near Tuzla. The International Tribunal names Karadžić and Mladić as suspected war criminals. The humanitarian airlift into Sarajevo is closed by the Serbs. Two French soldiers are killed by snipers; the possibility of UN withdrawal from Bosnia is raised by the French government.

May: Croats take western Slavonia, held by Serbs since 1991. Serbs flee into Bosnia. The military tide is turning. A Serb mortar round crashes into the western Sarajevo suburb of Butmir, killing eleven people. Smith calls for NATO air strikes, but is overruled by Akashi. Massive artillery exchanges in Sarajevo for the first time since the NATO threat of February 1994. Serbs now fire from so-called weapons-collection points, and remove weapons from them, as UN forces look on helplessly. Smith says firing and removal of these weapons must stop or NATO will bomb. NATO aircraft attack Serb ammunition depot near Pale. In response, Serbs shell Tuzla, killing seventy-one people, mainly youths, with one round. As usual they claim the Muslims have "bombed themselves." Serbs take UN forces hostage; some are chained to strategic sites as "human shields." NATO bombing stops after two days. Serbs take the UN's Vrbanja Bridge emplacement in Sarajevo. French UN forces counterattack and retake the position with the loss of two men. Four Serbs killed. Calls from senior UN officials for a radical change in the mandate, including possible abandonment of "safe areas," are ignored or overruled by Western governments.

June: UN hostages gradually released by Serbs. Release preceded by secret meetings between General Mladić and French generals, including Lieutenant General Bernard Janvier, the commander of UN forces in the former Yugoslavia. The possibility of further NATO air strikes is all but eliminated. At critical meeting in Split between Akashi, Janvier, and Smith, warnings from Smith about Serb plans to attack Srebrenica and other eastern enclaves are ignored; a statement says "UNPROFOR will strictly abide by peacekeeping principles" (such principles do not include use of air power). Fierce fighting around Sarajevo as Bosnian army embarks on offensive that fails with heavy casualties. UNPROFOR abandons weapons-collection sites, signaling formal end of attempt to stop the Serb bombardment of Sarajevo. Security Council approves the deployment of a 12,500-strong Rapid Reaction Force, to bolster the UN mission.

July: Serb assault on Srebrenica. Dutch United Nations soldiers stationed in the Srebrenica "safe area" are taken hostage by the Serbs. A Dutch soldier is killed by Bosnian forces as UNPROFOR retreats from the Serbs. As Serbs close in on the town, the Dutch forces are ordered to assume a blocking position "to prevent the further penetration" of Serb units and are promised NATO air support if this deterrence fails. Serb offensive does continue, but no air attacks are forthcoming as General Janvier hesitates. By the time a couple of sorties are flown, it is too late. Srebrenica falls. Muslim women and children are bused to Kladanj. Men taken prisoner or attempt trek to Tuzla area. Several thousand Muslim men killed by the Serbs in the worst single massacre of the war. Western governments, in London meeting, say they will use air power "on an unprecedented scale" to deter Serb attacks on Goražde. Žepa is not mentioned, and it falls to the Serbs. The Rapid Reaction Force deploys in the Sarajevo area, bringing 105-millimeter guns. Serbs begin an advance on Bihać. Tudjman and Izetbegović, meeting in Split, agree on "joint defense against Serb aggression." Croatian army takes Glamoč and Bosansko Grahovo, opening the way for an attack on the Serbs' Krajina stronghold of Knin. For the first time since 1992, front lines are shifting at speed.

August: In "Operation Storm," the Croatian army defeats the Krajina Serbs and captures Knin. The self-proclaimed Krajina Republic collapses, and over 150,000 Serbs flee eastward toward Serbia. In the second mortar attack on the Sarajevo market, a Serb shell kills thirty-seven people. As disaster follows disaster in the Balkans, and an election campaign looms, the Clinton administration bestirs itself at last. Tony Lake drafts a new peace proposal, pushed by Richard Holbrooke. His mission meets disaster as three senior American diplomats are killed in an accident on the Igman road. The war is now a physical fact to the Clinton administration at last. In a breakthrough in Belgrade, Holbrooke secures a commitment from Bosnian Serbs to defer to Milošević in negotiations. Milošević, weary of trade sanctions and unable to quell the cataclysmic tide he set in motion, is now desperate to end the war. NATO embarks on its first sweeping bombardment of Serbs in response to the marketplace attack. Air power is accompanied by the artillery of the Rapid Reaction Force. American-led diplomacy is finally backed by force. In this guise, and against the background of the almost-completed mass forced movement of populations to create largely ethnically homogeneous areas in the former Yugoslavia, the diplomacy quickly proves effective.

September: NATO bombardment continues. Tomahawk missiles are fired at Banja Luka. Bombing ends with Serb agreement to withdraw heavy weapons from around Sarajevo and allow free access to the city. Siege of Sarajevo ends. Meeting in Geneva, foreign ministers of Serbia, Croatia, and Bosnia recognize Karadžić's Republika Srpska as an entity within Bosnia and agree on a 51–49 split of territory between the Muslim-Croat federation and the Serbs, respectively. Croat and Bosnian forces advance rapidly against Serbs in western and central Bosnia. Croat forces take Jajce; Bosnian army takes Donji Vakuf and Ključ.

October: Bosnian army takes Sanski Most. Croat-Bosnian offensive against

Serbs ends with the proposed 51–49 territorial split roughly respected on the ground. Holbrooke's team secures a sixty-day cease-fire. Gas and electricity restored to Sarajevo. First convoy of Bosnian trucks to reach Goražde moves across Serb-held territory from Sarajevo under UNPROFOR escort.

November: Proximity peace talks at the Wright-Patterson airbase in Dayton, Ohio, bring together Milošević, Tudjman, and Izetbegović. After three weeks of talks an agreement is reached that is at once an ambitious blueprint for a single Bosnian state and a desperate compromise containing the lineaments of potential partition. Bosnia is split between the Muslim-Croat federation (51 percent of the territory) and the Republika Srpska (49 percent), with various overarching central institutions including a presidency and a legislature. The international community is represented by various institutions, including NATO, the United Nations, and a weak police force; this leads to confusion; promises to help the return of more than two million refugees remain largely empty. Undertakings to arrest indicted war criminals, including Mladić and Karadžić, are sufficiently nebulous to allow inaction by NATO and an ultra-cautious Pentagon.

December: The Dayton Peace Agreement is signed in Paris. Authority is transferred from the UNPROFOR to the NATO mission, known initially as IFOR (Implementation Force). Roadblocks come down. American soldiers thus take over from the lightly armed United Nations peacekeepers only when the war is over, and after the loss of about 200,000 lives. Bosnia's mottled society has been shredded and the hopes of knitting the country together again appear tenuous at best.

BOOK ONE

THE LOST CENTURY

CHAPTER I

MY FATHER'S WAR

SEAD MEHMEDOVIĆ GREW UP BELIEVING THAT HIS FATHER was dead, one of the more than one million Yugoslav victims of World War II. Where he had died, nobody knew, there was no grave, there was nothing, but Alija Mehmedović's death was a fact of Sead's childhood. So when Sead learned that this might not be true—that his father might be living outside Yugoslavia under an assumed name—the quest to find him naturally became an obsession. For years the search was fruitless, leading only to new riddles, but finally on December 15, 1970, Sead sat down in Belgrade to write to the father he had never known. With an address for his father at last in his possession, Sead could scarcely contain a tremulous excitement.

As he sat down to compose a letter, Sead confronted again the fact that he knew almost nothing of the dashing, dark-haired young man who appeared in the few surviving photographs of his father. Alija Mehmedović remained a shadowy figure. He had worked at the Belgrade daily newspaper *Politika;* had abandoned Sead's mother, Gaby, on the eve of World War II; had remarried in Sarajevo, the Bosnian capital; and had, it was long believed, been killed somewhere in his native Bosnia or in Croatia. This was the story on which Sead was raised. Such fragments, the shards of past conflict, were his inheritance.

Sead, like countless Yugoslavs, was a child of war. The Second World War took his father. The conflict had left him with confused memories. Certain images were always vivid, imbued with the particular luminosity of childhood. Others had faded. Of Hitler's bombardment of Belgrade, starting on April 6, 1941, when Sead was not quite three years old, he recalled only a dim sense of terror. He had found shelter in cellars as the Luftwaffe pounded the Yugoslav capital. Fear, the most instantly communicable of viruses, spread in a city that only days earlier had been full of defiant demonstrations against the Nazis that displayed a typical Serb bravura.

The crowds had poured into the streets to protest the Yugoslav prince regent Pavle's decision to enter into the Axis Pact with Hitler. "Better war than the pact" (*"Bolje rat nego pakt"*) and "Better the grave than a slave" (*"Bolje grob nego rob"*), the people of Belgrade chanted. A Serb officer, General Dušan Simović, who led a coup that ousted the regent, gave a rousing speech of defiance to Hitler in which he recalled the bones of Serbian military heroes and the Serbs' epic struggle, over many centuries, against the Turks.

Winston Churchill, the British prime minister, was delighted. "Yugoslavia," he declared, "has found its soul." But Hitler was enraged. By April 10, 1941, wide swaths of Belgrade had been leveled. The defiant crowds were silenced; the Yugoslav army crumbled; the Nazis quickly installed General Milan Nedić, a soldier who did the Nazis' bidding in Serbia as assiduously as Marshal Philippe Pétain's Vichy regime in France, and Yugoslavia disintegrated with the proclamation in Zagreb of an independent, puppet-Nazi Croatian state.

Belgrade was transformed by days of bombing. There were bodies piled in the streets and many dead and stray animals. A bomb hit the Belgrade Zoo, and Sead recalled animals roaming through the burning city. As if in a child's bedtime story, a polar bear made its way down to the River Sava.

A devastating conflict began on the fragmented Yugoslav lands, a conflict that was at once resistance battle against the Germans, revolutionary communist struggle aimed ultimately at the overthrow of the Serbian establishment that had ruled Yugoslavia, and civil war—violence laid layer upon layer.

Sead remembered the second bombardment of Belgrade with much greater clarity. In 1944, on the Orthodox Easter, the Anglo-American Balkan Air Force embarked on a campaign of heavy bombing against the Nazi occupiers of Belgrade. Once again there were scenes of mayhem. Sead, by now six years old, watched from what was then Kosmayaska Street as the Allied planes came swooping in. When the bombing started, he hid under the bed, until he was dragged down to the cellar by his mother. The Allies were doing to Belgrade what their Nazi enemies had done three years before.

Six months later, in October, Belgrade was again engulfed in fighting as the communist Partisan forces led by Josip Broz Tito and the Soviet army closed in on the Yugoslav capital. Sead saw the shabby, ragtag Yugoslav Partisans, rifles slung over their shoulders, red stars on their hats, moving up Kosovska Street in the center of the capital as a platoon of German troops—perhaps the last Germans in the city—took up a commanding position on the top of the central Albanija Building. The Germans were well stocked in two essential commodities for a last stand: ammunition and alcohol. They shot everything that moved on the square where Sead used to play. When the German snipers were finally silenced, Sead emerged from hiding to find his square littered with corpses and the bodies of dogs and cats. It was October 20, 1944, a beautiful, sunny day. He could not take his eyes off the small, splayed animals or shake from his nostrils the sweet, emetic smell of death. Some of the German corpses, still in uniform, had newspapers over their faces. Their boots had been removed by the scavenging Soviet forces and the equally deprived local population. After the mighty armored cars of the Germans, it was amazing to see Soviet soldiers sleeping on straw in the back of horse-drawn carts. This ramshackle army—through its mass, its momentum, and its morale—had triumphed over the Nazi war machine. He looked for a friend who used to sell tobacco on the square—his wooden leg, big mustache, and booming voice deeply impressed the young boy—but could not find him in the chaos.

The city still echoed to the intermittent crash of shells fired by the German troops retreating northward, and the cacophony of rifles, tommy guns, and—loudest and strangest of all—the Soviet Katyusha multiple-rocket launchers. Whether these were the sounds of battle, or of celebration of Tito's victory, was not always clear. The Germans had retreated to Zemun, on the other side of the Sava, the river whose confluence with the Danube provides Belgrade with the splendor of its setting. From Zemun they shelled the capital. Thirty years earlier, in 1914, and from the same positions, Austro-Hungarian troops in Zemun had fired the first salvos of World War I after the defiant Serbs rejected a demand from Vienna that Austro-Hungarian police be allowed into Serbia. The Austro-Hungarian government had demanded that the police be admitted to investigate the assassination by a Serb nationalist, Gavrilo Princip, of the Habsburg heir, Archduke Franz Ferdinand, and his wife in Sarajevo.

Belgrade was liberated, Sead free in the smoldering streets of the white and devastated city. Tito's forces took control amid the mixture of euphoria and terror that accompanies any revolution. It was not unusual to see a young man, denounced as an informer, being dragged off and summarily shot.

So it was that Sead, born on April 25, 1938, into a young country ruled by a conservative Serbian monarchy, found himself, at the age of seven, growing up a communist. A deeply wounded Yugoslav state was reconstituted under the unlikely banner of communism. Sead embraced this new religion, but he could not come to terms with the war that had led to its victory.

Sead was unable to walk through Belgrade without remembering that time. The wartime city and the modern city shared very little. Most street names had been changed several times and most of the town rebuilt after the war. But in Sead's mind they were superimposed on each other, like a house and its reflection in water. He lived in time present and in time past, trying, it seemed, to understand something that had escaped him.

CHURCHILL'S RESPONSE to Tito's communist victory was laconic. On January 18, 1945, he told the House of Commons, "We have no special interest in the political regime which prevails in Yugoslavia. Few people, in Britain, I imagine, are going to be more cheerful or more downcast because of the future constitution of Yugoslavia." Freedom for the Yugoslavs and the "Yugoslav soul," extolled by Churchill in 1941, had ceased to interest him greatly by 1945, when realpolitik and the exploits of Stalin's Red Army had come to dictate a carving-up of Europe.

For Western governments, the way the war in Yugoslavia was perceived was ultimately a question of interests. But for Sead it was an affair of the heart. The mystery, for Sead, centered on the disappearance of his father. Repeated attempts by his mother to discover where, and in what circumstances, Alija had died proved fruitless. As Sead grew older, the phantom of his father began to haunt him. Clues emerged that Alija Mehmedović, a Bosnian Muslim, had survived the war, fled Yugoslavia, and started a new life under a new identity in Turkey.

The fact that, by an odd concidence, Sead had, like his father, found work at the newspaper *Politika,* as a graphic artist in the advertising department, had only intensified his curiosity. Increasingly, the search to find his father seemed to Sead to hold the key to unlocking his own uprooted life, a life that struck Sead as eternally unresolved, a puzzle in which the pieces would not fit together.

"My dear old man," Sead began the letter in December 1970, *"I have been writing to you for several days now and have not found time to finish the letter. I come to my office very early in the morning, between five and six o'clock, although my working hours begin at seven. (Every time I get up, I move the alarm hand on the clock so that my wife does not notice how early I wake up—she would scold me.)*

"This is the only time when I am alone. It is still dark and there are no people around. That is when I write you a letter. But later, during the day, when I am bombarded by everyday life, things take on a different guise and however close to you I felt in those early mornings, you drift away from me and I become scared that I opened myself too much, that

in my unsent words I burden you with the thoughts of someone who is a stranger, and so I tear up what I wrote to you.

"Before, I fended off thoughts of you, but now that it seems I have found you, I am discovering how much I missed you as a Father—not so much in the formal, family sense, but as a friend, in whom I might completely, fully confide: the friend who would understand me. In a sense, perhaps it is better that I found you only now. In this way, we will avoid the barrier of a father's formal authority that is established in childhood and which has to be overcome later in order to establish real friendship, with no fences, between father and son.

"In some ways, as I grow older, I withdraw into myself. I try to hide from my surroundings because I have a growing number of thoughts that seem to me to be incomprehensible to others. There are ever more barriers and ever more secret spaces that I try to make unnoticeable to others, impossible for them to find. But then you appeared as someone in whom I can confide, someone who will understand me without the desire to cram me into a mold, into his way of thinking.

"Maybe you will be disappointed that you found a son who—instead of comforting you in all the misfortunes that have befallen you—burdens you with his own thoughts and dilemmas.

"Please do not misunderstand me. But I would prefer if people close to me, with whom I live, do not find out about our relationship, or, more accurately, about this part of me. I would like to keep it all to myself. These are all unselfish, wonderful, open and good people and maybe it is not right that I hide a part of me from them. But that part exists in me and I have to save its integrity. I think that I have a right to a part of you, a part that will be undivided and mine only.

"But I will tell you more about me when we finally meet and see each other. Still I am afraid that the meeting will not occur and we will pass like two ships in the night. I have a strong feeling that we two are alike and that we will understand each other. . . ."

Sead carefully folded the letter into an envelope and addressed it to Ali Erhan. Through an acquaintance, Sead knew this as the assumed name under which his father lived in Turkey, the better to shield himself from the past, the shadows of his former life in Yugoslavia. After a long search to understand the fragments of his life, Sead felt deliriously close to his goal.

THE STATE OF YUGOSLAVIA lived for seventy-three years, an average human lifespan. Its life, like that of Sead Mehmedović, was marked by a restless search for origins and identity. Thrown together in haste on the ruins of the Ottoman and Austro-Hungarian empires in 1918, Yugoslavia sought restlessly to reconcile differences within itself of religion, culture, and tradition. After 1945, in its second incarnation as a communist state, it sought also to overcome the deep divisions left by the violence that World War II ignited on Yugoslav territory.

This quest involved attempts to overcome many silences, blank spaces, pages deleted from history. People, like Sead's father, disappeared. Families knew who the executioners of their relatives were, but did not confront them. Vaclav Havel, the Czech president, has written that the "special union" between ancestors and descendants "is one of the foundations of the existence of every sound human community aware of its identity." Yugoslavia, by this standard, was never a "sound human community," for, in countless cases, the bridges across generations had been broken.

If this was the case, the savagery of Yugoslavia's destruction from within became more readily understandable. I came to see a bloody catharsis cynically willed by communist-turned-nationalist leaders, in the wars of Yugoslavia's destruction between 1991 and 1995; the catharsis of a seductive but repressed individual, one whose birth in 1918 from the marriage of loveless parents was flawed and whose midlife crisis in World War II left a residue of lies and fear that ruthless politicians were able to exploit.

Sead Mehmedović is a Yugoslav. He has the mixed blood of this Balkan crossroads state. His father was a Bosnian Muslim; his mother, Gaby, who was raised in Zagreb, is half Hungarian, one quarter Serb, and one quarter Austrian. Such mixtures on lands that were long part of the Austro-Hungarian or Ottoman empires are typically Yugoslav. But Sead is also a Yugoslav in another sense. His own family history was falsified.

Sead's smile is gentle: it begins and ends in his pale blue eyes, a smile that is never quite whole, for it contains, like a shadow, a suggestion of fatigue less physical than intellectual and emotional. The fatigue of a man in late middle age who has long sought, long questioned, before accepting with a wry abandon the absence of answers in any other form but riddles. "I have a very bad orientation in time and space," he said to me once. "I don't know if something happened three years ago or five years ago. When I go into some big home, I don't know the front from the back, the left from the right. It takes me a long time to orient myself. I am unable to navigate."

I, too, have experienced Sead's Balkan vertigo. There are moments when everything seems to lurch, like the listing white graves on the ridges above Sarajevo and Tuzla that march out to meet the surrounding houses, or what is left of them, in a visible dance of the living and the dead. Time, no longer an abstraction, becomes a palpable matter. The sheer accumulation of tombs turns the head, and a rational understanding of so much death seems not so much impossible as inadequate.

In the northwestern Bosnian town of Banja Luka, outside a stone fort, there are numerous black marble graves recalling Tito's "People's Heroes" who died in World War II. None of the dead—Muslim, Croat, or Serb—is older than thirty-five. On and on the names trail—Kazim Hadžić, Drago Lang, Ante Jakić—lives given for a Yugoslav state that is itself now dead. Beside the memorial stones flows the Vrbas River, gushing over rocks: this sound of water, an unquenchable sound, is the essence of Bosnia. On the far bank, in winter, children sled, their squeals of pleasure carrying out over the water. The cries spend themselves slowly over the ruins of the Roman fort, the tombs of the now forgotten or vilified World War II Partisan heroes, the battlefields of "ethnic cleansing" between re-born tribes that marked the last decade of the twentieth century, the soar-ing poplars and willows with silent ravens perched on the highest branches. The indifferent river swirls on, eddying past small promontories where grass peeks through the snow. Everything here appears to be in movement, defying a firm foothold.

Sead's search for his father was like Yugoslavia's search for its soul. In a fluid landscape, it was a quest for bearings, for an understanding of the past—the basis, for an individual, as for a state, of a sound existence. But on the unstable Balkan Peninsula, the quest was arduous.

IN 1995, some years after his quest to find his father had ended, Sead took me to a small room perched like an eagle's nest on the roof above his mother's Belgrade apartment. He unlocked the door and we walked into a cluttered space filled with boxes of papers. Casting a despairing glance at the disorder, he said, "When I'm old and my wife, who is much younger, leaves me, I will come up here and sort through all this."

But would he, I wondered, ever be able to bring order to this chaos? "Earlier," Sead said, "I had the feeling that there was so much time in front of me. Gauguin started to paint when he was forty. I could too. When I passed forty, this habit stayed, this feeling that I had time. Still, I don't re-ally register time passing. I don't pay much attention to my age, but just sometimes I feel this physical tiredness, a pressure at the back of my neck."

He reached into one of the boxes and pulled out an undeveloped roll of film. "This might interest you," he said. "I was given it by a friend of my father named Refik Cabi, but I never did develop it. You might find some pictures of my father."

Below us, the city stretched away, a beaten-up and shabby accumulation of masonry. Belgrade rises from the Sava and Danube rivers toward the handsome avenue of Terazije; it falls, a mound of crumbling gray stucco, sucked down toward the rivers' banks. The Serbs have a saying: *"Nema rata bez Srba"*—"No war without the Serbs." Belgrade, according to Serbian lore, has been destroyed and rebuilt forty times. Its obvious strategic importance, on a ridge at the confluence of two great rivers, at the entrance to the fertile plains of Vojvodina, Hungary, and eastern Slavonia, long ensured that it was battled over with a singular intensity. It stood, moreover, at the dividing line of the eastern and western Roman empires that ran along the Drina and the Sava; centuries later, it stood at another border, between the Austro-Hungarian and Ottoman empires.

Belgrade was, by turns, Celtic, Roman, Bulgar, Serb, Turkish, and Austro-Hungarian—to name but a few of its identities between the third century B.C., when the Celts built the "Round Fort" called Singidunum, and the Ottomans' recapture of the city in 1739. The crescent and the cross did battle atop buildings that were mosques, then churches, then mosques once more. The Orthodox Christian Serbs finally recaptured the city in 1813. Over the next hundred years they leveled every mosque but one.

I gazed out: the hill of Dedinje where Tito lies, the Sava River, the high-rises of Novi Beograd, and the fertile Serbian plains beyond. After the plains, I could see in my mind's eye the mountains of Bosnia emerging abruptly, shrouded by mist or haze. Clouds on rocks. Birds circling. The smell of pine and plum brandy. Beyond that the oleander and the heady, Dalmatian coast opening out like some lush dream from the backdrop of a stony hinterland. How beautiful and variegated the Yugoslav state had been! But like the undeveloped film in my hand, it had secrets that had been concealed for too long.

SEAD AND I WALKED past the villas of Dedinje Hill, the leafy suburb inhabited by Slobodan Milošević's Mercedes-driving mercenaries. The Serbian president's socialist party was the old Communist party dressed up in new clothes. Marxism had been dropped but Leninism maintained. The result was gangster capitalism with centralized control: call it Miloševic's Mafia-Leninism. Sead, who had believed in Tito and his revolution, was disgusted.

"These nouveaux riches put pressure on me," he said. "I have always wanted equality and social justice. I feel cheated by these people. When I was young, I thought it was enough to work and society would give you back what you gave to it. Maybe I am just envious because I have no idea how to make so much money and make it so fast. Here, there is no culture of making money slowly. It's fast or nothing.

"All my life, I thought that now it will be different, *now it will be different.* With my fifty-eight years, I am still naïve. I did not want to believe that they could be connected—the party I once supported and the massive crime of this wealth. But I have to bow to the evidence. Still, knowing this, I am divided between what I don't want to believe and what manifestly is—and I guess I will die with this division. I really wanted to live in a better world. I don't believe that the West is better. In America, capitalism can be a game for wolves. That is why I became a communist. I did not want that kind of society."

The towering house belonging to Željko Ražnatović, alias Arkan, one of the more murderous of Serbia's paramilitary leaders during the wars of Yugoslavia's destruction, loomed up beside us, with slitlike tinted windows. A Jeep was parked outside, its driver talking on a cellular phone. Sead shook his head. We walked on past the stadium of the Red Star soccer club, whose supporters' club provided an initial nucleus for Arkan's gangs. When we reached his apartment, Sead went into his bedroom and emerged carrying a battered suitcase. Smiling his enigmatic smile, he handed it to me. The case contained letters, diaries, photographs, and other material that provided a portrait of Alija Mehmedović's war and life and told the story of the terrible circumstances in which Sead ultimately found his father.

CHAPTER 2

THE PESSIMIST

THE SUITCASE CONTAINING ALIJA'S DOCUMENTS WAS A MESS, his story scattered through notebooks, papers, postcards, magazines, school reports, birth certificates, death certificates, medical reports, and pension slips. There were poems, love letters, address books, identity papers, bank statements; also newspapers and other bits and pieces piled together helter-skelter. There were notes and letters in Serbo-Croatian, in English, in French, in German, and in Turkish. Early letters displayed a fine flowing handwriting and a romantic streak. In later notebooks—recording every letter sent, every letter received, every cent earned and spent—the writing had shrunk to a spidery punctiliousness. Not only had the youthful journalist and musician assumed the new Turkish identity of Ali Erhan, he had become a pedant.

On scraps of paper, there were notes, apparently written to himself, that suggested the loneliness and fear that became part of Sead's father's life: "I now live like a hermit on the outskirts of Moscow. I communicate only with those who guard me from others—and guard others from me," one said.

I imagined Alija, alone, walking slowly through the narrow streets of some Turkish town, a hat drawn down over his eyes, making his way to some café where he would sit with a cigarette and a newspaper, as he had once sat in Sarajevo. When a stranger walked in he would avert his gaze until he was satisfied that the stranger was not also his designated killer.

There was another jotting, in English, evidently written to himself on his arrival in Turkey and entitled "Letter to a New Expatriate": " 'What a civilized city,' you said, as you stood on the doorstep of your house, your rented castle, looking up and down the quiet street. The mellow lamplight and the shadow of the trees combined to form a second dusk, in which the sounds of nearing footsteps and the noise of an approaching car brought only mild curiosity, not apprehension." For how long, I wondered, had Alija lived with this fear of "nearing footsteps" and "approaching cars"?

More wretched still, there was this cri de coeur that seemed to express Alija's anguish at his abandonment of his little boy, Sead: "He never found the boy. And now, said a neighbor, he raves like a madman, and in his eyes there is an expression beyond words." The boy in question was surely Sead; the madman, beneath a moderate exterior, was clearly Alija, pushed to the edge by exile and the pressure of a life split in two.

Details on Alija's childhood were scanty. His high-school diploma, which lay among the papers in the suitcase, revealed that he was born on December 16, 1911, in the northwestern Bosnian town of Prijedor, the son of Emina and Ahmed Mehmedović. He was thus born, like Tito, into the realm of Austria-Hungary, for the Habsburgs had formally annexed Bosnia-Herzegovina in 1908, having ruled it since 1878. The family was apparently one of modest means; Ahmed worked as a "technical clerk." Within three years, in 1914, the boy's life was engulfed by world war—just as that of his three-year-old son Sead would be in 1941.

There is no record of the family's movements during World War I, the conflict that destroyed the Austro-Hungarian and Ottoman empires and led to the creation of Yugoslavia on their former territories. But by the early 1930s, Alija Mehmedović was in the eastern Bosnian town of Bijeljina, attending the "royal state high-school." He was, to judge by a school report written in both the Latin and Cyrillic alphabets, an extremely gifted student. In Latin, history, biology, physics, mathematics, and chemistry, he was graded four, the second-highest mark, and described as a "very good" student. In religious instruction, French language, German language, conduct, and philosophy, he was deemed "excellent" and received fives. He also received a five for a subject called "Serbo-Croato-Slovenian language and literature." This hybrid subject was symbolic of the new Yugoslav state's striving to forge a shared national consciousness among its constituent peoples, a campaign that was crucial to the state's future.

YUGOSLAVIA OWED its birth in 1918 partly to ideals—ideals of America and ideals emergent in the Balkans. Woodrow Wilson, the American president and the chief architect of Europe's new order after World War I, dreamed of self-determination for European peoples. He wanted to seize on the collapse of the Austro-Hungarian, the Ottoman Turkish, the German, and the Tsarist Russian empires—the four great, multinational dominions that had been the pillars of the nineteenth-century European order—to build something new.

The liberation of European nations from imperial rule, Wilson believed, would be a step toward a more just world, one amenable to administration by his ill-fated creation, the League of Nations. The management of human affairs, Wilson insisted, could be raised from the messy balancing of conflicting interests to the enforcement of the rule of law in the name of the universal good. The sprawling dynasties of the Ottomans, the Habsburgs, the Hohenzollerns, and the Romanovs would give way to self-governing nations. In this way would the horrors of the Battle of the Somme, Verdun, and the western front be consigned to the past, the extinguished lamps of Europe be lit once more.

At the same time some South Slav intellectuals dreamed of the union in Yugoslavia of peoples linked by blood and language but long governed by the Ottoman Turkish or Austro-Hungarian empires and never previously gathered into a single state. These two distant currents, of the new and the old world, whose common professed wellspring was the idea of the liberation of peoples, merged. The Kingdom of Serbs, Croats, and Slovenes— later Yugoslavia—came into being in December 1918. Its existence was ratified at the Paris Peace Conference of 1919, where President Wilson played a decisive role.

Yugoslavia, like the United States, was thus an idea as well as a state. It was a marriage of interests, certainly, but it also coalesced around the notion of offering new freedom to long-subjugated peoples.

The ideals and the reality naturally stood some distance from each other. The Ottoman and the Habsburg empires had not been monuments to the oppression of their national minorities; tolerance was quite widespread. Moreover, Yugoslavia was itself quite clearly a multinational state; the fact that Sead's father had studied a subject called "Serbo-Croato-Slovenian language and literature" underscored this fact. Yet idealism, however deluded, informed the new state's creation.

The idea of Yugoslavia, the ideals that inspired it, were noble. The gamble inherent in "Yugoslavism" was that the many migrations across the land of the new state had left peoples marked by such miscegenation that no border could reasonably be drawn between them. The idea demanded that the Drina River, running through the middle of the new Yugoslav state, cease to be what it had long been—a line of fracture between the Western Catholic and the Eastern Orthodox worlds—and become instead the spinal cord of one Yugoslav body.

This ambition had some solid foundations: the South Slavs were all descended from tribes that came late in the long Indo-Iranian migration into Europe and that moved southward across the Danube into the Balkans in the sixth and seventh centuries. By the twentieth century, their blood was indistinguishable and their languages intimately related. The Corfu Declaration of July 1917, which laid the basis for the creation of Yugoslavia, stated that the Serbs, Croats, and Slovenes were one people, "the same by blood, by language, both spoken and written."

But there were also dangers. Whatever their many similarities, the historical and cultural experiences of the three peoples were distinct. The Corfu document understandably sidestepped the fact of protracted historical division. It also ignored the fact that Serbs, Croats, and Slovenes were not alone in Yugoslavia. There were also Macedonians, Albanians—and Bosnian Muslims. In the number of peoples and cultures it sought to embrace, Yugoslavia was, as the Slovenian president Milan Kučan once put it to me, "a very demanding conglomerate."

IT WAS a demanding conglomerate partly because, in the fifteenth century, the Ottoman Turks had added Islam to what later became the Yugoslav equation. The Turks captured Constantinople in 1453 and began the conquest of Bosnia nine years later. Bosnia had enjoyed the apogee of its independent power in the late fourteenth century, under King Tvrtko I. It was a land of distinct topology; its mountains, narrow valleys, and countless rivers tended to encourage parochial loyalties rather than the establishment of loyalty to a single authority.

Broadly, the Catholic church was stronger in the north and west of Bosnia, Orthodox Christianity stronger in the southern region of Herzegovina, and the heretical Church of Bosnia was strongest in the center. Firm historical evidence on the Church of Bosnia is scanty, but many Bosnians believe that their heretical forebears formed part of the Bogomil ("dear to God") sect that was active in Bulgaria.

What seems clear is that the Church of Bosnia represented a blend of Catholicism and the Bogomils' belief in a dualistic religious system where God and the Devil held equal power. It seems clear, also, that these ascetic Christian sectaries, having rejected the hierarchy of the Catholic church, saw in the Ottoman Turks and Islam a refuge from the twin pressures of the Catholic and the Orthodox worlds of which Croatia and Serbia were respectively a part.

Conversions to Islam were more widespread among followers of the Church of Bosnia than among the state's Christians, whether Orthodox or Catholic. But many Catholics and Orthodox Bosnians also became Muslims. The Turks, for their part, appear to have made more strenuous efforts in Bosnia than elsewhere in the Ottoman Empire to win the local population over to their religion. Because Bosnia represented the front line of the westward Turkish thrust into Europe, this proselytizing was of obvious strategic interest. The general weakness of the church in Bosnia—whether Catholic, Orthodox, or the local Bosnian sect—made the forces of Islam

916–1399: Middle Ages

AUSTRIA

Budapest

0   Kilometers   100

0   Miles   100

Drava

Danube

SLOVENIA

Ljubljana

Trieste

Drava

Zagreb

HUNGARY

CROATIA

VOJVODINA

ROMANIA

Sava

Zadar

DALMATIA

BOSNIA AND
HERZEGOVINA

Belgrade

Danube

Sarajevo

SERBIA

BULGARIA

ADRIATIC SEA

Niš

Sofia

Ragusa
(Dubrovnik)

KOSOVO

ITALY

MONTENEGRO

Uskub
(Skopje)

MACEDONIA

ALBANIA

GREECE

Boundary of Croatia under
King Tomislav, 916–928

Boundary of Serbia under
King Dušan, 1331–1355

Boundary of Bosnia under
King Tvrtko, 1371–1399

1945 international boundary

more seductive; there were also clear social and material advantages to be gained through conversion to Islam. These factors ensured that a large number of Bosnians—Alija Mehmedović's ancestors among them—became Muslims. Nowhere else in the great sprawl of the Ottoman Empire did such mass conversion occur.

So it was that the new Yugoslav state of 1918 came to straddle an exceptional number of borders. By its geography and its history, the state could only survive as a link between "Latins" and "Byzantines," between "Christians" and Muslim "infidels," between the "civilized" and the "barbarians." The towns that were the most eloquent expressions of its eclecticism—were as delicate as wafers, built from the sediment of countless migrations, their stones smoothed into an unlikely harmony by the passing of time. Only if this beauty was respected, and if Bosnia's Muslim-Orthodox-Catholic heart breathed, could Yugoslavia survive.

THE SERB-CROAT FLIRTATION that led to the state's birth began early in the nineteenth century. When Napoleon seized Slovenia and the Dalmatian coast from the Habsburgs in 1805, he gave the newly conquered Slavic lands the name "Illyrian Provinces," reviving a term used by the Romans for the people living in this part of the Balkan Peninsula. The name was intended to convey the French conviction that the South Slavs were all one "Illyrian" people speaking the same "Illyrian" language; the political intent of the designation was to strengthen the unity of the South Slavs and so their "liberation" from the Habsburg dominion. The term was inaccurate, in that the original Illyrian inhabitants had been largely superseded by the Slavs—Serbs and Croats—who had crossed the Danube and settled the Balkan Peninsula in the sixth and seventh centuries. The Illyrian Provinces, moreover, did not last long, because Napoleon was defeated in 1814. But the word and the idea proved politically fecund.

In the Illyrian Provinces lay the germ of the Illyrian movement, a gathering of Slovenian, Croatian, and Serb intellectuals committed to the assertion of the cultural and linguistic identity of the South Slavs and the pressing of their independent political rights. Some idea of the movement's importance may be gleaned from the fact that use of the word *Illyrian* was forbidden by the Austrian government in 1842.

The ban backfired. The term *Illyrian* was progressively replaced by the word *Yugoslav* as the banner of South Slav emancipation from the Habsburgs. *Jug* means "south" in the Slavic languages.

Language, as the embodiment of a national consciousness, was a cornerstone of the Yugoslav movement against Habsburg domination. At the beginning of the nineteenth century, the Slovenian scholar Jernej Kopitar, working in the Austrian capital, researched the past of the Slovenian language and revived its use; the Slovenian poet France Prešern captured its beauty. In Croatia, an important literary and linguistic renaissance was led by Illyrian leader Ljudevit Gaj, who edited a paper called *The Illyrian Morning Star* (*Danica Ilirska*).

Gaj and his followers made an important choice for the future of South Slav unity: they opted for the use of the Štokavski dialect in their paper, the dialect spoken by many Croats but also by all Serbs, rather than one of the dialects that was spoken only by Croats, the Kajkavski or Čakavski dialects. The Štokavski dialect had been codified and popularized by the Serbian scholar and writer Vuk Karadžić, who, before his death in 1864, popularized Serbian culture by publishing popular songs, poems, stories, and the Gospel in a language that was written as it was spoken. Vuk Karadžić himself was no "Yugoslav"; he assumed that almost all speakers of the Štokavski dialect were really Serbs. It was Serbian expansion, rather than Yugoslav integration, that interested him. Nevertheless, a common language became the basis for a shared South Slav movement. It was later invigorated by Josip Strossmayer, the influential Croatian bishop who founded the Yugoslav Academy in Zagreb in 1867, and by Dalmatian politicians.

But there were other currents that conflicted with the new spirit of Yugoslavism and these tended to set Croat against Serb. Each assumed the superiority, even the exclusive existence, of a Croat or a Serb nation. Rather than asserting what was shared between the two peoples, the creeds tended to stress their incompatibility.

THE ROOTS OF THIS FRICTION, fratricidal in intensity, went deep. In 395, after the death of the Roman emperor Theodosius, the border between the Western Roman Empire and the Eastern empire of Byzantium was set on the Drina River. The West became the province of the bishop of Rome, the East of the patriarch of Byzantium. Over centuries, the Orthodox Serbs to the east and the Catholic Croats to the west, South Slavs both of them, came to believe that they lived on the front line of a war of civilizations.

After the mission to the Balkans of the Greek monks Saints Cyril and Methodius in the ninth century, the Cyrillic alphabet and the Byzantine rites were generally adopted to the east of the river, the Latin alphabet and Roman rites to the west. This division was envenomed by the Great Schism of 1054, when the papal legate in Constantinople excommunicated the Byzantine heretics who worshiped at the altar of Santa Sofia.

The theological differences between East and West were not enormous: they centered on whether, as the Catholic church held, the Holy Spirit of the Trinity stemmed from the Father and the Son (*filioque*) or from God

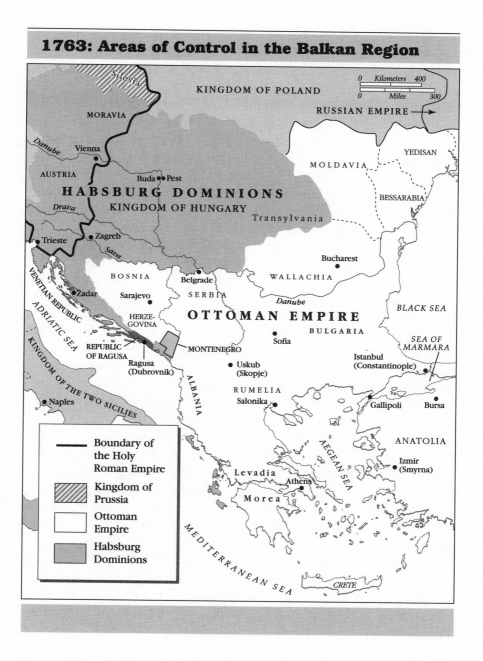

1763: Areas of Control in the Balkan Region

KINGDOM OF POLAND

Silesia

MORAVIA

RUSSIAN EMPIRE

0   Kilometers   400
0   Miles   300

Danube

Vienna

YEDISAN

MOLDAVIA

AUSTRIA

Buda • • Pest

BESSARABIA

HABSBURG DOMINIONS

KINGDOM OF HUNGARY

Drava

Transylvania

Zagreb

Trieste

Sava

BOSNIA

Bucharest

WALLACHIA

Belgrade

VENETIAN REPUBLIC

Zadar

Sarajevo

SERBIA

Danube

BLACK SEA

HERZE-
GOVINA

OTTOMAN EMPIRE

ADRIATIC SEA

REPUBLIC
OF RAGUSA

MONTENEGRO

BULGARIA

SEA OF
MARMARA

KINGDOM OF THE TWO SICILIES

Ragusa
(Dubrovnik)

Sofia

Istanbul
(Constantinople)

Uskub
(Skopje)

ALBANIA

Naples

RUMELIA

Salonika

Gallipoli

Bursa

ANATOLIA

AEGEAN SEA

Levadia

Izmir
(Smyrna)

Athens

Boundary of
the Holy
Roman Empire

Morea

Kingdom of
Prussia

Ottoman
Empire

Habsburg
Dominions

MEDITERRANEAN SEA

CRETE

the Father alone, as the Orthodox church to the east insisted. But these different interpretations were enough to lock the Serb and Croat representatives of what may be called the Eastern and Western civilizations in an intermittent antagonism.

Miroslav Krleža, the Croatian writer, once suggested that "Serbs and Croats come from the same manure, divided only by the wagon-wheel of history." The wagon wheel proved effective. The scant differences between Serbs and Croats were progressively accentuated by layers of sophistry about the frontiers between civilization and barbarism, between Western rigor and Eastern intrigue, between vulgar Oriental hordes and cultured Western Europeans. The Serbs will tell you that the East is a culture of grace, while the West is merely a culture of law. The Croats view the Serbs with a certain Mitteleuropäische hauteur. They will tell you that the Serbs are Byzantines—devious, slothful, vulgar.

These stereotypes emerged from the historical fact that Serbia fell for centuries under the Ottoman Turkish Empire, Croatia under the Austro-Hungarian. In the view of Serbs, the Croats were reduced to emasculated speechifiers by the long dominion of Hungary and later the Habsburgs. For Croats, the Serbs were turned into a nation of boorish brutes by the long dominion of the Ottomans. In fact much of Croatia had also been overrun and governed by the Turks for almost two centuries, and its Dalmatian coastline was long ruled by Venice. The shared history of both Serbs and Croats was one of adaptation to foreign rule.

Serbia began its emancipation from empire earlier than Croatia. The peasant uprisings of 1804 and 1815 opened the way for Serbian independence from the Ottoman Empire. By 1878, Serbia's status as an independent state had been formalized at the Congress of Berlin. In Vienna, Serbia's potential as a magnet to the restive South Slavs of the empire was quickly apparent. Relations between the Habsburgs and Belgrade were tense.

Serbia naturally tended to see itself as the leader of the South Slavs' struggle for independence and unification, the Piedmont of the Balkan Peninsula. It also tended to confound this unification and the territorial expansion of Serbia. For many politicians in Serbia, as for Vuk Karadžić, the "liberation" of the South Slavs—Serbs, Croats, Slovenes, Bosnian Muslims—and the extension of Serbian territory were synonymous. They saw no contradiction between the two ideas.

Such views were already apparent in a secret document simply called "Program" (*Načertanije*) prepared by a conservative Serbian stateman named Ilija Garašanin. This tract of 1844 called for the reinforcement of the nascent Serbian state and its extension to embrace all Serbs, including those living in Bosnia (then under Ottoman control) and in Croatia and

Vojvodina (then under the control of Vienna and Budapest). The assumption—widely shared in Serbia—was that these Serbs living beyond the Drina or the Sava rivers, who were known as *"prečani* Serbs," and other South Slavs would naturally welcome unification in an enlarged Serbian state.

The most extreme expression of such ideas came in the Union or Death movement, founded in Belgrade in 1911. Its constitution called for the "unification of Serbdom: all Serbs, regardless of sex, religion or place of birth can become members and anyone else who is prepared to serve this idea faithfully." In that Serbs were defined essentially by their Orthodox religion, the bizarre call to all Serbs "regardless of religion" betrayed the extremists' conviction that Bosnian Muslims or Croats were in reality Serbian Muslims or Serbian Catholics who had lost sight of their true identity. Among those influenced by the movement were Serb radicals in Bosnia, including Princip, who would assassinate the Habsburg heir in 1914.

This Greater Serbian idea was obviously a far cry from the "Yugoslavism" flowering among Croat and Serb intellectuals of the Austro-Hungarian empire, for whom any Yugoslav state was conceived as a marriage of equals rather than a collective bowing to a single national group.

CROATIA HAD a counterpart to expressions of Serbian fanaticism. Ante Starčević, a former adherent to Illyrianism, founded the Croatian Party of Rights in 1861. Starčević's argument was that all the South Slavs were Croats. The Serbs, Slovenes, and Bosnian Muslims were all Croatian in origin and essence. As a natural corollary, he believed that these people should all be included in any future Croatian state, which would embrace much of the land in the Balkan Peninsula. Starčević even proclaimed that the Serbian rulers, the Nemanjić dynasty, who took Serbia to the apogee of its medieval power in the thirteenth century, were Croats of "the purest blood."

Starčević's own blood, like that of many of the nationalist fanatics of the Balkan Peninsula, was mixed: his mother was a Serb. Nevertheless, he insisted that as long as the Serbs of Croatia did not grasp their essential Croat identity, they were inferior beings, virtual slaves. Indeed, in a tract published in 1868 called *The Name Serb* (*Ime Srb*), he argued that the word *Srb* came from the Latin *servus,* meaning a slave. The Serbs' only hope of salvation lay in abandoning their national consciousness (embodied in the Orthodox religion), converting to Catholicism, and so "becoming Croats." He developed his own version of the Croatian language, intended to distinguish Croatian completely from the language spoken in Serbia. Taking Tomislav's tenth-century Croatian state as his model, he assumed

that Bosnia-Herzegovina was part of Croatia and that the Bosnian Muslims were Croatian "blood brothers." A modern Croatian state, he believed, should harken back to past glory. Indeed it should be seen as a
continuation of the medieval state, for Croats had agreed on a union with
Hungary in 1102 and had not been formally annexed. As Aleksa Djilas,
the historian, has written: "Mystical and fanatical, intolerant and violent,
territorially expansionist and nationally homogenizing, Starčević's ideology contained all the important elements of the ideology of extreme Croatian nationalism in the twentieth century."

So it was that, long before World War I, the seed of Yugoslavia's subsequent agony existed. On the one hand was the Serbian desire for the "unification of Serbdom" and Greater Serbian dominion over the South Slavs.
On the other hand was the Croatian zealotry that held that virtually all the
South Slav peoples were really Croats belonging to a Greater Croatia. Between these poles was the fragile "Yugoslav" movement with its belief that
language, culture, and blood bound the South Slavs and that their union
would bring liberation.

In all these ideologies lurked the argument that the South Slavs were indistinguishable from one another and belonged in one state. But of the
three ideas, "Yugoslavism" was the only one that envisaged a marriage of
equals and did not carry within it an implicit violence, the seeds of a
twentieth-century fascism.

FROM THE AGE OF SEVEN, Alija Mehmedović lived in this new and
fractious country called Yugoslavia. His own marriage in 1937 was profoundly "Yugoslav" in that it involved a broad mixing of central and southeast European blood. His eighteen-year-old bride, Gabriella (Gaby)
Kovač, was a Catholic raised in Croatian Zagreb and Serbian Belgrade. She
was the daughter of a former Austro-Hungarian cavalry officer, Geza
Kovač, who had long been stationed in the Croatian capital and a woman
named Ruža Gostimirović, whose father was the Serb owner of Zagreb's
Palace Hotel and whose mother was Viennese.

Shortly after Gaby's birth in Zagreb in 1919, her parents' marriage collapsed. Her father, out of a job with the dissolution of the Austro-
Hungarian Empire, returned to his native Budapest; her mother refused to
follow. Gaby has only one memory of her father. He had returned to Zagreb to seek a divorce, and Gaby was taken to the station to say good-bye
to him. As they stood on the platform, Geza Kovač drew a revolver from
his pocket and tried to kidnap her. Police intervened. Gaby's last recollection is of her father hanging from the side of the train, waving to her. The
train took him across the new national borders of Wilsonian Europe. She
never heard from him again.

Gaby's relations with her mother were not good. They moved to Belgrade, where her mother took to a life of drinking and card-playing. Sometimes her mother would beat her, telling Gaby she was the image of her father. "She was beating me for looking like my father, she could not stand that," Gaby, a pale and fine-featured woman, told me.

In early 1937, a friend who knew the Ribnikar family, then the owners of *Politika,* took the eighteen-year-old Gaby to the newspaper, where she was given a job as a secretary. On her way to work she would pass a café terrace much frequented by *Politika* employees. One of them was the twenty-five-year-old Alija Mehmedović, then a hard-drinking young journalist and stenographer with a ready wit and a fine voice. Soon Alija had befriended her; she began bringing him to her mother's apartment to play cards. "I looked at Alija as a god," Gaby said, "an escape and relief from my domestic problems."

A story, perhaps apocryphal, surrounds the marriage of Gaby and Alija. One night the young man was playing cards with Gaby's mother and won a lot of money. In lieu of the debt he asked her to sign a piece of paper. Drunk, she did so without looking. When confronted with the paper the next morning she was appalled: she had promised her daughter's hand in marriage to Alija Mehmedović.

The wedding was celebrated on October 23, 1937, at the Bajrakli Mosque in Belgrade. Neither Gaby nor Alija wanted to convert to the other's religion, so the mufti said he could perform the ceremony in an adjacent office but not in the mosque itself. Gaby was already three months pregnant: the couple's son, Sead, was born the following April.

For their honeymoon, the couple went to Budapest. Gaby wanted to search for her father, and during the visit she discovered that Geza Kovač had died of pneumonia in September 1925. As a souvenir of her honeymoon, she collected his death certificate from the Budapest city hall. Throughout her life she would keep a framed photograph of the father she never knew on her wall. It shows him, a handsome upright man, in the full uniform of an Austro-Hungarian cavalry officer.

The marriage between Alija and Gaby was apparently passionate but flawed. It lasted less than two years. Gaby, just nineteen when her son was born, seems to have been in awe of the older Alija, who in turn seems to have been unready for the responsibilities of fatherhood. He enjoyed drinking and carousing; often he would disappear for one or two nights without explanation. When Sead was born, Gaby looked out the window of the hospital to find her husband drunk in the street below, serenading her with his fiddle.

Alija was clearly under pressure from his father, Ahmed, who repeatedly expressed disapproval of the hasty union. He appears to have been disap-

pointed that his Muslim son had married a Catholic. The relationship
with his overbearing father tormented Alija. Short of money and looking
after an aging mother in Sarajevo, Ahmed took it upon himself to fill Alija
with guilt for leading a reckless life in Belgrade. Increasingly, Alija's work
at *Politika,* where he was engaged principally as a stenographer at the Yugoslav parliament, seems to have held little interest for him. Gaby told me
that finally, after a three-night drinking spree, Alija declared that he could
no longer face the owner of *Politika.* He left his job at the paper. In late
1938, broke, he departed for Sarajevo to join his father, who had taken a
job at the Yugoslav Steel Company.

It was a decision he regretted. On November 18, 1938, Alija Mehmedović wrote a letter of passionate longing to his wife Gaby. "My only and
golden one," he began, "I received a letter of yours yesterday, and yet another one today. . . . I am crazy with joy that you are coming and because
of all the beautiful words you wrote to me. Your letter gave me a lot of
strength today, and I am beginning to believe that everything is not as horrible as I supposed it was. I am far from being a model husband (you can
see that from your position), and certainly not the best in the world, as you
wrote. You are exaggerating, but I am encouraged that you understand
me."

Three weeks later, on December 7, 1938, Alija wrote again, a much
darker letter. For reasons that are unclear, Gaby had not come to Sarajevo
after all. A reference to "cleaning weapons" suggests that Alija has been
called up for military service. The letter makes clear that his move to Sarajevo has not been easy. He is broke and suffering from the first of the illnesses that would steadily weaken him over the course of his life. Unable
to deal with married life, he appears to have been equally unable to deal
with the pain and remorse of separation from his wife and seven-month-
old son.

"My one and only," Alija wrote, *"you say that you feel completely broken. That is absolutely understandable because nobody else would have
endured even this much. I myself sometimes feel I cannot endure this and,
without the prospect of a visit, I'd just give up. Sometimes I am on the
verge of going crazy. Countless are the times that I have looked at your
and Sead's photograph. It is all creased already. My few friends, when I
show them your photo, comment: 'You really know what to live for!' And
it is so. But what they do not know is how it feels to be separated from
such a wonderful woman and one's kid.*

*"Sometimes I don't believe that everything is going to end well. I be-
come entirely depressed. I could cry with anger at the impossibility of
coming immediately to Belgrade to arrange things in some way. If I could*

*only get there I believe things would be easier for you also, wouldn't they?
But please don't think about how I feel. I have got used to my situation,
the one I deserved. Never in my life have things been particularly pleasant. That is one of the points over which I constantly quarrel with my
father. Thank God I will have nothing more to do with him. He is a perfectly impossible man and my nerves are weaker and weaker. I will be
calmer only when I see you. How wonderful that will be! But I feel a chill
when I think of what you endure. I often feel remorse because of you. I
have been so selfish. I had no right to marry you when I could not fulfill
my duties. It is horrible to ponder these things day and night.*

*"I feel very weak, especially today. For today I was given an injection
against typhus so my body temperature went up immediately. Anyway I
never feel well. Please write to me about everything, especially you and
Sead. This is the most important thing for me and, as for the rest, I will
deal with it or be ruined. Don't be angry that I am a pessimist. I can't be
different. I must go now because we are being called to assemble. For you
and Sead, many passionate hugs and kisses. . . ."*

When Alija returned to Belgrade nine months later, in September 1939,
it was to attend his divorce hearings in the district Islamic law (*Šerijat*)
court in Belgrade. The court session took place on September 12, 1939,
less than two weeks after Hitler's invasion of Poland and the outbreak of
World War II.

The court's decision stated that Alija Mehmedović no longer considered
Gaby to be his wife "in view of alleged discord and intolerance in their
marriage." He agreed to pay five hundred dinars a month in alimony and
a further five hundred for the support of Sead "for as long as the child is
being raised by his mother." The court concluded that, according to the
provisions of Islamic law, "the existing *Šerijat* marriage is divorced, regardless of whether the discord in the marriage was the wife's fault or not."

A month later, Alija's father Ahmed in Sarajevo wrote to Andjelko
Garović—a friend of the family at *Politika* in Belgrade, making clear that
a custody fight for Sead was about to begin and that he was furious with
his son over his failed marriage. "I reproach him for leaving *Politika* like
this. He fell into the claws of debauched women and he ruined himself,
besides inflicting shame not only on himself but on me as well. Despite his
lavish salary he never helped me with a penny. We suffered and these
women were robbing him. He does not deserve my help but I could not
be heartless toward him. He is a wretched and lost man. I ask you now to
take all his personal possessions from the apartment, as well as books and
dictionaries and small things and underwear, and send them to me in a
suitcase if necessary. I will return the case as soon as I can. If that former

wife of his refuses to give you any of his possessions, tell her to expect me and to expect a lecture on the way she lived with my son.

"Also please tell her that I intend to ask for custody of her son, Sead, because neither my son nor she can support him. . . ."

David Rousset, the French writer on Nazi camps, has noted that "normal people do not know that everything is possible." Until the moment when war intersects with the ebb and flow of private lives, people tend to try to look the other way. Their instinct to do so is natural in that the habits of peace are no preparation for the habits of war, and the collision of distant rumblings of conflict with private lives is never quite believable until it is too late. In 1939 and 1940, Ahmed Mehmedović devoted much energy to the single-minded quest to wrest his grandson Sead from Gaby. But in the tidal wave of World War II, this struggle over a small boy was quickly washed away.

THE TRAINS
OF HISTORY

An image I kept finding in the Balkans was included in a note in Alija Mehmedović's suitcase. Written in English, it said: "We can control the flood, but what can we do against *the cyclone?* We can only pray to Allah for mercy."

Alija was a Slavic Muslim born into the Habsburg Empire, bearing the religion of the Ottoman Empire; a man absorbed as a seven-year-old child into Yugoslavia, undone by Yugoslavia's destruction during World War II, and forced to slip away after the victory of Tito's communist forces in 1945. But who was he? I gazed at photographs of the young man—a life caught in the maw of a cruel century for the people of Central Europe. For Western Europeans, World War II had lasted six years, 1939 to 1945. For many Central Europeans, those on the wrong side of Yalta's cleavage, it would go on for five decades, until 1989. How, I wondered, would Alija have fared in Paris or London or New York?

The narrow, clean-cut face was dominated by intelligent eyes, a strong nose, and a sensuous mouth. That Alija could charm people was obvious. He was good-looking; the eyes suggested humor, a capacity for a clownish eccentricity. He wrote well; he was widely read. But he was also, by his own admission in a letter to his wife, a pessimist, a Bosnian more inclined to believe in fate than in the power of the individual, and it appeared from his dealings with Gaby, and from his relationship to his overbearing father, that his dashing demeanor masked weakness and cowardice. In the eyes there was not only intelligence; there was a wounded look, half-hidden, the lingering expression of a dog too often beaten. To imagine him veering between manic exuberance and black depression was not difficult. He had more charisma than confidence, more brilliance than ballast, more bravura than moral or financial security. In short, he looked vulnerable. It was this vulnerability, perhaps, that made him a conformist.

There was a yellowing Sarajevo newspaper, dated July 6, 1941, in Alija's suitcase. Three months had by then elapsed since the Nazis had entered Zagreb and installed the Croat fascist Ante Pavelić as the *Poglavnik,* or local Duce. Pavelić, an ultra-nationalist in the Starčević tradition, was the founder of the Ustasha (Uprising) movement, whose goal was defined in the 1930s as Croatian independence through terror.

Hitler helped the Ustasha achieve this aim. Under Nazi attack, Yugoslavia imploded. The Independent State of Croatia, or Nezavisna Država Hrvatska (NDH), was established. Croatia's obsessions, after more than nine centuries without sovereignty, may be understood from the fact that the word *independent* was included in the formal name of the quisling state. The country's sovereignty was in fact pitifully slight. Independent Croatia was an oxymoron, a puppet of Hitler's Berlin. It was divided into a German occupation zone in the north and a more tolerant Italian occupation zone in the south. The NDH, embracing Starčević's old vision, helped itself to a large chunk of Yugoslavia, including Sarajevo and all of Bosnia.

Alija's yellowing Sarajevo newspaper reflected these upheavals. Its name was *The New Sarajevo Newspaper, Croatian Information Daily.* Its Sarajevo address was 70 Ante Pavelić Street (later Marshal Tito Street). The top left-hand corner of its front page was emblazoned with the *šahovnica,* the red-and-white checkerboard shield that had long been a Croatian emblem and that Pavelić took as the symbol of his regime, adding a U for Ustasha to the center of the shield. So it was that the *šahovnica* became a symbol of terror for Serbs.

The paper's lead headline on July 6, 1941, was "Important Moves by the Leader." It referred to the "crystalline and untouchable" words of Pavelić, his legitimate contempt for the "greed, violence, corruption, bribery and exploitation" rampant in democratic states, and his unmasking of the conspiracies of "Jews and their plutocratic companions."

Advice to "Croats, Muslims and Catholics" renting property from Jews or Jewish organizations appeared on page three. They were told to pay rent only to an NDH government agency headed by one Josip Zubić, and refuse any payment to the Jews. A statement signed by Zubić read: "We have discovered that some Jewish real estate owners have dared to cancel rental contracts to Aryans because they received no rent from their lodgers. We are warning them *to stop with this nonsense.* We also notify all those who received such so-called cancellations from the Jews that these notifications are totally invalid."

On the next page, squeezed between the Domestic News section, listings for Sarajevo's five cinemas (three German films, one Hungarian, and one Mexican), and prices for textiles, I found a small announcement that

explained why Alija had kept this particular copy of the newspaper. "Mr. Alija Mehmedović, a contributor to our paper, and Miss Saima Kadić, daughter of Dr. Mustafa Kadić from Bosanska Dubica, got married," it said. "Cordial congratulations to the gentle bride and bridegroom."

Less than two years after his divorce from Gaby, Alija had married for a second time. His bride came from a prominent Bosnian Muslim family. He had also become a journalist for a paper peddling Pavelić's anti-Serb and anti-Semitic propaganda in Bosnia.

Most of page five of the paper was dedicated to the death and funeral of an Ustasha officer, Mijo Babić, who had died "heroically" on July 3, 1941, in a battle with "Serbian Chetniks." The Chetniks were originally irregular army units that played a role in Serbia's struggle for liberation from the Ottoman Turkish Empire. Later, during Yugoslavia's first royalist incarnation, they were associated with nationalist paramilitarism. During World War II, after Yugoslavia's temporary disintegration beneath the Nazi onslaught, the term *Chetnik* went through another semantic shift, coming to signify the mainly Serb guerrilla forces led by Draža Mihailović.

Babić was praised for his courage in confronting the Croats' "eternal enemy"—the Serbs. On the following page there were details of curfews in one Bosnian town: Jews were not allowed to leave their homes between 6:00 P.M. and 7:00 A.M. For Serbs, the restrictions were a little less stringent. They were confined to their homes between 8:00 P.M. and 7:00 A.M. Another article told the story of the imminent trial of a Serb "embezzler" and "murderer" from Banja Luka who had been an "exponent of the Serbian regime," "living in luxury while ordinary people suffered in poverty." The Contemporary Humor column offered this: "What does a Jew do when he catches his wife in bed with another man? He sells the bed."

How had Alija come to work for such a paper? Gaby had a copy of a money order she sent to Alija in Sarajevo two years earlier through one of his closest friends at the time, Abu Koen, a Jew who worked for *Politika*. (Koen was later hanged by the Ustasha.) The friendship with Koen, and Gaby's recollections of her husband in Belgrade before the war, suggested that he was not some visceral anti-Semite or Serb-hater. "I never heard him speaking against the Jews or the Serbs," Gaby said.

The couple had been in contact as late as November 1940, more than a year after their divorce. A letter in the suitcase revealed that on November 16 of that year, Gaby wrote to Alija, telling him that Sead was well, enclosing photographs of him, and making clear that she was ready to bring the boy to Sarajevo for a visit. She had been frustrated by Alija's failure to reply to two earlier letters, but she still felt goodwill toward her former husband. "My letters," she wrote, "concerned our agreement from October that I am to bring Sead to you so that you can see him and spend a few days with him. Not only did I keep my word; it was my wish to do so. But you did not reply. I really find that very strange."

Gaby did travel once to Sarajevo with the young Sead. But Alija finally appears to have given way to pressures from his father, the very man with whom he had earlier vowed to sever all contact. A letter sent by Ahmed to Gaby on December 14, 1940, and endorsed by Alija, was full of a new menace.

Ahmed urged her to give Sead up to his custody at once. It was "in the interest of the child to let us have him and raise him and take care of him." He was scornful of a lawyer that Gaby had contacted because "he should at least have been born a Muslim to know anything about *Šerijat* law." A thinly veiled threat followed: if Gaby refused to yield Sead immediately, he would come and get him. "Don't be surprised at anything, because I will have the child anytime I want, wherever you put him, and you will have neither the time nor the legal possibility to prevent that."

Alija, in a short postscript, urged Gaby to "treat this proposal as my own." The affair, he added, can "only be solved through my father, or my lawyer."

Three decades later, in a letter to a friend, Gaby reflected on the reasons for Alija's abandonment of her. "I can't understand that destiny has been so cruel to us," she wrote. "I believe that Alija only abandoned us under the pressure of his father's intolerance and his own self-criticism. At our parting he brought me violets and we were saying good-bye to each other for a painfully long time and we were both crying. We met once more in Sarajevo and it was painful again, but after that his father threatened me that he was going to take Sead away from me if I tried to see Alija again without his knowledge. Alija then gave up asking for the child. He said he did not need him without me."

Perhaps Alija had already met Saima Kadić and his ultimate estrangement from Gaby also reflected his desire to remarry. In any event, the war that engulfed Yugoslavia in April 1941 cut contacts between Belgrade and Sarajevo. Gaby, marking her distance from Alija and playing it safe in the tense climate of war, reverted to her maiden name of Kovać and had Sead baptized in late 1941. Her son's name was formally changed to the Serb-sounding Aleksandar.

Names and religions in the Balkan Peninsula have ever been so—flexible, susceptible to the ebb and flow of different armies. *"Može da bidne al ne mora da znaci"*—"It may be so, but not necessarily"—is a frequent saying along Serbia's Morava River. As fortunes changed, people hedged their bets. Pragmatism, not pride, has often greeted the invader. The fanatical attachment to ideas of nation has grown in inverse proportion to the provable authenticity of any national allegiance in the lands that made up Yugoslavia.

As soon as he took power, Pavelić made a determined attempt to co-opt Muslims like Alija Mehmedović. "Croat national consciousness never was extinguished in the Muslim element of Bosnia, and after the departure of the Turks has resurfaced," the *Poglavnik* declared in Zagreb. He called the Muslims "the flower" of the Croatian nation. The point was to persuade the Bosnian Muslims that they were really Croats of Islamic confession and to then win them over to the struggle against the Serbs. But many Muslims spoke out against the Ustasha, signing a Declaration of Sarajevo on October 12, 1941 that denounced massacres of the Serbs.

Alija, however, was seduced. Short of money, frustrated, out of a job, under the sway of an embittered father who found some solace in the Nazis' railing against the "plutocrats," engaged in a new romance, he may have seen a road to success and prosperity opening up before him with the arrival of the Ustasha. After he moved to Sarajevo, he had complained of being rebuffed when he approached the local office of *Politika:* resentment against its Serbian owners, even against his former wife in Belgrade, may also have played a part. I do not believe that Alija Mehmedović had any overwhelming predisposition to become a Nazi sympathizer. In other circumstances he might never have toyed with such ideas. He was a conformist, a bohemian only when drunk. There was fatalism and a kind of cowardice in him, but no evidence before 1941 of any attraction to fanatical violence. But just as Belgrade was swept by a revolutionary fever in the late 1980s, so was Sarajevo in 1941. It is but a small step to board such bandwagons; principled defiance, I came to believe in the Balkans, is not common. In his "Advice to a Young Writer," Danilo Kiš warned: "Do not be obsessed by historical urgency and do not believe the metaphor about the trains of history. So do not jump on the 'trains of history,' because that is just a stupid metaphor." Kiš knew well that such trains can have a monstrous momentum.

PAVELIĆ REPRESENTED the deranged expression of Croatian resentment at Serbian domination of Yugoslavia. He returned from exile in Benito Mussolini's Italy on April 16, 1941, wearing a black fascist tunic. The day after he was made ruler, a decree was passed stating that anyone who harmed the "honor and vital interests of the Croatian people or threatens in any way the existence of the Independent State of Croatia" faced the death penalty.

Among those considered to represent such a threat were Serbs and Jews. Like the Jews in Hitler's Germany, many were made to wear armbands. An exhibition was mounted in Zagreb, portraying the Jews as physically grotesque and morally vile. Use of the Cyrillic alphabet was banned on April 25, 1941. Pavelić's aim was clear: to head a religio-racial campaign that would solve the "Serbian question," ridding Croatia and Bosnia of the approximately two million Serbs or Orthodox Christians living there, as well as a much smaller population of Jews and Gypsies. Many Croats, including Vlatko Maček, the most influential prewar politicians, deplored such measures and were arrested. Other Croats went underground and joined Tito when his Partisan movement became active three months later. But Pavelić, backed by the Nazis and a hard core of fanatical Croats, was in a position to impose his will.

There were three methods for ridding Croatia of Serbs: slaughter, eviction, and forced conversion from Orthodoxy to Catholicism. Viktor Gutić, the Ustasha prefect of western Bosnia, coined a fertile term to describe the process; he called it "cleansing" (čišćenje). The numbers killed remain a matter of bitter dispute, but they were high enough, on any estimate, to classify Pavelić as a fascist killer of the first order.

The Ustasha terrorist movement grew out of the clash of expectations surrounding Yugoslavia's creation. Violence was inherent in so skewed a state. The assassination on June 20, 1928, in parliament in Belgrade of Stjepan Radić, the leader of the Croatian Peasant party and the most influential political figure in Croatia, intensified Croatian anger. Radić had always considered the formation of Yugoslavia precipitate. Croats, he warned, had rushed into union with Serbia "like drunken geese in the fog." There was insufficient basis for a Yugoslav state, Radić said, asserting that "it needs more to make a nation than an assimilation of tongues." His words proved prescient. The tenth anniversary, on December 1, 1928, of the founding of Yugoslavia was marked by rioting in Zagreb; twelve people were killed.

Soon afterward, on January 6, 1929, King Aleksandar, representing the Serbian dynasty, established a royal dictatorship. He abolished the political parties, dissolved the assembly, and inaugurated a period of personal rule aimed partly at forging a new Yugoslav identity through the eradication of national borders within the state and their replacement by nine "banovinas," or governorships. In the interests of reinforcing this gerrymandered unity, the Kingdom of Serbs, Croats, and Slovenes was formally renamed Yugoslavia.

Pavelić, then the secretary of Starčević's Croatian Party of Rights, fled into exile, where he founded the Ustasha movement. Its most audacious single act was the assassination, on October 9, 1934, of King Aleksandar, shortly after he arrived in Marseilles to begin a state visit to France. The assassin was a Macedonian, but he was in the pay of the Ustasha.

In the five years before World War II, a scramble ensued to patch up
Croat-Serb relations, but tensions had grown to the point where they were
essentially unbridgeable. A concordat designed to please the Croats was
signed in Rome in 1935. But opposition from the Serbian Orthodox
church led to its being withdrawn three years later. As tensions mounted
in Europe, and it became clear that the Yugoslav state would not hold together in a war, the Serbian prince regent, Pavle, encouraged negotiations
aimed at securing Croatian loyalty to Yugoslavia through the belated concession of sweeping autonomy.

But it was late in the day. Serbia had shown insensitivity toward the feelings of the other peoples gathered in Yugoslavia. One figure suggests how
far Serbian domination went: of 165 Yugoslav generals on the eve of
World War II, 161, or 97.5 percent, were Serb. Croats were virtually excluded from the top ranks of the royalist Yugoslav army despite the fact
that, of 375 generals in the Austro-Hungarian army at the outbreak of
World War I, 57, or 15 percent, were Croat.

The Croat-Serb talks resulted, on the eve of the war, in the *sporazum*
(agreement), signed for Croatia by Maček and for Serbia by Dragiša
Cvetković. The land accorded to a largely autonomous Croatia embraced
Slavonia, Dalmatia, and part of Bosnia and Herzegovina, including
Mostar and Travnik. In all, the agreement granted an autonomous Croatia about 30 percent of the population and territory of the Yugoslav state;
Bosnia and Herzegovina was to be largely dismembered, divided between
Zagreb and Belgrade. The Croatian entity was granted its own legislative
sabor, or parliament, but the governor, or *ban,* was to be appointed by the
king. The Serbian concessions were real. But for the Ustasha, this offer was
too little too late. Even among many more moderate Croats, Yugoslavia in
any configuration had become unacceptable after two decades of Serbian
political domination.

So IT WAS THAT when the Nazi panzer divisions bulldozed into Zagreb
on April 10, 1941, they were met by an enthusiastic crowd. For the Croats,
Hitler meant independence from Belgrade. To Pavelić and his followers,
Croatia's independence, its first since the medieval kingdom was absorbed
into Hungary in 1102, could only be consolidated through an assault on
the Serbs of Croatia and Bosnia that would wean the area permanently of
Serbian influence. They embarked on a campaign of intense brutality
against the Orthodox Serbs. The Catholic church, in whose name the crusade took place, was, at best, largely acquiescent.

The Ustashas drew strength from the fact that they viewed their campaign as a religious crusade. Mile Budak, a popular novelist, Pavelić's minister of religion and education, and the leading exponent of the regime's

1918–1939: The First Yugoslavia

AUSTRIA

Budapest ○

0 Kilometers 100

0 Miles 100

HUNGARY

SLOVENIA
DRAVA

ITALY

Ljubljana

Trieste •

• Zagreb

CROATIA *SAVA*

Srem

DUNAV

Novi Sad •

Prefecture of
Belgrade

ROMANIA

Banja Luka •

B O S N I A

VRBAS

DRINA

Belgrade ⊙

Zadar
(Italian)

D A L M A T I A

S E R B I A

Sarajevo •

MORAVA

Split •

PRIMORJE

HERZE-
GOVINA

ZETA

Niš •

A D R I A T I C   S E A

(Italian)

Dubrovnik •

MONTENEGRO

Cetinje •

Sofia ○

VARDAR

BULGARIA

Boundary of Yugoslavia, 1939

• Skopje

Banovinas, 1929

MACEDONIA
(SOUTHERN SERBIA)

Croatian *Banovina,* 1939

Tirana ⊙

Austro-Hungarian Empire
(until dissolution in 1918)

ALBANIA

Acquired from
Bulgaria, 1919

Former Ottoman Empire

GREECE

ideology, was unequivocal about the mission of Croatia. Serbs, those who had not been killed or evicted, were to be converted to Catholicism, because they would then "become Croats." "It should be remembered," Budak said, "that the Catholic church, which is neither a terrorist organization nor stupid, led six crusades to recover Christ's grave. Even children joined in crusading wars. If this was so in the eleventh and twelfth centuries, we can be sure that the Church understands our Ustasha struggle."

Some churchmen, among them Archbishop Ivan Šarić of Sarajevo, were outspoken supporters of the Ustasha; Šarić said that Pavelić was "a treasure from heaven." A former Franciscan priest, Tomislav Filipović, was a commander at the Jasenovac concentration camp.

On March 6, 1943, a meeting that exemplified Ustasha thinking took place in the Vatican between a Croatian emissary, Count Erwin Lobkowicz, and Francis Cardinal Spellman, the archbishop of New York. After quoting Archbishop Spellman as saying the Catholic and Orthodox worlds could not coexist in Yugoslavia, Count Lobkowicz laid out his thoughts on the importance of an independent, Catholic Croatia stretching to the Drina River. He sent the following message to the Pavelić regime in Zagreb:

"We pointed out that the present State is now in a very special position in the context of Catholicism and especially through its position between East and West, that the frontier of the Drina guarantees the maintenance of the Catholic position in that sector; and that the rebuilding of Yugoslavia would mean not only the destruction of the Croat people but also of Catholicism and Western culture in those regions. Instead of a western frontier on the Drina, we would have a Byzantine frontier on the Karavanke." The Karavanke Mountains lie between Slovenia and Austria, several hundred miles to the west of the Drina.

This note sent to a regime of murderers—with its facile references to "Western culture" and an encroaching "Byzantine frontier"—reveals the divisive charge concentrated in the Drina's waters and ever unresolved in the Yugoslav state. At the time, "Western culture" was being expressed by the Pavelić regime in the gouged-out eyes, slit throats, and smashed skulls of Serbs, Jews, and Gypsies.

THE BRUNT of the Ustasha onslaught focused on the long defensive strip running broadly along the western and northern borders of Bosnia that had long constituted the Vojna Krajina, or Military Frontier, of the Austro-Hungarian Empire. The southernmost part of this nine-hundred-mile-long line of battle set up by the Habsburgs against the infidel lies in the stark Dinaric Alps, not far from the Yugoslav railway-junction town of Knin. From there, it stretches north into Banija and Kordun, a region of hills and plains near the Sava River. Then the Krajina sprawls westward, embracing the wooded hills of western Slavonia and the flat, fertile farmland of eastern Slavonia. These areas, including towns like Glina, Pakrac, and Knin, were again to be the scene of fierce fighting during the wars of Yugoslavia's destruction.

In the era of the nation-state the Krajina, like the banks of the Drina, was always prone to violence because no neat ethno-national line could be drawn through it. These frontier marches were heavily populated with Serbs, while surrounding areas were Croat. Starting in the sixteenth century, Orthodox settlers had come to these regions. Many of the original settlers appear to have been Vlachs, a nomadic people who practiced the Orthodox religion but did not identify themselves as Serbs until Serbia's national identity became resurgent during the nineteenth century. Under an arrangement codified in 1630 by the Habsburg emperor Ferdinand II, the Krajina settlers enjoyed a large measure of autonomy, religious freedom, and ownership of their land, in exchange for military service on the front line against the Turks. They were ruled directly by the court in Vienna rather than by Zagreb or Budapest. The system was only abolished in 1881 when Austria-Hungary, having taken over the administration of Bosnia from the Ottomans, had no more military frontier to protect.

The Ustasha campaign against these Serbs began in earnest in the summer of 1941—that is, six months *before* the Nazis formally decided on the Final Solution. Entire Serb populations of many villages were rounded up and shot or hacked to death. At Glina, about sixty miles south of Zagreb, close to one thousand Serb peasants were packed into the Orthodox church and slaughtered; the church was then burned down. There were similar massacres at Pakrac, in western Slavonia. Serbs were marched off en masse to death camps of which the most famous is Jasenovac. There were others at Jadovno, Stara Gradiška, Laborgrad, and Djakovo, to name just a few. The focus of the onslaught was the Vojna Krajina. In June 1941, the German plenipotentiary general to the Independent State of Croatia, Glaise von Horstenau, recorded his impression that the Ustashas had gone "stark, raving mad." The barbarity, in short, was such that even a Nazi could claim to be shocked.

In the Kozara Mountain region, south of Jasenovac and north of Omarska, where the old Military Frontier runs east to west, the Krajina Serbs suffered a devastating attack by the Ustasha in the fall of 1942. The Serbs of Herzegovina were also hard hit. In a rare expression of outrage from a Catholic churchman, Alojzije Mišić, the bishop of Mostar, expressed his horror to Pavelić: "From Mostar and from Čapljina a train carried six wagons of mothers, girls and children under eight to the station at Šurmanci. There, they were taken out of the wagons, brought into the hills and thrown alive, mothers and children into deep ravines. In the parish of Klepci, seven hundred schismatics [Serbs] from the surrounding villages were assassinated. Must I continue? In the town of Mostar itself, they have been bound by the hundreds, taken in wagons to the edge of town and cut down like beasts."

How many people were killed in this genocidal assault? The issue has become the focus of much unsavory speculation. Milan Bulajić, a Serbian lawyer, has worked obsessively on this theme for years. In 1996, he completed a list of 19,554 children under the age of fourteen murdered in Jasenovac alone: 12,113 Serbs, 5,312 Gypsies, 1,927 Jews, 127 Croats, 66 Muslims, 2 Slovenes, and 7 unknown. In his view, the total number of victims in Jasenovac amounted to about 200,000; over 600,000 Serbs, he contended, were killed by the Pavelić regime.

At the other end of the spectrum, Franjo Tudjman has suggested that no more than 60,000 people were killed by the Ustasha. The most rigorous research, conducted independently by a Serb historian, Bogoljub Kocović, and a Croat, Vladimir Šerjavić, indicates that between 295,000 and 334,000 Serbs died on the territory of the Independent State of Croatia during the war. What proportion was killed in combat, what proportion in massacres and the camps, is unclear, but it seems that at least 100,000 Serb civilians were murdered by the Ustasha. This is well short of the more outlandish Serbian claims. But by any estimate, as the French writer Paul Garde has pointed out, Ustasha Croatia was the bloodiest regime of Hitler's Europe outside the territories controlled directly by Germany itself. Fascist Italy, Vichy France, Hungary, Romania, Bulgaria, and Slovakia did not come close.

WORLD WAR II MASSACRES, however, were by no means the exclusive preserve of the Ustasha. As Tito's Partisan movement gathered force, it sometimes used massacres and a scorched-earth policy to terrorize people in Bosnia into joining its march.

The Serbian Chetniks led by Draža Mihailović, a Serbian officer who wanted to restore the prewar kingdom of Yugoslavia ruled by the Karadjordjević dynasty, slaughtered thousands of Croats and Muslims in Bosnia.

Mihailović initially put up brave resistance to the Nazis. His movement predated that of Tito, who remained on the sidelines until Hitler attacked Stalin. But, after savage German reprisals against his followers in 1941, including the revenge shooting of over seven thousand Serbs—many of them schoolchildren—at Kragujevac in October, his approach changed. He came to see Tito's communist Partisans as a less formidable enemy than Hitler; he collaborated with the Germans in some operations against Tito's forces. The Chetniks also conducted an intermittent, often savage, cam-

1941: Occupation of Yugoslavia

AUSTRIA

Budapest

Drava

HUNGARY

ROMANIA

0   Kilometers   100

0   Miles   100

Trieste

Ljubljana

Zagreb

Sisak   *Sava*

Drava

Danube

Tisa

BAČKA

Vukovar

Novi Sad

BANAT

Controlled by Germany

Bihać

Banja Luka

GERMAN ZONE

Brčko

Belgrade

Zadar

Knin

ITALIAN ZONE

Sarajevo

INDEPENDENT STATE OF CROATIA

Drina

SERBIA
(Occupied by Germany)

Danube

ADRIATIC SEA

Split

Mostar

(Italian Protectorate)

Morava

Niš

Sofia

Dubrovnik

Prištinа
KOSOVO

BULGARIA

ITALY

MONTENEGRO

Skopje

Tirana

MACEDONIA

ALBANIA
(Occupied by Italy)

(Occupied by Germany)

GREECE

(Occupied by Italy)

—   Frontier of Yugoslavia before April 1941

·······   Italian-German line of division

Annexed by Bulgaria

Annexed by Germany

Annexed by Hungary

Annexed by Italy

Annexed by Italian-occupied Albania

paign against the Muslims of eastern Bosnia and Croats in the west. Initially supported by Yugoslavia's Western allies, including Churchill in Britain, Mihailović was progressively abandoned in favor of Tito on the pragmatic basis that Tito was killing more Nazis.

One Chetnik document called for "the creation and organization of a homogeneous Serbia that should include all the ethnic territory on which Serbs live." There were plans to "cleanse" wide swaths of Bosnia. The village of Foča, on the Drina, for example, was the scene of a Serbian massacre of Muslims in January 1942. Mass killing of Croats occurred in the Knin region and in western Bosnia. This rampage gathered pace in response to the Ustasha onslaught. The Chetniks targeted Muslims as well as Croats partly because of the old Serbian hatred for "the Turk" and partly because some Muslims supported the Ustasha. A unit of the Waffen SS, the Nazi party's elite military forces, formed largely of Muslims, was known as the "Handschar Division."

BETWEEN 1941 AND 1943, Alija Mehmedović appears to have prospered under the Pavelić regime. His second son, Džemal, Sead's half-brother, was born in Sarajevo on September 29, 1942. Soon afterward, the family moved to Zagreb, where Alija was active in the preparation of propaganda for the Pavelić government.

Details of his activities are scanty. Two decades after the war, as Gaby searched for Alija, she received this letter from Blaženka Kremešeć, a friend of Alija's second wife, Saima Kadić. "Saima was my best friend from childhood," Mrs. Kremešeć wrote. "We lived in houses next to each other and were inseparable. But later I went to secondary school in Split and Zagreb and naturally our paths diverged. We met again during the war in Zagreb, when she was already married to Alija. I hardly saw Alija because he spent very little time at home. Saima was always waiting for him for long periods and I would keep her company. Alija was a journalist and he moved in circles very close to the Pavelić government."

Just how close to Pavelić Alija was remains unclear. There is no record of Alija's name in the official Ustasha newspaper published in Zagreb during the war. One rumor suggested that Alija became Pavelić's personal stenographer, but there was no firm evidence of this. I knew from documents in Alija's suitcase that he had later received a pension from the German government in recognition of his services and "injuries" sustained during the war. So I wrote to the German federal archives in Berlin and eventually received a letter from the Bundesarchiv, dated October 10, 1996, that filled in part of Alija Mehmedović's war record. He had, according to official German records, joined the Croat SS Volunteer Division, the precursor of the Muslim Handschar Division, in Zagreb on June 16, 1943.

Hitler had ordered the establishment of this new Muslim division on February 10, 1943. Given the racial policies of the Waffen SS, the plan amounted to something of a revolution. It was one thing for Flemings, Scandinavians, and *Volksdeutsche* (ethnic German) to be recruited to the Aryan ranks of the SS; quite another for Muslims to be admitted. But war is a preeminent school of pragmatism. Increasingly tied down by Tito's Partisans, Hitler needed all the help he could find in Yugoslavia. He and Heinrich Himmler, the Nazi police chief and later interior minister, believed that Bosnian Muslims could be recruited en masse to fight their old Serb enemies.

The target was the recruitment of twenty-six thousand men by August 1943, but, despite a fairly lavish budget, this proved more difficult than they expected. The difficulties stemmed partly from Pavelić's hesitations over the creation of such a division and partly from the reluctance of the Muslims. The Muslims' religious leader, the mufti of Jerusalem, who had fled to Berlin in 1941, toured Croatia in April 1943 to promote the new unit. But his appeal appears to have had little resonance. Many Muslims in Bosnia were press-ganged into the Nazi forces; Alija's war record suggests that he was probably not among these reluctant recruits. The newly created SS oath for the division that Alija took said: "I swear to the Führer, Adolf Hitler, as Supreme Commander of the German Armed Forces, to be loyal and brave. I swear to the Führer, and to the leaders whom he may designate, obedience unto death. I swear to God the Almighty that I will always be loyal to the Croat State and its authorized representative, the *Poglavnik,* that I will always maintain the best interests of the Croat people and always respect the state constitution and laws of the Croat people."

The SS command decided to train the Muslim division at a location distant from the front. In early July 1943, the recruits were transferred to south-central France, near the town of Le Puy. Alija Mehmedović was among them. The letter from the Bundesarchiv said that he "accomplished his basic training as a noncommissioned officer in France."

The training, however, did not go as smoothly as hoped. Tensions were severe between the Muslims—referred to derisively as the "Mujos" by the Germans (a term later favored by nationalists in Zagreb and Belgrade)— and their mainly German or Yugoslav *Volksdeutsche* commanders. On August 6, 1943, Himmler tried to calm the situation by laying out the conditions in which the Muslim soldiers were to work and ordering respect for them:

"All Muslim members of the Waffen SS and police are to be afforded the inalienable right of their religious demands never to touch pork, pork sausages nor to drink alcohol," Himmler wrote. "In all cases a diet of equal value will be assured to them. I hold all commanders, company comman-

ders and other SS officers, especially those officers and NCOs involved
with economic administration, to be responsible for the most scrupulous
and loyal respect for this privilege especially granted to the Muslims. They
have answered the call of the Muslim chiefs and have come to us out of hatred for the common Jewish-Anglo-Bolshevik enemy and through respect
and fidelity for the man they respect above all, the Führer, Adolf Hitler. I
do not wish that through the folly and narrowness of mind of an isolated
person, a single one of the tens of thousands of these brave volunteers and
their families should suffer from ill humor. . . . I forbid jokes and facetious
remarks about the Muslim volunteers."

The appeal was largely unsuccessful. About one thousand members of
the division mutinied at Villefranche-de-Rouergue, about one hundred
miles southwest of Le Puy, on September 16, 1943. A number of noncommissioned officers were killed before the uprising was put down. Several Muslims were executed after conviction by an SS court. Once again
the mufti of Jerusalem was dispatched from Berlin in a bid to encourage
the force and restore discipline.

When training was completed in late September, the division moved to
lower Silesia and then on to Austria. Known by now as the "Bosnian-
Herzegovinian SS Volunteer Mountain-Division (Croat)," it counted 21,065
men at the beginning of 1944, according to German records. Of these, 360
were officers and 1,931—among them Alija Mehmedović—were noncommissioned officers.

In late 1943, however, Alija fell ill. Records from a German sanatorium,
dated December 7, 1970, gave a history of his illnesses: "Yellow fever in
childhood, from 1930 onwards frequent malaria, and in 1943 tuberculosis in the right lung. From 1943, two and a half years in a Vorarlberg sanatorium. Was operated twice. Two ribs were removed in front and four
behind. On the front right side the first and second ribs are missing. At the
back, ribs two through six are missing. Front top a horizontal scar. At the
back a vertical scar from the surgery. The right shoulder is lower. The right
side of the chest hardly moves when breathing. The left side of the di-
aphragm moves well. . . ."

When precisely the operation—aimed at treating tuberculosis through
reducing the volume of the rib cage—was conducted is not clear. On February 5, 1944, he was transferred to the Vorarlberg region of western Austria, where he entered a reserve field hospital called Valduna. His sojourn
there corresponds to the reference to a "Vorarlberg sanatorium" in the later
German medical report. In the Bundesarchiv, there are further records of
him in a Vorarlberg sanatorium dating from October 23, 1944, but none
after that. Whether, as he later told German doctors, Alija really stayed two
and a half years in Vorarlberg—that is, until the end of the war—is un-

clear. But it seems unlikely that Alija ever saw military action with his SS division.

The military action began in earnest in early 1944. By February, the division was at Brčko, the northern Bosnian town on the Sava River that would be the scene of Serb "cleansing" of Muslims in 1992. Between February and September, fighting between the Muslim unit and Tito's Partisans raged.

It was during this time, in May, that Alija's division received its final name of "Handschar." The war around Brčko was bitter, and Tito later accused the Handschar Division of a number of atrocities against the Partisans.

The war turned against the Axis during the Handschar Division's stay in the Brčko area, and the German forces began to withdraw from the southeastern theater in the fall of 1944. Himmler was not satisfied with the performance of his Muslim troops; many of them were released from the division as it pulled out in early October. But some Muslims remained and, with their mainly German or ethnic German officer corps, they fought on, first in Hungary against the advancing Soviet forces, finally in Austria. The remnants of the Handschar Division surrendered to the British on May 7, 1945, at St. Veit an der Glan in Austria, just north of Klagenfurt.

It appears certain that Alija Mehmedović was not with his division at this time. If he was still at the sanatorium in Vorarlberg, he might have been well placed to slip across the Swiss border. What is clear is that Alija was able to escape and in the general tumult of those spring months of 1945, he disappeared. When, later that year, Ahmed informed Gaby that Alija had been killed at the end of the war, she sent letters to Zagreb, Sarajevo, and Tuzla asking the municipal authorities if they had a death certificate for an Alija Mehmedović. She received no reply. Reluctantly she resigned herself to the likelihood that Alija had indeed been killed and that Sead would be raised fatherless, as she had been.

COLD WAR

WHEN HE FLED YUGOSLAVIA, ALIJA MEHMEDOVIĆ TOOK HIS fear with him. From correspondence and jottings, it is clear that he lived the rest of his life believing he was a hunted man. He had fought for the fascists in a country taken over by communists. His was a crime for which there was no statute of limitations. After the war Tito demanded that a number of Muslims and German officers of the Handschar Division be handed over for war-crimes trials. Alija remained convinced that Tito's agents were out to avenge his wartime role.

Leading Ustashas also escaped, among them Pavelić himself, the interior minister Andrija Artuković, the minister of religion Mile Budak, the commander of the Jasenovac camp Maks Luburić, and Archbishop Šarić of Sarajevo. Apparently Vatican connections helped them on their way and they eventually resurfaced, mainly in Franco's Spain or Péron's Argentina. Artuković made his way to Ireland and then California, where he lived for decades before being extradited in 1986 and tried for war crimes in Zagreb. Old and senile, he died in prison two years later.

But Pavelić, like most of his top officials, was never put on trial. In 1952, he was interviewed by *Epoca* magazine of Milan while lounging in the sun of Argentina with his wife, stroking a pet dog. He told how he had escaped through the Allied lines, pausing at the Vatican and Castel Gandolfo before going to South America. Having survived an assassination attempt in Buenos Aires in 1957, he died in Madrid in 1959. Like most of the top Ustasha officials, he expired in his own bed.

Less privileged followers of Pavelić did not fare as well. They decided to surrender to the Allies, rather than the Partisans, and they made their way, in May 1945, to the small Austrian border town of Bleiburg, not far from where Alija's Handschar Division made its last stand. Here they gave themselves up to British troops. The British, however, handed most of them back to Tito; thousands of people were killed in the ensuing massacres carried out by Partisan forces.

Bleiburg became a taboo word under Tito, but it was later turned into a sacred symbol in the postwar Croatian diaspora—for those, like Alija Mehmedović, who had fled the communist victory. For these people Bleiburg amounted to the onerous proof that the Ustasha battle was with the communists. It followed that the Pavelić regime's raison d'être was not the genocidal rampage against Orthodoxy and the Serbs but the defense of the Croatian independence that Tito denied. Bleiburg, in effect, became the moral counterweight to Jasenovac. The fact that Tito's forces brought some Pavelić supporters to Jasenovac to kill them abetted this obfuscation.

Tito's tendency to label all Croats who did not support him, and particularly all Croats in exile, as Ustashas, despite the fact that many were no more than Croatian patriots opposed to his regime, further served to obscure history and enrage diaspora Croats. To equate anyone who stood for an independent Croatia with the Ustasha was a provocation and a disservice to truth.

But truth was not really the issue in postwar Yugoslavia. Hitler had demolished Yugoslavia with a vengeance; the Yugoslavs had abetted his efforts. The state was reborn on the still-smoldering battlefields of a fratricidal war. Genocide, revolutionary terror, Nazi killing, and internecine "ethnic cleansing" had destroyed the first Yugoslavia. Deep wounds, entrenched suspicions remained.

TITO RESPONDED with the tight party discipline in which he had been trained in the Soviet Union and with the ubiquitous slogan of "Brotherhood and Unity." The first constitution of January 31, 1946, was heavily based on the 1936 constitution of the Soviet Union. It combined velleities about freedom of speech, religion, association, and assembly with a highly centralized state socialism that severely restricted private property and placed the means of production and foreign trade in state hands. Big hangars in Belgrade were full of the expropriated property of the bourgeoisie: Tito's new communist cadres were invited to go and help themselves in these self-service depots.

Interest in who killed whom between 1941 and 1945 was dictated by the degree to which it would serve the "Brotherhood and Unity" later symbolized by the construction of a Zagreb-Belgrade highway of the same name. Yugoslavs became victims of an undifferentiated "fascist aggression." The details of a civil war that was really fought were lost in the blanket of an "anti-fascist" war that was only part of the story. Partisan heroism obscured intra-Yugoslav horror. There was not, in Tito's Yugoslavia, the

political freedom, the justice system, or the independent press that could provide the remembrance that may lead eventually to healing.

The pits of Herzegovina were sealed; Bleiburg was never mentioned; Tito never visited Jasenovac. Just as Croat opponents of the communist state were all Ustashas, Serb opponents were all Chetniks. The old labels lived on. War crimes were equally shared and largely undifferentiated. Mihailović, the Chetnik leader, was arrested by Tito in March 1946 and sentenced to death on July 15 after what amounted to a show trial. His execution two days later illustrated how Tito proposed to deal with the Serbian ancien régime. The methods held Tito's state together—an immense achievement—but left old scores unsettled. Serbs and Croats, especially in exile, continued to nurse their wounds. For Alija Mehmedović and for many others, World War II was unfinished business.

THE ALLIES FOSTERED Tito's lies by allowing Pavelić—and the various crimes committed by all sides in Yugoslavia between 1941 and 1945— to be shunted into a largely forgotten historical siding, a place shadowy enough to incubate the ambiguity on which conflict in the Balkans has thrived.

The British historian A. J. P. Taylor has called this Allied approach the "Nuremberg Consensus." The Nuremberg Tribunal was set up to try crimes committed by the defeated German enemy. Yugoslavia, under Tito's control by 1945, did not qualify, for it was neither defeated nor an enemy. On the contrary, Britain and America had helped Tito to victory. What crimes had been committed there, just who had massacred whom in the great outpouring of blood, was not a matter for Allied governments to worry about, any more than they would concern themselves with the massacre of thousands of Polish officers at Katyn, for Stalin, like Tito, was on the right side at war's end. Thus were the manifold crimes of Pavelić pushed into relative obscurity. Postwar politics, Hitler's genocide against the Jews, and the fact that history is written by the victors eased the *Poglavnik* offstage.

The second factor in sidelining the Ustasha was an insidious historical conflation through which the Pavelić regime became synonymous not with a monstrous onslaught on the Orthodox Serb populations of Croatia and Bosnia, but with Catholic resistance to communism, or, by an acrobatic extension, the free Western world's resistance to communist dictatorship.

A central figure in this distortion was Archbishop Stepinac of Zagreb, the leading churchman in Croatia under Pavelić. Archbishop Stepinac immediately swore loyalty to the Pavelić regime—he met Pavelić on April 16, a day before Yugoslavia formally surrendered—and, in a circular to priests on April 28, 1941, the archbishop declared that Croatia had come "face to face with its age-old and ardently desired dream." He added that "the times are such that it is no longer the tongue which speaks but the blood, through mysterious union with the earth, in which we have glimpsed the light of God." For Archbishop Stepinac, it was "easy to see God's hand at work" in the "resurrected state of Croatia."

A day earlier, the official Catholic newspaper declared that God had given Croatia Pavelić as its leader, adding: "Glory be to God, our gratitude to Adolf Hitler, and infinite loyalty to our *Poglavnik,* Ante Pavelić." So began a campaign in which religion and nationality fused to run amok.

Later Archbishop Stepinac did protest to Pavelić over certain massacres and informed the Vatican of others. In 1942 he said that "one cannot exterminate Gypsies or Jews because one considers them an inferior race." He seems to have had little personal enthusiasm for Pavelić himself or for the brutality of his methods; indeed, he appears to have been increasingly troubled by what he saw. But never was there a formal renunciation by the Catholic church in Croatia of a religiously based campaign of persecution and genocide that was on a scale of the Spanish Inquisitors. If he was not himself a barbarian, the archbishop did not curb the barbarity of members of his clergy. There is no record of a statement by Archbishop Stepinac that comes close to the indignation of Bishop Mišić of Mostar.

Stepinac stayed on in Croatia after the war and began speaking out boldly against communism. He was arrested by Tito on September 30, 1946. The charges were collaboration with the enemy during the war and resistance to the communist government of Yugoslavia. At his trial he declared that he had never been an Ustasha supporter; he had merely responded to the yearnings for independence of the Croatian people. "The Croat nation unanimously declared itself for the Croatian state," he said, "and I would have been remiss had I not recognized and acknowledged the desire of the Croatian people enslaved in the former Yugoslavia."

Stepinac was sentenced to sixteen years' imprisonment. For many Catholics, he attained the status of a martyr. A Stepinac Institute was set up in New York, an apt symbol of the process by which the archbishop came to represent "freedom of thought" in Yugoslavia. Writing in 1956, the Irish essayist Hubert Butler said there seemed to be an agreement that "history should be falsified in Croatia in the interests of Catholic piety." He noted that the rehabilitation of Pavelić was well under way and that "one way or another the memory of a terrible crime against humanity is being confused and effaced, so that many people believe that it never happened at all or that it has been monstrously exaggerated."

In the great scale of the battle between the free world and the communist bloc that hardened in the 1950s, it was more useful to portray Stepinac as a lone fighter for liberty than to recall the central role of Pavelić in a squalid regional act of genocide, a pogrom broadly supported by the Catholic church. The first image was comforting, the second disquieting. Stepinac had represented the church in Croatia. His acts inevitably recalled the broad German sympathies of Pope Pius XII and his general silence before the Holocaust.

Besides, amid such a proliferation of killing the temptation was strong in the postwar years to lump the whole horror under the broad blanket of Balkan bloodshed, too visceral to comprehend, too varied to collate. The Allies generally preferred things this way. The safeguarding of Yugoslav unity, a central Allied aim, was thereby served. The difficulties Butler had in reporting on the Pavelić regime in the 1950s are illuminating: "I have been reproached several times," he wrote, "by sincere and civilized unbelievers for my efforts to find out the details of the vast campaign in Croatia to convert two and half million Orthodox to Catholicism. 'Why not let bygones be bygones?' they say. 'If we rake things up we'll merely start trouble at home and play into the hands of the Communists. And anyway they're always killing each other in the Balkans.' "

In this way, the selective memory of the victorious powers was established after World War II. During the decades of the cold war, the West could comfortably regard Pavelić and his regime as a sideshow to history's main events: the Allied victory over Nazism and the fall of the Iron Curtain across Europe. Obscurantism has always been the easy choice in the Balkans. It would be taken up as a central theme during the Bosnian war by General Sir Michael Rose, a British commander of United Nations forces in Bosnia, whose favorite dismissive phrase became "This is the Balkans, you know."

Like so much else that occurred in the principal killing fields of World War II in Central and Eastern Europe, the crimes of the Pavelić regime were swept under the carpet in the wholesale rewriting of history that came with acceptance of Stalin's dominion over half of a divided continent after 1945. When considered at all, the deeds of Pavelić were generally the object of ideological warfare. As Butler observed, "Truth, deferred, goes sour." Just how sour would not become apparent for a half century.

AFTER WORLD WAR II, Gaby found a job with the new Yugoslav national travel agency, Putnik. She and Sead moved first to Novi Sad in Vojvodina, then to Zagreb, then to the Croatian port city of Rijeka, then to Opatija, before returning to Belgrade in 1952. Sead, in his high-school years, was known as Aleksandar Mehmedović—his baptismal name of 1941. Only in 1955 did he revert to his original Muslim name of Sead because he needed identity papers and the only documents that identified him as Aleksandar were religious, and so not recognized by the communist authorities.

His reports show that, like his father, he was a good student. At his schools in Croatia, he was listed for some years as a "Catholic." Born to a Muslim father, baptized and admitted into the Orthodox church at the age of three, known for some years as a Catholic, Sead was a consummate Yugoslav. When, a few years after the war, Gaby married a Jewish Yugoslav of mainly Austrian descent named Egon Rozenblat, the potpourri—not atypical in the Balkans—was completed.

"I have no feeling for nationality," Sead told me. "I am nothing and I am everything. On the question of nationalities I am handicapped, I am color-blind, it means nothing to me. In Zagreb, as a boy, I was once teased for my high Serb accent, but I have no sense of national identity. And so of course I wonder if all those now who say it means so much to them are not suffering from an illusion."

Sead's eclectic upbringing was broadened when, after his return to Belgrade, he lived for two years with friends of his mother, Viktor and Kitty Starčić. In the tiny apartment that his mother and stepfather occupied on their return to the capital, there was no room for Sead.

Viktor Starčić was a famous actor, of mixed French and Serb descent; Kitty was a Russian aristocrat whose family had fled at the time of the Bolshevik revolution, moving first to Berlin and later to Belgrade. They had lost their infant daughter to diphtheria during the war, and they adopted Sead with love. He was thrust into an exotic, cultured milieu where the talk was often of the literature of France, Russia, and Britain and actors and actresses came and went. He played a number of small roles in plays in Novi Sad. Shakespeare and Soviet social realism were both in the boy's repertoire. He guided the blind and raving Lear on the dark cliffs; in rehearsals for a Soviet play, Sead was so upset by the sight of an "aunt" who had been strung up on a gallows, he could not stop crying. Starčić told him he would one day make a great actor, but Sead never liked the limelight.

In Belgrade, during vacations, he would go down to the River Sava with friends. There were barges full of watermelons during the summer. The boys would drive a nail with a string attached into the fruit; they would then dive into the water and drag the watermelon in with them. It was good to eat the succulent red fruit in the cool water and gaze up at the city.

He thought little about his father. The assumption was that Alija was dead. On February 7, 1952, Gaby signed the following statement in Belgrade: "By this I state that from the day of my official divorce in 1939, I had no contacts with Alija Mehmedović, the father of my son, Aleksandar. I am aware that in the same year he left Belgrade and *Politika* and went to

Croatia. Since then I have not seen him, nor did I receive any aid for my child. Unofficially I learned that he got married again in 1941 and went missing in 1943. In Zagreb, Sarajevo, and Tuzla I looked for any document that might reveal his whereabouts or his death certificate, but I never received any reply. I have maintained my child on my own since he was born and since 1940 I have been employed by the state and been receiving state aid for the child regularly."

The statement, made to ensure that state payments to her continued, was not quite accurate: Gaby had seen Alija after their divorce, he had left *Politika* in 1938 rather than 1939, and he had gone to Sarajevo, not Croatia. But it did accurately reflect the black hole into which Alija had disappeared.

This "disappearance" was a fact of life for Sead. It was also a wound. Much later, before finally setting out for Turkey to meet him, Sead would write: "You know, I'd be terribly interested in penetrating your feelings for me. To be honest, before I found you, I thought that I must mean more to you than you mean to me. I thought—you are going to be a stranger to me. But now I am haunted by the fear that it is the other way round. I am afraid that I am burdening you with love and intimacy that you do not want, that in fact I am a stranger to you. Whatever the truth, I do not want to impose myself on you by the mere formal fact that I am your son. Please feel no emotional obligation toward me. The only obligation I would ask you to fulfill is that you be open in regard to what you feel about me, if indeed after all these years you feel anything. But this again is my damn suspiciousness and fear of being abandoned like a fish out of water. This fear explains why I always leave some emotional bridges behind me."

LONELINESS AND FEAR lurked inside him, but Sead's childhood was happy enough. His mother and stepfather both had decent jobs at Putnik; later Rozenblat worked for the Foreign Ministry. Schooling reflected the first flush of Tito's revolution. Enthusiasm was widespread. Big estates—of collaborators, collapsed institutions, and the departed *Volksdeutsche*—were expropriated and land redistributed to peasants. Industry was largely taken over, and a Yugoslav "Great Leap Forward" planned. Initial achievements were considerable. Industrial output doubled between 1946 and 1952. Nationalities were carefully balanced among Tito's lieutenants—Tito the Croat was flanked by Milovan Djilas (a Montenegrin), Edvard Kardelj (Slovene), and Aleksandar Ranković (Serb)—and the "national question" held under control.

At first the revolution seemed wedded to Stalin and the Soviet Union. The Cominform (Communist Information Bureau), set up to replace the dissolved Comintern, chose Belgrade as the seat of its secretariat and held its first meeting there in 1947. But Tito's closeness to the British during the war, his occasional criticism of great powers in general, and his stubborn confidence born of having led his own army to victory, all made him a leader less pliant than Stalin would have liked. Tensions rose, fed by allegations about British spies in Belgrade and Yugoslav mistreatment of Soviet military advisers. On March 27, 1948, Stalin rebuked Tito sharply. He suggested that Yugoslavia had criticized the Soviet Communist party for repressive centralization and noted that Trotsky had also done so. "We think that the career of Trotsky is quite instructive," Stalin observed with his habitual subtlety.

Unbowed by such threats, aware that Churchill and Stalin had mapped out a fifty-fifty division of influence in Yugoslavia in 1944, Tito responded that "no matter how much each of us loves the land of socialism, the U.S.S.R., he can in no way love his own country less." He added that "we are developing socialism in our country in somewhat different forms." This Stalin could not tolerate. On June 28, 1948, the anniversary of the Battle of Kosovo, Tito's party was expelled from the Cominform. Milovan Djilas, a communist but also a proud Montenegrin, noted of this measure that "its promulgation on the anniversary of the tragic battle in 1389 at Kosovo, which had inaugurated five centuries of Turkish rule over the Serbian people, cut into the minds and hearts of all Serbs. Though neither religious nor mystical, we noted with a certain relish almost, the coincidence in dates between ancient calamities and living threats and onslaughts."

The Cominform's statement said that the Yugoslav party had placed itself "outside the united Communist front and consequently outside the ranks of the Information Bureau." It accused Tito and his cohorts of breaking with the "international traditions" of the Yugoslav Communist party and attempting to "curry favor with the Imperialist states." The aim was to strike a bargain with Western powers for Yugoslavia's independence and "gradually to get the people of Yugoslavia oriented toward these states, that is toward capitalism." Urging party members to overthrow Tito if he did not change course, the Cominform declared that "the Yugoslav leaders evidently do not understand, or, probably, pretend they do not understand, that such a nationalist line can only lead to Yugoslavia's degeneration into an ordinary bourgeois republic, to the loss of its independence and to its transformation into a colony of the imperialist countries."

In fact, Tito's intuition was unerring. A position between East and West gave him the scope to employ his enormous diplomatic skills, eventually gaining support from Washington, Moscow, and the Non-aligned Movement he came to personify. To have broken with Stalin was, inevitably, to become a friend of America. In the cold war, to paraphrase Roosevelt, there were sons of bitches and there were *our* sons of bitches. Tito, to some extent, joined the second category. As Madeleine K. Albright remarked to me, "A great deal of hallucination developed around him."

In 1948, the priority for Tito was the elimination of hard-line followers of Moscow, who became known as the Informbirovci. A climate of fear descended once again upon Belgrade. Disappearances were a daily occurrence as a purge led by Aleksandar Ranković's Yugoslav secret police, the OZNA (later UDBA), gathered pace.

Anybody who betrayed any sympathy for Stalin, or hesitation over Tito's infallibility, was removed. Sometimes people, under unbearable pressure from the UDBA, would finger an innocent man simply to be relieved of their interrogations. A casual comment that the Cominform might not be entirely wrong would quickly lead to another "disappearance." In general the "disappeared," in the tens of thousands, were taken to the barren Adriatic island of Goli Otok; the brutality there would be revived in the camps the Serbs set up in 1992. Those who returned from Goli Otok were too afraid to talk. By Stalin's standards, Tito's gulag was a very modest affair, but it was effective.

Sead, then a boy of ten, witnessed one of the effects of this purge. In 1948, he had been chosen to play the role of a messenger boy in a movie about the Partisans that was filmed in the Istrian coastal town of Pula. He was very excited about the role, but to his great chagrin the film never came out. Just as filming was nearing completion, the author of the screenplay was denounced as an Informbirovac and disappeared. Still, the boy's enthusiasm for Tito was undiminished.

"I JOINED Tito's youth groups," Sead told me as we took one of our walks through a crumbling Belgrade. "The first time, when I was fourteen or fifteen, I was the youngest in my brigade. We went to build the Vlasina hydroelectric plant somewhere in Macedonia. We built canals for the water. I don't even know if it was Macedonia. It was all Yugoslavia to me. Then we went to a place near the Prespa Lake in Macedonia to improve the irrigation system. We cleared the Ada Ciganlija island on the Sava in Belgrade—it was just a mass of vegetation before we started. And the fourth time I worked on the motorway connecting Belgrade to Niš. By then it was 1958; I was twenty.

"Of all that I have only beautiful memories. Not like Soviet camps. We were not pressured. We were socialist volunteers; we wanted to go. It was an honor. Many were refused. Being with young people, all of us enthusiastic, was an amazing feeling. I saw what I could do physically. That is an important part of growing up: to see what you can do physically. With drills. With tools. It was a kind of euphoria. We really believed we were building a socialist republic.

"For me, as a young man, the greatest thing, the purest idea, was to go and fight in another country for something you believed in. The International Brigades in the Spanish civil war—that was quite magnificent. It was the biggest thing possible. It was also a dream—I never went anywhere to fight—but one that never lost its luster.

"When it comes to ideology, I am still eighteen years old. I am an idealist. For me, it is a question of social justice. So in that sense, a romantic sense perhaps, I am still a communist. In the end communist ideology is Christian—take from the rich to give to the poor, the equality of everyone. Communism is Christianity for those from whom God has been amputated. The gulf that grew up between ideology and practice is a great disappointment to me. I feel cheated by it."

There was indeed a special quality to Tito's postwar state. A unique Yugoslav romanticism existed, part national trait and part Partisan dream: it was most vividly embodied in Djilas. The guiding idea was to hold fast to the principles of Marxism rather than surrender to the ruthless pragmatism of Lenin or its apotheosis, Stalin's terror. Just as the birth of Yugoslavia in 1918 had involved a South Slav idealism, a belief that what was shared in the new state outweighed what was not, so the first years of Yugoslavia's postwar rebirth involved the idealistic belief that the centralist, controlling role of a bureaucratic Communist party was not inevitable. Rather, it was a Soviet aberration. Such beliefs, combined with the sheer physical beauty of Yugoslavia, made it an extraordinarily seductive place for many people. Few Western diplomats who went there were unmoved. Military and economic aid from Washington and Western Europe began to flow in 1950. Countless youths, like Sead, gave their hearts to Tito, who appeared as the apostle of some new dream. Countless diplomats were seduced by him.

Tito declared in 1950 that "at the final stage of communism class differences will have disappeared entirely and the state itself, together with any repressive apparatus, will wither away." A blunt attack on Stalin followed: "What are the NKVD and the militia doing? Who is deporting millions of citizens to Siberia and the far North? Can anyone pretend that these are measures against the class enemy? Who is obstructing the free exchange of opinion in the Soviet Union? Isn't all this done by the most centralized and bureaucratic state apparatus, one that shows not the slightest trace of withering away?"

He went on to describe the outlines of a "Yugoslav way" that would lead to "workers' self-management" and the dreamed-of withering of the state apparatus. "First the decentralization of the state administration, particularly in economic matters. Second the transfer of factories and economic undertakings in general to self-administration through workers' collectives. The decentralization of the economic, political, cultural and other sectors of life is not only profoundly democratic, it also contains the germ of the withering-away process—the withering-away of centralism, and also of the state in general, of the state as an instrument of repression."

Kardelj, who became the leading theorist of the "Yugoslav way," put the choice succinctly in 1952. Socialist countries, he said, had to choose between "the Marxist teaching of the withering-away of the state and, with it, of any party system . . . and the Stalinist theory of the strengthening of the state." Yugoslavia's own choice, he claimed, was for the former—a decision symbolized by the replacement that year of the Communist party by the League of Communists of Yugoslavia (LCY). The notion of a league rather than a party was supposed to convey the advisory, consensual, nonautocratic role of Tito's communists, and their theoretical ability to disappear in the land of "democratic socialism."

But Yugoslavia, in effect, found itself trying to be half pregnant. If the LCY was to wither away, then so ultimately would Tito's command. If the self-managing class and the workers' councils were really to run things, then what were all the federal, republican, and local officials for? If centralized management of the economy was undone, then what would ultimately prevent the free play of market forces? If there was really a plurality of self-managing interests, then how could their political expression remain that of a one-party state rather than a democracy? Already, in late 1953, Djilas's open insistence that the "centralist role" of Tito's party was becoming a "hindrance to social development" led to a crisis that saw Djilas ousted from the LCY and imprisoned. Romanticism had its limits. Tito could not survive on the purity of Marxist ideas alone; he needed a party (even one called a "league") and he needed a security apparatus.

Captured by the Russians during World War I, a witness to the Bolshevik revolution, and an earnest student of its methods, Tito was never emotionally or politically inclined to abjure the Soviet model entirely. After Stalin's death in 1953, relations with the Soviet Union predictably improved once more. As the former British diplomat Duncan Wilson observed, "Wherever Tito's treasure was, his heart was in Moscow."

In the utopian factories of nascent "self-management," Ranković's UDBA agents were everywhere. Each enterprise had an agent assigned to it who would come every couple of days to ask if anything suspicious had been observed. There were also secret UDBA agents within the factory. In this way, if a director said he had nothing to report, he might be confronted and embarrassed by information provided by an internal agent. Any contact with foreigners had to be reported in writing. State security was ubiquitous. Perceived enemies of the regime, among them Andrija Hebrang, the wartime leader of the Croatian communists who was later suspected of favoring Croatian independence, disappeared.

THESE CONTRADICTIONS—between the self-management dream and the reality that Tito's party would not yield power—also affected the "national question." The theory, at least in the 1950s, was that a "socialist Yugoslav consciousness" would supplant old national loyalties. The specificity of the "Yugoslav way" would engender a peculiarly Yugoslav pride. In the development of a Yugoslav patriotism, Serb, Croat, Slovene, Albanian, Bosnian Muslim, Macedonian, and Montenegrin would be won over.

For many people, among them Sead Mehmedović, this was the case. Mixed marriages were frequent. But the fact was that the "Yugoslav way" was limited by its internal contradictions; so, too, was the Yugoslav consciousness that was supposed to emerge from it. Gibberish about "voluntarily united nations" took the place of the real freedom that might have forged a Yugoslav citizenship. Naturally Tito's Yugoslavia backed the "liberation" of Angola, of Ethiopia, of Cuba, and of other far-flung places, but its own "national question" festered under the dread mantle of Leninist prose, with its trumpeting of "the socialist friendship of peoples."

In fact, the only devolution that took place was bureaucratic rather than democratic in nature. The LCY, far from withering away, remained, steadily expanding its membership. The republican units of the party became the regional centers of economic power. Inevitably, rivalry grew up among them.

The friction was principally economic, but it became tinged with nationalism. Closer to Western Europe, richer, more developed, Croatia and Slovenia grew steadily more resentful of the central powers in Belgrade and of the high percentage of their income paid in taxes and then redistributed to poorer regions. Their intermittent calls for greater economic liberalization tended to look like a thinly veiled recasting of the old prewar Croatian and Slovenian invective against the domination of the Serbian dynasty.

These tensions came to a head in 1966 with the dismissal of Ranković, the most powerful Serb in Tito's entourage. He had been made vice-president and heir apparent in 1963; three years later, he was accused, in essence, of plotting Tito's overthrow and the reimposition of Serbian power through his control of UDBA. A Croat, Milan Mišković, was among those who engineered Ranković's downfall; Ranković passed, like Draža Mihailović, into the realm of Serbian lore. Beneath the surface, the old nationalist tensions were stirring, exacerbated by Tito's advancing age and reluctance to confront the question of a successor.

The year after Ranković fell, the main literary weekly in Zagreb published a declaration that the Croatian language was distinct from Serbian, suggesting that the Serbo-Croatian of Tito's Yugoslavia was in essence a political tool used to bolster a fictitious Yugoslav unity. It was signed by, among others, Croatia's leading writer, Miroslav Krleža. Forty-five Serbian writers immediately responded by calling for Cyrillic alone to be used on Belgrade television and requesting that the seven hundred thousand Serbs living in Croatia be taught Serb.

Tito's response was to embark on the gradual "confederalization" of Yugoslavia, a process that would culminate with the 1974 constitution— and ultimately the state's dismemberment. Talk of a Yugoslav socialist patriotism disappeared, replaced by the cumbersome balancing of national interests that led to the collective presidency. The bureaucracies within Slovenia, Croatia, Bosnia, Montenegro, Serbia, Macedonia, Vojvodina, and Kosovo gained power; even state security was no longer centralized, as it had been under Ranković. The process was largely an admission of failure. Tito had indeed become what the British historian A. J. P. Taylor called "the last of the Habsburgs," governing an array of peoples by dividing them and playing one off against the other. Rather than the withering-away of the state and the party, foreseen with such audacity in 1950, socialist dreams withered away, as did the Yugoslav idea associated with them.

A high idealism was always part of the Yugoslav dream. But the tumult of this century never allowed those ideals to be achieved, or even approached. Before World War II, the ideal was a unity that would allow all the South Slavs to unite their energies and subsume their differences in the construction of a new state. This ideal was frustrated by the misunderstandings that marked the country's birth and by Serbian inflexibility following it. After World War II, the ideal was a uniquely Yugoslav model of communism, one that would shun Stalinism, lead to "democratic socialism," and overcome the old national differences through a shared dream. This vision was enthralling and Tito maneuvered, often brilliantly, in its pursuit. But in the end the vision was frustrated by Tito's vanity, his Moscow training, and his need to maintain power through a one-party state. That party, ultimately, could never be a mere component of the so-called democratic pluralism of self-managing interests. It had to dictate and organize and monitor those interests.

As a result of these failures, Yugoslavia was left pursuing chimera and shadows, just as, for decades, Sead pursued the idealistic image of his lost father. Crisscrossing the ruins of the state, I would wonder at the range of its beauty—from the Alpine limpidity of the Slovene mountains to the splendor of Macedonia—and ask why such wealth and vigor could not be brought to sustainable life. History cannot be turned back, not even, it is said, by two seconds, but the sheer number of graves, the sheer volume of lives sacrificed for Yugoslavia seemed to me to demand that an exception be made to this rule, that some decisive moment of destructive folly be reconsidered so that the evident Yugoslav potential might at last be fulfilled. But it could not be. Yugoslavia, like some desolate beast, always tended toward its own destruction. The evidence was overwhelming, incontrovertible, repetitious. Yet I could not help thinking that the amount of blood that dismemberment ultimately involved suggested that Yugoslavia was not, as its many detractors insisted, a totally unnatural creation. Only something imbued with a measure of life could die with such difficulty. There were links; they had to be forcibly severed before Yugoslavia could finally wither. In the course of a cruel century, those bonds, the lifeblood of Yugoslavia, had never been nurtured by the equitable rule of law and a stable democracy. "One chooses democracy," Karl Popper wrote, "not because it abounds in virtues, but only in order to avoid tyranny." And if Yugoslavia had avoided tyranny, would the old cultural chasms have been bridged at last? Perhaps not, but at least the Yugoslav idea would not have been sold so cheaply.

Toward the end of his life, Kardelj tried to sum up the "Yugoslav way." But his painful probing only exposed his and Tito's failure. "Socialism," he wrote, "is not conceivable without democracy. It cannot make progress unless it fosters democratic relations among people. However, what a socialist society wants is democracy in socialism. Therefore we must preserve the class nature of our democracy. What this means is that the interests of the working class, closely aligned with all other working people, must be guaranteed undisputed predominance in this democracy, and that everyone acknowledging this fact will enjoy democratic rights."

Seldom have the contradictions of the elusive Marxist dream been more lucidly addressed. For who was to guarantee the "undisputed predominance" of the working class in Yugoslavia? Who would determine the people meriting democratic rights as opposed to those not qualified? What would happen to those excluded from the "democratic rights" of this socialist democracy? Ultimately, Kardelj's socialist democratic utopia required a single, centralized party and a police state to make it foolproof.

IN ALIJA MEHMEDOVIĆ'S SUITCASE, I found this odd jotting under the headline "Top Dogs and Underdogs": "Over lunch in a Washington restaurant, a senior Soviet diplomat turned to a U.S. acquaintance. 'You Americans are top dogs who are going down fast,' he said. 'We are underdogs coming up fast. We have Pompidou and Brandt going to Moscow. Heath is coming to get his astrakhan hat, and he might even get a keg of vodka too. They are turning our way. They are trying to strike bargains because they know we are moving up and you are moving down.' " Below this, with another pen, Alija had written again: "They are trying to strike bargains because they know we are moving up and you are moving down."

I imagined him, under his assumed name, in his Turkish town, watching the ins and outs of the cold war that had grown out of the war that undid his life. Tito's clash with Stalin. His reconciliation with Khrushchev. Beria's end. McCarthyism. Budapest. Sputnik. Berlin. Cuba. Kennedy. Prague. Alija's own place in this drama played out on either side of the Iron Curtain was clear enough. He was a fascist and a reactionary, fair game for Tito's UDBA. There were no bargains to be struck, no place for reconciliation, no returning home—unless Tito, his system, and perhaps even his country collapsed. For Alija, the past was frozen.

His lost war was his son's inheritance. Sead never gave up the communist idealism that grew out of the Partisan victory. He was not aware of the link between the system he believed in and his father's exile. *He had no father.* But abruptly, in 1966, he began to dream of an unimagined reconciliation. Just as his country began to splinter toward the impasse of confederalism, information surfaced that could make his own life whole. Alija was alive. And if he was living, surely no exile or alias could hide him forever.

CHAPTER 5

THE CAPITAL OF
THE OTTOMANS

BURSA, TURKEY, THE FIRST CAPITAL OF THE OTTOMAN TURKS, is a bustling boomtown that sprawls across a broad valley. New auto factories and supermarkets flank highways choked with trucks belching exhaust as they heave ungainly loads northward to Istanbul. In modern Turkey environmental concerns are inchoate at best. When the sun rises to its zenith the valley is smothered in a pall of dust, fumes, and industrial smoke. At such moments, it is pleasant to climb into the old town, where the air is cooler, fountains plash, and gardens flourish behind stone walls. In the shade of towering cypress trees the turban-topped gravestones of the Turks lean at angles that evoke the weight of time. These cemeteries have the hush of centuries past; their lurching tombs, fantastic as a dawn crop of wild mushrooms in a dewy meadow, have become part of the natural order of things. The frenetic movement of the valley seems distant; it is the spirit, not lucre, that resides in these shadows. Further up, above the mosques and the graves, where the solid trunk of the town splinters into narrow branches, the air is crystalline. Alleys twist or thrust upward into the foothills of what was known in antiquity as Mount Olympus of Mysia and is now known as the Ulu Dag. Byzantine monks once lived, studied, and took refuge on the mountain. Even in summer its peak is capped with snow.

It was to this town that Alija Mehmedović came after he fled Yugoslavia in 1945. And it was from this town, centuries earlier, that the great Ottoman wave rose, uniting Muslim Anatolia and the Christian Balkans in an uneasy symbiosis.

Osman Gazi, the founder of the Ottoman dynasty to which he gave his name, is buried in Bursa. He was the warrior-ruler of a small principality dedicated to holy war against Christian Byzantium. His death in 1326 coincided with the capture of Bursa from the Byzantines by his son Orhan.

A year later the first silver coins of the Ottomans were minted in Bursa. The city then became the first capital of a rapidly expanding dominion that, within two centuries, would stretch through Thessalonika and Bosnia to the gates of Vienna.

Visiting Bursa in 1333, the Arab traveler Ibn Battuta described it as "a great city with fine bazaars and broad streets." By the end of the fourteenth century, it had become the most important commercial city of Anatolia and a center of east-west trade. Silk caravans came to Bursa from Persia and the precious material was bought by Italian merchants; from the west came the cloths of Florence and Flanders. Even after the capture of Constantinople in 1453 and its conversion into the Ottoman capital of Istanbul, Bursa remained an important economic center, particularly for the silk trade.

The tombs of Osman and Orhan are placed side by side on a quiet, tree-lined ridge above Bursa's busy valley. In simple inscriptions Osman is described as "the founder of the Ottoman Empire that lasted 600 years." His son is accorded a longer tribute: "Sultan Orhan was a great organizer and the second ruler of the Ottoman Empire. During his reign Bursa was captured from the Byzantines. A few years later, the Ottomans crossed into Europe and the first silver coin was minted. He died in Bursa. His tomb was built on the old foundations of a Byzantine church." Kemal Atatürk's Turkish state is responsible for these laconic plaques. Founded in 1923 on lay principles that deliberately sought to wean modern Turkey from the weight of its Ottoman past, the republic has little taste for the ostentation of the sultans.

Not far from the tombs is a sign. It says that "the sister city of Sarajevo" is 980 kilometers distant. This serves as a reminder of the remarkable, and remarkably resilient, reach of Ottoman rule. From a frontier principality the Ottomans rapidly forged a frontier empire that, for more than five centuries, made Turkey a European power. Twice, in 1529 and 1683, the Turks besieged Vienna, only to be repulsed. During the reign of Süleyman I (1520–1566), the empire already stretched from central Europe to the Indian Ocean. Its decline was long and slow, tortuous as some Bosnian byway, marked by the very lethargy that came to characterize Ottoman rule. During much of the nineteenth century, Turkey-in-Europe, as it was sometimes known, clung on despite growing administrative decay. But in what Walter Bagehot called "the century of nation-building" its travails multiplied. Successive national uprisings in the Balkans slowly drove the empire back toward the Dardanelles, creating what became known to nineteenth-century European diplomats as "the Eastern question." A century later, a "Bosnian question" remains.

Bosnia feels close at hand in Bursa. The narrow alleys of the old town, the gardens with their makeshift trellises, the houses clinging to steep hills, the ubiquitous sound of water, the ramshackle rather than formal beauty, the contemplative groups of men gathered with cigarettes in the shade of trees, the sharp difference in temperature between the mountain and the nearby valley—all this is redolent of Sarajevo. Indeed, the similiarities suggest that Bosnia's special affinity to the Turks may also have been a question of terrain and climate. Many other factors—particularly the large heretical presence in Bosnia—explain the fact that conversion to Islam was more widespread in Bosnia than elsewhere in the vast Ottoman Empire. But the landscape at Bursa makes clear why the Turks built and clung to Sarajevo.

As Turkey retreated from Europe, ultimately abandoning all but eastern Thrace, Bursa was changed. The point of departure became a point of arrival. When Austria-Hungary took over the administration of Bosnia from the Turks in 1878, after the Congress of Berlin, many Muslim families fled. Leila Ilova, who lives in a crumbling cat-filled mansion in central Bursa, has hung a photograph of her great-grandfather in a place of honor in her living room. It shows a proud, straight-backed man, of fez and fiery gaze, standing on the Bosnian estate he lost when Austrian troops arrived. After his arrival in Bursa as a refugee, this Slavic Muslim went into the silk business and became a successful businessman.

A half century later another upheaval that coincided with the end of the Ottoman dynasty changed the population of Bursa more drastically. Greece, leading the Balkan push for liberation from the Turks, had won its independence from the Ottomans in 1830, and in the wake of World War I it sought to build a great Aegean power on the ruins of the Ottoman Empire. The Greek pursuit of the "Megali Idea"—a Greater Greece that would recover "the City," Constantinople, and embrace parts of Asia Minor, so re-creating the Greek world of Byzantium—ended in what has become known simply as the Katastrophe.

The irredentist "Great Idea" had been summed up by a speaker in the Greek parliament in 1844. "The kingdom of Greece is not Greece," he said. "It constitutes only one part, the smallest and the poorest. . . . A Greek is not only a man who lives within the Kingdom, but also one who lives in Yuoannina, Serrai, Adrianople, Constantinople, Smyrna, Trebizond, Crete and in any land associated with Greek history and the Greek race. . . . There are two main centers of Hellenism: Athens, the capital of the Greek kingdom, and the City, the dream and hope of all Greeks." In this way do demagogues attempt to project an ethnic-national consciousness onto far-flung people who may have little or no such awareness. Similarly, ever since the nineteenth century, Serbia sought intermittently to convince the Serbs of Bosnia and Croatia that they belonged inside Serbia, despite the fact that many of them were complete cultural strangers.

The campaign for Greater Greece, backed by Britain, began well in 1919. But initial Greek military successes slowly ground to a bloody halt before the determination of Kemal Atatürk's army, fighting quite literally for the life of Turkey. By 1922, the tide of battle had turned. On September 7 of that year, the archbishop of Smyrna (now the Turkish town of Izmir) addressed a desperate appeal to Eleutherios Venizelos, the Greek prime minister. "Hellenism in Asia Minor," he wrote, "the Greek state and the entire Greek Nation are descending now to a Hell from which no power will be able to raise them up and save them." He was right. A few days later, the archbishop was handed over to a Muslim mob who mutilated and killed him. The Greek and European quarters of Smyrna went up in flames; many of the hundreds of thousands of people who had lived in the Christian city were killed.

In late 1922, Ernest Hemingway, then a war correspondent for the *Toronto Star*, watched a twenty-mile-long line of Greek refugees trudging back from their ancestral homes in Asia Minor to a Greece utterly unfamiliar to them—the cowed masses that pay the price when nationalist folly ebbs or is defeated. Many of these Greeks, whose ancestors had lived under the Romans, under Byzantine emperors, under the emperors of Trebizond, and under the Ottomans, had never previously set foot in Europe. Greek nationality, in the modern sense, almost certainly meant nothing to them: it was imposed, with disastrous consequences, from afar. Bursa, whose population of ethnic Greeks was substantial, contributed many of its own sons and daughters to such grim processions westward. Ethnic cleansing, the attempt to sift some neat ethnic order from the variegated legacy of Ottoman rule, had begun in earnest. Woodrow Wilson's national states would not be birthed without barbarism on the mottled soil of Europe.

From its outset in 1919, the Greco-Turkish conflict had been marked by a singular brutality. Greek and Turkish nationalism sought to bury, finally, the multi-ethnic, decentralized, and sometimes tolerant world of the Ottoman Empire, where Byzantine Christian and Muslim traditions blended. Atatürk's "Turkey for the Turks" and Venizelos's "Greater Greece" could no more tolerate the places and the people in between than the nationalist discourse of Tudjman and Milošević. The universal caliphate—exotic, slothful, cruel, and eclectic—collapsed. The fault lines in old communities—fissures composed of differing religions, traditions, and folklore—stirred where they had long slumbered. Muslim and Christian communities traded atrocities. The Greek soldiers who landed in Smyrna in 1919 slaughtered unarmed Turkish civilians. Arnold Toynbee, the British historian who was then a correspondent for *The Manchester Guardian,* noted that in Greek villages destroyed by the Turks, each house had been burned to the ground, one by one. Similarly, in 1921, as they advanced toward Ankara, the Greeks drove whole villages of Turkish civilians from their homes. The techniques of Bosnia, 1992, were not new; indeed, they had consistently marked Balkan attempts in the twentieth century to draw new national borders.

The Greco-Turkish conflict was settled by the Treaty of Lausanne in 1923, an agreement that wrote "ethnic cleansing" into the formal language of diplomacy. Under its terms nearly half a million Muslims—often "Greeks" in every sense except their religion—were forced out of Greece and into Turkey. Many of them, particularly Muslims from Crete, made their way to Bursa and the nearby fishing village of Mudanya. At the same time over one million Christians—often "Turks" in every sense except their religion—were obliged to leave Turkey and go to Greece. The Greeks expelled from Mudanya founded another village called Mudanya in Crete. The unraveling of the Ottoman tapestry expressed itself in hordes carrying a few salvaged possessions on a long journey toward a new identity they had never imagined.

I WONDERED AGAIN, as I had wondered in Bosnia, why so much blood in a world long distinguished by its very capacity for intermingling? History is an irrational river, never more so than in the Balkans. Sometimes it seemed to me that I had been plunged into a madhouse, where life and death turned and turned about with all the significance of a Ferris wheel at a state fair. A scene from the Croatian director Lordan Zafranović's epic documentary *Decline of the Century* haunted me. There is a party. The gowns shimmer. The jewelry sparkles. The waltz begins. The figures sweep across the dance floor. The music suggests a world of heedless frivolity. But then the camera closes in. The faces of the dancers are swollen, gashed, suppurating, bloody. The thin smiles of the women dissolve into scars; the music dissolves into discord.

"Everything spins in a circle," says Zafranović. "The sky, the earth, the sun and moon, people and the waltz. So do sickness and humanity, interweaving."

What or who set the parameters of this Balkan circle? Ottoman conquest was founded on a religious ideology—that is, the expansion of the realm of Islam. But it was not accompanied by forced conversion. The idea was to subdue, not eradicate, the Christian infidel. Christian religious communities based on the *millet* system lived on, side by side with the Ottoman authorities. This principle was the basis of Ottoman tolerance.

But over time, this arrangement had a secondary effect. Religion and national awareness fused. Christian and Serb, Christian and Greek, Christian and Bulgarian—the two elements of identity under the long, increasingly immobile Ottoman domination became indissociable. Those who converted to Islam, by contrast, "became Turks."

When, after centuries, Ottoman rule was confronted by the uprisings of these national groups, the conflicts inevitably took on the intensity and cruelty of religious wars. The battles for new national boundaries were fought under the opposing banners of the cross and the crescent moon. The antagonists were peoples determined to shed enough blood to obscure their strong cultural resemblances to each other. Identity had been grasped and preserved essentially through autocephalous Orthodox religious communities in a backward, static Balkan world of sometimes random terror. The assertion of that identity against the Ottomans proved murderous. National liberation, so-called, became synonymous with butchering the unbeliever, the apostate, the infidel. There were no rules of war in such a world; there were only crusades.

In Bosnia, during World War II, the war against the Nazis and the revolutionary struggle of Tito were thus overlaid with the barbarous crusades of the Chetniks and the Ustashas against their respective "infidel" targets. As a result, the outpouring of blood was particularly large. When Alija Mehmedović fled from Tito's victory in this battle, he took the road of the ebbing Ottoman tide that had left his and so many other Slavic Muslim families behind it in Bosnia.

He came to Bursa and, in the old Ottoman capital, Alija met a man named Ali Bilir whose father had been forced out of Greece under the terms of the Treaty of Lausanne. During his life in Crete, Ali Bilir's father had been called Ibrahim Mesanaki. He was, in effect, a Greek Muslim. But the family name was "Turkified" to Bilir when, as part of the great Greco-Turkish population exchange, he arrived in Bursa in 1923. Upon reaching Bursa a quarter century later in 1948, Alija Mehmedović also changed his name. He became Ali Erhan, a Turk and no longer a Bosnian Muslim.

IN ALIJA'S BATTERED SUITCASE, with its emetic scent, I had found a letter dated September 1, 1970, from Ali Bilir to Alija, who was then undergoing treatment in a clinic. It was full of a moving devotion. "We await you, as always, with open arms, our hearts full of nostalgia. You are a member of our family, if of course you wish to be. I want you to know that you are not, and will never be, alone, unless you yourself feel that you are a foreigner. For us, you are somebody close and adored, a father, an older brother. You always have a room here with us in Bursa, or if you prefer to come to Mudanya, we have our house there, with two rooms, a kitchen and a bathroom. If you feel you need the sea air, and calm, you may wish to stay in the Mudanya house; from there it is easy to go to Yalova, or Istanbul or even Ankara. . . . I repeat to you: my house is yours, my children are yours, and I am like your son."

Other letters to Alija from Turkish friends were marked by a similar respect. He appeared, in his new life in Bursa, to have abandoned entirely the habits of his youth. The hard-drinking womanizer became a solitary man of learning, precise, quiet, ascetic, often depressive. Occasionally the old alcoholism would afflict him again and he would binge. But in general he lived almost silently with his secrets. An identity document issued in Bursa said that he was born in Bosnia in 1909. For the Turkish authorities, Alija had put back his date of birth by two years. He was afraid of prying Yugoslav eyes.

I found Ali Bilir in Mudanya, a small port town about fifteen miles from Bursa, at the small house he had mentioned to Alija. Set one block back from the Sea of Marmara, the house had belonged to a Greek family until 1923. When Bilir's father arrived in Mudanya from Crete, he took over the house. The family had lost a large estate in Crete. Ali Bilir told me his father was always embittered and his grandfather died of grief. But Bilir himself was full of good cheer.

He had the jaunty gait and bright eyes of a seafaring man. He wore a white sailor's cap; his blue eyes twinkled in the shadow of its peak. His slight, wiry frame exuded vigor. His brown skin was burnished to a golden hue by the sea air. His fine slender hands occupied themselves graciously with worry beads. His smile began in his eyes and buried itself in a brisk mustache. When I showed him a photograph of Alija Mehmedović, he pocketed the beads, grabbed the photograph from me, and kissed it repeatedly.

"You know, I would often invite Alija out here to Mudanya," Bilir said. "I thought the sea air would help him relax. But he would never come. He stayed in Bursa and stuck to his routine. He never went out at night. He never came to the sea. He preferred never to walk alone on the streets. If he had to give an address, he would use mine rather than his own. When I asked him if he really needed to be so afraid, he said that if Tito's people caught him they would kill him there and then."

I recalled the line in Alija's notes: *I now live like a hermit on the outskirts of Moscow. I communicate only with those who guard me from others—and who guard others from me.*

There is a café near the Green Mosque in Bursa with a commanding view out over the valley. Before the Turkish auto industry chose Bursa as its industrial base in the 1980s, the valley was still relatively peaceful, full of fruit trees and cereal crops. Alija would come to this café with Bilir and sit for a long time sipping tea, gazing out over his adopted country. There is a Turkish proverb that expresses the fatalism of the Ottoman soul: "It is not only the fault of the ax but the tree as well." In such a world, idle contemplation is as reasonable a course as any.

Bilir told me the story of Alija's escape from Yugoslavia. He said that Alija had arrived in Bursa with a small group of other Bosnian Muslims. He had made his way to France after World War II, but had been captured there and imprisoned. He escaped and went to Algeria, then part of France, where he was again held by French authorities. Only his knowledge of verses from the Koran enabled him to win the sympathy of a Muslim in charge of the prison and eventually secure release.

From Algeria, Alija made the short crossing to Spain and then spent some time in France, Italy, and Romania before reaching Turkey in 1948—a date confirmed by various Turkish identity documents. Leila Ilova, the woman whose great-grandfather had fled Bosnia for Bursa in 1878, told me that Alija had known a relative of hers in Bosnia before the war and that this acquaintance had probably led him to choose Bursa as his home-in-exile.

Alija Mehmedović—under his assumed name of Ali Erhan—found a job at the Bursa Chamber of Commerce as an interpreter. His excellent command of Serbo-Croatian, French, German, Italian, and English was widely appreciated. He also worked from time to time at the Bursa tourist office, where Bilir was employed. Alija wrote many of the letters sent by import and export companies based in Bursa. When, for example, silk cocoons were exported to Japan, he wrote the accompanying letter in English. A letter to Alija from the Mumin Gencoglu company—"import-export representatives"—suggested the deference that Alija inspired. Mr. Gencoglu wrote that it was an honor to know somebody as "honest, wise, and worthy of confidence as yourself." Like Ali Bilir, he declared himself always ready to help Alija in any way.

Only when a Yugoslav trade delegation came to Bursa would Alija decline to help. His anxiety increased, Bilir told me, after a visiting Yugoslav businessman recognized him, pointing a finger and declaring: "You're not Erhan, you're Mehmedović." He refused to even consider taking a flight that crossed Yugoslav territory because, he said, technical problems might force the plane to land. "He was implacably opposed to Tito," Bilir told me. "When I suggested that Tito had at least united Yugoslavia, he waved me away and said Tito's state was a nonsense. He insisted that Yugoslavia would disintegrate after Tito's death. He said he might not be around to see the disintegration, but it would come."

On one or two occasions, Bilir pressed Alija as to why he should be a target for Tito's UDBA. Alija replied that he had documents from the war

years that, if revealed, "would make Yugoslavia shake from top to bottom."
He never showed the documents, never revealed any significant details
from them, beyond saying that he had evidence that "Tito committed
every imaginable massacre." Bilir said that, on one occasion, Alija was offered a large sum for "the documents" by a man claiming to have contacts
with the Yugoslav government, but he rejected the offer. What had ultimately become of these documents, if they ever existed, was unclear.

Alija had also confided in Bilir about his Nazi past. He had shown his
sailor friend photographs of himself in the uniform of an SS officer and
talked about how soldiers would leap to their feet when he came into the
room. He had never expressed regret at fighting in Hitler's army; he had
insisted that the fight against Tito and communism was justified. When
Bilir objected and raised the subject of the Holocaust, Alija said he had
never taken part in any actions against the Jews and that, in the Yugoslav
war, atrocities were committed by all sides.

A LINGERING ALLEGIANCE had clearly tied Alija to the postwar German state, which sent him a regular pension in recognition of his war services. A "war-injured" identity card, issued by German authorities in
Calw-Hirsau, near Stuttgart, on April 22, 1966, confirmed that Alija had
been entitled to such payments. "The heavily disabled soldier's identification card is valid for disabled persons who, because of their decreased ability to earn a living, receive direct indemnity for 70 percent or more of their
living costs from the provisions of the federal social security law," it said.
On a few occasons, Bilir told me, a doctor had come from Germany to
check that Alija was still alive. In this way, the Federal Republic of Germany had supported ex–SS officers.

What part, I wondered, was fact and what fantasy in Alija's evident obsession with revenge by Tito? He had worked in circles close to Pavelić in
Zagreb in 1943. Might he then have had access to documents that somehow incriminated Tito? He was a trained stenographer. Was he ever employed to record Pavelić's private words? Could there have been secret
contacts between Tito and Pavelić, as there were between Tito and the
Nazis? Bosnia's war between 1941 and 1945, like Bosnia's war between
1992 and 1995, was not a two-way affair: on the principle that "the enemy
of my enemy is my friend," ephemeral alliances formed. Or perhaps, in the
scramble at the end of the war, Alija had somehow gained access to intelligence on Tito's sweeping revenge killings of his enemies at Bleiburg and
elsewhere? Or, to impress the likes of Bilir, had he merely inflated his
wartime role and wartime knowledge in order to justify his evident apprehension? Did the fact that Alija was once offered money for his documents

by an envoy from Belgrade not suggest that Tito's secret services knew where he was and could have killed him at will?

The only certainty was Alija's fear. I knew of another member of the Ustasha, a prominent officer in Pavelić's army, a man whose family had a large fortune before World War II. He had tried to escape at war's end, but had been handed back to Tito's Partisans by the British at Bleiburg, despite the fact that he knew one of the British officers who arrested him from his years of study in Britain. Only money saved his life. His wife offered a castle in Zagorje, a huge apartment in central Zagreb, and land in Slovenia to a senior Partisan official she had known in school. The Ustasha officer was then allowed to live in Zagreb but was never given a Yugoslav passport. He remained under surveillance until the end of his life in 1980; he could not even travel to the Dalmatian coast without permission. He was bitter, not so much at his treatment, but at his own errors. He had joined the Pavelić forces because he believed in an independent Croatia, never imagining the massacres that would follow. When the officer died, a communist official appeared at his Zagreb apartment the next morning and asked for his Ustasha uniform. He had been allowed to keep the uniform on the condition that it be handed back to the communist state on his demise. A decade later, after communism's fall, and just before the declaration of Croatian independence, the man's grandson, a journalist, interviewed the chief of police in Zagreb. The policeman offered him the UDBA file that had been kept on his Ustasha grandfather and his father. It was highly detailed, evidence of Yugoslavia's simmering underground wars, the pervasive silt deposited by the state's troubles.

About half a million opponents of Tito chose, like Alija Mehmedović, to leave Yugoslavia at the end of the war; a much larger number, like this Ustasha officer, remained in the country. The Ustasha remained active. When Pavelić reached Buenos Aires, he changed the Ustasha's name to the Croatian Liberation Movement (HOP). There were branches, and publications, in Argentina, North America, Sweden, Australia, and elsewhere. Maks Luburić, the former commander of Jasenovac, broke with Pavelić when he entered discussions with Chetnik organizations over an eventual carve-up of Bosnia if—as they planned—Tito's Yugoslavia fell apart. Luburić, convinced that all of Bosnia should be Croatian, helped set up Ustasha terrorist groups in West Germany and Australia. After a patient infiltration of Luburić's circle, Tito's UDBA agents tracked him to Spain, and on April 20, 1969, Luburić was found dead near his Valencia villa, stabbed and bludgeoned with an iron bar.

A former Yugoslav diplomat told me how preparation for Tito's trips abroad always involved painstaking prior attempts to identify any "Ustasha" or "Chetnik" groups that might attempt to assassinate the Yugoslav leader. In Buenos Aires, Yugoslav diplomacy involved dealing with the Ustashas. Their groups were infiltrated by Yugoslav agents. When, on a number of occasions, the Ustashas sprayed the Yugoslav embassy with machine-gun fire, or scrawled anti-Tito slogans across its walls, the embassy had masons and painters standing by to fix the damage by morning. A continuous cat-and-mouse game went on in the shadows of postwar Yugoslavia.

Alija's fear was not, then, entirely irrational. Perhaps he cultivated it as further insulation to the life and the son he had left behind. But it existed, one of the many fears that would eventually be resuscitated from the top down to destroy Yugoslavia in violence.

THAT FEAR WAS particularly prevalent in Bosnia. When the Ottoman Turks left after the 1875 uprising, the administration of Bosnia was handed over to another empire, the Austro-Hungarian. But Bosnia was a special case. When Serbia freed itself during the nineteenth century, the Turks pulled back; the same thing occurred in Bulgaria and in Greece. In Bosnia, however, such a "withdrawal" was impossible in that the Turkish dominion had become overwhelmingly indigenous. At the moment that Turkish rule ended, about a third of the population—and the vast majority of the landlords and urban bourgeoisie—were Slavic Muslims. Any government would clearly have to take account of this fact.

The British traveler Arthur Evans, visiting Bosnia in 1875, saw this clearly. "It is a favorite delusion," he wrote, "to suppose that the case of Bosnia finds a parallel in that of Serbia; that here, too, an independent Christian principality could be formed with the same ease, and that the independence of Bosnia has but to be proclaimed for the Muslim to take the hint and quit the soil, as he had already quit the soil of Serbia. . . . But, as I have said, the cases of the two provinces are altogether different; in Serbia the Mahometans were an infinitesimal minority of Osmanli foreigners, encamped; in Bosnia, on the contrary, they are native Slavs, rooted to the soil, and forming over a third of the population. Under whatever government Bosnia passes, it is safe to say that the Mahometans will still form a powerful minority, all the more important for having possession of the towns."

The issue was long finessed, first by the rule of the Habsburgs, then by Bosnia's absorption into the royalist Yugoslavia of the interwar years and the communist Yugoslavia that followed. But it was always clear that the establishment and reinforcement of Bosnian national identity would involve a compromise between Christianity and Islam, one not made anywhere else on such terms on the European continent. Moreover, the

Christianity was both Orthodox and Catholic. How was this understanding to be reached?

Tito paid special attention to Bosnia, the land where his Partisan struggle was largely waged and won. It was in the central Bosnian town of Jajce, in November 1943, that his Anti-Fascist Council of National Liberation of Yugoslavia (AVNOJ) laid the constitutional basis for the communist state. Bosnia was the birthplace of the new Yugoslavia; Tito knew it to be the heart of the state. He knew also what danger lay there because he had been a witness to the fact that a quarter of the Bosnian population had been killed during World War II, many of them in internecine massacres.

After the war, the rule of the communist authorities in Bosnia therefore tended to be harsher than in other republics to ensure that there should be no resurgence of "the national question." Between 1946 and 1949, there was a series of trials of the "Young Muslims," a group with strong links to the ulema, the Muslim clergy. Among the defendants was the future Bosnian president, Alija Izetbegović, who was sentenced to three years in prison. In 1983, Izetbegović would again be imprisoned after a political show trial mounted against "Muslim nationalism" by the communist authorities.

Djilas told me that, after the war, he and Tito believed that the "consciousness of the Muslims was primarily religious, rather than national, and with the fading of religion, they would split between Serbs and Croats." Official policy encouraged Muslim families to declare themselves as Serbs or Croats. In the new state's first official census of 1948, it was impossible to be a Muslim. There was no such category.

Nor could one simply declare oneself a Bosnian. Tito eschewed the course of asserting Bosnian nationhood as a means to heal the republic's wounds and overcome its divisions, apparently because such a policy would smack of the sort of rule by *diktat* exercised by the prewar Serbian monarchy after 1929, when the attempt to forge a Yugoslav identity was most aggressively pursued. Tito often referred scathingly to prewar Yugoslavia as "Versailles Yugoslavia" (after the treaty that created it), and as the realm of the "Great Serbian bourgeoisie"; his state would not be such a "prison" of nations.

In fact, of course, the prison merely took a different form. In Tito's Yugoslavia, there was one acceptable religion: communism. To call all Bosnians Bosnians, as they were, would then have raised the question of their differing religions: Muslim Bosnians, Orthodox Bosnians, Catholic Bosnians, and Jewish Bosnians. Such distinctions were ideologically unacceptable. He was also unable, for these ideological reasons, to allow the give-and-take of democracy to unite Bosnians as Bosnians. This despite the fact that everyone living in Bosnia—Muslim, Catholic, Orthodox, and

Jew—was marked by the same history, shaped by the same topology, infected, to a greater or lesser degree, by the same nostalgia and lethargy of a place where nature is hard and change slow.

Tito's tinkerings revived the old, often grotesque, debate about who the Bosnian Muslims really were. A religious group? An ethnic group? A nation?

The state of Bosnia existed in the Middle Ages, just as Croatia and Serbia did. It was distinct, although the degree of its independence from the Hungarian throne varied. Its most powerful ruler, King Tvrtko I, ruled over parts of what are now Serbia and Croatia. Some of the people living in Bosnia belonged to a heretical local church; they converted in unprecedented numbers to the Islam of the Ottomans. Others were Orthodox Christians or Catholics who either converted to Islam or did not. Many Catholics fled westward into what is now Croatia. As John V. A. Fine has written, "Throughout its long history (medieval, Ottoman and modern) Bosnia has had its own distinct history and culture, and this culture has been shared by people of all its religious denominations."

Later, migrations into Bosnia from east and west did bring people who might more plausibly describe themselves as Croats or Serbs. But the repeated claims from Zagreb and Belgrade, starting in the nineteenth century, that the Bosnian Muslims were simply renegade Serbs or Croats were tendentious, as far-fetched as, say, a claim that Muslims living in Serbia were really Bosnians. The claim that all Orthodox Bosnians were Serbs and all Catholic Bosnians Croats was also far-fetched, but it proved a politically effective slogan for the prophets of the Serbian and Croatian nation-states during the nineteenth century.

The Bosnian Muslims had their own customs, their own culture, their own collective memory. They were Muslims but they were not Anatolians. They were, in short, a distinct Slavic people, just as the Pontic Greeks in Asia Minor were not in any meaningful sense "really Greeks" as the nationalists in Athens claimed. The habits of the Bosnian Muslims and their way of practicing their religion were shaped by Bosnia, just as the Pontic Greeks absorbed the culture of the Black Sea. They could not be, or become, somebody else in the name of an ideology hatched in a faraway city.

Sarajevans have adopted a saying, borrowed from Krleža, the Croatian writer: "God save us from Croatian culture and Serbian heroism." It reflects the restless Serbian and Croatian appetites that have focused on Bosnia. By the time Yugoslavia was formed, Croatian "culture" was already tied to the idea of defending Catholic Europe. Croatia was the *Antemurale Christianitatis*—the ramparts of Christianity—a title first bestowed on Croatia by Pope Leo X in 1519. Beyond the Christian ramparts stood the Byzantine rabble of Serbia and the Islamic subclass of Bosnia (the latter

being intermittently co-optable, however, into the struggl
Serbs). Serbian "heroism" was indistinguishable from the id
ing Europe against the "Turkish scourge" and Islam—in s
camels from grazing on the Rhine or the Seine. Between t
ideas stood the Muslims of Bosnia, Slavs just like the Serbs and Croats,
and so particularly troubling to them.

Tito attempted, in his own way, to deny history in Bosnia. First he assumed, or hoped, that, as the single dogma of communism established itself, the Muslims would "disappear." Then, in 1971, he came up with
another answer. He recognized the separate identity of the Muslims, raising them to the level of a fully fledged national group. This was an awkward solution. He thereby acknowledged that the Bosnian Muslims were
not, as he had apparently believed after the war, putative Serbs and Croats.
The decision was also politically astute: it played well among the many Islamic countries of the Non-aligned Movement and, at a time of rising tensions between Serbs and Croats, gave Tito an additional card to play in the
elaborate balancing act that characterized his rule. From the 1970s, in
Tito's Socialist Republic of Bosnia-Herzegovina, Muslims, Serbs, and
Croats were all "constituent peoples"; none was a minority. In the interests
of parity, a loosely applied system of national quotas existed in official organizations.

But the creation of the Muslim "nation" in Bosnia was also divisive. It
did not serve the purpose of bringing Bosnians together as Bosnians: they
had to identify themselves on official documents as Muslims, Serbs, or
Croats. If they felt none of these labels appropriate, they could resort to
"Yugoslav." But they could not be Bosnians. Quotas, in the end, were an
artifice, part of the Leninist game of making the "liberation" of "nations"
a foundation of communist propaganda, while at the same time imposing
a repressive political system. However subliminally, quotas underscored
differences; they could thus give rise to grievances. Although Alija Mehmedović's Bosnia was calm in the postwar decades, the fact was that Tito overlaid the most delicate legacy of Ottoman rule in the Balkans with his
favorite balance-the-nations game. The tactic worked: Yugoslavia held together with Bosnia at its center. But, in the end, communism could only
exacerbate what the empires had left behind.

AFTER DECADES in his Turkish exile, Alija Mehmedović wrote to his
former wife, Gaby, who had found him at last and was about to travel to
Turkey with Sead to meet him.

"For a long time," he said, "I did not know that you were looking for
me. My own father, Ahmed, who died in Turkey in 1958, believed for
years that I was dead, unaware that I had been saved with the help of the

German army. Therefore, when he told you I was dead at the end of the war, he told you what he really thought." He went on: "I never really looked for Sead because I felt this was in keeping with our agreement that he belonged to you and because I believed that a past that had begun beautifully and ended badly should not be recalled."

That Alija had shunned Sead in keeping with some agreement with Gaby was not convincing to me. Rather, Sead had been abandoned because he was linked to a past Alija feared, and Ahmed's arrival in Turkey would certainly have encouraged Alija to distance himself forever from his life with Gaby. Ahmed, Bilir suggested, had even told Alija that Gaby and the infant Sead were killed during the Allied bombardment of Belgrade in 1944. Each would then have imagined the other to be dead, an apparently watertight insurance against reunion.

Another barrier to any meeting emerged with the arrival in Turkey of Alija's second wife, Saima, and their son, Džemal. They lived for several years in Banja Luka after the war, unsure of Alija's fate. In the end, Ahmed told them he was still alive. Only six years after the war, in 1951, were they able to leave Yugoslavia and rejoin Alija. Thus Džemal had spent much of his childhood in postwar Bosnia without his father and had shared, for a time, his older half-brother's ignorance about their father's fate. Bilir said that Saima was always very jealous and would tolerate no mention of Alija's life before their marriage. Alija later confided to his friend that the marriage to Saima had become an empty shell.

In the suitcase was a faded black-and-white photograph of Saima and Džemal, apparently taken in Bursa. Like his father, Džemal adopted the Turkish name of Erhan on his arrival in Bursa. His head shaven, his shoulders sloping, his smile sullen, Džemal appears to have none of the charm of his father in his youth. He clutches a cat as his mother—looking wan and tired—presses against him. The sun is shining, but there seems to be little sunlight in these two uprooted lives. Džemal's expression was familiar to me: he was yet another Balkan child of war.

CHAPTER 6

DEATH IN VIENNA

WHEN SEAD DRANK, A NOT INFREQUENT OCCURRENCE, HIS mother would often exclaim that his resemblance to his father was uncanny. Sead, like Alija, had the habit of running his hands across his face when the alcohol began to get to him, as if he were washing. He liked whiskey, as his father had, and he had the same difficulty in controlling his drinking. It was unreasonable, Sead thought, to control the pleasure of a moment in which the reserve he always felt toward people was overcome. His mother's comments about his father intrigued him, and they irritated him. Sead had thought of himself as a rational man. A Marxist. He believed that people's characters were determined by circumstances, class, and surroundings. Yet it seemed that he resembled, even in a small mannerism, a man he had never known. He began to suspect that there were other similarities, that his emotional reticence, his pessimism, and his sharp mood swings were also his father's.

In 1965, at the age of twenty-seven, Sead Mehmedović began to press his mother to resolve at last the mystery of his missing father. The feeling that Alija might be alive took hold of Gaby from time to time. It was true that many people "disappeared" in Yugoslavia, during the war and again at the time of the 1948 purge. The absence of any death certificate aroused her suspicions, and the fact that Ahmed, whom she never trusted, had given her the news that Alija was dead made the information almost worthless in her eyes. Sead's insistence bolstered her doubts.

After her second marriage, to Rozenblat, ended in divorce in 1962, she thought more and more about Alija. Their passion for each other, however hopeless, had a quality to it that proved resilient. Other events were weightless; they were discarded like theater programs after a show, but Alija remained. Time, she discovered as she grew older, had its intermittences; it did not flow steadily or in a single direction. She began to look

back at old letters. As she read his words, she developed an almost physical sense that Alija was living. At moments she felt the same sharp emptiness—like having her breath suddenly sucked out of her—that she had
experienced when thinking about her missing father. In Sead, whom she
adored, and whose resemblance to his father was so strong, she found a
proof that Alija had been the love of her life. Her own mother had despised
her for her resemblance to an absent father. But she only loved Sead more.

Sead told his mother they had to be more methodical in their search.
He began to write letters to the International Committee of the Red Cross.
In the spring of 1965, he wrote to the Bosnian and Croatian branches. The
Bosnian responded first. The letter, addressed to "Comrade Sead Mehmedović," said that the Red Cross was not competent to conduct such a
search and advised him to place a newspaper advertisement. The Croatian
branch, which addressed him as "Comrade Sead Mehmedović, a painter
with a university degree" said that inquiries about Alija with the Croatian
police had been fruitless: "He is not reported as a resident of Zagreb, and
it is not clear where he moved to from Zagreb."

Gaby sought information from anyone who might have known Alija in
Sarajevo or Zagreb during the war. She heard rumors that he had suffered
from a lung disease and that he might have slipped into Switzerland at
war's end. Somebody claimed to have seen him in a sanatorium in Slovenia. But it was only through a chance encounter in 1966 with Blaženka
Kremešeć, a woman living in Zagreb, that she began to learn more.

Mrs. Kremešeć was a childhood friend of Saima, Alija's second wife. She
offered to find out about Alija's fate through Saima's elder sister, Osima
Musanović, who had married a doctor and was living in Sarajevo. "Under
the pretext that I want to reestablish my childhood friendship with Saima,
I can try to find out where they live," she wrote to Gaby.

Osima Musanović, approached by Mrs. Kremešeć's sister in Sarajevo,
proved reticent. Her family included officers in the Jugoslovenska Narodna Armija (JNA), or Yugoslav People's Army. The fascist war record of
her sister's husband was a source of embarrassment. But Mrs. Kremešeć
eventually managed to glean that Alija was alive, had taken Turkish citizenship, adopted the name Erhan, and was living with his second wife and
son in Bursa, Turkey.

On March 25, 1966, more than a quarter century after her last correspondence with Alija, Gaby wrote to him again. "Alija, I believe that this
letter will come as a surprise to you. Although Ahmed told me in 1945
that you died a violent death, I did not believe it and I continued asking
around. But only now did I learn your address. I think that you will be
glad to know that your son is a good and industrious young man who
would make any parent proud. He graduated with the mark of nine, he is

a painter, a graphic artist, and the technical editor of a monthly. I believe that he will be happy to know that his father is alive and that he has a brother. All the best to you and your family, Gaby."

The registered letter elicited no reply. Alija later claimed that he never received it. Ali Bilir suggested that Saima, with her pathological jealousy, was quite capable of hiding Alija's mail. Another letter, sent by Mrs. Kremešeć, was returned with a note saying, "The recipient moved."

Documents in the suitcase revealed that Alija and Saima traveled to Europe in 1966. Both had health problems. Alija, according to later German health insurance claims, was suffering from heart and kidney ailments linked to his tuberculosis and the removal of several of his ribs. He was treated at the Rosenbach Clinic near Nagold, southeast of Stuttgart. Saima had begun to show symptoms of cancer and was also depressive. She went to stay with her family in Sarajevo. Alija later returned to Turkey alone. In May 1968, as a result of his earlier treatment, he was invited by the German consulate to the German hospital in Istanbul, where he underwent a week-long examination.

Osima Musanović, having provided the initial information, declined to give more. With her sister Saima in Sarajevo, she was almost certainly under pressure to conceal any news of Alija. Mrs. Kremešeć visited Sarajevo in the early summer of 1968. All that she was able to learn from Osima was that Alija "might be in Germany." Sead duly wrote to the German Red Cross. But on September 20, 1968, he received another disappointing reply. "With respect to your request to trace your father Alija Mehmedović-Erhan we have to inform you that it was not possible to establish any indication of his whereabouts."

A letter to the Turkish Red Cross was similarly unproductive. Increasingly desperate, Sead wrote directly to Osima, pleading for information, but received no reply. When a colleague of his mother's traveled to Sarajevo, he confronted Dr. Sinon Musanović, Osima's husband. But Dr. Musanović said they had not received Sead's letter, were unaware of Sead's existence, and knew nothing about Saima and her family. Sead had come to attach a critical importance to finding his father, only to hit a brick wall.

SEAD'S SEARCH WAS not only his; it was, it seemed to me, the search of all of Yugoslavia for reconciliation. Alija's was the first Yugoslavia, the creation of an American president, Wilson, and the realm of the Serbian monarchy. Sead's was the second Yugoslavia, the realm of a communist, Tito, and the hybrid fruit of compromise between East and West. Their state was shared, but its two incarnations were distinct, and between those incarnations lay a war.

There were many gulfs to overcome, of blood and ideology, but perhaps they were not unbridgeable. The two men would at least have a chance to grope across the chasms. The country had been betrayed, repeatedly betrayed, but perhaps the reunion of Sead and his father could unravel the web of violence and lies.

Betrayed by the short-sightedness of its first Serbian rulers, betrayed by the fury of the Croatian Ustashas, betrayed by Tito's mind games and secret police, betrayed by false history, betrayed by sealed pits full of unidentified bodies. And betrayed by the world.

Yugoslavia was born an orphan. Woodrow Wilson helped create Yugoslavia and remap Europe in the Treaty of Versailles, but then he quickly retreated. America contracted out of the unstable new order when the U.S. Congress refused to ratify the treaty. The League of Nations, and the new European states whose problems this world organization was supposed to resolve, were left to drift in an interwar Europe marked by an explosive mixture: economic depression, German revanchism, and the mutually sustaining Bolshevik and fascist ideologies.

David Lloyd George, the British prime minister, saw the fragility of Wilson's new European architecture quickly enough and wrote to the American president on March 25, 1919: "I cannot conceive of any greater cause of future war than that the German people, who have certainly proved themselves one of the most vigorous and powerful races in the world, should be surrounded by a number of small states, many of them consisting of people who have never previously set up a stable government themselves, but each of them containing large masses of Germans clamouring for reunion with their native land."

In other words "nations"—in the sense of communities of people with a distinctive, shared culture and language—did not always fit neatly into Wilson's "nations"—in the sense of the states established after World War I. That conundrum would dog Europe for the rest of the century. That another world war should follow in 1939, with devastating consequences for Yugoslavia, was not altogether unpredictable.

When war came, Yugoslavia was left to its fate once more. Churchill cheered on the defiant Yugoslavs, and the West's commitment to Yugoslavia was spelled out by the British historian Robert William Seton-Watson in a passionate radio message on March 27, 1941:

> *During the last week many friends have asked me what Yugoslavia would do in a situation whose danger and difficulty everyone here in London fully recognised. I always replied that Yugoslavia asked nothing better than to maintain an honorable neutrality within frontiers won by oceans of blood after long centuries of enslavement, but that if the mo-*

ment came when a foreign Power threatened those frontiers, her people would not submit to sabotage like unhappy Rumania or to intimidation like Bulgaria, but would rally to the last man in defence of independence.

There are many still in this country who remember with admiration and affection their Serbian comrades-in-arms in the World War and who proved by the hard test of experience that in spite of all the differences of race and education we and you have the same basic moral standards and the same belief in individual rights. We still believe that in the making of the new Europe after this war the Yugoslavs will range themselves not with the gangsters of the 30th June or the March on Rome, with their monstrous swindle of a so-called Neu-Ordnung, but with the democracies of Britain and America and the free overseas dominions, whose task it will be to bring back our unhappy world from Nazi forces and Fascist fraud to methods of peace, liberty and reconstruction. I salute you, my Yugoslav friends, true and trusty. We will not fail each other on the day of trial.

But when the war was over, Britain and America did fail Yugoslavia. The question of "individual rights" in Yugoslavia proved far less important than the support of Stalin's army in winning the war in Europe and in Asia. Churchill had made his calculations quite clear to Fitzroy Maclean, the dashing commander of the British military mission to Tito's Partisans: "Do you intend to make Yugoslavia your home after the war?" he asked in 1944. Maclean said he did not. To which Churchill replied, "Neither do I. And, that being so, the less you and I worry about the form of government they set up, the better."

The worrying was left to Sead and Alija, marooned on either side of an ideological chasm. And, much later, to those who witnessed what happened when the "form of government" in Yugoslavia that Churchill waved away unraveled as Europe's Iron Curtain was torn aside. Then the politicians and diplomats worried, at length and in circles. Once again, in the 1990s, the West would fail Yugoslavia and its people by failing to move quickly enough either to hold Yugoslavia together, perhaps in some looser form, or to ensure that its subtle heart in Bosnia was not crushed in a barbarous breakup.

IN 1968, Sead's half-brother Džemal Erhan took up residence in Vienna. He rented a room at 64 Taborstrasse, not far from the center of the city. The room, in the apartment of a Frau Hermine Meyer, was spacious, and Džemal had the use of a corner kitchen. Mrs. Meyer, who owned a large grocery store, was widowed and liked to have somebody in the apartment.

Džemal began studies for an engineering degree, and to earn money to supplement his father's allowance, he took a part-time job selling the newspaper *Kurier* on the corner of Taborstrasse.

The street appears to have changed little in the three decades since Džemal came to Vienna. It is a dowdy part of town. In fading cafés, rotating trays of uneaten cakes turn round and round. The buildings, with their peeling stucco, are shabby. Trams trundle past Doner Kebab restaurants, audio stores, and sleazy pubs. The tourists parading through the gilt-and-cream museum-palaces of the Habsburgs do not venture here. But the Habsburgs have left their trace in the Jewish, Slav, Magyar, and Germanic names of the people living at 64 Taborstrasse—Ruby, Drexler, Klvac, Trabka, Gussner, Gundel, Ulm, and Kaiser.

From Vienna, at different times over the four centuries before World War I, the Habsburgs ruled Slovenes, Croats, Germans, Magyars, Serbs, Carpatho-Ruthenians, Czechs, Slovaks, Italians, Poles, and Rumanians. Repeatedly, they did battle with another multinational empire, that of the Ottomans; the outcome of those battles set the border between Catholic Europe and Turkey-in-Europe. In Sarajevo—ruled for over four hundred years by the Ottomans and for forty years by the Habsburgs—the sharp break between the meandering alleys of the old Turkish town and the foursquare administrative buildings of the Austro-Hungarian section evokes the gulf between these two worlds that Yugoslavia sought to bridge. Bosnia, preserved, was that bridge between East and West; attacked, it was the inevitable fault line.

Karl Neustadter, a businessman, met Džemal Erhan in 1968 at his newspaper stand on Taborstrasse. Džemal, who spoke and wrote perfect German, liked to go out drinking. Neustadter would accompany him, and they became friends. "He told me that he was born in Bosnia and that he was anti-communist, but I never heard him vilify Tito," Neustadter said. "The Croats in Vienna were always violently anti-Tito, but he seemed more moderate. His main concerns were chasing girls and his studies, in that order. He also talked a lot about his Muslim religion. He seemed torn as to whether it was the right religion for him. We would talk about faith in general."

Džemal never mentioned his half brother, Sead Mehmedović, to Neustadter. He had a lot of Yugoslav émigré friends who would come to his room and drink late into the night. The noise was sometimes too much for Mrs. Meyer, who complained. Alija was also a frequent visitor to his son, sometimes staying for several weeks. He struck Neustadter as "a highly intelligent man, an intellectual, and extremely sympathetic." Alija spent a lot of time reading. But he was frail and clearly not well. He explained to Neustadter that he was often in Germany because, as a World

War II veteran of an SS unit, he had found that he was entitled to free medical treatment in German hospitals.

By now, Saima's condition was deteriorating and Džemal went regularly to Sarajevo to visit her. Some of his correspondence was in Alija's suitcase. On May 30, 1969, Džemal wrote from the Bosnian capital to Alija, who was then staying in Mrs. Meyer's room in Vienna: "Dear Daddy, I arrived happily in Sarajevo. Mother is better. But she insists on going to Germany because she has convinced herself that she cannot be cured in Yugoslavia. You are supposed to request 1,000 German marks against your pension. I have 1,000 marks with me which should be enough in any case to take her to the hospital in Germany. She has, after all, already paid everything in Germany for her treatment. . . . I think we will be in Vienna by Friday morning. Please drink less so that mummy does not get upset. Everyone sends their regards."

Alija himself appears to have toyed briefly with the idea of going to Sarajevo during this summer of 1969. His suitcase contained a letter, dated July 14, 1969, from a representative of the Center for Emigrants from Bosnia and Herzegovina in Sarajevo. Alija had written to the center, complimenting it on its publications, presumably brought to him by Džemal. The reply, from one Čedo Kapor, thanked Alija and said that it looked forward to "the visit you announce." It requested news from him on Bosnians working in Turkey and Austria. And it alluded to an important political connection that Alija still had in Yugoslavia: "I have not yet had a chance to deliver your regards to Cvijetin Mijatović, your school friend, because we have not met in Sarajevo or in Belgrade. He is very busy, constantly traveling all over Yugoslavia."

Mijatović was a prominent Bosnian politician who would later be the first president of the rotating presidency after Tito's death. He had been at high school with Alija. In 1969, as he pressed his quest to find his father, Sead asked Mijatović to look into whether there was really any reason why Alija should not return to Yugoslavia. The politician remembered Alija well from school days. "He liked Kant, and I liked Hegel," Mijatović told Sead. The idealist and the materialist had remained on different sides of the ideological spectrum. Mijatović replied in 1970 that, as far as he could ascertain, Alija was free to come back to Yugoslavia. But Alija did not return.

During his stay in Sarajevo in May 1969, Džemal discovered Sead's letter, written the previous year, requesting information about Alija. He angrily confronted his aunt Osima about her failure to reply. But Saima's family was set against any reunion with Sead. Džemal pocketed the letter and took it with him when he traveled with his mother to Vienna, arriving on June 6, 1969.

Later, in a letter to Sead dated November 21, 1970, Alija tried to explain why he did not respond to Sead's pressing request that he come forward. "Above all," Alija wrote, "I implore you to believe that I am deeply grateful to you for all your efforts to find me. I must explain to you how it was that I did not reply to the letter you wrote to Osima, the aunt of your brother Džemal. Actually Džemal frequently visited his very sick mother in Sarajevo and that is how he found out about your letter to Osima in which you implore her to give my address. Knowing that his aunt would not do that, he simply hid the letter and brought it with him when he came to Vienna with his mother on June 6, 1969.

"On June 10, 1969, we took her to hospital in Munich, *where she died four days later.* After that I returned to Vienna, where I stayed for a few weeks to recover. But instead of recovery came a throat cancer. In those very difficult moments, for me and Džemal, I could not bring myself to think about correspondence. Planning to answer later, I put the letter into one of Džemal's numerous files. After the diagnosis of cancer, I returned to Germany in the second half of August and began radiotherapy in Munich, at the Schwabing Hospital. In the beginning of November 1969, I was sent to the Schlosbergklinik, Oberstaufen, where the cancer was temporarily cured, but my old kidney disease worsened as well as my heart condition. At the Munich hospital and at the Schlosbergklinik, Džemal visited me several times and on each occasion we spoke about your letter which we could no longer find. He said that for him personally it was very important to find it because he was determined to visit you, but he believed, anyway, that he would find you easily, for he knew you were in Belgrade and a well-known painter. He insisted on how important it was that I write to you and promised to keep looking for the letter, but he did not find it."

SAIMA'S DEATH on June 14, 1969, clearly removed an obstacle to the long-awaited reunion between father and son. Alija was always susceptible. He had vowed to break with his father before World War II, only to give way to paternal pressure and instead sever all contacts with Gaby. Having never betrayed any fascist inclination, he had joined the Ustasha and the Nazis after their seizure of power. In the interest of avoiding confrontation, it seemed clear that, as long as Saima was living, Alija had avoided a serious search for Sead. Once his second wife was dead, however, finding Sead and Gaby became the priority of his waning life. But Alija's declining health and his refusal, in the end, to set foot in Yugoslavia made the closing stages of Sead's quest more complicated.

A YEAR AFTER his mother's death, Dzemal began his final exams in Vienna. His plan was to find an apartment in the city where he could live with his father. Alija was still in southern Germany, at the Schlosbergklinik in Oberstaufen, but was becoming impatient to leave. On July 3, 1970, Džemal wrote to his father. "My very dear old man," he began, "I received 300 German marks from you today. Thank you very much. I had already received your card and your letter. Above all, I am happy that you are not planning to leave the hospital, at least until July 8. As you know my last exam is on July 7. After that I will have to wait a few days, because there are some oral exams. When I know my exact date of arrival I will tell you. . . . For the moment I have already passed three of my exams. I was not satisfied with the first. I may have to take it again in a few months. The two others went much better. The fourth is on Monday or Tuesday. We'll see. Look after yourself. As soon as we find an apartment, you will come to Vienna and we will be together for two or three months. After that, we'll see."

Five days later, Džemal again wrote to Alija. His exams had been prolonged. He urged his father to be patient and not to sign his own discharge from the hospital. "I am doing a written exam on July 10," Džemal wrote, "and have some oral exams on July 14. After that I will come to Oberstaufen and we will talk everything over. For the moment, let's leave all plans aside. Next week I will tell you my exact date of arrival."

But Džemal Erhan never reached Oberstaufen. On July 14, 1970, there was a celebration of the end of exams. He returned home late. Mrs. Meyer's apartment was on the first floor. Džemal was found by Mrs. Meyer the next morning, unconscious at the bottom of the stairwell, the base of his skull fractured. He died later that day in the hospital. He was twenty-seven years old.

THE CAUSE OF DEATH was never established. Neustadter is convinced that Džemal Erhan was killed. "I went over the incident endlessly," he told me, "and I could never convince myself that a fit young man would die in such a so-called accident. He liked to drink but I never saw him drunk. How could he fall down the stairs in that way? If he had really fallen, would he not have made a noise that would have woken Mrs. Meyer? As it was, he lay there all night."

Mrs. Meyer, who has since died, also had her doubts, which she made clear in letters to Alija. On July 22, 1970, she wrote to the Schlosbergklinik, informing Alija that the funeral would take place on July 27 at Vienna's Central Cemetery. She continued: "Mr. Karl Neustadter called me and was of course horrified. His wife, too, was in floods of tears. Otherwise nobody has called until now which I find very curious. Where are these people that came continuously, so much so that I even got angry, saying it was like a café in Džemal's room? I have left the door to my room open ever since his death so that I do not miss the doorbell. But so far not one visit. I think day and night about how this could have happened. I am very sorry for him. My clients, who knew him from the newspaper stand, are very upset too. They say only good things about him." In a later letter, dated September 15, 1970, Mrs. Meyer returned to the doubts that plainly devoured her. "Not one of Džemal's friends who used to visit him so frequently has shown his face," she wrote. "I often still think about this mysterious incident."

ALIJA TRAVELED to Vienna. The only other person who came to the funeral was Neustadter. With his usual punctiliousness, Alija kept the invoice from the City of Vienna for the funeral costs: 1,880 schillings, the grave to be maintained by the city for a decade. He also procured and kept a copy of the *Kurier* from July 14, 1970. On it he wrote: "The last paper Džemal sold." Neustadter was amazed that nobody else, among the many "friends" who had surrounded Džemal, turned up. "It was so strange to me that there were only two of us at the funeral," he said. "Quite eerie."

Later, Alija told him bluntly that Džemal had been killed by Tito's Yugoslav agents. He said the same thing to Bilir when he returned, later that year, to Bursa. Exhausted, weak, he seemed to the two men to be quite unemotional in his assessment of what he saw as his son's murder.

Official inquiries into Džemal's death were inconclusive. On October 13, 1970, Neustadter wrote to Alija, who had returned to Oberstaufen, about various financial matters. "You have been granted the hospital costs of about 1,200 schillings," he said, "but not the burial costs, since it has not been established whether Džemal died of natural causes or foul play. The possibility of foul play is being actively considered." Neustadter continued to pursue the affair, but no formal conclusion was ever reached. Of Džemal, born in Sarajevo, raised in Banja Luka and Bursa, died in Vienna, not a trace remains. His grave, once the decade had elapsed in 1980, was no longer maintained by the Central Cemetery. Džemal Erhan, born Džemal Mehmedović, has simply disappeared.

But did Džemal suffer the fate that his father had long feared? The manner of his death, and the immediate disappearance of all the émigré Yugoslavs who had frequented his room, is suspicious. The year of his death, moreover, was one of mounting tension between the Yugoslav authorities and the Ustashas in exile. Luburić, the commander of Jasenovac, had been killed the previous year in Spain. In 1970, Vladimir Rolović, the Yugoslav assistant secretary for foreign affairs, traveled to Australia to give details to the Australian government of Ustasha organizations and involvement in terrorist actions. A year later, after his appointment as Yugoslav ambassador to Sweden, Rolović was murdered by the Ustasha. The UDBA was active at this time in dispatching agents to kill Ustashas in exile. If an envoy sent by Belgrade had indeed once tried to buy Alija's documents from him in Bursa, then the UDBA knew of his existence in Turkey and of his family. Džemal was not an Ustasha, but his father was, and he himself made no secret of his anti-communist feelings. It is possible, in this light, that Džemal Erhan was murdered.

LETTERS POURED IN to Alija from his Turkish friends, appalled at the loss, in such quick succession, of his wife and his son. They urged him to find consolation in God. A friend named Faik Dogan wrote: "From the Good Lord, we can only hope for clemency and for help for all our brothers in Islam. For us, sickness, accidents and death are always expected because they are expressions of the will of God, and we can only thank him, as much for the happiness as for the unhappiness that he gives us. We must not resist his will, must not importune him with questions about why we have been afflicted with some illness. It is useless. Above all—and you know this better than I do—we must remain calm and await with patience the days to come, be they good or bad. That is the way things are." Bilir and Alija's business friend, Gencoglu, also urged him to respect the will of God, however painful.

In September 1970, Mrs. Meyer rented Džemal's room to an Austrian student. She charged a reduced price because Džemal's possessions were still in the room. "Having washed all of your son's clothes," she wrote to Alija, "I realized how many things he had. It makes three suitcases full with laundry; the rest of the clothes I wrapped in blankets. The books and the rest of his things I put into cardboard boxes. Altogether it makes quite a sizable lot. If you have no other choice but to leave them here, I would be happy for you to do so. But I would ask you to pay 50 marks per month." Three months later, in December, Mrs. Meyer wrote again, to say that she was preparing to ship all the effects to Turkey. But something odd had happened at the shipping company. The man who had done the estimate had not contacted her for three weeks. Then she discovered that he had gone on holiday. In her last letter, she promised to keep pressing the matter.

It is not clear if any of these possessions were ever shipped. Sead did not find anything of Džemal's when he finally traveled to Turkey in January 1971 to meet his father. The shipment presumably included the lost letter that Sead had sent to Osima; perhaps it also included some of the sensitive documents about Tito that Alija claimed to have. In any event, Alija's attention, after Džemal's death, was on other matters. He had lost his second son, but he was about to recover his first.

CHAPTER 7

GOD AND
A BOTTLE OF GIN

IN THE CLEAR ALPINE AIR OF OBERSTAUFEN, WHERE THE clouds trace precise shadows on the meadows as they scurry across the sky, Alija spent a little more than one year. He arrived in the Schlosbergklinik on November 3, 1969, and departed on December 6, 1970. A certificate provided to him on his discharge says that he worked part-time as a translator and a janitor during his stay in the Bavarian town, southwest of Munich. But he seems to have spent much of the time in a state of nervous depression. Letters urge him to find comfort in nature, friends, love, God, and, finally, the imminent reunion with Sead. But his small notebooks, filled with neat handwriting, suggest a man in a state of near constant anxiety. Each vagary of his feeble appetite, each medicine sampled, each letter received and sent, each pfennig spent on a magazine or a postage stamp is recorded. The price of the copy of the *Kurier* bought to record Džemal's death appears in one of the debit columns, but there is not a word on his son. Alija, alone in a perfectly ordered place—where every path is manicured, every field fenced, every cow's udder swollen with milk, every gleaming room filled with the prospect of death—wanted a perfect order to his affairs.

There is a curious obstinacy to these notebooks. They suggest an orchestra that keeps playing as the ship goes down. Or a couple whose obsessive lovemaking in a closed apartment blinds them to the fact that their city has gone to war since they last bought the groceries.

Alija's life had been scattered to the wind. He was a stranger in Germany. He had changed his name. He had changed his nationality from Yugoslav to Turk. A quarter century earlier he had abandoned a wife and son; he had just lost another wife and son. He was seriously ill, being treated, according to medical reports, for cancer of the larynx, an extensive and chronic kidney infection, and weakness of the heart. Yet he lists every copy of *Le Figaro* or *Time* acquired. He notes every pair of pajamas bought. He lists every taxi fare paid. He records every yogurt consumed, every chocolate eaten, every apple juice drunk, every injection of cortisone and every new drug tried. The jottings are obsessive, but in the punishing weight of derisory detail Alija seems to have found some relief.

He struggled for spiritual peace, dabbling in Hindu disciplines and searching for some release from a decaying body. Certain phrases in Alija's writings suggest that he has embraced an Ottoman fatalism and found a consoling faith in God. "One should do his duty to God," he writes in English, "whatever that is—not what organized religion says it should be, but what one really believes."

At other moments, however, his old irreverence comes through and God seems no more comforting—only more insistent—than a bottle of gin. In one poem he penned in German and called "Discussion," Alija writes: "There were three of us: My friend, a bottle of Gin and I. Late at night the dear Lord joined us, as well as Immanuel Kant. The latter sat apart and looked over our shoulders. We had a long, excited conversation, my friend, the dear Lord, and I. Every now and then the bottle would get involved with clever jokes, and sometimes Kant made a biting remark, until late into the night, after a long altercation, the bottle fell silent. Immanuel Kant had already left. And only the dear Lord could not be gotten rid of again."

Whether it is gin or God or a godless world that brings on these ravings of a sick man, I cannot say. But Alija writes: "To invite—that was kind. I receive a pension in Germany, it would be better, but . . . Mentally I am not feeling worse. Most . . . thanks . . . why is the horror of the pictures: a memory. Mrs. Lorentz from Amsterdam. The air is bad. Mrs. Steinhort: her flowers are still blooming. I don't know anything about a female patient. . . . I can read. . . . And then enclosed: operation: being confused (with someone else?). Write at three in the morning. Insomnia. And the postcard: yes in the post-script he said thank you. To be reborn . . ." Reading this, another phrase of Alija's came back to me: "He never found the boy. 'And now,' said a neighbor, 'he raves like a madman, and in his eyes is an expression beyond words.'" What T. S. Eliot called the folly of old men: "Their fear of fear and frenzy, their fear of possession, / Of belonging to another, or to others, or to God."

Alija was not demonstrative. Whatever madness he had was held down within. Fear haunted him. Depression—he lost Džemal in the middle of the year—often paralyzed him. Another of his notes, in German, said: "You are afraid of life, but your fears are completely groundless." He had withdrawn from life in 1945, at the age of thirty-four, as some states withdraw from history. The rest was a Turkish coda, for he could never make his life whole. Fair punishment for a Nazi?

I developed the film that Sead had given me on his Belgrade rooftop, hoping to find an image of Alija in later life. There he was, in all his colossal banality. Tall, slim, a gray overcoat, a dark homburg, glasses, a glimmer to the eyes, and a certain weary kindness to the smile. A quality of shyness, a look slightly askance, intelligence and humility. Not a man who would turn the head; a face in the crowd, nothing more. I could not hate him. I tried but I could not. Soldier of Hitler, murderer of Jews—I tossed every insult at Alija, even some that were certainly groundless, but none would stick. That was the surprising fact. I had met too few heroes and heard too many hate-filled slogans thrown about in the Balkans—"Ustasha," "Chetnik," "fundamentalist"—to affix a label to Alija. Besides, there was too much of Sead in him, and I knew the generosity of Sead's soul. What a pair! The fascist father, the communist son: they were enemies then, cold warriors. But I found more truth in their shared habit of drawing their hands across their faces when drunk.

One hospital report from the Schlosbergklinik said of Alija: "He was not operated on in the clinic but was treated thirty times with Gammatron radiation. He feels exhausted, all of his bones ache. The voice got better after the X-ray treatment but he remains hoarse. No fever. No active tuberculous changes. We support the heart with Intensain, one tab three times a day, as well as one tab of DigiPersatin. Moreover we treat the patient with 500 millilitres of plasma twice a week." It described the fifty-nine-year-old patient as a "tall, slender, weak, lean figure."

A GERMAN NURSE named Heidi, aged twenty-six, fell in love with Alija. Her husband, a sick man, was in the clinic. He had tormented Heidi; she poured out her heart to Alija. "Dear Lord, I am behaving like a silly teenager, don't you think?" she wrote. "Like some young creature experiencing her first heartache. That is right. That is what I am saying. The only thing is that I am no longer a young teenager who is experiencing the joy and pain of love for the first time, but a young woman who . . . wants to make a small confession to a friend and is afraid that she is making a fool of herself."

Heidi's life was a mess. She had married for the first time because she was pregnant. She separated after a year and was granted custody of her son, Martin. But her former husband had engaged a lawyer to get Martin back. Her second husband, meanwhile, the one in the clinic, was violent and jealous.

"When I was married for the second time," Heidi continued, "everything seemed so wonderful and peaceful in spite of the illness. But the page quickly turned. Things became simply horrendous. I have never been so afraid as I have in this marriage. Everything happened—from beatings to death threats to being thrown out. I do not know how often I have had to hide at night in the clinic with colleagues. Dr. Kubelka helped me sometimes by giving my husband sleeping injections because he raged like a lunatic and threatened me. Every day there was something else, if you ignore the pathological jealousy. Finally, he has returned to his mother, and I do not want to have him back.

"Maybe you are shocked by the sober tone in which I tell you this. But perhaps you can imagine how it feels when someone makes you tremble with fear day after day. I am so happy that it is all over now. For Martin, too, who has already seen too much. You cannot imagine what a joy it was for me when you were able to join us briefly on my birthday. Until that moment things had been terribly dreary. . . . It was you who made this day special for me in every way. I was and am very grateful to you for this. I think that, although you did not know it, you did a lot for me. Please don't laugh at me but your necklace has become a sort of talisman which I treasure. . . ."

Alija duly recorded the arrival of the letter in his notebook. He also took note, without comment, of Heidi's telephone calls.

SEAD'S FRUSTRATION boiled over in the summer of 1970. On July 29 of that year he sat down to record the main elements of the story. It was a plea for help, addressed at once to himself and the world. He recorded his father's early career and work at *Politika*. Alija's second marriage to Saima Kadić in Sarajevo. His move to Zagreb. The disappearance in 1943. The first, ultimately fruitless breakthough of 1966, when contact was made with Saima's sister, Osima Musanović. Sead's letters to the Red Cross. His letter to Osima in Sarajevo. The refusal of the Musanović family to help. And the latest details:

"A few days ago when I inquired with Saima's friend as to whether she had heard anything new, she told me that Saima died some time ago and that she would try to learn more. She also told me that Osima had just received a telegram informing her that her nephew Džemal (my half brother) had been killed in a traffic accident, on his way to visit his father Alija in some specialized sanatorium, where he was being treated for his lung disease. She allegedly received the telegram from Munich. . . . I immediately made a phone call to Osima in Sarajevo. When I introduced myself, I pointed out that I had sent her a letter to which I never received a reply, and told her that I had accidentally received information about recent misfortunes in the family of my father. She answered that she did indeed receive a telegram, that she did not know from whom, that Džemal had been killed, that Alija was in a sanatorium, and that she knew nothing more. At my insistence she told me that the telegram came from Munich from a friend of Alija. As for my letter she told me that she had delivered it to Džemal when he was in Sarajevo, that he took it to Alija, and that Džemal wanted to go to Belgrade and look me up when he was here last year, but they had lost the address!

"My impression is that the family is trying to prevent me reaching my father. I am sure they knew something, certainly Alija's address, because they were being visited by both Saima and Džemal. I cannot believe that a father would resist the temptation—out of curiosity, if nothing else—to get in touch with a son whom, to judge by some of his letters to my mother, he loved. I have reasons to believe that my grandfather, Ahmed Mehmedović, who told my mother that my father was dead, also told my father that my mother and I were both killed in the bombardment of Belgrade. I cannot understand that any person of goodwill would not reply to a letter in which a son is looking for his father. At the very least tell me—'Your father is alive but does not want to get in touch with you'—or something of that sort. Therefore I have reason to believe that someone for some reason has deliberately stopped me from meeting my father. Whatever the truth may be, I want to learn EVERYTHING about my father. . . ."

Who, I wondered, had come up with the story of Džemal being killed in a traffic accident? Was that the first version of the story that reached Alija in Oberstaufen? Had he used it as a means to avoid tiresome explanations? Who was the friend in Munich? There was one in Alija's phone book—Petar Sokolov. I called the Munich number. Sokolov was dead.

The confabulations multiplied. When, a few days after writing his cri de coeur, Sead called Osima again in Sarajevo, she told him that Alija was dead. It was the second time that Alija's death had been announced. Gaby did not believe the news. Sead declared to his mother that he would not stop his inquiries until he had found his father's grave.

ON OCTOBER 10, 1970, Alija, still in Oberstaufen, made an unusually long entry in one of his notebooks. He was evidently experimenting with forms of yoga. "Breathe," he wrote, "with a strength that fills the room. Put body, soul and spirit in your breath. The kidneys, lungs and heart are to be cleared and strengthened by the vibrations of sound. Breathe in. Breathe out. Make an *Mmmmmm* vibration. The liver is cleansed of poison: circulation grows stronger. Through our will we can relax our nerves and muscles. But the only healer is God, who can work through us without hindrance. Walking and listening in peace and quiet:

God is at work here. Without breath no life. The healing effect of colors . . . of light . . . colorful flowers . . . yellow geraniums . . . heavy bleeding . . . light energy . . . irritation can make you sick . . . Let us heal ourselves with reconciliation . . . V=*Vergeben* [To forgive], *Vorbei* [Done with and over] . . . The Yogi raises your thoughts . . . not to quarrel but wait . . . in meditation what is experienced leads to the Divine. . . . They speak like mystics in the Middle Ages. . . . The spirit emerges from the eyes. We fly without wings. . . ."

His condition was deteriorating. Five days later, on October 15, he recorded his weight as 62.3 kilograms. By October 22, it was 57.9 kilograms. He had no appetite. He took to reading the horoscopes and, on November 15, he recorded the following prediction: "You find success through active, self-confident, purposeful activity. Don't start anything new on a Wednesday."

In November, Alija took a new approach. He at last sent a messenger to try to find Sead. She was a Yugoslav nurse named Gorana Boljević who had worked at the Schlosbergklinik. Her research in Belgrade was successful, and she found Sead at *Politika* in the middle of November 1970. She told Sead his father was not well; she brought photographs of Alija; she gave the address in Oberstaufen. Alija, she said, was now anxious to meet his son.

GABY SENDS the first letter on November 17, 1970. "Finally, after 30 years of persistent search, we got news and pictures," she writes. "Since 1945, the year that Ahmed told me you were not alive, I have been searching through various institutions and finally, by accident, I got your address in Bursa. I wrote a registered letter but never received a reply. I did not give up looking further and three years ago I even visited Munich. From the family of Osima Musanović I received a message in July of this year that you were dead and I should not look for you any further. It is not clear to me why everyone so persistently hid you, Sead's father, from him. I hope that you will meet each other and that you will like each other and, although late, it will not be too late to offer each other a friendly hand. Thank you for giving me such a wonderful son; you will be grateful to me for looking after him and for the fact that he has become such a wonderful man. I wish you a speedy recovery and I would like very much to see you. . . ."

Alija notes the arrival of the letter on November 19, beneath entries recording that he has taken three doses of "multivitamin," received a transfusion, and been administered a new drug. The following day, he writes back to Gaby, his first letter to her since 1940: "Your letter dated November 17 arrived yesterday. I can sincerely say that it surprised me pleasantly.

An intelligent letter, bereft of sentimentality or probing of the past. . . . Your registered letter sent to my Bursa address was never delivered. If I had received it, there would have been no reason not to answer."

He turns to Osima Musanović. She is a liar, a meddler, a terrible woman. To try to hide a boy from his father is abnormal, Alija writes. His rage against her masks his own guilt.

"Thank you for your information about Sead," Alija continues. "Although brief, it was precious to me. I am glad that you are so proud of him, although I have not contributed at all to his upbringing. Rest assured that I am sincerely grateful to you that, through your efforts, he became such a wonderful man, much better than his father, just as it is supposed to be.

"Thank you for your wishes concerning my recovery. But, to put it bluntly, there is no hope because my kidneys are incurably ill. Cancer has not reappeared after the first treatment, but my kidneys and heart cannot endure for much longer. On December the 1st or 2nd, I plan to leave the clinic and set off, if possible by sea, for Turkey, and from there I will of course get in touch with you.

"As for your wish to see me, I am in agreement, but I think we had better leave that to the future for the time being and see first how Sead and I will meet. I have nobody in the world anymore who would be closer to me than he is. So you may imagine that I certainly want to see him—of course, on the condition that he wants it also."

Gaby immediately replies. She says she hesitated to write again so soon because she wanted to leave time for a letter from Sead to arrive and for arrangements to be made for the two men to meet. But a sense that time is short impels her, and she puts things to Alija with her customary straightforwardness: "You are the father of our child. As long as I live nothing else, as far as you are concerned, will matter to me. I have always thought about you and I have passed that feeling on to our son. Blood is thicker than water and he has so many of your traits."

She goes on to describe some of her attempts to find him, only to dismiss them as unimportant now. "Let all that go, don't be upset," she urges Alija. "You've had enough hard times this year, many shocks. Pull yourself together if you possibly can and gain consolation from Sead. If I can help you in some way tell me, I'll do anything I can with all my heart."

Alija's decision to return to Turkey by boat leaves Gaby perplexed. She urges him to reconsider. To come to Belgrade and get some rest, so they can talk—talk, as she puts it, "so nicely." She wants to offer him moments of peace; she is worried about who will care for him in Turkey. "Come on, old boy, raise your head," she concludes. "For as long as we live things will go on somehow and when we get a passport to the other world, we will live in our child. Now get some rest. Good-bye and take care. Gaby."

• • •

AT THE SAME TIME as this letter, just a few weeks before the letter he sent with tremulous hand to Turkey, Sead writes to his father for the first time. There is no greeting at the top of the letter. "As you see I don't know how to address you," he says, "so I am leaving that to time to solve. Gaby told me she wrote to you yesterday. I am a bit confused. It is certainly easier for her—she knows you and I only know of you. . . .

"I hear that, like me, you are hesitant and you don't know how I will react now, after all these years. Please don't worry about that—I know that life is strange and that it often puts people in circumstances that cannot be changed or overcome in any way. You know, I always thought that I would have so many things to tell you about myself, and now I am avoiding them, because it seems that I want this first contact of ours to somehow be a continuation, not a beginning. I am sure that you will understand.

"I will not tell you about my attempts to find you—there will be time for that. But anything that we managed to find out was always so unclear and contradictory, as if somebody did not want us to meet. I wish I had known Džemal and I am sorry that so much misfortune has befallen you. I will be happy if I can alleviate that even a little bit."

An attempt at a self-portrait follows. But Sead labors to describe himself in more than the most basic terms. He is a painter, a graphic designer. A strange coincidence has brought him to *Politika,* not the newspaper, but the company's advertising agency. He is married, for the second time, happily. Anyway, he writes, abandoning the effort, they will soon get to know each other well.

Sead, too, is worried by the journey to Turkey, where he has heard that there is a cholera epidemic. It would be easier if Alija remained in Germany. "I am very happy that I have found you," he says, "and here, now, as I finish this letter, I have the impression that you are close to me and that we have been reunited rather than found each other for the first time. . . . Love, Sead."

ALIJA'S FIRST LETTER to his son, written before Sead's letter arrived, is a long, tangled, defensive explanation of why he has not found him earlier. Depression, Džemal's death, cancer, and other diseases are all invoked. The letter begins: "Dear Sead, it is not easy for me as a father to write to the son whom he last saw when he was hardly a year and half old. Since then, almost half of your life has passed and, for me, the second half is drawing to a close. Whatever the situation is now, this correspondence was bound to happen because there was a mutual desire and had you not come up with the initiative, your brother Džemal would have. His death in an accident in July this year was the only thing that stopped him looking for you. He would certainly have found you easily because he knew you were in Belgrade. . . ."

The awkwardness between father and son is evident. They spoke once on the telephone. Later, in a letter, Sead described his feelings. "You know, when I called you for the first time (when we actually spoke for the first time) I wanted to tell you that I would come immediately to Oberstaufen and I was waiting for some sign from you that you wanted me to come. However it seems that we are both a bit constrained and we don't open up easily. The circumstances were not too favorable either. Gaby and my wife Mina were present and I don't like to open myself completely even before the people closest to me, and people usually do not understand what kind of 'secrets' I might have and they want to participate and sympathize with me in everything."

In a letter sent from the clinic to Gaby, Alija is more forthcoming and less painfully disingenuous. He says he can walk but he is not well (his health seems to have rallied—his weight is recorded as 61.54 kilos on November 25). He thanks her for the invitation to Belgrade, but says he must return to Turkey and get organized first—"if this disorganized head of mine can get organized at all." Not to return to Turkey, he says, "would mean, for me, death in solitude and a state of nervous depression in a foreign country." He would like to come to Yugoslavia, not least, he says, to go to Sarajevo and introduce himself to Osima Musanović as "Alija from the other world!" But at least in Turkey, there are "a few good friends." His costs will be much lower. He will not feel lonely and "in the spring I will move to some village by the sea and wait for the end."

Alija explains his fears. He favors taking the boat to Turkey because he is afraid of airplanes. Planes and elevators are the things he fears most. He used to sedate himself with whiskey and fly in a stupor, but now he has been told not to drink, especially as he is incapable of drinking in moderation. So he will go by boat. But what if there is a heavy swell on the winter sea? He may catch a cold on the boat. If he gets a fever his kidneys will ache terribly. So, after all, he may go by plane.

He tries to express his feelings about Sead. He is "very happy" that they will finally meet. The meeting is an immense consolation, "although I have no moral right to seek consolation in the son that I did not try to find for so long a time." He gives an address in Ankara—that of a friend, Refik Cabi, whose apartment he notes has central heating—and says that he will be in touch as soon as he arrives in Turkey.

ALI BILIR TOLD ME that Alija came back to Turkey in December 1970 because he did not want to die and be buried in *gavur* land—that is, in the

land of the infidel or the nonbeliever. "He was not a very religious man,"
he said, "but he wanted to die in the Muslim world."

It was a long, difficult journey for a sick man to undertake. It took him
farther from the son with whom he had just made contact. Perhaps he was
not thinking clearly at all. He had referred to his muddled head. There were
references in his diary to yellow geraniums and to flight without wings. Or
perhaps his motives really were simple. He did not want to die alone or in
Christian Europe. He saw himself in the spring in a village by the Sea of
Marmara, where the breeze is sweet and the pace slow. Familiar smells and
familiar sounds—the muezzin calling the faithful to prayer, the bustle of
the market—in place of the sanitized order of the Bavarian Alps. He would
be reunited with his books and papers, which were to be dispatched from
Vienna. With people like Bilir, conversation was straightforward, less demanding than in the clinic, where suffering was all around him.

All this no doubt affected Alija's decision. But he was also afraid, to the
last, of a return to Tito's Yugoslavia. His own conviction was that Džemal
had been murdered. If he was to tell the story of his life to his other son,
Sead, it would be in Turkey, where he had found refuge.

Alija left the clinic on December 6 for Munich, where he took a room
at the Hotel Eder. He had talked to his friends at the clinic of his imminent reunion with Sead. They all wished him well. Some wrote him poems
full of a cloying German romanticism: the lofty peaks, the green pastures,
the blue lakes, the vast glaciers, the mountains shimmering blue and white
and yellow and offering the eternal consolation of nature. Heidi asked
whether Sead and Gaby would now live with him permanently in Turkey.
She implored him to give her a photograph. In her last letter, she wrote:
"My dear fatherly friend, I beg you wholeheartedly not to lose courage and
to contact me if things seem hopeless. I cannot bear to watch someone destroy himself. Please don't do this, for me, because as a friend I never want
to lose you. Think of us occasionally. Maybe that will help you a little."

On December 10, 1970, Alija boarded a Turkish Airlines flight from
Munich to Istanbul. In his notebook, he recorded the time of arrival: 2:15
A.M. on December 11 (3:15 A.M. Turkish time). He checked into a hotel in
Istanbul and proceded the next morning to Bursa. Apparently lacking the
strength to go on, he changed his original plan to go on to Ankara. Instead
he took a room at the Cinarli Hotel in Bursa. He wrote a first postcard to
Sead on December 13. On December 26, he wrote a second postcard to
Gaby and gave her Ali Bilir's address. Each of the cards took more than ten
days to reach Belgrade. He said that his appetite was fading and that he
would probably move to a hospital on December 29. Gaby and Sead made
immediate plans to travel to Bursa for the long-awaited reunion.

CHAPTER 8

THE CYPRESS TREE

SEAD FELT THAT HE HAD BEEN OFFERED, SUDDENLY, A CANVAS vaster and more inviting than any he had known. It was his now to fill. His defenses had been up. They would be removed. A wound would heal. He would be braver. Relations between fathers and sons always involved the issue of authority; he dreamed that by discovering his father so late in life he would bypass this barrier, opening the way to a different relationship. They would talk, widely and freely. His vision would be made whole.

Panic seized him. He wrote repeatedly to his father as he awaited news from Turkey. Would Alija remain in Bursa or Ankara? Why had he left Germany? "It would be too absurd a twist of destiny," Sead said, "if I was to lose touch with you again so soon. . . . I want to write to you about the job I do, the people I live with, but it all seems so unimportant to me now. . . . I feel insignificant and tiny before the forces of life and circumstances that cannot be influenced. I hate this feeling of helpless writhing! The more I think of you, the closer you are to me. . . . Perhaps this is a reality or perhaps just a reflection of my wish that we be close. . . . Based on the precious little I know, I constantly dig out similarities between the two of us. . . . I am discovering the strange influences of lineage. . . ."

There were practical problems that caused delays. Sead had wanted to go alone to meet his father, but Gaby was so insistent she come that he finally acquiesced. They were about to book one of the two weekly flights to Istanbul when they learned that a cholera epidemic in Turkey obliged them to be vaccinated. After that, they had to wait a few days for the vaccination to take full effect.

Before leaving, Sead wrote another letter to his father. He dwelt on his hopes for their nascent relationship. Noting that the love of other people always gave him the feeling of finding himself in chains, he said, "I am fighting tooth and nail to save a part of myself because we are free only within ourselves. Maybe this feeling of mine—that we are imprisoned and fettered by some loves—made me cautious in relation to you at the beginning. I did not want to be a burden to you, with my need for you; I did not want to impose on you an obligation to love me. But now, despite everything, I am entangling you in my unease. This is selfish, but you are the only one I can talk to so openly. And of course, I want you to be completely frank, although somewhere deep inside me there lurks the fear that you will not understand. I try constantly to suppress that fear and to persuade myself that I am similar to you and that, after all, you are, quite naturally, the only person who can understand me without reproach. I am entitled to that small amount of inner freedom and selfishness, am I not?"

Sead urged his father to be discreet about all that he had written in conversation with Gaby, and he added, "I am panic-stricken that I might lose you before I find you."

At last, on January 18, 1971, they were ready to leave. There were no flights that day so they took an overnight train that brought them to Istanbul on January 19. They were booked on a flight to Bursa that day, but it was canceled. So Gaby and Sead stayed the night in Istanbul. On January 20, they proceeded to the first capital of the Ottomans.

IT WAS ALI BILIR who looked after Alija. Every morning he brought him a hot meal that his wife had cooked. But Alija had little appetite. His weight fell steadily and he complained of fatigue. He was reading Confucius. The only time he seemed animated was when he talked of Sead. Alija and Bilir went together to a tailor and ordered a new suit to be ready in time for Sead's arrival.

To Bilir, Alija seemed very excited at the prospect of the imminent reunion. He talked of losing one son and finding another. He told Bilir that "they" had killed Džemal, but nobody would prevent him from being with Sead. He had come home to die, but he was not quite ready yet.

In late December, Alija's health deteriorated. He ate nothing. Still he itemized each expense—a copy, for example, of *Time and Life* on December 31, 1970, for fifteen Turkish lire—and listed each medicine taken. There were some odd entries in his last notebook—definitions in English of words for fabric and clothing. For "tweed," he wrote: "A coarse wool cloth in a variety of weaves and colors, either hand-spun and hand-woven in Scotland, or reproduced, often by machine, and domestically."

Bilir put Alija in touch with a doctor, Cahit Yidiz, who suggested that he be hospitalized. Alija was taken on December 29, 1970, to the Bursa State Hospital, just a few hundred yards from the tombs of Osman and Orhan, the founders of the Ottoman dynasty, on the ridge above the broad valley. From his hospital window, he could see the cypress trees that dot the ridge and the minarets of Bursa's many mosques. He continued to read.

In the early morning of January 20, 1971, as Sead and Gaby began the last leg of the journey that would bring them to Bursa, Bilir went to see Alija at the hospital. Alija was bleeding from the nose and mouth; the doctors told Bilir there was nothing to be done. Alija was still conscious. He took off his wedding ring and requested that Bilir give it to Gaby when she arrived. Soon afterward, Ali Erhan, born Alija Mehmedović, died in the arms of his last friend, Bilir. He was fifty-nine years old.

Just three hours later, Sead and Gaby arrived.

As ARRANGED, Sead and Gaby went to the Bursa tourist office where Bilir worked. He broke the news of Alija's death to them and asked if they wanted to go to the morgue to identify the body. Sead felt that life itself had been sucked from him: he was empty, powerless, stunned. The canvas had been ripped before he even began to paint. The search had taken so long, only to end in this great void at the point of arrival.

He said that no, he would not go to the morgue, he did not want to see his father in that way, he wanted to preserve a certain image of him. But Gaby went. Empirical proof mattered to her. She said she had heard so many times, and for so long, that Alija was dead, she wanted to see for herself. Bilir accompanied Gaby to the mortuary; a sheet was pulled back to reveal Alija's face. Gaby nodded in silence.

The next day, January 21, 1971, a short article appeared on the front page of the local newspaper, *Hakimiyet*. Beneath a photograph of the young man—in suit and tie, with his dark hair combed back—the death of Ali Erhan was announced. The article noted that he had worked as a translator with the Chamber of Commerce, that he had arrived in 1949 as a "refugee" from Yugoslavia, and that soon after he had brought "all his family" to Bursa. It said that he had left to be treated in Europe and that, during that time, he had lost his wife in Germany and, "four months later," his son had died "in an accident in Vienna." He had returned to Turkey a month earlier but "could not be saved despite hospital care." Thus, with a few factual errors, some minor, some fundamental, was Alija Mehmedović's broken life rendered whole.

The burial took place the same day. The Chamber of Commerce offered to pay all the costs, but Bilir had been given some money from Alija and he used it. The funeral took place in a cemetery near the hospital, high up in the old town. The weather was cold and a mist drifted in over the old graves leaning this way and that. Sead came with Gaby and Bilir and Leila Ilova, the friend of Alija's whose family had fled Bosnia in 1878. The women had to remain outside the walled cemetery in conformity with Islamic tradition. Sead entered. It was then that he saw his father.

But even before his eyes, his father remained invisible. Alija Mehmedović was swaddled from head to foot in ten yards of white cloth. "He was in an open coffin," Sead said. "When I saw him he was wrapped in white cloth. As is the Muslim tradition, I climbed down into the grave. Then the body of my father was passed to me. It was the first physical contact I had with him. And I laid him in the earth."

There were prayers, incomprehensible to Sead. But Leila had explained their drift. This was not an end but another beginning. The brief, earthly interlude was over and the soul liberated. All striving and longing put to rest, a paradise awaited Alija, in accord with the wishes of God. As a seed is laid in the earth, so was the body of Alija, in preparation for new life. He would return, just as the sun and the moon disappear only to come back again.

Sead could find no consolation in the beauty of the ceremony. He did not believe, and he did not believe that his father believed. Alija had searched for God, but his God, if he found one, was his own—"not what organized religion says it should be." His father had died more than a quarter century earlier, only to reincarnate himself in Turkey as a man of the shadows. Alija would have no second afterlife.

A corpse was not what Sead had come for. He had not searched for a dead body or dreamed of so cold a touch. He had no desire to linger in this foreign place. All the interest, the fascination, the obsession that had built up over so many months and years evaporated. From Bilir he collected what papers and possessions there were, bundled them into Alija's battered leather suitcase, and carried them back to Belgrade. The case was seldom opened. When he later met Alija's friend Refik Cabi, who gave him a roll of film containing pictures of his father, Sead did not even develop the film. He heard of Alija's other possessions that were supposedly en route from Vienna, but he could not find the energy to investigate their whereabouts.

"After what had happened, I lost interest," Sead told me. "I never tried to find his books or his so-called documents. I am not a man who lives for the past or the future. I like the present. When something ends, I cut completely. I don't like plans."

The day after the funeral, Sead and Gaby traveled back to Belgrade. Gaby took the ring. She was inconsolable. When she reached the Yugoslav capital, she wrote to Leila Ilova: "When I at last found Alija in Germany, I wanted to go to him at once and, knowing that he was seriously sick, offer to take care of him and make his last days nicer for him. But always some obstacle sprang up and it was not destined that we meet. But if fate wanted to punish Alija for abandoning us and not trying to find us for so many years—why was I denied the last consolation and why was a son denied the chance to be with a father he longed for so much? It was a horrible shock for Sead and now he is completely withdrawn. I do not know if he blames me for something. He does not talk. He does not ask questions. It is hard for me to watch him like that. I have always done everything I could to help him become the young man he is, and I was so proud that I was going to show him to Alija, and I believed that he would be happy and praise me before our son. And now, my cheerful and inspired young man has become a moody and inapproachable figure. And so it is that many things remain untold."

SEAD FELT PARALYZED on his return. He lay on his bed, completely empty for several weeks. "I had expected to find some answers, I don't even know to which questions, but answers, answers," he said. In their place he felt, again and again, the dead, silent weight of his father's body being lowered into the ground.

Two years after his father's death, Sead had a dream. There was a knock on his door. He opened it. Before him was a man swaddled in white cloth. The man said nothing. Sead reached toward him but he disappeared. The dream was particularly vivid. Sead talked about it with a psychoanalyst he had started seeing. She told him that the man was his father. Such was Sead's rejection of Alija after the visit to Bursa that he had failed to make the obvious connection himself.

Bilir had planted a cypress tree—known in Turkish as a *selvi*—at the spot where Alija was buried. Twenty-five years later, his wooden casket had rotted and disappeared. Only weeds and nettles and scattered stones covered the earth. He was gone, as completely as Džemal on the ground of the rival empire in Vienna. But the cypress tree had prospered, growing to a stature that offered a pleasing shade from the summer heat. Cats slithered among the graves, as silent as shadows. From the mountains where Byzantine monks once hid from the Ottomans a cool wind carried the scent of pine down into the cemetery. Its capricious gusts seemed to mock the lugubrious dance of human desire and longing that had found its unhappy resolution at this spot.

SEAD AND ALIJA had passed within an inch of each other. But their hands, outstretched at last like those of God and Adam in Michelangelo's *Creation,* had never touched. What life that touch might have engendered, and what reconciliation, will remain forever in the realm of useless speculation.

Yet I could not help dreaming of what might have been. The majesty of the country compelled such dreams. It often seemed to me that Yugoslavia had come as close as Sead and his father, just missing some lasting reconciliation, divided always by some further misunderstanding. In the end the breath in the country's lungs was extinguished. No place could survive such repeated blundering, such senseless battering. But just as it was easy enough to imagine that Sead and Alija might, over time, have understood many things about their two Yugoslavias, royalist and communist, and about the silences occupying the space between these two incarnations of the state, so it was not difficult to imagine a free Yugoslavia in the post-communist world, a big country in every sense, profoundly European in its mixed composition, unlike the small Balkan states that have taken its place.

Yugoslavia was already crumbling by the mid-1980s. But the brutal Milošević in Serbia, the impatient Slovenes, the dismally myopic Franjo Tudjman in Croatia, the killers of every caste marauding under their new tribal banners—they, between them, ensured that the old wounds Sead knew so well would be reopened and the state finally drowned in blood.

Was all the destruction inevitable? Could the mottled beauty of the country have found some lasting bloom? To dream amid the splendor of Yugoslavia, even one in ruins, was inevitable. It was also worthless and stupid. In the end, there were only the hard facts. The ruins of Vukovar. The soaring Ottoman bridge of Mostar, blasted to stumps of stone jutting grotesquely into space like amputated limbs. The blood of a child on the streets of Sarajevo and the last expression of vacant wonder in the eyes. The young man Sead lowering the father he never knew into the ground and watching the earth fall slowly on a lifeless body.

CHAPTER 9

THE TOMB

Alija Mehmedović hated Tito's state and believed it would not live long. Within six months of his death, Tito uttered these words: "Under the cover of national interest, all hell is collecting . . . even to the point of counterrevolution. . . . In some villages, the Serbs, out of nervousness, are drilling and arming themselves. . . . Do we want to have 1941 again?"

The speech was made in July 1971 to the Executive Committee of the Croatian Communists. The circumstances were the great stirring of Croatian patriotism that became known as "the Croatian Spring." The nervous Serbs in question were those in the Krajina border marches whose families had suffered the brunt of Pavelić's onslaught during World War II.

Croatian resentment was expressed in all sorts of ways—economic, linguistic, historical—but at root it represented a longing for independence. Šime Djodan, a Croatian economist, wrote in 1971 that "in old Yugoslavia 46 percent of our income was used outside Croatia, under Austria-Hungary 55 percent and today it is 63 percent. Thus for the Croats the Socialist Federal Republic of Yugoslavia is a bigger exploiter and less acceptable than Austria-Hungary or old Yugoslavia."

The theme was an old one: Belgrade, whether royalist or communist, as worse tyranny for the Croats than the Habsburgs and Vienna. It had been sounded as early as 1918. The creation of Yugoslavia bred a hatred between Croats and Serbs that had not existed before.

Incidents spread throughout 1971. Signs in the Cyrillic alphabet were destroyed. Croatian emblems, such as the red-and-white checkered shield, appeared, stripped of the communist red star that had always adorned them under Tito—the very emblems that Alija Mehmedović had served. There were riots in mixed Serb and Croat areas. The cult of Stjepan Radić, the Croat political leader murdered in Belgrade in 1928, was revived. At schools, Serb children were taunted and sometimes attacked.

A chief vehicle for Croatia's reborn nationalism was the Matica Hrvatska (Croatian Queen Bee Society). Ironically, its predecessor in the nineteenth century had been one of the main backers of the Illyrian movement toward a Yugoslav consciousness. Branches spread throughout Croatia, in predominantly Croat areas of Bosnia, and among Croatian laborers, or *Gastarbeiters,* in Germany. One of its members who was particularly active in cultivating links with diaspora Croats was Franjo Tudjman, who had abandoned a brilliant military career—he was Tito's youngest general—to become a historian at Zagreb University.

On the basis of his research, Tudjman began to talk of the "Jasenovac myth," suggesting that the number of victims under Pavelić had been wildly exaggerated, and pressing the view—like Archbishop Stepinac—that the Independent State of Croatia (1941–1945) was less a criminal regime than a legitimate expression of the Croatian quest for sovereignty. In 1971, he suggested that Serb-Croat relations would best be handled within a "Confederation or League of States" rather than within the Federal Republic of Yugoslavia.

In his July speech, Tito lambasted the Croats for such views. "Are you aware," he said, "that others would immediately be present if there were disorder? I would sooner restore order with our army than allow others to do it. We have lost prestige abroad and it will be hard to get it back. They are speculating that, when Tito goes, the whole thing will collapse, and some are seriously waiting for that. The internal enemy has plenty of support from outside. The great powers will use any devil that will work for them, whether he is a Communist or not."

The Croats were unbowed by these admonishments. Tito was seventy-nine years old. He had begun the move toward a "confederalization" of Yugoslavia by proposing a "collegiate presidency" in 1970—it originally had twenty-three members!—and by stipulating that territorial militia, established under a new defense law in 1969, should fall under republican rather than federal control. A statement from the League of Communists in 1970 said that "there is an urgent need for a further step in the direction of reconstructing the federation as a function of the statehood and sovereignty of every republic and the autonomy of the provinces, as the basis of the equality of the nations and nationalities of Yugoslavia." The guiding principle was that all powers, except those specifically delegated to federal authorities, would now go to the six republics and two autonomous provinces.

In these circumstances, the Croats naturally felt entitled to dream. In November 1971, the Croatian Queen Bee Society published its proposals for revising the constitution of Croatia. They fell little short of a declaration of independence. The definition of Croatia was "the sovereign national state of the Croatian nation with the right to self-determination, including the right to secession." It was to have full control of revenues collected on its territory and would make only "voluntary contributions" to federal Yugoslavia, on the basis of interrepublic agreements. Croatia would have its own central bank and issue its own money. The Croatian territorial army would be autonomous and Croatian recruits to the Yugoslav army would generally perform their service in Croatia. Even more sweeping ideas were put forward at student meetings held to support these amendments: the revision of Croatian frontiers to embrace parts of Bosnia, separate Croatian membership in the United Nations, and the breakup of the federal Yugoslav army.

Tito had let the movement in his native Croatia go a very long way. An ambivalence was evident: several times he traveled to Zagreb to upbraid the Croats, only to modify his tone. It was, apparently, the same ambivalence about Croatia that had led Tito to grant Archbishop Stepinac what amounted to a state funeral in Zagreb Cathedral in 1960. Only on December 2, 1971, did Tito finally act. Croatia's communist leaders—Miko Tripalo and Savka Dabčević-Kučar—were forced to resign; nationalist students were arrested; the army put on a show of force in Zagreb. Within a month the Croatian Queen Bee Society had been banned, and four hundred nationalist leaders, among them Tudjman, arrested.

Yugoslav unity was shored up. Alija Mehmedović's predicted breakup was postponed. For the sake of balance, Tito naturally proceeded the next year to a purge of the Serbian Communist party, one that appeared to have much less basis in any separatist or nationalist movement. But the ghosts only retreated, and within two decades, Tudjman would be back to arouse the same fears among the Krajina Serbs.

DID TITO CARE what would happen after his death? Did he worry about all that remained unsaid and unresolved in his state? Did he fear that the secrets of Yugoslavia, the countless sagas of separation like that of Sead and Alija Mehmedović, would lead to some grim reprisal?

I visited his tomb. The iconography of the Belgrade mausoleum is interesting. A staircase winds up a hill toward the grave. On either side of the stairs are sculptures by artists from all the former Yugoslav republics representing moments in Tito's heroic struggle. Images of war, of suffering, transcended by the compassion of the great leader; images arranged in a carefully calibrated equilibrium to denote the "brotherhood and unity" of

Slovenia, Croatia, Bosnia, Serbia, Montenegro, and Macedonia; images that lead the visitor *upward*, as befits a place of pilgrimage leading to a communist shrine.

But the place is going to seed: ferns are dying, the brownish grass is increasingly patchy. There used to be ten thousand visitors a day. In 1996, there are virtually none. A couple of soldiers guard the great emptiness— Tito's residence, above the mausoleum, is vacant, as is an adjacent museum. All the shutters are down. A guard slouches about in jeans carrying a radio. He has one instruction: it is obligatory to circle the tomb clockwise rather than counter-clockwise. Some vestige, this order, of the days when there were crowds? The guard is unforthcoming. When asked how long he has worked here, a shadow of suspicion falls across his face and he refuses to answer.

Among the many rumors about the longtime leader there is one, strangely persistent, that says that Tito is not really buried in Belgrade. When I once protested that in that case he must be buried elsewhere, I was met by the reply that people in the West have "tiresome logical minds."

The tomb—or cenotaph?—consists of a huge slab of white marble on which the following inscription is engraved in gold lettering: JOZIP BROZ TITO, 1892–1980. Perhaps the terseness reflects the fact that, after the great hagiographical outpourings during his lifetime, there was nothing more to say. But the absence even of the five-pointed Partisan star, the symbol of Tito's life and work, of postwar Yugoslavia itself, is surprising. The lacuna has given rise to comment that in the last months of his life Tito reverted to the religion of his birth, Catholicism, and renounced the religion symbolized by the star.

But then the man who was never questioned in his lifetime has since been called into question about everything. The Serbs argue passionately that Tito the Croat—he was in fact half Slovenian—set out to emasculate them. Weak Serbia, strong Yugoslavia: this, they now claim, was Tito's philosophy.

The Serbs have an arsenal of arguments: the Serbian monarchy, which governed the first Yugoslavia, was the regime that Tito's communist revolution overthrew. Tito, whose initial power base in Serbia was weaker than elsewhere, was worried that the Serbs, accounting for close to 40 percent of the population, were almost twice as numerous as the Croats, the next largest nation. He responded by circumscribing Serbian power in the first postwar Yugoslav constitution of 1946: a new Macedonian republic was detached from Serbia and two autonomous provinces created within it. The first was Kosovo, the heart of medieval Serbia but an area populated mainly by ethnic Albanians; the second was Vojvodina, with its Hungarian minority. Thus, Serbs say, was their influence cut down.

For Dobrica Ćosić, the Serbian author most closely identified with the rise of Serbian nationalism in the 1980s, these steps were merely the first in a consistent campaign by Tito to weaken the Serbs. Others were the elimination of the Serbian strongman and head of the secret police, Aleksandar Ranković, in 1966; the reinforcement of the independent powers of Kosovo and Vojvodina in 1974; and the effective house arrest of Tito's wife, Jovanka, a Serb, in the years before his death. "Tito," Ćosić insisted to me, "was always afraid of the Serbs. I know that personally. In 1961 and 1962, he was paranoid about the Serbs, telling me they would try to take his life."

WHEN TITO DIED in 1980, the enduring volatility of the "national question" was evident in the unworkable collective presidency set up to inherit his power. The creation of this many-headed beast allowed Tito to avoid designating a successor, a decision that might have inflamed national feelings in that a single ruler could not possibly hail from all six republics and two autonomous provinces at once. But it also made an already extremely cumbersome state even more cumbersome.

Djilas, Tito's closest lieutenant during World War II, told me in an interview shortly before his death in 1995 that "to the end, Tito was afraid that Yugoslavia would break up. But he was always against any strong leader, excluding himself. So he came up with the collective leadership, which was a nonsense." The rotating presidency was comprised of representatives from the six republics—Slovenia, Croatia, Bosnia-Herzegovina, Serbia, Montenegro, and Macedonia—and Kosovo and Vojvodina, the two autonomous provinces whose powers had been raised almost to the level of the republics by the 1974 constitution. Each representative headed the presidency for one year.

The dilution of the presidency was ominous in that all power had been vested in Tito. The Orwellian 310-page Yugoslav constitution of 1974 laid out, in 406 articles, just how a utopia of democratic, socialist self-management, bereft of nationalist divisiveness, should be organized, only to make clear in Article 333 that all the provisions were almost meaningless because Tito could ignore them. This privilege, the constitution noted, was granted in view of "the historic role of Josip Broz Tito in the National Liberation War and the Socialist Revolution, in the creation and development of the Socialist Federal Republic of Yugoslavia, the development of Yugoslav socialist self-management society, the achievement of the brotherhood and unity of the nations and nationalities of Yugoslavia, the consolidation of the independence of the country and of its position in international relations and in the struggle for peace in the world."

Sic transit gloria mundi. Encomiums aside, the world's longest and perhaps most complicated constitution—the fourth one promulgated by Tito's Yugoslavia—was a recipe for chaos, disintegration, and economic decline, saved only by the declaration of one man's absolute rule. It was so long precisely because bogus democracy takes a long time to explain.

But as long as Tito, the master juggler, was there, its labyrinthine provisions were not critically important. Once he was gone, there was no basis on which to run a state subject to growing external and internal pressure. As General Veljko Kadijević, Yugoslavia's last defense minister, once remarked, "The constitution is a monster pregnant with its own destruction. It is neither federal nor confederal. The center of power is not defined."

If there was a theory behind the constitution, it was that power should be devolved from the state to the republican and district levels, a process conceived in part to head off nationalist tendencies by satisfying the national ambitions of each Yugoslav republic. Communist idealists saw in it a withering-away of the state and the empowerment of the people; in practice, its provisions led to the withering-away of Yugoslavia. As Ivan Stambolić, the former leader of the Serbian Communist party, put it to me, "We devolved power to the republics and the provinces and the republics were supposed to devolve to the enterprises. Instead the republics became the real units of economic power. So warring economic systems and warring communist bureaucracies grew up in each republic and this contributed to the crisis."

Certainly, such a system was ill-equipped to head off Yugoslavia's economic decline, which began in the late 1970s. Inflation spiraled, reaching over 2,500 percent in 1989. Debt grew, output fell, and unemployment, particularly among the young, was only masked by the increasingly strained artifices of "socialist self-management," a system that in theory gave all workers a share in the ownership of their enterprises but in practice turned slowly into a bureaucratic morass. The British economist Harold Lydall noted in 1989 that "the decline in the living standards has been so great that it is difficult to imagine another country that would not have reacted to such a situation through radical political change or even through a revolution."

The vulnerability of Yugoslavia was greater because Tito was never unequivocal in his support for the emergence of a Yugoslav consciousness. Colonel Jozef Pilsudski, the liberator of Poland, said that "it is the state which makes the nation and not the nation the state." Another nineteenth-century soldier-statesman, Italy's Massimo d'Azeglio, put the same idea a different way: "We have made Italy," he declared at the first parliamentary

session of a united Italy. "Now we have to make Italians." But Tito had little interest in making Yugoslavs. He preferred to consolidate his power
through *divide et impera.*

Indeed, because the one determined attempt to impose a Yugoslav identity, through the creation of administrative units that cut across republican
borders, was associated with the dictatorship of the Serbian monarchy in
the 1930s, such a course was anathema. Prewar Yugoslavia was dismissed
as a period of "Serb bourgeois hegemonism." In its place had emerged a
"socialist federation of free and equal peoples." This change was symbolized in the replacement of the royalist slogan of *"Narodno Jedinstvo"*
("National Unity") by *"Bratstvo i Jedinstvo"* ("Brotherhood and Unity").
Yugoslavia was formally defined, in the bureaucratic verbiage of communism, as "a federal state having the form of a state community of voluntarily united nations and their Socialist republics." As the Leninist
prolixity suggested, the unity was fragile. If Tito was good for the world,
it is far less clear that he was good for Yugoslavia.

An alternative road to consolidating a Yugoslav identity might have lain
in a real democratization giving Yugoslavs a direct participation in the
functioning of their state and a forum for the airing and resolution of their
differences. Tito's Yugoslav society was more free than its communist
neighbors. People traveled outside the country, dissident books were published, the cultural scene was lively and open. There were no Soviet troops
on its soil, you could read Orwell and Solzhenitsyn. These differences were
substantial. But fear was there, manipulated as necessary by the regime. In
the end Lenin's principle—*"Kto kovo?"* ("Who comes out on top?")—was
also Tito's.

AT KUMROVEC in Croatia, the birthplace of Tito, the scene is desolate,
a reflection of the Croats' own misgivings about the man who refounded
Yugoslavia in 1945. There is a vast parking lot for buses that no longer
come and a large hotel for visitors who no longer appear. A Croatian flag,
of all things, now flutters over the site; just up the road there is, of all
things, Croatia's international border with Slovenia.

The little cottages that house the museum of Tito's childhood and
evoked to millions of Yugoslavs the poverty from which he rose are deserted. A sickly sweet pathos, indigestible as treacle, pervades the weaving
room, the ironsmith's shop, and the pottery kiln where busloads of Yugoslav schoolchildren once stood. The waxwork model of a merry peasants' wedding represents the apogee of this kitsch display. The children
would be brought here at least once a year to behold these exhibits—
Marxist-Leninist nativity scenes—and to learn how Tito fed the animals

and looked after his little sisters and struggled to make his way in life, first as a waiter and then as a locksmith and metalworker.

Croats have their own arsenal to prove that, in reality, Tito was pro-Serb. Under him, most high-level bureaucratic posts went to Serbs—some accounts put the figure higher than 75 percent. Over 60 percent of officers in the army were Serb. In Croatia, where Serbs accounted for 11.5 percent of the population in 1981, they were disproportionately represented in the police and the Ministry of Defense. Over 21 percent of local political posts went to Serbs. Tito, moreover, chose to govern Yugoslavia from Belgrade—a symbol of the enduring Serbian domination of the Croats.

It has ever been so between Serbs and Croats: they talk past each other. Observing them in their new state in 1928, Robert William Seton-Watson observed, "My own inclination is to leave the Serbs and Croats to stew in their juice! I think they are both mad and cannot see beyond the ends of their noses!"

THE TRUTH, of course, lies somewhere between the conflicting Serb and Croat revisions of history. Tito knew that Yugoslavia's existence hinged on the relationship between Serbs and Croats, South Slav brothers settled uneasily on either side of the Theodosian line dividing the Roman Empire into East and West. Between them, the two peoples accounted for 66 percent of the population at the state's foundation in 1918; they represented about 56 percent at its death.

They had both borne the burden of statelessness, the Croats for almost a millennium, the Serbs for 350 years; they stood, or at least saw themselves standing, on the front line of the Latin and Orthodox worlds; their histories, in the Austro-Hungarian and Ottoman dominions, were divergent. They were different but scarcely so, cousins scattered by circumstance but united by blood. From the outset, the Bosnian Muslims, 6 percent of the Yugoslav population in 1921 and 9 percent in 1991, were less protagonists than bystanders, caught in the gyre of Serb and Croatian violence that accompanied these two peoples' flailing attempts to come to terms.

Tito had a visceral sense of these realties, one so acute that he preserved Yugoslavia against all the odds. As a soldier in the Austro-Hungarian army he had fought against Serbia in World War I; as a Partisan in World War II he gained much of his initial support in Bosnia from Serbs and did battle with the Croatian Ustasha of Ante Pavelić. He knew in how much blood and recrimination the Serb-Croat relationship was bathed during World War II.

His artful response was to circumscribe Serbia, staff Croatia with Serb officials, and use Bosnia as the glue to bind them. The Muslims of Bosnia, whom Tito always favored and supported, accounted for a relatively small part of the population, but they were a useful element in playing Serbs and Croats off against each other. If royalist Yugoslavia was plainly ruled and dominated by the Serbs, communist Yugoslavia was not. The skillful balancing act worked with Tito at the fulcrum. He extended the same formula to international relations. With considerable acuity, he played one side off against the other. To have tinkered with communist orthodoxy was to be assured of a measure of indulgence from Washington, especially in light of Yugoslavia's position between the Soviet Empire and the warm waters of the Mediterranean. Tito alternated condemnations of "bureaucratic, dogmatic" tendencies, a reference to Moscow, with diatribes against "anarcho–petit bourgeois and pseudo-liberal trends," a reference to the West. He toured the world so tirelessly in his role as Non-aligned leader that Yugoslavs joked that rumors of a man on the moon could not be true because, if he existed, Tito would have visited him. But what would happen without him?

Shortly before his death in 1980, Tito was visited by W. Averell Harriman, the former United States undersecretary of state, and his wife, Pamela Harriman. The meeting took place on the Adriatic island of Brioni, where Tito gave full expression to his extravagant tastes. There were polar bears, giraffes, and a wonderful collection of lions descended from one offered to him by the Ethiopian emperor Haile Selassie. Tito loved to talk about the war years, but Harriman tried to press him about the future and his succession. Tito was irritated; this was not the world that interested the old man. His reply, as Mrs. Harriman recalled, was brusque: "You don't understand. When I came to power, as the leader of the Partisans, I had the whole country behind me. This will never happen again. I could only exercise such power because of the war. It is quite impossible for me to name a single successor. In the end, there is no way to protect this country from its divisions."

At what used to be the Tito Museum in Belgrade, I asked a historian, Nevenka Kovandžić, if she believed that Tito had foreseen Yugoslavia's violent end. "I don't know if he foresaw this—I doubt it—but he must have been aware of the dangers he left hanging in the air. What concerns me is that we are already wiping away the facts of Tito's life. Look at this museum. All the objects have been moved into depots, all Tito's gifts stashed in basements. We are creating another gap in history. What we should remember is that we worshiped this man. We turned him into a satrap, a god. We allowed him to forge his own myth and to hide certain historical facts. There were gaps. And then the horrors of World War II came back to haunt us. So now we should know how dangerous these historical gaps are."

SEAD LIVED MUCH much of his life with one such gap. Now he is bereaved. He has lost his country. "I can't manage in this world now," he said. "There are so many *feuilletons* about the past—what the Chetniks did, what the Partisans did. What is in all that, what it is supposed to mean, I do not know. I do know that I want to believe in something, something decent. I have a need to believe in something. But in this time of breaking apart, I cannot believe in anything. I don't know *what* to believe. I am like a boat on the sea, battered one minute one way, and the next another.

"I suppose you would have to say that I am an old internationalist. Between 1945 and 1960, never mind romanticism, never mind idealism, people believed—maybe they believed wrong, but they believed. I believed in the dictatorship of the proletariat. I still believe in it. I would not kill a million people for that, but perhaps a hundred! I would take it as an honor to be persecuted for such ideas. Some of my friends at school were against Tito. I think now they knew more than I did. But they also missed something. Something quite special.

"The problem, in the end, with any utopia is that you have to organize it. And once you start organizing, the organization becomes the heart of the affair, rather than the utopia itself. And within any organization, of course, you find ambition, corruption, pettiness, and rigidity: precisely what the dream had set out to abolish. The only possibility is for individuals, each one of them, to act in concert with the ideals set out by the utopia, but to imagine that would ever happen is utterly far-fetched. I see in myself that I have lacked courage; in 1968, for example, I did nothing when Paris rose and Prague fell. I have a terrible fear that, like my father, I am a conformist."

IT WAS ONLY after his return from Bursa that Sead came to understand fully his father's mortal fear of Tito. The evidence was there in the brown suitcase. But he did not judge his father, any more than he revised his own beliefs. What had happened had happened. The chapter was closed. There was nothing more to say.

Slowly he recovered from the blow. At his fourth marriage—he divorced twice more after his return from Bursa—he at last got it right, and had two children, a girl and a boy, who are now the light of his life. They are children who know their father.

"We have only one life," Sead said. "It is a crime to spend it reckoning what you have done or not done, or what might have been. Just live it. I do not understand the need to leave something behind you. Why this need? For what? I would say to an artist who has had three shows and no critical response, fine, now it is time for something else. For myself, I will leave my children and, I hope, something of me in them."

He has not traveled in ten years. His salary as a teacher has fallen steadily and is usually paid late, but it is just enough to survive until the next tardy payment. He rarely paints. He had dreamed of taking a house in the country, but in these times in Serbia a Muslim name such as his might cause problems in a small village, so he has put off his plans. But Sead still cannot feel any affinity with the "nationalities" of Balkanization ad absurdum. He is neither Muslim nor Serb. He is a stateless Yugoslav.

When Yugoslavia began to die in violence, Sead was stunned. The Ustashas, the Chetniks—they belonged in the past's grubby suitcases and undeveloped rolls of film. His father's story was old stuff, or so he had come to believe. "All this has been a strange war for me," he said. "All I can really note is that we became poor, very poor, and that our so-called nations were pushed into a state of amok where they did not even need guns, all they needed was alcohol, knives, and axes. The real war for me was 1941 to 1945. The bombardments, Belgrade destroyed, that was war. This war was impoverishment, division, desperation, and emptiness, the dismal end to a lost century."

BOOK TWO

INTIMATE BETRAYALS

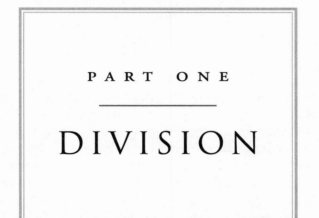

PART ONE

DIVISION

CHAPTER 10

A DEATH
IN THE FAMILY

To the people of Sarajevo, mountains like Trebević assumed intolerable proportions. In their woods and on their ridges lurked the artillery trained on the city below. Gradually, through an inevitable transference, the peaks themselves were imbued with the power of oppression. They bore down on the people in the city, taunted them with their indifferent beauty, left them naked. Sarajevans felt herded toward a collective scream. Their sense of suffocation was expressed through a gesture of self-strangulation. Once synonymous with the 1984 Winter Olympics—Trebević was home to the bobsled track—and weekend homes, the mountains were transformed by war into towering fonts of death. Looking at them became physically painful. To gaze upward was to be stripped to the bone.

When shells fell on Sarajevo, the sound waves, caught between the mountains, seemed palpable. They met the frozen immobility of a town abruptly deserted, its people in shock. The effect was disorienting, like suddenly inhabiting a field of radiation. It was no illusion, surely, that the sunlit air shimmered after the rending detonation of a shell's impact or that the reverberation assumed physical form as it coursed around the hills into hidden corners of the city. Humdrum scenes—women in high heels hitching skirts to flee in awkward terror, men burdened like mules, children at play among the graves—were then seen as if through a distorting glass. They faded only to return more vividly, like the insistent echoes in this Balkan valley.

Sarajevo is a city of echoes. Below Trebević Mountain, which rises south of the city center to over five thousand feet, it is laid out like Eliot's "patient etherised upon a table." The city's limbs climb over hills in attitudes of lazy abandon. Certain cities can make people mad. Sarajevo, like Istanbul and Jerusalem, is a place of confluence, imbued, by the slow interaction of man and nature and the creeping ebb and flow of civilizations, with a strange fascination.

Its Ottoman center, narrow streets that snake around hills, is a labyrinth; its soul, like that of Bosnia, liquid. The Turks, who captured the small settlement called Vrhbosna in 1451 and made of it a flowering city, gave Sarajevo a name that means "palace in the fields." Ottoman culture is nomadic rather than settled, accommodating itself to beauty as much as imposing its own. The barriers between metropolis and nature remain evanescent in Sarajevo, like the mists that constantly drift across Bosnia, shifting the familiar into ephemeral new patterns.

A shadowy alley opens out abruptly to reveal tumbledown houses sprawling over the hills, a minaret reaching piercingly for the light, the mountains beyond. A window in the heart of town looks out, quite unexpectedly, on cascades of cherry blossoms and a snowcapped peak. The town invites contemplation rather than dissection, for its character is allusive. It dissolves as readily as the grains in the coffee sipped on its every corner.

Sarajevo ranges capriciously along a valley that gradually opens out as it runs from east to west. The old Turkish town of Baščaršija, situated at the narrowest and most easterly point of the valley, is a maze of coffeehouses, coppersmiths, and other artisans' stores. It retains the intimacy of the bazaar; the conversation it encourages is as meandering as its alleys. Baščaršija gives way to the mainly Austro-Hungarian center of Sarajevo, whose wider streets, rectilinear crossroads, and solid administrative buildings betray a Habsburg attempt to bring a touch of Viennese order—but scarcely grandeur—to the Balkan Peninsula after taking over the administration of Bosnia and Herzegovina from the Turks under terms agreed to at the Congress of Berlin in 1878. This attempt was ended thirty-six years later when the shots of Gavrilo Princip, the Bosnian Serb nationalist opposed to Austro-Hungarian rule of Bosnia, killed the Habsburg heir Archduke Franz Ferdinand and his wife during a visit to Sarajevo. The slaying ushered in World War I.

Farther west, as the valley becomes a plain wide enough to accommodate an airport, dismal evidence of Sarajevo's more recent history abounds. The legacy of empire, Ottoman and Austro-Hungarian, gives way to the legacy of a twentieth-century imperium, communism. Shabby residential blocks, suggestive of the outskirts of Warsaw, reflect the efforts of Tito's town planners to accommodate the massive exodus from the countryside to the cities after World War II. The population of Sarajevo grew to 526,000 in 1991 from 99,000 in 1948.

Through the middle of the city flows the Miljacka, less river than gurgling stream. Rivers are always at hand in Bosnia. They rush through steep mountain passes or stir lazily between banks disputed by rival armies. Water informs the Bosnian imagination; water saps the striving of the rational mind. Rivers, not the earth, run red with blood. Corpses, in the collective memory, do not lie still. They float eternally on the Sava, the Una, the Bosna, the Neretva, or the Drina.

The Miljacka flows beside the mosques of Baščaršija; it runs on past the Catholic and Orthodox cathedrals on the north bank and the city's main synagogue to the south; it continues through the new town, beside the broad avenue that became known during the war as "Sniper's Alley." It is never majestic, but it is always the bubbling artery of the city. When Tito's communist authorities tried to introduce the new greeting *"Zdravo Druže"* ("Hail Comrade") after World War II, Sarajevans twisted it into the nonsensical *"Vozdra Žedru."* The town's spirit is fluid. In it lurks a ludic irreverence that saps rigidity and mocks outside attempts to impose a new order.

At the core of the military campaign embarked on by the Serbs in April 1992 lay an attempt to break this city's spirit. The campaign was imported. It was led by a cobbler's son from Montenegro named Radovan Karadžić; it was financed and directed from Belgrade. The thrust of the Serb offensive was to deny, through force of arms, that the people living together in Bosnia and Herzegovina—44 percent of them Muslim, 31 percent Serb, 17 percent Croat, and the rest of sufficiently mixed descent to call themselves simply "Yugoslavs"—could continue to coexist as a society and a community. Because Sarajevo, with its intensely variegated gravestones and its Muslim, Catholic, Orthodox, and Jewish places of worship, was the most eloquent symbol of that coexistence, it had to be destroyed.

The Serbs, led by Karadžić, took to the mountains surrounding the city. They ensconced themselves in the gabled chalets of a modest ski resort called Pale, about eight miles southeast of the center, and began shelling Sarajevo. The sun still rose and set and the moon still slipped across the sky, but the ends of the world, in the Bosnian capital, shrank to the confines of an encircled valley.

Trebević, rising so steeply from a point so close to the city center, was the most troubling peak. Such untamed beauty close to the heart of urban life had been an inspiration; now the mountain was a wall. It had been turned on its head by Karadžić, like so many things. Sarajevans laughed, sometimes hysterically, at their upside-down lives. Candles, once predictably romantic, became hated symbols of the degradation of so many days lived without electricity. Skis, once synonymous with pleasurable weekends in the surrounding mountains, came to connote the inaccessible Serb-held hills and death. Old shoes and old clothes became the subject of debate between intelligent people as to which burned better in the ubiquitous woodstoves. Children's toy cars, their tops removed, became the base for wheeled contraptions on which to carry containers of water from wells to homes. Parks became cemeteries, then parks again, because the only place to play was among the spreading graves.

FOR HARIS ZEČEVIĆ and his squad of Bosnian soldiers, it was in the late afternoon of August 3, 1992, that the firing became ominous. The squad had advanced up the steep slope of Trebević Mountain to a position beside the old Austro-Hungarian observatory. They had been there several days, in a position to interdict the road linking the Serb headquarters of Pale with the main Bosnian Serb garrison near Sarajevo at Lukavica. The sun was shining and, in certain photographs, Haris, his brother Muris Zečević, and some friends were laughing and making faces.

From his position at the observatory, Haris watched the Serb shells going in, detonating near his brother's trench. There was so much dust rising he could not see much. Each rending impact knotted his stomach. He thought of the trench, strong, big logs laid one on top of the other, some rocks, some blankets, piles of earth. Muris should be all right. No way of getting there: the fire was too intense.

Nightfall came before the shelling eased and Haris could make his way over to the trench. He took the hand of the first man. It was cold. Somehow he knew, there was no life left there in the dark. Then he made out Tarik Kapetanović's head—with a gaping hole in the middle of it. He tried to pull Tarik out, but a log had fallen over him. Haris, his heart thumping in his throat, called for help, and some other men took over. He never did see his brother. Later they told him there was not much left of him to see.

The night Muris died Haris could not sleep. He had thought that this was not his war. After all, he had not sought it. But when they attack you, the war is delivered to you and you cannot send it back. Still, it had taken him a long time to reach this point, much longer than his brother. Methodical by nature, less inclined to caprice than Muris, heavier in his movements and slower in his instincts, Haris had taken a while to understand the new reality of Bosnian life: kill or be killed. For a while it had all seemed no more than a sick joke. Carnival time had come, but out of season. The masks looked deformed, the costumes lurid, the music was deafeningly loud. But the guns were real enough, Sarajevo was sealed, and Serbs who had been neighbors for years were suddenly ready to kill Muslims.

At the front line, sometimes, the neighbors-turned-enemies tuned into one another's radios and the old banter of Sarajevo bars resumed with a new tone. Haris said, "You're Bulgarians, not Serbs, we killed all the Serbs five hundred years ago." A voice came back: "There are ten thousand of us, your days are numbered." "Ten thousand? What a pity. We only have five thousand fezzes!" Then the Serb shelling began. What was this war? Some Serb playing cards sitting on an anti-aircraft gun listening to a soccer game on the radio, swigging a beer and firing another round every time Red Star Belgrade scored a goal.

But now the situation had hardened. He saw quite clearly, on that mountain, with its familiar smells of grass and timber and its unfamiliar pain, that near-death is a passage to some other state. There was intense gunfire below him on the left and right and Haris imagined for a moment that he was surrounded. Ready to go down, he grabbed his rifle. The knots in his stomach unraveled. There is a point, he noted with mild surprise, when you just do not care anymore.

Like most inhabitants of a city more given to pleasure than to industry, Haris had taken his prewar life in Sarajevo pretty much for granted. He was not the unrequited kind. He was clever enough to do well enough not to have to exert himself unduly. Girls liked him. Winters on Jahorina Mountain, summers with the cool stones of Dubrovnik beneath his feet, Sarajevo evenings of beer and music. Odd jobs here and there, some study, vague plans to become an engineer. Then everything—homes, friendships, lives—was carried away like debris on a windswept beach at dusk.

When the Bosnian war began on April 6, 1992, Haris Zečević was twenty-three years old. He had hardly fired a shot before. It was Muris, two years his junior, who shared their father's passion for hunting. He would skin and clean the pheasants they killed together in the forests near Sarajevo. He was at one with a weapon in a way that was foreign to Haris. He had told Haris the war was coming. Unlike most Bosnians, Muris had been ready to see and to believe the myriad signs. Not Haris. But in the end, there was little choice. It was not a question of loving Bosnia. Or hating Bosnia. It was a question of survival. There were two possibilities for a Muslim in Sarajevo: confront the Serbs or let them in and get killed. Haris took a rifle.

He was out on patrol, a month after the war began, looking for Serb snipers. He identified a window in the center of town, near the parliament building, where the fire seemed to originate. When he reached the apartment, he found an old lady living with her cats. He apologized for disturbing her. But the firing resumed the next day, and when Haris went up there again he found a stash of AK-47 assault rifles under the bed. After that, he began to understand that anything was possible.

War is not credible until it is on your doorstep and then it is too late. Its mechanism is largely incommunicable. It is a vast machine churning out fear and fog that can only be understood from within. Haris met Muslim refugees in Sarajevo who had remained in their homes because of the livestock, the retiled roof, or the newly installed kitchen; remained despite tales of horror from towns just a few miles away; only to wonder, after the loss of a son's life, how such trivia could ever have mattered to them. Haris resolved to stay ahead of the game.

But there was this strange feeling. Of the gun conferring authority. Of adrenaline; being invulnerable. The rational world receded like a neatly ordered Alpine village sinking into low-lying cloud. How else to explain that they were up there, Haris and Muris, on Trebević Mountain, above Sarajevo, pushing their luck? All they had were automatic weapons and one 12.7-millimeter machine gun. A group of Sarajevo youths—what passed for the Bosnian army—facing Serb artillery and tanks.

The day Muris died, their commander, Bego Poturić, a mountain man, a hunter, went down to the city. They had been up on Trebević too long; the Serbs knew their position. They were expecting an order to withdraw. But Poturić returned with an order to hold the trench overlooking the road from the Serbs' headquarters in the mountain village of Pale to the Serbs' main barracks at Lukavica. It was madness to stay there. Poturić had given the Zečević boys one piece of advice: never fire two shots from the same spot. But they had been in the same, increasingly vulnerable emplacement for three days.

Haris wanted to demand an explanation from Poturić. An explanation! Sarajevo was under attack from Serbs who used to live in the town, neighbors-turned-strangers ready to shell their own former homes. The city was being run partly by former leaders of its criminal underworld, thugs who had been among the first to take up guns and organize the city's defense.

Responsibility for the duty roster on August 3 lay with Haris. His was the decision that determined who should go to the exposed trench, who should remain at their base in the old observatory, built a century ago during Austro-Hungarian rule. Haris had wanted to keep Muris out, but his brother kept insisting on going to the trench with his friend, Kapetanović. When Muris wanted something it was hard to stand in his way. He was highly strung, like their mother Bisera, a woman in whom laughter and tears were never far apart.

Haris watched his younger brother make his way over to the trench—that vigorous, lithe gait. He saw him take up his position with Poturić and Kapetanović and six others. Up on these pine-clad hills, a few months earlier, they had still come to clubs, or had skied, with the enemy they now confronted. You could feel the suspicion rising, the violence in the air; you could see the flags of separation unfurling and hear the songs of the new tribes rising; but you could not imagine the implacable way that war puts the time before it beyond reach and friendships formed in that time beyond recovery.

When his brother died in that trench, Haris's life snapped. There was the time before and there was the time after. In some way, even on that first night, cornered on Trebević, Haris knew that he would spend the rest of his life trying to reconcile the fragments. Layers of guilt began to form in him. Muris was younger, he did not have to be in that trench, Haris had sent him there.

There was another element to his guilt. Zoran Suša, a young Serb from Sarajevo, died in the same trench as Muris. Haris had never trusted him, although Zoran swore loyalty to the Bosnian government and fought in the same squad. "Kill some Serbs first, go on, *kill somebody*, and then I'll trust you," Haris used to say, taunting the twenty-one-year-old Serb who said he was a Sarajevan first and wanted nothing to do with the Serb separatists who denied Bosnia's existence. Haris would not let Zoran get behind him; he wanted the Serb in his sights. Zoran responded by fighting like a madman, volunteering for every dangerous mission, pushing his luck. He had wanted to go to that trench to prove to Haris that he was a Bosnian patriot, a Bosnian soldier, a Bosnian citizen as much as any Muslim or Croat. To prove to Radovan Karadžić, the leader of the separatist Serbs, that there was an alternative to the dismemberment of Bosnia. Haris began to feel that he had pushed Zoran to die.

When the dawn came at last, Haris gazed down at Sarajevo, trailing along its valley, shimmering in the haze of its mountainous amphitheater. For the first time he looked on his city as a stranger. What he now knew he would take with him everywhere, a knowledge inimical to comfort.

THE ZEČEVIĆ FAMILY lived in a spacious apartment in central Sarajevo, just off Sniper's Alley, a few hundred yards from the hideous mustard-colored block known as the Holiday Inn. During the war the hotel, built for the 1984 Olympics, acquired the distinction of being the only Holiday Inn in the world where you could step outside and stand a fair chance of being shot. Beirut's Commodore Hotel was once aptly described as a functioning telex machine surrounded by four hundred broken toilets. The Sarajevo Holiday Inn—four hundred broken windows appended to a vast crepuscular atrium designed, it seemed, with the overriding aim of chilling the soul—made me nostalgic for the Commodore.

Before the war, the Zečevićs were completing the construction of a weekend house in Butmir, a suburb beneath Mount Igman, just west of Sarajevo Airport. Every summer they vacationed on the Dalmatian coast. Asim, a mild-mannered man with a typically Bosnian passion for fishing and hunting, worked as a dentist; his wife, Bisera, worked in an import-export company. The conjuring trick of Sarajevo life, one that somehow permitted more leisure than had really been earned, continued: hard currency still flowed in from the Yugoslav *Gastarbeiters* in Germany, from tourism, and from the International Monetary Fund. The security of the Zečevićs in Yugoslav society was not something anybody questioned, any more than they discussed the origin, religion, or ethnicity of this ordinary Sarajevan family.

Ordinary because mixed: Asim's sister, Fida, had married a Bosnian Serb. Ordinary because secular: the family's mainly Muslim religious and cultural identity had been eroded by more than four decades of communist rule in Bosnia. Asim's father, Safet, had been a devout Muslim who attended mosque every day and donated 2.5 percent of his salary every month to the poor. But Asim himself was less devout; only on a few special occasions would he go to mosque.

Bisera was hostile to religion. She had been born in 1941 into a family that fought from the outset in Tito's communist Partisan movement. Her father was a Partisan throughout the war, until the Serbian royalists known as Chetniks killed him in 1945. His daughter was raised in the faith for which her father died. The élan of Tito's revolution after World War II was irresistible, and both Asim and Bisera believed it had at last conjured away Yugoslavia's ethnic differences.

Like most Bosnians of their generation, Muris and Haris therefore had a secular upbringing. Religious observation was officially reprobate because it tended to be identified with nationalist ambitions. The religious education of Muris and Haris Zečević was confined to occasional visits to the mosque with their father, usually on Bairam, the Bosnian Muslim feast that marks the end of the Ramadan period of fasting. The boys' faith, insofar as it extended beyond a commitment to the languorous pleasures of Sarajevo life, was to Tito, the state he had forged, and the *"Bratstvo i Jedinstvo"*—"Brotherhood and Unity"—that was his slogan. That they could be attacked for being Muslims was an idea so remote as to be unthinkable, especially as Bosnia was characterized by an apparently inextricable mingling of religions and peoples.

FROM EARLY CHILDHOOD, Haris and Muris had been studying Tito's doctrine of "total national defense." This was the chief medium through which the unity of Yugoslavs was impressed on children. The Yugoslav People's Army (JNA), the direct descendant of Tito's struggle during World War II, amounted to the strongest single symbol of the triumph of a Yugoslav identity. The army grew out of a Partisan movement that, by war's end, included members of all Yugoslavia's main national groups.

There were Serbs, Croats, Muslims, Slovenes, Macedonians, Montenegrins, and Albanians fighting with Tito, united in their embrace of communist ideology. The JNA took on this mantle.

The "total defense" learned in school was that of the united Yugoslav
peoples. The boys' first contact with grenades and other weapons was in
fifth grade, at the age of ten. The subject was called *"Opšte Narodna
Odbrana,"* or "General People's Defense." In seventh grade, their textbook
told them, "The Socialist Federal Republic of Yugoslavia is an association
of equal peoples and minorities. They all live in a brotherly, united association. The Brotherhood and Unity of our Peoples and minorities were
forged in the course of the war for liberation [World War II]."

The same textbooks that taught the glory of the Partisans and the importance of the JNA also gave students an unstinting indoctrination in the
evil of the Partisans' enemies inside and outside Yugoslavia. The boys
learned that "the Communists loved their people. They loved all the people in the world—all the working people. The Communists wished a
peaceful and good life to all the nations of the world. That is why the
Communists hated the Fascists as the biggest enemies of the working people. However, there were some people in our country who were helping
the Fascists. Those were the rich men who intended to preserve their fortunes with the help of the Germans and to get even richer. Fascists were
also being helped by various lazy squires who intended, together with the
Germans and their aid, to preserve their carefree and easy way of life. The
Fascists were also helped by policemen, who, even before, in old Yugoslavia, had been servants of the rich men and gentlemen. All those traitors entered the German service, they became servants of our enemies."

World War II was officially known as the *"Narodna Oslobodilačka
Borba,"* or "People's Liberation Struggle." Another official description was
the "War of the Yugoslav Peoples Against Fascist Aggression." Such descriptions suggested a unity among Yugoslav peoples that did not exist.
During World War II more Yugoslavs were killed by other Yugoslavs than
by external enemies. The label "fascist aggression" conveniently confounded Nazis, Serbian Chetniks, and Croatian Ustashas.

The basic premise of the boys' textbooks was that constant vigilance was
needed, from all Yugoslavs, against enemies, and that a decentralized defense system—involving both the Yugoslav People's Army and local Territorial Defense Forces—was required to protect the country and deter
attack. Everyone, in Yugoslav army doctrine, had to be ready to fight,
using a mixture of conventional warfare and the guerrilla tactics employed
by Tito's Partisans in the forests of Bosnia.

The boys learned about Yugoslavia's highly sensitive position between
East and West, how the country was vulnerable to Soviet forces seeking a

warm-weather port, and how seriously that threat should be taken after the Soviet invasions of Hungary in 1956 and Czechoslovakia in 1968. They learned that NATO troops just across the Adriatic in Italy might pounce at any moment. They learned how these powers had repeatedly sought to devour Yugoslavia, how Tito had been brave enough to say no to Stalin in 1948 and astute enough to say no to the West's Marshall Plan, thereby preserving Yugoslav sovereignty.

The message was crude, but it had one kernel of truth. The postwar Yugoslav state always stood delicately poised between East and West. The country's status was symbolized by its leadership of the Non-aligned Movement and by Tito's simultaneous access to billions of dollars in Western credits and to support, material and ideological, from the Soviet bloc. Important to both blocs, communist Yugoslavia was uniquely placed to benefit from their continued confrontation. Conversely, the arrival of perestroika and the fall of the Berlin Wall in 1989 were certain to affect the foundations of the state.

Unless freedom exists in a multinational state, any release from political oppression tends to be seen at first by each nation, or ethnic group, not as an invitation to gain liberty through democracy but, above all, as an invitation to be "free." The casting-off of chains involves the assertion of claims to national rights and independence. The process, as the breakup of Czechoslovakia in 1993 illustrated, need not be violent. But in Yugoslavia, the collapse of an ossified communist system coincided with a deliberate stirring-up of all that was violent in the past of the South Slav state.

HARIS CAME DOWN from Trebević Mountain the morning after his brother died wondering how to tell his mother and father what had happened. He was looking for somebody with a sedative when he met a friend who told him that word of Muris's death was already out. His mother, when she saw the faces of the men who had come to inform her, simply asked, "Which one of them is dead?" His father, Asim, was at work in his dental office when the same two men arrived. They sat down, speechless. Asim could not bring himself to ask "Which one?"

Sarajevo was a middle-class city. People had washers, dishwashers, toasters, electric stoves, mixers. A lot of the people getting killed there had video cameras. They filmed the destruction of their lives as they once filmed vacations on the Dalmatian coast. Until the film, like the food, ran out.

There is a video of Muris's funeral. It shows a hurried affair in one of the cemeteries that rise above Baščaršija, the old Turkish quarter. The sun is shining, the shadows are sharply delineated, the shells are coming down, the mourners exposed, the sound of falling earth competes with the dull echo of exploding rounds. In prayer the grieving hold out their arms. They turn their palms upward, a gesture of humility and supplication, a signal of acceptance.

The hands that are clasped in Christian prayer are directed outward, to God, but, in their pressure on each other they also seem to express self-awareness and the power of volition. But these upturned and separate hands, offered to God in the prayer of Islam, appear to express nothing so much as the absence of volition and the abandonment of self to the mystery of God. This faith, and this fatalism, implanted by the Ottomans, found a natural home in Bosnia. Perhaps it was because the mountains— each, in the words of the Bosnian historian Omer Effendi, "an eyesore to the foe"—already provided a natural home for the conviction that there is no refuge from the storm.

Asim Zečević is a precise man, punctual, never raising his voice, holding the storms down within him. Dignity and principle and acceptance of one's fate before God—these, his father taught him, were the rudiments of life. Just once, two days after the funeral, he cried. The tears crept up with an unexpected force. They were brought on by a simple thought that had somehow escaped him. Muris, the boy whose smile could dissolve any parental anger, was gone.

The first years of Asim's life had been passed in wartime. He was nine years old when World War II ended. He had considered his boys' generation a favored one, ignorant of war, more oblivious to the divisions that had devoured Yugoslavia between 1941 and 1945 than could ever have been imagined. For all his personal misgivings about Tito's regime, this thought consoled him. He knew what was hidden by the official accounts of the "People's Liberation Struggle" during World War II, but those times had seemed distant and increasingly irrelevant. Who could imagine these boys exchanging their basketball shoes for soldiers' boots, their skis for guns? But now the Balkan gyre had come about.

Asim had seen the storm rising. Still, the gradual convergence of a violent movement leading to war and a family with no obvious tie to the tumult resembles the collision, in the immensity of space, of two meteors. It is too improbable to believe.

After his younger brother died, Haris never had a dream he remembered. When he looked at photographs of Muris, he wondered how his body looked in the ground. This was not the way he wanted to think of his brother, but he found that morbid speculation had a force of its own.

CHAPTER II

MARCH
ON THE DRINA

THEY WERE A MOTLEY BAND, THE WEEKEND WARRIORS FROM Serbia who pulled over the Drina into the Bosnian border town of Zvornik in that August of 1992. Unshaven and largely unhinged, they appeared to have spent the previous days digging through wardrobes and old trunks in an atavistic frenzy aimed at unearthing the apparel of their ancestors. Or perhaps they had simply acquired the military uniforms, insignia, and badges they now wore from one of the countless stands peddling the memorabilia of Serbian heroism in the streets of Belgrade. In any event, the source of these soldiers' kit was irrelevant because the actual deeds of their forebears and the counterfeit symbols of past Serbian military glory then on sale for a dime had coalesced to produce a fever of exalted indignation in which reality and illusion were one.

The Serbs, as they explained, were on their way to fight "Turks" in Bosnia. The fact that there were probably no Turks in Bosnia did not seem to bother them. The Muslims of the independent Bosnian state—people like the Zečević family in Sarajevo—had already been collectively transfigured into the lingering Turkish ghoul of the Serbian psyche.

In reality, the enemy in Bosnia was scarcely a foreigner at all. But among the Serb warriors on the Drina's banks there seemed to be no question that some latter-day Ottoman power, in the form of an independent Bosnian state led by a devout Muslim named Alija Izetbegović, had mustered on Serbia's western doorstep. Hence the contention, expressed to me later by Radovan Karadžić, that he was fighting Europe's last "anti-imperialist war."

The Ottoman Turkish Empire, as a political force, had in fact been beaten back by the Serbs during an earlier Balkan war, that of 1912, and had lost all but a toehold in Europe at the time. The empire—Gladstone's "sick man of Europe"—collapsed entirely shortly afterward, dismembered during World War I. By the end of World War I, the Serbs had already fought three wars this century: the Balkan wars of 1912 and 1913, when Serbia pushed southward to absorb Macedonia, and the conflagration that began in Sarajevo in 1914. Scarcely more than a generation passed before the outbreak of World War II, whose toll on the Serbs was particularly heavy. And now this war. I made a quick calculation: a war every seventeen years, on average, since 1912. No wonder these Serbian men seemed haunted by shadows.

One thing was clear in the town of Zvornik: if this was a Serbian catharsis, it was a ramshackle one. The Serbs headed for the Bosnian killing fields in the late summer of 1992 were not traveling in tanks. Armies have tanks; these volunteers were a wilder bunch. They had opted to go to war on the morning bus from Belgrade to Pale, the ski resort that had been converted into the impromptu headquarters of those Serbs who denied Bosnia's existence and were determined to carve out their own state on much of its territory.

Riding a bus to Bosnia was appropriate enough at this time because the war, in its initial months, had certain recreational aspects. One Serbian paramilitary unit, active in the Brčko area of northern Bosnia, was called the *"Vikendaši"* ("The Weekenders"); another, active in Prijedor, was called "The Rambos."

For the Serbs, with overwhelming superiority in weapons inherited from the JNA, the war was mainly about the slaughter, eviction, or incarceration in concentration camps of Muslim civilians, a process necessary to ensure that wide swaths of Bosnia became ethnically pure. The task was essentially the work of units manned by the likes of the boys on the bus. Resistance was slight because President Izetbegović had not bothered to organize a Bosnian army as he pushed for independence, and the rewards of the attacks were sometimes considerable. The Serbs' "cleansing" of towns and villages was followed by the collection of booty from prisoners and abandoned homes: German marks, jewelry, furniture, kitchen fittings, parquet floors, even toilet seats.

Complete power is a heady thing. You grab an assault rifle and a packet of Marlboros, down a quick drink to steady the nerves, and watch the world change before your eyes. Neighbors suddenly look like sheep, heads cowed, meek, lined up against walls, pupils dilated and awaiting your word. The early months of the war were part boozy outing—a Sunday in the country with Muslims as lambs—part post-communist society reinterpreted as a license to steal at gunpoint.

In the first months of the war, about 70 percent of Bosnia was captured by the Serbs. The territory ran broadly from Sanski Most in northeastern Bosnia along the Sava River toward Serbia and then south along the Drina through Zvornik, Višegrad, and Foča to Trebinje in the southeast. Muslims were herded into concentration camps or toward government-held territory in central Bosnia and into a few enclaves—Bihać in western Bosnia, and Goražde, Žepa, and Srebrenica in the east. After this initial onslaught failed to bring the surrender of the Bosnian government, the war settled into something of a stalemate. Front lines did not change dramatically until the summer of 1995.

I gazed from the bus at the murky waters of the Drina, which, in the epic Serbian imagination, are always tinged with blood. The Drina has great resonance for the Serbs, a people, like the Armenians, who long lived without a state and so took to sustaining the life of their homeland in poetry, epic tales, religious liturgy, and myth. For centuries Serbia was more idea than reality. Words therefore came to carry as much weight as physical facts, which were painful. In words the nation resided. Indeed, only the passion of language—in verse, prayer, and song—could fill the void of statelessness. Faith and nation merged in a mystical way, at once compelling and dangerous.

The song *"Marš na Drinu"* ("March on the Drina") was composed in 1914, a little more than a century after Serbia began clawing back territory from the Turks. The march was inspired by initial Serbian victories against the Austro-Hungarian army that had swept across the Drina from Bosnia and Herzegovina at the beginning of World War I; it became a much-loved symbol of Serbian defiance of greater powers and of the notion of irrational valor with which Serbs identify so strongly. In 1992, Milošević adopted the song as the soundtrack for a television spot about his Serbian Socialist Party (the renamed Serbian League of Communists). The caption, which summed up all the stunning vacuity of nationalism as political philosophy, was simply, "This is Serbia."

The lyrics of the song catch the theme of the hero that is central to Serbia's vision of itself:

Sing, sing, Drina, you cold water
Remember and retell how they were falling,
Remember the brave soldiers
Who, full of fire and overwhelming force
Expelled the foreigner from our dear river.
Sing, sing, Drina, tell to my kinsmen
How bravely we fought.
The soldiers sang, the battle was fought near the cold water

Blood was shed
Blood was spilled down the Drina for freedom

But the freedom was short-lived. Within a year, the Austro-Hungarian army had overrun Serbia. This army included Croats and Muslims from Croatia and Bosnia, which then formed part of the Habsburg Empire. But the Austro-Hungarian Empire also had a large Serb minority: according to the military census of 1851, there were 1.4 million Serbs in the empire. The Austro-Hungarian forces naturally included some of them.

So it was that in World War I, Serb battled Serb. Indeed at the Battle of Mačkov Kamen in September 1914, the Serbian Fourth Regiment from Užice fought a mainly Serb Habsburg regiment from the Lika area in the Krajina. The battle was long and bloody, to the point that an exasperated Commander Purić of the Užice Regiment urged his brothers not to die so stupidly. They replied, "Have you ever heard of Serbs surrendering?"

In World War II, there was another variant on this strife. Serb royalists, dedicated to the reinstatement of the Serbian monarchy, fought Serb Partisans who supported the communist goals of Tito. Indeed, according to Tito's history books, his uprising officially began on July 7, 1941, when a Serb communist, Žikica Jovanović, killed a Serb policeman in the Serbian village of Bela Crkva.

The most conspicuous symbol of Serbdom is the symmetrical Orthodox cross adorned with four *C*'s (the Cyrillic letter *S*) and standing for *"Samo Sloga Srbina Spasava"*—"Only Unity Saves the Serb." Another rendering, however, is *"Srbin Srbina Sekirom Seče"*—"Serb Cuts Serb with an Axe." The Serb obsession with unity is one rooted in a history of disunity.

A REPORT UPON the Atrocities Committed by the Austro-Hungarian Army During the First Invasion of Serbia, written by Dr. R. A. Reiss of the University of Lausanne and published in 1916, chronicles some of the bloodletting of the Austro-Hungarian campaign. The book, based on a report submitted to the Royal Serbian government in 1915, is interspersed with photographs of dead Serbs that have a familiar look: decomposing corpses piled high, teenage boys with their eyes gouged out, women with their breasts hacked off and vaginas slashed.

In Šabac, a town on the road from Zvornik to Belgrade, more than sixty Serbian civilians were killed beside the church, according to a corporal of the Twenty-eighth Landwehr Regiment whose deposition was taken by Dr. Reiss. The victims had previously been confined in the church. "They were butchered with the bayonet," Dr. Reiss writes, "in order to save ammunition." An account of events in Breziak lists the fifty-four victims. The first seven are Anica Jezdić, aged thirty-two, eyes put out, nose and ears cut off; Simo Jezdić, nose and ears cut off; Jelka Domić, aged thirteen, nose and ears cut off; Cvetko Pavlović, eyes put out; Krsman Kalabić, aged fifty-six, eyes put out, nose and ears cut off; Smiliana Vasilijević, aged forty-eight, eyes put out; Miroslava Vasilijević, aged twenty-one, violated by about forty soldiers, genital organs cut off, her hair pushed down the vagina. She was finally disemboweled.

Survivors in the Serbian army, flanked by monks carrying the relics of Serbian kings, retreated southeastward in the dead of winter through the Albanian mountains to Greece, where a Serbian government-in-exile was established in Corfu. From exile, supported by French troops in a three-hundred-thousand-man allied force, the Serbs would eventually return, up through Macedonia, winning victories that led in 1918 to the creation of Yugoslavia on the debris of the Austro-Hungarian and Ottoman empires.

The retreat to Albania, which took a terrible toll, was immortalized by another song, composed in 1916, and now as resonant to Serbs as "March on the Drina." Called *"Tamo Daleko,"* or "There Far Away," it is the lament of a people uprooted. It ends with the verses

There, far away, where yellow lemons blossom
There lay the only way for the Serbian army.
Without a fatherland, on Corfu I lay
But I always chanted "Long Live Serbia."

Both these songs from another conflict—"March on the Drina" and "There Far Away"—were well known to the volunteers, and over the forty-three months of the war I heard many different renderings of them. They represented two sides of the coin Serbs had forged during their long Balkan trials and migrations: the bravery of the Drina victories and the pathos of the vanquished in Corfu.

Indeed, at times it seemed that victory and defeat, defiance and loss, were equally attractive to the Serbs, to the point where I was not sure that they perceived a real difference between them. Both were a vindication of some sort; both reinforced the Serbs' view of themselves and their imper-viousness to criticism. As Danilo Kiš, the sprightly literary saboteur of Stalinism, observed a decade before Milošević's revolution, "Nationalism is the ideology of hopelessness, the ideology of feasible victory, victory which is guaranteed and defeat which is never final."

Often, in the meandering justifications of the war offered in Belgrade and Pale, the heroic and pathetic modes merged. The result was not up-lifting: a mawkish mélange of loud-mouthed defiance and cloying self-pity in which events were simply turned on their head. A clearly well-planned war in Bosnia became a desperate act of self-defense; mass persecution of the innocent became preemptive resistance to Muslim plans to annihilate the Serbs; the use of overwhelming power became a proud circling of the wagons by a small, beleaguered Serbian people alone, yet again, against the world. In such arguments reason was inverted in much the same way as the Serb defeat to the Ottoman Turks at Kosovo on June 28, 1389, was transfigured into a victory.

Kosovo is more myth than battle. It did not, as Serbs often insist, mark the end of the medieval Serbian state. That state, much reduced, persisted for seventy more years; its rulers fought *alongside* the Turks on several military campaigns. Serbia only ceased to exist when the Turks took Smederevo, a Serbian fortress on the Danube, in 1459. But *peu importe.* Through fable and legend, the Serbs have transformed their defeat to the Turks in 1389 into a kind of victory and the single most potent symbol of their nationhood.

The folly of their leader, Prince Lazar, in joining battle with vastly superior Turkish forces at Kosovo has been transfigured into the wisdom of his choice of the Kingdom of Heaven over mere earthly power. Serbian legend holds that, before the battle, Saint Elijah came with a message for Lazar from the Mother of God. Lazar then saw that "if I choose an earthly kingdom, / An earthly kingdom lasts only a little time, / But a heavenly kingdom will last for eternity." He opted for a hopeless battle and "all was holy, all was honorable, / and the goodness of God was fulfilled."

Thus did physical disaster become a source of spiritual pride. In Serbian myth, the blood spilled on Kosovo field is transformed every year into the poppies that bloom across the bleak plain where the battle was fought. In suffering lay salvation; in being the victim lay the consolatory, transcendent stigma of Serbdom. Defeat and victory achieved an extraordinary synthesis, one evident in the fact that the Serbs are the only people who have chosen a calamity to mark their national day.

BUT IT WAS not merely Kosovo that weighed on the Serbs. Sometimes, listening to a diatribe in Belgrade, I wondered if the sheer accumulation of war in this century had not simply unhinged people. France was so drained, morally and physically, by World War I that it put up virtually no resistance to Hitler's invasion a generation later. Yet before the long struggle of World War II, Serbia's per-capita battle casualties between 1914 and 1918 were two and a half times those of France. It suffered a greater loss of men and wealth than any other participant in the war. The state lost one fifth of its population. About 275,000 Serbian men, or 40 percent of those mobilized, perished. The devastation, moreover, came on top of Serbia's losses in the two Balkan wars of 1912 and 1913, respectively fought against Turkey and Bulgaria.

1830–1918: The Formation of Serbia

HUNGARY

Drava

Tisa

CROATIA

Sava

ROMANIA

VOJVODINA

● Novi Sad

Danube

Sava

BOSNIA AND
HERZEGOVINA

Belgrade

Morava

SERBIA
(autonomous 1830,
independent 1878)

Danube

Sarajevo

Drina

Mostar

Niš ●

MONTENEGRO

Priština ●

Sofia ●

Dubrovnik

Podgorica ●

KOSOVO

BULGARIA

ADRIATIC SEA

Skopje ●

Tirana ●

MACEDONIA

Acquired, 1878
Acquired, 1913
Acquired, 1918
Boundary of Serbia, 1914
Current boundary of Serbia

ALBANIA

GREECE

0 Kilometers 100
0   Miles   100

By comparison, the peoples of the southern Slav areas of the Habsburg Empire—those who joined in 1918 with Serbia in the Kingdom of Serbs, Croats, and Slovenes (later renamed Yugoslavia)—had been relatively spared. Serbia's sense of carnage and tribulation was overwhelming. There was inevitably a tendency for Serbs to view Yugoslavia as the just reward for these trials and see the claims of the Croats joining the state as no more than the grumbling of a defeated people saved from ruin by Serbia.

In effect, World War I exacerbated tensions surrounding the Yugoslav idea. For when the new state came into being in December 1918, it was a union of the victorious and the vanquished. The Serbian army, after its crippling retreat to Albania, had emerged triumphant. Slovenia, Croatia, and Bosnia fought on the Austro-Hungarian side and were defeated.

Serbia could do without Yugoslavia. It already had an independent national territory. Its long-lived premier, Nikola Pašić, initially favored taking Bosnia and part of the Adriatic coast as the fruits of battlefield victory. Serbia might simply have extended its borders at the expense of the defeated in much the same way as Romania acquired land from Hungary. But the United States and France, among others, pressed for a broader Yugoslav solution.

The situation for the Croats, Slovenes, and Bosnians, the South Slavs of the imploding Habsburg Empire, was more critical. The secret Treaty of London of April 26, 1915, offered Italy the entire Dalmatian coast, as far south as Split, as an inducement to bring the Italians into the war on the allied side. Beyond Split the coast would be Serbian; all of Bosnia would go to Serbia too. Article Five of the treaty said, "Italy shall be given the province of Dalmatia within its present boundaries."

If Croatia was not to lose its coastline, long the dominion of the Venetian Empire, and perhaps more, an alternative resolution to the collapse of the Austro-Hungarian Empire needed to be agreed to quickly. Slovenia was also vulnerable to Italian claims. Ante Trumbić and Franjo Supilo, the two Croatian politicians most supportive of the Yugoslav idea, led the push for a rapid union with the Kingdom of Serbia that would serve the pragmatic purpose of heading off Italy's territorial demands. This was the thrust behind the initial agreement reached between Pašić and a Yugoslav committee headed by Trumbić and Supilo and later signed in Corfu. It called for the establishment of a Yugoslav state as a constitutional monarchy under the Serbian Karadjordjević dynasty.

Yugoslavia thus rested on a confusion of interests. On the Serbian side, it represented a risky gamble on a maximization of territorial gains: the new Yugoslavia was more than four times larger than prewar Serbia. On the Croatian and Slovene sides, it most immediately reflected a desire to head off possible dismemberment at the hands of the victorious powers.

The Habsburg Empire no longer existed in 1918. Neither Bosnia nor Croatia had known independent existence for several hundred years. Serbia, independent since 1878, saw itself as coming to their rescue. But the other peoples gathered in Yugoslavia, particularly the Croats, tended to see things differently. For them, "liberation" from empire meant little if it involved no more than the exchange of domination by Vienna or Budapest for domination by Belgrade.

This confusion inevitably weighed on constitutional questions. For Serbia, it was natural that the new state be unitary in that Yugoslavia was old Serbia expanded by certain postwar annexations. For the Croats and Slovenes it was natural that Yugoslavia be a federal state in that it was a new entity created jointly by all its constituent parts. The Yugoslav marriage was hastily consummated, with each partner viewing it differently, and there was no prenuptial agreement to cover an eventual divorce.

Serb feelings are powerfully conveyed in *The Time of Evil,* a novel by Dobrica Ćosić, Yugoslav president from 1992 to 1993. One of the characters is a Serb soldier returning from the World War I front, who says, "For the decimated Serbian people, the unification [of Yugoslavia], at least as I felt it, was a brutal manifestation of an instinct for survival. From a psychological point of view, it was the only moral and historical compensation accorded to what remained of the Serbian people for all their victims, the only tangible proof that the defiance of the Austro-Hungarian ultimatum of 1914 and the retreat across Albania had a sense for the future. And all the demands, the speculation and the political intrigue of the Croats seemed to me, as to all the soldiers who had survived, like an insult to our military victory, and a terrible injustice toward the suffering and the sacrifices of the Serbs."

As a result of such sentiments, the Kingdom of Serbs, Croats, and Slovenes was a skewed creation. Its first constitution was a triumph for Serbian centralism. All the Croatian parties and the Slovenian delegates opposed the constitution; the main Bosnian Muslim party was only won over with some last-minute blandishments. In the final vote, boycotted by all the Croatian parties and the Slovenian delegates, just 258 representatives of a total of 419 were present. For a state supposed to embody South Slav unity and a Wilsonian liberation from the oppression of the old European order, it was an ignominious debut. The idea that Yugoslavia was an expansion of Serbia had triumphed, but at the expense of alienating a wide swath of the people living in the new state.

The abbreviation for the Kingdom of Serbs, Croats, and Slovenes was SHS.

For many Croats, the initials stood for *"Srbi hoće sve"*—"Serbs want it all." For the Serbs, there was another meaning, *"Samo Hrvati smetaju"*—"Only the Croats spoil it." There were many Yugoslav patriots—but there were also simmering resentments between the two dominant national groups.

These, then, were the manifold ambiguities in the flawed birth of the South Slav state. This much always seemed clear to me: the majority of Serbs viewed Yugoslavia as their creation, because they suffered the most to bring it into being, because they were united by it, because they saw themselves as the victors succoring the defeated, and because their manifold myths mauled reasoned judgment. "Without Serbia's acts at the end of World War I, the Adriatic coast would be Serbian and Italian," Ćosić told me. "Yugoslavia was the incubator of Croatian and Slovenian independence. But from the national point of view of the Serbs, opting for Yugoslavia was a mistake. A grave and fatal historical mistake."

This conviction—that they had erred in 1918 and been repaid with scant gratitude by the other peoples of the Yugoslav state—redoubled the Serbs' frustration and fury as Yugoslavia was undone. In counterpoint, playing off the initial Serbian frenzy whipped up by Slobodan Milošević, Croats led by Franjo Tudjman vented all their grievances and rage at the way Belgrade had "imprisoned" the Croatian nation from Yugoslavia's precipitate birth in 1918 onward.

MY MUSINGS beside the bridge at Zvornik were interrupted by the realization that the Serbian males on the bus—some teenagers, some middle-aged men—had disappeared. They soon returned, in high spirits. The source of their good humor was apparent in the array of hand grenades, cartridge belts, and Zastava rifles (a Yugoslav version of the Soviet Kalashnikov) now appended to them.

All this weaponry for the boys crossing the border was intriguing in that General Života Panić, the Serbian chief of staff, had told me during a meeting in August 1992 that there was not a soldier from Serbia left in Bosnia. "Since May nineteenth, there has not been one left. Not a single one. We look at Bosnia as a quite distinct place, like America!" Throughout a war directed largely from Belgrade, Milošević and the Serbs would never abandon this fiction.

One weekend warrior informed me that he did not need a gun for aggressive purposes—Serbs, he explained, were merely defending their own homes in Bosnia—but to kill himself in case he was captured. Accounts of Muslim atrocities, particularly an alleged propensity for impaling captured Serbs and then roasting them on a spit, were rife at the time. I never saw any evidence of such acts, but the Ottoman practice of impaling victims and putting them on public display—*pour encourager les autres*—had passed into Serbian lore long before the latest fighting in the Balkans began. The pointed oak stave topped with a Christian head is a symbol lying deep in the Serbian psyche.

What was most striking in these Serbian warriors was the enormous distance between the stirring images of the past that seemed to inspire them and the dismal reality of which they were part. This was a recurrent theme of Yugoslavia's wars. Few sights were as emblematic as a bleary-eyed soldier, the worse for the previous night's plum brandy, gazing out over a Balkan vista of unmitigated destruction and rhapsodizing—in the case of a Croat—about the greatness of King Tomislav or—in the case of a Serb— the glory of Emperor Dušan.

Tomislav, dead for over a millennium, and Dušan, dead for more than six hundred years, had one thing in common: they represented the ephemeral apogee of the power of two nations whose states later ceased to exist for several centuries. Under them, Croatia and Serbia were *very big,* as big indeed as they have ever been. Subsequent subjugation had frozen history at this moment. All that followed—the long Hungarian and then Habsburg rule over Croatia; the Turkish conquest of Serbia, Bosnia, and wide swaths of Croatia; the centuries of Venetian rule over Dalmatia; the drawing and redrawing of borders in the light of these events—all this was no more than a perversion of an immutable truth, one embodied in the states of Tomislav and Dušan. As the Bosnian war was largely about making Serbia and Croatia bigger, the long-dead rulers were the symbols that could best justify the destructive fever.

Here in Zvornik, the bus rattled and lurched; overburdened women huddled in the aisle clutching children, food, and belongings; the early morning breath of the troops was already heavy with alcohol; and none of the ragged uniforms on display matched. I had never seen such a proliferation of different military hats cocked at various angles in what looked like a comic-book historical guide to Serbian military accoutrements. Yet the heads beneath the hats seemed to brim with atavistic images: Prince Lazar, the Battle of Kosovo, the defense of the Drina, the desperate retreat through Albania.

Amid all the military gear from the itinerant history of the Serbs, a particular penchant was evident, in these wild early days of the Bosnian war, for the Chetnik look: long beards, straggly hair, royalist insignia, conical hats with badges of the Serbian double-headed eagle pinned to them.

Long taboo under Tito, the term *Chetnik* was, by 1987, beginning to enjoy a revival, becoming linked to what many Serbs viewed as the quest for the recovery of their identity as the communist system unraveled. The reemergence of the word involved the rehabilitation of Mihailović, the Chetnik leader executed by Tito. No longer a Yugoslav traitor, he resurfaced as a Serbian hero.

Still, on the bus headed over the Drina, it was strange to see latter-day Chetniks seated beside other Serbs attired in the Partisan uniforms and caps of the communist executioners of Mihailović. The double-headed eagle and the Partisan five-pointed star were both on display. This extraordinary, and, as it proved, fleeting fusion of the royalist-nationalist and Partisan-communist currents in Serbia was the singular achievement of Milošević. Unity for the Serbs had been achieved at last. It fortified the collective folly that seized Belgrade between 1987 and 1992 and shattered the delicate mosaic of Yugoslavia.

Shortly after the bus moved over the Drina into Bosnia, a soldier pulled his hat down over his eyes and dozed off. The grenade on his lap then fell onto the floor. All eyes were fixed on it as it rolled, but there was no detonation. As the befuddled warrior pointed out with a toothless grin on emerging from his slumber, he had been astute enough not to pull the pin.

This, then, was what Serbia's past military glory had been reduced to: a coarse, violent, sometimes farcical parody in which men dressed up as Chetniks and men dressed up as Partisans sat side by side on a lurching bus to Bosnia. All of them had subsumed their fragile, long-repressed, postcommunist individuality into the embrace of a resurgent folklore. If history underpinned these endeavors, it seemed to be a history perverted, transformed into a source of kitsch, the kind of history peddled over a half century in the classrooms of communist Yugoslavia, where facts were malleable things, grist for the greater glory of Josip Broz Tito, ruler for life.

CHAPTER 12

HISTORY AS AXE

A FEW WEEKS AFTER MURIS ZEČEVIĆ WAS KILLED, I FOUND myself on Trebević Mountain near the trench in which he died. I was with Serb forces in a bunker overlooking Sarajevo. The place was a converted nightclub called the Osmica, in which Serbs, Muslims, and Croats from the Bosnian capital had gathered to enjoy live music. But five months into the war, the club was a charred ruin hung with pinups and ammunition belts, packed with the Serbs' 7.9-millimeter machine guns and shoulder-mounted grenade launchers, protected by sandbags and timber cut from the towering pines on the ridges of Trebević.

Sarajevans, throughout the war, felt they were living in the telescopic sights of a gun. They were the wildlife in a city-cum-sniper-safari-park: pay a dollar, take a shot. From the bunker, known as position "number eight," it was evident that their impression was no illusion. Each window of the yellowish hulk of the Holiday Inn, each minaret of Baščaršija, each twist of the city's streets was visible. Sarajevo's beauty, its mountain fastness, had become its trap.

The Serbs manning the gun position included former residents of Sarajevo and others who, like the boys on the bus, had traveled from Serbia itself. One man said he was from Novi Sad; he had volunteered because a relative was killed by Croatian forces near Derventa early in the war. They were convinced, all of them, despite the obvious superiority of their position above the encircled city, that they were defending themselves. "Sniper, sniper," they said amid the occasional crackle of fire and the regular, but distant, boom of *outgoing* mortars, warning me to keep down.

Ranko Ćosović called himself a sergeant. He had lived in Sarajevo all his life. He worked at the Famos mechanical factory until he joined Karadžić's forces on April 17, eleven days after the war began. He had decided to attack his own city because the alternative was to live in "a Muslim state, governed by Izetbegović, in the heart of Europe." Sarajevo, he said, would eventually have to be divided into distinct areas for each religious group. Another Serb soldier, who had abandoned his import-export business in Sarajevo, said his parents were still living in the city, near the Skenderija sports complex. It was therefore possible, he conceded, that he was firing on his own family.

But then, I realized, the idea that they were *attacking* anyone, that the civilians in the town below were a target, was foreign to these men. Like the boys on the bus, who had dispersed to their units around Sarajevo, these Serb soldiers were impervious to the notion that their actions might be construed as aggressive, that the shells lobbed from these hills were killing women and children. They were secure in their post-communist religious conviction that all this amounted to a defense against the infidel.

NATIONALISM INVOLVES NUMBERS. The nationalist declares not only that there are a lot of us, enough to impose our will, but also that there would have been a lot *more* of us if we had not, in the past, faced war, persecution, eviction, mistreatment, abuse, and other misfortunes at the hands of the enemy. A nationalist movement seeks to change the present in the name of the past in order to create a future vague in all respects except its glory. This luminous future, portrayed as a natural right, is, in the nationalist's discourse, the one that would have occurred were it not for history's aberrations. A paradise lost is never lost to the nationalist leader. It can always be regained or at least exploited.

The outlandish Serbian accusations that rained forth in the *Memorandum of the Serbian Academy of Sciences and Arts,* made public in 1986, were in essence complaints about history. They in turn formed the basis for Slobodan Milošević's rise to power in 1987, for the subsequent Serbian revolution, and for the war that these men were fighting on the hills above Sarajevo.

The Memorandum, paranoid, self-pitying, and aggressive, was certainly the single document most influential in establishing the drumbeat of Serbian bombast and pathos that led inexorably to Yugoslavia's dismemberment. Noting the decline in the population of Serbs in the southeastern Serbian province of Kosovo, it accused the Kosovo Albanians, who by the 1980s accounted for 90 percent of the province's population, of "neofascist aggression"; establishing a "physical, moral and psychological reign of terror"; practicing arson, murder, and rape; attacking "the cradle of the Serbs' historical existence"; and waging "open and total war" against the Serbs. It added that "the physical, political, legal and cultural genocide of the Serbian population in Kosovo and Metohija" amounted to the worst defeat for the Serbs since they rose against the Turks in 1804.

War and *genocide* are strong words, especially so in the absence of fighting. Throughout the 1980s, no more than five Serbs died in violent incidents in Kosovo. Imagined war, imagined genocide, of which the majority of a nation becomes convinced, may in time come to inspire real war, real genocide, it hardly matters where.

Moving on from Kosovo to Croatia, the Memorandum noted that in 1948, there were 543,795 Serbs living in Croatia, or 14.8 percent of the population. By 1981, the number has fallen to 531,502, or 11.5 percent of the population. This development, the Memorandum suggested, was the result of cultural and political pressure, including attempts to forge a separate Croatian language, limit use of the Cyrillic alphabet, and prohibit Serbian associations or cultural institutions.

The Serbian intellectuals then made a leap similar to the one made in their discussion of Kosovo, transforming grievances with some limited basis in fact into wild allegations calling forth the ghosts of genocide. Other than in the time of the Croatian fascist dictator Ante Pavelić, they declared, "the Serbs in Croatia have never before been as jeopardized as they are today."

Pavelić's policy on the Croatian Serbs during World War II had been clear: kill a third, convert a third to Catholicism, and evict the remaining third. To draw a parallel between the situation of the Serbs in Croatia in 1986 and the genocidal onslaught they faced in 1941 was to foster the most dangerous of illusions. But it served a clear purpose: *to couch an aggressive project in defensive terms.*

Serbs, the Memorandum claimed, were threatened, genocidally threatened, in Kosovo, in Croatia, indeed throughout Yugoslavia. Their need to unite preemptively was therefore overwhelming. "The integrity of the Serbian nation and its culture throughout Yugoslavia presents itself as the most crucial question of its survival and progress."

But there was a problem, one that would become the central conundrum of Yugoslavia's violent dissolution. This Serbian "culture" was widely spread. The authors noted that, according to the 1981 census, 1,958,000 Serbs, or 24 percent of all Serbs, lived outside the territory of the Socialist Republic of Serbia. The dispersion of these Serbs in Croatia, Bosnia, and elsewhere in Yugoslavia had the effect, the Memorandum claimed, of "completely breaking up the national unity of the Serbian nation" and exposing Serbs to "chauvinism," "Serbophobia," "denigration," and "an imposed guilt complex."

What to do? The dangers are pressing: "Serbia must not be passive and wait to see what the others will say, as it has done so many times in the past." To begin with, the autonomous status of Kosovo and Vojvodina within Serbia must be ended in order to make them a "genuinely integral

1992: Predominant Ethnic Groups

AUSTRIA

ITALY

SLOVENIA
(Slovenes)

Ljubljana ⭐

Trieste ●

Sava

Zagreb ⭐

CROATIA

Karlovac ●

● Rijeka

Sisak ●

● Pakrac

Dvor ●

Bihać ●

Prijedor ●

● Banja Luka

BOSNIA AN
HERZEGOVI

A D R I A T I C   S E A

● Zadar

Knin ●

Sara

Split ●

Mostar ●

Dubrovnik ●

Tre

Legend

Croat majority

Muslim majority

Serb majority

Without any one ethnic
group over 50 percent

part of the Republic of Serbia." This will ensure that "Serbia ceases to be the only republic whose internal affairs are ordered by others." Beyond this first step, all Serbs must unite. In short, "the Serbian people must be allowed to find themselves again and become an historical personality in their own right, to regain a sense of their historical and spiritual being."

The words *Greater Serbia* never appear in this tract. But in its assiduous cultivation of a Serbian persecution complex, in its warnings that Yugoslavia is fragmenting and that dangers are pressing, in its quasi-mystical references to the lost "spiritual being" of the Serbs, in its deliberate cultivation of fear through the wild exaggeration of threats, in its references to economic discrimination against the Serbs, and in its relentless impeachment of an allegedly unjust history, the pamphlet amounted to an irredentist appeal of incendiary power in a society whose governing ideology, long embodied by Tito, was fraying, and whose push for "democratic socialism" had reached the limit of its internal contradictions.

As LONG AS the authority of the League of Communists remained, buttressed by Europe's division into rival blocs, the flawed legacy of Tito could be papered over. But the league, leading the headlong rush of central and southeastern Europe's communist parties into extinction or irrelevance, survived just two months after the fall of the Berlin Wall. The implosion came on January 23, 1990, when the Slovenes walked out of the Fourteenth Extraordinary Party Congress.

The Slovenes always tended to look askance at the rest of Yugoslavia in much the same way as the people of Milan and Turin find it hard to hide their disdain for southern Italians. Richer than other Yugoslavs, and closer to Western Europe, the Slovenes tended increasingly to identify with Vienna just as the Milanesi feel more in common with Geneva than with Rome or Naples. There is always an element of hypocrisy in such attitudes—the wealth of Slovenia depended largely on a captive Yugoslav market. But Serbia's nationalist crescendo of the late 1980s naturally increased Slovenia's discomfort and provided a pretext for its progressive separation. The Slovenes' departure from the party made Yugoslavia's demise likely. But violence was still far from inevitable.

Bloodshed was always possible, however, because of fear and because history's wounds had not been addressed.

It has become axiomatic to say that communism was a freezer that congealed old historical tensions. In many ways, however, it was more of a cauldron. That which is frozen is immobilized but not essentially altered. But communism was not neutral about the past. It mixed the past around; it stirred history up; it did heated violence to memory, the kind of violence that is not quickly forgotten. The reason was evident. Communist systems had their gods. Those gods were demanding. They required certain versions of history to explain, justify, and bolster their deification.

In postwar Yugoslavia, before and after his death in 1980, the god's name was Tito, who was born to a Croat peasant father and a Slovene mother in the Slavic dominions of the Austro-Hungarian Empire and died a communist deity. Yugoslav schoolchildren, presented with the conundrum of what would happen after Tito, were taught *"Posle Tita, Tito"*— "After Tito, Tito." Thus was expressed the idea that gods, even the mortal ones who bestride this earth, do not die.

I know of a man in the Serbian town formerly called Titovo Užice (now just plain Užice), who was imprisoned for putting a coil of rope around the neck of a bust of Tito while attempting to hoist it onto a pedestal in the town square. I learned from Ryszard Kapuscinski's *Imperium* that a man in Moldavia spent ten years in a camp after "coiling a thick rope around the neck of Lenin" as he tried to maneuver it over a balcony into a second-floor common room. The methods of rule in the Soviet Union and communist Yugoslavia were not identical. Tito exploited his country's unique position between East and West to indulge, at times, in experiments with liberalization. But, just as in the Soviet Union, where Tito spent many formative years, certain things never changed: the one-party state, the deification of an untouchable ruler, the selective use of terror and intimidation, the exploitation of fear to still the inquiring mind. In both states, a rope around the neck of a bust of the regime's god—even one placed in the interests of hoisting the bust higher—was not a mere coil of rope. It was a counterrevolutionary noose punishable by the gulag.

The imposition of such a repressive system begins in the physical world but must quickly be extended to the mind, which is where it really takes root. Curiosity must be beaten down, bearings eliminated. An uprooted man is far more vulnerable than a rooted man, a vagrant is more ready to serve some new order than one who knows where he belongs. Tampering with history is an effective tool for both these missions. The effect of an invented past is both stifling and disorienting.

In the Soviet Union, for example, the Second World War became the "Great Patriotic War of 1941–1945." As Norman Davies has pointed out, this suggests that nothing happened until the Nazis invaded the Soviet Union. In fact, there had been Stalin's pact with Hitler, the invasion of the eastern half of Poland, the Katyn massacre, and the invasion of the Baltic states and Finland. These acts were hard to square with the supposed neutrality of the Red Army, and so they literally disappeared from official histories.

In Yugoslavia, the "People's Liberation Struggle" tended to obscure manifold horrors. Far from a natural precursor of the *"Bratstvo i Jedinstvo"* that became the slogan of Tito's Yugoslavia, the events of World War II foretold, in many respects, the state's violent destruction that began in 1991. Like the events of 1939–1941 in the Soviet Union, the real war in Yugoslavia was too sensitive to be related; so it, too, disappeared. Or rather it was relegated to one of those silent archives where facts gather dust and await the avenging moment of their revelation.

It was the suppressed ghosts of these internal wars that Slobodan Milošević of Serbia and then Franjo Tudjman of Croatia raised in order to cement their power and ensure that Yugoslavia died in violence. The day of reckoning in Yugoslavia came in 1991. As Atif Dudaković, one of the most resourceful Bosnian army officers, once told me, "This Balkan guest house had been open since 1918 and the check was sure to be big."

Yugoslavia's destruction coincided with the end of the cold war, steep economic decline, and the pervasively poisonous rhetoric of nationalist leaders determined to use fear as a political tool. The cumulative effect of these three factors was disastrous. The first made the United States relatively indifferent to Yugoslavia's fate; the second provided a disaffected youth that could be whipped, often with the help of outright criminals, into a murderous frenzy; the third used old wounds to create new enemies and set neighbors on one another.

ONCE AGAIN, the outside world proved no help to Yugoslavia. James Baker, the American secretary of state in the years of Europe's latest transformation, the representative of an administration with something like the power of Wilson in 1918 or Roosevelt in 1945, came to Yugoslavia on June 21, 1991. American prestige had been greatly boosted, and American interests consumed, by the Gulf War, a victory that seemed in mid-1991 to have ensured the reelection of George Bush. Baker, representing the leadership of the "free world," as well as Bush's electoral calculations (which did not include any messy involvement in the Balkans), held eleven meetings, with all the republican presidents and with members of the federal government. The message, according to Jim Swigert, a U.S. diplomat present, was quixotic: America opposed the breakup of Yugoslavia, but also opposed the use of force to hold it together. This approach was supposed to represent a compromise between two conflicting principles: the inviolability of borders and the right to self-determination of peoples. "But it was a little too subtle for these guys," Swigert observed.

Baker warned Slovenia and Croatia against "preemptive unilateral actions." But the republics took the measure of America's commitment to the post–cold war Yugoslav state. No longer a likely point of ignition for World War III, Yugoslavia had become an unlikely structure perched on a nonexistent foundation. No overriding American interest resided there.

Four days after Baker left, Slovenia and Croatia declared independence; fighting that was to last for more than four years began.

The reaction of the Bush administration was to huff at the bad faith of the Slovenes and Croats, which confirmed every prejudice about the Balkan snake pit. The upshot was that the problem was passed to the Europeans, who wanted to use the Balkans to test the diplomatic muscle of a united Europe but were hobbled by a basic problem: the European Union does not have an army. In the Balkans diplomacy without military backing is dithering.

Thus, with a whirlwind one-day visit, America betrayed its essential indifference to the state whose two incarnations it had buttressed so decisively. The Bush administration failed to make a basic decision: it might have concluded that Yugoslavia was moribund and assisted in its peaceful dismantling, or it might have committed itself energetically to the preservation of the state, perhaps in some looser form. The failure to do either was an act of irresponsibility. The Balkan wars then fell between Europe and America, passed back and forth like a poisoned chalice. NATO became, for several years, a bitter alliance and one demonstrably in need of rethinking.

MILOŠEVIĆ, THE APOSTLE of the Serbian Memorandum, became a man of extraordinary power because he was prepared to exploit the cathartic shifts of the late 1980s. A communist bureaucrat, he was briefly seduced by nationalist myth and the heady whiff of deification that went with it. In a disoriented Yugoslav society, he saw clearly the power of nationalism as what Miroslav Hroch has called "a substitute for factors of integration in a disintegrating society." His message was simple: a glorious, and avenging, future on the basis of a supposedly glorious past. In Serbia, as a nationalist and a communist, Milošević contrived to represent and unite the warring traditions of the country. He was at once a Chetnik and a Partisan—a miraculous, a divine achievement. Ex-communists and long-frustrated Serbian conservatives plastered his poster over their rooms with equal enthusiasm. Of course, the combination was impossible, oil in water. It could not endure. But for a time that did not matter and the irreconcilable was reconciled in an orgy of euphoria followed by wave upon wave of violence.

His revolution combined some of the methods of the well-trained apparatchik (particularly in the highly effective use of televised propaganda designed to instill fear) with the exploitation of the very Serbian national icons that communism had suppressed. The bones of Prince Lazar—symbolizing the Serbs' "historical and spiritual being" forged at Kosovo—were wheeled out and taken on a tour of Serbian monasteries, where they attracted huge crowds in 1989. Secular Serbs lined up in the streets to be baptized. The mass appeal of the Milošević movement, in an economically depressed Serbia, lay in the adept utilization of the transcendent moments of the Serbs' troubled history, spiced with a keen sense of the way Tito's *Homo yugoslavus* had developed an easily exploitable craving for terrestrial gods.

The Serbian revolution was in fact an object lesson in the dangers of the post-communist world. For nationalism, as Lenin failed to predict and the Polish writer Adam Michnik noted, is to communism as imperialism was supposed to be to capitalism: its last stage. The nation is cathartically released from certain constraints but is still controlled and channeled through variants on the methods of Leninist dicatorship. In the place of the system and its secular god, it is the nation and its long-suppressed icons that are portrayed as being under threat from insidious enemies, internal and external. That much changes. But the power to cow people and herd them is preserved.

Milošević is a closed man who does not make many speeches and does not often venture into the limelight. He understands the compelling mystique of hidden power, an art honed in the Kremlin, that high academy of fear where invisible leaders refined the quintessentially twentieth-century technique of terror: the mass disappearance of people. In this way was it demonstrated that the unseen had the power to cause nonexistence— surely a godly attribute. Milošević's father, Svetozar, was an Orthodox priest who abandoned the family when Milošević was a young boy, returned to his native Montenegro, and committed suicide. His mother, Stanislava, was a teacher and a dedicated communist activist. She too committed suicide, by hanging herself, as did her brother.

Milošević's family background thus offers a macabre reflection of an image dear to the Serbs: that of a people with a tendency, even a predilection, for self-destruction. Certainly destruction, of his own people and others, has been a central theme—indeed, the overriding characteristic— of Milošević's oeuvre. His small, shifting eyes and jutting chin reflect his personality: a craven, clever bully. He was not made to stand before people and hold them; he was made to manipulate them from afar. His is a world of calculation rather than feeling. I never saw a smile cross his face that did not have the painful aspect of a rictus, nor have I often seen such a troubling mix of timidity and assertiveness as in his features. The eyes and chin, like his squat thug's body and tailored lounge suits, are forever in search of some elusive reconciliation.

It was in Kosovo, scene of the Serbs' defeat to the Ottoman Turks, that the revolution was ignited. Milošević's declaration to the Serbs of Kosovo, on April 24, 1987, that "no one should dare to beat you" was the first statement that, as he later put it, the "fatherland" took precedence over mere politics. Because politics in Yugoslavia would have meant support of the communist authorities—and the Kosovo authorities allegedly doing the "beating" were mainly ethnic Albanians—this was a revolutionary declaration.

Revolutionary in its language. No longer the vapid bureaucratic formalism of communist speech, whose aim is not to clarify but to convey an impenetrable authority. Rather, the direct appeal to the blood of the nationalist demagogue. Already, in Kosovo in April 1987, Milošević had found his tone: "It was never part of the Serbian and Montenegrin character to give up in the face of obstacles, to demobilize when it's time to fight. You should stay here for the sake of your ancestors and descendants. Otherwise your ancestors would be defiled and descendants disappointed."

Ancestors, descendants, national character: blood. The rest followed naturally enough: the ousting, at the Eighth Session of the Serbian Central Committee in September 1987, of Stambolić, the leader of the Serbian Communist party, Milošević's former mentor, and the man who first said that the Serbian Memorandum should be renamed "In Memoriam, Yugoslavia"; the development of the tumultuous cult of Milošević's personality; the crushing, as prescribed in the Memorandum, of the autonomy of Vojvodina and Kosovo in 1988 and 1989; the installation of a subservient Montenegrin leadership; the stirring of a Serb rebellion in Croatia; the steady disintegration of Yugoslavia, where, by 1990, Milošević effectively controlled four votes in the eight-man collective presidency (those of Serbia, Kosovo, Vojvodina, and Montenegro) instead of one.

Tito's balance had been upset. In Europe, where the blocs he played so adeptly against each other had disappeared, and in Yugoslavia, where soil, blood, and history had gained the upper hand in an atrophied system whose unifying god, in his creamy marshal's uniforms and endless gold braid, had been replaced by the ungainly eight-headed monster of a collective presidency. Sirens still wailed all over Yugoslavia at 3:05 P.M. on May 4, the anniversary of Tito's death; the country still fell silent for two minutes at that moment; commanders of the JNA still referred to Tito after his death as "our supreme commander." But the torch had passed.

The enshrinement of Milošević as a Serbian god, and the new Serbian domination of Yugoslav politics, inevitably invited the question among other republics of whether they wanted to remain in Yugoslavia—or, as some of them now called it, "Serboslavia." When they eventually made clear that they did not, Milošević responded that the Serbs were on the defensive because they merely wanted to remain in the Yugoslav state. This approach was suggestive of a man who has smashed all the furniture and then insults people for not sitting down with him.

Here, not in a distant Balkan past as impenetrable as some Transylvanian night, were the sparks of the war. The Serbs, delirious in the illusion of a rediscovered unity, were pushed to the frenzied pursuit of an aggressive design framed in defensive terms. The dissolution of Yugoslavia—always a danger in the aftermath of communism and in light of the state's anguished history—was thus set on a path of violence. Others, led by Franjo Tudjman of Croatia, soon leapt on the nationalist bandwagon. Milošević's revolution provided a wonderful pretext, and precedent, for other expressions of nationalism that sought to settle, finally, the painful Balkan legacy of the Austro-Hungarian and Ottoman empires in blood rather than diplomacy.

THE SERB SOLDIERS above Sarajevo had grenades strapped to their belts, symmetrical Orthodox crosses strung around their necks. Their weapons, inherited from Tito's atheist army, protected them; their rediscovered faith buttressed them. The Serbian Orthodox church, the ultimate repository and guardian of the Serbs' nationhood during their myriad migrations across the Balkans, had given its support to Milošević's initial message that the Serbs were only acting in defense of their rights and their homes. A few weeks before I reached position eight above Sarajevo, the Holy Assembly of Bishops said of the war that "this is not the first time in their history that the Serbian people have experienced crucifixion." It went on to speak of Pavelić's "genocide" against the Serbs during World War II and to defend the idea of a Greater Serbia. "Our church is for the unity of the Serbian people and Serbian lands."

The Serbs of Croatia and Bosnia did suffer a genocidal attack from Pavelić during World War II; some Bosnian Muslims, like Alija Mehmedović, joined the fascist forces; other Muslims fought against the Fascists. Izetbegović's devotion to his religion was evident in a tract called the "Islamic Declaration" in 1970 that was pushed on me insistently in 1992 in Belgrade and Pale as proof of his "fundamentalist" designs for Bosnia. It is an attempt to reconcile the precepts of the Koran with the organization of a modern state. It contains several ominous reflections, such as this one: "The media should not be allowed—as so often happens—to fall into the hands of perverted and degenerate people who then transmit the aimlessness and emptiness of their own lives to others. What are we to expect if mosque and TV transmitter aim contradictory messages at the people?"

But Izetbegović had no army or plans for war. He had, before the fighting, led a coalition government in Bosnia made up of the three national parties. His seven-man presidency—three Muslims, two Serbs, two Croats—was a rotating one. The president of the parliament was a Serb and the prime minister a Croat. He had committed himself to a Bosnia respectful of all its peoples and he had stated that the Islamic Declaration was no blueprint for Bosnia. What possible "crucifixion" did the Serbs of Bosnia really face? And at whose hands?

But by the time Bosnia was moving toward independence, the cultivation of the Serbs' grand delusion had been in progress for several years. It began in Kosovo. The alleged "genocide" by Albanians against Serbs in Kosovo provided, from 1986 onward, the central cog in Belgrade's galloping generator of paranoia. The so-called Martinović case played a key role in the Serb allegations.

The first reference to Djordje Martinović, a fifty-six-year-old Serbian farmer in Kosovo, appeared in the Belgrade newspaper *Politika* on May 4, 1985. The article said that he had been attacked by two people, who tied him down, beat him, and finally thrust a bottle into his anus. It quoted his family as being especially bitter because, before the attack, Albanians had come several times to ask if his land was for sale and had been rebuffed.

Eight months later, *Ilustrovana Politika,* a more popular version of *Politika,* took up the story, saying that Serbs and Montenegrins were leaving Kosovo because of the Martinović case and the "pressure of the Albanian irredentists." Later in 1986, the Serbian Memorandum itself examined the case, saying the attack was "reminiscent of the darkest days of the Turkish practice of impalement." By December 1988, Martinović was the object of a program on Radio Belgrade, *Searching for the Truth,* in which Miodrag Bulatović, a member of Milošević's Serbian Socialist Party, said the attack was a crime against the Serb nation committed by a "bullying and terrorist nation."

In February 1989, the weekly magazine *Nin* felt moved to expound on the wider significance of the attack: "Here, we are dealing with the remains of the Ottoman Empire, in the use of a stake, but this time one wrapped in a bottle. In the time of the Turks, Serbs were also fixed to stakes, but even then the Turks used their servants—the Albanians." Finally, in 1991, the Belgrade magazine *Politikin Svet* declared that the attack was "a Jasenovac for one man"—a reference to the most notorious of Pavelić's concentration camps.

Thus an incident in which nobody was killed was used by Milošević's media to awaken the darkest specters in the Serbian psyche. Serbs had been killed in rioting in Kosovo in 1968 and 1981. But in the six years between the attack on Martinović and the beginning of Yugoslavia's bloody disintegration in 1991 this humiliation of a single Serb in a Kosovo field became synonymous with five centuries of Turkish oppression, impalement, genocide, and the concentration camps of Pavelić's Ustasha regime in Croatia.

Listening to those gunners above Sarajevo, it was clear enough that the Martinović model had been reapplied in Bosnia. All the specters of past Serb suffering had been deliberately raised and exaggerated here in Bosnia to justify a war in which the Serbs, consciously or unconsciously, used precisely the methods of their past torturers.

In March 1991, Patriarch Pavle of Belgrade had dwelt on this painful past in a menacing tone. He chose to quote the words of Archbishop Nikolaj, uttered in 1958: "If the Serbs avenged themselves in proportion to all the crimes committed against them in this century, what would they have to do? They would have to bury people alive, roast people alive, skin them alive, chop up children in front of their parents. This Serbs have never done, not to wild animals, much less to humans."

Memory is necessary. But so is the ability to forget. When memory is everything it devours the rational mind. Then memory spills over into myth, justifying the unjustifiable, releasing murderous demons that claim impunity and blindness in the very name of the innocent victims of the past.

DUŠKO KORNJAČA, a thirty-two-year-old doctor commanding Serb forces in southeastern Bosnia and leading the Serb assault on Goražde at this early stage in the war, wore two crosses around his neck. He had opted for the Chetnik look, and his shaggy black beard was one of the more impressive I saw. When I met him in the late summer of 1992 in the village of Čajnice, about thirty miles from Sarajevo, he was about to attend a Sunday banquet with the local bishop, Nikolaj Mrda, and invited me to join him.

The bearded churchman in his vestments and the bearded warrior in his khaki uniform sat side by side before a table laden with food. Beside them soldiers and priests mingled. The pageant was medieval, lifted, it seemed, from some luminous Gozzoli fresco in a dark Florentine chapel, and the battle under way just a few miles away was also of another time. Its sounds reached us occasionally. Cannons boomed, machine guns chattered, and I imagined the muddied soldiers in their trenches or pushing through the dense woods. This war, in its weaponry, was little different from Tito's, fought a half century earlier in these very same woods. The war that all Yugoslav boys, like Haris and Muris Zečević, had studied as an example and an inspiration. Sophisticated weaponry played little part; young boys were pushed through the mud into the face of machine guns; scorched-earth tactics and barbaric cruelty played their part in forcing the conversion of minds. And although there were now American spy satellites in the skies

overhead, they had little interest in seeing what was happening, for to understand was to be invited to act.

This war, too, no doubt, like Tito's war, would be remembered by each
side for some moment of heroism. But the histories would tell us less of
the boys pushed forward across the snow into positions where they were
marooned and deprived of artillery support. Of the terrified teenagers
shooting themselves in the arm or calf to avoid taking part in the attack.
Of the old men and homosexuals forced to dig trenches, trembling, hesi-
tating to light a cigarette for fear of being seen and then lighting one at the
wrong moment and having their heads blown off. Of the terror of plunging into a minefield and being pinned down by artillery fire. Of the sheer
stupidity and tragedy of an improvised war, where a hill of little or no
strategic value, far from the cameras of CNN, could cost a thousand
young lives.

The feast began with the rich veal soup known as *čorba;* there was roast
lamb; there was a lot of excellent slivovitz, the plum brandy brewed in
every self-respecting Bosnian's backyard. The bishop said grace and gave
what amounted to a brief sermon in which he accused Izetbegović of wanting to deprive the Serbs of their rights. Commander Kornjača noted that
before us lay good and simple things, for this was not a time for indulgence, this was a time of struggle for "a better Yugoslavia." Of course, Yugoslavia had ceased to exist by then, but the fiction of its preservation
allowed the Serbs to say they were merely fighting to defend the state in
which they had all lived.

After the food had been eaten, the commander and the bishop embraced *à la Serbe,* kissing each other three times on the cheek. Some girls
in white sang folksongs. The struggle was pure; the struggle was blessed.
The Serbs, it was clear, had been elected by God. The corollary was equally
clear: other peoples had not. There cannot be two chosen people on the
same land.

We went to Commander Kornjača's office, decorated with the usual
Balkan ethnological maps. These are works of cartographical ingenuity.
They all use subtle tones to suggest that the religious group to which the
owner of the maps belongs is dominant. In Kornjača's case, the whole map
of Bosnia appeared as a more or less intense shade of red, the color denot-
ing the Serbs; in Sarajevo, such maps tend to appear in various shades of
green, the color of the Muslims; in west Mostar, Bosnia is a blue sea of
Croats. The commander pointed to the map and went straight into a battery of statistics that proved that every town of any significance in Bosnia
had a Serb majority.

"This is our land," he said. "We cannot accept that Islam imposes itself.
If we don't stop Islam now, in ten or twenty years it will be in France and

England and dominating Europe. The West wanted to carve up Yugoslavia for itself, the Americans wanted to break up any significant power in the Balkans, but in fact the West is not in danger from Orthodox Christians, it is in danger from the Muslims."

The commander, whose unlikely nickname was "The Turtle," beamed at me. He knew his lines. They amounted to the rote of Serb aggression: Serbs sacrificing themselves selflessly on the eastern ramparts of Europe to save Paris and London from seeing Notre Dame and Westminster Abbey dwarfed by the minarets of a thousand mosques. He had about him the verve, the open-armed garrulousness, of many Serbs, and he offered me a signed pass that he said would enable me to move about Serb-held Bosnia with absolute ease. It was taken from me, at gunpoint, at the first Serb checkpoint.

Back at Trebević, with Sarajevo stretched out below, it was hard to see any "danger from the Muslims." The steep, scarred slope that Muris Zečević and his squad had fought their way up a month before, only to die on this hillside, amounted to a formidable emplacement for the Serb artillery. But at Lukavica barracks, the Serbs' military headquarters in the area, the message was the same: the Serbs were only acting in self-defense.

The Muslims, with weapons from Turkey, Saudi Arabia, and Austria, had been attacking in strength, and all the outgoing artillery fire we could hear was merely a "defense" against this threat. Colonel Ljuba Kosovac, the commander of the barracks, told me that "the aim of the Serbian side in the war is to liberate and protect the lands that belong to the Serbian people according to the property papers that we possess. That is all we want, nothing more."

And what of the Serb sweep through much of Bosnia and the rounding up of tens of thousands of Muslim civilians? "We have not done ethnic cleansing," Colonel Kosovac, a former officer in the JNA, said. "The other side began with ethnic cleansing of Serbs and imposed the war on us. In wars, people flee. So our regions became ethnically clear because of the wishes of the Muslim people."

CHAPTER 13

WHITE CITY

VESNA KARIŠIK, A FIRST COUSIN OF HARIS ZEČEVIĆ, FLED from Sarajevo to Belgrade. Early in the war she ran from a conflict that left no room for people like her, the children of Bosnia's mixed marriages.

A pale, slender young woman, she has the vivid green eyes and long, expressive hands that distinguish many Bosnians. I see in these traits a magnetic vitality somehow transmitted from Bosnia's mineral-rich land. She is a true Bosnian. Her mother, Fida, the sister of Haris's father, is a Muslim; her father, Slobodan Karišik, is a Serb. Hers is the middle ground war relentlessly erodes; hers the Bosnian distinctivness that the fanaticism of nation-as-tribe must destroy.

Bosnia has always been distinguished by its heterodoxy. In Bosnia, in the late Middle Ages, heretics gathered. These people opposed the asceticism of their beliefs and mores to the established authority of the churches of Rome and Byzantium. For their defiance, the sectaries, who, like the Bogomils, saw the material world as an expression of the Devil, were repeatedly persecuted.

But Bosnia is a sheltering land for the outlaw. Even some of the Albigensians of Provence, who saw the world in the same stark terms as the Bosnian heretics, sought refuge here. When the Turks came in the fifteenth century, a strange phenomenon occurred: the heretics found an accommodation with Islam. In effect, a new people was created: Slavic Muslims inhabiting Europe, speaking the language of their Christian neighbors, influenced but hardly dominated by Istanbul, asserting, in a new guise, the distinctiveness of Bosnia. A Bosnian difference that neighboring powers would repeatedly seek to obliterate, yet a difference obstinate enough to persist and to show itself—or so I came to believe—in the slender hand and transparent green eye of a girl like Vesna.

It was she, then aged fourteen, who took the call about Muris's death in

August 1992. A man from Sarajevo wanted Vesna's father. Vesna was afraid, thinking her mother, Fida, was dead. Muris Zečević is dead: that was the message. She could not say anything. She felt the strength in her legs going, the color draining from her face, and she fell. Her older sister, Jasna, aged sixteen, was watching and was terrified, in her turn, that her mother had been killed.

Death approached the girls before they were ready for it. They felt its bleak caress for the first time. Their grandfather, Safet Zečević, had died in 1983. They remembered their mother lying on the floor beside the phone and crying. But they could not understand, then, what was happening.

Just a few months before, Vesna had been skiing on Jahorina Mountain, near Sarajevo, and she had seen her cousin Muris, sitting in a café on the slopes, drinking a beer, laughing with friends, and she had waved to him—*waved to him.* This was the image she had of Muris now as she sat alone with her sister in Belgrade, far from her mother and all that Sarajevo life that was so unquestioningly theirs until the war began. When her father returned from the office to their dingy apartment that evening, they sat in silence, alone even in this grieving.

That evening, Vesna wondered what she would have said to her uncle, Asim Zečević, her aunt Bisera, or to her cousin Haris if she had still been in Sarajevo. She could not imagine what words she would have found. Indeed, it was hard to imagine her home at all, so completely and so quickly had war swept away the settled Sarajevo life her family had known.

WHEN, ON APRIL 12, 1992, six days after the war began, Vesna and Jasna left the Bosnian capital, they were Sarajevans and Bosnians. But from that day on, the backdrop to the lives of Haris's two cousins was Serbia, plunged in its isolation and illusions. They had expected to stay in Serbia for ten days. But days became months, months years, and naturally Serbia became a part of them. The two girls, aged fourteen and sixteen when they departed from Sarajevo, could not be impervious to Belgrade's view of the war.

That view was presented mainly on Radio-Televizija Beograd, the principal Serbian television station and most effective conduit for the vitriol of Serbian president Slobodan Milošević. Milošević's control of television was critical to his government—and to the stirring-up of war—because the evening news, called *Dnevnik 2,* was watched by about 60 percent of the population over ten years of age. As a result, for most Serbs, reality was what Belgrade Television served up to them.

In Bosnia, Serbs were "unarmed defenders of centuries-old hearths," "fighting for freedom" and the right to protect their "native soil" from the Muslims. These Muslims were variously referred to as "evildoers," "cut-throats," "Ustashas," "Islamic Ustashas," "Islamic chauvinists," "Islamic fundamentalists," "mujahedin," "jihad warriors," and "commando-terrorist groups." On Milošević's television no town was ever taken by the Serbs; it was liberated. If there was an atrocity, it was committed by the Muslims against themselves. An immense, impenetrable fog was assidu-ously cultivated. There were no maps. There were no diagrams to show which army had taken what towns. There was no attempt to illustrate the strategic aims of a war never declared or explained. Live footage was rare, scenes of destruction perpetrated by Serb forces nonexistent. The sole focus of the coverage was on Serb victims.

On one occasion, when the girls walked up to Knez Mihailova, Bel-grade's central pedestrian avenue, they found it full of patriotic songs, the insignia and memorabilia of the Chetniks, and banners denouncing "the rape of Serbia" or demanding "media justice." Milošević's revolution was in full swing. People roused themselves to rages over the "anti-Serbian plots" of Germany, the Vatican, and the United States. They dwelled in lurid detail on the atrocities of "Alija's fundamentalists"—a reference to Bosnia's Muslim president, Alija Izetbegović. After an international trade embargo was imposed on Serbia on May 30, 1992, in response to its in-volvement in the fighting in Bosnia, anger mounted further. The convic-tion that a worldwide anti-Serb conspiracy existed grew.

Yet their cousin, Muris, was dead, killed by a Serb round. Their city, with their mother inside it, was under Serb siege and shelling.

It was difficult to talk to anyone at school about what had happened to them. The general view of the war, insofar as it interested other pupils, was the one presented on Belgrade Television. Families had their own prob-lems: how to survive as the embargo took hold and how to raise their chil-dren. Sarajevo was far away. But the thoughts of Vesna and Jasna about the war were insistent and complex, full of contradictory feelings growing out of their position on the eroded middle ground of a Bosnian mixed mar-riage. In a fundamental sense it was impossible to blame anyone because to do so was to blame either their father or their mother.

When their father arrived in Serbia, two weeks after them, he left the girls with a family in Sremska Mitrovica, about fifty miles west of Bel-grade, while he looked for a job. But when he found one at the Serbian state telecommunications company in Belgrade, there were no places left in the schools, so the girls were sent to stay with distant cousins in Vršac, near the Romanian border, for the 1992–1993 school year. Their Muslim mother, Fida, remained in Sarajevo.

It was a difficult time. At school they heard that Muslims have bad teeth. Friends would go off to their families for Christmas, New Year's, Easter, and birthdays; Vesna and Jasna watched.

Their father's position seemed to harden. Fida was unrealistic, he suggested, driven by her emotions, which blinded her to the reality of the war. The world's "demonization" of Serbs, made manifest by the embargo, incensed him. If there was any truth to the charges leveled against the Serbs, it was only because the Muslims had done the same or worse to them. What about the hundreds of thousands of Serb refugees from Croatia and Bosnia in Serbia? He concluded that the world's problems were in some way linked to Islam. America, its military-industrial complex now deprived of any obvious enemy, seemed to him to have some interest in stirring up these problems. A small war, a weakened Europe—that suited America. As for the talk of a multi-ethnic society in Bosnia, it made him laugh. He, a Serb, was supposed to feel himself represented in Izetbegović, a man whose core was Islam! When he left Sarajevo he had thought that he might one day return. But within months he felt that the game was up. There was no choice now: Serbs, Muslims, and Croats had to be separated once and for all and the borders of Bosnia redrawn.

THE GIRLS' MOTHER, Fida, had been convinced that the fighting would be over within a matter of days: Bosnia could not be prized apart, its population could not be unscrambled, so they would have to negotiate. In fact she would not see her children for more than two years.

Fida Karišik is a handsome woman with a strong, upright bearing and bold, sensuous features dominated by luminous eyes. She shares with her brother Asim the tendency to suppress powerful feelings to the point where they sometimes well up uncontrollably, filling her eyes with tears, causing her lips to tremble. Her face is deeply marked, not merely, it seems, by war.

In 1974, she fell in love with a Serb, a man raised in poverty in the countryside of eastern Bosnia, single-mindedly devoted to the study of electronics. Slobodan Karišik had little in common with Fida, whose comfortable Sarajevo home was dominated by the Muslim faith of her father, Safet. But Slobodan was brilliant and he attracted her. When he asked Fida to marry him, she did not hesitate.

Her father was outraged. Safet Zečević had based his life around observance of the Koran and he had raised his children to scorn the atheism of Tito's communist regime. For his daughter to marry outside the Muslim faith was unconscionable. Marry Slobodan, he said, and we will never talk again.

It was a question of religious principle rather than of personality—he never spoke ill of Slobodan. Moreover, although he had a strong sense of the violence that could erupt between the ethnic groups in Bosnia, his objections were not political. He never expressed hatred for the Serbs. But such a mixed marriage amounted to a transgression of the Koran's laws. Fida's generation, the first to be raised under Tito, naturally viewed things differently. By the time she was contemplating marrying Slobodan, about 30 percent of marriages in Bosnia were mixed. She saw no reason to change her mind.

For the nine years between her marriage in 1974 and Safet Zečević's death in 1983, Fida and her father never spoke. When the girls, Jasna and Vesna, were born, she brought them to her parents' house, and Safet treated them with kindness. But his disappointment in his daughter, and his conviction that she had erred, remained. There was no reconciliation.

Slobodan and Fida did not talk about this family rift. As a couple, they tended to avoid painful subjects. He had a way of making her feel that her emotions were foolish and should be kept under control. She was always struck by her husband's closed nature. He liked to say that there was nothing that satisfied him like inventing a machine that worked. His brilliance in his field was exclusive. When she or Jasna would read a work of literature, by Tolstoy or Dostoyevsky, he would ask why they did not prefer to read a technical manual.

There was, it seemed, a darkness in him, a loneliness formed in his childhood, that was indelible. He came from the Drina borderlands, the eastern town of Rogatica, where life was hard and knives drawn easily. He had put together his first homemade radio when he was fourteen and left home shortly after that. In Sarajevo, and then Belgrade, where he studied, he had made his way on his own, struggling to make ends meet. Once, visiting Switzerland, they had seen a group of young children playing and laughing by the lake in Geneva. Slobodan said, "These children do not realize that the reason they are so happy is that they had the luck to be born in this country." To be born in Rogatica in 1941, to see blood spilled on the Drina's water and know the penury of the postwar years, was not to share that luck.

Slobodan's talent was exceptional. He rose quickly in the Bosnian telephone service, designing the main Sarajevo switching exchange; he taught electrical engineering at Sarajevo University; he took a series of temporary assignments with the United Nations, designing and installing telecommunications facilities in developing countries, including Burundi and Sri Lanka. One such assignment took him to Sudan throughout 1991. He only returned to Sarajevo and his family four months before the war broke out.

The tensions in the city had grown sharply since his departure for Khartoum. Military trucks could now be seen almost every day on the mountain roads around the city. *Slobodna Bosna,* a weekly newspaper started in the autumn of 1991, had just published an article of uncanny prescience.

The issue of November 21, 1991, carried a banner headline: "Sarajevo in the Chetniks' Sights—Secret Plan to Attack Sarajevo." Apparently leaked by an officer in the JNA, the article described how Karadžić's Srpska Demokratska Stranka (Serb Democratic party) was planning to employ paramilitary forces armed and trained by the JNA to blockade Sarajevo. But Slobodan escaped from the indications of war, as he once escaped his poverty, by concentrating on his work.

Fida came to understand, as the war approached, that it was possible for people whose friendships went back many years to find an abyss of suspicion opening between them. Even her closest friend, Ranka Brkić, a Serb who had been born on the same Sarajevo street as her, whose husband, Mićo, had been the best man at their wedding, even Ranka was becoming a stranger. When they talked of a Bosnian state and Bosnian independence, Ranka would laugh. "That, Fida, will never happen."

Ranka and Mićo went to Belgrade soon after the war began. *They knew it was coming, they kept it secret even as they went on living and working with us:* it was this thought that Fida found most devastating.

OF SUCH ESTRANGEMENTS was the decomposition of Bosnia made. Containment, for the outside world, meant preventing the war from spreading or intensifying. Seen from within, however, the policy of containment was about the spread and intensification, over a period of years, of the divisions that destroyed Bosnian society.

Everybody had prewar photographs. In black and white. In color. Full of smiles. The company photograph. The football-club photograph. The school photograph. The family photograph. The friends who met every Sunday to go fishing, or hunting, or skiing. The house on the Dalmatian coast. The birthday. The wedding. No matter how intimate the photo there was always somebody who was now dead, or disappeared, or departed over to the other side. The war was a giant threshing machine that tore those photographs to pieces.

Early on, however, people knew more or less where the pieces had fallen. They still thought in the same way; their frame of reference, however shaken, was still those photographs. But for Haris and Bisera and Fida and Asim in Sarajevo—and Slobodan, Jasna, and Vesna in Belgrade—it became harder and harder to recall the world that had once placed them in the same photographic frame. With time it became impossible. Containment and international inaction were a death sentence for Bosnia.

Throughout Bosnia, during the early part of the war, there were piles of photographs and photograph albums in the garbage. This was natural. When you move into somebody else's abandoned home the photographs and the family albums are among the things first tossed out the window.

• • •

AND WHAT OF FIDA'S MARRIAGE, the most intimate of bonds? When Fida was at a loss to know what Slobodan was thinking, she had formed the habit of telling herself that scientists are a little strange. She did not like to press him. Was Slobodan a Serb or a Bosnian first? Was he a Sarajevan first, a cosmopolitan man, or a man of the harsh rural area where he had lived his childhood? He had been out of Bosnia; he was, in some sense, a man of the world; she was sure that he had not given his support to Karadžić; but beyond that she could not say. They had long ago formed the habit of avoiding difficult subjects, and so it was in their approach to a war that did not admit of a Serb-Muslim relationship such as theirs.

Slobodan Karišik is a tall man with a slightly stooping gait and eyes half-hidden behind thick spectacles. The eyes are evasive but kind. I ask him why he never talked about the war with his wife. He says he never believed it was coming. He was raised in the postwar years, in the first proud embrace of Tito's revolution, when any talk of the nationalities in Bosnia was taboo. He was taught at school to prepare for war as if it could break out tomorrow but to act in the conviction that there would be no war for the next one hundred years. He smiles at me, a bland smile, as if to say: what would you have done, as a Serb in Sarajevo, suspected by a growing number of Muslims, shelled by other Serbs? He has made his choices. He has cared for his daughters in Belgrade. He has inflicted great pain on his wife. His move to the Serbian capital has enraged his nephew, Haris. He has come to see the war as a kind of inevitable disaster, manipulated from afar, bereft of right or wrong, as ineluctable as the laws of science. It seems to me that he has made some cold compromises, accepted small betrayals, set aside his critical faculties. But perhaps he has merely sought to survive, physically and emotionally. Perhaps, indeed, that is what each person does, consistent with his or her moral stature, in the course of a war.

Slobodan was not a soldier. He did not have the eyesight or the inclination for things military. He saw no reason to imagine anything other than a century of peace. He had been on assignment in Lagos in 1980 when Tito died and was astonished when a British engineer asked him if Yugoslavia would hold together. "Of course it will," he said, and never gave the question another thought.

But now, a decade later, as his country fragmented, he tended to see dark forces at work. It was a conspiracy, this turmoil, engineered by outside powers, principally America, that no longer set great store by the Yugoslav state.

The day the shelling began, Slobodan listened to the radio and watched television. The radio said shells were falling on Sarajevo—not who was firing them. Like rain, they were simply falling. The news made no sense because it made no attempt to describe what was happening. To do so, for the official Bosnian media, would involve identifying an enemy—the former Yugoslav army—that was still supposed to be protecting all the people of Bosnia. Slobodan, too, felt unable to confront the war.

Fida and Vesna were out when the shelling began. They found that the family car had been stolen in the chaos and went to a police station to file a report. There were young men running in and out collecting weapons. They were ordered to go home but, with shooting on all sides, they could not pass the Holiday Inn. Fida threw her daughter on the sidewalk and lay on top of her to protect her. When they reached home, Vesna was struck by her father's ashen appearance. "From now on," he said, "nobody leaves this house except me."

As a child Vesna had watched the war games the boys in her neighborhood used to play. One group would act out the role of the Partisan heroes, the other the Nazi villains. They would race between the apartment blocks firing at one another. It was an honor to be Tito. At school, where a photograph of Tito hung in every classroom, they were asked, *"Koga voliš najviše?"* ("Who do you love best of all?"). Unthinkingly, she would say, *"Tita"* ("Tito"). She was once selected to take part in the annual *Štafeta Mladosti,* or Youth Relays, when youths carried a baton through the whole country, over a period of one month, finally entering Belgrade on May 25, Tito's birthday. While Tito was alive the relays ended with the baton being handed to him in the Red Star Stadium. Even after his death, the official make-believe held that his presence endured, and it was glorious to carry that baton through the streets of Sarajevo with people cheering as she went. The baton symbolized the connectedness of all Yugoslavs. It was their bond to Tito, alive even in death. When, in 1986, the Communist Youth Organization of Slovenia declined to take part in the Štafeta, it broke that increasingly illusory bond.

Vesna's education went further. She was asked in class whom she hated the most and was taught to respond, "Hitler." So it seemed to her that the boys who acted the role of the Nazis in the street game of her youth must find that very difficult, even if it was just a game. And it *was* no more than that, for real war belonged to another time.

Now Vesna's parents explained that all this would soon be over. They did not say what "this" was, but they wanted Vesna and Jasna away from it. A few days, they would be in Belgrade, safe. A huge crowd was shoving and screaming at Sarajevo Airport, placid people pushed to panic. Her father knew somebody in the air force. They got in through a back entrance and onto the plane. The city fell away like the disjointed fragments of a dream, longed for but unattainable and finally invisible.

The shooting continued. Still Sarajevo television would not say who was shelling the city. For how could units of the JNA shell their own? One thing was clear to Fida: they could not leave the children alone indefinitely. She began to press her Serb husband to leave, to be with the children in Serbia. Then, if the war really continued, they could all move somewhere else, anywhere in the world. It would not be difficult to find another assignment with the United Nations.

Slobodan was hesitant. Finally, on April 30, 1992, he agreed to go. That night, he called from Novi Sad: he had reached Serbia but had been obliged to pay hard currency to get through the Serb lines. The Bosnian Serbs were rounding up all Serbs to fight.

Two days later, on May 2, 1992, the central Sarajevo post office was blown up, with the loss of thousands of phone lines. Bosnian authorities suspected somebody with inside knowledge. Police came to the Karišik apartment and interrogated Fida about her Serb husband. She defended him, convinced that Slobodan would never destroy something he had created. Haris Zečević, however, suspected that his uncle had sabotaged the exchange. When, three months later, Muris died on Trebević Mountain, Haris's anger at Slobodan Karišik began to harden into hatred.

THE IDENTITY OF any Bosnian today is not much more than an accident of history: a Serb may be a Bosnian Catholic who converted to Orthodoxy; a Muslim may once have been a follower of the Eastern rites; a Catholic may have been a heretic who adopted his faith under the suasion of Franciscan missionaries who arrived in Bosnia in the thirteenth and fourteenth centuries. In this land nothing is immaculate.

On all sides of the battle lines, I found similar scenes. The lambs were skewered in the same way, with a stake driven down through the whole length of the carcass, and then turned slowly over embers; they were eaten in similar settings, at makeshift tables perched above valleys where the sound of wood being chopped could be heard and fruit trees blossomed in abundance. There was the same hard-drinking culture on every side; the same kismet, or fatalistic impassivity, of people used to distant or autocratic rulers; the same simple pleasure in nature; the same ubiquitous *vulkanizers,* tire shops that, like the cafés beside them, amounted to the summit of private enterprise in Bosnian village life; the same sudden, unpredictable flaring to anger of a people that counts its sheep by the number of necks and never speaks of killing without an accompanying throat-slitting gesture. Bosnia was whole enough, a place where life was always pretty cheap, a land of melancholy stoicism, of sullen passion, of patient longing, of sheep-breeding men who, whatever their religion, were quick with the knife.

There was the same note of yearning in the music, the same mingling in all things of the gentle and the harsh, a feature of the Bosnian landscape that has passed to its people. There was the same preference for reflection over the illusions of action, the same pronounced taste for meditation and observation.

There were the same outlandish contrasts of the modern and the medieval—a man walking his goat past a massive thermoelectric power plant, women pickling vats of cabbage in houses with satellite dishes, horse-drawn carts loaded with timber beside outsized soccer stadiums with towering floodlights—images, these, of a society long arrested in its development, far from its Ottoman, its royal, or its communist rulers.

Arthur J. Evans, the British writer who traveled through Bosnia and Herzegovina in 1875, arrived at another moment of conflict in the country. The Christian peasantry—or *rayah*—had risen against their Turkish overlords. Early in his journey, he came upon a crowd of several thousand Christians, mainly Catholics, who had gathered by a shrine midway between Doboj and Travnik in north-central Bosnia.

"What was most striking," he writes, "was the thoroughly Mahometan appearance of so many of these Christian devotees. The influence of Islam seemed to have infected even their ritual; for many grovelled on the ground and kissed the earth, as in a mosque. There was one man whom I should have mistaken for a Hadji or Turkish pilgrim; there were others with the shaven crown of a true-believing Moslem, and the single pig-tail, so thoughtfully preserved by the Faithful to aid the Angel Gabriel in dragging them into Paradise. There were women with faces so nearly eclipsed that they seemed in fear of the injunctions of the Koran; and even the monks who had come up from the monastery of Comusina might be mistaken at a little distance for Turkish officials. There was something pathetic in the sight of so many Christians, dressed indeed in the garb of Mahometans, but still clinging to the faith of their fathers."

As Evans's observations demonstrate, even religious differences were long blurred by the syncretic impact of the lengthy Turkish presence. More than two centuries earlier, another British traveler, Henry Blount, had noted how the Turks converted Bosnian churches into mosques, "much suppressing the public exercise of religion, especially of the Romish, so that many who profess themselves Christian scarcely know what it means."

There was a French United Nations officer in Bosnia during the war that began in 1992. He came from the Basque country in southwestern France. He traveled back and forth across the lines and was fascinated by Karadžić's insistence that "Turkish" or "Islamic" culture threatened to engulf not only his people, the Serbs, but all of Europe. What he found so intriguing was that, in fact, there was no discernible difference in the way of life of the people on the Bosnian government side and those on the Serb side: they had both been touched equally by "Turkish culture." One day the officer tried to explain this to Karadžić, and to suggest that the only advancing culture in the world, the only one he should worry about, was the American one that led his young French children to forsake Basque culture in favor of collecting photographs of Sylvester Stallone. But he was met by a blank stare of incomprehension.

Evans, in 1875, had understood the essential unity of the country: "We have in Bosnia a common language and a common national character born of the blood; and that national character, whatever may be said to the contrary, is not prone to revolution . . . it is slow, it is stubborn." He declared himself convinced that "fanatic as are the Christians as well as the Mahometans," there existed "elements of union in this unhappy country which can be moulded together by wise hands."

Karadžić did not understand this Bosnia, any more than he could perceive that his rantings about rampant "Islamic culture" were, in essence, nonsense. He was living in another time, one that left him blind to the fact that his imagined position on Europe's cultural barricades was a fiction. But his sweeping violence inevitably pushed people away from their shared Bosnian culture toward new divisions. That, indeed, was the essence of his campaign.

WHEN VESNA AND JASNA came to Belgrade from Vršac to visit their father the girls were struck by how distant the war seemed. They wanted to remember it, to feel it, to rage over it, but it seeped from them like water into sand. A growing passivity, as dense as Danubian mist, seemed to permeate Belgrade. Economic collapse, international isolation, the relentless propaganda of Milošević, a secretive political system, an influx of refugees, and the fog of wars on its doorstep all played a part in Serbia's progressive disorientation. Wars prepared by illusionism—specifically the myth of a new genocide against the Serbs—were in turn sustained by illusionism. Belgrade was eerie.

For this was the war that Beograd—the white city—avoided. Few conflicts in the Balkan vicinity had previously passed it by. Much ransacked, much rebuilt, the Turks called Belgrade "Darol-i-Jihad"—the home of Holy Wars. But as the state of which it had been the capital died, no corpses floated on the lazy confluence of the Sava and Danube rivers beneath the Ottoman fortress of Kalemegdan. No buildings lost their roofs. No street was stained with blood. No smashing shell on Terazije or volley of fire on the leafy Bulevar Revolucije undid the spell of Milošević the illusionist.

The city at the still eye of the storm was marked, after the initial fever of Milošević's nationalist revolution, by a somnolent moroseness. Over-crowded buses heaved and belched their blighted smoke. On once elegant buildings—the work of the late, lamented Serbian bourgeoisie—bruised caryatids supported mounds of crumbling stone. From basement windows, widows in black stared with hawklike eyes. Over the cobblestones of Skadarlija, where the once bustling cafés were empty, cats scurried and young women stepped awkwardly in high heels. Thigh-length black boots, short red dresses, and crucifixes buried in plunging cleavages betrayed a kind of desperate vampishness. Retired professionals, on pensions of forty dollars a month, lined up at markets to sell off family heirlooms. When they could find them, they lugged home sacks of flour and sugar and stored them behind the living-room sofa. Graffiti spread: SEX AND VIO-LENCE, NIRVANA, UNITED PUNKS, GRAVEDIGGERS, SOUTHERN FORCE, YOU NEVER WALK ALONE, even the hated swastika. Gypsy bands with raw faces and wind instruments stood on street corners. The city was full of a quiet desperation and a dull, gray violence as explosive as repressed sexuality.

Passive lines of pensioners, winding around a city block, waited to hand their German marks to banks offering 15 percent monthly interest rates on hard-currency deposits; then waited once more, in even longer lines, after these pyramid schemes that financed the early campaigns of Milošević's wars collapsed, to try to recover capital they would never see again. On the Danube and the Sava, empty barges bobbed and rotted on the murky water.

The outlandish gifts to Tito from visiting dignitaries, aligned and non-aligned, had been shunted off from their museum to a warehouse or a basement—nobody seemed to know. Only Colonel Muammar Gadhafi's camels were still on display at the zoo. Officials sat at the end of cavernous corridors staring into smoke-filled space. They still called themselves Yu-goslavs, representatives of the truncated federation of Serbia and Mon-tenegro, but just down the road, as every inhabitant of Belgrade knew but could not see, Yugoslavia, the only one worth its name, had gone up in smoke.

The middle classes virtually disappeared. Milovan Djilas called the ap-paratchiks who made it after World War II the "New Class." The war brought a new "New Class" of smugglers and traders operating with the acquiescence of Milošević and growing fabulously rich. Stalin liked to quote a Russian proverb, "Out of filth you can make a prince." The Bos-nian war produced many filthy princes, murderers in maroon suits eating big slabs of meat with their cellular phones propped on the table.

Their mores were most eloquently symbolized by the towering mansion with tiny windows like reflector glasses Arkan had built near his thriving bakery and the Red Star soccer stadium. Other mansions nearby affected green roof tiles, turretlike chimneys, and immense wrought-iron gates. Gleaming Ferraris and Mitsubishis, as unlikely as spaceships in the general grime, glided past rows of now penniless professionals or redundant workers hawking plastic containers of reddish gasoline by the roadside.

Cocooned, shadowy, Belgrade seemed peopled by ghosts. Immobile cranes hovered over abandoned building sites and the shells of buildings. Grand boulevards were abruptly out of scale in a diminished city. Some elementary schools warned that they would close in a few years because nobody was having children. The vast federal edifices and conference centers of Novi Beograd (New Belgrade), built after World War II on the swamps north of the Sava River, were transformed into bloated monuments to the death of a state and the irrelevance of the Non-aligned Movement in a world without alignments.

This wounded city became the point of reference for the Muslim-Serb girls from Sarajevo. Their secret was inside them, incommunicable. They looked for some tangible sign of the fighting that had taken their cousin Muris. At the bottom of the elegant Topčider Hill, home now to the war's profiteers as well as to diplomats, there was a hospital called Rudo specializing in prosthetics. A lot of men hung around there, propped against the wall, smoking. A blond woman, quite beautiful, on crutches, stared through the fence in fierce desperation. She was missing a leg. *They were all missing legs.* Oh yes, *the war,* out there, somewhere, beyond the Drina.

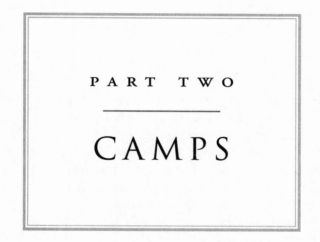

PART TWO

CAMPS

CHAPTER 14

DISAPPEARANCES

THE SERB BOMBARDMENT OF SARAJEVO LOOKED LIKE MIND-less barbarity in that, over more than three years, it took thousands of in-nocent lives and was a colossal public-relations disaster. In the early months of the conflict, however, it served one important purpose. It dis-tracted international attention from the real business of the war.

That business was brutal, venal, and rural. It involved the eviction or slaughter of Muslims living in the provincial towns and villages of much of Bosnia during the spring, summer, and fall of 1992. The process had a ramshackle air. Serbian fascism was never slick or monolithic. Its uniforms never matched; its executions were on the advanced artisanal rather than the industrial scale. A ghoulish savagery rather than cold-blooded effi-ciency drove the boozy killing. Ears and sexual organs were sliced off; some people were beaten to death, a relatively time-consuming business. Bull-dozers or ploughs rather than made-to-measure incinerators disposed of the victims. Ruthlessness was tempered by slovenliness. If the organizers of the Serb terror in Bosnia had been running the Nazi death camps they would have sold off the Zyklon B gas as soon as they were able to dispose of it for a profit.

Still, the solution was final enough. In a great arc from Sanski Most in northwestern Bosnia to Trebinje in the southeast the Serb terror unfurled. War, traditionally, is a term describing a conflict between armies. In this sense, the Bosnian war did not really start until after its defining horror was over.

Muslim civilians were taken from their homes, herded into concentra-tion camps, and selectively killed. Surviving males, generally those with-out political influence or professional qualifications, were made to dig trenches until they dropped; they were bundled from camp to bestial camp, and, if they were lucky, or could somehow find a thousand German marks to buy their freedom, they were eventually pushed over the lines. Women, often raped, and children were also gathered in the camps. They huddled in silence on the floors of disused mining complexes, military depots, factories, stadiums, gymnasiums, schools before being prodded like recalcitrant cattle over the hills into territory controlled by the Bosnian government.

In a sharp burst of Serbian violence more than three quarters of a million Muslims were ousted from a swath of territory covering 70 percent of the country. Once the fabric of a society has been cut so comprehensively, it is virtually impossible to piece it together again. Once a crime is unpunished its effects fester. Fear takes root; divisions harden. Herein lay the essence, and the accuracy, of the Serbian calculation.

The United Nations Convention defines genocide as certain "acts committed with intent to destroy in whole or in part a national, ethnical, racial or religious group, as such." This is a sober description of the Serbian rampage against the Muslims in the first six months of the Bosnian conflict. To avoid use of the term, or argue against its aptness, is to allow the Nazis a posthumous victory: the establishment of a proprietary right to "genocide" just because the scale of the Holocaust is unmatched.

It is also to grant the Serbs a victory. Throughout the wars of Yugoslavia's destruction, *genocide* was perhaps the most overused word in the Serbian vocabulary. The refrain of arguments emanating from Belgrade was that of the repetitive "genocide" suffered by the Serbian people—in Croatia, in Kosovo, in Bosnia, in Serbia itself. Deployed in this way, "genocide" was no longer a horror but a form of immunity. It was a *passe-partout* allowing the eternal Serbian victim to butcher with impunity.

Milošević loved the word. At the opening of the peace conference in The Hague on September 7, 1991, he accused Croatia of "a policy of genocide." His speech to representatives of the European Union in Geneva on December 9, 1993, went even further and typified a well-honed Serbian genre. Attacking international trade sanctions on Serbia, he declared, "I do not know how you will explain to your children, on the day when they discover the truth, why you killed our children, why you led a war against three million of our children, and with what right you turned twelve million inhabitants of Europe into a test site for the application of what is, I hope, the last genocide of this century."

As Pascal Bruckner, the French sociologist, has pointed out, we are confronted by two dangers: the enshrinement of Auschwitz in a place of memory so sacred that we are inured to the perhaps lesser, but nonetheless real, horrors of the late twentieth century, and, conversely, the reductio ad ab-

1991–1995: The Height of Serb Conquest

surdum of *genocide* through overuse of the term to the point where "henceforth any people that has massacred or annihilated another can claim to have suffered genocide."

The Bosnian genocide took place before our eyes. Many of the Serb camps were less than two hundred miles from the Austrian and Italian borders. Refugees were pouring westward with stories to tell. Reports from the International Committee of the Red Cross, survivors, and informers were reaching the State Department: they were not comprehensive but they painted a picture. It was summer, the skies were clear, good weather for photography. Yet, for three months, we claimed we saw nothing.

Stalin chose Kolyma as the setting for one of the most savage experiments in his gulag in part because it was a very long way from anywhere. Auschwitz was a fair distance from Berlin. What happened in Bosnia therefore suggests a remarkable phenomenon: that as our capacity to see has increased to the point where any spot on the globe can be instantaneously photographed, any image instantaneously transmitted, so the necessity to conceal horror has diminished. I once pressed an American intelligence officer in Washington about this paradox. His reply was instructive. "Yes," he conceded, "in July 1992, we had pictures of Bosnia. But what is a crowd and what is a group of people about to be executed?"

Here we stand at the heart of things. *What is a crowd and what is a group of people about to be executed?* It depends, of course, on the viewer's willingness to see, capacity to discern, readiness to understand. Our age has made it easier to look without seeing. It is the age of the indifferent spectator. Useless knowledge accumulates. The Bosnian war was much looked at, little seen. It was one image amid a flood of others.

I would come away from the war with the fetid smell of misery still in my nostrils, the last knots of fear still unraveling in my gut, the last images of desolation still clutching at my mind, and find myself quite quickly in some place like Frankfurt airport looking at vending machines selling Billy Boy condoms in packages emblazoned with German blondes, and Paloma Picasso ads about how accessories are essential, and American girls with outsized backpacks complaining about their need for a shower, and brightly illuminated windows full of sophisticated alarm clocks and photographic equipment and salamis and every designer label under the sun, and I would wonder if this onslaught did not amount to the end of experience. It was not easy, in such a place, to be sentient—to remember, feel, be angry, think straight. I thought more and more about the war. I did not want it to slip from me. I did not want to be gathered back into the numbness of comfort. The more I thought about it, the more it seemed to me that, yes, Bosnia had been worth fighting for and the fascism that destroyed it worth confronting and defeating, but although the place was just a few hundred miles away, it seemed scarcely to impinge on a world in which appearance had eaten away at substance to the point where the two had become virtually indistinguishable. The most powerful images have weight; they resist the instantaneousness, and insubstantiality, of zapping. But what confronted me everywhere in our global culture was an eerie weightlessness: an R.E.M. video clip, a pile of Tutsi bodies in Rwanda (or were they Hutu?), a Coca-Cola advertisement, and a woman gazing at her severed arm in Sarajevo were all part of the same undifferentiated stream. In this morass, awareness and awakening were unconnected. Life and death, right and wrong, had become disembodied issues, matters of indifference, no more than questions of management.

Managing Bosnia, for the Bush and then the Clinton administrations, meant staying out of it. That, in turn, meant a refusal to see, or acknowledge, the true gravity of the war. Its gravity—as opposed to its importance—lay precisely in the fact that the issues it raised were not primarily economic or strategic. They were moral.

The cold war victory was framed in moral terms, suggesting that it amounted to more than an opportunity to mall Central and Eastern Europe. It was about freedom overcoming walls, dignity oppression. It was, in a broad sense, about America. It was an American victory, fought for and won by Americans, for what America represents. After Bosnia, however, these truisms began to ring hollow. That summer of 1992, in the villages and small towns of Bosnia, a crowd and a group of people waiting to be executed were generally synonymous. But nobody wanted to see the photographs, listen to the fragments of testimony, piece together the manifold horror.

Ron Neitzke, an American diplomat still trying to recover from the way Bosnia shattered his life, said to me, "There were photographs. We had them in 1992. If you looked you could see a little outbuilding suddenly blimping into a circus full of people. You would have reports, perhaps fragmentary, about a concentration camp at site X, and it would have been possible to look at site X and see. Somebody simply had to collate the fragmentary evidence from refugees and intercepts with the photographs. But we were determined not to see it because all this could lead to pressure for intervention. *We are learning not to see.* If a human crisis looms that we do not want to face, we withdraw resources. During the cold war, for forty-five years, we obsessed about Yugoslavia. It was one of the top three potential tinderboxes for World War III. The resources focused on that country were enormous. It was not a technical screwup that we did not see the camps. This was willed. In the end, the Central Intelligence Agency is a political tool of the administration."

The people in the doomed crowds were Europeans, Slavic Muslims recently "liberated" from communist rule. However, they became part not of some longed-for sliver of the American dream, but of a sordid calculation. The calculation became clear in the early days of August 1992, after reports by Roy Gutman of *Newsday* about boxcars carrying Muslims to concentration camps in Bosnia finally pushed the Bush administration into saying something.

IT WAS AUGUST 3, 1992, the day that Muris Zečević was killed on Trebević Mountain. A State Department spokesman, Richard Boucher, confirmed that "abuses, torture, and killings" had taken place in Serbian "detention centers" throughout Bosnia. But a day later, Boucher was contradicted. Thomas M. T. Niles, then assistant secretary of state, said such reports could not be confirmed. Niles's claim to a House foreign affairs subcommittee that he could not confirm torture and killing in Serbian camps was tendentious; it served the overall political purpose—a coverup. For if genocide was indeed being committed against these Muslims, and was unambiguously acknowledged in Washington, how could America, a signatory of the Prevention of Genocide Treaty, just stand by?

Tom Lantos, a Democrat from California, put the issue succinctly. "Either Mr. Boucher is lying or you are lying," he told Niles, adding that "Munich and appeasement" kept echoing in his mind. To which Niles replied, "To say that somebody is lying or trying to cover this up, I have to take very strong exception to that because Richard did not say yesterday that we have information. He said we have reports."

This claim, too, was false. Boucher had said that the State Department had its "own reports—information similar to press reports" of "torture and killings in these Serbian camps." The "information," in other words, was from the State Department's own sources.

The man in charge at the State Department when Niles spoke was Lawrence S. Eagleburger, a former ambassador to Yugoslavia who took over as acting secretary of state on August 3, 1992, after Baker left on a vacation. Eagleburger, a man with a lifelong fascination with Yugoslavia, later said to me in a telephone conversation that "I don't recall trying to look the other way. But the fact is that there was nothing I could conceive of, in the realm of the possible, that would lead the president to put our troops there. The president's view and the chiefs' was that military intervention was the worst possible thing to do and would involve substantial losses on our part with little public support. I doubt that even full knowledge of the camps—which we did not have then—would have made any difference. The costs of correcting this moral disaster were greater than we were prepared to pay."

Of course the "moral disaster" was in fact something more specific: Serb

Portraits of Tito, Yugoslavia's longtime communist ruler, still
adorned many Sarajevo offices at the outset of the Bosnian
war in 1992. A bullet through this one sums up the fate of the
state that Tito miraculously held together from the end of
World War II until his death in 1980. (© *Milomir Kovacević*)

Alija Mehmedović and his wife, Gaby Kovač, stroll through the streets of Belgrade in 1938. They had been married just a year, but there were already tensions between them. Alija would soon leave for Sarajevo. *(family photograph)*

Having fled Tito's Yugoslavia, Alija Mehmedović changed his name to Ali Erhan on arrival in Turkey in 1948. Here is a portrait of him on an identity card issued in Bursa, Turkey, his adopted home after World War II. Erhan lived in fear that Tito's agents might kill him. *(family photograph)*

Gaby Kovač, Alija's first wife, with their infant son, Sead. After the war, Sead initially believed his father was dead, before beginning a long search to find him. *(family photograph)*

Sead Mehmedović as a pensive young art student in Belgrade. Like his father, he later went to work at the Belgrade daily newspaper, *Politika. (family photograph)*

Alija was born in the northwestern Bosnian town of Prijedor, the scene of the brutal killing of Muslims by the Serbs in 1992. This photograph was taken after his return to Bosnia shortly before World War II. *(family photograph)*

Shrapnel from a shell has just killed this young woman on a Sarajevo street. A passerby tries to rouse her, but her eyes are already unseeing. In the besieged Bosnian capital, death often came suddenly out of a clear blue sky. (© *Milomir Kovacević*)

Winter in Sarajevo. People scavenge for firewood. Electric or gas cookers gave way to wood-burning stoves during the forty-month war. The city, surrounded by Serb forces, was often without gas and electricity. (© *Milomir Kovacević*)

The Bosnian army was hurriedly formed amid chaos after the Serb onslaught on Sarajevo and wide areas of Bosnia began in April 1992. Young and old were bundled into the ranks of the makeshift force from which a professional army would only gradually evolve. (© *Luc Delahaye, Magnum*)

Before the myriad dead and the devastation of Yugoslavia's dissolution, the peacekeepers of the United Nations often found themselves looking on helplessly. The Yugoslav wars were the graveyard of any "new world order." *(© Luc Delahaye, Magnum)*

genocide against the Muslim community of Bosnia. But public precision—verbal or analytical—over Bosnia was never truly deemed to be in America's interest. The pattern of American obfuscation of the war, in which the single consistent aim was to keep U.S. troops out of the area, was established during those first days of August 1992. The only unequivocal voice at this time came from Bill Clinton, then a Democratic candidate for president. "I am outraged by the revelations of concentration camps in Bosnia and urge immediate action to stop this slaughter," he said on August 4, 1992. "If the horror of the Holocaust taught us anything, it is the high cost of remaining silent and paralyzed in the face of genocide." On August 5, Clinton followed this statement up by saying, "We cannot afford to ignore what appears to be a deliberate and systematic extermination of human beings based on their ethnic origin. I would begin with air power, against the Serbs, to try to restore the basic conditions of humanity."

These were stirring words from the then governor of Arkansas, but, to the enduring cost to Bosnia, they were to prove hollow.

UNLIKE THE ZEČEVIĆ and Karišik families of Sarajevo, the Šestovićs were from one of the myriad small towns that dot the Bosnian countryside. It was in such places that the highest price was paid for America's decision to look the other way and for Europe's incapacity to do anything without American leadership.

Vlasenica sits astride the main Belgrade-to-Sarajevo road. It is a timber town, like many in Bosnia, and it never made any claims to sophistication. There are coffee bars and hairdressing salons and *vulkanizers* and small stores all selling the same wan state-produced staple goods. Before the war the local economy was bolstered by the steady trundle of trucks bearing goods from the Bosnian to the Serbian capital, the bauxite mine at Milići, and the important Yugoslav army base at the nearby town of Han Pijesak.

But Vlasenica, about twenty-five miles west of Srebrenica, was always a hard place, a mountain town, fiercely cold in winter, where eyes are often bleary from alcohol and faces unshaved. The town changed hands several times during World War II as Chetniks, Partisans, and Muslim sympathizers with the Ustasha engaged in a cycle of massacres and revenge killings. It was known then as "the windiest place." Perched, like many Bosnian settlements, in a narrow valley, it is still a town where the light shifts suddenly and the nearby forests can appear idyllic or darkly menacing by turns. It is also a town of such modest dimensions that a walk on the main street is almost certain to yield an encounter. In Bosnia, chance meetings are the ineluctable occasion for a coffee, and around this gentle custom the rhythms of provincial life unfolded. Until the killing began.

. . .

ERMIN ŠESTOVIĆ, a Muslim from Vlasenica, is trying to remember the events of that summer of 1992. He is seated in the John P. Fisk fish restaurant in Malmo, Sweden, a bustling establishment run with brisk Scandinavian efficiency. Its clientele is affluent, its herring plump and succulent, its waiters good-humored. So when Šestović begins to sob uncontrollably, his anguish is doubly shocking.

Šestović, a refugee in Sweden, is recalling his father, Ruzdija Šestović, who has disappeared. He was rounded up on June 20, 1992, in his apartment in Vlasenica, by Serb forces. This disappearance has spawned a grief more intractable than bereavement because it is tinged with a tenuous hope.

"I hope my father is alive," Šestović says. "Some days it seems good that I don't know anything. But then I realize I have to know. Because there is a block inside me. I cannot concentrate. When I am happy, I feel I do not have the right to be. I want to know."

Šestović, a young man with soft eyes over which a shadow had fallen, buries his head in his hands. Waiters pass. Cutlery tinkles. Herring is dissected. Businessmen discuss Swedish exports. The gulf separating the Bosnian war from the rest of Europe—and at the same time their inextricable proximity—are fleetingly palpable. Chekhov noted that "your elbow is near but you cannot bite it." I want Šestović to bite these nearby diners, shake them from their pampered insouciance, holler his agony, *bring a European war home,* but quickly enough the moment passes.

History scarcely records the sumptuous meals enjoyed, the fine paintings bought and sold, the outings to the races and the opera that also occur during wars. Evelyn Waugh wrote that even as "the Halberdiers and their guests sat bemused by wine and harmony" during World War II, the trains of central Europe were "rolling east and west with their innocent loads." These gulfs, these walls of silence, are the very stuff of war.

A few days later I meet Šestović's mother, Muska, a refugee in Germany. She is living—or more accurately camping—in a hostel on the eastern outskirts of Berlin. She is surrounded by other refugees. Cigarette smoke, Turkish coffee, and early morning liquor reproduce the darkness and intimacy of Bosnia in the cold former communist suburbs of the city. Muska cries a lot. Her one solace is that she has been dreaming often of her missing husband. A sign, she believes, that he is alive.

Muska says she was held in a concentration camp called Sušica in Vlasenica during the summer of 1992. But the Red Cross has no record of such a camp. She has nothing to prove her incarceration. She therefore receives no special benefits or aid from the German state.

So, the facts: a man, Ruzdija Šestović, fifty years old in 1992, who has "disappeared"; a concentration camp that has "disappeared"; an intimate Bosnian town, where everyone knew everyone, but nobody knows what happened to the Muslims. Unlike his family, I am convinced that Ruzdija Šestović is dead. But I believe he can still tell a story. One I want to drag back from oblivion.

I FIRST PASSED through Vlasenica in the late summer of 1992 aboard the Pale bus. I came back, eighteen months later, in February 1994, to find out what had happened to the 18,699 Muslims who, according to the 1991 census, had lived there, alongside 14,356 Serbs, 40 Croats, and 336 "Yugoslavs." That the Muslims were gone there was no doubt, but of the manner of their disappearance there was no certainty: they left not a trace.

Less than a mile from the southern edge of town, just visible through the dense pine trees, stood a military depot surrounded by barbed wire. The road to it was barred and guarded; a sign at the entrance to Vlasenica said, "Any loitering by foreigners is forbidden." I made my way to the town hall to try to find out why.

A crowd was milling around, looking to obtain favors. A Palermo scene without the Sicilian sun, darker and more hard-edged. When I asked to see the mayor I was met by a look from a thin bearded man that embedded itself in my gut like an arrow. There was terror in that look and its other face, murder. I was about to turn and leave when a man I had not seen presented himself as Mihajlo Bajagić, the president of the town council, and invited me to come upstairs.

His office was spacious, dominated by a large desk, overseen by the bushy-browed gaze of Radovan Karadžić in a framed photograph. The conversation meandered. There were housing problems, Bajagić said, because of the Serb refugees who had fled from the Muslim-held towns of Zenica and Goražde and Srebrenica. He was doing the best he could for them. But the war was taking a toll. This war, he added sorrowfully, that the Serbs had never wanted, that they had been driven into, that they only wished to end. Did I know, the town president asked, that in the 1990–1992 period, not a single proposal from the Serbs of Vlasenica was approved in the Muslim-dominated town council?

I had not, I confessed, been aware of that. And, by the way, what had happened to those Muslims? Bajagić looked wistful. "We lived together," he said, "but was it superficial. Was it a mirage?"

A mirage? Bajagić began to develop his thoughts. At the beginning of the war, he said, everyone ran away. Later, however, the Serbs returned. But, after all that had happened, it was hard to imagine living together with the Muslims again.

But what, I pressed him, had happened? "The Muslim families of

Vlasenica ran away of their own accord when the war broke out," he said. "But, for a period of time, there were some who were imprisoned, there were some who were confined." I asked what had happened to those who were imprisoned or confined. "They were exchanged," he said, "against Serbian prisoners."

A look of panic flitted across his face. It lingered there, the uneasy shadow of something suppressed, the abrupt intuition, perhaps, of some retribution to come. "What I say may not be completely accurate. It is probably not accurate at all. I did not have this job at the start of the war. I really have no idea what was going on."

I decided, in that the conversation was clearly drawing to a close, to venture a last, blunt question. When and where were these Muslims "imprisoned or confined"? His look hardened. "I told you that I don't know what was going on."

RUZDIJA ŠESTOVIĆ, Ermin's father, was twenty-four years old when, in 1966, he moved from the mainly Muslim Sandžak area of northern Montenegro to the eastern Bosnian town of Milići. A bauxite mine, Boksit Milići, was beginning operations, and Šestović was employed to operate earth-moving equipment. Soon after he arrived he met a local Muslim girl, Muska, whom he married. They had two children—Ermin and a daughter, Nada.

Milići, about thirteen miles east of Vlasenica, is today a medium-sized town that does not hide its debt to bauxite, the principal ore in aluminum. The supermarket is called Boksit. The bus station is called Boksit Trans. There is a Boksit Sports Center. The dowdy high-rise blocks scattered around town house Boksit workers. But when Ruzdija arrived, the mine had no more than seventy employees.

Among them was a Serb named Rajko Dukić, who was destined to play a central role in the life of Ruzdija Šestović. Their parallel and then sharply divergent lives reflect a central fact of the Bosnian war: the conversion of friends and neighbors into foes. A mining engineer born in Milići, Dukić joined Boksit Milići in 1967. For more than two decades the two men worked together closely at the mine. The business diversified into timber, poultry, hotels, and restaurants; the number of employees rose to three thousand and sales reached $100 million a year. Dukić became a director; Ruzdija Šestović took charge of the maintenance of mining equipment.

But as Yugoslavia began to unravel in 1990, the lives of the two friends took different paths. Ruzdija showed little interest in the nationalist parties emerging in Bosnia. He never joined Alija Izetbegović's Stranka Demokratske Akcije (SDA), the first nationalist party in Bosnia, founded on May 26, 1990, although, like most Muslims, he did dutifully vote for it in the November 1990 elections. He never went to SDA rallies. He never showed any inclination to go to mosque.

Dukić, however, was active in the emergent Serb nationalist movement. On July 12, 1992, six weeks after the formation of the SDA, he became a founding member of Karadžić's SDS party. He was the first president of the executive committee of the SDS, and it was he who ordered the erection of the first barricades in Sarajevo in March 1992. After the war began, however, he gradually moved from a conspicuous political role to become an éminence grise of Karadžić's movement.

I began my search for Dukić at the stark, redbrick headquarters of Boksit Milići in Lukić Polje, a village on the outskirts of Milići. The mine had clearly been immobilized by the war. The only people in the director's office were a couple of Bosnian Serb soldiers in uniform who suggested that Dukić was more likely to be found in Belgrade.

Everyone knows the offices of Boksit Trade in Belgrade, located in the center of the Serbian capital, at the crest of the hill that rises between the Sava and Danube rivers. It is prime real estate and the windows of the offices suggest the reasons for the company's notoriety. The collective fantasies of Milošević's Serbia are on display: Sony Trinitron televisions, Sony Walkmans, Johnny Walker whiskey, Ray-Bans, Reeboks, Calvin Klein colognes, Yves Saint Laurent's Opium scent, and other accoutrements of the Belgrade nouveaux riches for whom the wars of Yugoslavia's demise were not hell but opportunity.

These windows of Boksit Trade, in fact, bear witness to a revolution that took place under the cover of the war. The revolution involved the fabulous enrichment of the politicians who fomented the wars and of their often murderous lieutenants. Conversely, it involved the impoverishment of almost everyone else and the defeat of the last serious attempt to bring economic and political reform to Yugoslavia.

The proposed reforms of Ante Marković, the last federal prime minister of Yugoslavia, would have amounted to a remarkable innovation if they had succeeded in empowering the individual within a functioning democratic system and the credible framework of the rule of law. In the Balkans, the arbitrary or autocratic rule of distant authorities has bred deeply ingrained habits of passivity and petty corruption. Notions of personal responsibility and initiative, and of the collective political power of individuals, scarcely have a foothold. It was therefore not difficult for a politician like Milošević to ensure that the old system, in which personal enrichment and political influence were inseparable, prevailed.

Marković, who took office in March 1989, tried to push through the reforms needed to create what he called "an undivided Yugoslavia with a market economy, political pluralism, democratic rights and freedoms for all citizens." He curbed the high inflation of 1989; he made the dinar convertible. But the chief political implication of his reforms in Serbia—the dilution of the power of the governing class of communists-turned-socialists led by Milošević—was unacceptable. Milošević unleashed his nationalist propaganda on Marković's League of Reform Forces; he attacked Marković as an American stooge; he made sure enough dinars were printed to wreck Marković's economic plans; he stole $1.6 billion from the Yugoslav National Bank. By the time Marković resigned in December 1991, he was a meaningless figure, the prime minister of a state that no longer existed, the leader of a party that proved mere flotsam on the nationalist tide in Bosnia and Serbia. In the place of Marković's reform came the revolution that propelled Rajko Dukić and his ilk to riches, creating a class that thrived on the fear and foggy mechanisms of war, dressed in Western clothes, aping Western mores, reinterpreting capitalism as thuggery.

DUKIĆ, LIKE KARADŽIĆ, was not wealthy before the Bosnian war broke out. But Boksit Milići, which, like all big businesses, was state-owned, had a lot of cash. Once the war was under way, Karadžić, Dukić, and other leaders of the Serb separatist movement gathered in the SDS were in a position to grab all the previously state-controlled assets in the 70 percent of Bosnian territory that rapidly came under Serb control.

In the case of Dukić and the Boksit Milići company, money was transferred to banks and shell corporations in Cyprus—a center of Serbian economic activity that mushroomed during the war, especially after the imposition of the United Nations trade embargo on Serbia and Montenegro two months after the conflict began.

The embargo had many loopholes, but the most conspicuous at the outset was that it did not cover the Republika Srpska (Serb Republic) of Karadžić and Dukić. This self-styled republic was in Bosnia and was thus not under sanctions. This omission created opportunities that, as Dukić once remarked, only a fool could miss. Oil and cigarette smuggling were particularly lucrative. The papers of companies like Boksit Milići, registered in Serb-held Bosnia, could be used to buy oil. Officially, this oil would be bought for the use of a Bosnian company (Boksit Milići), but in practice most of it was sold in Serbia for huge profits.

For Boksit Milići, the trafficking was facilitated by the establishment of a shell company called BOMIL, with branches in the Macedonian capital of Skopje and in Limassol, Cyprus. This company acquired oil, mainly in Macedonia and Greece. In exchange for a commission of about 30 percent, Macedonian authorities would allow the oil to pass through the Macedonian-Serbian frontier. The cash profits were then carried back by hand to Macedonia or Cyprus, where the bank accounts of Boksit Milići and the other entrepreneurs of Serbia's war swelled.

It was not difficult, then, to diversify from oil into the Western status symbols—from Ray-Bans to Mitsubishi Pajeros to cellular telephones— avidly sought by the few winners in the war's revolution. Hence the gleaming Belgrade windows of Boksit Trade, the BMWs of Dukić, the Limassol apartment of Dukić's son, the Mercedes of Karadžić, the English courses in London for Dukić's wife, the fast cars of Milošević's flamboyant son Marko, and all the gaudy new villas of Belgrade with their slabs of marble, their big gates, their Range Rovers parked outside, their guard dogs, and their insidious whiff of blood. This was the gaudy underside of the war, once encapsulated by Karadžić in a memorably artless phrase: "We would rather drive Mercedes than tanks." Behind all the Greater Serb rhetoric, all the talk of "good Serbs" and "traitors," there lurked thievery and impoverishment on an epic scale.

When I found Dukić in his Belgrade office, he proved affable enough. He had the well-heeled air of a successful provincial businessman and a methodical manner that I attributed to his engineer's training. His small eyes were shrewd, his mustache neatly trimmed; his tweedy jacket would not have looked out of place at the races in Britain. What I wanted to know from Dukić is how he could betray his friend, Ruzdija Šestović; I also wanted to know where and when this former Muslim employee of Boksit Milići was killed. Of such intimate betrayals the war was made.

But Dukić, in the Balkan manner, began by evoking what he called the tragic history of Bosnia and the moment he first grew alarmed because he felt threatened by the Muslims.

The occasion was the inaugural meeting, in June 1990, of the Vlasenica branch of Izetbegović's SDA party. "It was very frightening," said Dukić. "Izetbegović was there, but Muslim religious leaders did most of the talking. The message was that the Drina River from Zvornik to Foča had to be dominated by Muslims. They said the Serbs could live there, but would have to accept life in Bosnia as a dominated minority. They said it was time the Muslims were released. I wondered: Released from what?"

As a prominent local businessman, Dukić addressed the meeting—a fact that is in itself curious if his own account of the Muslims' mood is accurate. He said that he told the crowd that their Muslim leaders were offering them a return to the fifteenth century, apparently a reference to the conquest of Bosnia by the Ottoman Turks. He pointed to the buildings, hotels, and businesses of Vlasenica, many of them built with the profits of Boksit Milići, and urged the Muslims not to "throw this all away" and return to the violence of World War II. It was clear, Dukić insisted, that the Serbs would have to organize and defend themselves. Many "problematic people"—alcoholics and gang members in the Vlasenica and Milići areas—had already joined the SDA party. The Muslim design, he told me, was clear: take over the top jobs in government, in industry, in education, in the police, and gradually squeeze the Serbs out of Bosnia, as they had been pushed out of Kosovo, through political pressure and isolated acts of intimidation. "I felt," he said, "the smell of danger in the air."

CHAPTER 15

CELESTIAL PEOPLE

HERE I WAS, AGAIN, FACE TO FACE WITH A SERB, DUKIĆ, whom I believed to be responsible, directly or indirectly, for the death or dispersion of tens of thousands of Muslims, people like the Šestović family who had once lived alongside him in eastern Bosnia. But what preoccupied Rajko Dukić was the fact that he, as a Serb, felt threatened by the Muslims. This was a central issue of the war: the Serb, as perennial victim, could not see himself as executioner; the Serb, as eternal liberator, could not see himself as enslaver; the Serb, as concentration camp survivor, could not see the concentration camps he built.

The first dead bodies I saw in the Bosnian war were in fact Serb civilians. Their corpses, charred and putrid, lay sprawled beside overturned cars, scraps of clothing, and broken glass. The blackened skull from another victim had fallen from a vehicle onto the road. The remains lay baking in the sun, marking a no-man's-land between the Bosnian-government-held town of Goražde and the Serb-held town of Rogatica. A convoy of Serb civilians pulling back in buses and cars from rural areas just north of Goražde on August 27, 1992, had been ambushed by Bosnian government forces. Several days later, the bodies still lay where they had fallen.

A sixty-four-year-old survivor, Veljko Lasica, whose left leg had been amputated in the Sokolac hospital, near Pale, said the attack occurred in the early afternoon. Just north of the village of Kukavice, the road from Goražde passes into a gully bordered by steep embankments. From the tops of the banks, mainly Muslim Bosnian forces opened fire with automatic weapons. "It was like hail," Mr. Lasica said.

Most of the Serb victims in the hospital had leg injuries—consistent with fire from above into the windows of cars and buses. One of them, an emaciated ten-year-old boy named Bogdan Pljevaljić, had also lost a leg. He looked limp—like a puppet abandoned by its puppeteer.

His mother told me he would not eat. He was having recurrent nightmares about the ambush. What haunted Bogdan was not so much his own injury but the death of an eleven-year-old school friend named Dalibor Matović. "Boro," as Bogdan used to call his friend, had been sitting just two seats away on the bus. Bogdan would awaken screaming. His dark eyes looked enormous in his sallow face. He never looked me in the eye but stared straight ahead and said that all this was insanity.

In the five months since the start of the conflict, Serb forces had gradually tightened their noose on Goražde, a town with a prewar population of thirty-seven thousand people that was 70 percent Muslim. Its underfed population had been swollen by thousands of Muslim refugees who had fled the Serb terror in surrounding towns in eastern Bosnia. Now, as Serb forces pulled back a few miles in partial compliance with an undertaking made at a conference in London—but never fulfilled—to lift the siege of all Bosnian towns, these civilians had followed and been killed.

There were hundreds of thousands of such Serb sufferers from the war. Nobody could reasonably suggest that Bogdan Pljevaljić, aged ten and one-legged, or Dalibor Matović, aged eleven and dead, were anything other than innocent. Nor could I perceive anything but innocence in a Serb boy named Milomir, aged eleven, who once peered down on Sarajevo from the surrounding hills, listened to the sound of the mortars, and gave me the most laconic description of the war I heard: "Boom boom, no good." But were they victims of the Muslim fundamentalist "danger" that Dukić claimed to have descried in Vlasenica in June 1990, or of a moment of untrammeled, collective, and sanguinary dementia that seized the Serb people?

WAR IN BOSNIA had by no means been a complete surprise to Washington. The inevitable focus of the bellicose rhetoric of Serbia and Croatia was the very heart of the Yugoslav state, the place of greatest confluence and miscegenation—Bosnia. As early as the fall of 1990, the Central Intelligence Agency predicted in a report that Yugoslavia could not hold together. Ron Neitzke, the American diplomat who served as chargé d'affaires and then deputy chief of mission in Zagreb between 1992 and 1995, looked at that report in early 1991 and then gazed at the extraordinarily mottled hues of a Bosnian ethnological map. His conclusion was that the CIA might have it wrong, because a breakup of Yugoslavia, involving the unraveling of the Bosnian knot, would require a degree of barbarity that the United States and the West would never tolerate.

Many had such illusions about the limits of the West's tolerance. They believed that a century of horror on a scale hitherto unknown had put an end, at least in Europe, to tolerance of the intolerable.

Bosnia, moreover, was the third war of Yugoslavia's breakup. Fighting only reached the republic after a brief war in Slovenia and a six-month conflict in Croatia that raged during 1991. The wars followed the two republics' declaration of independence on June 26, 1991.

In Slovenia, the JNA fought a halfhearted ten-day war, supposedly in the name of Yugoslav unity. Forty-four JNA soldiers were killed, almost two hundred injured. Thousands deserted. Slovene casualties were light. This bizarre outcome of a war pitting a tiny newborn state against Europe's fourth-largest army reflected the fact that the Yugoslav unity the JNA supposedly represented had already become a fiction; unity was no longer the strategic aim of Belgrade. Milošević was interested in the construction of an enlarged Serbia on Yugoslavia's remains. Slovenia had no Serb minority; it was Serb free; it could go.

In Croatia, where there was a substantial Serb minority and where Serbia had real territorial ambitions, the JNA quickly became a fully fledged Serbian army when war erupted in July 1991. The Memorandum of 1986 had laid out the Serb goals: "The establishment of the Serbian people's complete national and cultural integrity, regardless of which republic or province they might be living in, is their historical and democratic right." The fighting pitted the Serbs of the Krajina and their JNA backers against the nascent, initially weak forces of the Croatian National Guard. At the Croatian village of Kijevo near Knin in August 1991; at Vukovar beginning in September; and at Dubrovnik in October, JNA officers demonstrated how the Soviet doctrine of blanket artillery bombardment might have been applied in a European war.

The JNA's conversion of Vukovar, a once gracious town on the Danube, into a latter-day Dresden became the symbol of the most devastating fighting in Europe since Hitler's war. To prove that Vukovar was Serbian—the town's population was 37.4 percent Serb and 39 percent Croat before the war—the JNA destroyed it. About two thousand people were killed, many in massacres as the Serbs mopped up. The action was then described by the Serbs as a "liberation."

These methods, which would be taken up again in Bosnia, did much to alienate public sympathy for the Serbs, whose case in Croatia was potentially compelling. By comparison, the Croatian slaughter of Serb civilians and conscripts in towns, including Gospic and Sisak, tended to pale. Tudjman proved a master of committing his atrocities in the shadow of larger Serb ones. By November 1991, about 500,000 Croats and close to 250,000 Serbs had been displaced by a war that claimed more than 10,000 lives before a tenuous truce took hold on January 3, 1992, with Serbs holding about 27 percent of Croatian territory. They called the land they held the *Republika Srpska Krajina,* or Serb Republic of the Krajina.

DUKIĆ TOLD ME about a meeting he had held with Izetbegović in Sarajevo shortly after the 1990 Bosnian elections. The nationalist parties had triumphed, winning 202 of the 240 seats in the bicameral parliament. Of these, Izetbegović's SDA won 87 seats, Karadžić's SDS 71, and the Bosnian branch of Croatian president Franjo Tudjman's Hrvatska Demokratska Zajednica (Croatian Democratic Union) 44. The meeting was called to discuss how power should be divided among these parties that had quashed both the former communist rulers of Bosnia and Marković's supranational party with its pale program of market reforms.

In Dukić's recollection, Izetbegović suggested the SDA should hold two of the three top government positions. Dukić and the Croat representative, Stjepan Kljuić, countered by saying each of the three national communities should have one of the posts. Then Izetbegović developed his argument. The Serbs had their own country, Serbia; the Croats had Croatia; the Slovenes, Slovenia. But the Muslims had no country other than Bosnia, where they were a relative majority, with 44 percent of the population. It was therefore natural that Bosnia should be a state of Muslim people. All other people would be welcome. But Bosnia would be a state of Muslims with other peoples living in it.

"I responded with the idea that a Swiss cantonal system could be established in Bosnia, but Izetbegović did not like that," Dukić said. "He was confident that his vision of Bosnia would prevail. The Islamic philosophy is based in the idea that time is on your side, you do not have to hurry. For the Muslims, time has a very different dimension than for Christians in the West."

Dukić, like many Serbs, saw Bosnian Muslims in stereotypes. But he had a point about Izetbegović, who is, without question, a man of patience, a quality no doubt reinforced both by his faith and by the eight years he spent in prison for his Islamic beliefs under the communist rulers of Yugoslavia. On the occasions I met him, I found his mild-mannered azure gaze fixed on the middle distance, suggestive of a man less moved by his immediate surroundings than by the beckoning glimmer of a dream. Early in the war, he told General Philippe Morillon, then the commander of United Nations forces in Bosnia, "I am prepared to sacrifice a generation to stop the Serbs." His voice can contain a curious deadness on which emotion, even before tragedy, does not appear to impinge. His major work, *Islam Between East and West,* argues that "Islam is more than a religion" and suggests ways to reconcile Western material progress with the spiritual values of Islam. Certainly, he hoped to see Bosnia characterized by such a reconciliation.

But as the founder of the first nationalist party in Bosnia in May 1990, he chose a treacherous path, one more inclined to rouse the flames of nation-as-tribe than lay the foundations of a citizen-state. He knew his Muslim movement was dangerous, but, with the examples of Milošević and Tudjman before him, he also saw no other way to gather votes. With a dark lucidity, he described nationalism as a "minefield" that had to be passed through; later, he said, civil society in Bosnia could be established.

His calculation proved accurate. The abject failure, in the 1990 elections, of Ante Marković's League of Reform Forces, the one serious party that tried to appeal to all Bosnian nationalities, showed the immaturity of a political system in which the drumbeat of tribal allegiance quickly drowned out the pale call of a Yugoslav democracy. The "minefield" foreseen by Izetbegović proved to be a four-year war.

On February 27, 1991, just two months after the meeting with Dukić and Kljuić, Izetbegović told parliament, "I would sacrifice peace for a sovereign Bosnia-Herzegovina, but for that peace in Bosnia-Herzegovina I would not sacrifice sovereignty." The statement was provocative to the Serbs; it was also an explicit acknowledgment that Izetbegović, aged sixty-six when the war broke out, was ready to see blood shed for the achievement of a long-held dream.

There were other provocations. In the summer of 1991 Izetbegović traveled to Turkey and applied to join the Organization of the Islamic Conference. In February 1992, he accepted, along with Croat and Serb leaders, a European-brokered accord dividing Bosnia into three national cantons, only to change his mind about this so-called Lisbon Agreement a few days later. Dukić, like Karadžić, insisted to me that this document, prepared by the Portuguese diplomat José Cutileiro, would have averted war, despite its vagueness on the allocation of territory. Izetbegović, he argued, thus bore responsibility for a conflict in which Serbs had been obliged to defend their scattered homes against a Muslim takeover.

By the time I listened to Dukić I had heard this Serb argument in myriad guises. It had a veneer of logic to it, usually driven home by a question like, How would Americans react if the governor of Texas suddenly announced that the state was going to secede? The basic message was that the Serbs had merely wanted to remain in their country, Yugoslavia; they were the passive party, forced into wars by the Slovene, Croatian, and Muslim secessionists; their desire for unity was natural given the scarcely reassuring history of minorities in the Balkans.

The longer I covered the war, however, the more impatient I became with this bogus case. The Serb tragedy, and the Serb folly, of this fin de siècle began in Kosovo. Milošević and the ideologues of his Serbian revolution took their people back to the womb of their unreason. A place where defeat was victory, death a kingdom of heaven, suicide redemption, suffering vindication, and exile a homeland. Having reverted, with a kind of primal scream, to this upside-down world of life-in-death myth, the Serbs, in their flailing catharsis, could justify almost anything and turn any horror on its head. Having destroyed Yugoslavia, they set out to remake a smaller one with a host of subject peoples—Kosovo Albanians and Bosnian Muslims among them—only to express outrage when these peoples objected, whether passively or with swords.

Throughout the year leading to the first fighting in mid-1991, Izetbegović cast around for solutions that would avoid bloodshed. He and Kiro Gligorov, the Macedonian president, put forward a plan for a loose Yugoslav confederation—sovereign states within a sovereign state. Later, after the fighting broke out in Slovenia and then Croatia, he called for the preemptive dispatch of United Nations peacekeepers to Bosnia. His appeal went unanswered. It was not Muslim nationalism that lacerated Bosnia; it was the Serb and Croat nationalism that preceded it in Serbia and Croatia. If Izetbegović was ready to countenance war, he seems to have had no enthusiasm for it. Violence, however, was always part of Milošević's equation.

Tom Nairn, the British historian, has written that "nationalism is the pathology of modern developmental history, as inescapable as 'neurosis' in the individual, with much the same essential ambiguity attaching to it, a similar built-in capacity for descent into dementia." In the Serb case, I believe, the "descent" was particularly precipitous because, at the time that communist Yugoslavia became vulnerable, the Serbs had been casting around for the stable borders of a modern nation-state for almost two hundred years.

A SERBIAN PIG FARMER named Djordje Petrović, known as Karadjordje or Black George, first rose against the Ottoman Turks in 1804. Karadjordje thus became a pioneer for a century of nascent nationalisms; his campaign became known as the First Serbian Uprising. As the hold on humanity of the sacred and the dynastic began to weaken in the nineteenth century, undermining the transnational imperia of Christendom and Islam, the "imagined communities," to borrow Benedict Anderson's phrase, of nationalism emerged with their solace of a glorious past and their mirage of a glorious future. In an era of eroding certainties the consoling chimera of the nation took hold. Nowhere, perhaps, were these national communities more "imagined" than in the Balkan Peninsula, where the very notion of ethnic homogeneity had been nullified by centuries of miscegenation, migration, and religious conversion.

But legend gained strength from the very precariousness of Balkan national identity. The belief of the Serbs in their national liberation became entirely concrete as the nineteenth century progressed: they fought hard, and repeatedly, for the independence that was recognized at the Congress of Berlin in 1878. They fought again and again and were decimated, but victorious, in World War I. Then, as the philosopher Mihailo Marković once said to me in Belgrade, "We Serbs sacrificed our identity in 1918 for the Yugoslav identity. We had already been liberated and recognized in Berlin. But we threw away our coat of arms and our national anthem. We marched in the face of the historical truth that the modern supranational community cannot be built until the first stage of the nation-state has been passed through."

As the communist Yugoslav state eroded, Milošević and the authors of the Serbian Memorandum tried to rectify this perceived error by dragging the Serbs back in time, not merely to 1918, but to 1389 and the charged symbolism of the Kosovo battle. Six hundred years after their defeat, they used an imagined "genocide" against the Serbs of Kosovo to justify the dispatch of tanks to the Kosovo capital of Priština, the slaying of Kosovo Albanians, and the crushing of the autonomous rights of the almost two million ethnic Albanians living there. Then, having thus unmoored Yugoslavia, they elaborated their expansionary program in the name of the autonomous rights of the Serbs of Croatia and Bosnia.

The inconsistency was flagrant. Milošević used the argument of Serbian historic frontiers to claim Kosovo *against* the argument of nationality—for Albanians accounted for about 90 percent of the population. He then turned around and used the argument of nationality *against* that of historic frontiers to claim Serb-populated areas of Croatia and Bosnia. Milošević wanted to have his cake and eat it.

In much the same way, Czech leaders had used the argument of historic frontiers to claim German- and Polish-occupied areas of Bohemia and Moravia after World War I, and arguments of nationality to claim Slovakia, which historically had been part of Hungary. The results were equally disastrous.

But Milošević fever in Serbia was such that, by the time the war broke out, the Serbs had come to perceive themselves as "celestial people," descendants of Saint Sava, the great shaper of the medieval Serbian empire, the man who bound church and state in close union, and Prince Lazar, who chose defeat at Kosovo and "the kingdom of heaven."

I once stood with a Serb soldier, a young woman named Dragana Nosić, in an exposed area of the Serb-held Sarajevo suburb of Grbavica.

She had an AK-47 assault rifle slung over her shoulder and, with a radiant smile, she said, "Serbs are a celestial people, protected by God. We want to regain our history before 1918. We lived happily enough in Yugoslavia but all the others wanted the state to break up. We tried to help others in 1918, and again in 1941. There will not be a third time." She paused, gazed across the Miljacka River at the government-held part of the city, and declared that the Muslims could shoot her at any moment. "But I can defy destiny," she added, "because we are celestial."

TO THE CELESTIAL, rules of reason do not apply; they are blessed with a bulletproof halo. A battle—Kosovo—defined Milošević's movement in Serbia and, in the end, further battles were its corollary. Negotiation presupposes a minimum of coherence, but Milošević had cemented his power precisely by unleashing the irrational. The diaries of Borisav Jović, a close associate of Milošević and Serbia's last representative on the Yugoslav federal presidency, are illuminating in this regard.

Jović is a small, dapper man who takes himself very seriously. His tinted hair and manicured nails, his monogrammed shirts and his gleaming patent leather shoes betray his vanity. When I met him during the summer of 1994, he was ensconced in a comfortable office on an upper floor of the New Belgrade high-rise that houses Milošević's Serbian Socialist party; a red flag still fluttered on the roof, and Jović had all the trappings and mannerisms of a high communist functionary: heavily padded doors, selected coffee-table books, somber wood paneling, averted gaze, and deadpan delivery. Jović, as president of the rotating Yugoslav presidency during the critical years leading to the Slovenian and Croatian declarations of independence, had played an important role in destroying Yugoslavia, always preferring Serb bombast to the quest for compromise. His position had not budged. "The Serbs fought for centuries to live in one state," he told me, "and that state was Yugoslavia. We suffered great injustices in it— economic and political—but it was ours, and we have only sought to protect it."

Jović always viewed the Serbs as blameless. But later, peeved at being excluded from Milošević's inner circle, he published diaries that showed the scrupulous Serb preparations for war. On October 13, 1989, Jović quotes Milošević as saying that a true multiparty democracy in Serbia was impossible because, in that case, there would be an Albanian party and "we would lose Kosovo." War has always been a splendid distraction from internal political impasse and, on February 13, 1990, as tensions in Yugoslavia mounted, Milošević exclaimed, "By God, there will be war."

On March 9, 1991, Milošević crushed his internal opposition, using tanks to break up a Belgrade demonstration against his stranglehold on the media. But there were still two schools in a Serbia divided: that of the federal army, under the defense minister General Veljko Kadijević, and that of the prominent writer Dobrica Ćosić. Kadijević and the JNA wanted initially to fight to defend Tito's Yugoslavia against the growing secessionist movements in Croatia and Slovenia. They had not yet entirely abandoned the communist Yugoslav state. But Ćosić, by late 1990, had concluded that Yugoslavia was dead, its communist ideology moribund, its raison d'être destroyed, its unity no more than an illusion. Given this fact, the cause to be fought for was the one lost in 1918: a Serbian nation-state.

The ideological buttress produced by Serbian intellectuals was that Yugoslavia came into being as a union of nations, not republics. Therefore nations (read: "Croats" or "Muslims" or "Slovenes") could secede (unless they were Albanians), but republics (read "Croatia" or "Bosnia") could not. The internal republican borders of Tito's Yugoslavia were therefore to be thrown out as mere administrative lines and replaced by the new borders of an enlarged Serbia covering any ground where a Serb lived or could be unearthed.

In fact, of course, the republican borders were much older than Tito; they broadly reflected the ebb and flow of armies, administrations, and cultures across the Balkan Peninsula over centuries. Only at the height of the medieval empire did Serbia embrace any land west of the Drina River. The border between Croatia and Bosnia corresponds broadly with the extent of Ottoman penetration into Europe after the seventeenth century. Vukovar, just across the Danube in Croatia, or Zvornik and Višegrad, just across the Drina in Bosnia, could not be made "Serb" without terror on a massive scale against their large non-Serb populations.

Milošević appears to have wavered for some months over which course to take: the defense of Tito's Yugoslavia or a Greater Serbia carved out of its ruins. In other words, he was unsure whether to wear his Partisan or his Chetnik hat.

On January 10, 1991, he said, "If Yugoslavia were to become a confederation of independent states, Serbia would demand territories from neighboring republics so that all eight and half million Serbs would be in the same state." But until March 12, 1991—when Jović unsuccessfully pressed for a majority within the eight-man presidency to vote for a preemptive coup by the JNA against the secessionist movements in Croatia and Slovenia—Milošević had apparently not abandoned the preservation of Tito's Yugoslavia. The condition, however, was that he would dominate it.

This hesitation ended on March 16, 1991, after the JNA coup was marginally rejected by the presidency. Milošević announced that "Yugoslavia is finished" and that he had "ordered the mobilization of special reservists and the urgent formation of additional Serbian militia units." He warned Croatia that if it continued to push for independence, "it should not occur to anyone that a part of the Serbian nation will be allowed to go with them." He let it be known to the Slovenes that they could go because there was no Serb minority there. He said that "if we have to, we'll fight. I hope they won't be so crazy as to fight against us. Because if we don't know how to work and do business, at least we know how to fight."

Arms started flowing to Serbs in Croatia and Bosnia to prepare them to fight this war for a Greater Serbia. The militias of Željko Ražnatović, alias Arkan, and other longtime operatives of the Serbian secret police were prepared; extreme nationalist politicians like Vojislav Šešelj were allowed to form their own Chetnik militias (Arkan's militia, formed in October 1991 was known as "the Tigers"; Šešelj's, also formed in late 1991, the "Šešeljovci"). Hand-picked agents with the Serbian Department of State Security—the Služba Državne Bezbednosti or SDB—became the vehicle for the secret financing, arming, and organization of undeclared wars.

The dirtiness of Serbia's wars owed much to Milošević. Faced by a re-luctant army he chose to use his security police—part of the Serbian Inte-rior Ministry, widely known by its acronym of MUP—to arm whatever wild bunch would volunteer to fight in Croatia and Bosnia. Criminals were released en masse from Serbian jails on the condition that they would go to fight. This method had the additional advantage for Milošević of blurring chains of command, a considerable attraction to a man who sets immense store by always placing himself in a position to deny responsi-bility—what Ian Traynor of *The Guardian* has called the doctrine of "plau-sible deniability."

A wiretap of a conversation between Milošević and Karadžić in Sep-tember 1991, released by the office of Prime Minister Marković, reveals Milošević telling his Bosnian Serb surrogate that he can collect the weapons and assistance he needs from General Nikola Uzelac, then the commander of the Banja Luka Corps. In January 1992, as Jović revealed in a BBC documentary made by Brian Lapping Associates, Milošević or-dered the redeployment to Bosnia of all JNA forces born in Bosnia. By this time, the Croatian war had turned the JNA into what was essentially a Ser-bian army. The Yugoslav state that General Kadijević initially sought to de-fend had gone. When the Bosnian war broke out, Jović estimated, 85 percent of the ninety thousand JNA troops in Bosnia were Bosnian Serbs. The war could scarcely have been better prepared.

DUKIĆ, AS A TOP MAN in the SDS, was aware of these preparations. In the nine months leading to the Bosnian war the drumbeat of bellicosity from the SDS was unrelenting. The Serbs' intention to contest Bosnian independence by force of arms, just as they did in the Croatian war, was clear enough. From September 1991, they began to establish "Serb autonomous regions" within Bosnia. On October 14, 1991, their leader, Karadžić, said Bosnian independence would open "a highway of hell" in which the Muslim people risked "annihilation."

Preparations for such an annihilation proceeded apace. Arms poured in from Serbia; a "Serb Republic of Bosnia-Herzegovina" (later abridged to "Serb Republic") was proclaimed on December 21, 1991; Serb militias were formed, with the weapons of the Serbian-dominated JNA, to "cleanse" this self-styled republic of Muslims.

The party seized its first television transmitter in the region covering Banja Luka, Prijedor, and Sanski Most in August 1991 and began to nourish the people of northwestern Bosnia with a diet of ghoulish horror stories about Izetbegović's "fundamentalists." Other transmitters were seized as the year progressed. By December 1991, with the proclamation of the "Serb Republic of Bosnia-Herzegovina," the SDS had formally established its parallel state in waiting and the military power to bring that state into being was being readied.

The day after a March 1, 1992, referendum on Bosnian independence, which was boycotted by the Serbs, Dukić's barricades went up around Sarajevo. The Serbs said the barricades were a spontaneous response to the killing of the bride's father at a Serb wedding party in the old Baščaršija section of Sarajevo. But the military organization behind them suggested a well-prepared response to the massive vote in favor of Bosnian independence. Of the 64 percent of the electorate that took part in the referendum, 99.5 percent voted for "a sovereign and independent Bosnia-Herzegovina, a state of equal citizens and nations of Muslims, Serbs and Croats and others who live in it."

By the time the independent state of Bosnia was recognized by the European Union on April 6, 1992, and by the United States a day later, the Serbs were ready to start the war. To destroy Bosnia, to kill the very idea of the place, the Serb followers of Karadžić immediately began to shell Sarajevo, a city in which over one hundred thousand Serbs still lived.

The "fear" of the Muslims professed by Dukić was thus cynically fomented by Milošević's media and then used as a pretext, artfully manipulated, to justify a Serbian war of aggression. After that December 1990 meeting, Izetbegović accepted the division of power that Dukić had proposed. A Serb, Momčilo Krajišnik, became speaker of the Bosnian parliament, and a Croat, Jure Pelivan, became prime minister. The presidency was to rotate among the national communities; a system of balances existed; the rudiments of a multinational state, albeit a crude one, were in place.

Izetbegović made compromises and tried, on several occasions, to reassure the Bosnian Serb community. He was headstrong in his quest for independence, but his options by January 1992 were stark: either independence from Milošević's truncated Yugoslavia or a life within it offering no guarantees that life for Bosnia's Muslims might not quickly resemble that of Kosovo's Albanians.

Izetbegović chose independence, aware that bloodshed could follow, yet he was unprepared to fight a war. By any estimate it was a perilous course, that of a visionary rather than a statesman. He took his people down to the Neretva River in the depths of winter and asked them to swim. But it was Milošević and Karadžić and Dukić who assiduously made the preparations for war. Indeed, Dukić and his wife abandoned their Sarajevo home just a few days before war broke out on April 6, 1992. They knew exactly what had been prepared for the Bosnian capital.

The enemy the Serbs created through their propaganda had two faces: that of the Ottoman Turks killing and plundering the subjugated Serbs over centuries, and that of the Ustasha Croats pursuing their čišćenje (cleansing) and throwing Serbs into the genocidal concentration camps of World War II. The Serbs proceeded to step into the shoes of these reincarnated, conflated enemies. They killed, raped, and plundered Muslims, and they "cleansed" them by throwing them into concentration camps. Whatever the arguments on their side—and, however flawed, they had some—the Serbs trampled them into the Bosnian mud with this vicious campaign that flouted all the principles on which Europe had been rebuilt since 1945. As a people, the Serbs cannot escape responsibility: they massively backed Milošević's nationalist upheaval and they voted him into office in the first "free" elections of December 1990. Only as the war progressed, spreading its misery like a virus, did the number of Serbs claiming "innocence" increase. In their majority, they were scarcely innocent; they were victims of themselves.

But acting in the distorting glow of the Kosovo myth, magnetized by the apotheosis of Milošević, dazed by the incandescent reapparition of the anthems and symbols they had cast away in 1918, they were blind. In murder the Serbs remained victims, in aggression they remained on the defensive, in cleansing they remained the cleansed. As love is close to hatred, so in a moment of madness the specters most repellent to the Serbs proved close to their repressed desires. It was the Šestović family—and those Serb children killed and maimed near Rogatica—who could not deny what they saw or escape from what they suffered. They and countless others paid the price for this Serbian convulsion, conceived on a bleak medieval battlefield, orchestrated in the white city of Belgrade, consummated on the hills of Bosnia.

• • •

BY THE SECOND HALF of 1991, as fighting raged in Croatia after its secession from Yugoslavia, politics in the small town of Milići had become
impossible for the Šestović family to ignore. As the only Muslims in an
apartment building full of Serbs their position became increasingly uncomfortable. They were pointedly excluded from meetings of Serb residents in the basement. Serb insignia appeared everywhere; Chetnik songs
became daily taunts to the Muslims.

Muska Šestović was particularly alarmed. She persuaded her husband to
swap apartments with a Serb named Ratko Kandić who lived in Vlasenica,
about twenty miles away. Because Vlasenica, unlike Milići, had a Muslim
majority, and because it is a larger town, she was convinced the family
would be safe there. The swap took placed in October 1991. At about the
same time, Mrs. Šestović told me, Ruzdija, as a Muslim, lost his job at the
Boksit mine company.

Ermin Šestović was in Rogatica at the time that his parents moved. He
had finished his military service in the JNA in the summer of 1990, having served in the southeastern Serbian town of Niš and in Sarajevo. His father's brother died that year, leaving a house in Rogatica. With financial
help from his father, Ermin opened a café in the town, whose prewar population of about twenty-one thousand was 60 percent Muslim and 40 percent Serb.

The café offered a vantage point from which to observe the fissuring of
Bosnian society. Initially, its clientele was mixed. But during the course of
1991, Serbs stopped frequenting Ermin's café. There were now Serb cafés
and Muslim cafés. In another eastern Bosnian town, Bijeljina, whose population of ninety-eight thousand was 58.8 percent Serb and 31 percent
Muslim, some of the first violent incidents occurred in 1991 between the
clients of the newly opened Istanbul and Serbia cafés.

In late 1991, the situation became increasingly tense; Ruzdija felt that
the family should be together. Ermin reluctantly closed his Rogatica café
and found a job as a waiter in a Vlasenica restaurant, the Panorama. Nada
opened a hairdressing shop called "Salon Nada." On January 7, 1992, the
Serbian New Year, there were celebrations outside the Orthodox church in
Vlasenica: Chetnik songs were sung and Serbs paraded openly with
Kalashnikovs. The Šestović family tried to look past these signs and remake their lives.

But after the Serb-boycotted referendum on Bosnian independence, the
indications of looming war were too insistent to ignore. Nada noted how
many Serb women who used to frequent her salon were packed off to Belgrade by husbands and fathers. Ermin listened to clients of the Panorama
talking about the nocturnal delivery of weapons to Serb apartments in
Vlasenica. He heard about the Serb attack on Bijeljina on April 2, 1992,

when Arkan and his Serb paramilitary forces began the "cleansing" of this town just fifty miles north of Vlasenica. At night, growing numbers of Serbs came into Vlasenica from outlying villages, getting drunk and firing shots in the air. On April 5, 1992, Ermin saw a truck near the restaurant unload a cache of automatic weapons for the Serbs. He called the police, but when they came they said they found nothing. It was then that he decided to leave.

On April 6, with Bosnia's recognition as an independent state by the European Union, the war began in Sarajevo. On April 7, Ermin spoke to his parents.

"I told them, 'Let's get out of here.' I said, 'How are we going to defend ourselves?' I urged them to come to Zagreb where my mother's sisters live. But my father said nothing can happen here. We're all together. We're with people we've known a long time. They can't hurt us." This was the grand illusion. Tens of thousands of Muslims paid for it. They did not imagine that their neighbors might turn on them; they conceived of enemies as outsiders; they refused to believe what was literally before their eyes.

"We hesitated," said Mrs. Šestović. "We had our flat, our hairdressing salon, even our Serb friends. We had no weapons, we had never been in the SDA. We had not done anything wrong." Their sense of invulnerability was reinforced by the fact that they had become friendly with Dukić's brother-in-law, Mladen Čojnić, and his wife, Spomenka, who lived downstairs and told them not to worry about anything.

Ruzdija insisted there was no real danger, but his wife wanted the children to leave. On April 10, 1992, Ruzdija borrowed a friend's car and drove westward with his two children toward Kladanj, a town about twenty miles away. Two miles from Vlasenica they were stopped at a roadblock by Serb paramilitary forces with machine guns. "Are you trying to escape?" they asked. The Šestović family said they intended to return to Vlasenica and they were allowed through.

Ruzdija drove his children to Tuzla, where he left them. The parting was the last time Ermin and Nada saw their father. They did not understand, then, their father's illusions. He had grown up amid the euphoria that accompanied the reconstruction of Yugoslavia under Tito. Having been part of that postwar generation, having seen the new communist Yugoslavia take form, having identified with and served its single most powerful symbol, the armed forces of the JNA, he could not believe that the JNA would not protect him. He could not see that, by April 1992, the JNA was in essence a Serbian army.

FOR THE OLDER ŠESTOVIĆS, life in Vlasenica quickly became infernal. The Serbian noose tightened. On April 21, soldiers from the Novi Sad

Corps of the JNA surrounded the city. Tanks were installed in key positions. The bus station was patrolled. Soldiers moved through the streets with megaphones declaring that Vlasenica was "liberated" and people could come out on the streets. But the message was only for the Serbs. Arrests of Muslims became frequent, usually based on allegations that SDA lists of Serbs to be killed had been found in their homes. It became impossible for Muslims to leave. In mid-May the JNA formally departed, but by then this departure amounted largely to a fiction: all their weaponry had been transferred to the emergent Bosnian Serb army and local militias.

The Šestovićs never left their apartment. At night, afraid to put the light on, they sat in the dark. A Serb acquaintance, Goran Visković, searched their home for weapons, found none, and warned the Šestovićs not to go out. What food they needed was brought to them by friendly Serbs, particularly the Čojnić couple downstairs, who supplied them with coffee. A twenty-year-old niece and thirteen-year-old nephew, Vahda and Salih Ibišević, were entrusted to them in late April. The children's parents were convinced that their own small eastern Bosnian village, Gerovi, was more dangerous than Vlasenica.

Until late May, the phone worked. Then the lines were cut. During their last conversation with Nada and Ermin, who had reached Zagreb from Tuzla, Muska Šestović cried incessantly. Ruzdija said just two words: *"Save yourselves."*

On June 20, around midnight, three men in black masks and gloves, armed with automatic weapons and knives, came for Ruzdija Šestović. Trembling he raised his arms. They grabbed him and started to drag him out of the apartment. Muska pleaded with them to allow her husband to put on his shoes. She said that if her husband had to die she wanted to die with him. They said she should not worry, her husband would be back in a couple of hours. He merely had to sign a document stating that he accepted the exchange of his apartment for another one in Kladanj, a town held by the Bosnian government. Ruzdija said to his wife that he would go because then she and the children would be safe. Muska tried to call the Čojnić couple downstairs, but they had just left for Belgrade.

After a sleepless night pacing the apartment, Muska Šestović went to see a Serb friend, Ranko Ivanović, who lived in Vlasenica and had worked at the Milići mine. Ivanović said it was not possible that Ruzdija had been taken. There must be a mistake. He advised her to see the chief of police, Branimir Sokanović.

The police chief received Muska in his home at about 10:00 A.M. on June 21, 1992. He asked his wife to make some coffee. Muska had heard a rumor that gold could buy a relative back from the Serb authorities. She offered one thousand German marks, a gold necklace, and three rings.

Sokanović accepted this bounty. The two drank coffee to consummate what Muska imagined to be an agreement for her husband's release.

Sokanović took her to the police station. In a windowless room crammed with about fifty local Muslims from the town she found her husband. They were able to talk briefly. There was a camera focused on Muska.

After the meeting, Sokanović posed a question: Would she rather her husband went to prison or to the Sušica camp? Muska had not heard of the camp. She said she would rather her husband came home. Sokanović explained that this was impossible because the Bosnian Serb authorities had given orders to remove all Muslims from Vlasenica. He recommended, however, that Ruzdija Šestović not go to the Sušica camp "because people are being killed there."

For almost a month after this meeting, Muska Šestović was able to bring food to her husband daily in Vlasenica prison. Other Muslims were severely beaten, but Šestović was spared, apparently on Sokanović's orders. One day, Šestović gave his wife his wedding ring and said, "Even if we die, at least we know our children are safe. We cannot be sorry." On another day he asked her to contact Dukić. Despite his lost job at the mine, Šestović had some vestigial faith in Dukić. He believed that Dukić's influence alone might save them.

But with telephones cut and the road to Milići barred to Muslims, Muska could not reach their powerful former Serb colleague. The last time she saw her husband was on July 19, 1992. Later that day, Muska Šestović herself was arrested, along with her niece and nephew, and taken to the Sušica concentration camp.

CHAPTER 16

USELESS VIOLENCE

Pero Popović wanted to talk. He said it was his conscience. One memory in particular was bothering him. He once beat Muslim prisoners of the Sušica concentration camp. Beat them with pieces of timber. The worst was this: he knew some of the people getting beaten, like Amir Berbić, the Vlasenica locksmith with whom he used to play soccer before the war. They really went for Berbić's left ear.

But Popović, a former guard at the camp, wanted one thing clear. He had never beaten anyone to death. That happened to some Muslims, like Durmo Handžić and Redžo Hatunić, who were suspected of hiding weapons and were battered with metal rods, but he did not take part himself. Nor had he participated in the firing squads that killed groups of Muslims up on the hill called Debelo Brdo, about six miles south of Vlasenica. In fact, he said, he was always reluctant to be there, at Sušica, but if he had tried to run away he would have been shot by his commanders.

Time passes but does not necessarily heal. Memories fester, the past's weight grows. In the end somebody cracks. Twenty years go by and a former Argentine navy captain comes forward and talks for the first time about how the military disposed of political prisoners by throwing them, alive but unconscious, into the Atlantic Ocean from aircraft. That starts the ball rolling. An Argentine army sergeant decides to tell his story—how the prisoners at the Campo de Mayo barracks were injected with tranquilizers before being taken to the planes, how they flew so low he could see sharks, how the stripped bodies—enemies, real or imagined, of the military junta—plunged into the water. Then a general concedes that the army used "illegitimate methods" because it did not know how to fight its enemies "by legal means." Two decades on, the *desparecidos* of Argentina's "dirty war" reappear. In the Bosnian dirty war, at least eighteen thousand people "disappeared." A similar symmetry must lurk: between the disquiet of people, like the Šestovićs, who have lost a relative, and the executioner, nagged by some compunction, whose composure snaps.

Popović is the Everyman of the Serb onslaught. An ordinary man, neither bright nor stupid, neither particularly brave nor particularly cowardly, living at a time when things fall apart, borne along by the tide. Before the war, he lived on the fringes of the law, trading in timber and other goods. The provenance of some of his merchandise was suspect; it had somehow been lost on the road between Sarajevo and Belgrade. He knew a truck driver who worked the route. It was not difficult to deposit part of the loads—a few hundred yards of cable, a hundred pounds of coffee—in a cache in Vlasenica and, on delivery, spin some yarn about how the inventory was wrong. Then, the proceeds from the sale of the pilfered goods could be split between them. They would hit the bars, buy drinks for the girls—"the high life," Popović called it. The system seems to have worked well enough. Popović, who was thirty-four years old when the war started in 1992, had built himself a house, bought himself a heavy gold chain that dangled from his neck, and set up two trading companies that did whatever business they could.

For a man like Popović, with a high-school education, a native shrewdness, and a knowledge of the angles, there were always deals to be made. The activities of the big state companies, principally in timber, steel, mining, and arms production, left a lot of margin in Bosnia for small-time private enterprise operating in the gray zone between creative entrepreneurship and petty theft. Survival and the circumvention of authority had long overlapped in Bosnia, as was natural for a backward province of imperial, royal, or communist bureaucracy. Out of this tradition grew the hectic trafficking of the war: the sales, across the lines, of cigarettes, fuel, coffee, and food; the elaborate networks, usually charging at least two thousand German marks—about $1,200—a head for smuggling Serbs out of government-held territory or Muslims out of Serb-held territory.

Popović saw opportunities in the war; it was a free-for-all at the outset and his side had the guns. Besides, the bosses said it would all be over in a couple of months. But then things got out of hand.

I found him in Loznica, a Serbian town just a few miles from the Bosnian border on the Drina. The war was still evident in Popović's troubled green eyes and his tics. He tugged at his beard, he fiddled with his chain, he was subject to involuntary grimaces. He had deserted from the Bosnian Serb army at the start of 1993, abandoning everything in Vlasenica, and he was living in fear of being found and drafted.

Down on his luck in 1994, he seemed pliant in the hands of his willful

Serb girlfriend, Milica, who had an infant child by a first marriage and was pushing him to get out of the country. A case, perhaps, of torturer turned mommy's boy. This much was clear: more than a troubled conscience was at play in Popović's decision to talk about the Sušica camp. He had the dim notion that what he had to say might ultimately interest international investigators of war crimes and so help him leave Serbia. But his banal progress into hell was illuminating, and the more I looked into it, the more credible his story became.

Money: Popović saw the conflict not so much as an eruption of nationalist hatred as a savage capitalist spree filling the vacuum left by the collapse of the old communist system. In this upheaval, thugs had a field day, wealth changed hands as fast as in any revolution. Throughout early 1992, he observed what he called a steady influx of "gangsters and criminals from Serbia, and others who saw a chance to make money." He had been a member of the fan club of the Red Star Belgrade soccer club—the nucleus of much of Arkan's initial support—and he knew some of the hooligans now marching or busing into Bosnia. "With a mass of unemployed people under twenty-five, you can do what you like," he said. "These people from Serbia were longing for action and a chance to loot Muslims. The madness had to be imported into Bosnia." The offer of a hundred marks and a Zastava rifle was enough to bring kids to the action.

Money flowed at the start of the war. Popović, who had been a sergeant in the JNA, rejoined the army in April 1992. At the time, ordinary soldiers were earning close to five hundred marks ($330) a month in salaries paid from Belgrade—a decent wage at the time. In addition, they had free food and lodging and, most important, a steady supply of Marlboros. As the promised two-month victory turned into a forty-month war against an increasingly well organized enemy, Serb morale fell with the disappearing Marlboros.

Popović said groups of Muslims had behaved provocatively in Vlasenica before the war. They had thrown stones at Serbs; they had translated their rapid population growth—a 22 percent increase in the 1981–1991 period—into growing domination of the local political scene. But he seems to have drifted into the army as much through acquiescence as animus.

The extent of his loyalty to the Serb cause was, however, quickly tested. At the beginning of May 1992, he was told by his commander, Captain Boban Kukić, to prepare for work in a prison camp that would be housed in a former JNA military depot called Sušica. During the month of May, Popović said, one of the two hangars at the depot was emptied and the camp surrounded with thick coils of barbed wire. "Fifteen of us were chosen as guards. We were all over thirty; they wanted people with some experience. The alternative was to be shot or sent to the front line. But I still did not believe that there would be massacres of civilians."

THE VOLKSWAGEN GOLF was the Serb war trophy par excellence. Karadžić's forces grabbed and cleansed the northwestern Sarajevo suburb of Vogošća early in the war and helped themselves to the large Volkswagen factory there. Inside, they found two thousand assembled Golfs and another three thousand in parts.

On May 31, 1992, a Volkswagen Golf approached the Vlasenica home of Hiba Mehmedović, a widow then aged forty-eight. Inside the vehicle were three Serbs in military uniforms. She knew one of them, a local named Dragan Basta who went by the nickname of "Tsar." All the men had automatic weapons.

They stormed into her house and arrested her two sons, Kemal Mehmedović, a twenty-seven-year-old driver, and Nedzad Mehmedović, a twenty-five-year-old mechanic. "Why are you taking my boys?" she asked. The men replied that the arrests were an administrative procedure. Her sons would return shortly, after "reports" had been filed. Mrs. Mehmedović never saw her boys again.

On the day of their arrest, she went to the local doctor, a Serb named Nedeljko Kipić. He said she should not worry, her boys were not troublemakers, and he would try to help. She went to see the police, who also said she should not worry, the worst that might happen was that her boys would be "exchanged." Returning in tears to her home that night, she met a neighbor, a Serb named Obrad Kovaćević.

"What happened?" Kovaćević asked.

"They took my boys."

"Oh, don't worry, they'll just beat them a bit."

"What?"

"And, by the way, why don't you come over for a coffee? My wife is away in Belgrade."

Power, the unlimited power of the Serbs in the first months of the war, conferred the ability to humiliate, with a gun, a club, an iron rod, or a penis, it hardly mattered. The Muslims, so excruciatingly similar to the Serbs in appearance, in habits, in tastes, had to understand their treason, or that of their ancestors, in not "remaining Serbs." That was the basic assumption: all the Muslims had once been Serbs. So they had to pay for this act of separation by being made separate, reduced, that is, to the state of vermin, creatures whose bodies could as usefully be lined up to be shot on the edge of a ravine or possessed in exquisite revulsion. The mass Serb killing of Muslims in Bosnia was also a form of sexual inebriation.

Too afraid to go home, Mrs. Mehmedović went to stay with a friend.

Two days later, on June 2, 1992, she learned of the systematic Serb cleansing of Zildžići Mahala, the most densely populated Muslim street in Vlasenica. After that, she scarcely moved from her apartment, eking out an existence in Vlasenica until July 18. On that day she was told that Ratko Ostojić, a Serb refugee from the government-held town of Olovo, would move into her house; soldiers forced her onto a bus and she was taken to a village on the front line. From there she walked down into the Bosnian town of Kladanj. Her home became a classroom in the local kindergarten.

The refugee is a pathetic figure. As Yugoslavia unraveled, human flotsam was tossed about on the floors of empty buildings, gathered in chicken coops or idle factories, discarded by the roadside. The remains of the country were awash in such human debris. Mrs. Mehmedović, a big woman, was obliged to use toilets built for four-year-old children.

She slept on a thin mattress on the floor. Two faded black-and-white photographs of her sons were hidden under the mattress. Kemal's showed a young man in JNA uniform—the proudest moment for most parents of the postwar generation, who had seen Tito rebuild Yugoslavia. Mrs. Mehmedović was still touched by that JNA uniform in the same perverse way that some Jewish survivors of the Holocaust clung to photographs of themselves as proud German officers during World War I.

"Like any mother," Mrs. Mehmedović said, "I have to believe my boys are alive."

She gave me one of the photographs. Kladanj is just twenty miles west of Vlasenica, but the war placed it at a great distance. Every road sign of the former Yugoslavia was the forlorn memento of a lost state. Those that survived pointed the way to unreachable places. Others were removed in a deliberate attempt to change the mental geography of people. Croatia, attempting to consolidate the process of separation, pulled down every sign that might suggest the existence of Serbia. A black hole lay beyond its eastern border. The sign in Kladanj that once indicated the way east to Vlasenica had survived. It was the only accurate signpost I saw during the war. The word VLASENICA had been scratched out and replaced by a single word: DEATH.

I made the long journey around the lines—south to Split, from Split to the Croatian capital of Zagreb, from Zagreb to Hungary, from there to Serbia. Popović took a look at the photograph and his expression of recognition was unmistakable. He said, "The two Mehmedović boys were executed in June 1992, after being taken to the Sušica camp."

POPOVIĆ DREW ME a diagram of the concentration camp: the creek along the south side, the barbed-wire fences, a few trees at the eastern end, the electrical pylon against which Muslims were sometimes shot, the small cottage where the commander was lodged, a garbage shed, two toilets, the hangar that had been converted into a storage room, and the other that served as the prisoners' barracks.

At least six hundred Muslims—men, women, and children—were generally held inside the hangar, which was about forty yards long and twenty wide. They were not allowed to wash; in the midsummer heat, the stench was sometimes overwhelming. They were not allowed to talk. On the concrete floor, piled together like slaves in a cargo hold, they sat in silence. The heads of men were shaved. When the guards beat them, they called them *"balija,"* a racial insult for Muslims.

Twice a day, prisoners were allowed to file out of the hangar, in groups of ten, to get a bowl of thin soup and use a toilet. When one of the guards entered, the prisoners had to bow their heads. Dragan Nikolić, the commander, who affected the nickname of "Yankee," liked to hold up a cigarette butt and declare, "This is now worth more than all of your Muslim lives put together."

Nikolić's own net worth was increasing daily. Everything of value was taken from the Muslims. "One woman offered me eighteen thousand German marks to arrange her release," Popović said. "There were nearly twenty thousand Muslims in the county. So you can imagine the money that was being made."

A thin man with a nasal voice who worked in an aluminum plant before the war, Nikolić was not a professional soldier. He joined the Bosnian Serb movement early on and appears to have taken delight in his duties. Muslims were made to sing Serbian songs as they were stripped to the waist and beaten, inside or just outside the hangar; some had Orthodox crosses slashed in their backs with knives. Often, at night, Nikolić would come in drunk with his cronies and pick out a few prisoners at random, who were then shot dead just outside the barracks.

At other times, Popović said, the selection of victims was more systematic. Men suspected of links with the SDA or trafficking in arms were not taken for exchange, but generally executed. Other men who seemed more innocuous were often transported to Batković camp, near Bijeljina, which opened in late June. Once at Batković, a camp that, unlike Sušica, did eventually become known to the International Committee of the Red Cross, they were sometimes exchanged for Serbs in government-held Tuzla. Women and children were held in Sušica for as long as it took to organize their transport to the front line a few miles to the west, where they were abandoned and ordered to walk "to their Alija Izetbegović" in Kladanj.

The whole operation was under the control of the army, represented in Vlasenica by Major Mile Jaćimović, who oversaw the camp. "There is no question that orders came from the highest level," Popović told me. "Our army had a strict chain of command from the outset. Jaćimović received orders from above."

The function of Sušica was spelled out to Popović: the removal, through death or dispersion, of the almost twenty thousand Muslims in the Vlasenica area. The camp formed part of a wider archipelago of perhaps three hundred detention centers whose function was equally clear: the destruction of the non-Serb communities on large swaths of territory running broadly along the Drina River in the east and the Sava River in the north and west.

In the east, the Serb purpose was a double one: the severing of links between the Muslim communities of Bosnia and the Sandžak area of Serbia, elements of what Serb commanders called the "Green Transversal," an allegedly menacing Muslim front running from Turkey up through Albania to Bosnia; and the creation of a seamless expanse of Serb-held and Serb-inhabited territory on either side of the Drina. Along the Sava, the strategic aim was to forge a link with the Serb-held Krajina area of Croatia, taken by force of arms during the Croatian war of 1991. Without this artery, the western lands of Greater Serbia would not be viable.

Because the Serb campaign was always portrayed as defensive, no such plan could ever be avowed. But Marković, the federal prime minister in 1991, did reveal the existence of a plan known by the acronym RAM that involved the arming of Serbs on precisely the territory that was seized in the first months of the Bosnian war.

In this overall pattern, Sušica played its part. It was an organized operation with a precise purpose. All the evidence suggests that the camps in the Prijedor area, in Brčko, in Zvornik, in Bijeljina, in Višegrad, in Foča, and in every other region where "cleansing" took place were substantially similar, in their conditions and their purpose, to Sušica. This coordinated campaign of genocide will take its modest place among the manifold horrors of this century.

EVERYWHERE THERE WAS the swaggering randomness and sadism of Nikolić's nocturnal executions—what Primo Levi, recording his experiences at Auschwitz, called "useless violence"—but equally there was the design that alone produced the contiguity of Serb-held land stretching from Knin in southern Croatia through western and northern Bosnia to Belgrade.

Karadžić always scoffed at any notion of a plan or command structure existing behind the death or exodus of hundreds of thousands of Muslims from this territory. "In the first few months of the war," he told me, "there was no command. Chaos was commanding. What happened was coordinated only by years and years of antagonism and fear. Fear from the Serbs that they would be killed by these Muslim people as they had in the past. Nobody could control it. Our police and our army were not doing this. There was a spontaneous shifting of population."

He smiled his bland smile and ran his manicured hand through his mane of hair. I thought he had finished but, apparently, the thesis that *the complete absence of volition* could explain the movement of hundreds of thousands of people needed further elucidation. "Ethnic cleansing was not our policy. It happened because of fear. Fear and chaos. I was not informed on a daily basis. We received some information from our troops. But civilians were doing all this."

So, the organization that created Sušica and Omarska and Keraterm and Trnopolje and Manjača and Batković and numberless other Serb concentration camps did not exist. The argument had its own twisted logic. The camps were used precisely to reduce the Muslim population of wide areas of Bosnia to nonexistence. They were run by Serbs inebriated by a propaganda suggesting that past and present genocides against them (the former real, the latter imagined) had imbued, for all time, the Serbian people with qualities incompatible with any such crime against humanity. By placing the Serb in the realm of the sacred, the design that created the camps tended to make the torturer immune and the victim invisible. In this overall scheme, of course, the "useless violence" was not entirely gratuitous, for it served the purpose of dehumanizing the Muslim victim, making of him a plaything, the inflatable doll of sadism.

Popović was one of Karadžić's troops. Karadžić coordinated the preparations for war with Milošević. Popović, like all the Bosnian Serb army, was paid through the Ministry of Defense in Belgrade. His orders were clear enough. There was a logistical problem at Sušica. It could only hold about six hundred people at any one time. Inmates had to be moved out to make room for newcomers. So, on a regular basis, men were loaded onto the back of a truck, taken up to the Debelo Brdo hill, and shot. Groups of young soldiers were brought in to perform the executions. The bodies fell into a ravine and bulldozers were later used to cover them over.

During the period of Yugoslavia's dissolution, Serbian newspapers and television had been full of stories from World War II about the Serb bodies buried in the pits of Herzegovina after execution by the Croatian Ustasha. Some of the bones had been exhumed in elaborate ceremonies.

A friend of Popović once took me up to the ravine during the war. Some rubble was evident—remains, he said, of the Vlasenica mosque, which was razed early in the conflict. We did not stay long: the area was closely monitored. I did not see any bones and I cannot say how many may lie beneath the surface or whether one day, like those Serb bones in Herzegovina, they may be exhumed.

Popović had one particular memory. In mid-June 1992, a group of twenty-six people were taken up to the ravine to be executed. A man escaped, he said, running into the woods. His own estimate was that over one thousand Muslims were executed at that one site and close to three thousand people killed during the camp's four-month existence. This estimate seems to be at the high end of what may reasonably be deduced from the evidence.

ZIJAD ZEMIĆ, a Muslim from Vlasenica, entered the camp on the day it opened, June 2, 1992. I found him in Tuzla in northern Bosnia, a city of salt mines and common sense, a town at the heart of the old Yugoslavia, the one place that did not vote for the nationalist parties in 1990. Zemić, who was seventeen years old when he entered the camp, had an earring in his left ear and a stutter. Two Serbs—he knew them as Milan and Mišo—had taken him from his home. It was raining that day and he recalled that he had wanted to get a coat.

Outside a group of about two hundred Muslim men had been rounded up in the surrounding Vlasenica streets. Zemić was thrust into the midst of them and led, head bowed, down to the Sušica camp. There he was searched by Serbs in military and police uniforms; all his documents were taken. He was thrust into the hangar, which was already so crowded there was scarcely a place to sit. Some people were wounded; others, who had apparently been forced to crawl, were filthy.

Nikolić, the camp commander, arrived at the camp about ten days later. Conditions worsened. He would come into the barracks at night, point to men, or read out a list of names. Usually, there were four or five people. They were taken outside. Zemić heard shooting. In the morning he saw blood, later covered by sand. Others were beaten to death inside the hangar—an old man called Asim Zildić, and Durmo Handžić, who had once worked at the post office in Vlasenica.

On July 1, 1992, after almost a month in the camp, Zemić was transferred to Batković camp. On his way out, he had to file through two columns of Serb soldiers lined up on either side of him. They beat him and the other prisoners. This punishment was borrowed from Tito's arsenal. Political prisoners had been sent to the barren Adriatic island of Goli Otok, where thousands disappeared. Newcomers to Goli Otok, a vast labor camp, were made to pass through the so-called *topli zec* (literally "warm rabbit"). They had to run, like rabbits, through a path flanked on either side by other prisoners who were obliged to beat them as they went. Prisoners who failed to beat hard enough were themselves severely beaten by the guards. The idea was clear enough: everyone is watching everyone on the road to physical submission and mental conformity. Survivors later whispered stories of this treatment in Goli Otok, a place that, officially, did not exist. The *topli zec* lived on, to be revived at Sušica.

At Batković, conditions were a little better for Zemić, but random killing continued. On September 8, 1992, he was told that he would be released. He was put on a bus with a group of old people and fifty-three children and told they would be taken to the front line near Tuzla. But they were arrested on the way by a unit of Serb soldiers and imprisoned at Janja, a town between Bijeljina and Zvornik. Later, he was transferred to Zvornik Prison, where he spent five months before being taken back to Batković. The International Committee of the Red Cross registered him as a prisoner of war in March 1993. On May 7, 1993, almost a year after his arrest, he was allowed to cross the lines between Bijeljina and Tuzla.

Hajrudin Merić was also frog-marched from his home on June 2, 1992, and taken to Sušica. His wife and three children were arrested with him, but were released two days later and taken by bus to the front line near Kladanj. Merić stayed in the camp for twenty-eight days before being transferred to Batković on June 30, 1992. However, his older brother, Muharem, stayed on in Sušica; he was never heard of again. A mentally handicapped younger brother, Fadil, also vanished. Merić's father-in-law, Mujo Jusić, and his two sons, Mensur and Mevludin Jusić, remained in Sušica. They, too, "disappeared."

Merić slept in stables at Batković and was made to dig trenches on the Serb front line. There were about thirty-five hundred inmates in the camp, he said. Of a prisoner who had been badly beaten, the Serbs liked to say *"On je našminkan"*—"He has makeup on." When officials from the International Committee of the Red Cross visited the camp, old people, children, and those with "makeup" were hidden by the Serbs, just as the Nazis hid the unpresentable inmates of the Terezin ghetto in Czechoslovakia when they showed it off to the Red Cross in 1944. Those who were shown to the Red Cross officials were presented as "soldiers captured in battle."

Merić was released July 21, 1993, and crossed the lines to Tuzla. He gave me a photograph of his older brother, Muharem, who had been a carpenter. Popović told me he had been executed.

The International Committee of the Red Cross has a book of Bosnian "disappeared." By 1997, there were 18,406 names in it. Muharem Merić carries Red Cross identification number BAZ-102500. Fadil Merić, his younger brother, has the same number. Mujo Jusić is number BAZ-101911. Mensur Jusić, his older son, is number BAZ-102033. Mevludin Jusić, his younger son, is number BAZ-102460. There is, in fact, a whole page of Jusićs. Some of them "disappeared" during the Serb attack on Srebrenica in July 1995. It was to Srebrenica, through the woods to the east of town, that some Muslims who managed to escape Vlasenica and the Sušica camp fled.

CHAPTER 17

BROKEN BRIDGES

THE INTIMACY OF A CAMP LIKE SUŠICA IS EXTRAORDINARY. When the boxcars arrived in Auschwitz, they carried loads from Budapest or Novi Sad. But Popović dealt with his neighbors. "I grew up there," he told me. "I was watching all these people I knew who could not take a shower." Such intimacy provokes a question: Were the Serbs trying to destroy a suppressed image of themselves?

When the Ottoman Turks took Constantinople in 1453, one of the first acts of the sultan, Mehmed II, was to issue a decree qualifying the Byzantine church as untaxable and guaranteeing to it all the privileges it had previously enjoyed. The measure confirmed Mehmed's ambition to take on the multiconfessional imperial mantle of Byzantium, whose capital he had just conquered. The image of the *ghazi,* or warrior against the Christian infidel, that had inspired the first conquests of the Ottomans was dropped. This was a natural step in that Mehmed himself was the son of a mixed marriage: his mother, Mara, the wife of Murad II, was a Serb.

The Ottoman Empire was multinational and multiconfessional. Its existence frustrated a deep-seated ambition of medieval Serbia: to become the successor to the fragmenting Byzantine Empire. Yet the Ottoman dominion was a nuanced world in which a Serb could rise to be the grand vizier or become the wife of the sultan.

The system of *devsirme,* or forced recruitment and conversion of young Christians to serve in the sultan's army, court, or administration, was a cornerstone of the Ottoman system. The Janissary corps, initially formed from prisoners of war, constituted its elite guard. In conversion to Islam lay the possibility of advancement to the summit of the administration; at the same time, the liberty to practice the Christian faith remained. The Ottoman world was often cruel, increasingly so as the centuries passed, the empire began to crumble, and rule became more arbitrary. The rampages of the bashibazouks, or Turkish irregulars, in the nineteenth century provided an archetype for the world's image of Balkan carnage. Nonetheless, to the end, the empire was far from uniform. Yet it was in the undifferentiated terms of the oppressor that the Serbs came to see it, the better to define their own nationhood.

THE EMERGENT NATION-STATES of the nineteenth century all had to invent histories that served to consolidate the new national consciousness of broad masses of people who had not previously thought in such terms. The Serbs were no exception. The Battle of Kosovo, lost to the Turks, became the primary source of the myths that sustained them. In Miloš Obilić, the Serb who supposedly slipped into the tent of Sultan Murad I and stabbed him, a hero was found. To this day, "How shall we meet our Miloš?" is a Serbian expression, used to ask how an individual can rise to become a paladin of Serbian honor. (Ottoman and some Bulgarian versions of the battle, however, state that Murad was not killed by Miloš but while leading an attack on the Serbs.)

An archetypal villain, the Judas of Serb legend, was found in Vuk Branković, whose abandonment of the Kosovo battle at the head of twelve thousand followers allegedly led to defeat and the slaying of Prince Lazar. (Ottoman versions of the battle state that it was the brilliance of Murad's son and successor, Bayezid, that led to victory.) Kosovo, for the Serbs, was entire and luminous. It identified the enemy, it illustrated the power of heroism, it exposed the baseness of treachery.

But Kosovo, portrayed in these terms, was myth. The Serbs had in fact suffered a first crippling defeat to the Ottomans in 1371. At Kosovo, they were flanked by the Bosnian troops of King Tvrtko I in the fight against the Turks. After the defeat, Serbia's relations with the Ottomans were ambiguous. As a vassal Christian principality of the Ottomans, Serbia survived the Battle of Kosovo. Indeed, the son of Prince Lazar, known as Stefan the Despot, offered his daughter to the harem of the sultan.

When, six years after Kosovo, the Turkish sultan Bayezid crossed the Danube in 1395 to take on the Wallachs, Stefan and Marko Kraljević, a hero of Serbian folksongs, fought victoriously by the sultan's side. Kraljević was killed in the battle. A man loved by all Serbs died in the ranks of the Ottomans.

Stefan's successor as despot of Serbia, Djurad Branković, navigated a meandering course between support of the Ottomans and an alliance with Catholic Hungary. He died in 1456, three years before the medieval Serbian state really collapsed with the loss to the Ottomans of the fortress of

Smederevo. At the time, the commander of the Serbian forces, Mihailo Andjelović, was the brother of the grand vizier, a Serb whom the practice of *devsirme* had raised to the highest rank of the Ottoman court.

Another grand vizier of Serb descent, Mehmed Pasha Sokollu (in Serbian, Sokolović) hailed from the village of Sokolovići, near the Drina. Ivo Andrić, the Bosnian novelist, attributes to him the decision to begin work in 1516 on the great stone bridge on the Drina at Višegrad. In *The Bridge on the Drina,* Andrić writes that the vizier was driven by the desire to "bridge the steep banks and the evil water between them, join the two ends of the road which was broken by the Drina and thus link safely and forever Bosnia and the East, the place of his origin and the places of his life."

Such links were possible. The Ottoman order, imposed on Bosnia for more than four centuries after the conquest of 1462, was not monolithic. Advancement in the Ottoman administration was generally contingent on conversion to Islam, but a measure of religious tolerance was guaranteed through the *millet,* self-governing Christian communities that were a basic unit of the empire's structure. There was no Bosnian Inquisition. Jews from Spain fled to the more tolerant universe of the Ottoman Empire. Peoples and religions coexisted, not joyfully, not without mutual suspicion, but in a way that secured long periods of relative tranquility.

The Ottoman regime, particularly in so distant a province, was often a harsh world of sloth and administrative decay, a place of sometimes overwhelming fatalism, cut off from its surroundings, locked in a quasi-feudal immobility. But backwardness did not always equal bigotry. Bosnia was a realm of osmosis rather than exclusion. It was not impossible, for example, for an Orthodox convert to Islam to rise to the top of the sultan's court in Istanbul even as his brother became an Orthodox monk.

Indeed, throughout the early years of Ottoman dominion in the Balkans, Orthodox inhabitants of the Ottoman Empire tended to fare better than the Catholics, for it was the Catholic world and the pope that periodically issued calls to arms against the Turks, not the Orthodox patriarch, who was vulnerable in that he continued to exercise his functions in Istanbul. The Orthodox Serbs could at times find allies in the Ottomans against the Western church. This only ceased to be true during the nineteenth century when the Serbs' push for emancipation from Istanbul turned the Catholic population of Bosnia into natural allies of the Turks in confronting the Serbs.

The nineteenth century was a time of growing violence. Tensions between the mainly Muslim big landowners and the mainly Christian sharecroppers and peasantry rose. This was the period of national uprisings against Ottoman rule in the Balkans: Greeks, Serbs, and Bulgarians all sought, and ultimately gained, liberation. Bosnia could not remain untouched by these stirrings.

Nationalist movements in Serbia and Croatia saw potential followers, and the source of territorial expansion, in the Orthodox and Catholic populations of Bosnia. Serbia would gain a coastline, Croatia a coherent shape, if Bosnia could be absorbed. In Belgrade and Zagreb claims that the Orthodox and Catholic Bosnians were "Serbs" and "Croats" became more insistent.

Often these claims proved fruitful because social and national tensions overlapped. The sharecroppers and serfs (*kmets*) were generally Christians; economic hardship made them natural candidates for co-option by the Serbs or Croats. In 1870, Ottoman statistics of approximate value estimated that 49.8 percent of the Bosnian population was Muslim, 36.4 percent Orthodox or Serb, and 12.8 percent Croat or Catholic. Other estimates put the Christian population much higher.

It was a Serb peasant uprising against Ottoman rule in 1875 that foreshadowed the collapse of the Turkish administration in 1878 and the handover of control of Bosnia to Austria-Hungary. The fierce fighting during the 1875 uprising, followed by a slight redrawing of Bosnia's borders at the Congress of Berlin and the departure of many Muslims to Turkey with the end of Ottoman rule, changed the Bosnian population balance. By 1879, according to Austro-Hungarian figures, 38.8 percent of the population was Muslim, 43 percent Serb, and 18 percent Croat.

Population ratios changed, but Bosnia's multiconfessional nature did not. In the emergent era of the European nation-state, the problem with Bosnia was that there was no titular "nation." Indeed, the essence of Bosnian identity lay precisely in its heterogeneity. As Tito conceded, "Bosnia is one, because of centuries-old common life, regardless of confession."

For centuries, in this Balkan world, symbiosis and antagonism coexisted in the relationship of Turk and Serb. Many Serbs wore fezzes; Turkish expressions littered their language. Miloš Obrenović, the Serb who led the second uprising against the Turks in 1815, had a Turkish mansion, complete with a divan, built for himself in the middle of Belgrade to celebrate his capture of the town. Belgrade, at the beginning of the nineteenth century, was a city dotted with mosques.

The Serbianization of Serbia required first the separation and then the elimination of the Ottomans; it required the destruction of the mosques and of all the "bridges," physical and emotional, of the likes of Mehmed Pasha Sokollu. The Muslims of Bosnia were a reminder of the mottled reality and mutable past that had no place in Serbia's nation-forming myths. Converts to another faith, these Bosnian Muslims awakened a suppressed, anti-heroic image of Serbia, the image least tolerable to a nation on the march under the banner of Milošević's apotheosis at Kosovo field.

The Serbianization of Bosnia, like the Serbianization of Serbia before it, required the obliteration of this image. It required the most intimate form of destruction—that of the person in the mirror, that closest to suicide.

THE PACE OF KILLING accelerated in the Sušica camp after a local Serb hero was killed on July 5, 1992, in a Muslim ambush at a village called Barica, a few miles from Vlasenica. The hero, Dragoljub Stojišić, was known as "Kalimeiro," a popular Serb cartoon character. He was revered for his bravery and skills as an auto mechanic. Heavy reprisals were exacted for his death. Popović told me that about three hundred Muslim prisoners at Sušica were killed by firing squad.

Refija Hadžić was rounded up three days later. A Serb soldier came to her Vlasenica apartment and ordered her to undress in front of her eight-year-old daughter. She was beaten with the butt of his gun and cut with a knife. Her husband, Ejub Hadžić, had been taken away half an hour earlier. She has never seen him again. He is among the "disappeared," bearing Red Cross number BAZ-102453.

Mrs. Hadžić was held for ten days in Sušica. Certain memories remain: a man who had his ear cut off; the killing of Ismet Dedić; the way dead bodies would lie inside the hangar for several hours before a guard would come with bags and remove them. On July 18, she was put on a bus with other women and driven westward toward Kladanj. But the bus was stopped on the way and several younger women—including twenty-seven-year-old Aida Karac (BAZ-102208)—were removed by Serb soldiers.

I found Hadžira Hodžić, another Vlasenica refugee, in the same kindergarten as Mrs. Mehmedović. She and her two children were surviving on the soup and bread distributed twice a day by the local authorities. Her husband, Rasim Hodžić, was taken from their apartment on July 1, 1992, along with several other Muslims who lived in the building, among them Mahmut Ambesković (BAZ-101015) and Murat Dautović (BAZ-102400). Mrs. Hodžić was able to see her husband at the police station for five days, but on July 6, 1992, the day after Kalimeiro was killed, she was told he had been taken away. She never saw him again.

BY SEPTEMBER 1992, the only Muslims left in Vlasenica were old people or invalids whom the Serbs had refrained from shifting before. Their turn now came. On September 15, 1992, a Serb soldier came to the Vlasenica home of Tima Handžić. Aged ninety-three, she was lying in bed when the soldier kicked in the door and ordered her to come with him.

"Kill me at my door," she said. "I can't move."

The soldier replied, "I don't want to kill you but you have to come with me."

Mrs. Handžić's daughter, Meira, was also in the house. "We had no shoes on," she said, "and we were not allowed to put them on."

The two women were driven to Sušica, where they found several hundred people sprawled on the concrete floor of the hangar. A surprise awaited Meira Handžić. Among the prisoners was her son, Suljo, who had been arrested on June 1. Her son embraced her and said, "Now that you are here, I see that it's finished. There is no hope."

Tima and Meira Handžić were loaded onto a bus the following afternoon and driven, in the usual procedure, to a village near Kladanj. "Go to your Alija," was the parting order from their Serb guard.

In Kladanj, Meira Handžić found another of her sons, Abdulah Handžić, a passionate chess player whose friendship with the Serb president of the Vlasenica chess club had saved him. On May 17, 1992, armed with a special pass provided to him by the president of the chess club, Abdulah Handžić had escaped from Vlasenica. By 1994, he was a soldier of the First Muslim Brigade of the II Corps of the Bosnian army, walking with a limp after stepping on a mine. He was driven by twin hopes: that Vlasenica might be "liberated" and that Suljo might be alive.

But Popović told me that Suljo Handžić had been executed after the closure of the Sušica camp. The camp closed in late September 1992, when Major Jaćimović determined that its task had been completed. At the time, there were about two hundred Muslim prisoners left in the camp. About half were executed on the spot, Popović said. The rest, including Suljo Handzić (BAZ-102435), were taken up to the front lines to the west and used to dig trenches until they, too, were killed.

By the time Vlasenica closed, two months had passed since the discovery in early August of Omarska, Trnopolje, Manjača, and the other camps used in the cleansing of the Banja Luka and Prijedor areas. Unlike these camps in northwestern Bosnia that were uncovered by Roy Gutman and then visited for the first time by Ed Vulliamy of the British daily newspaper *The Guardian,* and a television crew from Britain's ITN channel, Sušica was never found. It had gone on functioning for more than two months after the photograph of a skeletal Bosnian Muslim prisoner named Fikret Alić, standing behind barbed wire at the Trnopolje camp in sunken-eyed bewilderment, his ribs pressing through his skin, had at last stirred Europe to the realization that its ghosts had risen.

I asked Popović if there had been any concern that Sušica would be discovered by the United States government or other Western powers. "None," he said. "We went on functioning as before. When we closed, it was simply that there were no more Muslims left in the Vlasenica area."

Of course, it was not merely the Vlasenica area that had been "cleansed," but 70 percent of Bosnia. As at Sušica, the conditions were everywhere unspeakable. In 1993, one State Department official recorded this testimony from a Muslim, a highly credible professional man, who survived the Serbs' Luka camp at Brčko and went to live as a Luka refugee in Scandinavia.

> *"After his initial interrogation in the office building near the docks, he was taken with other prisoners to hangar 2 of the loading dock. The prisoners were forced to look into the interior of hangar 2. Inside he saw a pile of more than 200 corpses, or torsos, all bloodied. Most of the body parts had been chopped off: hands, arms and genitals. He recalled noticing a head rolling toward him out of hangar 2. The quantity of mostly coagulated blood visible in the hangar was so great, in his words, that three barrels would not have sufficed to hold it. The prisoners standing outside hangar 2 were told that that was how they would end up if they told lies while being interrogated. When a 13-year-old boy tried to protect his father from the sight, one of the 'Chetniks' hit the boy with the butt of a gun, shattering his face. The guard killed the boy's father with three shots when he went after him for what he had done to the boy."*

IT WAS NOT EASY to get such detailed information on Bosnia during the summer of 1992. Frederic Maurice, the head of the International Committee of the Red Cross in Sarajevo, was killed on May 18, and the organization pulled out of the country for several weeks. The United States embassy in Belgrade, chiefly responsible for monitoring the area, lost many of its contacts in eastern Bosnia in May because the situation became too dangerous and telephone lines were cut.

Muslim refugees were going the other way—westward toward Croatia, where the American consulate of Yugoslav days was replaced by an American embassy on August 24, 1992. Even then, however, it amounted to a fledgling operation. Ron Neitzke, who arrived as Consul General on August 1 and became chargé d'affaires when the embassy opened, said that reporting on Bosnia remained a "jealously-guarded prerogative of Embassy Belgrade, and the specific testimonies of refugees fleeing into Croatia went untapped." Until well into August, despite a mounting volume of testimony about the genocide proceeding apace, "the State Department was still referring, even in private communication, to 'alleged camps' in Bosnia," Neitzke told me.

George Kenney was then the Yugoslav desk officer in Washington. "By June," he told me in 1994, "and certainly by July, we were getting reports from northern Bosnia that, if we had wanted to look closely, would have been very disturbing. In July, we had maybe a dozen reports of really barbaric things being done by the Serbs. The reports were anecdotal, but they came from good local contacts who had proved reliable in the past." Kenney said that he tried several times to introduce the word *genocide* into official accounts of what was happening in Bosnia-Herzegovina. "I thought it was warranted, but there was absolutely no acceptance of that."

The Bosnian government says that it first used the word on July 19, when Izetbegović wrote to President Bush complaining of "genocide" being perpetrated by the Serbs against the Muslims of Bosnia. Before that, in mid-June, the government had presented a list of 161 "concentration camps," including Omarska, to international officials in Zagreb. But the list was widely dismissed as propaganda.

When President François Mitterrand came to Sarajevo on June 28, 1992, Izetbegović informed him of the camps, but there was no reaction. On July 3, United Nations staff in Croatia drafted an internal memorandum noting the probable existence of four Serbian "concentration camps" in northern and western Bosnian and the "concerted action of local Serbian authorities to establish a Serbian Republic of Bosnia-Herzegovina free of Muslims." The report had no visible impact.

On July 29, 1992, the president of the International Committee of the Red Cross, Cornelio Sommaruga, came as close as anyone to making the facts public at last. Referring to the war in Bosnia, he said, "Behind this nightmare situation, nourished by revenge and hate, there is a deliberate plan based on the exclusion of other groups." The plan, he continued, involved "the terrible ravages of ethnic cleansing, in whose name whole populations are being terrorized, minorities intimidated and harassed, civilians interned on a massive scale, hostages taken, and torture, deportation, and summary executions are rife." The methods, he said, recalled "the horrors of the Second World War." Then, displaying the prudence of an organization that must operate on all sides of the lines, he added that the methods "are used by all the parties involved, to an extent determined by the means at their disposal." The message, for those interested, was clear enough: the means to execute a deliberate plan recalling World War II were overwhelmingly in the hands of the Serbs, who had inherited the JNA's weapons.

"As I've read the definition of genocide, this was genocide," Jim Swigert, then the chief political officer in the Belgrade embassy, told me. "But we did not want to say that. The marching orders from President Bush were that Yugoslavia was essentially a European problem and we were to stay out of it." Kenney said the basic approach was to "stonewall" in the face of information about the Serb camps.

• • •

How much did the Bush administration know about the systematic Serb killing of Muslims between April and October 1992, an act of genocide that, by most estimates, accounted for between 75 and 80 percent of the total slaughter in Bosnia throughout the forty-month war? Neitzke, now a senior State Department official in Washington, has looked into the matter closely and concluded: "The Bush administration's attitude toward genocide in Bosnia was a combination of willful ignorance and determined indifference. If they did not know precisely how many were being killed in the death camps in real time, nonetheless they knew from multiple sources a good deal more than they were comfortable knowing—given their fixed policy—about what was happening at very close to the time it was happening."

With the Gulf War triumphantly concluded and the election just a few months away, President Bush had no interest in building the case for an American-led intervention in Bosnia. His "fixed policy," in essence, was: no American intervention, whatever may be happening. Bush had the means to build an argument for action: the American people are not insensitive to images seemingly lifted whole from Treblinka, and such images, in early August 1992, existed. Their potential political resonance was immense.

But this potential was deliberately squandered because its consequence might be an intervention that the administration did not want on the eve of an election it thought it could win. Neitzke said, "The Bush State Department on Bosnia distinguished itself for the sheer audacity of its efforts to misinform and confuse a partly roused and further rousable American public as to the nature, extent, and one-sidedness of the slaughter and the potential utility of an American military response. The tone of their approach changed only slightly for the better in their waning months in office."

The expertise on Yugoslavia in 1992 at senior levels of government was extraordinary. Eagleburger, the deputy secretary of state and later secretary of state, had been ambassador in Belgrade; Brent Scowcroft, Bush's national security adviser, had also served in Yugoslavia; so, too, had Tom Niles, the assistant secretary of state for European affairs. At their disposal was an intelligence-gathering system built up over forty-five years of intermittent American obsession with a country poised perilously between East and West. Yet, like the Joint Chiefs of Staff, who, as Neitzke said, "moved decisively into the realm of national security and foreign policy decision-making on Bosnia," these men concerned themselves not with the genocide taking place but with a pitiful attempt to find evidence for wrongdoing on all sides, to portray Bosnia as an intractable morass that had defeated the Wehrmacht during World War II, and to reinforce vague notions of the Balkans as a focus of ancient blood feuds. In testimony to the Committee on Armed Services on August 11, 1992, General Barry McCaffrey, representing the Joint Chiefs of Staff, estimated he would need four hundred thousand troops to quell the violence—an astonishing figure.

Yet the basic nature of this "violence" was clear enough: marauding Serb military and paramilitary forces herding unarmed Muslim civilians into concentration camps in order to "cleanse" entire areas of Bosnia of their non-Serb populations. It is true that Muslims also killed Serb civilians, notably in Sarajevo, in these early months of the war. But the scale, the intensity, the consistency, and the brutality of the Serb campaign at this time were quite without equal. Moreover, the thugs leading the campaign were almost certainly vulnerable to even a limited display of American resolve.

But rather than confront the genocide, an attempt was made to pretend it was not happening. As late as August 21, 1992, Eagleburger declared of the genocide in Bosnia that, "On the basis of what we have so far, I think it's best to say the evidence is unpleasant conditions." He added that the term "death camp" was inappropriate for the Serb-run camps in Bosnia, if what was meant by that was "an Auschwitz or a Belsen." He thus appeared to justify America's inaction on the basis that what the Serbs were doing to the Muslims was horrific but not quite as bad as what the Nazis had done to the Jews.

Neitzke, who was in a position to know, says that from early in the summer of 1992 "numerous cables were sent in conveying (of necessity) secondhand reports of massive 'ethnic cleansing,' torture and killing and a network of Serb-run 'detention centers.' " Moreover, Neitzke confirmed to me that "the administration had at its disposal, well before Eagleburger's late August denials, satellite imagery showing the progressive enlargement of camps in exact places reported in other channels." His conclusion is that either Eagleburger was "wittingly dissembling" or the intelligence community was still unaware of the corroboration the imagery might reveal. "What is clear," says Neitzke, "is that in order to preserve at least a fig leaf of U.S. government deniability of awareness of death camps, precious few resources were devoted to the task of ascertaining what the intelligence already on hand would substantiate, and no effort was made to obtain the supposedly vital on-site verification—other than through hoped-for but predictably constrained International Committee of the Red Cross visits."

A COMPELLING ARGUMENT for intervention, at the head of a multilateral force, might have been built around the photographs of Omarska and Trnopolje, just as a case for the intervention in Kuwait was built at the

United Nations in 1991. The flouting of the basic principles of the United Nations Charter, of the rules of war and of international law was incontrovertibly evident in the existence of the camps and in the consistent bombardment of the civilian population of towns. The existence of a "threat to international peace and security," to quote the United Nations Charter, was also manifest. But the will, in this instance, was absent. From that moment, in the summer of 1992, the unraveling of Bosnia gained an irresistible momentum.

For a half century, the world lived with a division into rival blocs and the nuclear threat. Mutual assured destruction was a simple concept. A world no longer bipolar is more nuanced. Limited military intervention is possible.

There are no friends in foreign policy, the saying goes, only interests. The determination therefore had to be made that Serb genocide against the Muslims of Bosnia, daily terror against civilians, the flouting of international law, the dismemberment of an internationally recognized state situated in the inflammatory midst of a Europe in transition—that all this, cumulatively, represented an unacceptable affront to American interests. Using the narrowest possible definition of the American interest, one that turned its back both on the history of the American idea and on the history of Europe in the twentieth century, that determination was not made in 1992.

After the contradictory and belated acknowledgment in early August that something horrendous might be happening, President Bush said he was ordering U.S. intelligence agencies to use "every last asset" in an attempt to discover what was really happening in Bosnia. A few weeks later, officials said these efforts did not confirm "institutionalized killing." But Kenney said the "new resources" that had been deployed were, in fact, "nonexistent."

On August 25, 1992, Kenney resigned in protest at American policy. In his formal letter of resignation, he wrote, "I can no longer in clear conscience support the administration's ineffective, indeed counterproductive, handling of the Yugoslav crisis. I am therefore resigning in order to help develop a stronger public consensus that the U.S. must act immediately to stop the genocide in Bosnia and prevent this conflict from spreading throughout the Balkans."

Peter Galbraith, then on the staff of the Senate Foreign Relations Committee and later the Clinton administration's ambassador to Zagreb, was also appalled. In Bosnia between August 7 and August 14, 1992, he concluded that America's record in the face of the Serb onslaught was "sorry and sordid." He noted that there was not one addition to the staff of the Zagreb embassy in August 1992. This was an odd omission. The embassy would have been the obvious base from which to gather intelligence if a desire to do so had existed. Muslim refugees were fleeing, in large numbers, westward toward Croatia.

"We did not want to know what was going on, did not want to confront it, and did not want to act," Galbraith said. "This was the last issue the Bush administration wanted to deal with in August 1992."

Only months later, on December 16, 1992, did Eagleburger acknowledge publicly the terrible scale of what had occurred in Bosnia, speaking of the events there in the same breath as the Holocaust. Naming Milošević, Karadžić, and Mladić as men potentially responsible for war crimes, he said: "We have, on the one hand, a moral and historical obligation not to stand back a second time in this century while a people faced obliteration. The fact of the matter is that we know what crimes against humanity have occurred, and we know when and where they occurred. We know, moreover, which forces committed those crimes, and under whose command they operated. And we know, finally, who the political leaders are to whom those military commanders were—and still are—responsible."

By then, however, it was much too late for the prisoners of Sušica and other camps. Indeed, for fully two months after the early-August outcry over Omarska, Sušica was able to continue administering death to the Muslims of eastern Bosnia without the least disturbance.

AN AMERICAN DETERMINATION to confront the concentration camps in Bosnia might have helped Muska Šestović, the wife of Ruzdija, for she was not finally removed from her Vlasenica home until July 29, 1992. On July 19, there was a knock on the door of her apartment. It was her neighbor, Goran Visković, who had earlier searched the apartment and warned the family not to go out. His mood had changed. He pointed a Kalashnikov at Mrs. Seštović and her terrified niece and nephew, Vahda and Salih Ibišević. Flanking him were four other armed men whom Mrs. Šestović did not know.

"I said to Visković, 'You know me, you know my husband,' " Mrs. Šestović recalled. " 'How can you do this to me?'

" 'That time is over,' Visković replied. 'I no longer know you. You chose your Alija Izetbegović.' "

Outside, Visković pointed his weapon at Mrs. Šestović and made her lie on the road. Then he ordered her to crawl along the street. He kicked her at his leisure. Finally, she and the two teenagers were pushed into a small bus filled with Muslims and taken to Sušica camp. There, she was particularly repulsed by the severing of one man's ear, and by Nikolić's habit of forcing children to kneel and kiss his feet.

After ten days in the camp, Mrs. Šestović and her niece and nephew were bundled onto a bus along with other women and children and driven up toward the front line about ten miles from Kladanj. On the way, a group of Serb soldiers blocked the road and lined up the passengers outside the bus. They took thirteen young women, aged between fourteen and twenty, including her niece, Vahda Ibišević (BAZ-101955), who was never seen again.

Vahda was twenty years old when she disappeared. To what sexual use, I wonder, was she put?

THE SERB OBSESSION with the sexuality, fertility, and promiscuity of the Muslims was striking to me. It was a young Serb soldier named Milomir who first drew my attention to this.

We were standing, early in the war, in the Lukavica barracks, near Sarajevo, and he was explaining, in heated terms, the Serb case in Bosnia: "The Muslims expelled us from Kosovo with their sexual organs," he said. "They want to do the same here. The way they reproduce, they need room. You will soon feel that elsewhere in Europe." He pointed to a poster, then popular in Serb barracks, showing the blue flag of the European Union with green paint dripping all over it. Green is the color of Islam. The caption read, "This is not a paint commercial. This is the future."

Biljana Plavšić, the former professor of biology from Sarajevo University who became the deputy leader of Karadžić's movement and later a most unlikely standard-bearer of the Dayton Peace Agreement, liked to expound on the Muslims sexual proclivities. In September 1993, she wrote in the Belgrade newspaper *Borba* (*Struggle*) that "alas, rape is the war strategy of Muslims and some Croats against the Serbs. Islam considers this something normal since this religion tolerates polygamy. Historically, during the five centuries of the Turkish occupation, it was quite normal for Muslim notables to enjoy the *jus primae noctis* with Christian women. It should be stressed that Islam considers that the national identity of the child is determined by the father." Summing up, Ms. Plavšić described the Muslims as pursuing a form of "sexual terror" that was "genocidal in character."

Throughout the war, there was a mirror at work in the Serb mind. Their psyche had become infected, like that of the policeman who has worked all his career on wiretaps and goes insane because he is convinced that people are listening to him at every moment. Whatever the Serbs had suffered, at any time in history or merely in their imaginations, was what they inflicted. Genocide, concentration camps, and rape were the perennial lot of the Serb people; so they imposed them on others. Thousands of Muslim women were systematically raped by the Serbs in 1992.

In the case of rape, part of the "cleansing" of 1992, there may have been a double incentive at work: the circumcised penis of the Muslim male was the most visible symbol of his imagined "treason" in converting from Christianity to Islam. Sexual humiliation of the Muslim was thus a form of all-embracing revenge, a visible reassertion of Serbdom that would people Bosnia with "little Serbs" and so check the advance of the Islamic hordes. Mrs. Šestović's twenty-year-old niece, I suspect, paid the price for this particular delirium.

ONCE IN BOSNIAN GOVERNMENT TERRITORY, Mrs. Šestović made her way to Tuzla, because she had heard that the city was a center for prisoner exchanges and she was convinced that her husband, Ruzdija, would eventually appear there. Ermin Šestović, her son, did odd jobs in Zagreb until March 1993, when he joined the ranks of the 121,000 people from the former Yugoslavia seeking asylum in Sweden. The asylum was granted. But by the time Ermin tried to bring his mother and sister to join him in Sweden in the late summer of 1993, the Swedish government had stopped admitting refugees from the area.

So Ermin decided to try to get his mother to Germany, which had already accepted more than four hundred thousand refugees from the former Yugoslavia. He needed money. His family had never set foot in a mosque. It seemed to Ermin that the mosque in Göteborg, Sweden, might prove the best source for the funds he needed. So it was that the first time Ermin Šestović went to a mosque was in the fall of 1993, in Göteborg.

Over a week-long period he managed to raise five hundred marks, mainly from Pakistani families. This was enough to get his mother and sister to Berlin in December 1993. Muska Šestović had been seeing a medium in Croatia before her departure, and the medium suggested that Ruzdija was alive.

I thought that Popović might be able to throw some light on Ruzdija's fate, but he knew nothing of the Šestović family. So I tried asking Karadžić himself if he could find out anything about Ruzdija. He brushed off my inquiry. "I do not know this individual, Šestović," he told me. "The experience of past wars suggests that it can take up to ten years for individuals to appear. We are searching for seven thousand missing Serbs from Sarajevo. Many of the Muslim missing have left." He waved his arm in a dismissive gesture and added, "Some are even in Pakistan."

So I was left with Dukić, the former colleague of Ruzdija Šestović and cofounder of the SDS. My conversation with him in Belgrade meandered for several hours. His conscience was clearly nagging him. In 1988, when Dukić was briefly detained in Belgrade on embezzlement charges, Šestović had traveled to the Yugoslav capital to try to obtain his release. Thus Dukić has a debt to his Muslim friend.

Dukić told me he believed that Šestović might have reached Tuzla. But informed that Mrs. Šestović waited there for many months, he conceded that this was very unlikely. Then he told the story of another Muslim employee of the Milići mine, Mehmed Mlaćo (BAZ-100095), who had been a friend of his and disappeared in Vlasenica in September 1992. "I looked for Mlaćo for many months," Dukić said, "and I found out he was taken by a paramilitary group between Vlasenica and Kladanj and killed."

He looked at me, as if to ask if things were becoming clear. I looked back, wanting him to go on inching toward what he really wanted to say.

Then, at last, he gathered himself and said, "Look, Ruzdija Šestović was an innocent man, caught up in uncontrollable things. There were a lot of paramilitary groups in the Vlasenica area, and they were killing Muslims. I feel very bad for Mrs. Šestović and if I can do anything to help the family, I would like to. I understand the need the Serbs felt for protection but not this madness. There was no reason at all for Ruzdija Šestović to get killed. Tell his wife I send my regards and I will try to find out more."

Dukić had circled endlessly, like a vulture waiting for a prone animal's last agony to end. Finally, he had made it fairly clear that Ruzdija Šestović (BAZ-105810) was dead, while leaving the faintest glimmer of hope. As I left, he confided that his attempts to find out more would be delicate. "If you ask questions, people want to know why you want to know. They are afraid of war-crimes trials."

UNITED NATIONS SECURITY COUNCIL Resolution 827 of May 25, 1993, established the International Criminal Tribunal for the Former Yugoslavia. The resolution cited "reports of mass killings, massive, organized and systematic detention and rape of women, and the continuance of the practice of 'ethnic cleansing,' including for the acquisition and holding of territory." The pious hope was expressed that the court would contribute to the "restoration and maintenance of peace" in the region.

But it took another four months for eleven judges to be confirmed by the United Nations. It took more than a year of wrangling among member states to find a chief prosecutor, the South African judge Richard Goldstone, who accepted the job on July 6, 1994. Only then could work finally begin in earnest on developing cases from the sixty-eight thousand pages of evidence submitted by a United Nations–appointed commission of experts headed by Cherif Bassiouni, a law professor at Chicago's DePaul University.

It was late in the day. The world had belatedly decided to try to judge acts that it had not sought to stop, acts committed, in their overwhelming majority, by Serb forces it was not ready to confront or defeat. The undertaking was, in its very essence, flawed—a worthy battle but also a surrogate one and, as such, largely unwinnable.

Popović got his wishes. Having talked to him three times, I put him in touch with American officials. Eventually, he was questioned by investigators from the Yugoslav War Crimes Tribunal in The Hague and granted asylum in the United States. His testimony was apparently of value: On November 7, 1994, Dragan Nikolić, the Sušica commander, became the first man indicted by the tribunal. But, like so many of his prisoners, Nikolić was nowhere to be found.

PART THREE

BLEEDING
HEARTS

CHAPTER 18

A DEATH OBSERVED

THE MOUNTAINS TAUNTED BISERA ZEČEVIĆ WITH THEIR MOR-
tars and their memories. Devoured by the loss of her son Muris she gazed
at them. By the summer of 1993 tears welled constantly. She smoked and
stared from the window of the family apartment in central Sarajevo. She
became so thin that she had to spend time in the hospital. Asim could not
comfort her. His placidness was unbearable at times.

She would go to the western suburb of Butmir, where the family had
built a summer house shortly before the war broke out. The whole Zečević family had gone in 1991 to celebrate Bairam. Bisera was never religious; the celebration was her concession to her husband. For the party
Asim had bought a lamb and his sons had helped him skewer it on a spit
and cook it over a fire. Butmir now lay beyond the Serb lines to the southwest of the city, and getting there was hazardous. She wanted to be inhabited by the memories of that place and find release, even fleeting, from a
slow extinction.

Escape from Sarajevo, in the summer of 1993, meant running across
the exposed airport. Haris had got away in February, crossing the airport
at night; Bisera would follow him. With one son dead and another gone,
there was little to hold her back. She wanted to go in July but spilled boil-
ing water on her leg and was unable to walk for twenty days. Asim tried to
stop her from taking the risk, but she was adamant. Her sister-in-law, Fida
Karišik, tried to dissuade her and was met by a sharp reply: "Don't make
conflict in my home. I have decided to go and that is the end of it."

A friend of Muris's named Anan agreed to go with her. She had been
happy about the thought of going, inhabited by a new lightness. But as they
started across the airfield in the early hours of August 11, 1993, she was
suddenly scared. The two ran side by side, until United Nations soldiers
beamed a spotlight on them. There were shots from the Serb forces on the

Ilidža side of the airport. Bisera, a bullet in her stomach, fell to her knees. Anan urged her on, telling her she could still move. But she could not.

The airport had been under United Nations control for just over a year, since June 29, 1992. UNPROFOR—the United Nations Protection Force—had been created four months earlier, on February 21, 1992, but its mission was initially unrelated to Bosnia. The force was to consolidate the ceasefire in the Croatian war, secured at the beginning of 1992, by policing and demilitarizing certain "protected areas" that had been seized by Serb paramilitary forces, backed by the JNA, during the six-month conflict. But, with an eerie maladroitness that was to prove enduring, Sarajevo was chosen as the headquarters for this Croatian mission. It was seen as neutral ground between Belgrade and Zagreb!

So it was that there were already a few UN personnel in Bosnia at the time the Bosnian war broke out in April. Many withdrew in May as the situation became increasingly dangerous, but by early June UNPROFOR had a mission in Bosnia: to secure the airport, then held by Serb forces, and ensure its reopening for the "unimpeded delivery of humanitarian supplies to Sarajevo." The United Nations presence in Bosnia was to grow steadily. By June 1995, there were 19,756 troops in Bosnia out of a total of over 44,000 deployed in the former Yugoslavia.

When President François Mitterrand of France came to Sarajevo on June 28, 1992, it was St. Vitus Day, the anniversary of the Kosovo battle in 1389 and of the provocative, fatal visit to Sarajevo in 1914 by the Habsburg heir Franz Ferdinand. Mitterrand met Izetbegović in Sarajevo and was told about the Serb camps. However, he appears to be have been looking at the war through another lens, one he had explained to the *Frankfurter Allgemeine Zeitung:* "As you know, Croatia was part of the Nazi bloc, not Serbia." Serb concentration camps were unthinkable. It was a case of history blinding, rather than enlightening, an old man.

Later, and in secret, Mitterrand met Karadžić at the airport. The immediate upshot was the Serb handover, the following day, of the airport to the United Nations; General Lewis Mackenzie of Canada raised the flag. The longer-term upshot was that "humanitarianism"—in this case the delivery of aid to the three hundred thousand people encircled in Sarajevo—became the world's agreed response to the bombardment of the Bosnian capital and the camps of which Izetbegović had informed Mitterrand.

The humanitarianism of the late twentieth century sees victims on all sides; succoring them involves neutrality. As expressed at Sarajevo Airport, this "neutrality" meant stopping Sarajevans like Bisera Zečević from escaping across the airfield. To do otherwise, United Nations commanders argued, was to stray from impartiality and the agreement with Karadžić that gave them control of the airport.

An unspeakable chasm existed between the facts and the pious tone of the ninety-eight resolutions on the former Yugoslavia that emanated from the UN in New York. I would sometimes imagine how a truthful resolution might read: *"Recalling that the borders of Bosnia and Herzegovina are inviolable; deploring further that its call for the immediate cessation of forcible expulsions and attempts to change the ethnic composition of the population has not been heeded; dismayed that conditions have not been established for the unhindered delivery of humanitarian assistance; recalling its primary responsibility under the Charter of the United Nations for the maintenance of international peace and security; the Security Council has decided to request UNPROFOR to beam a spotlight on a fifty-two-year-old Muslim woman trying to escape from the city of Sarajevo following the death of her son and sixteen months under siege."*

When Bisera Zečević fell, a victim now desperately in need of humanitarian assistance, the UN came to her aid. A transporter picked her and Anan up. He was dropped off on the Sarajevo side and she was taken, still alive, to a field hospital. The next day Asim Zečević went to the Koševo Hospital to look for her.

His wife was not at the hospital, so he went to the morgue. He found her naked. Adnan Hodžić, the blue-eyed guardian of the morgue, told him she had been delivered by UN personnel. Bundled in a plastic bag, she arrived at the mortuary stripped of her clothes, her rings and other jewelry, none of which was ever recovered.

On the bag a single word was written: UNKNOWN.

ALMOST A YEAR before Bisera Zečević died in the cool gleam of international humanitarianism, I had an early insight into the fatal ambiguities of the UN mission to Bosnia.

The scene was a gentle one, full of a breezy late-summer lushness and lethargy: plum trees, sheep, cottages with red-tiled roofs and neat piles of timber stacked outside. Horse-drawn carts loaded with more wood for the approaching winter wound up narrow lanes. In the midst of a field stood a dozen 122-millimeter Serb artillery pieces with their barrels pointing toward Sarajevo.

The guns, in their ungainliness, might have passed for forgotten relics—were it not for the distant boom of artillery. But their oddity in this bucolic setting on a hill called Tilava about eight miles from the Bosnian capital was surpassed by that of three onlookers: young men sitting beside a wooden shack and wearing the light blue berets of UNPROFOR. They had binoculars and notebooks and light arms and very detailed maps and they were as crisply turned out as any soldier awaiting inspection on the parade ground. Captain Patrick von Hoorebeke of Belgium introduced himself. He was flanked by Captain Rolf Sainsbury of Switzerland and a Major Ibrahim of Jordan, who thought it more prudent not to give his last name.

It was September 14, 1992, early in a long war. We sat down in the hut; coffee was prepared; we exchanged pleasantries. Then I asked them the obvious question: What were they doing on this Bosnian hillside? They gave this some thought. "We can't control the situation," Captain von Hoorebeke said, "but we do monitor it."

That day, for example, they had monitored the fact that Captain Savo Simić, the commander of the Serb unit at Tilava, had fired a few rounds at Sarajevo. The fire, Captain Simić had explained, was defensive—directed at Bosnian government forces attacking the Serb-held suburb of Ilidža. The Serb action, and explanation, were duly noted.

"We have to take care of all our units," Captain Simić, a former officer in the JNA, later told me. "Our forces in Ilidža need our cover and the Muslims continue to attack." It was only logical, he continued, that the Serb guns surrounding Sarajevo should be used when the Serbs were on the defensive.

By any estimate, the situation was bizarre. After much bluster, the response of the Western powers to the discovery of the Serb concentration camps had been to convoke an international conference in London under the auspices of the UN and the European Union. Slobodan Milošević and Radovan Karadžić, the men responsible for the "cleansing" of Bosnia's Muslims, were invited. The scene for the ensuing debacle was thereby set. But the hospitality offered to Milošević and Karadžić had the advantage of obviating the alternative: meeting force with force in Bosnia in order to demonstrate that history's lessons in Europe had been learned.

The London Conference ended on August 27, 1992, with an agreement signed by the Serb leaders. They promised to dismantle the camps immediately, lift the siege of Sarajevo and other Bosnian cities, and turn over all their heavy weapons to "international supervision." It was decided that the International Conference on the Former Yugoslavia (ICFY) should become a moveable feast, entering continuous session in Geneva and elsewhere to pursue a peace settlement. Cyrus Vance, the former American secretary of state, and Lord Owen, the former British foreign secretary, would lead that quest.

There was trumpeting; there were threats. John Major, the British prime minister, declared that "the Yugoslav parties have pledged themselves in front of the world to a code of conduct." Eagleburger, then acting secretary of state, noted, without being more specific, that Karadžić had been warned of the dangers of not surrendering Serb heavy weapons that had already been bombarding Sarajevo for several months.

Near Sarajevo, eighteen days after the London Conference, the vacuity of the Serb promises was clear. "International supervision" was three young men in light blue berets in a hut in the middle of a field. The heavy weapons were still in the Serbs' hands. The siege of Sarajevo continued. Out in eastern Bosnia it was business as usual at the Sušica concentration camp despite the Serb commitment in London to the "unconditional and unilateral release under international supervision of all civilians detained, and the closure without delay of the detention camps."

I did not realize it at the time, but the germ of the catastrophe was there on that hillside near Sarajevo in 1992. It was encapsulated in the pathos of Captain von Hoorebeke's avowal: "We can't control the situation, but we do monitor it." As I walked away something prompted me to turn back. I saw the United Nations troops and Serb soldiers preparing to cook the spitted carcass of a lamb—just like the Zečevićs in Butmir. Serb hospitality can be generous and engaging; the feast would no doubt be memorable. In the week ending September 20, 1992, Sarajevo suffered its heaviest bombardment of the six-month-old war, with 925 civilian casualties.

AT THE TIME Bisera was shot, Sarajevo had officially been a United Nations "safe area" for three months. Five other Bosnian towns threatened by Serb forces—Srebrenica, Goražde, Žepa, Tuzla, and Bihać—were also declared "safe." In the Security Council resolution of May 6, 1993, which conferred this status on these Bosnian towns, UN diplomats in New York chose to remark on Sarajevo's "unique character" as a "multicultural, multi-ethnic and pluri-religious center which exemplifies the viability of coexistence and interrelations between all the communities of the Republic of Bosnia and Herzegovina." These were the velleities of the war. The reality was another: the preservation of Bosnian society, to adapt Otto von Bismarck's dismissive remark on the Balkans, was not "worth the healthy bones of a single Pomeranian grenadier."

The idea of the "safe areas" grew out of the Serb attack on the eastern Bosnian town of Srebrenica that gathered pace in February 1993. Many Muslim refugees from surrounding Bosnian towns—including Zvornik, Vlasenica, and Rogatica—had taken refuge in Srebrenica the previous year. The population of the town and its immediate surroundings had swollen from about thirty-seven thousand—72 percent Muslim and 25 percent Serbs in the prewar years—to over fifty thousand.

Among them was Naser Orić, a former bodyguard to Milošević, who placed himself at the head of an increasingly effective Bosnian guerrilla force that, in the fall and winter of 1992, wreaked havoc on surrounding Serb villages. Orić liked to show visitors videos of piles of Serb bodies. He would boast about the number killed in a succession of lightning raids in the Bratunac area in which Serb communities were massacred and buildings torched. Orić was a nasty piece of work. He illustrated the effectiveness of the Serb terror of 1992: the Serbs' methods were reproduced in revenge killings and Bosnia's dismemberment advanced.

General Ratko Mladić, the former JNA colonel who took over command of Bosnian Serb forces on May 9, 1992, has an obsession with the dead. Orić, because he killed a lot of Serbs, became the object of such an obsession. Mladić liked to usher United Nations officials into desecrated Serb cemeteries in Bosnia in order to explain why he could never trust "the Turk." When, early in the war, the commander of United Nations forces, Lieutenant General Lars Eric Wahlgren, asked Mladić why he continued to bombard Sarajevo, Mladić responded by asking, "General, do you remember your father?" Wahlgren said that he did. "In my case," Mladić continued, "my son is the first in many generations to know his father. Because there have been so many attacks on the Serb people, children do not know their fathers."

Mladić, born in the Bosnian village of Božinovići in 1943, lost his father in 1945 to the combined forces of Nazism and Croatian fascism. It was through this prism that he saw the war.

When, in December 1991, the European Union was browbeaten by Germany into recognition of Croatia, Mladić called the decision "a second Munich." In the barracks of the Bosnian Serb army posters showed soldiers wearing Nazi uniforms above a screaming slogan—"Are you ready for Deutschmocracy?"

At the time of Croatia's declaration of independence, Mladić was a lieutenant colonel in the JNA, commanding a corps at Knin, the headquarters of the Serb revolt in Croatia. His methods there—illustrated in the flattening of the Croatian village of Kijevo in a twelve-hour bombardment on August 26, 1991—reflected a basic philosophy that talk was cheap and force effective. His goal never wavered, and he expressed it with a lapidary bluntness: "the protection of Serbian territory and the people who have lived there for centuries."

Tant pis for the other people—like the Croats in Kijevo—who might be living there alongside the Serbs. By mid-March, Mladić was closing in on his nemesis, Orić. Serb forces had overrun much of the Srebrenica area, including Konjević Polje, and were approaching the town itself, with its mass of terrified Muslim refugees. General Philippe Morillon, the commander of United Nations forces in Bosnia, decided to make a stand. He forced his way into Srebrenica and, on March 12, declared, "You are now under the protection of United Nations forces. . . . I will never abandon you." The commitment was improvised—Morillon had no instruction to make such a promise—but solemn nonetheless.

"I wanted to avert a catastrophe," Morillon told me. "Orić was responsible for several massacres in which dozens of women and children had been killed, and it seemed to me there was more hatred in that one small corner of Bosnia than anywhere else. Mladić wanted to avenge his dead. As for the Muslim refugees from Serb terror, they were in a desperate state."

Morillon managed to bring a temporary halt to the Serb assault and arrange for the evacuation of Muslim refugees to Tuzla. It was one of the rare instances in the war of a UN commander averting a disaster through an act of personal initiative rooted in a sense of military honor. Soon afterward, fearing that their general had gone native, the French government announced that Morillon would be withdrawn.

I saw the French general and Mladić in Belgrade on March 26, 1993. They announced a Bosnian cease-fire and the establishment of a "corridor" for the ferrying of aid into Srebrenica. Mladić, his pale blue eyes gleaming, was full of ribaldry and a booming defiance. He said "Muslim forces" had destroyed 113 Serb villages in Bosnia since the war began. He said over fifteen hundred Serb civilians had been killed by "Muslim forces" in recent months. He accused the world of using a double standard for Serb and Muslim victims. He said the sole aim of "the Muslims" was to bring about a Western military intervention in the war. With each assertion he banged the table with his fist. He laughed, exuding an overwhelming self-confidence.

Morillon's analysis of the Serb general was succinct: "A Greater Serbian patriot who thinks of himself as Napoleon." He told Mladić as much. He also reminded him that Napoleon was fine as long as he was winning his battles, but he had ended his days in exile on Elba and then in bleaker exile, as a prisoner of the British on the windswept South Atlantic island of St. Helena. Mladić laughed.

The accords announced in Belgrade proved predictably meaningless. Serb shelling of Srebrenica resumed in April. With the Serbs about to take the town, a United Nations–brokered accord was hammered out between Mladić and General Sefer Halilović, then the commander of the Bosnian army. Signed in Sarajevo on April 17, 1993, it called for a total cease-fire to begin the next day, the deployment of a United Nations company in the town, and the demilitarization of Srebrenica within seventy-two hours.

The agreement said: "All weapons, ammunition, mines, explosives and combat supplies (except medicines) inside Srebrenica will be submitted/handed over to UNPROFOR under the supervision of three officers from each side with control carried out by UNPROFOR. No armed persons or units except UNPROFOR will remain within the city once the demilitarization process is complete."

Thus this agreement called for *Bosnian and Serb forces* in Srebrenica to be disarmed. The Muslim refugees from past Serb assaults were to be left without weapons. Karadžić announced the "surrender" of the Muslims and the handover of their weapons to the UN. It never happened.

On its way through the Security Council, the "safe area" concept was changed. Resolution 824, passed just over two weeks after the Srebrenica demilitarization accord, said that Srebrenica, Sarajevo, Goražde, Žepa, Tuzla, and Bihać should "be treated as safe areas, free from armed attacks and from any other hostile acts which endanger the wellbeing and the safety of their inhabitants." All *Bosnian Serb* military or paramilitary units were to withdraw "from these towns to a distance wherefrom they cease to constitute a menace to their security and that of their inhabitants." *No mention was made of Bosnian army forces.* The right of UNPROFOR and "international humanitarian agencies" to have "free and unimpeded access to all safe areas" was spelled out.

A few weeks later, the means to achieve these aims were outlined in Resolution 836, which extended UNPROFOR's mandate. Asserting, as ever, "the need to restore the sovereignty, territorial integrity and political independence of the Republic of Bosnia and Herzegovina," the Security Council expressed its determination to "deter attacks against the safe areas" and ensure the protection of civilians there, through the removal from the safe areas of all forces *"other than those of the Government of the Republic of Bosnia and Herzegovina."* Contradicting the Sarajevo agreement of April 17, the right of Bosnian forces to remain in the safe areas, including Srebrenica, was made explicit.

UNPROFOR, "acting in self-defense," was now authorized to use force, including NATO air power, "in reply to bombardments against the safe areas by any of the parties or to armed incursion into them or in the event of any deliberate obstruction in or around those areas to the freedom of movement of UNPROFOR or of protected humanitarian convoys."

This, by any measure, was a robust mandate to protect Sarajevo, Srebrenica, and other cities. The measures, moreover, were specifically adopted under Chapter VII of the United Nations Charter, which, unlike Chapter VI, does not require the consent of the parties to the dispute and allows the Security Council to authorize the United Nations or member states to take action—including military operations—to restore international peace and security. The mandate to go beyond conventional peacekeeping into the realm of peace enforcement was clear.

The "Mogadishu line" so persistently invoked by General Sir Michael Rose, the British commander of UN forces in Bosnia through most of 1994, was thus a creation of his own fertile imagination. In fact the line between neutral peacekeeping and peace enforcement had already been crossed by the people in New York who gave him his job. In effect, Rose used Somalia and Mogadishu—where a UN peacekeeping mission developed into the disastrous American-led bid to capture Mohammed Farah Aidid—to buttress the most conservative possible interpretation of his mandate. In so doing he served the cautious designs of the British government.

The transference that ensued was intriguing: United Nations officials came increasingly to blame the Bosnian army for their failure to carry out their mandate to protect the "safe areas" from the Serbs. They criticized the Bosnian government for rendering the "safe-area" concept unworkable by leaving its forces within them, despite the fact that the resolution establishing the "safe areas" specifically stated that such troops could remain.

Rather than referring to the resolution that bound them, these officials referred to the Srebrenica demilitarization accord and insisted that it represented the true intentions of the Security Council. There was a stubborn blindness in such protestations. The only mandate the UN troops were bound to follow was that of the Security Council. Disarming the Bosnian troops in Sarajevo and Tuzla would have amounted to declaring outright victory for the Serbs in Bosnia. It was unthinkable.

Morillon's successors talked incessantly of the thirty-four thousand extra troops they had requested (and never obtained) who alone could make the "safe areas" work. Language was turned on its head. The phrase "deter attack" was subjected to tremendous semantic contortion as officials tried to explain that the two words did not mean that the "safe areas" would be defended if deterrence failed. This despite the fact that Resolution 836 explicitly called for the use of force in reply to "armed incursions" or "bombardment"—situations, in other words, that already demand "defense" rather than "deterrence" because an attack is under way.

Like the upside-down rhetoric of the Battle of Kosovo, where defeat became victory and attack defense, the realities of the war slowly got inverted as the "international community" tried to portray the conflict in terms that justified its paralysis. In this skewed world the killing of Bisera Zečević with the compliance of the UN became part of the natural order of things, as did the killing of Hakija Turajlić, the Bosnian deputy prime minister, shot by Serb police in January 1993, as he traveled in the supposed safety of a United Nations armored personnel carrier.

Two months before Bisera was killed, as he was about to leave Bosnia, Morillon toyed with an idea. His stand in Srebrenica had turned him into a hero with unprecedented sway over the Bosnian population. He had also earned a grudging respect from the Serbs. He was taken by the notion that he could gather the citizens of Sarajevo and, like some Pied Piper of the New World Order, lead them out through the Serb lines at Ilidža toward the sea. "At that moment," he told me, "they would have followed me and the siege, I believe, would have been ended. I was close to doing it. But there was a risk. As a soldier, and not a politician, I felt in the end that I could not assume that responsibility. But the thought of what I might have done then has never left me."

IT WAS a twisted conflict. In the midst of the fighting there was a host of international folk, most of them in the light blue berets or helmets of the UN. They were a motley crew: a Kenyan with a wide smile basking in the sun on a ridge above Knin and waving a peace sign at passersby; a French officer who had set himself the Herculean task of writing an encyclopedia of Bosnian checkpoints; a British officer for whom the password of the UN in Bosnia was BOHICA—an acronym for "Bend over, here it comes again"; a Russian officer, a veteran of the KGB, inspired by every third vodka to rhapsodize on the historic opportunity presented by the war for Moscow to secure, at last, an Adriatic "warm-weather port" through its Serb allies; a Nepalese platoon cooking curry beside a smashed-up gas station on the deserted Brotherhood and Unity Highway connecting Belgrade to Zagreb; military observers from the European Union whose "observations" were always gleaned far enough from any action to ensure that their uniforms remained so spotlessly white they were known, not so tenderly, as "the ice-cream salesmen."

These people were so pervasive—as much a part of the Bosnian war scenery as roofless homes or graffiti on ruins saying OVO JE SRBIJA ("This is Serbia")—that the sheer outlandishness of having tens of thousands of foreign spectators to a war was often forgotten, as was the overriding question of what they were doing there. Besides, the response from United Nations civilians and military officers was always confused. On the one hand, they were peacekeepers whose shibboleth was neutrality. On the other, they were soldiers whose mission was anything but neutral. For they were supposed, at the very least, to be upholding the sovereignty and "territorial integrity" of Bosnia-Herzegovina, a state whose territory had been carved up by Serb and Croat separatists; ensuring the delivery of food to encircled towns like Sarajevo and Srebrenica; and, from mid-1993, protecting Muslim civilians in various "safe areas" from Serb attack.

The doublespeak inherent in trying to be two different things at once—defenders of a savaged Bosnia and disinterested agents of humanitarianism—often assumed Orwellian proportions. The security situation was "not very conducive to security"; the siege of Sarajevo was not really a siege but a "militarily advantageous encirclement" for the Serbs and a "tactical disadvantage" for the Bosnian army; the airport at Sarajevo was "open" although there were no flights coming in and no flights going out; ditto Tuzla airport; trams in Sarajevo were "running" although their service was temporarily suspended. The outlook for the Bosnian army was described in such memorable terms as, "This war is going to be full of surprises and they are not going to be the surprises we all expect." Or, "We do not know if they are in a position to change their position." On the overall situation in the war, there were such incisive observations as, "If this continues, we are going to have more of the same." All in the name of balanced treatment. It was outlandish, this straining for neutrality or the completely anodyne, and plain ludicrous at times—Monty Python meets genocide, live and in English, on CNN.

But then the horror far outweighed the farce. Compassion, in its officially orchestrated international form, is a modern scourge. Its concomitant is what the French intellectual Alain Finkielkraut has called *"le dogme de l'équidistance."* In the world of "humanitarianism," there are no more enemies; there are only victims. Indeed, it is no coincidence that "humanitarianism" has spread precisely as critical threats to American security have diminished with the cold war's end.

The wars of the 1990s, then, are seen not so much as conflicts in which there may indeed be butchers and victims and a need for resolve, but as "humanitarian disasters" with victims on all sides, requiring the rapid dispatch of aid and the creation of "safe areas" in which some of the more severely disaster-struck folk may be gathered and fed, usually by representatives of the UN. The way to this sweeping view of the world's conflicts was opened by the fall of the Berlin Wall. Bosnia then became the consummate illustration of the ugliness of post–cold war weltschmerz. The Bosnian war broke out as a result of a Serbian decision, made in Belgrade, to dismember the nascent state; it was later bolstered by designs, drawn up in Zagreb, for a Greater Croatia. Yet it was increasingly portrayed in Western capitals as a messy civil war full of unfortunate "victims" because this description best justified the international response. As Clifford Orwin has observed, humanitarianism, for millions of North Americans, "implies the limits of the desirable commitment to a given situation in which their nation has no interests of a more pressing sort."

The Bosnian war could never have continued for as long as it did, or in such restricted form, if the rival blocs of East and West had still existed in Europe. In a cold-war setting, Bosnia would have been explosive—Chile or Angola an hour from Rome. War there would almost certainly have been stopped fast or become a prelude, as in 1914, to something far wider. The Bush and Clinton administrations would not have been able to hide behind "multilateralism" and "humanitarianism."

But in the post-ideological world of the 1990s, the strategic importance of Bosnia appeared limited: a small place, it had no large oil reserves or other compelling economic claim to America's interest or involvement.

Given Clinton's problems with the U.S. military and his administration's trade-dominated, trade-manipulated, and seemingly traded-in view of foreign policy, this was an obvious handicap. Clinton opted to fudge. The way was thereby opened to humanitarianism—that is, the placing of a cordon sanitaire around a war and the treatment of everyone in it as victims, as helpless as the survivors of a flash flood. Those who contributed to the United Nations High Commissioner for Refugees (UNHCR) aid effort in Bosnia were often heroic. Many, like Monique Tuffarelli, a Frenchwoman in the western Muslim enclave of Bihać, stood by the people they fed and sustained even when shelling was intense and they had been urged to leave. But the international policy behind their presence was not edifying: it involved feeding the victims as a substitute for stopping the butchers.

The humanitarian approach has several attractions. It assuages consciences: there is no question that the delivery of an average of almost one thousand metric tons of food aid a day to 2.7 million beneficiaries in Bosnia saved lives. It gives the impression that something is being done while circumventing the risks of military intervention. It is well suited to "multilateralism," that other splendid mechanism for the dilution of risk. It allows the continued smooth functioning of the world that counts: the increasingly undifferentiated global market where Bosnia and Rwanda and Zaire and Chechnya and 23 million stateless Kurds glide fleetingly across a screen, or perhaps no more than some small corner of a screen. It conforms, moreover, to the psychology of a world marked by what Robert Hughes has called a "culture of complaint," one distinguished by the widespread cultivation of the status of victim: a world where a president like Bill Clinton more often looks lachrymose than pugnacious, more often wipes his eyes than bangs his fist. After the Berlin Wall, a teary American president plays pretty well. In this sentimental culture, bereft of an obvious enemy or an obvious dialectic, other victims are natural objects of empathy. It is far easier to understand "victims" than to work out who is responsible for creating them. Victimhood attracts emotion and dulls intelligence. Like the weather, that unfailing source of modern drama, it has a facile appeal to the television viewer.

In the case of Bosnia, "victimhood" was doubly guaranteed by the preservation of a United Nations arms embargo, imposed on all the states of the former Yugoslavia on September 25, 1991. In early 1991, the JNA had about two thousand tanks, two thousand heavy guns, and seven hundred fighter aircraft; this matériel was overwhelmingly inherited by the Serbs. The embargo thus placed Bosnian forces at a crippling disadvantage at the outset of the war. By denying Bosnia-Herzegovina the right to self-defense, it also appeared to contravene the United Nations Charter.

But the embargo buttressed the philosophy of humanitarianism, as interpreted by the likes of Lord Owen, for whom it was not immoral because "it ensured the continuation of UNPROFOR's humanitarian mandate for the first few years, when it saved hundreds of thousands of lives." In other words, to deny a people the right to defend themselves is morally defensible, even desirable, if it enables you to have the satisfaction of "saving their lives" with free beans. Margaret Thatcher, the former British prime minister, had a different view. She said support for the embargo made the European Union "accomplices to a massacre."

That was how the Bosnian war began: as a massacre of European Muslims, one prepared, coordinated, and made possible by political and military leaders in Belgrade. Once the Serb concentration camps had been found, four months after the war began, this fact was flagrant enough. But the United Nations chose not to distinguish between killer and victim, between concentration-camp guard and prisoner. This was the tainted essence of the international response to the war. An indefensible neutrality was adopted from which a flawed humanitarianism flowed.

The Universal Declaration of Human Rights passed by the United Nations General Assembly in 1948 talks about the right to freedom of thought and religion and the right to life and liberty. There was nothing new about these rights being flouted. What was new, in Bosnia, after the end of the cold war, was the way the United Nations itself became the political and moral focus of a failure that made a mockery of the organization's founding charters.

In the old practice of foreign affairs, the relationship between policy and military power was close. In the new world, it is policy and televised Samaritanism that must cleave to each other. Nuclear bombs generally have little relevance to regional, tribal wars. Alas, unlike military power, compassion and containment can be no more than palliatives. They cannot change situations. They can only place them in a holding pattern that acts as a distorting lens because it may be increasingly agonizing to those inside it—the Zečevićs, the Šestovićs—even as it is increasingly soothing to the onlooker steadily numbed by seemingly interchangeable images of faraway wars.

IN MACEDONIA, in the summer of 1994, I met American soldiers wearing the uniforms of the United Nations who were in the new world "containment" business. They were from the Second Battalion of the Fifteenth Infantry Division, based in Schweinfurt, Germany. In Macedonia, their presence was designed to act as a deterrent to anyone with a notion to ignite the ethnic tensions between Albanians and Slavs in the new state and so spread Yugoslavia's wars southeastward toward America's uneasy NATO allies, Greece and Turkey. But their precise task, on the day I came across them, was to count donkeys. The donkeys were crossing the border between Macedonia and Serbia and the burdens on their backs were therefore suspect. They might have constituted infringements of the United Nations trade sanctions on Serbia. So Sergeant Scott Culver was recording their passage—and his own from soldier to Samaritan.

"I am a combat soldier," he told me, "and I was not trained to be a peacekeeper. Here, on a patrol, you wanna be seen. That's new to me. The norm I know is stealth. We're trained to do everything at night. But here you drive during the day in white vehicles with your headlights on! You have to wave and be nice and shake everyone's hand. It's weird! If the other guy raises his rifle, I'm allowed to mimic his action, but not before, so I guess you just hope he's not a good shot. Right now, I monitor donkeys, which I guess is part of being a soldier of the future."

Corporal Heribert Agusto had not yet adjusted to that future. A former Marine, pure sinew, tattooed from top to bottom, he was all of a piece with his gleaming M16A1 assault rifle. Simple, he said: one shot, one dead. "Unfortunately, we're not here to kick butt," he added in a tone of mild disgust. "We're here to be *friendly.*"

Several hundred American troops were sent to Macedonia in 1993, on a preventive peacekeeping mission that has been a success. The Bosnian war did not spread to Macedonia. But they were kept out of Bosnia, where there was a war on and where they might have made a far more decisive difference, because the danger clearly existed that some of them might come back seriously dead.

This was another important aspect of putting a cordon sanitaire around the Bosnian war. American body bags might demand more than Clinton's watery eyes; they might require the unleashing of American power. So Bosnia could be a slippery slope. The obsession of the military establishment in Washington, led by General Colin Powell, the chairman of the Joint Chiefs of Staff, became "mission creep" and "Bosnian quagmires"— what Richard Holbrooke, a former assistant secretary of state, has described as "the Vietmalia syndrome." The "quagmire" was Vietnam, 1961–1973; the "mission creep," and ensuing death of eighteen American soldiers, was Somalia, 1993. Munich, 1938, and the cost of not calling aggressors by their name, appeared peripheral, if that, to Powell's calculation.

An odd paradox crystallized. The boys in the armed forces, like those I met in Macedonia, were ready to kill or be killed; indeed, they had volunteered for the armed forces precisely because they wanted to be soldiers in the conventional sense. But their masters in the Pentagon had developed an approach that redefined televised soldiering around what amounted to a zero-risk, zero-body-bag doctrine in which Bosnia had no place. Zero killed is a military perversion. A soldier is paid to fulfill his mission, not to save his skin. No soldier worth his salt is ready to kill but not ready to die.

An irony of the Bosnian war was that it broke out at a time when the end of superpower rivalry had opened new, fluid possibilities for limited intervention, but also at a time when the Gulf War had given new credence to the Powell Doctrine—the notion that the United States should act militarily only when its vital interests are clearly threatened and overwhelming force can be used, preferably with impunity.

Bosnia probably required limited force. Karadžić later acknowledged that five thousand NATO troops on the Serbian border in Zvornik and five thousand more at Brčko to cut the Posavina corridor to western Bosnia would have ended his campaign early in the conflict. The vital interests threatened by the Bosnian war were rather more subtle in their nature than in Kuwait. Europe's stability was undermined; Western relations with the moderate Islamic world affected. These were important issues for any American administration. But America is also an idea, and Bosnia was above all a moral issue. On every count—the case for limited use of force in a post–cold war setting, and the American interests threatened by the 1992 genocide in Bosnia—General Powell was dismissive. He did not get it. As Charles Thomas, one of many American diplomats demoralized by the war and the Western response to it, said to me in 1995, when the disaster was already consummated, "Foreign policy is like the old kiss formula: Keep it simple, stupid. We should have told them when the war broke out, You reach an accommodation, you stop the shelling of Sarajevo, or we'll kill you."

THE CLINTON ADMINISTRATION was not ready for such bluntness. It adjusted its rhetoric accordingly. Weakened by the furor over gays in the military and by his record on (and lack of record in) Vietnam, the president was in no position to take on Powell's Joint Chiefs when he came into office in early 1993. The "genocide" alluded to so forcefully on the campaign trail in 1992, and the unequivocal calls for air strikes against the Serbs, quickly gave way to prevarication.

Warren Christopher, the secretary of state, was assertive enough in his first statement on Bosnia on February 10, 1993: "Serbian ethnic cleansing has been pursued through mass murders, systematic beatings, and the rapes of Muslims and others, prolonged shellings of innocents in Sarajevo and elsewhere, forced displacement of entire villages, inhumane treatment of prisoners in detention camps." But by March 28, just six weeks later, the tone had changed.

Speaking on the CBS news program *Face the Nation,* Christopher said,

"Let me put that situation in Bosnia in just a little broader framework. It's really a tragic problem. The hatred between all three groups—the Bosnians and the Serbs and the Croatians—is almost unbelievable. It's almost terrifying, and it's centuries old. That really is a problem from hell."

Thus was signaled the steady march toward the abject view of the Bosnian war as a kind of natural disaster. If it was rooted in ancient tribal hatreds, and a product of "hell," the war became "inevitable," like a hurricane. Stripped of specific causes, anodized by vagueness, spewed into the maw of some made-to-measure history, the war could be approached with the neutrality that UN representatives in Bosnia constantly described as essential.

By May 1993, Christopher's tone was straining yet further to present the war as a conflict in which everyone was bad and discriminating thought therefore futile. After an unsuccessful visit to Western Europe aimed at convincing the allies that the administration's professed initial policy—lift the arms embargo and use air strikes against the Serbs—was the right one, Christopher quickly retreated. On May 18, 1993, he made clear that a new policy had been born: "Containing the conflict in the Bosnian area is one of the prime goals of President Clinton," he told the House Foreign Affairs Committee.

Descriptions of the war naturally had to be changed to buttress this new objective of containment. Above all, any moral imperative to intervene had to be removed. No longer "genocide" or even "ethnic cleansing," the war was now a "morass." In the morass, insofar as it was penetrable to the human eye, there appeared to be "atrocities on all sides," Christopher declared.

Asked by Representative Gary L. Ackerman, a New York Democrat, whether "ethnic cleansing" was not the same as genocide, Christopher uttered one of the stangest official pronouncements on the conflict: "It's been easy to analogize this to the Holocaust, but I never heard of any genocide by the Jews against the German people." In this hallucinogenic phrase, Christopher came close to defending the Serbs' view of themselves as the real victims of genocide.

In effect, within four months of taking office, the administration's arguments had come to resemble those of the first UN commander in Bosnia, General Mackenzie, who compared the Serbs, Croats, and Muslims to serial killers who happened to have killed a different number of people and asked whether it made sense to help the one who had murdered fewest. The best response, Christopher intimated, echoing Bush and Baker, was to take refuge in distance: "At heart," he said, "this is a European problem."

President Clinton's language also shifted steadily from the lapidary clarity of 1992. On Bosnia he became the protean president. In April 1993, he had already seized on the comforting fact for opponents of intervention that "Hitler sent tens of thousands of soldiers to that area" during World War II but failed to subdue Tito's guerrillas. By May, he was talking about the "process" and "the map"—ominous words for a region where processes do not exist and everyone has his own map.

In June, he abjured the powers of his office: "Let me tell you something about Bosnia. On Bosnia, I made a decision. The United Nations controls what happens in Bosnia." In early 1994, Clinton said the following: "What happened in Yugoslavia was when Mr. Tito died and then the central government's authority began to erode and then all the various parts of Yugoslavia began to try to be more independent, Bosnia-Herzegovina, which always had these three different factions, basically degenerated back to the conflict which had been there for hundreds of years. And you can— there is no perfect solution to any of life's problems, you know. But in this case, the truth is, people there keep killing each other."

He continued: "If you don't have an imperial army, if you don't just go and take people over and tell them what to do, then you have to make some allowances for the fact that on occasion they'll do the stupid thing and keep on killing each other even when it doesn't make any sense. And there are some areas where you can stop it and some where you can't."

America, however, does have an imperial army sustained at an annual cost of about $250 billion. But by mid-1995, Clinton appeared to have thrown in the towel before *these people who just keep killing each other.* Wars such as the one in Bosnia only stop when those involved "get tired of fighting each other." The chances of the three sides doing that were remote, the president suggested at the economic summit meeting in Halifax, Nova Scotia, on June 16, 1995, because they had been engaged in a continuous brawl "at least, at least going back to the eleventh century."

This was the background drone, as meaningless as that of the NATO planes that circled endlessly through Bosnian skies during the war, which steadily drove Sarajevans crazy. There was a colonial undertone: *These Balkan natives are just uncontrollable.*

But Sarajevo is an island of sophistication in Bosnia. The inhabitants knew, with painful lucidity, what their city had been. They could see what had been allowed to happen to it. They listened, day after day, to the verbal contrivances with which these events were colored. They took to calling Clinton "Bil? Ne Bil? Clinton"—"Will I? Won't I? Clinton." When, on May 3, 1994, they heard the president say of Bosnia that "I did the best I could," they were incredulous, for they had rejoiced at his election, expecting much more. Boutros Boutros-Ghali, the Secretary-General of the

United Nations who said on his first visit to Sarajevo that he could think of ten worse places in the world, became the "Egyptian mummy."

Increasingly, I met people who appeared driven to the verge of madness as much by the mind-bending international declarations on the war as by Sarajevo's plight. Ljerka Subašić, a Croat woman living in Sarajevo, was typical. She told me that she was "terribly angry and desperate" because of what "the outside world" had done to her: impose an arms embargo, dispatch occasional food packages, and deplore the irrational Balkan proclivity for slaughter. Her eyes glistened, her fists were clenched, she was ready, I believe, to kill the first identifiable representative of the international order she could lay her hands on.

Others relapsed into inertia. At most they tilled their tiny war gardens, planted with seeds provided by the UN, created from any available patch of soil, a piece of sidewalk, a patch of park, and watched the carrots, garlic, spinach, and lettuce grow. There was no future because no plans could be made. There was no past because a normal life in the city became so infinitely distant as to appear unreal. There was only the present moment, because a Sarajevan life could be extinguished at any instant.

CHAPTER 19

MOJA BOSNA

Asim Zečević buried his wife about a hundred yards from his son Muris in one of the cemeteries that rise above the old Turkish quarter of Baščaršija. The wooden grave marker says simply BISERA ZEČEVIĆ 1941–1993. Born into a war that took her father, she died in its sequel having lost her son.

Habits held Asim together. On the third of every month, he would go to Muris's grave; on the eleventh to Bisera's. He never changed his pace as he walked through town. What difference would it make? "If you run," the Sarajevo saying went, "you hit the bullet. If you walk the bullet hits you."

Bisera was running. She was about eighty yards from the far side of the airport when the spotlight fell on her and the bullet followed. Another saying held, "You do not hear the bullet that's for you." Before leaving, when Asim pressed her as to why she insisted on taking the risk, she had told him simply, "I want to put my feet down in our garden." To that he had found no reply.

The city gradually became a stranger to him. There was the destruction, of course. Baleful towers of shattered glass, mounds of ancient stone, garbage smoldering or skittering in the wind, graves and sprouting onions where city parks used to be. Lurching pylons and cables dangling like forgotten props over a deserted stage. Upended trucks and cars pointing their splayed innards to the sky like dying animals. Sheets of plastic for windows, woodstoves for electric cookers. White men in white vehicles and blue helmets hurtling around with a colonial effrontery.

But it was not all that, so much. War brings home the fact that physical things count for little. What mattered was the destruction of Sarajevo's culture, a skein of yarn so fine as to be invisible and now utterly unraveled. The vast influx of refugees had no notion of the city's manners. Something violent in their ways, and uncouth, made Asim despair for his Bosnia. There was a cri de coeur scrawled on a wall in the center of Sarajevo— MOJA BOSNA ("My Bosnia")—that almost made him weep.

His sister Fida, deserted by her husband Slobodan, moved in with him and his old mother, Hasnja. For a while, he took to drinking a brandy or two at breakfast. He gazed at family photographs and sometimes, to his sister, seemed very far away. He pinned a Bosnian fleur-de-lis to the wall of the living room. "A man can suffer a lot," he said to himself. "The outer limit of what a man can stand is not yet known."

SIX MONTHS AFTER Bisera died, and almost two years into the war and the siege, sixty-nine Sarajevans were killed at the central marketplace when a 120-millimeter mortar round plunged into the tight maze of makeshift stalls. It was February 5, 1994. The day before, a shell had slammed into the suburb of Dobrinja, killing ten Sarajevo children. At a rough estimate, six hundred thousand Serb shells had landed on the city since the start of the war.

A debate ensued at UNPROFOR. It focused on whether the Serbs had fired the mortar at the Sarajevo market, or whether the Bosnian government forces had shelled their own people with the aim of bringing NATO into the war on their side. As the conflict dragged on, the notion that a devious Bosnian government might lure NATO into the war through acts of provocation became an overriding preoccupation of several United Nations officials and officers, including General Rose. Their chief mission became to avoid being tricked by the Muslims. Consciously or unconsciously, this preoccupation reinforced a stereotype dear to the Serbs: the Muslim as turncoat finding fortune in treachery.

Senior UN officials told me that a first, sketchy report by one of the mission's ballistics experts suggested that the mortar, fired from the northeast of the market, had come from nearby government positions. The central question was the range. There were Bosnian and Serb troops deployed in the same line of fire, with the government forces closer, the Serbs a little farther out. A second, more detailed investigation concluded, however, that the vestiges of a market stall did not provide clear enough evidence of the angle of impact for the range—and so the source of fire—to be determined with accuracy. Neither report, the first accusatory, the second inconclusive, was made public by United Nations headquarters in New York.

Lord Owen, however, chose to include in a cable to European capitals an extract from a report by the Yugoslav news agency Tanjug, based in Belgrade, blaming the shelling on the Muslims and citing a leaked version of the findings of the first, suppressed United Nations inquiry. This odd de-

cision naturally tended to give a dispatch by Tanjug—effectively Milošević's official organ throughout the war—Owen's personal imprimatur and,
through him, that of the European Union.

Owen's own view, as he made clear to me in Geneva a few days after the
attack, was that anybody in Bosnia was capable of anything. "It's almost
impossible to describe how difficult it is to deal with these people, what a
truly corrosive effect communism has had," he said. "They can say anything, sign anything, and it makes no difference." He was still visibly angry
with the Clinton administration for having ditched the Vance-Owen
Peace Plan in May 1993; he attributed the decision largely to the fact
that the plan would have required a commitment of American troops to
police it.

The plan's proposals centered on obliging the Serbs to give up 40 percent of the territory they held in order to piece Bosnia together as a decentralized state with ten largely autonomous provinces. "The Americans
are terrified of the military commitment involved in reversing ethnic
cleansing, and that is what Vance-Owen required," he said. "If Clinton is
willing to send five brigades of infantry to reverse ethnic cleansing, fine,
but don't keep telling us what to do from the air."

Owen certainly had a point. His plan had the great misfortune to col-
lide with the incoming Clinton administration, whose disarray over the
Balkans was then at one of its periodic apogees. However, he had not
helped his case by declaring, in an interview with *The New York Times,* that
Christopher was a touch gaga on Bosnia, just as he was getting to know
the new secretary of state.

What was interesting, nine months later and in the aftermath of a murderous attack on Sarajevo, was the way Owen's spleen had spilled out in all
directions. It was, after all, the Serbs, moved by Mladić's blunt suasion,
who had rejected the Vance-Owen Plan on May 5, 1993, voting against
acceptance in a tumultuous parliamentary session in Pale. They had done
so despite the presence of Milošević, who traveled from Belgrade to Pale
to try to convince Karadžić and General Mladić to accept it. This was the
only time that Milošević crossed the Drina. How unreal the ruins must
have seemed to him!

The Serbian president had already made his calculation: a fair slice of
Bosnia and Croatia—protected by the dithering presence of United Nations forces—would amount to an adequate outcome and allow him to ex-
tricate Serbia from international sanctions. But he had not reckoned on
the power of the ghosts he had unleashed. General Mladić, for whom
Greater Serbia was a thing of flesh and blood rather than political calculation, quashed his plea; Milošević slouched back across the Drina, never to
return.

1993: Vance–Owen Plan

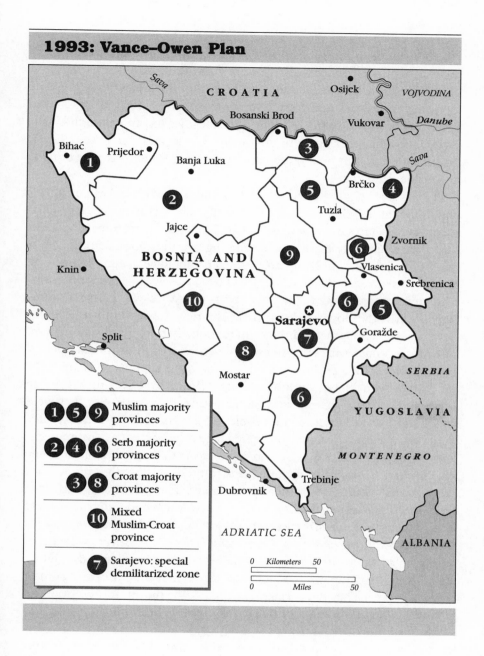

Owen appreciated Milošević's gesture; he felt he could work with him. His irritation was not directed at the Serbs. It was now focused on Clinton and Christopher for walking away from the plan after its rejection (made final in a Serb referendum on May 16, 1993) and on Izetbegović for using shifting assurances of American support to avoid any coherent commitment to peace. "As long as Izetbegović has an appeal in Washington, he will never agree to anything," Owen said. "If U.S. policy is Bosnian government policy, then all we get from Sarajevo is a lot of nonnegotiable demands."

History kept getting rewritten during the war. Memory was astonishingly short and, when it existed at all, malleable. Horrors became mere subordinate clauses in the sophistry that garnished international cynicism. Elaborate diplomatic constructs emanating from European capitals often did a poor job of concealing an unspoken prejudice against Islam. The Muslims were victims, *agreed*. They had been thrown by the tens of thousands into camps, *agreed*. They had been massacred, *OK*. An arms embargo denied the Bosnian government the right to buy arms legally and resist the dismemberment of their internationally recognized state, *agreed*. The West's values were surely best represented by a Muslim-led government, however unappealing, that also enjoyed the support of many Serbs and Croats who thought of themselves as Bosnians, *OK*. The Serb siege and bombardment of Sarajevo was unconscionable, *agreed*. But they were so difficult, these government people. They would not go away, they would not sue for peace, they intimated they might accept a Muslim ministate on, say, a third of Bosnia and then *perversely* ditched the idea. They set up *illegal* channels to acquire arms, forging links with Turkey, Iran, Saudi Arabia, Sudan, and other Islamic allies. These links suggested that *the Muslims were indeed fundamentalists*. Their Muslim identity, under persecution, became increasingly sharp, suggesting they *never had any real interest in a multi-ethnic society*. They *really besieged themselves* in Sarajevo, setting up administrative barriers to the departure of people and so refusing to assist the complete depopulation, through death or dispersal, of the Bosnian capital. They did *devious things* like firing mortar rounds from the grounds of hospitals in order to provoke return fire from the Serbs that would yield horrifying images for CNN and so increase the pressure on Washington, London, and Paris to do something. Their word was *worth nothing*. They were quite capable, *these unscrupulous Muslim victims*, of slaughtering their own people in the streets of Sarajevo if that would get other people to fight their Balkan war for them.

Such ideas were sometimes explicit, more often implied. Behind them lurked a fascinating shift: the so-called parties in Bosnia were no longer judged by their acts in the war itself. They were judged by their degree of cooperation with the UN mission.

The arguments always left me troubled, as if I had been watching the expression on the face of a murderer who is trying to cover his tracks. The international flight from the war's uncomfortable facts had begun in its first horrific months. This plunge into obfuscation was symbolized, and given institutional form, by the London Conference in August 1992. The conference evolved into the diplomatic equivalent of a Russian doll: there was always another peace plan, yet smaller, yet more modest, lurking inside the one on the table. A moral and political failure of such significance inevitably has lingering effects. Making the war a morass, intensifying its fog, muddying its origins, clouding its central issues—these were also ways of blurring the mind and so resisting the reproach of memory.

NONETHELESS, CERTAIN FACTS existed as the only ballast in this disconcerting storm. The Serbs bombarded Sarajevo steadily from the outset of the war. Hundreds of thousands of shells fell on the city. On February 4, 1994, for example, the fact that it was a Serb shell that killed ten children in Dobrinja was undisputed.

In such a consistent deluge of shelling unpleasant incidents are inevitable. Most Sarajevo streets are marked with the imprint of a mortar round's impact. Yet in the case of the three bloodiest single attacks—the bread-line massacre of May 27, 1992, in which sixteen people were killed, the marketplace attack of February 5, 1994, and the second marketplace attack of August 28, 1995, in which thirty-eight people were killed—the Serbs declared that it was obvious that the Muslims had shelled themselves. Indeed, it was impossible to find anyone in Pale or Banja Luka who did not wave away these incidents as "Muslim propaganda." They mocked the amateurish way in which the incidents had been "staged."

UNPROFOR was the translucent screen through which these claims and counterclaims were refracted. In general, United Nations officials and officers found the Serbs more amenable than the Bosnian government. Karadžić, Plavšić, and Nikola Koljević, the Shakespeare scholar who became a leading theorist of the Bosnian Serb campaign, all spoke excellent English. The lamb they offered was succulent, their hospitality generous, their manners good. The senior officers of the Bosnian Serb army, including General Mladić, had all served in the JNA. They knew about saluting and wearing hats and firm handshakes and the appropriate toasts and the rituals of officer-to-officer camaraderie.

By comparison, the Bosnians were a bunch of hillbillies. Their soldiers called themselves members of special units if they had two boots that

matched. Their officers were local capos who looked like they were
scratching their heads when they tried to salute. Moreover, the Serbs had
grabbed the territory they wanted—70 percent of Bosnia—in the first few
months of the war. Time was not in the Serbs' favor, because the army of
Bosnia-Herzegovina could only improve. The Serbs therefore tended to
show more active interest in the so-called peace process that the United
Nations persistently sought to foster. By comparison, the Izetbegović government was shifty, worse than traders in a Turkish bazaar. So it was that
UNPROFOR came to look with a certain sympathy on Serb claims, even
the more outlandish ones.

Yasushi Akashi, the Japanese diplomat who was the chief UN representative in the former Yugoslavia during much of the war, told me that "as
an observed phenomenon, it is true that sympathy tended to lie more with
the Serbs." He saw his role as irrevocably rooted in the impartiality that,
he believed, would alone allow aid to be delivered and doors to be kept
open to both sides. He liked the notion of what he called "classical peacekeeping" and had a deep aversion, perhaps rooted in the experience of Hi-
roshima, to the use of force. To Akashi, the British and French were
"realistic" while the United States was "affected by an overdose of morality" that was utterly unpragmatic—and ultimately hypocritical—in that it
was not backed by a willingness to put men on the ground in Bosnia. "The
tragedy," he told me, "was that the Americans wanted to stay only in the
air and that exasperated me. If the United States had come in, perhaps in
early 1994, I believe we could have advanced toward peace."

Akashi had a point about America. But his stubborn refusal to confront
the Serbs proved disastrous. Keeping doors open—a favorite expression—
meant engaging Karadžić even as the Serbs repeatedly ran circles around
UNPROFOR. "You can bring a horse to water but you cannot make him
drink"—another favorite expression—meant never threatening the horse.
Akashi was intrigued by the Bosnian Serb leader, in whom he observed the
suicidal and deluded traits, but whose sanity he must ultimately have believed in, for he negotiated endlessly with him. Karadžić told Akashi that
the spirit and soul of the Serbs would in the end prevail over the material
superiority of the United States. Akashi retorted that Karadžić's words reminded him of what Japanese leaders said in World War II. They, too, believed in the mystical nature of Japan and were convinced that its material
inferiority would be overcome by Japanese spiritual superiority. Their illusions plunged Japan and other Asian nations into what Akashi called "an
abyss of very deep suffering." He cautioned Karadžić against the romantic
belief in a nation's destiny. When Karadžić told Akashi of his admiration
for the Japanese writer Yukio Mishima—whom Akashi had known before

his ritual suicide—the Japanese diplomat again tried to caution him against excess.

Akashi believed that he could wear Karadžić down, bring him around. He believed that he should never give up. In Cambodia, where he had served on his previous assignment, he had been told repeatedly that the mission was impossible, but the results in the end had been positive. Persistence, Akashi thought, would also pay in Bosnia. He told me that Karadžić was "a good, astute politician, with a lot of emotion, of pride and defiance." At one point he told the Serb leader that the word *crisis* in Chinese is made up of two characters—the first meaning danger, the second opportunity. At times of danger there were opportunities (for peace) that should be seized.

Karadžić, Akashi told me, was excited by this notion because, as a psychiatrist, he believed that crises for individuals were also moments of danger and opportunity. Akashi clearly believed he could reason with the man. "There have been disappointments in the past in my dealings with the Serb leadership," he said, "but I feel this should not deter me from negotiating. I do not have the luxury of conforming to high moral or ethical standards. I have to negotiate to the end." When, on November 30, 1994, Boutros Boutros-Ghali came to Sarajevo in an attempt to salvage the floundering United Nations missions and Karadžić refused even to see him, Akashi told me, "I am disappointed and a little bit mad with Karadžić." That "little bit" was about as far as he ever went.

True to his word, Akashi negotiated to the end. This was the course that coincided with his perception of his mission, and, no doubt, his own intimate convictions. But, with a kind of implacable dedication that became a form of blindness, he failed to avert the debacle that was Bosnia.

ALTHOUGH UNPROFOR's PORING OVER the marketplace crater of February 1994 produced nothing conclusive, NATO's patience with the impasse in Sarajevo was running out. Like any long, sick marriage, the United Nations–NATO relationship over Bosnia had a remarkable capacity for inertia. Indeed, the ability to look very busy yet remain quite inert may have been the relationship's ultimate raison d'être. But every now and again, with a kind of seismic rumbling, something shifted. The shifts could prove illusory, momentary convulsions before relapse into the bog known to weary United Nations spokesmen as the *status quo ante*. But they were remarkable nonetheless.

Manfred Wörner, the German secretary-general of NATO, was dying of cancer. He came to the NATO meeting of February 9, 1994, in Brussels against the advice of his doctors; he would live just five months longer.

But Wörner wanted to be there because he believed in the alliance's obligation to draw a line, however belated, in the Bosnian mud and stop the Serb bombardment of civilians.

A cadaverous figure, his cheeks drawn, his eyes unnaturally fervid, he was visibly elated after the fourteen-hour meeting. "This is a historic moment, a decisive moment in the life of our alliance," he said. "We will use our air power to stop the appalling loss of life in Bosnia. We hope our warning will be heeded. We are not looking to use force. We prefer a negotiated solution. But we will not hesitate to use force if we have to."

The warning—never called an ultimatum because that is what Austria-Hungary issued to Serbia in 1914—stipulated that the Serbs withdraw their artillery and mortars to a distance of 20 kilometers, or about 12.4 miles, from the center of the Bosnian capital by 1:00 A.M. local time on February 21, 1994. The Bosnian government was to hand over its heavy weapons in the city to the control of UN peacekeepers. After the deadline, the statement said, there would be bombing if guns remained within the designated zone: "Heavy weapons of any of the parties found within the Sarajevo exclusion zone, unless controlled by UNPROFOR, will, along with direct and essential military support facilities, be subject to NATO air strikes which will be conducted in close coordination with the United Nations Secretary-General."

Clinton, who had been silent on Bosnia for months, said, "Nobody should doubt NATO's resolve. NATO is now ready to act." The message seemed clear: an alliance that had confronted and deterred and overcome the Soviet threat without ever firing a shot in anger was ready to be transformed into an attacking force.

The resolve was the fruit of a momentary resolution of the differences between the United States and its European allies that had made coherent policy so elusive in Bosnia. France and Britain had the largest, most influential contingents in the United Nations force. The United States had no troops in UNPROFOR, but, starting in April 1993, had pilots patrolling the Bosnian skies in a NATO operation code-named "Deny Flight" that was supposed to stop all helicopter and fixed-wing flights by the belligerents. UNPROFOR thus reflected French and British thinking on Bosnia; NATO, the American. The visions were naturally different: the former ground level, intimate, and cautious; the latter aerial, sweeping, and nominally bold. It was an ingenious scaffolding for paralysis and for interminable obfuscation. The buck stopped in midair.

But confronted by the killing at Markala, the Sarajevo marketplace, the French foreign minister, Alain Juppé, suffered a surge of statesmanship. His calls for the need to act in order to "preserve the values of civilization" amounted to a thunderbolt. Lord Owen, among others, was discomfited.

He insisted that it was technically incorrect to call the situation at Sarajevo a siege. Owen was worried about what the Russians would think if NATO became more assertive. But a fleeting Franco-American alliance was enough to carry NATO to what looked like a new purposefulness.

It was in these circumstances that I returned to Tilava Hill on February 21, 1994, almost one and a half years after my first visit. A fierce winter now gripped the hillside near the Bosnian capital. A cold wind sliced down from the peaks. On such days, the long, frozen isolation of Bosnia, cut off from the mainstream of European history, was palpable.

ON TILAVA, nothing had moved. The Serb guns, more numerous now, were still there, with Sarajevo in their sights. There were eight mortars, four 122-millimeter field guns, two multiple-rocket launchers, and four anti-aircraft guns. United Nations soldiers were still there. But the confusion, already evident in 1992, had eased from the realm of the bizarre into that of the surreal.

The deadline for the ultimatum that would not speak its name had expired about twelve hours before my visit. Technically, the Tilava battery should have been subject to immediate NATO air attack. Any weaponry within 12.4 miles of the city was supposed to have been "regrouped" and placed under United Nations control. But the closest United Nations soldier to these guns was Sergeant Robert Monneret of France, who was standing half a mile away and peering at them through binoculars.

"My mission," he told me, "is to survey the Serb weapons and prevent any use of them. For us, it would have been much easier to regroup these artillery pieces and mortars in a UN collection site lower down, but the Serbs say they have orders not to budge from this position. The guns are operational, but we try to keep them under our visual control."

As we spoke, two NATO F-14 Tomcat fighters raced overhead. They circled the area, swooping ever lower over the Serb guns, descending to about one thousand feet with an intimidating roar. Sergeant Monneret looked up at them with an expression in which a soldier's impassivity mingled with a man's apprehension. "If they dropped a bomb it would amaze me," he said. "But, in any case, if they do, we're pretty badly placed."

Monneret was a master of understatement. Any NATO bombing would probably have wiped out his platoon of French United Nations soldiers. I considered this odd situation. The "safe areas," including that around Sarajevo, were avowedly maintained through deterrence; deterrence, as NATO had proved in staring down the Soviet threat over four decades, is about the ability and readiness to escalate; the potential escalation must be limitless to be credible. Yet here, almost two years into the war, was the kernel of the West's response in Bosnia: a deployment of allied forces that made one group a potential target of the other and so made a nonsense of deterrence.

The "targets" wore the light blue helmets of the United Nations and drove around Bosnia in white vehicles. The deterrent forces, dressed in combat fatigues, swooped overhead in NATO jets. The former included British, French, Dutch, Belgian, and other allied soldiers, but no Americans; the latter was an operation dominated by the United States. The lunacy was reinforced by the fact that most of the tactical air control teams on the ground—those theoretically guiding the NATO pilots to their targets—were under UN control; they could thus be manipulated by the likes of General Rose. In that the flawed nature of this setup was blindingly obvious to anyone who spent more than a few days in Bosnia, the question must be asked why it was allowed to arise and, once arisen, fester for more than three years.

The Bosnian war broke out at a time of flux. The security architecture established in Europe over the postwar decades had just been rendered obsolete by the ending of the Soviet Union, an ending only made completely clear by the failed putsch in Moscow of August 19–21, 1991. Western Europe was thus relieved of the supreme threat that locked its military alliance with the United States in place. NATO no longer constituted an inevitable marriage of interests.

At the same time, Western Europe's slow march toward economic and political union was gathering pace. Its pretentions toward union and a degree of strategic emancipation from the United States were symbolized by the confident assertion that "the hour of Europe has dawned," uttered by the foreign minister of Luxembourg, Jacques Poos, before the first of numberless futile European peace missions to the Balkans in June 1991. But the fact was that Europe, even after the agreement on the Maastricht Treaty in December 1991, had no army and its most powerful state, Germany, was constitutionally barred from projecting power militarily. The diplomacy of Europe therefore amounted, in the phrase of the American diplomat Herb Okun, to "baseball without a bat." When Bush and Baker left the Yugoslav question to Europe they handed power to an orphaned minor. The chaos that ensued demonstrated the extent to which the Soviet Union's demise had set NATO adrift. The Bosnian war was to France as Chicago is to New York. The United States had a buffer called the Atlantic Ocean. This geographical fact, in a war that did not threaten the use of intercontinental weaponry, tended to make Western European countries more pragmatic and less willing to countenance any use of force by NATO. In this, their position was often closer to Russia's than to America's.

The United States, meanwhile, took a distinct strategic view of Islam in

the Balkans. It tended to see the defense of moderate Islam as a way to bolster—or at least not alienate—moderate Islamic countries generally, particularly three crucial, and vulnerable, allies: Egypt, Turkey, and Saudi
Arabia. Moreover, the moral high ground at least offered Clinton an appearance of solidarity with Izetbegović even if he was not ready to defend
his government or his country with even a platoon of American soldiers.
By contrast, Britain and France, with strong historical ties to Serbia forged
through two world wars, were inclined, sotto voce, to equate the arrival of
a mainly Muslim state in the Balkans with the establishment of a fundamentalist terrorist threat. For France particularly, Sarajevo loomed as a potential Algiers in the midst of the continent.

These differences were the basis for endless transatlantic arguments that
were real in the sense that outlooks differed but fake in the sense that the
resulting impasse suited everyone. Washington, London, and Paris all preferred arguing about the future of Atlanticism to going to war for Bosnia.

The Clinton administration could blame the Europeans for weak-
kneed cynicism in not lifting the arms embargo and backing air strikes.
The Europeans could blame Clinton for keeping American boys safely off
Bosnian soil and wanting to "fight the war there down to the last European." They could all worry together about what an obviously self-
absorbed and incapacitated Russia might think about Western actions in
the Balkans. Bosnian society, meanwhile, could, and did, pay the irrepara-
ble price.

All this discombobulation spawned a stunning disarray. NATO, unhinged, deferred to the UN. The Security Council, where it could agree,
contracted out certain tasks to NATO—first a maritime blockade in the
Adriatic, then Operation Deny Flight, finally the protection of the "safe
areas." The two organizations then bound themselves through an unworkable compromise known as the "dual key" that, in its most burlesque
expression, could leave a military decision on a shifting situation in Bosnia
dangling from the tergiversations of a half-dozen people in Goražde, Sarajevo, Zagreb, New York, and Naples (where NATO's southern command
is based). Akashi came away from the war with a wooden carving of two
keys pointing in opposite directions and inscribed with the words DUEL
KEY. But the unfunny thing was that the duel between NATO and UN-
PROFOR was one in which Bosnians died.

At bottom, the "dual key" subjected any NATO action to the approval
of Akashi and the United Nations military command in the former Yugoslavia—that is, to the people who were responsible for men like Sergeant
Monneret and his platoon on Tilava Hill. The upshot was a devilish mechanism for *immobilisme*. Rose pinned up a photograph in his Sarajevo office that summed up the mess and the simmering ill feeling between his

UN command and NATO. It showed a Red Cross vehicle that had been flattened by a bomb. The caption read, "Nice one, NATO." Akashi told me straightforwardly, "NATO is too blunt an instrument to use in diplomacy. In these small wars, it is simply too big to be effective."

What was interesting was the way the individuals who had the power to put an end to this paralysis remarked constantly that their actions were no more than the reflection of what the world or the "international community" wanted. They presented themselves as the physical embodiment of the Security Council's lowest common denominator. The corrosiveness of modern multilateralism lies in the fact that it creates not only botched compromises but also people who have abjured their power to make a difference. The result is muddle presided over by mediocrity. Initiative is abjured: Morillon *requiescat in pace.*

I heard the arguments in countless guises. Akashi: "Our deterrence function has not been realized in a perfect way. But we have to carry on. We have to be aware of the danger of escalation. In such a tight confrontation, how can you use air power? It sends the wrong signal on impartiality. The use of force in peacekeeping is a fascinating subject, and there are real and genuine differences of view. But what I see is that with force we may pass one checkpoint, but what happens at the next one? And we have to feed close to two million people."

Rose: "NATO principles are not the same as ours. NATO doctrine was based on the massive application of force for the total destruction of the enemy. Now we have no enemy. I must maintain dialogue with both sides, because the alternative is war. If someone wants to fight a war here on moral or political grounds, fine, great, but count us out. Hitting one tank is peacekeeping. Command and control, infrastructure, logistics, that is war."

The inexorable effect of these ideas was appeasement of the Serbs, the prolongation of the war, and the exacerbation of Bosnia's divisions. With each day the country died a bit. UN officials still paid lip service to a "multi-multi-pluri" society in Bosnia, but their eyes glazed over as they did so. "Multi-multi-pluri" stood for "multi-ethnic, multicultural, pluri-religious." However, the glib shorthand became a term that captured the West's essential cynicism over Bosnia's fate.

Respect was also proffered to the "suffering of the people," but I believe this suffering remained largely abstract. Akashi, ensconced in Zagreb, disliked being obliged to spend a night in Sarajevo and tried to limit his stays there to a few hours. I never saw Rose venturing into one of the countless hostels for refugees in Sarajevo.

Even after the massively flawed initial response to the war, the worst was not inevitable. Given the United Nations deployment, escalation required courage, but the bluff of the Serbs could certainly have been called long before it was. Likewise, the deployment in Bosnia of American troops would have required courage. But it would also have focused the minds of the Serbs in an entirely new way and eased divisions by ensuring that the major Western powers finally viewed the situation in Bosnia from the same standpoint.

SERGEANT MONNERET WAS right. The F-14s did not bomb on February 21, 1994. Nor did any other NATO aircraft. Akashi concluded that the work of United Nations peacekeepers "up to this point assures us that there is no need for air strikes." The deployment of about four hundred Russian troops in United Nations uniform in the Sarajevo area gave Karadžić a way of saying that he had not blinked to the forces of NATO.

The day the deadline passed, the Serb leader echoed his reflections at the London Conference of August 1992: "We are separate ethnic groups and we are separate states. Why should we make some hybrid creation that would not work? It is not a good solution." So much for Bosnia-Herzegovina. As for the Serb guns trained on Sarajevo, Karadžić told me there were some artillery pieces still "stuck in the snow," but they were under United Nations control.

The day after the ultimatum took effect, February 22, 1994, I went to another Serb artillery emplacement within the exclusion zone. This one was at Osijek, to the west of the capital. There were nineteen Serb cannons and howitzers dotted around. A platoon of British troops had tried, and failed, to take control of the guns. There was no question that NATO, by the terms of its own statement of February 9, was bound to bomb the position. But Lieutenant Simon Coldrick summed up the problem: "The Serbs are an undefeated army. They see their cause as legitimate. The war is not over. So we have to try to accommodate them."

In the end the accommodation rewrote NATO's terms. The Serb heavy weapons that failed to leave the exclusion zone were not, in general, placed in collection sites; rather, those "sites" were improvised around the gun emplacements themselves, to which groups of UN soldiers were dispatched to engage in yet more monitoring. This arrangement made many United Nations troops easy targets for Serb hostage-taking. Another contribution to the final disaster of the summer of 1995 was thereby made.

But there was a moment of elation. Shelling stopped completely for the first time in 676 days; trams started running again on March 12, 1994; Sarajevans ventured out into the streets. On March 17, a road was secured across the airport and over Mount Igman. Rose was delighted and squashed any suggestion that the improvement might be temporary with a sweeping rebuff: "If you don't have a sensible question, don't ask it."

• • •

SOON AFTER Rose got the trams running, I watched four Sarajevo boys play a war game in the spring sunshine. They were darting back and forth behind pockmarked walls, firing slender paper darts at one another out of blowpipes fashioned from metal tubes. They said they were less frightened than before. One of them, Almir Plećo, aged eleven, told me how his stomach would seize up under shelling. Their happy faces suggested a time of relief for the city.

But the scene darkened as Emin Kapo, also aged eleven, began to talk about his life. He had lived, until August 3, 1992, in a predominantly Muslim village called Kramer, near Rogatica in eastern Bosnia. Then Serbs attacked and took his entire family prisoner, marching them off to a nearby school that had been converted into a prison. "The day we were captured," he said, "my father and my older brother were taken away and I have never seen them again."

His mother, Hanifa Kapo, took up the story. When the family entered the school, her husband, Ramiz Kapo, and her twenty-two-year-old son, Ramo, were separated from the rest of the family and grouped with other men, the usual pattern during the Serb rampage that summer. "My husband knew one of the Serbs who captured us from his school days, and he was begging him to be allowed to stay with us," she said. "But they kept him and the boy. The last time I saw them, later that day, they had blood all over their hands."

That night, Mrs. Kapo, her young son Emin, and four daughters were put on a bus and taken to the mountains near Sarajevo. They were told to start walking toward the town. The Serbs' last words were: "Go to your Alija." Since then, Mrs. Kapo and her five children had been living in a small room in a building that was formerly a residence for students at Sarajevo University. She kept breaking into tears. The parents of the other boys, also refugees, lived in adjoining rooms. Almir Plećo's father, Husein, also from Rogatica, had recently been hit by a Serb sniper. With a bullet in his leg, he had been discharged from the Bosnian army.

I came away from the hostel thinking that there was too much unresolved pain on the one hand, too little international coherence on the other for it to be likely that the lull would be lasting.

THE SERBS TOOK the measure of Rose and Akashi. On March 31, 1994, they attacked another "safe area": Goražde. This time, NATO bombed. On April 10, in NATO's first offensive action, two United States Air Force F-16s dropped three bombs on a Serb artillery command bunker. There was another attack the following day. On April 14, a British

Sea Harrier was shot down by the Serbs. Overall, however, the bombing was so limited in scope that it amounted to a gesture with no deterrent effect on the Serbs.

Muddle ensued. On April 20, NATO said that unless there was an immediate ceasefire, a Serb troop withdrawal to a distance of three kilometers from Goražde town center by April 23, and a withdrawal of all Serb heavy weapons to a distance of twenty kilometers by April 26, there would be air strikes. When the conditions were not fully met by the Serbs on April 23, Akashi prevaricated, prompting a furious telephone exchange between him and Wörner, for whom NATO's credibility had been compromised.

Rose drew one central conclusions from events in Goražde: the Muslims were perifidious because, he believed, they had folded their front line and so opened the way for the killing of a British officer who had gone into Goražde to direct air strikes. The officer was from the elite unconventional-warfare unit of the British army, the Special Air Service, or SAS, which Rose had once commanded. When the radio report came in from Goražde, Rose exploded. "We are being stitched up," he said. "The Muslims are doing a dirty to get us to fight their war." Later, of the Bosnian action that led to his colleague's death, he commented, "One bloke with a crowbar could have stopped them, but they turned and ran."

After the Serb assault on Goražde on April 29, Rose called me into his office in Sarajevo. "Reports on Goražde were deliberately exaggerated in order to shame the world into doing something," he said. "The attacks were not of the dimension suggested. A false impression was given to the international community to help stir the vision of the Bosnian Serbs as the enemy and, unfortunately, all this very nearly went out of control. A big problem is that the Muslims believe they can bring the Americans into this war. They are living in an unreal world. A dangerous overreaction was stirred up in international capitals. There's an awful danger that we'll come to see Mladić like Aidid in Mogadishu. And then, who will feed the two point seven million? Who'll stop Sarajevo being hammered again?"

The general meandered on. Yes, he said, there were still some Serb weapons within the Goražde exclusion zone, but "I'm not about to start a third world war for three rusty pieces of metal." Goražde hospital never was a working hospital and, contrary to reports that it had been destroyed, it only had a "shell through the roof" and "two or three tank rounds into the stairwell." The Serb aim had never been to take Goražde but merely to apply a "chosen level of pressure." In any event, Rose added, "it is very hard to believe that the Muslim enclaves are viable in the long run."

In short, journalists had got it wrong and almost started World War III.

On the day Rose spoke, Ryan Grist, a relief worker who had just left Goražde after the three-week Serb assault on the town, described a quite different scene. "There was complete terror and horror in the town and the place is basically a ghetto," he said. "It's a Srebrenica-type situation." The death toll became a matter of sharp dispute—was it three hundred or seven hundred?—but subsequent investigations showed that, whatever its precise dimension, the Serb attack had been damaging. As time and slaughter would prove, it was the United Nations "safe areas" that were a fiction, not the reporting on what happened in them.

Goražde completed Rose's conversion. He had arrived in Bosnia in January 1994, convinced that he could at least end Sarajevo's agony. "Who dares, wins" is the motto of the SAS, and Rose talked boldly of restoring electricity, collecting the garbage, establishing a postal service, and opening up routes in and out of the city. But the élan evaporated. Rose's favorite refrain became, "This is the Balkans, you know." It was a form of renunciation.

He became obsessed with what he saw as the perfidy of the Muslims. They had one 82-millimeter gun that they would sometimes bring on a truck into the Koševo hospital, in order to draw Serb fire. Such desperate and despicable acts disgusted Rose. But he stopped asking why the Bosnian government had been pushed toward such actions.

Barking scattershot responses to questions, pouring scorn on what he viewed as America's guilt-driven attachment to Bosnia's Muslims," muttering about Muslim plots to lure NATO into the war, threatening NATO air strikes on government forces if they continued their "provocations," he appeared an increasingly unbalanced figure. His unblinking pale blue eyes gleamed. So did those of his tight entourage of SAS folk and romantic Irish Guardsmen, quoting late into the boozy night from commonplace books and discussing what T. E. Lawrence called "the irrational tenth"— the intuitive flash that points the way to victory. Meanwhile Rose's interpreter, a British officer of Serb descent, took to spewing scorn on all those in the "international community" who misunderstood the Serbs.

Rose found Mladić and Karadžić congenial but was roused to fury by the endless maneuvering of Ejup Ganić, the Bosnian vice president. His relations with the American ambassador to Bosnia, Victor Jackovich, were poisonous: "You're only accredited to one of the warring factions," he told the ambassador scathingly.

Insisting that he had "a very logical mind," Rose liked to talk about how he got visitors "squared away"—that is, fully apprised of the fact that the Muslims were professional victims. When, on July 27, 1994, the Serbs forced the closure of the road across the airport and over Mount Igman that had temporarily provided Sarajevo with a lifeline, and then shot at a British United Nations convoy, killing one soldier, Rose declined to call in

NATO air strikes or reopen the road. He described the Serb action as a "misunderstanding." The noose around Sarajevo tightened once more.

A lot of misunderstandings happened. When Rose's vision of the war was jarred by some uncomfortable fact he waved it away with an expression that drove American diplomats mad: "That," he would declare, "is of no importance." Akashi kept trying to do business with the Serbs. On May 2, 1994, he allowed seven Serb tanks to cross the area around Sarajevo from which heavy weapons were banned. In exchange, he obtained a Serb "promise" that convoys carrying food and aid would be allowed into Goražde. Later Akashi acknowledged that this was perhaps his sole mistake.

One of the most persistent "misunderstandings" concerned the Serb theft of United Nations property—particularly jeeps, armored personnel carriers, and fuel. In effect, the Serbs were confident enough of the impotence of the United Nations to help themselves to whatever matériel they needed.

On December 10, 1994, for example, Serb forces stole two Mercedes jeeps from a Dutch convoy from Srebrenica as it passed through the Serb-held Sarajevo suburb of Ilidža. That day, Victor Andreev, a Russian official who was chief of civilian affairs at Rose's Sarajevo headquarters, wrote to Koljević, the Bosnian Serb vice president: "If you wish to cooperate with the United Nations, then I am sure that you will find a way to guarantee the early return of the two stolen jeeps. I am sure also that you will be able to identify and return the three other jeeps of the same kind that were stolen recently in Vlasenica and Podromanija." By way of a threat, Andreev added that he was forwarding a copy of the letter to Akashi, who would "bring this matter to the attention of the foreign and defense ministers presently deliberating the future of this mission."

Later that day, Koljević spoke to a senior United Nations official in Sarajevo and told him the theft of the jeeps was a "misunderstanding." The official forwarded this information to Akashi along with some other observations on the routine woes of the United Nations mission:

1. *The Serbs have informed us that no Armored Personnel Carriers will be allowed to cross Serb-held territory at all. The United Nations High Commissioner for Refugees has advised us that they will not run convoys to Sarajevo without such escort. Thus, no aid convoys will come into the city, even from the airport.*
2. *All convoys from the eastern part of the country are blocked, and several are being held up on Serb-held territory between Sarajevo and the enclaves. Even the convoy bringing mail and fresh food to the UNPROFOR troops in Goražde has been refused.*

3.   *Danish convoy has been hijacked. Three tanker trucks carrying fuel for this*
     headquarters have been seized and are currently being unloaded some-
     where near the main road to the west of the city.

The report to Akashi concluded with the following reflection: "One
cannot help wondering whether the contempt with which we are treated
by the Serbs is not the natural by-product of a policy of endless appeasement."

This last phrase—with its pointed reference to appeasement—roused
Akashi to an unusual fury.

CHAPTER 20

THE TANGLED
ROADS OF GOD

In Sarajevo, I would sometimes watch a video made by Bosnian television on April 5, 1992, the day before full-scale war broke out and Bosnia was recognized as an independent state. It seemed to capture the naïve hopes of Muris Zečević and of many Bosnian people. A mixed group of Sarajevans is milling on the central Vrbanja Bridge, when shots ring out, fired by Serb paramilitary forces who that morning had attacked the Sarajevo police academy on the south side of the city. The shots took the first casualty of the war, Suada Dilberović, a twenty-one-year-old medical student from Dubrovnik, on Croatia's Dalmatian coast.

Abruptly, Muris appears, wearing a beret and dark glasses, brandishing an automatic weapon, the only armed man. He fires into the air; the people shout, "Cowards!" and "Terrorists!" to the Serbs shooting from a high-rise building. Jet fighters from the Serbian-dominated Yugoslav air force pass overhead. Muris joins the people on the bridge in jeering, shaking their fists, and chanting, "Bosna! Bosna! Bosna! Bosna!"

On the video, the people surrounding Muris—Muslims, Serbs, and Croats—look vulnerable. At first it appears that the fighters swooping overhead create this impression. The Sarajevans, Bosnians all, stand on the bridge in the middle of their city, demonstrating for a straightforward idea: that Bosnia—a community of Muslims, Serbs, and Croats—need not be torn to shreds; that the city, in its cosmopolitanism, is worth preserving. But the shots keep ringing out, scattering these people, breaking their bonds, pushing them toward new, as yet unimagined, hatreds, and it slowly becomes clear to me that it is not just the fighter planes bearing down on these Sarajevans that make them look so utterly helpless. It is Alija Mehmedović and the whole bungled history of Yugoslavia with its unspeakable maw of misapprehensions.

Vojna Adamović, a Bosnian Serb, was at Muris Zečević's side on

Vrbanja Bridge in Sarajevo on April 5, 1992, demonstrating against war
and in favor of a united Bosnia. The Serb and the Muslim stood together.

"We tried, we really tried, we tried from the bottom of our hearts,"
Vojna said. "All together. And what did it gain for us? You cannot fight
with your bare hands. The worst thing that we lost was not our apartments, not our clothes, not our cars, but our entire lives. I loved Yugoslavia
a lot. Then I had my other little Yugoslavia, Bosnia, and that went too.
Now I just don't care. I am a Bosnian. I had everything in Sarajevo. Great
friends. The sea three hours away. The mountains twenty minutes away.
Tell me: What did I need Greater Serbia for?"

WHEN THE SHELLS of Karadžić's forces started to fall on Sarajevo the
day after the demonstration, Vojna was terrified. She had never taken
Karadžić seriously. A Montenegrin poet-psychiatrist who had come to
Bosnia to tell the Bosnian Serbs they were endangered by the Muslims!
Her husband, Miloš Jelić, also a Montenegrin, had warned her for several
years that war might come, but Vojna waved away his fears. Montenegrins
were known for stories that were a mix of fantasy, fact, and folly.

Jelić had political ambitions when Vojna met him in the early 1980s.
He had joined the Communist party in 1980, two months before Tito
died, and risen to be leader of the Communist Youth in Bosnia. There was
a mixture of idealism and obstinacy and honesty about him that appealed
to Vojna.

She had joined the Communist party in Tuzla simply because she was a
good student; the crowning accolade for students such as she was party
membership. She would go to boring meetings once a month and sit chat-
ting or doing crosswords while she was informed that there was a threat
from the west, a threat from the east, and Yugoslavia in the middle. Her
musings on Pink Floyd and the Doors were considerably more intense
than on such strategic issues. But Miloš was different. He believed; he
thought that the party could be an instrument of political change. After
Tito's death, he was convinced of the possibility of, and need for, democratic evolution. He was also convinced that, in the long run, a multi-ethnic
state without democracy could not survive. For Yugoslavia, change was a
question of survival.

But at every turn Jelić found himself blocked. The political and economic climate in Bosnia soured throughout the 1980s. In 1987, the trial
for embezzlement of a leading Muslim businessman, Fikret Abdić, was
used by the Belgrade security services as a means to ruin the most prominent Bosnian Muslim politician, Hamdija Pozderac, and his family.
Pozderac, who had been set to head the Yugoslav presidency and was op-

posed to Milošević's demands that Albanian autonomy in Kosovo be curtailed, resigned and died of a stroke shortly afterward.

The tone of the affair was set by the Belgrade daily *Politika* when it remarked that the ground pepper called Mujo Hrnjica produced by Abdić's firm Agrokomerc bore the name of a "medieval Turkish oppressor." Jelić attended a party meeting in Sarajevo at the time and was astounded when a veteran of World War II, Rudi Kozak, declared, *"Idemo u gradjanski rat"*—"We are heading toward civil war." He was so surprised that he jotted the phrase down and showed it to Vojna. She laughed.

Jelić went to the party congress in Belgrade in 1989 and suggested the creation of a new Social Democratic party that could compete with the communists and open the way for meaningful elections. But Milošević's revolution was already in full swing and nationalism had taken an irrepressible hold.

After the congress, he told Vojna that Milošević was dangerous. She was amazed. She had been touched, albeit at a distance, by the Milošević cult. "We had assumed that Milošević was protecting us Serbs," she told me. "I was sure of that. And Miloš said no, he's going to drive us to disaster."

To Jelić, the rudiments of the catastrophe were apparent in 1989. Milošević's nationalism was an instrument with which to beat back democratic reform, yet such reform was the only hope for a multinational state such as Yugoslavia. If he was not to be allowed to remain a Yugoslav, Jelić asked himself what he could be. A Montenegrin? A Serb? A Bosnian? He felt Bosnia in his heart: a Bosnian then. But none of the nationalist parties that triumphed in the 1990 elections represented his Bosnia. How could he feel himself represented by Izetbegović, the leader of a Muslim nationalist party who made no secret of his religious views? In despair he said to Vojna, "We produce history all day, every day, and yet we never learn." He plunged into work at a timber company and abandoned the political scene entirely.

Vojna thought her husband too pessimistic. She had traveled to the United States four times in the late 1980s as an interpreter for delegations of Yugoslav mining engineers and scientists. She had developed a sense of the esteem in which Yugoslavia was held and, she thought, a deeper understanding than Miloš of Bosnia's indivisible position at the heart of that state. Look at your own family, she told him, pointing to the mixed marriages of most of her husband's relatives. Yugoslavia, she insisted, was not an impossible country; it was an emotional reality, like Bosnia. That was why, even after the unraveling of Yugoslavia began in 1991, she was on Vrbanja Bridge with Muris Zečević on April 5, 1992.

But then Karadžić left Sarajevo, climbed the hills, declared a "Serb Sarajevo" in Pale, and began shelling the over one hundred thousand Serbs who were still in the Bosnian capital. Not just Serbs, of course. Muslims, Croats, children, pregnant women. Karadžić's immediate readiness to shell his own people brought home to Vojna the naïveté of her reasoning, whose fault, she now saw, was that it was rooted in some basic humanity. But what was an Adamović, a Hadžić, or a Babić to the gunners and their ideological backers in Belgrade?

VOJNA LEFT THE CITY on April 12, 1992, the same day as Vesna and Jasna Karišik. She went to Belgrade and then Tuzla. She wanted to convince her parents, Mišo and Milena Adamović, to abandon Tuzla immediately. She also wanted to convince her pregnant sister, Aleksandra, who had just married a Croat, to leave.

Miloš Jelić refused to accompany his wife. Sarajevo was his city, he insisted; he was not about to abandon it. He was quickly drafted into the Bosnian army, where he was made to dig trenches. The first thing was to dig a hole for yourself deep enough to afford some cover. Then you could edge out from there. It was important, Miloš found, not to think. Dig, don't think, he told himself.

On August 2, 1992, the day before Muris Zečević was killed, Miloš Jelić was injured by shelling as he sat in his apartment. Shrapnel pierced his elbow. The injury brought home the absurdity of a war fought to trace ethnic lines across territory where no such frontiers could be drawn. As a Montenegrin and a member of the Orthodox church, Miloš was regarded with suspicion by many Muslims in the Bosnian army. In their eyes he was a Serb. Yet he had almost been killed by Karadžić. Like anyone in the wars who had a shred of Yugoslav patriotism, he had nowhere to go.

THE MINGLED MINARETS and church spires of Sarajevo offered a facile emblem of a multi-ethnic Bosnia. Tuzla, a city of power plants, chemical factories, and salt mines, provided no such facile imagery. It boasted only different shades of smoke—white, black, brown, and gray. The air of the city was thick with the dust of coal and the detritus of smokestacks. But the reality of civic tolerance was perhaps stronger in this gritty town than anywhere else in Bosnia.

In the last Yugoslav census of 1991, almost 17 percent of the population of 131,861 declared themselves to be Yugoslavs. They had, in other words, come to identify their nationality with their state, just as every citizen of the United States is an American. The corresponding figure for Sarajevo was 10.5 percent. Tuzla, as its lone rejection of the nationalist parties in the 1990 Bosnian elections underlined, was a city unprepared for tribal rupture.

Vojna Adamović's aunt, Kosa Hegeduš, lives in Tuzla. Before the fighting started Kosa was a Tuzlan, a Bosnian, a Yugoslav. She still puts her
clenched fist to her heart and says simply: "Bosnia is in your heart." Her
expression says the rest: Bosnia is in the generosity, the nostalgia, the longing, the unpredictability, the rages, and the intimacy of the heart. These
are qualities not easily grasped in the corridors of national chancelleries.

She is a Tuzlan, a Bosnian, a Yugoslav. She is also a Serb. Her parents
were both Bosnian Serbs. She is married to Zoly Hegeduš, a Slovene pho-
tographer of mainly Hungarian descent. She minds a small photographic
shop in the middle of Tuzla, beside the market, where she uses a hair dryer
to dry photographs. Her right eye has been dimmed by illness, but her left
eye still has a blue clarity to which suspicion is a stranger. Photographs
under glass on the counter in front of her portray a world scattered to the
winds. She says in her mild and considered way, "There is no Croat that
can say he is a pure Croat, no Serb that can say he is a pure Serb, no Muslim a pure Muslim. My great-grandfather, a Bosnian Serb, served in the
Austro-Hungarian army in Vienna and met my great-grandmother, an
Austrian, there. In this part of the world the roads of God are tangled. A
Bobić, a Kovačević, a Filipović—these are names that can be Muslim,
Serb, or Croat. We are mixed. The mistake in Yugoslavia was not to do
away with the republics, as was done before World War II. I respected Tito
but he made a small Soviet Union here. Our republics were upheld in the
grand tradition of Leninism. Why could the model not be the United
States or France? We would all have been Yugoslavs. Tito's motto was 'Preserve Brotherhood and Unity as preciously as your eyes,' but the reality
was different. I was in the party, I believed in it—and the hardest thing is
when you believe in something and then you lose your ideals. But you
could not help seeing that the differences between rich and poor were supposed to fade and were growing bigger and the same with the national differences. We were lied to, unfortunately; the truth was not told; in the end
people made frontiers in their minds."

Kosa's disillusionment with the party grew after Tito's 1974 constitution bestowed increased power on the republics and formalized their right
to secede. She had joined a party that represented the union of Yugoslavs,
a party that embodied the will to rebuild and reconcile in the postwar
years. But after the Croatian Spring of 1971, Tito, already an old man, appeared to Kosa to acquiesce to the notion of Yugoslavia's fragmentation.
There were now six parties, one in each republic. The parties amounted to
six bureaucracies, each bent on furthering its economic power.

Kosa clashed twice with the Tuzla party leadership after the new constitution appeared. In 1977, she argued against a growing preoccupation
with the "nationality" of new party members. If there were six posts open,

the new dogma held that two must go to Serbs, two to Croats, and two to Muslims. She was formally reprimanded for insisting that the only criterion for picking new members of the party should be talent. Two years later a conflict developed at her school over new provisions according teachers who were members of the party higher pay than those who were not. To Kosa, the party's growing role as a regional economic machine was symbolized by this proposal. She objected but was overruled.

When, in January 1990, the Slovenes walked out of the Fourteenth Extraordinary Congress of the League of Communists of Yugoslavia, Kosa was on vacation in Slovenia. She saw the party's dissolution as the logical consequence of Tito's Leninist tinkering with the "national question." She returned to Tuzla and resigned, declaring at a meeting that the party no longer had any sense.

Just as the party had fragmented as its idealism was eroded, so the country it had governed now fell apart. But still Kosa refused to believe that war could come to her city. For six weeks after the fighting broke out in Sarajevo, Tuzla was quiet. On May 14, 1992, there were announcements on television assuring people that war did not threaten Tuzla. The next day, Kosa went, as usual, to the school where she taught mathematics. At 2:45 P.M. the school bells sounded. The teachers were told to inform their students that the school year, which would normally have continued until June 10, was over. The bus service had mysteriously stopped, so Kosa walked home. At about 6:00 P.M., she started to hear waves of machine-gun fire and explosions.

On May 15, in what appears to have been a carefully prepared ambush, mainly Muslim militia units attacked a convoy of JNA troops leaving the city. Trucks filled with ammunition exploded; shells hurled balls of fire into apartment buildings; mayhem engulfed the streets. Dobrica Simić, a Serb doctor who was out walking with his wife, Amalia, who is half Croat and half Jewish, said the chaos was terrifying. Sounds of battle that would become banal still had the power of the unthinkable. Estimates vary of the number of JNA troops, most of them young Serb cadets, killed in the attack, but it seems clear that between 150 and 200 soldiers died. Still in the service of a fictional Yugoslav state, they appear to have believed that an agreement existed ensuring that their departure would be unhindered, for they were neither deployed nor disposed to fight. Aleksandar Soborović, a Serb doctor married to a Croat, was on duty at Tuzla hospital that day and estimated the JNA dead at about 200.

The city was 47.6 percent Muslim before the war, with the rest divided roughly equally among Serbs, Croats, and "Yugoslavs." By May 15, that balance had already begun to change. Muslim refugees were arriving in Tuzla from Bijeljina, Zvornik, Brčko, and other surrounding towns that were the first targets of Arkan, Šešelj, and the Belgrade thugs dedicated to the "cleansing" of Bosnia. Tensions naturally mounted in the city and finally became uncontrollable.

That night, Serbs in the surrounding hills began shelling Tuzla. The encirclement of the city started to harden. Serbs like Kosa Hegeduš and Dobrica Simić and Aleksandar Soborović, all of them living in their mixed marriages, found themselves doubly isolated. Rather than citizens they were now potential traitors, condemned to spend their time explaining that all Chetniks are Serbs but not all Serbs are Chetniks. May 15 came to be officially celebrated as the date of "the liberation of Tuzla." For them, however, it was the day that the gray light of confinement enveloped their city.

Six weeks earlier, Brčko, a similarly mixed town, had died at the hands of rural Serb extremists and units from Serbia. The Muslims of Brčko bore the brunt of this onslaught, but the urban Serbs of Tuzla later suffered the consequences of the inevitable reprisals. The breakup of Bosnia was thereby advanced. Lavrenty Beria, Stalin's police chief and one of the principal architects of his terror, once remarked that he no longer needed police. The system that had been put in motion had become self-sustaining. The central problem with what Milošević had started by brainwashing, arming, and backing the Serbs who ripped Brčko, Zvornik, and Bijeljina apart at the outset of the war was that there was no obvious way to stop the progressive Bosnian fracture that ensued.

KOSA HAD NOT HEARD gunfire since World War II. She was born in 1940 shortly after her father, Miloš Jović, was captured by the Nazis and taken to Mauthausen concentration camp in Germany, where he spent the rest of the war. Her mother, Vojna Jović, then took care of her and two older sisters. They lived in Priboj, about ten miles east of Tuzla, where Vojna was active in a communist Partisan cell. She would take salt from Tuzla to Partisan followers of Tito hiding out in the woods.

In 1943, Vojna Jović, then aged twenty-six, was captured by Serbian royalist forces opposed to Tito's Partisans. A Serb, but a communist, Vojna was taken before a Serbian Chetnik court and sentenced to death.

Kosa remembers: "My mother called me and my sister Radisava and she was walking close to us. And I was in my mother's arms. And we were flanked by Chetniks who were escorting us. My mother did not want to leave me, she wanted to be with me until the last possible moment. Although I was only three, I still remember . . . that one man snatched me out of my mother's arms and, perhaps fifty meters from there, they killed my mother. I heard the shots; I remember this. At the time I did not immediately realize that my mother was dead. I was told by my grandmother that she had gone to heaven and would come back and when we were not good my grandmother said my mother would cry up in heaven and would certainly not return and it was only later that my aunt explained to me. I missed my mother a lot. I had no mother and so I read a lot and tried to develop my own world."

THE USTASHAS HAD a saying, *"Srbe na vrbe"*—"Serbs on the gallows." But Kosa has another version: *"Srbe na Srbe"*—"Serbs against Serbs." Karadjordje, the leader of the first Serbian uprising, was beheaded in 1817 by an agent of Miloš Obrenović, the leader of the second uprising in 1815. Kosa's own Serb mother was executed by the Serbs in 1943. Almost a half century later in Tuzla, Kosa found herself running from Serb shells.

If there was a central theme to the Serb convulsion that precipitated and accompanied the destruction of Yugoslavia, it was that of Serb unity. The outlandish idea that—after centuries of migration, separation, cultural division, and internecine killing—all Serbs could be unified in a homogeneous new state defined by that unity was at once an illusion and an obsession. In this irreconcilable tension between illusion and obsession lay the Serb disaster.

The theme was already evident in Milošević's speech at Kosovo field in 1989, where Branković's desertion during the Kosovo battle, six hundred years earlier, provided a central theme.

"The disunity and treason at Kosovo," Milošević said, "would follow the Serbian people like an evil omen throughout its history. In the latest war, that disunity and treason brought the Serbian people and Serbia into an agony whose consequences, in a historical and moral sense, exceeded that of fascist aggression. Even later, when socialist Yugoslavia was formed, the Serbian leadership in that new country remained divided, prone to compromises at the expense of their own people."

Milošević continued: "These concessions that many Serbian leaders made at the expense of their own people could not be accepted—ethically or historically—by any nation in the world. Especially since, throughout their history, Serbs never conquered or exploited others. Their national and historical being throughout history was a liberating one. They were perennially liberating themselves and, whenever they had a chance, helping others to be liberated. And the fact that we are a big nation in this region is not a Serbian sin or source of shame. It is an advantage that the Serbs never used against others. But I have to say on this great legendary field of Kosovo that the Serbs did not use the advantage of being big for themselves either. Due to the vassal mentality of their leaders and politicians, Serbs felt guilty before others and even before themselves. The disunity of Serbian politicians was pulling Serbia backwards and their inferiority was a humiliation to Serbia. It has been so for decades, for years. *Here we are today on the field of Kosovo to say that it is not so any longer."*

THREE YEARS AFTER Milošević's speech, as part of the campaign to attain this elusive unity, Serb forces began to shell Sarajevo and then Tuzla. There were almost 180,000 Serbs in the two cities before the war. There were another 45,000 Serbs in two other principal Bosnian cities—Mostar and Zenica. This great mass of urban Bosnian Serbs—almost a quarter of a million of them in all—were placed in an untenable position.

In the countryside and smaller towns it was easier to break Bosnia. Villages always tended to be Muslim, Serb, or Croat. There was an old rural resentment of the city—particularly that of the Serb peasant farmer toward the predominantly Muslim bourgeoisie—that Karadžić could exploit. But his task was more difficult in the big towns. Still, the war, spewing fog, breaking bonds, did its work. Caught between the barbarity of Mladić and Karadžić and the growing suspicion or harassment of their Muslim neighbors, many urban Serbs fled to Serbia. In Mostar and Zenica few Serbs remained. Those who stayed in Tuzla or Sarajevo had to grow accustomed to being shelled by fellow Serbs.

Kosa's son Predrag, an artist whose longtime girlfriend Suada is a Muslim, was in Belgrade when the shooting started in Tuzla. He never returned. Kosa's sister Milena, the mother of Vojna Adamović, was at her weekend home in Priboj. She and her husband, a prominent Serb mining engineer named Mišo Adamović, had refused to listen to Vojna's warnings about leaving Tuzla. But now they also abandoned their home and possessions rather than return to a city at war.

For some time, Mišo had felt his Muslim and Croat colleagues at work retreating behind new barriers. When, a year before the war, a Muslim friend approached him as he read the Belgrade daily *Politika*—which he had read for the past twenty years—and asked him angrily why he was still reading that "Chetnik rag," he told his family that conflict was coming. But his wife would not believe him.

The only one of Kosa's close relatives to remain in Tuzla was her sister Radisava. Of the twenty thousand Serbs in the city before the war, twelve thousand had left by 1994. It was not easy to escape, but for between three thousand and four thousand German marks you could be accompanied across the lines. Kosa paid for her cousin, Djordje Blagojević, to escape that way with his wife after he was fired from the mining institute and she from the school of economics. Serbs were often dismissed from their jobs without explanation.

After midnight, there would be telephone calls and anonymous voices screaming, "When are you Chetniks leaving?" Sometimes Muslims with papers authorizing them to enter apartments would come and look their places over. It was fascinating to observe the acquisitive instincts of people even in the midst of a war, their eyes lighting up at the sight of a dishwasher or a television when their blood could be on the street the next day.

At Kosa's school there were progressive changes in the syllabus that tended to glorify the Ottoman history of Bosnia. Turkisms were introduced: *merhaba* instead of *zdravo* for "hello"; *duvar* instead of *zid* for "wall"; *pendžer* instead of *prozor* for "window"; *sahan* instead of *tanjir* for "plate." Kosa was saddened, but she saw the tens of thousands of Muslim refugees in the city and compared her hardship to theirs. Nobody had put a gun to her head.

DOBRICA SIMIĆ, the Serb doctor, was drafted into the Bosnian army soon after the fighting began and was sent to the front line near Brčko in 1993. It was tense being a Serb in the Bosnian army. Dobrica always tried to be amusing, to be good-humored, to avoid confrontation. All that was exhausting, and at night they would sit and drink and somebody would get aggressive. He saw some Croats blown away by drunken Muslims. Once an officer suggested that the Chetnik doctor was poisoning the troops, and some Muslim soldiers set out to get him, but they were drunk and they never found him. He saw what misery the heroic fight for Bosnia could harbor. Many young Muslim soldiers were brought to him after they had shot themselves in the arm or calf to avoid having to push forward as fodder for the Serb artillery. Other soldiers were injured in accidents. They would leave their trench to defecate and when they took their pants down a grenade would fall from their belts and explode. The wounds were particularly difficult to treat because there were feces mixed with the blood.

He thought a lot about the war. He did not want to leave his town and, as a Serb married to a Croat, saw no obvious place to go. At the same time Dobrica saw no future in Bosnia for his family. After World War II Germany was destroyed, but Germany still existed. Here, he felt increasingly, there would be no country, there would be nothing but potholed, overgrown roads and corn withering in the mined, untilled fields of new and meaningless national corrals.

His instinct was to blame the Americans. The CIA knew that Yugoslavia was doomed; they encouraged the nationalists in order to weaken a Europe moving toward unification. That, at least, was his theory. Beyond that, he was not sure whom to blame. He could not join Karadžić but neither could he understand Izetbegović's stance. Why could Izetbegović not have said we will have independence, but in a year or two, when some questions have been worked out? After all the accumulated bloodshed of the Serbs in this century Izetbegović should have known that he was lighting a tinderbox of irrational fear.

His colleague, Soborović, left for America with his wife. At times Dobrica felt he would go crazy if he remained in the Bosnian army, a Serb, yet again, fighting Serbs. The stupidity of so much death overwhelmed him.

At Tuzla hospital, a colleague, Kasim Muminhodžić, became increasingly prominent as the local head of Izetbegović's SDA party. By 1994 he had become a font of theories that justified the Turkification of the language. When I saw him, he explained to me that if communism had persisted for another decade, the Bosnian Muslims would have disappeared. "But now we have returned to our own language," he said, "and that is the language from which Serbo-Croatian was developed. Why should this return to our language be a problem? It is only a problem because the Serbs and Croats do not want a Bosnia. This war is God's blessing and punishment. It is his blessing because, without it, we may have died out. But now we have discovered our Muslim identity. It is his punishment because so many people have died. But the blessing is stronger because now we know ourselves and we will fight to the last man to get our homes back."

Muminhodžić was scathing about Selim Bešlagić, the secular mayor of Tuzla, who, since the start of the war, had been fighting a rearguard action to preserve the mixed community of the city. He said Bešlagić was a communist and all communists were Chetniks. This was nonsense; so, too, I felt, was Muminhodžić's odd theory on the Bosnian language. To me Bešlagić simply looked tired and marooned, a man left behind. At our meeting in May 1994, he told me that he had been fighting for two years for the survival of Bosnia. This fight involved trying to explain to everyone that polarization was exactly what Karadžić wanted. "If the soul of Bosnia is to survive," he said, "it must rise above this pressure."

On the day we spoke, a twenty-two-year-old Serb woman in Tuzla, Nataša Ćorak, was killed by Serb shelling.

VOJNA ADAMOVIĆ is named after her executed Partisan grandmother Vojna Jelić. After leaving Sarajevo, she went with her parents and sister to Subotica in northern Serbia, near the Hungarian border, where the family had distant relatives. Mišo Adamović, her father, began a life of humiliation. He would join lines of cars waiting—often for more than twelve hours—to cross into Hungary. There he would buy a full tank of gasoline. When he returned to Subotica, he would empty the tank into jerricans (bringing the cans across the border was not allowed because of international sanctions). After several trips, he would take 150 liters of gasoline to Belgrade, where it sold for 3 marks a liter, compared to the 1.3 marks a liter Mišo paid in Hungary. On these laboriously amassed profits the family eked out an existence.

Vojna's sister, Aleksandra, had a son named Filip. But a year after his birth, her marriage broke up. Darko Krančević, Aleksandra's Croat husband, declared that he could no longer live with the Chetniks and left for Croatia. He never contacted his wife again. Filip, soon after he began to talk, would ask about his father. His mother replied that he was "far away."

Vojna and her sister moved to Belgrade at the beginning of 1993. Vojna, desperate for money, found a job in February as a translator and secretary for Rajko Dukić, the Boksit trade executive who had worked closely with Karadžić and knew a lot about the disappearance of Muslims—including Ruzdija Šestović—in Vlasenica. Dukić told Vojna that her husband, Miloš, was a "traitor" because he had remained in Sarajevo.

She watched the shelling of Sarajevo on television and prayed that her husband would survive. Initially, her rage against Karadžić was paramount. Then she started to feel an overwhelming anger against America—for allowing this to happen and for lumping all Serbs in the category of villains. Finally, her anger was replaced by disgust for all the politicians who had engineered Yugoslavia's destruction and now profited from the war. Dukić was rich, her father ruined: that was the simple equation of war. Before the conflict both had been mining executives whose pay was roughly equal, but Dukić had hitched his sail to the nationalist wind.

"Of course we might have had different opinions in the run-up to the war," she said. "But that was not a reason to kill each other. We were forced to kill each other, to kill and be killed, so that they could retain office and go on making money."

MILOŠ HUNG ON in Sarajevo for eighteen months. But in the end it appeared there was nothing left. His family had gone. His friends had gone. His country had gone, replaced by a great emptiness, a wasteland of discarded cartridge cases. His city was disappearing before his eyes. His wife was in Belgrade, his mother in Ilidža; he could not speak to either of them. Some friends tried to escape across the Miljacka River into the Serb-held district of Grbavica, but they were captured, imprisoned, and tortured by Bosnian government forces. The suspicion that he was a spy always seemed to hang over him; it was exhausting. He had remained in the city and been injured in the fight for it because he believed for a moment that the new barriers were ephemeral and the soldiers in the rival trenches would soon be playing soccer again on the same fields. But he could not resist the relentless fissuring of his country. He grew angry at the West: Why did it wait so long and so ensure that the destruction of Bosnia was irreversible? Six months after the war began, Miloš found he could no longer convince himself that this was a war for a multinational Bosnia, the only Bosnia in which he and Vojna belonged.

Vojna traveled to Pale. A network operating there in collusion with Muslims in the city would spirit people across the lines for a payment of about one thousand dollars. But the arrangement fell through. A month later, on September 19, 1993, Miloš escaped with the help of a Serb liaison officer working at the United Nations office in the Sarajevo suburb of Nedžarići. The officer brought him across Sarajevo Airport to Serb-held territory.

When Miloš reached the Serbs' main barracks in the Sarajevo area, at Lukavica, he was detained. The Serbs there, like Dukić, accused him of being a traitor for remaining in the city. They put him in a Bosnian Serb army uniform. They interrogated him as to his activities in the Bosnian capital. They told him he would have to fight for the Bosnian Serbs and assist in the shelling of Sarajevo. When Miloš objected—and pointed to the traces of his injury from that very shelling—he was put in prison.

Vojna, through an official in Pale, was eventually able to secure his release. When, after an eighteen-month separation, Miloš was reunited with Vojna in Belgrade, he could not stop crying. The vacant, shattered look in his eye, bottomless as muddied water, was one she had already seen in her once-proud father. Miloš kept repeating a single phrase—*"Sta nam uradiše? Sta nam uradiše?"* "What have they done to us? What have they done to us?"

CHAPTER 21

HIGHWAY TO
TOMORROW

THE MARLBORO MAN, LASSO READIED, GAZES DOWN AT Haris Zečević as he cruises the Detroit freeway. Land of the free! The American icon, all taut, rugged assurance, seems to mock the Bosnian refugee whose loose belly and unwashed hair suggest a young man going to seed. Haris's hair is pulled back in a ponytail; stubble darkens his face. He has just bought the car with a bank loan; driving it fast gives him a kick, nothing like the war's adrenaline, but still. Before him on an urban plain is a wasteland of audio stores and eateries, auto dealerships and repair shops stretching into the featureless distance. Anybody on foot is strange. There could scarcely be a place farther removed from the intimacy of Sarajevo.

Since he reached Detroit Haris has been trying to forget Bosnia. But the violence and loss lived there are wound tight inside him and will not let him be. The passage from Bosnia to the United States was a passage from animal to human: "I was in the war for a time and you have to change or you ain't going to survive. You have to learn to bite, to fight for whatever you can get. Here, you still feel like you felt before in Bosnia. That is, anyone messes with you and you take out a gun. You kill 'em, turn 'em into meat. *You ever thought of taking a bite out of someone?* But you know that you try any of that stuff here and you're in trouble."

It has been a long road. Haris came down Trebević Mountain after his brother Muris's death and found that all his squad's ammunition, back at the Sarajevo headquarters, had been stolen. He'd been up there risking his life and down in the city some self-styled Bosnian soldier was helping himself to Haris's things. A period of swirling disillusionment began.

Haris tried repeatedly to find out who had given the order that they remain at the trench where Muris was killed. But trying to establish a line of responsibility in Sarajevo in the late summer of 1992 was as futile as looking for a pattern in the way shrapnel sprayed from a mortar blast. The government never offered any formal acknowledgment of Muris's death in the Bosnian ranks, much less a tribute to him.

Haris saw Muris's girlfriend, Sanja Mrehić. She said that the last time she was with Muris, she had begged him not to go back up Trebević, but he had dismissed her concerns, mocking the idea that the Chetniks could ever touch him. She was furious. The last thing she said was, "Don't you ever come back to me." But he had, in dreams, repeatedly.

Asim and Bisera Zečević wanted Haris to leave the army immediately. But he stayed on for a few weeks. What he saw troubled him. The Armija Bosne i Hercegovine (ABH) had come together haphazardly over the summer months, formed from a host of paramilitary units. These included the Patriotic League volunteer militia that Muris had frequented before the war; the official Territorial Defense; an SDA militia called the Green Berets; elements of the police force; and leaders of the Sarajevo underworld who knew how to handle a Magnum.

It was an army born in desperation, initially facing Serb tanks and artillery with AK-47s, hunting rifles, and pistols. The first coup for Bosnian forces followed the kidnapping of Izetbegović by the Serbs at Sarajevo Airport on May 2, 1992: when an exchange was negotiated through UN-PROFOR, involving Izetbegović's return in exchange for permission for a convoy of JNA soldiers to leave the city, Bosnian paramilitaries reneged, killing six JNA soldiers and seizing weaponry. Some elements of the JNA, under General Milutin Kukanjac, had tried to play a moderating role in the first weeks of the war, but this ambush ended that attempt. As the attack by the emergent Bosnian Serb army grew in the following weeks, intensifying with the heat of the summer months, defense of the city center was often heroic.

But war also meant stores to be emptied, cars to be commandeered, luxury apartments to be taken over, and fuel to be traded across the lines. Haris had cooks who couldn't cook; he had commanders who ordered him to clean the latrines while they worried about whether the color of their lighters matched that of their stolen Audis.

After Muris's death, he was confronted on the street by two policemen who pointed to his gun and asked him where his permit was. Haris showed the permit issued by his commander. They said it was no longer valid, there were new permits now, and they needed the rifle for their patrol. So Haris laughed and said his gun was not a gun, it was a violin, and did they want to see him play? The policemen stared at him. So he put the rifle on the ground and he took a grenade from his belt and he pulled the pin and he said, "Go on, take my violin."

Uneducated guys who had been small-time crooks before the war were suddenly responsible for hundreds of people. They had secret caches of weapons, they had been the first to come to the city's defense, they knew their way around the black market, and so they had their way. They inevitably formed ties, and interests, with a weak government that needed their services.

Among them were Ramiz Delalić (known as "Ćelo"), who had done several years in prison for rape; a former nightclub singer called Musan Topalović (known as "Caco"); and Jusuf Prazina (known as "Juka"). On three occasions Haris felt that the Bosnian forces might have the momentum to push through the Serb siege lines at Ilidža and end the encirclement of Sarajevo. There were enough desperate people. But unexplained countermanding orders came at the last minute. The notion crossed his mind a few weeks after Muris's death: Did the money being made through trafficking now mean the siege of Sarajevo was in somebody's interest? *What the hell am I fighting for if these guys, who have crept out of the basements, are making a million on me?* He suppressed the thoughts, but they gnawed at him.

Haris changed. He came to see that nothing could surprise him any longer, nothing impress him, nobody convince him of anybody's good faith. Muris was gone: that was all he knew. All that had happened to him was his own fault because he had allowed it. That was the bottom line. His Serb friends, they just needed a couple of lunatics as leaders and they all went berserk. He could not explain that. If, then, there was no reason for what they had taken from him, the only recourse he could see was revenge. The alternative, as far as he could judge, was to attribute it all to a higher power, become religious, or mystical, or some bullshit. His laughter became hollow. At the age of twenty-three, he became incapable of enthusiasms. When people talked to him about ideals or about beauty he found that he could only snicker to himself.

His maternal great-grandmother, Pasa Gagić, died in the weeks after Muris's death, at the age of 105. His mother kept telling him to get out of Sarajevo. His father's silence weighed heavily. Scared, guilty, and angry, his will to fight for Bosnia evaporated. Through a family friend, he found a job in the police and served for a few months as a bodyguard to an SDA politician.

Then, on February 26, 1993, six months after Muris was killed, he decided to risk escape across the airport. There were about one hundred of them that night. The shooting started soon after they set out across the airfield. In the scramble, Haris stepped on a man's head. Patches of snow, patches without snow. *A man's head.* And the ubiquitous white vehicles of the United Nations patrolling.

Haris made his way to the family home in Butmir. In the basement he found a cache of arms and explosives, apparently hidden there by the Bosnian army. He decided it was wiser to sleep at the neighbor's house, where, that night, he ate meat for the first time in a year. He had always said his favorite vegetable was meat.

From Butmir, Haris went down to Split, on the Croatian coast, to stay with his maternal grandmother. He was a refugee, one of the 2.7 million.

The family had a friend, Nino Crnovršanin, living in Detroit who, before the war, had offered to help Haris study engineering in the United States. Crnovršanin, a Bosnian Muslim opposed to communist rule, had fled Tito's Yugoslavia. He had made money in the metals business and, since the war began, had been trying to help the Bosnian government in whatever way he could. He had set up a branch of the SDA in Detroit and raised money to help Bosnian soldiers injured in the war. Now, he came to Croatia to try to help Haris secure an American visa.

Despite an invitation from Crnovršanin, Haris's initial application for a visa was refused. His situation became increasingly uncomfortable after the tenuous alliance between Croats and Muslims in Bosnia collapsed and full-scale war erupted between them in April 1993.

There was never much more than the old principle that the enemy of my enemy is my friend behind the Croats' initial understanding with the Muslims. Tudjman's Bosnian appetites were always as voracious as Miloševic's, but the military means at the Croatian president's disposal were at first comparatively meager. By 1993, however, the Croats were ready to attack in central Bosnia, using a bogus interpretation of the Vance-Owen Plan's map to justify an attempt to push Muslims out of the Travnik-Vitez area of central Bosnia.

For the first time, the Muslims fought back. It was an indication of the gradually turning tide of the war. But Haris had already opted out, and, as a Muslim refugee, he suffered growing harassment in Croatia. He decided to press his visa application by approaching the United States Refugee Resettlement Office. After three months, his application was at last approved and, on July 27, 1993, he flew from Split to New York and then on to Detroit.

THE CITY is weird. You drive seventy miles in a day on highways that cross one another at right angles, and that's normal. But Haris soon understands what is essential. He has to get a job so that he can get some money so that he can get a credit rating and get off welfare. With a credit rating, he can get a car and a television. Without a car, he is lost.

Detroit is busy. People are always going somewhere with a purpose.

There is, without question, a deep-seated assumption that a purpose exists. Strange, Haris reflects, that this fundamental premise has never gained much of a foothold in Bosnia. Part of the purpose, in Detroit, is to get places as fast as possible. So walking is not an option. Nor is public transport, because, in essence, there is none.

Besides, there are the distances. Between places—Clinton Township, where Haris starts out, and Dearborn and downtown Detroit where, the Bosnian refugees say, *"pojesti će te mrak"*—"the darkness will eat you." But also between people. That distance, between people, is strange to Haris. It has a hermetic quality, a sharpness, and a certain pain. Everyone is on his own here, sealed inside a car, a job, a home.

Haris is impressed by these American distances. Life seems to have been disentangled here in a way that is cruel but that also springs people loose from the vengeful coil of history into a present that is bland and plentiful. He is used to a past that crowds in on you. It is there across the dinner table in the face of your grandmother, there across the street in the crumbling mosque, in the ramshackle Sarajevo streets that curl and straighten like question marks, in the white graves that lace the Bosnian landscape the way gas stations litter the land in America. Here he sits in a café on a highway that hurtles only toward tomorrow and watches the old women, some with blue hair, sitting alone eating waffles and reading some publication like *Modern Maturity*. These women seem to have been left alone by their families. Their home is "a Home." They are sad but scarcely menacing. In Bosnia, he learned too late, each family was an extended history lesson pregnant with violence.

He goes to work for Crnovršanin in a metal-processing shop, making components for Ford. He persuades Crnovršanin's brother to cosign a loan of three thousand dollars for the purchase of an '85 Thunderbird. Crnovršanin introduces him to some of the other Bosnian refugees—a couple of hundred have already come to Detroit. Many have gathered in Hamtramck, a Polish-dominated township in northeastern Detroit. Their places smell of Bosnia: cigarette smoke, beer, plum brandy, lamb, and an ineffable pall of rancid weariness. They talk about green cards and, eventually, getting citizenship.

Here, strangely, citizenship *is* nationality. Once a citizen you are an American. You have obligations but you also have rights. The American nation, therefore, is something willed; it has nothing to do with blood or religion or whether you came from Lodz, Bratislava, or Sarajevo. All the Stars and Stripes fluttering in people's yards, hanging from factories, adorning fast-food restaurants—all these national flags are therefore about that choice, the choice of the nation as a rational rather than a blood-driven thing.

The nations of the French and the American revolutions were just that: inclusive, not exclusionary, ideas. But at home in Bosnia, nationalism had been precisely about the absence of choice. *You're* a Serb, *you're* a Muslim, *you're* a Croat: the drumbeat became inexorable. In the end, you could not exercise your mind, could not choose to be a Bosnian or a Yugoslav. You could not abandon, or relegate, the primal loyalty of the tribe and embrace some more generous, or simply more rational, ideal of humanity. The flags became no more than symbols of crassness and cruelty. Yet how much more similar were all the South Slavs, how apparently more suited to forming a living nation, than the people gathered in the flat, flat sprawl of Detroit alone!

In Hamtramck, Haris meets Dragan Vraneš. He is a Serb from the Krajina area. His family, living in Petrinja, was wiped out by the Croatian Ustasha during World War II. He got out of Yugoslavia in the early 1970s and came to the United States with a suitcase and a few dollars. In Hamtramck, over the years, he has put together a company that does building and decorating and he has made enough money to live well.

He owns six houses in Hamtramck, knows all the cops well enough to fix a parking ticket or a speeding fine, likes to give a hand to the Bosnians, show them around General Foods, resolve things when they get in a scrape. Likes to rent them his property, too. His message is clear enough. Forget *that thing over there.* You don't need the stress and there's nothing you can do about it. Roll up your sleeves and remember, over there it's cash, cash, and over here it's credit, credit. So don't make a late-life start on the mortgage.

Vraneš is an American. The United States, over two decades, has stripped him of his family's tragedy, now all part of *that thing over there.* They are fighting in Petrinja again. It's a front-line town where the Serb survivors of the onslaught in which his parents died have defied Croatian independence and set up a self-styled Krajina republic. But Vraneš does not care. He has become a rather simple man. The painful knots of his fate have been unraveled by the neutral backdrop of the American Midwest. His English is broken, basic, commonsensical. He cares nothing for, knows nothing about, the epic Serb tradition of oral poetry that moved Goethe to learn Serbian. Directness, rather than the grand rhetorical sweep of the Balkan history lesson, is the manner of communication that interests him now.

I don't care who is who, he says. It's not my thing. What have I got against the Bosnian Muslims or anybody? There are no refugees in the United States. Everyone is the same. Working, making money, getting that first mortgage, building some collateral. The first two years are hard, but then you make your way. Everybody has the same opportunity over here, no matter who you are, that's why this is the greatest country in the world. He smiles. *"I'm doing good."*

Among those lodged in one of Vraneš's houses is the Sorguč family from Hadžići, about twenty miles southwest of Sarajevo. *That thing over there* is still part of their lives. The Serbs rounded up all the Muslims in Hadžići on May 14, 1992, and took them down to the sports center. Ekrem Sorguč, a mechanic, was taken to the sports-center camp. His younger son, Mirza, then aged sixteen, was only saved by a Serb neighbor, Obren Krstić, who told the Serb paramilitaries, "Leave that kid, he's mine."

Ekrem stayed in the camp for over a month. He saw a Serb guard trying to prize off the gold wedding ring from one man's finger and, losing patience, slice off the finger and pocket it. He saw bleeding men forced to suck their blood from the floor without leaving a drop. He was forced to perform fellatio on another prisoner while the guards chanted, "This is Serbia." *You are not Muslims, you are converts, fuck your mother, fuck your mother, tell us you are Serbs.*

On June 24, 1992, Ekrem Sorguč was transferred from the Hadžići camp to Lukavica. He kept his nerve by sitting in a corner and thinking of his family and telling himself, You're gonna make it. As it happened, his older son, Adnan Sorguč, who was in Sarajevo at the beginning of the war, had been making it big.

When war broke out in Croatia in 1991, Adnan was a lieutenant in the JNA. He was injured near Zadar. His JNA contacts enabled him to know war was coming to Bosnia and so, in March 1992, he teamed up with Ćelo in Sarajevo and began training a unit to fight. There were only about twenty Muslims in it, but, over the summer months, the number grew to about forty-five hundred. Adnan Sorguč gained the nickname "Führer"; he was one of Ćelo's deputies. He had his own personal bodyguard, the title of brigade commander, and a new Magnum. He also had the prestige to get his father out of Serb captivity.

Adnan Sorguč contacted the Serb police chief in Ilidža, Tomislav Kovač, and suggested the exchange of his father for two prominent Serb prisoners in Sarajevo. The exchange eventually took place in the late summer of 1992 at the Delminium Café in the Sarajevo district of Stup, then an area controlled by the Croats. Ekrem Sorguč was saved but broken. As for Adnan, he gradually tired of being what he calls "a tool of politics" and of a sense he shared with Haris that the siege might have been broken if the political will had really been there. In April 1993, two months after Haris, he escaped from Sarajevo by running across the airfield.

Haris listens to these stories. To each his wound. The funny thing is they are lucky. They are *alive*, all of them, and they have been let loose on the big American continent. But they are also maimed, confronted with the new even as they are consumed by the old.

FIFTEEN DAYS AFTER Haris arrives in the United States, his mother is killed at Sarajevo Airport. Asim gets word to Crnovršanin, but he chooses not to tell Haris.

A month later, Crnovršanin calls him in after work and tells him there has been a "big tragedy" in the family. *Tragedy* is already a big word, and Muris has been dead for a full year now. There are only two of them left, Asim and Bisera. So, again, the old question: Which one?

Haris cried for his brother. He wants to cry for his mother. But all he can do is gasp for air. Nothing will come out of his eyes. He has been emptied. There is only the pain and the armor of rage and cynicism that tries to hide it. He wants to know when, where, how, but Crnovršanin does not know and there is perhaps one telephone line into Sarajevo.

Eventually he talks to his father and learns about the airfield and the UN beam on Bisera and something crashes in Haris's head and he wants to go back, no matter what, and kill the first Serb he can lay his hands on, kill them all, until there is nothing left beyond the Drina, just a great blackness, and, in the killing and his own death that would surely follow, atone for the guilt that is mounting in him because, he believes, if he had been there in Sarajevo his mother would never have tried that and if he had gone to the trench in the place of Muris, his brother would still be alive. His mother was in a cage. She was not guilty of anything. She had her memories. She wanted to get over there to Butmir. He could understand. But that the "international community" would turn her into a target was beyond his comprehension.

It is not easy to get back. Crnovršanin and the other refugees try to calm him. Rage slowly gives way to a confusion in which anger is mingled with guilt; sometimes there is nothing, just a dead void. "That's a strange thing about my feelings. I don't have them too much anymore. Sarajevo left me with that. But from time to time—this is weird, this is sick—one thing comes into my mind and it hurts me. I'm looking at pictures of my mom and my brother and I start wondering, what's happening to their bodies now, what do they look like in the ground. And that is something that is killing me."

Thoughts of revenge do not leave him. With renewed intensity he focuses on his Bosnian Serb uncle, Slobodan Karišik. The suspicion that Karišik helped blow up Sarajevo's central post office and most of its phone lines on May 2, 1992, becomes a blind conviction. Karišik is in Belgrade, the heart of darkness. He had money, a Swiss bank account stashed with funds from his UN work, he might have helped Haris's mother if he had stayed in Sarajevo. Haris feels with a growing clarity that he would kill his Belgrade uncle if he had half a chance.

AT THE BEGINNING of the 1993–1994 school year, shortly after they heard about Bisera's death in Sarajevo, Haris's cousins Vesna and Jasna Karišik moved to Belgrade to a small apartment in an outlying suburb, part of the city's northern sprawl into the plains that form the Serbian breadbasket. They had been saddened by their aunt's death, of which they learned in a letter from their mother, but it made nothing like the impression of Muris's. Perhaps it was their familiarity with death, perhaps their growing distance from the war. Their father, Slobodan, also seemed unmoved. Although the girls' new home was a dowdy ground-floor apartment, they were happier in it, pleased to be with their father and to be exposed to a bigger, more tolerant city like Belgrade.

For Vesna, Sarajevo became a place of sadness. She had been a girl there; in Belgrade she was a young woman. She was tired of moving and found it increasingly hard to imagine ever returning to Sarajevo. The city would reject her, she felt, for having left it. She did not want to confront the rebuke of so much ruin.

Jasna, who had known Sarajevo longer, was more ambivalent. There was something that nauseated her in the material obsessions of the young men who pursued her in Belgrade. She grew thinner, tenser; sometimes she trembled like a leaf. Faster cars, paging systems, Rifle jeans. It was all part of some great delusion, one that she could not undividedly join.

For the war's winners, she noted, money was no object. Dafina Milanović, the founder of the biggest of all the Serbian pyramid schemes, the Dafiment Bank, tossed five thousand German marks into the foundations of a new shopping mall. Just for luck. She was a pillar of the Milošević regime. Known for a time as "the Serbian mother," she described Milošević as "the real man that Serbs need." Before its collapse in 1994, her bank bilked hundreds of millions of dollars in hard-currency savings, enough to modernize several SAM missile systems and bankroll a war. Another financier of the regime, a self-styled "mystery man" named Jezdimir Vasiljević whose interests included the Belgrade horse-racing track, ran another pyramid-scheme bank, Jugoskandik, that defrauded seventy or eighty million dollars before he fled in 1993 to Israel and finally Quito, Ecuador.

In fashionable Belgrade clubs, a cellular phone and a first-class revolver became de rigueur. Dresses with zip-up fronts and big zippers, très décolleté, were en vogue. The revelers drank to the sounds of turbo-folk, the mélange of traditional Serbian tunes, hypnotic bass-guitar rhythms, and heavy Oriental lilts that took an isolated Serbia by storm. The most celebrated exponent was Svetlana Veličković, known as "Ceca," whose romance and then marriage with Arkan filled the gossip pages. The lyrics of turbo-folk—"Coca-Cola, Marlboro, Suzuki, discothèques, guitars, and bouzouki"—were scarcely uplifting, but they captured the obsessions of Serbia's heavily armed arrivistes.

Inflation spiraled—a million percent a year, a billion percent a year for a while in 1993. Then, as abruptly, it abated. The international trade embargo on Serbia, imposed two months after the Bosnian war began, was like that: permeable enough for an absolutely devastating crisis to be circumvented. At the worst moments, there was blood on the streets of Belgrade—the blood of pigs. I saw a bank employee named Vida Milivojević prop a seventy-pound side of pork on a sidewalk bench and hack it into pieces small enough to fit into her bag. Beside her, other bank employees were chopping flanks of pork. The scene evoked the wrong side of the Styx. Because there was no meat in Belgrade stores, Mrs. Milivojević had subscribed, for just over one hundred dollars, to a pork purchase arranged between her bank and a farm. She was, she said, deeply humiliated.

At times Jasna could not get her bearings in Belgrade. Roads in the city changed their names so often it was hard to describe where one was. Marshal Tito Street became Ulica Srpskih Vladara (Serbian Leaders' Street), an odd formulation apparently conceived to withstand the next twist of Balkan history. July 7 Street, which recorded the official date of the start of Tito's uprising in 1941, reverted to Kralja Petra (King Peter) Street, its name before World War II. But as the divisions between Serbian royalist Chetniks and Titoist Partisans were still unresolved, the change caused a row and the street was split in two. One part was called Ulica 7 Jula, the other Kralja Petra; naturally nobody knew which part was which.

One of the few thriving enterprises in the city's miasma was the Belgrade Zoo. It prospered on the basis of the shrewd nationalist marketing devised by its popular director, Vukosav Bojović. The zoo's chief attraction was the Serbian Defense Dog, a monster that prowled a prominent cage. Take a wolf, add a part or two of Nepalese mastiff, mix in some Doberman and a touch of Bosnian sheepdog, and this is what you get. It had the flanks of a horse and weighed over 130 pounds. "We call the dog Gari," Bojović told me. "He's well suited to Bosnia."

Crowds were also drawn by a tiger that had grown from a cub presented to Arkan by Bojović early in the wars; the cub became the symbol of Arkan's Tigers militia. Near the tiger, there was a cage with a light brown, cuddly looking bear called Knindza. It came from the Knin region of the Krajina and had been the mascot of another paramilitary brigade, led by Dragan Vasiljković, an Australian mercenary of Serbian descent who was known as Captain Dragan.

The virile symbols offered by the zoo stood in opposition to what Serbian publications liked to call the "Mickey Mouse" culture of Haris Zečević's adopted home in America. On the one side there was a real big dog; on the other a cartoon mouse. Serbia was authentic, wholesome, unbowed; it confronted what Serbian television portrayed as an uprooted mass of Western people awash in commerce, Americana, and hypocrisy.

The Serbian Defense Dog was grotesque. But there was also a certain pride in Belgrade's reaction to the war. In the endless patience of the long lines of people waiting outside banks, at bus stops, and at stores, in the gentility of much hospitality, in the care with which children were clothed and fed even in times of hardship, in the obstinacy of evidently broken men clinging to old habits of dress and comportment and reading, there was a dignity and a unity that revealed the lineaments of an old culture. But this old Serbian decency and sense of honor amounted to a culture defeated. Caught in the midst of a nationalist catharsis and a post-communist yearning for Western status symbols, Serbia was a black hole.

Jasna Karišik groped her way. "I see the war as a revolution," she told me. "What happened was a revolution. It had to happen, like the French Revolution. Tito's system was rotten, it had to change. It was a bad system, and it had to go. It went in a lot of blood and my family was caught in the middle. One thing strikes me, though. I've seen many Serb refugees here complaining about how they were treated by the Muslims. But the fact is that, unlike Muris, they are alive."

CHAPTER 22

THE BELL

By 1994, MORE THAN TWO MILLION PEOPLE WERE LOOKING for answers in the same way as Jasna Karišik or Vojna Adamović or Ermin Šestović. Over half the Bosnian population were refugees. The West's unwillingness to commit military power for purposes other than the containment of the Bosnian conflict had become overwhelmingly clear. Contained but unresolved, the war continued and, with it, the polarization of Bosnian society.

The Bosnian army, avowedly multi-ethnic, became increasingly marked by the use of Islamic symbols, quotations from the Koran, and other religious insignia alongside the fleur-de-lis emblem of a lay Bosnia. Mujahedin—self-styled holy warriors from Iran, Egypt, Algeria, Afghanistan, Sudan, and the Persian Gulf states—arrived by the dozen to bolster the Bosnian army in the center of the country. Izetbegović's SDA, always a Muslim nationalist party, became increasingly authoritarian, with influential members attempting to ban "aggressor" music (that is, Serb songs) from Sarajevo radio stations and inveighing against mixed marriages as "mostly ruined marriages."

All this, naturally, delighted the Serb followers of Karadžić, who had argued from the outset that the Muslims were "fundamentalists." They were not. But once persecuted, the expression of their identity naturally became more strident. In Bosnian army ranks, a new self-confidence that was also a new self-awareness became increasingly evident.

On May 6, 1994, I stood with a Bosnian officer, Mevludin Hasanović, in a small, green-walled mosque, flanked by the imam. Hasanović spoke of a Muslim soldier killed a few days earlier who, before his death near the town of Kladanj, had been blessed with a vision of the Bosnian army's ultimate victory over the Serbs.

"His vision will come true," Hasanović declared. "Today is an Orthodox holiday and normally the Serb girls bathe in a creek, but the weather is so bad they cannot. On the Orthodox Christmas there was a crescent moon in the sky. We gather strength from these signs. It has taken some time but now we know that the world will not help us. Not Akashi. Not Rose. Not Clinton. Not Boutros-Ghali. We must fight for victory alone. There are Croats on our side, and some Serbs, but we Muslims are the majority here so we must give the most and fight the most. Muhammad wants you to give all you can for the battle. So pray for the Muslims—in Arabic if you know how, or in your own language."

The mosque was packed, its rug-covered stone floor a sea of prostrate devotion. Hasanović was a compelling orator. After the service, held in the small northern Bosnian village of Ogradenjovac, he invited me to his office at a nearby Bosnian army building, located just south of the most critical single front in the war. The narrow corridor at Brčko amounted to the Serbs' umbilical cord. Linking Serbia to Banja Luka, the largest Serb-held town in Bosnia, it was the channel through which logistical support from Belgrade reached the Serb territories in Croatia and in northwestern Bosnia, seized respectively in 1991 and 1992. Without this support the territories would wither and die. The strip of land, about twelve miles wide, had initially been secured early in the war when a combined JNA and Serb militia onslaught on Brčko, in April and early May of 1992, cleared the town and its immediate surroundings of a large Muslim population; later, in further Serb assaults, it was widened.

Hasanović's small room was adorned with a poster of Alija Izetbegović bearing the slogan "I would call the day night if there was no Alija." A student of neuropsychology before the war, Hasanović was now a Bosnian warrior, his life wedded to a cause. His family had been hounded out of Brčko by the Serbs on April 30, 1992; he was wounded on November 15, 1992, trying to fight his way back into his hometown on the southern bank of the Sava River. These experiences had coalesced into a kernel of hatred.

"We have to clean our brains of the idea that somebody will come to help us," Hasanović said. "Only God will help us. We have to be cool. We have to kill more Chetniks than they kill among us. It's a very simple count. You have to shoot the Chetnik before he shoots you. Time is working on our side and, at the right moment, we shall cut the corridor."

I gazed into Hasanović's determined eyes and the French expression *"Les guerres sont dures et durent longtemps"* flitted through my mind. This war would be long and hard and, even after the fighting stopped, its residue would surely poison a generation or more. Perhaps it would lie latent like a recessive illness, but this pain would not be quickly spent.

Two years had passed since the Serbs stormed Brčko. The town of

87,332 people had been 45 percent Muslim, 25 percent Croat, 20 percent Serb. The rest called themselves Yugoslavs. Between May 1 and June 7, 1992, the Serbs herded several thousand Muslims and Croats into a concentration camp at Luka, a complex consisting of an old brick factory and a pig farm. Prisoners were held in three hangars, one so crowded that people were forced to sleep standing up. Sušica-on-the-Sava. Perhaps three thousand people were killed; surviving males, as at the Sušica camp, were taken to Batković camp near Bijeljina. Many women were driven over the lines into the northern Bosnian city of Tuzla.

The harvest of hatred from this Serb killing had now come in. A virus had embedded itself in the gut of Bosnia and was eating at every last artery of tolerance. In his talk at the mosque Hasanović had allowed himself a perfunctory mention of the Croats and Serbs in the Bosnian army. But the setting for his exhortation, and its thrust, spoke more of a Muslim Bosnia than a mixed state of Orthodox, Catholic, and Muslim citizens.

I recalled a young Muslim woman from a village close to Tuzla gazing at a photograph of her eighteenth birthday party, pointing to a Muslim girl, her best friend, who had since lost her arm in the war and saying, with a tone that impressed me with the lucidity of its rage, "That kind of thing limits your ability to think with your rational mind."

To unknit Bosnia, where a third of marriages were mixed, it had been necessary, early on, to unhinge the rational minds. That, in essence, was the military logic of Sušica, of Luka, of Omarska; of the berserk marauding in Višegrad and other towns; and of shelling Sarajevo from day one of the war. These deranged acts had a sense after all. They served to destroy the realm of reason in which tolerance—and any hope for Bosnian society—resided.

Hasanović, having come through this Serb onslaught, believed in the power of God. But he also believed in the power of mathematics.

The Muslims of Bosnia had to organize themselves into a strong army and kill Serbs at a faster rate than Serbs killed Muslims. That was the lesson of 1992, the arithmetic of a Bosnian "Never Again." It was a lesson I could not contest. But, as the war entered its third year, I became increasingly unsure what room, if any, its application would leave for Bosnia's once mottled society.

I MADE MY WAY up to the front line at Boderiste, looking out across the corridor. The scene—rural, intimate, curiously soft—was typical of the war. Just a few hundred yards behind the line, looking as placid as peasants in a Millet painting, Muslim refugees from Brčko were planting potatoes, tomatoes, onions, and peppers in recently tilled soil. Beside them a couple of Bosnian soldiers were twining lengths of wire together as they built a rudimentary communications link. They would not have looked out of place on the Somme.

From a distance came the sound of occasional mortar rounds, the dry hammering of heavy machine-gun bursts and light arms fire. At the front, dug into a narrow labyrinth of trenches that twisted around the blackened, roofless vestiges of a small settlement, there was a group of Bosnian soldiers. The Serbs, about two hundred yards away beyond a grove of fruit trees, were close enough to talk to. When things were quiet, the enemies traded in cigarettes and gasoline. At night there was banter about soccer teams or arguments about history. If somebody was injured, the person who shot him might even inquire later about his health. War, this was called. But the barriers sometimes seemed ludicrously insubstantial, and the fighters often had the impression that it would be enough for the politicians in Zagreb, Belgrade, and Sarajevo to be bundled into a spacecraft and they would settle matters themselves within days. The impression was an illusion: the world that had united these enemies and given them a common language had been blasted to pieces.

The silos of Brčko, the town from which some of these soldiers came, were just visible in the afternoon haze. In the Bosnian army most soldiers had some equivalent of the Brčko silos—distant beacons glimpsed through the shifting mists. These beacons justified the fight. For some it was the bridge over the Drina at Foča, for others the old fort at Banja Luka, for others the market at Ključ. It was a war to go home. It was a war of longing, of gazing across minefields at the familiar terrain of the heart. Therein lay its intensity. Muslim refugees from the Serb rampage of 1992 gave the Bosnian army its backbone. Muslim national identity, never strong, was born; its midwife was Karadžić.

In Travnik, the old Ottoman capital in central Bosnia, the refugees formed the Seventeenth Krajiška Brigade, commanded by Colonel Mehmet Alagić, himself a refugee from Sanski Most; the brigade became a legend. Here on the Brčko front, the Second Corps of the army was full of refugees from eastern and northern Bosnia. They had a shared belief in the power of time. "When the watch breaks down, that does not end our belief in time," one of them said to me. Nedžad Okičić, a soldier, had lost his family home in Brčko in late April 1992. "On some days, I can actually see my own house," he said. "I am here because I know we will get Brčko back one day."

I doubt that Okičić could really see his home out there across the plain. But he could see it in his mind's eye. That was all that mattered.

PRESIDENT CLINTON liked to say that 1994 was a comparatively good year in Bosnia. He once remarked that, in 1992, about 130,000 people were killed in Bosnia. In 1994, he went on, less than 3,000 people were killed there. "That's still tragic," he said. "But I hardly think that constitutes a colossal failure."

The failure was there, however, palpable and corrosive. Cleansing, unchecked and unconfronted, had become a way of life. The two-way division of Bosnian society in 1992 had become a three-way division in 1993, as Croats and Muslims in central Bosnia fought their own war. One of the sparks to this secondary conflict was provided by rumors that Muslim refugees from Srebrenica might flood into central Bosnia. Fear and the massive displacement of people had a momentum of their own.

The Croats committed manifold atrocities, throwing Muslims into camps around Mostar that scarcely differed from those of the Serbs. Muslim units, made up of refugees from the initial Serb onslaught, rampaged through towns like Visoko, Travnik, Kakanj, and Zenica, driving out the Croats. The magnificent old Ottoman bridge at Mostar, a soaring symbol of the once-linked communities of Bosnia, was destroyed by the Croats on November 9, 1993. When the Clinton administration helped put an end to this conflict in early 1994, creating a "federation" between Muslims and Croats, it calmed the waters in Bosnia and held forth the hope of a credible military challenge to the Serbs. But the federation was always hollow—the Croats' contempt for the Muslims was never far beneath the surface—and its inevitable corollary was a divided Bosnia: Croats and Muslims on one side, uneasily bound by American and German diplomatic pressure; Serbs, increasingly isolated, on the other.

The divisions hardened throughout 1994. The ponderous diplomatic game had lumbered on, marked by convoluted equations for territorial divisions (what price 0.25 percent of Bosnia?), proposals for inland waterways and ports, and odd schemes for border changes that appealed particularly to Lord Owen. The Vance-Owen Plan, summarily ditched by the Clinton administration on May 22, 1993, had given way to a Joint Action Program that was neither joint nor active. This in turn had yielded a plan for the partition of Bosnia, presented as a union of republics (Muslims 33.3 percent of the land, Croats 17.5 percent, Serbs the rest), and hammered out in talks on the British aircraft carrier HMS *Invincible* in September 1993. Ultimately rejected by Izetbegović, this gave way in 1994 to a new map for Bosnia, known as the "Contact Group map." Devised by diplomats from the United States, Russia, Britain, France, and Germany, it offered 51 percent of Bosnia to the Muslim-Croat federation and 49 percent to the Serbs. In July 1994, the Bosnian Serbs, ignoring Milošević's pressure yet again, rejected this map. As with the Vance-Owen Plan, Milošević thought he had convinced his erstwhile surrogates in Bosnia, but the game, to his fury, had escaped him.

1994: Contact Group Plan

Front line

Proposed Muslim-Croat territory

Proposed Serb territory

Sarajevo area under UN control

The Serbs, inhabiting a world of destruction, were increasingly marooned. I returned to the Drina valley. On its banks were the ruins of Bosnia's mixed society. The mosque at Konjević Polje had been razed; its minaret lay in a twisted coil atop the rubble. Nearby, the former houses of Muslims still smoldered. To pass the time on cold weekends, Serbs came out to the rubble and made fires. These forlorn figures, warming themselves in a ghostly landscape, were suggestive of soldiers defeated by the Russian winter on the long march to Moscow. How remote they seemed from those wildly enthusiastic Serbian volunteers with whom I crossed the Drina in the summer of 1992. The tide was turning, slowly but quite visibly, against the Serbs.

The Muslims, and their mosques, were gone from the Drina borderland. But two years after the war began, there was a hole in the heart of the monstrous Serbian project. Milošević, its instigator and architect, had lost interest in pursuing the war. His power consolidated, but his economy shattered, he was looking to disembark from the nationalist bandwagon. His influential, but deeply deluded, wife Mira had begun to indulge in Yugo-nostalgia; to this end, the rhetoric of Serbdom was ditched. Milošević had neither the courage to pursue an outright military victory nor the honesty to speak plainly to the Serbs marooned amid the ruins by his aborted campaign. He was a nationalist all right, albeit a calculating one, but he did not have the courage of his convictions. The boozy inertia and slowly sagging morale of the Bosnian and Krajina Serbs were the inevitable upshot of this obfuscation.

The unity of the Serbs proved a fleeting thing. On April 8, 1992, when Arkan's Tigers militia moved on the Drina border town of Zvornik, there was singleness of purpose. The JNA shelled Zvornik from the Serbian side of the river while the militia moved through the town evicting and killing its forty-eight thousand Muslims. The idea was simple enough: Serbia, for the Serbs alone, on both sides of the Drina.

But this Serbian community obstinately refused to be born. Not even the death and dispersal of hundreds of thousands of Muslims, the destruction of their mosques, the eradication of all trace of their culture, could bring it to life. The rubble on the Bosnian bank of the Drina rebuked the neat houses on the Serbian side just as General Mladić's passionate involvement in the Serbs' struggle rebuked Milošević's calculated, ephemeral interest in a Greater Serbia.

Milošević had no emotional tie to Bosnia: his family is from central Serbia. General Mladić, through his own birth in Bosnia and his father's death there in World War II, was bonded by blood to the country. This division was mirrored countless times. As the war dragged on, it became increasingly clear that the Serbs were chasing the unifying chimera of their myths even as a divisive reality confounded them.

The reality was that the Serbs of Bosnia and Croatia had scant shared culture with the people of Serbia. Many of their forebears, as members of the Austro-Hungarian army, had fought against Serbia in 1914. Men of the mountains, men of the Military Frontier, they tended to dismiss the Serbian Serbs as emasculated. Even after Yugoslavia was formed, Serbs out-side Serbia, led by Svetozar Pribičević, were often angry and embittered by the centralizing policies of the government in Belgrade, whose disastrous effect on the new state they accurately perceived. Conversely, people in Serbia tended to view the Bosnian and Krajina Serbs as hicks, the refugees pouring in as a tide of flotsam from the boondocks. Mutual incompre-hension was reinforced by the fact that the Cyrillic alphabet was univer-sally understood in Serbia, whereas the Serbs of Bosnia and Croatia favored the Latin script. No violence, no thunderous evocation of myth, no "cleansing" of the other, could conjure away these differences.

The Serbs, in truth, were at war with their own history. The battle was condemned to be lost because history cannot be defeated. It can be sup-pressed, with enough force, for a time, but it will have its say. As the bat-tle unfolded lives were carried away: the Muslim Šestovićs from Vlasenica to Sweden and Germany, burdened with their memories of Ruzdija and his disappearance; the mixed Zečević family, with their deaths and unspo-ken divisions, to Detroit and to Belgrade; the mixed Hegeduš and Adamović families to Subotica, Bijeljina, Croatia, and Belgrade. These families—the product of centuries of migration and intermarriage—existed, but the history in whose name they were destroyed was largely in-vented. It was because history's myths and history's reality were in such violent conflict among the South Slavs that Yugoslavia died amid so much blood.

IN 1994, Zvornik had a Serb mayor, Branko Grujić, who wanted, above all, to set history straight. He was the chief official in a small, traumatized town whose Muslims—59 percent of the population—had been killed or evicted in 1992 and whose beautiful Rejecanska Mosque had been razed. A rumpled figure in a ragged place, he contrived to see his role in exalted terms. Bosnia, for Grujić, was the center of the world, the nexus of all in-ternational intrigue. And Christianity was about to win a conclusive vic-tory, of global significance, over Islam and the Turk.

Grujić extended an invitation to me. Would I accompany him to the top of the escarpment overlooking Zvornik and the Drina where his pet project was taking form? He would be honored, he said, if I would bear

witness to what he called his crowning achievement. His elaborate politeness and his evident paranoia were disturbingly juxtaposed.

Any journey of any length in Bosnia inevitably involved the spectacle of
villages not merely deserted but systematically destroyed. The possibility
of *the other's* return had to be eliminated, as far as possible, by the destruction of his dwelling. A house with a roof spoke of comfort, warmth,
reason, conversation—all the elements of any possible conciliation. In the
same way, a corpse simply dead but not mutilated spoke of the rules of war,
whereas the body of a man with his genitals severed and stuffed in his
mouth conveyed a terror sufficiently savage to make the reconstitution of
Bosnian society unimaginable. Even by the standards of this war, however,
Grujić's intinerary was striking for its landscape of lunar desolation.
Charred walls and piles of rubble, resembling homes only as carrion resembles living flesh, were all that remained of the houses that once lined
the road.

When the Serbs attacked Zvornik at the start of the war, surviving Muslims fled in terror up the hill where Grujić led me. Gathered around the
old Ottoman fortress of Kula Grad, they held out for several days against
the Serb assault. Finally, they were massacred amid the ruins I now saw.
Kjasif Smailović, the Zvornik correspondent of the Sarajevo-based Bosnian daily *Oslobodjenje*, filed a dispatch during the attack which ended
with the words: "This will probably be my last report." He was right. A
Muslim, the journalist was killed by the Serbs just outside his office. In
Belgrade the regime's faithful newspaper, *Politika*, announced the heroic
Serbian "liberation" of Zvornik from "Muslim extremists."

At the summit of the hill, Grujić clambered out of his car and hurried
to kiss a wooden cross recently erected at the site. "The Turks," he said,
"destroyed the Serbian church that was here when they arrived in Zvornik
in 1463. Now we are rebuilding the church and reclaiming this as Serbian
land forever and ever." His back turned to the ruins, he gazed out over the
waters of the Drina, evidently basking in the messianic glow of his imagined campaign.

Watching that disturbed official gaze out over the Drina, I thought of a
favorite Bosnian expression: *"Teško narodu kad pametni ućute, budale pro-
govore, a fukare se obogate"*—"It is difficult for the people when the smart
keep quiet, fools speak out, and thugs get rich."

"Look at the bell tower," said Grujić, pointing upward to his pride and
joy, a makeshift structure of metal girders topped by a large bell that he described as the precursor of the Orthodox church he was building. Then he
grabbed a rope and began ringing the bell, whose mighty clang echoed out
across the glistening valley before him and the charred destruction behind

him as he intoned: "I am praying to God to give President Clinton the wisdom to abandon the Muslims and return to his true allies, the Christians."

The bell rang and rang. During the long Ottoman occupation of Serbia and Bosnia, Christians had generally been allowed to practice their faith. But no church bell could be rung. I do not know if Grujić was consciously ringing that bell to avenge those centuries of silence or if he was merely driven by some subliminal force. In drawings and paintings across Serb-held Bosnia, there was an obsession with the bell. Like birds or kites bells floated out across the landscapes and villages portrayed by local artists.

At last he stopped and looked down at the deserted, formerly Muslim village of Divić on a lip of land on the Drina and announced that he had renamed it Sveti Stefan, after the Christian Saint Stephen. Then he turned to the devastation behind him on Kula Hill and announced that the area would be renamed Djuradj Hill, after Djuradj Branković, the medieval Serbian ruler who built the first church on the site in 1410. Finally, he rang the big bell once more, gazed out at the indigo waters of the Drina, and declared, "We are liberating our beautiful land. Tell Serbs in America it is their duty to send us money for the church."

As I watched Grujić—a man quite evidently deranged—I was unsure what was happening. Was he ringing the bell? Or was the bell propelling him? He clung to the rope as if it were beyond his control, with the intensity of a man suspended over a rock face. History, it seemed, had him in its grasp and would not let go.

THERE WERE myriad people emptied by the folly of men like Grujić. Their land was Bosnia and its ending left a vacuum inside them. Haris Zečević in Detroit. Fida Karišik in Sarajevo. Vojna Adamović and her husband Miloš Jelić in Belgrade. Mere names—meaningless to UNPROFOR, or the Contact Group, or any of the national governments serving up daily velleities on the war—but also the very substance of Bosnia. When he reached Belgrade from Sarajevo, Miloš Jelić said a terrible thing to Vojna: "History blew through me and now there is nothing left. I am empty."

This image—of people tossed about like scraps of paper in a gale—was, I found, a recurrent one in the Balkans. At his show trial in 1946, Draža Mihailović, the leader of the Chetniks, declared simply that he was a man "carried away by the gale of the world." That gale brought the first destruction of Yugoslavia, later papered over by Tito.

Earlier, in the nineteenth century, the Serbian view of the Turk and of Islam in the Balkans was captured in the epic poem *Gorski Vijenac* (*The Mountain Wreath*) written by Petar II Petrović Njegoš, the prince-bishop of Montenegro. Although a Montenegrin, Njegoš fought flanked by Serbian knights in his battle against Islam in the Balkans and, as an Orthodox Christian confronting the Turks, was spiritually adopted by the Serbs.

The poem describes a campaign, known as "the extermination of the Turkicized ones," conducted in Montenegro in the late eighteenth century against Montenegrins who had converted to Islam. It thus portended the Serbian campaign against the "Turkicized ones" of Bosnia that marked the breakup of Yugoslavia. The opening lines capture the epic's central theme, referring to the "damned brood" of the Turks, planning to "ravish the entire earth, like locusts ravishing the fields."

Montenegro was then the only free territory in the Balkans, surrounded on all sides by the Turkish Empire, and the Montenegrin prince-bishop, named Danilo, compares himself to "a straw caught between whirlwinds."

Through much of the epic, Danilo hesitates to attack the Montenegrin converts to Islam because he is afraid that fratricidal war will make it easier for the Turkish army to conquer Montenegro. But ultimately he is persuaded to make no distinction between the "Turkicized ones" and the Turks themselves. "Let there be a ceaseless struggle, let there be what cannot be, let the inferno devour us, let Satan mow us down, On our graves flowers will spring for some distant descendants." Every Muslim house in the Montenegrin capital of Cetinje is burned, the mosque is razed, and those Montenegrin Muslims who refuse to be baptized are killed. A leader of the campaign reports to Danilo that "not a single eye-witness escaped, they will not have as much as someone to tell how it was."

FOR THE SCATTERED PEOPLE of Bosnia, it seemed to me important that there be eyewitnesses, to tell how it was in Bosnia, at the ending of Yugoslavia. Without witnesses, there would surely be a greater chance that the Balkan gyre would come about once again, to take another generation.

It seemed to me, in the agonized vestiges of Yugoslavia that I saw, that memory and understanding were inextricably linked. At times, in Sarajevo, I could not sleep and would watch diamonds of light flicker across the ceiling of my room: mirrors within mirrors, like the layers of Yugoslavia's fraught history. From a distance came the thud of tank fire or the rumble of a machine gun, followed by the sharper, much closer, crack of sniper fire. I imagined them in their bunkers, up at Sarajevo's old Jewish cemetery, firing at shadows across the ancient, lurching stones. Even if they had once known what they were fighting for, I was not sure, as the war progressed, that they still did. Far away in the night, down in Butmir perhaps, the mortars kept booming, sending their enveloping echo up the valley into the winding recesses of the old town, where the sound spent itself, like a black cat slithering into the shadows to rest. What were these destructive echoes in the hills and valleys of Bosnia? Where did their origin lie?

The war was a labyrinth in which each clearing only led into the next maze. The dawn, I knew, would come, but would bring only the first, throaty burst of machine-gun fire followed by the foul flapping of pigeons scattering over deserted streets; the reek of plum brandy and international hypocrisy; and, on some meaningless mountain, yet more unsung young lives blotted out like bugs on the windshield of a hurtling car.

In the narrow gullies of Bosnia, I often shuddered: empty hotels, incinerated discos, stray dogs attacking the carcasses of cows, and, at the end of a twisting road, some cross-eyed Serb commander in a "liberated" town of roofless, smashed-up Muslim dwellings standing beneath a picture of Saint Sava with his twitchy finger on the trigger and a stash of Kalashnikovs on a shelf behind him.

I dreamed once in Sarajevo of four men hanging from the rafters of a roof. They were bearded, ascetic figures, as I imagined the Bogomil heretics, whose shadow, real or imagined, hung over Bosnia. Their crime was, in some way, to have defied authority. The sun was shining and the empty house in which they hung was open on one side—its wall simply peeled away—allowing a large, rapt crowd to watch. What was not clear, and what I wanted in my dream to know, was who the hangmen were and who the silent onlookers.

After a time in Bosnia, I felt that the story before my eyes, compelling as it was, amounted to the epilogue of something older. To see clearly in the Balkan morass, to understand the executioner, it was necessary to seek the source of the gale, the center of the returning whirlwind. As people in Bosnia say, *"Drvo ne raste s neba"*—"A tree does not grow from the sky." It has roots. The roots were not only in Serbia. They were in the Croatia that Alija Mehmedović had served during World War II, and the Croatia that Franjo Tudjman had revived.

BOOK THREE

THE

GILDED

HEARSE

Redeem
The time. Redeem
The unread vision in the higher dream
While jewelled unicorns draw
    by the gilded hearse.

T. S. ELIOT, "ASH WEDNESDAY"

CHAPTER 23

OUR CROATIAN
FRIENDS

THE WAR WAS A CIRCLE. IT KEPT RETURNING TO ITS TRUE point of departure: the attempt, as in Alija Mehmedović's time, to disentangle Croats and Serbs. But as it turned, the balance of forces changed. On the Serb side there was confusion at the most basic level: Milošević, constantly hedging his bets, never identified the goal for which the Serbs were fighting. On the Croat side there was clarity: Tudjman did not want to be the father of three quarters of an independent Croatia. The Croatian commitment to taking back the land seized by the Serbs in 1991 was firm; this objective was a galvanizing force, bolstered by the presence of three hundred thousand Croatian refugees pressing to go home.

A central figure in the Croatian campaign was Gojko Šušak, a former Ottawa pizza-parlor owner. As Croatian defense minister, he brought his North American commercial skills to the world arms bazaar. On October 17, 1994, he invited me over to his spacious Zagreb office. Between offers of games of tennis and other blandishments, Šušak scoffed at the international arms embargo imposed in 1991 on the states of the former Yugoslavia, describing it as a complete joke.

Buying weapons was easy, Šušak explained with the brisk directness he had acquired during his émigré years in Canada. Former eastern bloc countries from Poland to Slovakia were itching to sell; controls were virtually nonexistent. Not only did Croatia have access to all the anti-tank weapons, artillery, multiple-rocket launchers, and ammunition it wanted, it had begun to build the T-72 tank in Slavonski Brod and assemble MiG fighters! "Frankly, we couldn't care less if the embargo is lifted or not," Šušak told me with his discomfiting grin. "What I need I get. The arms market is saturated, so saturated you would pay three times the price if you got things legally."

Some of the weaponry—what Šušak called "lighter things"—was

passed on to the Bosnian army, Croatia's nominal allies since the American-sponsored Muslim-Croat federation was established in Washington on March 18, 1994. These "lighter things" included anti-tank weapons and ammunition for mortars, cannons, and machine guns. But, Šušak cautioned, Croatia was not inclined to be generous to "the Muslims" because it did not trust them after fighting a war against them in 1993 and because, in any event, the Bosnian state amounted to little more than a fiction.

"With a free Croatia and a free Serbia," he exclaimed, "Bosnia does not make much sense. Under Tito, when none of us were free, perhaps it had a role, but not now. Izetbegović tells us he does not want an Islamic state but a Muslim state. What is that and how is it possible in Europe?"

It was easy enough to find Šušak risible. With his brazen manner, his broken English, his priggish contempt for Muslims, his glad-handing crudeness, and his almost childlike enthusiasm for all things American, he could come across as an unsavory buffoon—a pizza-peddler out of his depth, a hungry kid in a candy store with a bulging wallet. But he was smart, and America underestimated him. The Bush national security team, with its visceral contempt for the Croats, dismissed him as a joke. Both Lawrence J. Eagleburger and Bush's national security adviser, Brent Scowcroft, had served in Belgrade; they had trouble taking Croatia seriously. Šušak loved to tell the story of a visit to the Pentagon in 1990 during which he was told that not he, not his children, not his grandchildren, would ever live in an independent Croatia. But Croatia had declared independence on June 25, 1991, and been recognized by the United States nine months later. Šušak was a driving force in this emancipation. In his origins and prejudices, he was also an emblematic figure of Tudjman's Croatia. Šušak hailed from Široki Brijeg, in western Herzegovina, an area that sits astride the Dinaric Alps, which rise with unlikely harshness from the scented shores of Dalmatia. The umbrella pines and vines of the coast quickly give way to rocks and snakes, two of the three principal features of these mountains. Ustashas also abound here. Artuković, Pavelić's interior minister, came from Široki Brijeg; the town's Franciscan monastery and seminary played a role in giving some ideological backbone to the quisling regime. Several other leading Ustashas—including Pavelić himself, Mile Budak, the minister of religion, and Viktor Gutić, the prefect of western Bosnia—were also from western Herzegovina or neighboring Lika. At the end of World War II, Tito's Partisans exacted sweeping revenge on Široki Brijeg. After the town was captured in May 1945, several friars were doused in gasoline and set on fire.

The town was renamed Lištica. But this communist attempt to suppress bad history failed. Poverty and isolation on Balkan borderlands breed extremism. Western Herzegovina had them in abundance. It also had a difficult past, one marked by the shifting tides of Orthodoxy, Islam, and Catholicism. The sense of constituting a Catholic frontier, present in much of Croatia, was at its most rabid and proseletyzing in the area of Široki Brijeg. Under Pavelić the Catholic frontier had been pushed far eastward across Bosnia to the Drina River. Šušak, who fled Tito's regime for Canada in the 1960s, took with him the fanatical nostalgia of his birthplace.

CROATIA'S ODD SHAPE is no more than history incarnated as geography. The country curls, like some unfortunate hollowed-out cheese, around the edges of Turkish penetration into Europe. Not the farthest point of that daggerlike penetration, for the Turks occupied much of present-day Croatia for almost two centuries, but the borders of Turkey-in-Europe as they were set in 1699 at the Treaty of Sremski Karlovci and lasted, with occasional buffeting, until the Austro-Hungarian occupation of Bosnia in 1878.

This shape—with its suggestion of something missing, of a hole in the heart—bothers many Croats. They like to recall *povijesna Hrvatska*—historic Croatia. The one, that is, brought to its apogee by King Tomislav, a shadowy figure who ruled between about 916 and 928 over territories that embraced all of Bosnia and the coast of Montenegro as well as the land that now constitutes the state of Croatia. Stretching from the Adriatic to the Drina River, this Tomislavian Croatia had the blocklike physical coherence that modern Croatia lacks.

After Tomislav there was a long lacuna. Disjointed, lacking a central city, Croatia grew weak. By the terms of the Pacta Conventa signed with King Kalman of Hungary in 1102, the Croats recognized Kalman as king. They were granted substantial self-government under a *ban,* or viceroy. Nevertheless, for the next eight centuries, Croatia became part of the kingdom of Hungary. Croats still make much of the fact that they were not entirely subjugated when they entered voluntarily into the pact of 1102, and so constituted an associated rather than a vassal kingdom, but the fact is that they lost their independence. An eight-hundred-year hiatus began. Tomislav and his realm were placed in formaldehyde, preserved as a greater truth than all the dismal truths of progressive etiolation that followed.

The Croatia of Tomislav fragmented, fissuring unrelentingly like parched earth, leaving not much more than a memory. Bosnia went its own way, under increasingly independent *bans,* then kings, and then the Turks. Northern Croatia was governed separately by the Hungarians as the

Kingdom of Slavonia ("land of the Slavs"). By the early fifteenth century, all of Dalmatia, from Zadar to Dubrovnik, had been lost, either through sale or conquest, and was under the control of Venice.

When the Ottoman wave reached its height in the sixteenth century, Slavonia fell and the Turks pushed close to Zagreb. With most of Hungary, including its capital, occupied by the Turks, the Croats elected a Habsburg, Ferdinand, as king of Croatia in 1527. This maneuver, aimed at gaining support in driving back the Turks, only created further complications. The Habsburgs encouraged Orthodox settlers to establish themselves on what became the Vojna Krajina, or Military Frontier, with Turkey. Vienna governed these marches as a separate entity. Croatia was thus carved up four ways: Ottoman Croatia, Venetian-ruled Dalmatia, the Habsburg-administered Krajina, and a sliver of territory around Zagreb sometimes known as "Civil Croatia," where a measure of self-government under Habsburg suzerainty persisted. In short, it was reduced to what the Croatian *sabor,* or legislative assembly, called the *"reliquiae reliquiarium,"* or "the remains of the remains." The *sabor* was the symbol of the continuing life of Croatia. But legislating in Latin, representing a largely moribund class of landowning bishops and Magyarized aristocrats, it had, by the eighteenth century, become an apt symbol of the exiguity of that life.

The nineteenth century brought a Croatian revival. It took two essential forms: Strossmayer's Illyrianism and Starčević's nationalism. But statehood remained elusive. When the Habsburg-Hungarian yoke was finally cast off in 1918, Croatia fell into Serbian-dominated Yugoslavia. Then, miraculously, in 1941, with the decisive help of Hitler, an independent Croatian state of almost Tomislavian proportions, *one embracing all of Bosnia,* was resurrected under the fascist Ante Pavelić.

The miracle turned into a murderous spree. So, as I traveled through the country, I never grew entirely accustomed to the sight of photographs and busts of the Ustasha leader Pavelić on sale at souvenir stands alongside bars of chocolate, bottles of Croatian eau-de-vie, and portraits of President Franjo Tudjman. What, I wondered, would Alija Mehmedović have made of this unlikely revival? I tried to imagine pulling off the *autostrada* for a cappuccino and finding a portrait of Mussolini, or stumbling on postcards of Hitler at the duty-free in Frankfurt Airport. But I could never conjure up a convincing image. The Croatian case, however, was different. Or so Tudjman and Šušak insisted.

Tudjman is a prickly man. When he gets exercised, a frequent occurrence, he is given to disarming facial twitches. He has, like Tito, a soft spot for pomp and sartorial indulgence. His tastes run to white military uniforms bedecked in gold braid; he takes great pride in his mounted Praetorian Guard; he likes nothing better than to hold court on Brioni, the Adriatic island that was home to Tito's menagerie. He tries to keep his bigotry down, but every now and then, like Dr. Strangelove's arm, it pops up. During his first election campaign in Croatia, he remarked that he was relieved not to be "married to a Serb or a Jew." Of Izetbegović, a devout Muslim who shuns alcohol, he liked to comment that "if only he would sit down and have a drink like a civilized human being, we could do business with him."

After his involvement in the Croatian Spring of 1971, Tudjman spent two spells in jail. These naturally reinforced his essential conviction, reached in middle age, that Tito had conceived a version of history designed to discredit, for all time, the idea of an independent Croatia. Tito's historiography held that Croatian opponents of Yugoslavia were all Ustashas. Tudjman fought back with his own extravagant claims.

In 1978, for example, Tudjman told *The American Croat* review, aimed at the large Croatian diaspora in North America, that "no ethnic minority, and especially not an ancient historical nation, will endure any national restraint, but desires to be sovereign in the international community." He added the singular thesis that "conservative and reactionary, not to mention fascist currents, were never present in Croatian political life." The publication was emblazoned with a map showing a Croatian state encompassing all of Bosnia and Herzegovina, just as in the time of Tomislav and Pavelić and Alija Mehmedović's *New Sarajevo Newspaper, Croatian Information Daily.*

As the communist system crumbled in Yugoslavia under the pressures of perestroika, economic decay, and Milošević's rampant Serbian nationalism, Tudjman emerged at the head of the Hrvatska Demokratska Zajednica (HDZ), or Croatian Democratic Union. The party was one of those legalized in December 1989, in preparation for the first multiparty elections in Croatia. Funds came largely from Croatian expatriates like Šušak, many of them in North America, Australia, and Sweden, who were driven by anti-communism. Šušak organized the raising of money. Through off-budget accounts, filled mainly by Croats in exile, he also helped buy arms for the nascent Croatian state—a system that would later be expanded.

These émigrés, some of them former Ustashas, were invited back en masse to the first HDZ congress on February 24, 1990. There, Tudjman declared, "Our opponents see nothing in our program but the claim for the restoration of the independent Croatian Ustasha state. These people fail to see that the state was not the creation of fascist criminals; it also stood for the historic aspirations of the Croatian people for an independent state."

• • •

AMBIVALENCE ABOUT PAVELIĆ'S USTASHA state continued to distinguish Tudjman's politics. He reminded people of his Partisan past and
went through perfunctory condemnations of fascism. But in the name of
what he liked to call "national reconciliation," he repeatedly contorted history, belittling or glossing over the crimes of the Pavelić regime. Distortion
met distortion. Tito had lied by calling all Croatian patriots Ustashas;
Tudjman lied by twisting the murderous campaign conducted between
1941 and 1945 into a form of Croatian patriotism, regrettable perhaps,
but at heart a noble inspiration. Hence those pervasive portraits of Pavelić
and other memorabilia of the Ustasha; hence all the Partisan monuments
in Croatia with the Ustasha *U* scrawled over them.

One thing was always clear. Tudjman's "national reconciliation" was
never intended to embrace the large Serb minority in Croatia, concentrated in the Krajina region and accounting in 1991 for 12.2 percent of
the Croatian population. After winning Croatia's first democratic elections
in April 1990, Tudjman took a series of provocative steps. He amended the
Croatian constitution to end the Serbs' status as a "constituent people" of
the republic, purged the police force and the judiciary of its large Serb
presence, severely restricted the use of Cyrillic, and revived the *šahovnica*—
the red-and-white checkerboard shield—as the Croatian national flag.
The *šahovnica* is a Croatian emblem dating back several hundred years,
but its use as the national flag by the Pavelić regime turned it into a symbol of menace for the Serbs.

Tudjman and Šušak determined that their interest was not in laying to
rest the ghosts of Pavelić but in selectively reviving them. They were
helped by the great unfurling of Serb nationalism, beginning in 1986, that
inevitably provoked a Croat reaction. Milošević served Tudjman. Serbia's
nationalist frenzy gave the Croatian president the ammunition he needed
for his push for independence.

Theirs was truly a macabre dance. At times I imagined Milošević and
Tudjman in their gray suits, turning in circles to the tune of a waltz. They
clasped each other. They did not like the proximity; it was repellent; but
at the same time they thrived on it and were irresistibly bound. An energy,
one they had scarcely imagined, was released. As the music built to a
crescendo, the other people on the floor were jostled, thrust aside, and
crushed by the two men, who seemed oblivious to the mayhem. As the last
chords faded, the two men strode away, making their way over piles of
bodies and pools of blood, their silver hair neatly groomed, their nails
manicured, and their black shoes gleaming. As they took their leave, they
shook hands with a stiff formality and a slight awkwardness. They did not
look back.

Primed by Milošević's propaganda, the Krajina Serbs could only see Tudjman in the most drastic light. Their fears were relentlessly fed by Belgrade from the moment the Serbian Memorandum of 1986 first referred, with no justification, to Pavelić and the Ustasha. In line with the policy he applied in Kosovo, where the Albanians were transformed into monsters before they were suppressed, Milošević served the Serbs of the Krajina a diet of fear-mongering propaganda about the Croats that complemented and tended to justify Tudjman's bigotry. Milošević's aim was to make the Krajina Serbs part of a Greater Serbia. It backfired. The effect was to provide Tudjman with a convincing camouflage for an anti-Serb campaign. By identifying Tudjman with Pavelić, Milošević ultimately allowed Tudjman to succeed where Pavelić had failed.

The stoking of a Serb revolt by Milošević's media was relentless. References to the Ustasha rising again abounded. In the summer of 1990, the main Belgrade paper, *Politika,* carried six pages on Ustasha crimes. The birth, in early 1990, of a political movement for Krajina Serb autonomy, initially led by a Knin psychiatrist named Jovan Rašković and later by Milan Babić, the mayor of Knin, was hailed as an uprising against the Ustasha. It took the name Srpska Demokratska Stranka, or Serb Democratic party, the same party name that Karadžić would use. Links, political and later military, were steadily tightened between the Krajina Serbs and Belgrade.

Equally, Tudjman's acts were insensitive. A firm condemnation of the Ustasha, a genuflection at Jasenovac, assurances to the Serbs of a degree of regional autonomy—these were among the gestures that might have helped ease tensions. Instead, the *šahovnica* was everywhere after his election victory and a deliberate ambiguity over the Ustasha maintained.

WHEN VIOLENT INCIDENTS erupted in Pakrac, in western Slavonia, on March 2, 1991, a few weeks before the first casualties were recorded in Plitvice, Rašković announced "the beginning of a new genocide" against the Krajina Serbs. Milošević's and Tudjman's first casualties were recorded soon after: one was a Serb, one a Croat. They died in gunfire at the beautiful Plitvice Lakes, in the Krajina, on March 31, 1991. Local Serbs, driven by Milošević's propaganda and Tudjman's provocations to believe that the Ustasha had risen again, clashed with Croatian police. An old war started a new one in the very place where it had been fought in 1941.

Two months later, Yugoslavia was dead. Its death came with the collapse of the eight-man collective presidency that was Tito's barbed legacy to his people. The final disintegration occurred on May 17, 1991, when no agreement on the normal rotation from the Serb member, Borisav Jović, to the Croat member, Stipe Mesić, could be reached. Mesić, a member of

Tudjman's HDZ, had been branded as an Ustasha, along with most of his party, by the Serbian media.

The end of the presidency—the federal unit on which all else, including the JNA, depended—left Yugoslavia headless. The presidency's brief revival in July 1991, at the insistence of the European Union, was risible and essentially meaningless. By then, Slovenia and Croatia had declared independence and fighting had begun.

The Serb barbarism during the war of 1991—the flattening of Vukovar, the bombardment of Dubrovnik, the destruction of many Croat villages—then united the long disunited Croats in outrage, just as the Muslim identity in Bosnia was forged by Serb aggression.

Unlike Milošević, Tudjman's nationalism was uncompromising, more than a bending to the winds of change. But Tudjman resembled Milošević in two essential respects: he wielded history with the potency and subtlety of an axe, and he placed a far higher priority on the preservation of power than the avoidance of violence. His interest in compromise with the Croatian Serbs was always slight. "If there were to be any Serbs in Tudjman's Croatia, it was always clear that they had to be a small, humble, contrite, quiet, and second-class minority," said Ron Neitzke, America's deputy chief of mission in Zagreb during the wars of Yugoslavia's destruction. "We kept hearing official reports of the number of Serbs in Croatia, and there was always a certain relish as those numbers went down."

Like Starčević and Pavelić before him, Tudjman started tinkering with language in order to make Croatian more distinct from Serbian. An *"aerodrom,"* for example, became a *"zrakoplovna luka,"* literally an airswimmer-port. It was a mouthful, but it *was* Croatian. The square of the "Victims of Fascism" in Zagreb became the Trg Velikana, or Square of the Croatian Great Ones. The change inevitably raised the question of whether the "Great Ones" were fascists. In 1994, after much discussion, the Croatian currency was renamed the kuna, the very name used by the Pavelić regime. This choice was defended by Tudjman as "proof of Croatian sovereignty."

THE GOVERNMENT CASE for the kuna was set out in a sixty-eight-page illustrated pamphlet published by the National Bank of Croatia and written by Dalibor Brozović, a founding member of Tudjman's party. In its mixture of extravagant historical claims, defensiveness, and pomposity, it reflected Croatian traits that appeared to stem from an uncomfortable fact: more than eight hundred years of statelessness ended in 1941 with the birth of a criminal regime. In effect, the chalice, long sought, proved poisoned. It therefore became necessary to explain that the poison (Pavelić) was the aberration, not the chalice (Croatia) itself. These explanations could be tiresomely arcane. The urge, in Zagreb or west Mostar, before torrents of Jesuitical sophistry about Croatian civilization and history, was often to retort: "Thou doth protest too much."

Brozović was master of the convoluted Balkan historical argument. He explained to me that the kuna—the word is Croatian for "marten," a small forest animal with a valuable fur—had a thousand-year history as a Croatian unit of exchange in that the marten's skin was used as a form of payment in the Middle Ages! The oldest mention of the marten skin in Croatian regions, he said, dated back to 1018, when on the island of Cres, "the town of Osor paid at Christmas a tribute of 40 marten skins."

Reeling off every allusion to the kuna over the ensuing thousand years, Mr. Brozović described the Ustasha regime as an "insignificantly short four-year period otherwise lost in the sequence of centuries." The fact that, in the period from 1102 to 1991, these four years were the only time in which Croatia was independent was dismissed as irrelevant. "Minority groups, such as the Jews and the Serbs, cannot dictate Croatian policy," he told me. "The average Croat is happy with the kuna. We cannot allow the quisling Pavelić regime to have a monopoly over Croatian symbols that date back to the Middle Ages."

The Middle Ages played a disproportionate part in Croatian discourse. Zagreb was modest, faintly dreary, sad; it could not quite shake off the air of a Habsburg outpost, picturesque but provincial. A piano was always tinkling in some distant room, expressing a genteel and melancholic longing. By contrast, distant history carried with it the beating of drums and the vivid colors of heraldic ceremony; it was glorious. Thus did the exchange of marten skins in 1018 become more important than the sensibilities of Serb citizens of Croatia whose immediate forebears had suffered the onslaught of 1941. Thus was a fortune spent restoring—or, more accurately, building—a medieval fort just north of Zagreb called Medvedgrad that Tudjman renamed "the Altar of the Homeland."

In the tenth century that Croatian homeland had included Bosnia; Tudjman's intimate conviction was always that it still should. Against the often moderate views of the Croats of central Bosnia—those living in Sarajevo, Zenica, and Vitez—he favored Šušak's Herzegovinian lobby with its attachment to a Greater Croatia rooted in readings of early medieval history.

The first leader of the HDZ in Bosnia, Stjepan Kljuić, a Sarajevan and a believer in a multi-ethnic Bosnia, was replaced in late 1992 by the Herzegovinian Mate Boban. The meeting that approved the change took place, fittingly enough, at Široki Brijeg. The horrors then committed by the Hrvatsko Vijeće Obrane (Croatian Defense Council), Tudjman's surrogate army in Bosnia, during the Muslim-Croat war—the Croat slaughter of more than one hundred Muslim civilians at the village of Ahmići in 1993, the bestial Croat camps near Mostar, the destruction of Mostar's Ottoman bridge—reflected the election of Boban. Even when the war ended, the Muslim-Croat federation was formed, and Boban was finally dropped, Tudjman's thinking, like Šušak's, reflected contempt for Bosnia and the Muslims. The meaning of the federation, Tudjman told *Der Spiegel,* was "to prevent an Islamic state arising in the middle of Europe." At stake was "not only a matter of the territorial division of Bosnia among Serbs, Croats, and Muslims but of the delineation of civilizations." The old Ustasha notion of "a Catholic frontier on the Drina" was never far beneath the surface of such bigotry.

One American official who dealt with Tudjman extensively was reminded of "those Soviet diplomats who slope up to you and make some really racist remark about the blacks, convinced that deep down, underneath the veneer of civility, you are a racist too: that was Tudjman on the Muslims."

Such attitudes were part and parcel of the myth of Croatian superiority to its Balkan neighbors. In this mythology, only some historical aberration had lumped Croatia with the Balkan Peninsula, rather than in Western Europe where it belonged. Toward its Balkan neighbors Croatia displayed the prim and irritating disdain of a cashier receiving a crumpled bank note.

Serb myth was clear enough: Kosovo and the heroic fight of a misunderstood people against the stronger enemy. The fabric of Croatian myth was more elusive, slipping from the grasp like the texture of Zagreb itself, eternally divided between the quaint Gornji Grad, or upper town, with its whiff of provincial self-importance, and the handsome but strangely heartless lower town. Yet it was equally pervasive and dangerous.

It involved the elimination of Croatia's Turkish past (the many mosques of Slavonia were leveled when the Turks retreated at the end of the seventeenth century) and the placing of Croatia in Western Europe rather than the Balkans; the portrayal of long dismemberment as less humiliation and military subjugation than clever rearguard action by the legislators of the Croatian *sabor;* the cultivation of the romantic idea that Croatia fought constantly on the "ramparts of Christendom"; and the embalming of Tomislav's Greater Croatia in the most hallowed halls of memory.

Croatia, of course, was much less whole, much less Western European, and rather less heroic than it liked to claim. Its history was squarely Balkan, one of conquest and miscegenation, and much of it—including subjugation to the Turks—was shared with the Serbs. Even Croatia's nineteenth-century military hero, Ban Josip Jelačić, led a force that was formed as much by Serbs from the Krajina as by Croats. They stormed into Hungary not to demand Croatian independence but to fight Hungarian rebels against the Habsburgs. Jelačić's patriotism lay essentially in a conviction that the Catholic and Orthodox Slavs—Croats and Serbs—of the Habsburg Empire would be stronger united than divided. There was indeed much that united them. But Croatian independence, when it came a century later in 1941, was constructed around an anti-Serb crusade. Tudjman and Šušak, decisively abetted by Milošević, could never quite see the second independence of 1991 in any other terms.

ŠUŠAK WAS in an exuberant mood that late fall of 1994. "Every day," he said, "we are better organized and better equipped. Every day the Serbs are in a worse position. They have more tanks than they have people to man them." But it was not merely his sense of an approaching victory that explained his elation. It was above all the fact that he had the United States and the Clinton administration firmly on his side.

The defense minister told me that, just a week before, he had taken Colonel Richard Herrick, the military attaché at the American embassy in Zagreb, to a demonstration of Croatian air power. Among the aircraft on show were twelve MiG fighter planes—Croatia had no more than four when the arms embargo was imposed—and several Mi-24 armored assault helicopters that fired guided anti-tank missiles. Croatia had none of these helicopters or missiles before the embargo took effect. "Herrick," Šušak declared, "was enormously impressed."

Herrick did not want to talk. But it was an open secret at the American embassy in Zagreb that the United States was turning a blind eye to the Croatian arms buildup. Peter Galbraith, the ambassador, liked to say, with a twinkle in his eye, that he would be "shocked, I repeat, shocked" to learn that arms were getting into Croatia. American policy toward Croatia was largely one of covert inaction. The embargo was to be ignored; the formal American decision, on November 11, 1994, to stop the use of its ships to monitor the weapons ban was therefore largely irrelevant.

There were other elements to America's rapprochement with Croatia. On March 24, 1994, just six days after the agreement on the Muslim-Croat federation was signed, Šušak had written to John M. Deutsch, then the deputy secretary of defense. "Our goal," he wrote, "is the peaceful transition of our previously Moscow-Belgrade dominated military to one which follows the model of the United States. . . . To accomplish this goal we need assistance in advising our past and future leadership on military-civilian matters, programs and budgeting and legislation relating to democratic military institutions." The letter was couched in mild enough terms, but it was essentially an appeal for American assistance in getting the Croatian army to a level where it could smash the Serbs.

Direct government assistance to the Croatian army, however, would vio-
late the arms embargo. So Šušak's letter was referred to a company called
Military Professional Resources Inc., based in Alexandria, Virginia, and
run by retired American officers. Ed Soyster, a retired lieutenant general
and one of the company's vice presidents, told me, with engaging exuberance, that he and his colleagues constituted "the greatest corporate assem-
blage of military expertise in the world."

After some back and forth with the State Department, during which
the company formally undertook not to provide direct military planning
or advice on strategy, Military Professional Resources Inc. signed a contract with Croatia on September 23, 1994, just three weeks before I saw
Šušak. It was Šušak himself who signed the contract and, during our meeting, he bubbled over with enthusiasm about his upcoming appointments
with "American officers." The officers were in fact retired, but they wielded
clout. Among those dispatched to Croatia in November 1994 were General Carl E. Vuono, who from 1987 to 1992 was the army chief of staff,
and General Crosbie E. Saint, who from 1988 until 1992 was the commander of the United States Army in Europe.

In theory, activities were limited to courses on leadership, the training
of noncommissioned officers, the place of an army in an emergent democracy, and other subjects unrelated to the Croatian army's single obsession
at that time: the fact that 27 percent of Croatia was held by Serb rebels. In
practice, the dividing line between abstract theory and practical military
advice appears—as was probably inevitable in such a situation—to have
been flimsy.

Within the American embassy in Zagreb, by the second half of 1994,
there was growing concern over the extent to which the United States had
become the de facto diplomatic and military ally of the Croatian government. The logic behind the Clinton administration's position was that
only a strong Muslim-Croat federation could stand up to the Serbs, create
a balance of power in Bosnia, and so open the way to peace. There were
some strengths to this argument. Its flaw, however, was that one of the primary goals of Tudjman's government—the control of a substantial chunk
of Bosnia—was anathema to the American government; another Croatian
goal—the removal of most, if not all, of the Serb population of Croatia—
made Washington queasy. At the very least these two priorities meant that
Bosnia would never be made whole again and that another massive wave
of "ethnic cleansing"—of Serbs this time—might take place.

"Tudjman took our measure," said Neitzke. "He became well aware
that Washington did not really have a policy, other than the avoidance of
direct involvement. We knew about his contempt for the Muslims. His
aim, and we knew this too, was always to gut Croatia of Serbs. But the fact

was that for three years, from 1992, Washington was largely brain-dead, engaged in a day-to-day battle to portray our fecklessness as positively as possible."

FECKLESSNESS IN TURN opened the way for the "Iranian pipeline" into Croatia. In effect, the Iranians became America's surrogates in providing the military assistance to the Bosnian Muslims that the Clinton administration refused to give directly. A first Iranian plane loaded with thousands of rifles and millions of rounds of ammunition had landed at Zagreb's Pleso Airport on Labor Day weekend 1992, but its load was seized by the United Nations under heavy pressure from the Bush administration. From that time, Iran had been pressing insistently to provide arms through Croatia to the Bosnian government. With the establishment of the federation, and Washington's willingness to pay any price to avoid such direct involvement itself, this question again came to the fore.

Throughout late 1994, there were insistent rumors of Iranian flights going into the island of Krk, in southwestern Croatia. Once again, it was clear that America was turning a blind eye. What was not clear, until a *Los Angeles Times* report published on April 5, 1996, was that Tudjman had formally asked for America's view on these shipments and that, on April 27, 1994, Clinton's national security adviser, Anthony Lake, had advised Clinton how to give a green light to Tudjman. Accordingly, Galbraith saw the Croatian president and told him that he had "no instructions" about the Iranian shipments. Tudjman was well versed in such "amber lights"; he always saw green unless he was made to see red.

THIS EXTRAORDINARY AMERICAN DECISION—to allow Iran to arm Bosnia—reflected the fact that anything, quite literally anything, was viewed by Clinton's White House as preferable to direct involvement in Bosnia. The decision was made in highly unusual circumstances, made clear in a confidential memo that Peter Galbraith, the American ambassador to Zagreb, wrote for his files on May 6, 1994. The memo was written, at the time of the events in question, to afford the ambassador some protection and to try to ensure that what had happened not be subsequently obscured by others. Among the officials involved in the decision were Tony Lake, Clinton's national security adviser; Charles E. (Chuck) Redman, the special American envoy to the Balkans in 1993 and 1994; Strobe Talbott, the deputy secretary of state; Alexander (Sandy) R. Vershbow, then the principal assistant secretary of state for European and Canadian affairs; and Jennone Walker, the senior director for Europe at the National Security Council.

Galbraith's "Memorandum to the File" reads: "During an April 29 evening meeting with President Tudjman and Ambassador Redman, President Tudjman sought for the second time U.S. advice as whether Croatia should facilitate arms transfers from Islamic countries, principally Iran, to the government of Bosnia-Herzegovina.

"In reply, I told Tudjman what I said the day before still stood, that I had no instructions from Washington on how to advise on this issue. I urged Tudjman to focus not only on what I had said yesterday, but on what I had not said.

"Ambassador Redman told Tudjman, 'It is your decision to make. We don't want to be in a position of saying no.'

"In response to several requests for guidance, I was told by Sandy Vershbow that I was to tell Tudjman I did not have instructions at this time. On April 29, at 9:30 P.M., in a conversation with Jennone Walker, Jennone conveyed a message from Tony Lake that my instructions were to say 'I had no instructions' but that Tony had said this 'with raised eyebrows and a smile.' On April 30, Sandy Vershbow again told me to relay a no-instructions message to Tudjman, clearly drawing his attention to the idea we were not saying no. Finally in a May 2 telephone conversation, Ambassador Redman conveyed to me an instruction from Tony Lake that I not report the conversation with Tudjman. In a May 5 conversation, Vershbow said, after I recounted Redman's and my conversation with Tudjman that 'you and Chuck have taken it exactly where we want to be.'

"In a May 6 conversation with Deputy Secretary Talbott, Talbott said the instructions were no instructions. I explained that anything short of a statement that the Croats should not facilitate the flow of Iranian arms to the Bosnians would be understood as a U.S. green light.

"Talbott said we did not want to be seen as undermining the embargo.

"I told him of the order not to report the April 29 conversation and asked if he wanted it reported. He said the answer is almost certainly yes, but Steve Oxman or Sandy Vershbow would be in touch."

But Galbraith was never told to report what had happened through official channels to the State Department. The private memorandum was duly signed by Galbraith and witnessed by Neitzke, who had been alarmed by the irregularity of the circumstances—including the way the decision was conveyed and the order not to put it in writing. Neitzke had therefore urged Galbraith to write the memorandum, which was kept in a safe in the embassy in Zagreb. Neitzke's understanding was the order from Lake not to put what had happened in writing reflected the fact that the decision had been taken without coordination with the Pentagon or the CIA. This was indeed the case, and would become a source of growing tension. In the long trail of sloppy policy that marked America's approach to Bosnia, this was a conspicuous nadir.

• • •

THE SHIPMENTS—which made Iran the largest arms supplier to Bosnia—came at a price. To begin with, Croatia took a cut of over 30 percent; the Bosnian army became deeply dependent on Croatia. Groups like Abu Nidal, Hamas, and Hezbollah moved into the Balkans. A worried CIA official told me in 1995 that this terrorist presence was "a real concern, an area a lot of people are looking at. You dance with the devil and you run the risk of getting burned. They have moved some way toward their goal of an Iranian foothold in Europe. But our options were difficult. Stalin sent twenty million people to the gulag and we worked with him in World War II."

America was not prepared to take on the Serbs. It gradually found other ways to counter them, and a regional balance of power was thus advanced. But the alternatives amounted to bad policy and came at high cost: American support for a Croatian government with no interest in a united Bosnia and an open door to Iran from a State Department headed by a man, Warren Christopher, who had led a diplomatic and economic crusade against Iran.

Direct and prompt American confrontation of the Serbs might have made Bosnia whole; indirect confrontation of the Serbs, through Tudjman and Iran, could do nothing for the avowed American goal of a united Bosnia. As they had been from the outset, American actions were craven and clouded with hypocrisy. The protracted debate in Congress and the Senate over the embargo was, in the end, a phony one, like so many of the transatlantic arguments over Bosnia. The bottom line, for Clinton and the Pentagon, was the avoidance of direct American intervention in the Bosnian war (with its risk of body bags) and the safeguarding of NATO despite sometimes bitter differences over Bosnian policy between Washington and its European allies. In this light, the Iranian pipeline had a double merit: it provided arms to Bosnia without putting Americans at risk, and it circumvented a clash with the Europeans over a lifting of the arms embargo. The British and French governments, with troops on the ground in Bosnia, argued that ending the embargo would merely, in the words of the British foreign secretary Douglas Hurd, "level the killing field."

Šušak was a pragmatist. The contortions of American policy bothered him not a whit. All that he cared about was that Croatia was procuring arms and the Hrvatska Vojska, or Croatian army, was growing stronger by the day. He invited me to take a look at his arms factory, called Djuro Djaković, in Slavonski Brod, the principal town in Slavonia, squeezed between the Serb-held territory in western and eastern Slavonia. A polite manager, Bartol Jerković, showed me around. He explained that components were easy to find in Eastern Europe because the tank manufactured there was an improved version of a Soviet model. The gleaming green hulls of five battle tanks stood waiting for turrets and 125-millimeter cannons to be installed. Production of ammunition and various automatic weapons was also brisk. Mr. Jerković suggested that tanks might soon be exported to Kuwait.

One of his colleagues took me to lunch. A man in his sixties, marked by a gentle civility, he had none of the zealotry of the other factory managers. After a few drinks he explained, with slight embarrassment, that he was part Serb, part Croatian. With a look of utter weariness, he said, "I am a cosmopolitan but these are not the times for people like me. You know, one of the most surprising things in life is age."

As I drove back toward Zagreb down the short stretch of the Brotherhood and Unity motorway in Croatian hands, a horse abruptly cantered across a bridge over the highway, followed by a foal. It was an arresting image of freedom in a landscape heavy with war's shadow. Another, contrasting image came into my head, one related by a friend in the Bosnian army. He had been watching two horses drinking at a pond. A shell came in. He ducked and, a few second later, looked up. The two horses were standing there still, frozen. Then, very slowly, one of them keeled over. At that moment, he noticed that the second horse had no head. Blood was gushing, *gushing,* from its neck. After a moment, the headless horse fell to the ground. Like Haris Zečević with his vision of his brother Muris in the earth, he was never able to get that image out of his mind.

The wild free horse and foal or the headless horse of battle? As the war moved into its fourth year in 1995, I could see no freedom for Bosnia, only more blood. Croatia was plainly rising, its fortunes bolstered by a messy marriage of interests with America. But I saw little or nothing in Tudjman's Croatia to suggest that the forces of reason, reconciliation, and ethnic tolerance in Bosnia would be bolstered by this trend, or that the way might be opened for Haris Zečević, Vesna and Jasna Karišik, Ermin Šestović, or Vojna Adamović to go home.

CHAPTER 24

FRAGMENTS
OF A LIFE

HARIS ZEČEVIĆ, THE REFUGEE, KEEPS MOVING ACROSS THE
flat sprawl of Detroit. From Clinton Township to Dearborn to Hamtramck to Madison Heights to Warren. One drab apartment after another,
too hot in summer, too cold in winter. He lets his hair grow; he puts on
weight; he is often unshaven. On one occasion he asks a barber to shave
him. "The only thing we shave here," the guy says, "is necks." The tone is
roughly that of a man saying, "The only thing we slit here is throats."

In Sarajevo, his barber would shave him with the devotion of the arti-
san. The sure, swift sweeps of the blade spoke of a world in which time was
something to be savored, not overcome. Life as riddle in the place of life
as race. Old habits in an old world gone forever. *To hell with all that.*

But his mother's grave is over there. When Haris thinks about Sarajevo
he dwells on the grave that he has not seen. His father has told him that
Bisera is buried close to Muris, in full view of Trebević Mountain, where
Haris's life came apart in the fourth month of the war.

To Haris, there is no point in thinking about home because he no
longer has one. The way he sees it, you feel good in any place where you
can do what you like. To do what you like you need money. The equation
is simple enough. Without money, Sarajevo or Mostar or Dubrovnik are
just old stones piled in a certain way. Or, at least, that is what he proclaims.
"People think about their lives," he likes to say, "but I don't have a life. So
I don't think."

He goes through cars. First the '85 Thunderbird, bought for three thousand dollars and smashed two weeks later. Then a two-hundred-dollar
Buick that worked for two weeks. Then a period of walking to work or,
when it was freezing, finding lifts with friends. Then an old Mazda. Finally, the first car that satisfies him, a twelve-thousand-dollar Ford Probe
bought, as Dragan Vraneš always urged him, on credit. He builds up a lot

of credit. A television, some furniture, the stereo system, all bought with borrowed money. In America, he discovers, letters are bills—from American Express, Montgomery Ward, the electric utility, the phone company, Mervyn's, Visa. Haris learns to juggle them, pay a bit here, a bit there, enough to stay out of trouble. As a reminder of his former life, he, like his father in Sarajevo, pins up the Bosnian fleur-de-lis on a wall. As a rebuke to the insufferable flatness of Detroit, he adds a photograph of the snow-capped peaks around the Bosnian capital. That is all.

To talk to Haris is to confront a series of walls. They have been erected against his wounds. Against guilt also. He says the war was no longer his war and that is why he left. But it was his war and he knows it. His with a vengeance. Part posture, part desperation writ large, his attitude now is like a big prison spotlight sweeping back and forth across empty terrain.

The expression in his eyes stands on the uneasy border between defiance and pain. His laugh is hollow, like the refugee's life. When he grows a beard it is out of laziness, and when he shaves it off he cuts his face and neck. He tugs his hair back into a ponytail and declines to wash it. He gazes, absently, at the television. He has stopped reading. He smokes incessantly, sixty cigarettes a day. The lean, fit Sarajevo soldier is cocooned in the flaccid flab of too much fast food.

When reports appear on TV about the shelling of Sarajevo or lifting the arms embargo, he snickers to himself. Clinton, with his false sincerity, sickens him. Virtually nobody here knows about Bosnia. Fewer care. He watches Americans try to explain to fellow refugees how a dishwasher works: *They think we are savages.* "This war has gone too far now," he says. "Unless the United States is ready to give us Muslims two million green cards the end will only come when one of the armies is beaten."

Work in the metal shop of Nino Crnovršanin, the old family friend, becomes increasingly strained. Nino is fanatical about Bosnia. He hated Tito's Yugoslavia, the communist state that he fled. Now he feels for the first time that he has a homeland. He devotes most of his time to raising money for Izetbegović's SDA party and to looking after the more than one thousand Bosnian Muslim refugees in Detroit. He introduces Haris to other survivors—Nedžad Stukan, who lost one of his legs at Mostar; Ramiz Gigić, who got shrapnel in his eyes in Sarajevo and now has 20 percent vision left in one eye. His diatribes against the American betrayal of Bosnia, and against the perfidy of Britain and France and the United States, are relentless. Nino wants Haris to join him in all these campaigns; he wants to control Haris's life. Haris is not going to let anybody do that.

At a company called QQC, run by Crnovršanin's son-in-law, Haris eventually finds another job. The company, inspired by its Anglo-Indian founder, Previn Mistry, invents advanced materials that reduce manufacturing costs for anything from auto batteries to beverage cans. Haris works with lasers precise enough to cut a hole in a human hair without burning the hair. He programs robots that use computer-directed lasers to weld car parts. He is computer literate and Mistry, throughout 1994, tries to encourage him to study. But Haris cannot find the discipline or patience to embark on an engineering degree.

The idea of doing anything slowly—and a degree, he calculates, would take him at least four years—has become foreign to him. He wants to move fast. Adrenaline is a need. When he is sent on a business trip to California and takes a day off to go to Bear Mountain, he is thrown off the piste for reckless skiing. Back in Michigan, he is badly cut in a Jet Ski accident.

Hurrying helps Haris not to think. Not to remember. But sometimes his mind drifts back. Then he asks why this happened to his family, to the Muslims in general. And he comes to the conclusion that the killing happened because he did not respect himself. The Muslims did not respect themselves. Sometimes Muslims would give their children Serb or Croat names. But it was very rare for a Croat or Serb to gave their child a Muslim name. That he now finds to be an interesting fact.

His father, Asim, had wanted to give him a sense of his Muslim identity. He had encouraged him to come to the mosque on Bairam. But that meant getting up early; it meant swimming against Tito's tide. He saw no sense in it. His father talked about pride in his roots, but Haris did not understand him. He worshiped Tito, the man who had consigned prejudice to the past.

Haris was eleven when Tito died in 1980. He cried. Everybody else was crying, and it seemed like the thing to do. He was frightened. Without Tito, all the outside enemies were suddenly more threatening. He repeated the phrase he had learned by rote—*"Posle Tito, Tita"* ("After Tito, Tito")—but it brought scant comfort. Everything had depended on Tito; everyone was asking what would happen in his absence. He did not really understand. So he kept crying. He sobbed.

Visitors to Yugoslavia used to ask, What will you do you after Tito dies? The tour guides were taught to reply, "Tito will never die." So the visitors, rational people from the West with their linear minds, asked why. And the guides said, "Because Tito is all of us." But it was a lie. In Germany, when Tito died, the children of the Yugoslav *Gastarbeiters* were given several days off school. Many of them were naturally delighted. Some of them were beaten by their parents for their lack of respect. It was incumbent to cry; even a child should understand that.

Stalin, that first Commissar of National Minorities, with whom Tito clashed but whose methods he never truly disavowed, had died thirty-seven years earlier, in 1953. The Russian poet, Joseph Brodsky, was a boy then, aged twelve, a year older than Haris at Tito's death. He and his schoolmates were called into the auditorium, and the "class mentor" gave them the news. "She began a funeral oration," Brodsky told the writer Solomon Volkov, "and suddenly cried out in wild voice: 'On your knees! On your knees!' Pandemonium broke out. Everyone was howling and weeping and it was somehow expected of me to cry, too, but—to my shame then; now, I think, to my honor—I couldn't. I looked at her with some astonishment, until my father suddenly gave me a wink. Then I realized for sure that there was no particular reason for me to get upset over Stalin's death."

Tito was different from Stalin. He clashed with him. Collectivization in Yugoslavia was less severe; the Yugoslav gulag an insignificant thing. There was a Yugoslav way. Several years after Tito's death Haris experienced Tito's democracy for the first and only time. He was finishing high school. He had learned about self-management and elections—all the differences between the Yugoslav system and the Soviet. The whole democratic structure seemed quite elaborate. But when it came to voting, the system proved crude and his knowledge useless. The vote was public. Somebody stood there and told him which names to circle. "Circle this, circle this, circle this." That was democracy in action in Tito's Yugoslavia.

Yet he had believed in that system. No other identity but the Yugoslav had mattered or seemed relevant to him. Haris feels now that he was cowed by fear. A subtle fear. He could travel anywhere he liked. So he was free. But he knew, even as a young man, the price of that freedom. He could not say certain things; he could not be a good Yugoslav *and* a good Muslim.

Haris was fourteen when the trial of thirteen Muslims, including Izetbegović, began in Sarajevo in 1983. They were accused of "spreading hostile propaganda" against Yugoslavia and the Communist party and of promoting Muslim nationalism. The trial had been well prepared by UDBA agents; it was designed to demonstrate the resilience of "Brotherhood and Unity" in Tito's absence. One of the defendants was interviewed and asked what he had done. He said he had *done* nothing; he had only thought and said certain things. That was enough. This made an impression on Haris. He is angry now that he did not think more about that. He is angry at missing so many signs of the sickness beneath the surface of Yugoslavia in the 1980s. If he had been more vigilant, he keeps telling himself, his mother and brother would be alive.

In the summer of 1987, as Milošević rose to power, Haris began his military service in the northern Bosnian town of Tuzla. He thereby began the rite of passage designed to cement awareness of the unity of Yugoslav peoples. But even within the army, the tensions generated by Milošević's rumblings in Serbia were clear. One day Haris and a group of other conscripts were called in by their commanding officer. They were told that there had been a serious infringement of army discipline that was under investigation and in which they were suspects. Chetnik songs had been overheard in the bathrooms. It was inadmissible, and a crime, to sing Chetnik songs on a base of the Yugoslav People's Army, for this amounted to an attack on Yugoslavia.

Haris was completely bewildered by the charges, which were later dropped. He had not heard the songs, much less sung them. He was a Muslim. What would he be doing singing Chetnik songs? It seems to him now, in Detroit, that he had to be blind not to see the paranoia mounting.

He wants to atone for his blindness. In memory of his mother and his brother. He tries, for the first time in his life, to fast for Ramadan. He wants to be a better Muslim. But after the first twenty-four hours he has a terrible headache and he stops. Besides, he has to smoke. He consoles himself: some of the most devout Muslims of independent Bosnia used to be communists. He does not want to exchange one lie for another. Or that, at least, is what he tells himself.

HARIS IS LONELY. He does not like to admit it. But in the end he gives in. After the encirclement of Sarajevo is eased in February 1994, by the first serious NATO threat to the Serbs, he manages to get his girlfriend, Vildana Vranić, out of Sarajevo through a humanitarian agency. She leaves on April 21, 1994. Their relationship had started a month before the war. She was so scared, by the second month of the war, she lay in bed for six weeks. She would think about which route to take to get to Haris's place. But she could not move. Mental games to beat the shells had a way of leading nowhere. Her ex-boyfriend lost his leg in December 1992 to a mortar. Her brother, Nihad, was imprisoned for trying to desert. Vildana, after two years of war, felt that she was losing her mind.

She arrives in Detroit on June 21, 1994, almost a year after Haris. A strong girl, big eyed, determined. Their agreement is that she has come to marry him. But there is an ambivalence in Haris. She comforts him, soothes the rawness in him. At the same time, when she calls him at the office, he feels she is trying to trap him. She does not understand his need for speed and for adrenaline, or his American obsession with making more money.

After the first passion of their reunion, he feels that she pesters him. Vildana sees the situation clearly enough. His youth has been ripped from him so he does not want to admit that he is no longer eighteen. He wants to have the right to go out and get drunk. She understands that her lone-

liness in America, and her poor English, weigh on him. But there is also a
limit to her understanding.

They talk about having a child. There is a side in Haris that wants a
child desperately. After so much death, a life. After such loneliness, a family. After such rupture, a connection. But there is another side that says no.
He cannot afford a child. His life will be ensnared. He is not ready. Vildana, in Sarajevo, has seen the corpses of Muris and Bisera. She wants to
give him a child. They will work everything out, she tells him.

By October Vildana is pregnant and the next month they get married.
The ceremony is perfunctory, witnessed by other refugees from the war.
Vildana goes to work in an auto-component factory on the production
line. She works six days a week and earns $7.25 an hour. When she needs
to go the bathroom, she has to find somebody to replace her on the line.

It is strange how hard he and Vildana have to work just to survive. In
Sarajevo, before the war, they did nothing and there was always money
around. Haris had a friend called Slobodan Djokić, half Serb, half Croat.
When the war broke out, he, like Haris, was thrust into the Bosnian army.
Slobodan had a theory. In essence, it was that if people had been obliged
to work harder in Bosnia, there would have been no war. "We would have
come home from the factory tired and we would have had no time to talk
our way into a war!" Djokić said.

He was half joking, but he had a point. In America, the toughest thing
was to get your first credit. No history, no credit rating, no nothing: that
was the first barrier to overcome. But look at Tito! Haris, when he arrived
in Detroit, could lie all day and get nothing from the banks. But Tito lied
throughout his life, reinvented a state, and received close to thirty billion
dollars from Western banks! He bought peace—and to hell with the future. The credit went a long way. Throughout Yugoslavia nobody worked
excessively hard and everyone lived well enough. There was job security,
and, if you needed some extra cash, you could always go off to Sweden or
Germany and come back with hard currency that went a long way.

Now most of the solid, red-tiled Yugoslav houses built with all that cash
are roofless. His father, Asim, back in Sarajevo, lives without water or electricity. His uncle Slobodan, in Belgrade with his cousins, sides with and
abets the killers of his mother and brother. It was all a lie then: the money,
the brotherhood, the unity, the good life. Haris watches Vildana's belly
grow. Amid all his ambivalence he is sure of one thing. Never will he take
this child back to live in Sarajevo. Not if there are twenty years of peace.

A LOW-KEY RADIO WAR exists in Detroit, pitting Muslims against
Serbs. Many of the Serb refugees from the Bosnian war have gone to
Windsor, just over the Detroit River in Canada. They have what Haris

calls a "Chetnik radio." He tunes in sometimes, with disgust. The Muslims, in Detroit, have a radio station too. In the New World, old battles continue: the radios trade opposing versions of the war.

At the start of the Bosnian war, in April 1992, Muslim and Serb stood side by side. Haris's brother, Muris Zečević, had been on Vrbanja Bridge in the center of Sarajevo with Vojna Adamović, a Serb, demonstrating for a united Bosnia. Their efforts drew only gunfire from Karadžić's separatist Serbs. Now, almost three years later, Muris was dead and Vojna in Belgrade. Haris was in Detroit, and Vojna's Sarajevan cousins, Mladen and Mira Elazar, were over the river in Windsor, Canada.

The Elazars had been close to Vojna in Sarajevo. Mira's mother and Vojna's grandmother were sisters. But, soon after the Serb shelling began, Mira, like Vojna, fled from Sarajevo, Serbs running from Serb shells. Mira took the couple's two young boys, Bojan and Roman, to Croatia. Her husband Mladen remained, initially confident that the Bosnian capital would resist Karadžić's attempt to dismember it. Married to a Serb, he was the son of a Croatian mother and a Jewish father. He was, in short, typically Bosnian in his mixed blood. And blood, Mladen reasoned, could not be unmixed, however many shells rained down from the hills.

Like most Bosnian Jews, Mladen's ancestors had fled Spain in the 1490s, at the time of the Inquisition, and made their way to the more tolerant realm of the Ottoman Empire. This was also the route taken by the Sarajevo Haggadah, one of the world's most beautiful illustrated Jewish manuscripts. The Elazars eventually settled in northern Bosnia.

When World War II began, Mladen's grandparents, Joseph and Miriam Elazar, were successful merchants, with a retail business at Modriča, near Brčko. Pavelić's Croatian Ustasha killed Joseph and Miriam at the Jasenovac concentration camp, along with their six daughters and a son called David, whose wife and nine-month-old child were also butchered. Mladen's father, Meyer, was the only survivor. He jumped into a freezing river near Modriča as a squad of Ustashas, who were inspecting the fur-lined coat that they had just taken from him as booty, prepared to execute him. Later Meyer Elazar joined Tito's Partisans, ending the war as an officer. He always had nightmares about the war, and Mladen, as a child, recalled waking to the sound of his father's screams.

Mladen's mother was a Croat. His father, sole survivor in his family of the Ustasha slaughter, married Štefica Topić, who had been raised by the brother of a leading Ustasha. The marriage was a fitting symbol of Tito's postwar reconciliation. In fact, Štefica was not entirely Croat. Her father was a Bosnian Muslim named Halil Topić, who converted to Catholicism and changed his name to Hinko Topić in order to marry Stefica's mother. Bosnian names, so poisonous during the war, had in fact been interchanged in this way over centuries: they were virtually meaningless. Mladen was perhaps the ultimate Sarajevan: part Croat, part Muslim, part Jewish, and married to a Serb.

He tried to hang on in Sarajevo. It was his city and he did not want to give it up. He had a private business in equipment for oil and gas pipelines. Just before the war, the company had been working on a big project, a gas pipeline between Zenica in central Bosnia and Bosanski Brod. Two months before the fighting started, Mladen invested one million dollars on material. A friend told him he was mad. She had not even bothered to plant her seeds that year, so convinced was she that war was coming. Mladen waved her fears away and lost everything. He pulls out a prewar photograph of some of his employees: Nijaz Logo, a Muslim, dead; Milenko Morača, a Serb, who long served in the Bosnian army before escaping to Italy; Mijo Marković, a Croat, somewhere in Herzeg-Bosna. Lives, friends, scattered to the winds.

"We were all Bosnians," Mladen says. "We were the hospitable, generous, amusing, simpleminded Bosnians. Then the madness started. You see what is happening, but you are in the middle of the stream and how do you resist? We, the educated people, should have resisted. It was our mistake. We let the priests and the imams dictate how simple people voted. Nobody told those people how they would feel when their sons' legs were gone. Karadžić did monstrous things. But Izetbegović made mistakes. From the start, next to the Bosnian flag, we had the green flag with the crescent moon of his Muslim SDA party, the first nationalist party in Bosnia. When I reported to the Bosnian army in Hrasno at the start of the war, there was the flag of the SDA next to that of Bosnia. What incentive did that give the Bosnian Serbs, Croats, and Jews to fight for a united Bosnia? Then the Izetbegović government tried to use me. Somebody I knew in Bosnian national television called me in May 1992 to do an interview with Spanish television, because Izetbegović was quickly aware that the way Jews were treated would be critical to world opinion. The week before they had accused me of using my business as a shield to help the Serbs dig trenches!

"I wanted to stay, for the city and for the business. But then I began to see that Sarajevo was gone. It was not a matter of the buildings. It was the people: God takes the best people first. And, hiding in cellars those first months, I changed. I saw what my life was worth: precisely one bullet. All the running to build the business suddenly seemed absurd. In the end, after six months, I got out with precisely three hundred dollars."

Mladen was reunited with his family and found a temporary job running a small hotel on the Croatian coast. He considered remaining in Croatia. But, after Sarajevo, he was looking for a place where nobody

asked, Who is your father? Who is your mother? What is your religion?
Tudjman's Croatia was not such a place. At his sons' school, Mladen had
to provide a written explanation of why Bojan and Roman were not
Catholic and would not be attending religious classes. When his father,
who had also fled Sarajevo, died at the age of eighty, the Croatian authorities wanted to bury him in a communal grave for refugees at Split because
he was a "foreigner." Finally, with the help of a Jewish agency in Croatia,
Mladen was able to bury Meyer Elazar in Rijeka.

As a Croat, Mladen tried to find his place. But Tudjman's Croatia exasperated him with its desire to be different, to be Western, to prove its distinct identity and its appurtenance to the West. All sorts of new words
appeared on television, the rudiments of a reinvented Croatian language
as distinct as possible from Serbian. But the culture was self-evidently the
same. Mladen watched Croatian television and then the Krajina television
of the rebel Serbs. The broadcasts were interchangeable: only the words
Serb and *Croat* needed to be swapped.

In 1994, the Elazars made their decision to emigrate. Windsor, Ontario, is a long way from home. The Elazars have a small apartment provided by the municipality. A Polish nun lives opposite and takes
scrupulous care of her lawn. There is a Ukrainian church on the corner.
The wisteria blooms on a leafy street where as many bicycles pass as cars.
At his school of English, there are students from China, Somalia, and Vietnam: all the escapees. Windsor is far quieter than Haris's Detroit. The
boys, Bojan and Roman, are also learning English. Bojan, the older boy,
does the Sunday paper route and earns fifteen Canadian dollars. He has a
poster in his room of Michael Jordan and another of the Royal Canadian
Mounted Police.

It is a shock, for Mladen, to live in an organized state such as Canada,
one where he makes an appointment for social security or health care and
does not stand in lines and everything is done in a day. But with the improved organization, he finds, there comes a diminished generosity.

Canada is dull, but Mladen prefers this dullness, this quieting of the
blood. He has been drained of ambition and identity in equal measure.
Happiness is a bicycle ride along the river with his boys. Jasenovac, where
his grandparents were killed; Sarajevo, where his own life came apart: these
towns are symbols now of a cycle from which Mladen wants his boys to be
freed. He never listens to the radio.

CHAPTER 25

MORE GUNS
THAN PIGS

Vojna Adamović's parents, Mišo and Milena, the Serb refugees from Tuzla, had no desire to move to Karadžić's Republika Srpska. But life was cheaper in the Serb-held part of Bosnia than in the Serbian town of Subotica where they had taken refuge, and Milošević would not grant identity papers to Bosnian Serbs, making it impossible for Mišo to get a pension. Mišo's long waits at the Hungarian border on trips to buy gasoline became unbearable.

In 1994, broke, the couple moved to Bijeljina, where Arkan's Tigers had started the "cleansing" of Bosnia in the first days of April 1992. The town lies just thirty miles west of Tuzla. But the front line of the war ran through the Majevica foothills between the two towns, and there was no communication between them. Milena was unable to contact her sisters, Kosa and Radisava, who remained in Tuzla.

The couple brought their two-year-old grandson, Filip, with them. Their younger daughter, Aleksandra, did not have enough money to look after him, and Filip's Croat father had disappeared. Having declared that he would have nothing more to do with a Chetnik family, Darko Krančević was true to his word. The family learned that he might be living in the Gospic area of Croatia, but never heard from him again.

In Bijeljina, the Adamović family found accommodation with one of the few surviving Muslims in a town that had had more than thirty thousand Muslim inhabitants before the war began. His name was Sead Delagić, and he welcomed the presence of the Adamovićs in his small house because he saw it as insurance against being "ethnically cleansed."

Mišo was advised by the Bijeljina municipal authorities during the summer of 1994 that he could ask for Delagić to be removed at any time; the Muslim owner of the house would then be thrown across the lines to Tuzla. Mišo was dismayed. He had lost his own home in Tuzla and he knew what such loss meant. He said he preferred that Delagić remain. Because of the presence of a Muslim, the Adamovićs were told they would never be accorded a telephone line.

Delagić, the solitary Muslim, was silent. He spent his time tending a pear and apple orchard behind the house and pacing slowly among the trees, his hands clasped behind his back. He was single. In one room hung a photograph of his parents. His father, with neatly trimmed mustache, stood upright in his fez. Beneath the photograph the possessions of the Serb Adamović family were piled in a few bags. "That way," said Mišo, "we are always ready to move on."

The once-proud engineer of the Tuzla Mining Institute faded. Mišo's eyes were sunken, his face unshaven. After protracted negotiations with the authorities of Karadžić's self-styled mini-state, he was accorded a pension of about ten dollars a month—enough to buy a kilo of coffee. When he retired in Tuzla in 1991, his pension had been close to one thousand dollars a month. He had a mild stroke. He liked to quote a friend who said that refugees such as they had at least one prospect nobody could take away: the grave. "Bosnia," Mišo told me, "is destroyed. From now on, it will live only in people's hearts."

THE FAMILY WAS joined by Milena's sister Radisava, a kindergarten teacher, who decided late in 1994 that she could no longer live as a Serb in Tuzla. Harassed, tired of Muslims entering her apartment with "papers" that allowed them to inspect the premises, she and her husband paid thirty-five hundred German marks to escape across the lines. They were taken on a fifteen-day journey through the Croat-held town of Kiseljak in central Bosnia, to Serb-held Ilidža, and finally to Bijeljina. Radisava laughed at the fact that those who took the money from her—Croats and Serbs—were the same people who had fomented the fighting. Such trafficking was an essential source of money for those making a killing out of the war. "We were not thrown out of Tuzla in the stupid, brutal way that Serbs used with Muslims," Radisava told me, "but we were forced out all the same." Kosa, her sister, had a laconic description for the times: *"ružno i tužno"* ("sad and ugly").

The only solace for Mišo was Filip—his pert little face and eyes full of curiosity. He loved him but he wanted him to leave. The only hope for his daughters, Vojna and Aleksandra, lay in emigration. He urged them to look into going to Canada, where their cousins, Mladen and Mira Elazar, had gone from Sarajevo. The first years in North America might be hard. But once established, your efforts were safeguarded by the rule of law; thirty years of work could not be whisked away at the whim of a handful of madmen.

Mišo strolled the streets of Bijeljina. The town was flat and dull after Tuzla. People drifted. Some profiteer was building a gas station; it was odd how even gas stations could look corrupt and threatening. There was something in the air, something you could not put your finger on, something rotten. Even in an ordinary-looking street it stuck to you. You came away dirty. What was it? A mixture of decay and menace. You never knew when you were talking to a murderer. Occasionally a Mercedes belonging to Karadžić or Dukić or one of their people would sweep through on the way from Pale to Banja Luka or Belgrade. The hospital was full of the injured—young men missing limbs. It was a small war, run by small-minded people, and this was a small town in the hands of gangsters. But it had been enough, this little war, to destroy his life.

Greater Serbia! Kosovo field! The fundamentalist hordes! The resurrected Ustasha! Who could have dreamed this up? For twenty years, every week, he had met with his friends in Tuzla at the Hotel Bristol, then at the Hotel Tuzla, and they played cards and drank and laughed. Serbs, Muslims, Croats: there was nothing between them, around that table, but friendship. It had not been an illusion—he clung to that belief—but it already seemed part of a faraway world. Now all that was left to him and Milena was survival. Mišo preferred that his clothes remain in those bags. Serbs had long migrated westward away from the advancing Turks, but the tide now seemed to him to be flowing the other way. For all Karadžić's predictions of imminent victory and union with the Serbs of Croatia, it was not hard for Mišo to imagine that his future might eventually hold an eastward passage over a Drina bridge to Serbia.

BY 1995, there was not a trace of the drunken Serbian fever that had accompanied the volunteers crossing the Drina in 1992. In its place there was a hangover. Nebulous, contested, the broad objective of Serb unity in Greater Serbia was visibly frayed. As one United Nations official observed of the vast, increasingly depopulated sprawl of Serb-held lands in Croatia, "More pigs than people, more guns than pigs."

In truth, the vastly superior arsenal of the Serbs at the start of the fighting had always masked a limited willingness to fight. During the Croatian campaign of 1991, General Kadijević, the last Yugoslav defense minister, complained about the number of deserters and Milošević's limited success in mobilizing Serbs. The craven long-range bombardment of Vukovar and other towns reflected the reluctance of the Serbs to take casualties and engage in fighting at close quarters. In Bosnia, at Sarajevo, the pattern was repeated. The Serb army never justified the exaggerated—and self-serving—respect accorded it by Eagleburger, Scowcroft, and the Pentagon;

the only occasion on which the inheritors of Europe's fourth-largest army proved really effective was against defenseless civilians.

The Serbs were also ill served by Milošević's constant failure to tell his people what his objectives were. After the fall of Vukovar on November 17, 1991, the Serbs' momentum appeared to open the possibility of crushing the Croats. At the time, the international response to Yugoslavia's breakup was so muddled that military victory might have allowed Serbia to dictate terms before Croatia's borders were internationally recognized. But Milošević was too much of a coward ever to go for the jugular. The fate of the Romanian dictator Nicolae Ceauşescu haunted him; conviction eluded him because to state his aims was to be accountable if they were not attained or if the methods used in their pursuit were criminal. He was a Greater Serb with half an eye on Western capitals.

In Croatia, as later in Bosnia, he favored the deployment of United Nations peacekeeping troops along the front lines of Serb territorial gains rather than the pursuit of an unambiguous victory. The Serbs beyond the Drina were left in a halfway house; moreover, this house had no foundations—it trailed hundreds of miles westward from Belgrade in a pattern dictated by the presence of Serb settlements or graves but not by even the remotest economic logic.

Milošević did not care. After he lost patience with Karadžić in mid-1994, the war simply disappeared from the television screens of Serbia. Even events of some importance were relegated to terse, colorless items at the bottom of the news, preceded by endless dispatches on such shattering developments as the arrival of a Russian trade delegation in Kragujevac, Serbian ambitions to export do-it-yourself furniture, and skiing conditions in the south Serbian Kopaonik Mountains.

The Bosnian and Croatian Serbs sat in bars and trenches; they drank; they played cards; they tried to learn the Cyrillic alphabet; they stared at their handiwork of 1991 and 1992—the charred ruins of Catholic churches, parking lots where mosques had once stood, villages reduced to Paleolithic mounds of stone. The whiff of plum brandy, unwashed military fatigues, and cigarette smoke seeped from the sleepy outposts of the Serbian *Anschluss*. Markets offered children's shoes the color of army camouflage. Factories stood idle. Roads were empty. Unused railway lines disappeared under advancing vegetation. Lamb carcasses hung from butchers' hooks, but few had the means to buy meat; people ate potatoes, peppers, cabbage, and the beans doled out by the UN High Commissioner for Refugees. They baked their own bread because it was cheaper. "Good Serbs," one caustic saying went, "must learn to eat roots." The only worthwhile employment was at one of the UNPROFOR camps. Those who could leave did: a Serb population of 1.3 million in Bosnia on the eve of the war had fallen to no more than 700,000 after two years of fighting.

The nine-hundred-mile-long front line in Bosnia barely moved after the initial Serb attack in the first months of the war. Increasingly, the huge Serb superiority in tanks and artillery was offset by the stronger, more motivated infantry of the Bosnian army. Mladić's artillery could resist most Bosnian attacks and inflict heavy losses on the more uncoordinated offensives. Often Bosnian infantry were thrown forward into indefensible positions where an accurate Serb artillery barrage decimated them. Life in the Bosnian army was cheap. There were young men sacrificed to a warped game that seemed to involve keeping offensives far from television cameras and contained enough not to threaten the first truth of the war: that of the Muslims as victims. But the Serbs were not in a position to do more than defend. They did not have the men or the morale to take and hold new ground. The Muslims were buttressed by their new sense of identity; the Serbs sapped by the chimera of myth. Only the eastern Muslim enclaves— Srebrenica, Žepa, and Goražde—were obviously vulnerable, but the Serbs hesitated to overrun their small United Nations garrisons. A stalemate, more wearying to the Serbs than the Bosnian army, set in.

By early 1995, American analysts estimated that Izetbegović had between 130,000 and 150,000 men under arms, compared to 85,000 in Karadžić's army, despite the fact that the Serbs had called up men over sixty. Serb officers still received salaries from Belgrade, but regular soldiers received no more than basic rations and an irregular supply of cigarettes. Through domestic arms production in Bugojno, Travnik, Bihać, and other towns, strong financial support from Malaysia, Saudi Arabia, and other Islamic countries, and clandestine arms imports from Iran and Turkey, the Bosnian army gradually grew in stature as the Serb war effort frayed. However, it was still not an army that could defeat the Serbs without Croatian support.

Milošević formalized his abandonment of the lurching Greater Serbian ship on August 3, 1994, after Karadžić's rejection of the Contact Group map. He tried to advance his rehabilitation in the West by imposing a porous embargo on the Drina River border with Serb-held Bosnia. Thus were the old Serb divisions that Milošević had attacked so vehemently at Kosovo field in 1989 reborn. Matériel still went to Mladić's forces, often delivered through nocturnal helicopter flights, but other supplies were more limited. The misery of the Bosnian and Krajina Serbs increased. Greater Serbia was a bog: the rhetoric of Serb valor seeped in; misery oozed out.

THE SERB UPRISING that ultimately dumped Mišo Adamović in Bijeljina had begun in the railway-junction town of Knin, a bleak little Croatian industrial town forty miles inland from the Dalmatian coast. It was here, beneath a medieval castle on a hill and beside a sprawling screw factory, that Milošević's propaganda and Tudjman's provocations coalesced. The poison produced took the form of a revolt among Serbs, who accounted for 88 percent of Knin's prewar population. In August 1990, two months after Tudjman's election, a Serb National Council meeting in Knin adopted the Declaration on the Sovereignty and Autonomy of the Serb People, which laid the basis for the self-proclaimed Serb state in Croatia, the Republika Srpska Krajina (Serb Republic of the Krajina).

The Croatian war of 1991 left this separatist republic occupying 27 percent of Croatian territory in an arc ranging north and east from Knin all the way to the fertile plains of eastern Slavonia on the Serbian border. Added to the 70 percent of Bosnia occupied by the Serbs in 1992, this territory made up the Greater Serbia taken by Milošević from Yugoslavia's ruins. Knin, more than three hundred miles west of Belgrade, was always a touchstone of this Serbian project. It was strategically vital in that it was the rail junction connecting Zagreb with the Dalmatian coast towns of Split and Zadar, and it was vulnerable because distant from the Serbian capital. Whatever was discernible in Bijeljina, less than one hundred miles from Belgrade, was writ large in Knin.

By late October 1994, the train station at Knin amounted to an emblem of the impasse into which Milošević had led the Serbs. Miloš Petrović, the stationmaster, came to work every day. Work was a relative term, however; he did nothing and he had done nothing for more than three years. About four hundred rusting wagons stood in front of him on the tracks where they had stood since June 30, 1991, the date that fighting between Serbs and Croats stopped the trains. Once, 120 trains a day from all over Yugoslavia, and 20 international train services, had passed through Knin. Now a single train a day lumbered a few miles up the track.

The line to Zagreb was cut by the Croats; the line to Belgrade cut by the Bosnian army. Greater Serbia, in short, was in a state of ineluctable atrophy. "We used to be the fourth-largest station in Yugoslavia after Belgrade, Zagreb, and Vinkovci," Petrović said with an admirable matter-of-factness. "Now we are nothing." Knin had become a junction to nowhere. Its train station was as useless as Yugoslavia's road signs and as outsized as the Yugoslav federal buildings in New Belgrade built to serve a nonexistent state. Milošević should have come to Knin to see what he had wrought, but he never liked to link himself to the destruction, physical or moral, that flowed from him.

Petrović, the stationmaster, had earned about fifteen hundred German marks a month when Yugoslavia existed; he now earned fifty marks. Almost all his former colleagues had either left or been forced into the army.

He said he saw no future for himself but still believed that the Serbs had been right to resist joining Tudjman's independent Croatia. "It is better for Serbs to suffer in this hole than be part of Croatia and dead," he said.

This was also the view of Branko Kurilić, a television producer in Knin, who saw the choice for the Serbs as one between being massacred by the Croats and union with Serbia. He was equally troubled by the Muslims. He had recently been in Glasgow, where he had suffered a disturbing experience. "You would not believe what I saw," he told me. "A mosque. A mosque in the middle of Glasgow! Can you believe it?" I stared at him in wonder. "The Muslim tide is advancing. We Serbs are really fighting a war for the West here. You know that Paris is now the second largest Muslim city after Cairo?"

I WANDERED UP from the station to the offices of Milan Martić, the former Knin police chief who had become a leader of the Serb rebellion and, after the fall of Milan Babić in 1992, the self-styled president of the Serb Republic of the Krajina. The self-important heads of the various mini-states that emerged from Yugoslavia's destruction all liked to surround themselves with elaborate trappings of power and an arsenal of "democratic" institutions and verbiage that stood in inverse proportion to the amount of democracy that actually existed. Ministries, parliaments, referendums, committees, and subcommittees abounded: there was a pathological desire to ape the West. But these were tin-pot dictatorships all the same, and they were led by crooks who had little interest in change because they controlled all the lucrative trafficking across the lines of their latter-day Ruritanias. Martić, a puffed-up little man, and quite stupid, amounted to a paragon of these tendencies. Any meeting with him involved a struggle to penetrate an army of acolytes dedicated to the preparation of the agenda of the "president."

Martić sat at the end of a long, long table beside his flag. He exuded a confidence that smacked more of bravura than conviction. "For four years," he declared, "we have been a state. We have seventeen thousand square kilometers of land and five hundred thousand citizens. We have everything except international recognition: a territory, a people, a democracy. In the end, the world will change its view of us. The facts are all on our side and so is military strength. If necessary, we can defend ourselves even without Belgrade."

The world's view of Knin was in fact that the most the Krajina Serbs could hope for was autonomy within Croatia. The American ambassador to Zagreb, Peter Galbraith, was pushing something called the "Z-4 Plan," which offered the Serbs their own police, their own flag, their own education, and their own money—what he called "everything they can possibly

achieve in the real world." But the real world was not the one inhabited by
Martić. Another bleak Balkan equation was this one: The more remote the
outpost, the more the local honcho ruling it believed he sat squarely at the
center of the universe. Martić did not believe the world's—or Croatia's—
patience with him could ever run out.

It was highly unlikely that Tudjman could ever be persuaded to accept
the Serb autonomy contained in Galbraith's plan, which was privately
mocked in several Western capitals. But, like Karadžić in Bosnia, Martić
never confronted his enemies with tough diplomatic choices. His defiance
was bad diplomacy. All Martić needed to do was to take one look at the
Knin railway station to see that time was running out for his republic on
the old Austro-Hungarian Military Frontier, but, like many Serbs, he was
more interested in history lessons than getting the trains to run. "Of
course I will allow my people to decide in a referendum," he said mag-
nanimously, "but my personal opinion is that we will never accept being
part of the Republic of Croatia."

There were good reasons, of course, for the Serbs' anxiety—many more
than had ever existed in Bosnia. Savo Štrbac, a lawyer in Knin, put his people's case as concisely and articulately as anyone I met. "We do not want
to live with Croats because of Pavelić's genocide," he said. "Tudjman does
not want to live with Serbs, he only wants the land where we are living.
On December 22, 1990, we ceased to be a constituent nation of Croatia
under Tudjman's constitution. Nobody consulted us about that, any more
than they asked us about Croatia's secession. We had lived for the previous
seventy years with other Serbs, and we believe we have the right to go on
doing so. Croats and Serbs have to trust each other. It took eighty years
and three wars for France and Germany to begin to trust each other. Because of recent history, and because of Tudjman's ambivalence about the
Ustasha, we do not trust each other and so we cannot be together. If the
choice is between a return to Croatia and economic isolation, we prefer
isolation. We prefer war. There is no solution. That is the way it is. We are
in an impasse plotted by Germany."

SERB ANGER AGAINST Germany for its forthright support of Croatian
independence was always vehement. The conviction is deep among Serbs
that there have been two basic thrusts to Serbian policy since the early
nineteenth century: the removal of the Turks from the Balkans and the
prevention of German penetration of the area. The vehicle for German expansionism was first the Austro-Hungarian annexation of Bosnia in 1908
and the world war of 1914 that followed; then it was Nazism. In the plot-
filled atmosphere of Milošević's Belgrade, and in the bars of Knin, German
support for Croatian independence was portrayed as a third, thinly dis-

guised push for a warm-weather Adriatic port. It betrayed Bonn's irresponsible desire to solve "the Croatian question" at the expense of creating a much larger "Serbian question."

In fact, by the time Germany decided to recognize Croatia in 1991, there were no good options. War had been raging in Croatia for several months, and Milošević had resisted all of the European Union's peace proposals. His obstinacy was clearly serving as a shield for Serb territorial gains in Croatia. The presence in Germany of a powerful Croatian lobby, the murderous Serb flattening of Vukovar, the Serb attack on Dubrovnik, the steady spread of Serb-held land in Croatia, and the awakening of old historical and religious sympathies led Germany to act.

Hans-Dietrich Genscher, then Germany's foreign minister, presented his country's ultimatum at a European Union meeting in Brussels on December 15, 1991: Germany would recognize Croatia unilaterally in the absence of rapid joint progress toward recognition. The French were furious; so were the British; so was Lord Carrington, who had been leading the European Union's efforts to bring peace. The old power of the Balkans to split Europe had manifested itself once more.

If the European Union meant anything the fissuring had to be stopped. A hasty compromise was worked out. All Yugoslav republics that wanted to be recognized had to apply, by December 24, to an arbitration commission headed by Judge Robert Badinter of France; the commission would report its findings by January 15, 1992. It was an absurdly precipitate timetable that helped usher Bosnia toward war, and it removed the only real leverage Carrington had for an overall settlement of Yugoslavia's dissolution: the bait of international recognition if real safeguards for minorities were in place. The United States, still piqued by the Croatian and Slovenian secessions, withheld recognition for a few more months, but, in essence, the United States had opted out of an active role in Yugoslav diplomacy.

Croatia won its recognition from the European Union on January 15, 1992, despite the fact that the Badinter Commission found that conditions there were not yet appropriate. The Croatian war was thus brought to an end, albeit by a truce that was tenuous. It is unlikely that the war could have been stopped so quickly without Germany's action. But rampant Serb theories about world plots against them and German expansionism gained an enormous shot in the arm. Croatia discovered a new hymn—"*Danke Deutschland*"—as Serbia discovered the notion of the Fourth Reich.

Štrbac, the Knin refugee, was from Benkovac, near the coastal town of Zadar. He had fled Croatian harassment in October 1991 and come to Knin. Miroslav Gutesa, a translator, was another refugee in Knin, from

Gospić in the Lika region of Croatia. Married to a Croat, he had worked in a tourist company called Jadran for fifteen years. On August 23, 1991, he was severely beaten by Croat thugs. He fled a month later, leaving everything. A friend had sent him a photograph of his house, which had been blown up. He also had a photograph of his closest friend, Rajko Barac, who had been mutilated by Croats in Gospić. His ears were cut off and his beard burned. Gutesa's travails had not begun with this war. He had lost most of his mother's family to the Ustasha; his father, a Serbian royalist, was killed by Tito's secret police in Stuttgart in 1947. He seemed to carry with him the weight of Serb suffering in this century.

I looked at Gutesa, a man obviously in pain and indignant at what he rightly saw as America's cosseting of Tudjman. I looked at Štrbac, with his understandable anger against Germany. It was an unhappy fact of the Yugoslav wars that the sheer scale, and maladroitness, of the Serbs' crimes tended to dwarf Tudjman's violence. While Serb shells fell on Vukovar or Dubrovnik, while the Albanians of Kosovo lived under Serb repression, while Muslims were terrorized in Bosnia, Tudjman could pursue his sinister designs for the Serbs of Croatia with a reasonable assurance that little international outrage would be left over for him. This is precisely what happened. The West became an ally of Croatia, prodded in that direction by the Serb leadership. Seldom has a people been as ill served by their leaders as the Serbs during the period of Yugoslavia's destruction.

A case for Gutesa and Štrbac could be made. It seemed to me that they deserved autonomous status within Croatia over a period of years while tensions eased. But Martić and Milošević were not the men who could make such a case effectively. The former was a small-town policeman with no notion of diplomacy; the latter interested only in his own hold on power. "My policy, and it will never shift," Martić told me, "is for my people to remain on their land."

IN FACT, as Martić and I spoke on October 31, 1994, several thousand Serbs had just lost their land in the first major military setback for Serb forces since the start of the war. On October 26, the V Corps of the Bosnian army, based in the western Bosnian enclave and "safe area" of Bihać, north of Knin, had embarked on a surprise offensive, sweeping across the Grabež Plateau south and east of the town. Having broken through the Serb front line, they met little resistance from Serb soldiers, whose morale had evidently sunk through thirty-one months of war. Greeting this first victory, Haris Silajdžić, the Bosnian prime minister, said, "The Serbs are fleeing because it's not a picnic anymore. It's not plunder. It's not rape. It's not taking gold from women. It's not easy. It's merely a bullet in the forehead."

Serbs who had fled this offensive gathered in the village of Donji Lapac, in the Serb-held part of Croatia. A platoon of ragged Serb soldiers was trying to regroup, but when I started talking to them, their enraged commander came at me with his Kalashnikov, ramming its butt into my back. I came back two days later and managed to avoid him. Refugees huddled on the floor of the elementary school, just as, two years earlier, Muslims from Vlasenica had found refuge in the kindergarten in Kladanj. The Balkan gyre was turning.

The Serbs told their stories of arson, looting, and terror by the Muslim-led Bosnian forces; some of the older people had lost their parents to the Ustasha and described their flight as "evil coming around for the second time." The evil coming around was in fact that of the Serb marauders in 1992 who, by persecuting Muslims in western Bosnian towns like Ključ, Prijedor, and Sanski Most, had stirred the anger around which the Bosnian V Corps was built. But, whatever its source, the suffering of these people was real enough.

A Muslim woman named Edina Zeč was sprawled on the floor in Donji Lapac with her two young children. She was married to a Serb and had stayed throughout the war on the Serb side of the lines, in the village of Kulen Vakuf, southeast of Bihać. When the village had been overrun by the Bosnian army, she had fled. Her husband was fighting with Mladić's Serb forces in Bosnia. Her two Muslim brothers were with the Bosnian army that had just burst out of Bihać. She, a Muslim in flight from Muslims, was in the middle, with nowhere to go. Quite possibly, as we spoke, her brothers confronted her husband on the battlefield.

It was this absurdity, this pain, that Milošević and Tudjman had wrought and to which the world had acquiesced. By the time I met Edina Zeč, I had seen the pain in myriad guises among the ruins of Yugoslavia: people marooned, existences unmoored as if gravity itself had been removed, the living dead. People standing in smoldering towns, hanging their washing, shirt by shirt, sock by sock, as the shrapnel flew; hanging their washing because the only flight available was to some ethnic corral that would never welcome them, the countless Yugoslavs of mixed blood or marriage. In the name of Lazar, or Dušan, or some imagined historical injustice, Milošević and Tudjman had destroyed millions of lives, but, ensconced behind their desks in faraway capitals, they had, I believe, little notion of the sea of suffering on which they floated. So it ever was with the folly of nationalist convulsion.

The Bihać Muslim pocket, from which Edina Zeč had fled, was surrounded by Mladić's Bosnian Serb forces to the east and Martić's Krajina Serb forces to the west; it represented a kernel of this suffering. It was steadily shelled back into the nineteenth century. When the sun set on

Bihać and the 190,000 Muslims living in the pocket, the area was plunged into blackness. Nobody moved, and there was scarcely a sound, save that of howling dogs and desultory machine-gun fire. Faintly visible were the silhouettes of nearby mountains, where Serb forces were perched. Cut off from Sarajevo, largely forgotten by the world, the town was virtually ruined by 1994. On the main street, there were more horse-drawn carts than cars. They moved slowly past sandbagged storefronts, carrying loads of firewood, the sole source of heat. Cattle and goats grazed by the roadside.

From its base in this town, the hastily formed V Corps of the Bosnian army had, since the start of the war, fought a remarkable rearguard action under its commander, Atif Dudaković. Its approximately fourteen thousand men were made up largely of Muslim refugees from the Serb onslaught of 1992. When I met Dudaković a few months before the retaliatory offensive that drove those Serbs into Donji Lapac, he already appeared quietly confident.

A makeshift factory for the production of ammunition and mortars had been resurrected in the town, and Dudaković seemed untroubled by his isolation. His military objective was clear enough—ensuring that every Bosnian be allowed to return to his home—and he was ready to pursue it for as long as necessary. In such determination lay the core of the Bosnian army's strength. Martić had bombast, but Dudaković had ballast; over time this was a telling difference. "There is a cosmic rule of justice," Dudaković told me. "Whoever started this war will pay a high price. The Serbs attacked us and drove us back here because they were stronger. But the chickens will come home to roost."

DUDAKOVIĆ WAS NOT only fighting the Serbs. From September 1993, he was also fighting a war within a war against Muslims who had rebelled against the Izetbegović government and given their support to Fikret Abdić, a wealthy local businessman known to his adoring following as "Babo" ("Daddy").

Abdić had emerged as a local hero from the Agrokomerc trial of the late 1980s—he was charged with embezzlement at the company, but the case was largely political—and won more votes than any other Muslim in the 1990 Bosnian elections. A stocky wheeler-dealer, he had tired of war, thrown in his lot with Martić's Krajina Serbs, accused the Izetbegović government of destructive nationalism, and ensconced himself in a castle on a hill beside the town of Velika Kladuša in the northern part of the Bihać pocket. Needless to say, he, too, declared "independence," named himself "president," enveloped his breakaway government in all the trappings of "democracy," and grew richer on the sale of everything from coffee to papers allowing Bosnians to escape to Zagreb. His castle, in mid-1994, was adorned with oak beams, stone walls, Oriental rugs, and discreet spot-lights. It would not have looked out of place in *Town and Country.*

Abdić was a sleazy figure and his mini-state ridiculous, but the war be-tween Muslims in the Bihać pocket was real enough and it took hundreds of lives. One of them was that of Colonel Nevzet Derić, a dashing figure who, like the refugee Edina Zeč, embodied all the ambiguities of the fight-ing.

There was right and wrong in the war, but that did not mean that choices were ever easy on the inside of the conflict. Dudaković told me that Derić, a Bosnian Muslim who fought with Abdić, was a "traitor." But I could not see him in such straightforward terms, any more than I could simply hate Alija Mehmedović, the Muslim who became an Ustasha in an earlier war and then "disappeared" in Turkey.

When I met Colonel Derić in June 1994, a few weeks before his death, he was sitting in a small bar in Pećigrad that doubled as his military head-quarters. The bar stood close to the front line of the intra-Muslim war in Bihać. Through the window, we could see mortar shells from Dudaković's army crashing regularly into the lush fields, sending black plumes up into the heady summer air. Their detonation was distant and dull. How strangely soft, almost bucolic, the Bosnian war could look! Peasants de-fending their pigs and goats among the apple groves. The V Corps was closing in. When I stepped outside, accompanied by one of Derić's sol-diers, a sniper's bullet whistled by, uncomfortably close, and we ducked behind a stone wall. The softness was an illusion.

Derić, who had risen early, was weary. Radio messages poured in. But he scarcely appeared to be listening. He was a handsome man, with an en-gaging smile, caught in a fight he clearly loathed—one in which Muslims killed Muslims. "Instead of enjoying this lovely warm weather," he said, "we have to chase each other through the hills. Instead of listening to music, or having coffee with beautiful women, I have to listen to these messages about meaningless victories and defeats. But everything has two sides—the bright and the dark—and perhaps we cannot have one without the other."

This former Yugoslav army officer was nearing the end of a long odyssey. He had become alarmed about Bosnia's future when the Croatian war broke out in 1991. If the Serbs were so ferocious in the defense of their people in Croatia, he reasoned, how would the large Serb minority in Bosnia react to independence? As a military adviser to Izetbegović's SDA party in Banja Luka, and in his home town of Ključ, Derić had spent much of 1991 urging the party to arm Muslims and arrange the defection of Muslims in the Yugoslav army. But Izetbegović, who was deluded enough to tell Sarajevans they could sleep peacefully on the eve of the war, had rejected the idea.

"I was labeled an extremist for saying that we must get armed," Derić told me. "Izetbegović ordered us to stay in the JNA. Then he ordered us to leave, but without weapons, and those weapons were used against us. The fact is the Serbs of Bosnia were fighting for their national interests in 1991 and preparing for war at the same time. We Muslims were fighting for our national interests and *not* preparing for war. That was stupid."

When war broke out, Derić's hometown of Ključ was quickly "cleansed" of its more than seventeen thousand Muslims by the Serbs. Derić fled to Bihać; his wife and daughter fled to Slovenia. In Bihać, Derić became commander of the 504th Brigade of the V Corps and earned a reputation for unusual bravery. Dudaković himself conceded that Derić was an "extraordinary fighter."

Between June 1992 and June 1993, Derić was, it seems, possessed by a ferocious determination to drive back the Serbs. He spent every night in the hills, regaining some territory, holding the line, plotting a break-through to Banja Luka. Then, suffering from what he called "a complete nervous and physical breakdown," he collapsed and spent two months in Bihać hospital.

"I lay there," Derić told me, "and started thinking. And two things became clear to me. The first was that I would never reach Ključ or Banja Luka by fighting, and political compromise with the Serbs was the only way. The second was that if my pleas to push forward were so often rejected, it was because many officers in V Corps just wanted to keep their comfortable position, their money, and their Mercedes." And so, when Abdić declared autonomy on September 27, 1993, Derić followed him because, he said, "not even the Serbs can do as much harm as Izetbegović, who has pushed us into a battle against a well-armed enemy."

Doubtless Derić had been well paid by Abdić for his defection; doubt-less there was personal animosity within V Corps that helped explain his decision. But I believed him when he said, "My conscience is absolutely clear. I do not think that I am a traitor." Derić, aged just twenty-six, had reached the end of his own road. He had been "ethnically cleansed"; he had fought for Izetbegović's Bosnia; he had decided that the fight could lead nowhere. "For a long time," he told me, "my conclusion has been that nothing can be solved by this war. Nothing. It would be easier for me to fight these battles if I was not convinced of that."

A few weeks after we spoke, a shell crashed into that bar at Pećigrad and Derić was killed. Instantly, I hope. The Abdić forces, who had depended on Derić's leadership, folded; thousands of his followers fled into Serb-held Croatia. Dudaković's corps enjoyed a steady ascendancy, culminating in its victories over the Serbs of October 1994. Martić was enraged by Dudaković. When I saw him, the Krajina Serb leader declared that he was about to dispatch "special police and military units" over the border into Bosnia in order to recapture the lost land. An aide nudged him; it was clearly illegal to send troops over an "international border" into Bosnia; Martić should not make his purpose so plain. But the Krajina Serb was nothing if not blunt. "We will see," he said, "if the Bihać pocket ends up smaller than it was." The last "safe-area" crisis before the denouement of the war at Srebrenica in July 1995 was about to begin.

THE BATTLE FOR BIHAĆ in November 1994 amounted to a shambles. The steady unraveling of the NATO alliance, torn by strategic difference between Europe and America over Bosnia, was laid bare. The confusion surrounding the creation of UN "safe areas" was evident. International vows to protect one of those areas, Bihać, proved empty. More than one thousand Bangladeshi troops in the service of the United Nations, with perhaps three hundred automatic rifles between them, were left marooned in the pocket through weeks of fighting. Several hundred UN soldiers, including dozens of Canadians, were taken as hostages by the Serbs.

The forces of Martić attacking Bihać from Serb-held Croatia, of Muslim renegades under Abdić attacking from the north, and of Mladić attacking from the east converged on the supposedly protected enclave without any coherent international response. More than sixty thousand people, including refugees from outlying villages, huddled in Bihać. A host of new Serb SAM-2 and SAM-6 air-defense systems, fresh from Belgrade despite Milošević's supposed embargo on the Drina, were "discovered." Akashi muttered about unacceptable humiliations for the United Nations. There was even talk of a UN withdrawal from Bosnia. An elaborate departure plan was drawn up. But leaving, after all the billions of dollars spent, was never an attractive prospect: it would be a humiliation, it would take months, and presumably somebody would have to turn out the lights.

The Serbs' attack on Bihać was a response to the offensive out of the "safe area" by Dudaković's forces. This fact exposed the ambiguities of the "safe-area" concept and complicated efforts to forge a common response. General Rose, the commander of UN forces in Bosnia, was resolutely opposed to using NATO force to stop the Serb riposte. "If one side or the other, and in this case both sides, have chosen to go into the area to fight then there's very little we can do by force of arms to stop that happening," he said. Rose was supported by General Bertrand de Lapresle, the French commander of all United Nations forces in the former Yugoslavia.

On November 21, two weeks after the Serb attack began and three days after Martić's Krajina Serb aircraft dropped napalm and cluster bombs on the Bihać area, NATO did bomb the Udbina airfield in Serb-held Croatia from which the Serb planes had taken off. But at Lapresle's insistence, the bombing did not hit the fifteen planes themselves, only the runways, which were quickly repaired. Yet again, it was a case of NATO shackled in the interests of the doctrine of impartiality. That day, Douglas Hurd, the British foreign secretary, said, "We don't see a victory for one side or another in this war and we are not involved in helping one side or another to a military victory as we think it is impossible." This was also Rose's view: *There is no solution.* It was intellectually and ethically flawed. It brought great, and needlessly prolonged, suffering. Its corollaries were containment and, where possible, amelioration, but never an attempt to strike at the core of the problem.

As the Serbs advanced, and Bihać tottered, there was endless wrangling within the alliance as to which area of the pocket should be protected. Where, in other words, should a line be drawn in the Bosnian *glina*—the cloying mud in which so many armies had stuck?

The Bihać "safe area" gradually shrank until, on November 21, the United Nations and NATO decided on a sliver of territory, four miles wide and six miles long, that covered the town of Bihać and its immediate environs. Kofi Annan, then the United Nations undersecretary for peacekeeping, sent a firm cable that day to Rose: "All members made it very clear that any direct attack against the safe area as defined by UNPROFOR should be responded to by the use of air power. I confirmed that this was UNPROFOR's understanding as well and I would appreciate you ensuring that the policy is firmly pressed."

The next day, the Serbs took a hill immediately overlooking Bihać that was well within the area defined by Annan. Clearly Rose was committed to resist this advance. He had a meeting with General Zdravko Tolimir, a leading Serb general, at Sarajevo Airport. "Unfortunately," Rose told Tolimir, "your troops have moved in. This is probably a *misunderstanding*." He added his own interpretation: that the "safe area" concept was "flexible," and a reasonable solution could no doubt be found.

Acrimony within the alliance was at a high pitch. America's public position was that it wanted bombing. On November 23, NATO jets hit three Serb missile batteries within a fifty-mile radius of Bihać, but this did nothing to help the town or slow the Serb advance. The international commitment to protect "safe areas" was transparently empty.

When there was further Serb shelling of Bihać on November 25, Rose, under pressure from Madeleine K. Albright, the American envoy to the United Nations, did call in NATO planes. But then he made sure that the

British officers on the ground who were supposed to guide the planes to their targets did nothing. "We assembled a strike team. We had about ten planes over the area. But we never got a target from the guy on the ground," said Jim Mitchell, a spokesman at NATO's southern command in Naples.

In the protracted Bosnian farce that saw the British and French governments in one corner wearing the colors of the United Nations and the American government in the other wearing the colors of NATO, this was a culminating moment. Perceiving the alliance at risk, Anthony Lake, Clinton's national security adviser, called an end to the phony fight. Phony not because it lacked genuine bitterness, but utterly phony because both sides, in their differences, claimed to be battling for the good of Bosnia. If this had been even remotely true, the transatlantic tensions would have been resolved almost three years earlier.

Lake's somber, if long-obvious, conclusion from the Bihać debacle was contained in a memo for the president drafted on November 27, 1994, with the help of Alexander R. Vershbow, his top aide for European affairs. Lake noted that an American effort "to use NATO air strikes to prevent the fall of Bihać has only intensified transatlantic frictions." And he concluded, "Bihać's fall has exposed the inherent contradictions in trying to use NATO air power coercively against the Bosnian Serbs when our allies have troops on the ground attempting to maintain impartiality in performing a humanitarian mission. The stick of military pressure seems no longer viable."

In other words, NATO unity, increasingly an oxymoron, was more important than saving a small town in Bosnia. For the American interest this was unquestionably true. But Lake's memo raised several old questions. If the British and French troops on the ground "attempting to maintain impartiality" in pursuit of a United Nations mission were vulnerable to NATO bombs, should not the most vulnerable be placed out of harm's way in order to make the NATO threat credible? If the international commitment to the Muslim "safe areas" was an empty one, should not their protection either be boldly reinforced or abandoned? If America put any real store by the safeguarding of Bosnia, should it not dispatch troops to flank its European allies on the ground and so bring unity to Western efforts?

All the questions had been around for some time. All were difficult but critical. All were fudged over the ensuing months. Nothing of substance changed. There is a fairly basic rule in life: If something does not work, do the opposite. For years in Bosnia, the rule was ignored. Disaster ensued in the summer of 1995.

DUDAKOVIĆ, IN THE END, held on to Bihać itself. In Velika Kladuša, in the north of the pocket, fighting long raged. I watched a battle from the ruins of Abdić's castle on a hill. The place had been gutted by V Corps after they took it over in August 1994. No more Oriental rugs or discreet spotlights; no more neatly planted geraniums outside. Now, in early December 1994, Abdić, backed by the artillery of the Krajina Serbs, had taken the castle back and was closing in on the town of Velika Kladuša itself. Shelling and heavy machine-gun fire reverberated through the mist-filled valley. A single man ran for cover across the deserted town. I wondered if Abdić would set about restoring the castle if he ever consolidated his position. Back and forth, back and forth, like some pendulum with no clock to give its movement sense, the war went, and, equally deprived of sense, the West's reaction moved with it. I looked down at the smashed-up town from which black smoke billowed. A small, quaint provincial place—until the Balkan winds rose.

Not far from Velika Kladuša, there was a chicken farm where about seventeen thousand Bosnian Muslim refugees, followers of Abdić, sheltered, waiting to know the result of the fight. Where once sixty thousand chickens had clucked and fed, hordes of Bosnia's ragged dispossessed mingled in the mud, lugging containers of water and bundles of washing through a landscape awash with sewage and misery. Children played among stinking piles of garbage, women crouched in vast chicken coops stirring soup over makeshift fires, men chopped firewood in the gloom. In each of twenty-four fetid sheds that were once home to the chickens, about 750 refugees lived. By the shifting light of candles or small stoves, some played cards, some stirred cauldrons of cabbage, some lay slumped on mattresses provided by the UNHCR. Babies screamed and children played while the old just stared from hollow eyes across a shadowy, seething expanse suggestive of the netherworld. The distinction between these people's lives and those of animals was not easy to discern.

"For me this is the shame of Europe," said Wycliffe Songwa, the Kenyan UNHCR official who was striving to conjure some decency from the morass. "If I was back in Africa, I would understand, because the poverty is such that these situations arise. But in the middle of Europe, this is unacceptable."

In the middle of Europe, this is unacceptable. But it had been for so long! We stood, Songwa and I, perhaps two hundred miles from Venice. More than thirty months earlier, the Serb concentration camps had done their execrable business at the same distance from centers of Western civilization. Nothing had been done. Lake and Vershbow, for whom this had long been mainly a war of position papers, drafted their memos. The Pentagon explained the impossibility of military action. Clinton looked sorrowful, or tearful, or plain helpless. Orphaned children skipped amid the sewage in former chicken coops.

I would get out from time to time and go to Paris and watch the people on the rue de Montorgeuil choosing their cherries, their strawberries, their glistening golden haddock, their pink salmon filets, their oozing Camemberts. What were two million Slavic Muslims to them? The European Union had kept the war safely distant; another continent-wide conflagration had been avoided. But no European soldier had planted the blue-and-gold European flag on the roof of the Presidency Building in a liberated Sarajevo. Europe had lost a chance to give itself a soul, lift itself above the mere calculations of economic integration. A price would be paid, I was sure of that; Dudaković's chickens would come home to roost.

CHAPTER 26

THE DARK SIDE OF
THE MIRROR

THERE IS A WHISPERING BEFORE A STORM. IN A PLACID LAND-scape a sudden fluttering of a leaf, a slight darkening of the sky, a rustling in the grass, a tremor in the air bespeak the turbulence to come. The still-ness of Sarajevo, in quieter times, always had this quality: a gathering-in of energy whose release, it seemed, would be violent.

Before the angry spring of 1995 came, I would watch the children on sleds glide noiselessly over the snow, the trams slipping by, and, at night, the lights on the hills climbing silently toward the stars. Not a mortar round or a sniper's shot disturbed the peace. The miracle of electricity sometimes lasted for weeks.

Some Sarajevo cafés reopened between April 1994 and April 1995. Cer-tain days were so peaceful that the sound of coffee being ground in the cafés was audible. To watch the handle being patiently turned on the old Ottoman grinders was to understand something of the Oriental rhythms of Sarajevo life. A take-out pizza service did a reasonable business. Food was never abundant, or cheap, but there was enough to eat. Among the United Nations armored personnel carriers on the streets, a few private cars appeared. Sarajevans repainted their rooms, saying to themselves that even if this was only a time-out in the killing they would take advantage of it. At times the twilight zone of muted war even looked a little like peace.

For General Rose and his United Nations entourage, as for many West-ern politicians, this pause in the horror was cause for hope. The improve-ments in the conditions of a city still encircled were viewed as a likely precursor of the peace that had eluded Bosnia since its independence was recognized on April 6, 1992. A cease-fire and a real peace—as distinct as a palliative and a cure—were conflated.

Such views involved being seduced by the surface of things. Sarajevo, even when life looked least unbearable, was full of an implacable outrage.

This was a quality, gemlike in intensity, that the politicians looking at the war from the outside missed. Their calculations were thus flawed. Silajdžić once said to me, "Tanks are hard. Bullets are hard. Bombs are hard. But the spirit is an elusive, defiant power and the politicians did not reckon with it."

One woman, Amra Džaferović, an accountant and mother of a three-year-old boy, told me, "I am a very normal person and I do not wish harm to anyone. But if I were ordered to go up to Pale and shoot the Serbs up there, I would do it. They have taken my son's childhood away and nobody has the right to do that." On January 17, 1995, her son Adi watched images of destruction from the earthquake in Kobe, Japan. "Mom," he asked, "did the Chetniks do that?" For this boy of three, destruction equaled Serbs: that was the only reality he had known.

In Dobrinja, down by the western front lines, lived a sixteen-year-old Muslim girl named Azra Obuća. Like Haris Zečević's mother, she had tried to escape across the airport, setting out with a friend, Emir Subašić, on the night of April 15, 1993. As with Bisera Zečević, UNPROFOR obliged the Serbs by pointing the beam of a spotlight at the young pair. Emir, aged seventeen, was killed; Azra survived but was severely injured. Her mother, Vasfija Obuća, was wounded soon afterward by a shell. She became afraid of any sound; the phone made her jump. "When a snake has bitten you," said her husband, Rasim, "you are afraid of a lizard."

He went into a back room of their small apartment and returned holding a bullet, the one that had lodged in the stomach of his daughter as she tried to run across the airport. It had been removed in the Koševo Hospital. He fondled the bullet that had almost killed his daughter: a talisman of sorts. "This," he said simply, "is the worst feeling. The feeling that I want to give this bullet back to somebody in revenge. Back to the Serb who did this. I never believed I was capable of such feelings. But now I could kill."

Occasionally, across the so-called Bridge of Brotherhood and Unity linking Serb-held Grbavica with the government-held part of Sarajevo, would trudge another dazed and frightened group of evicted Muslims. The NATO ultimatum of February 1994 temporarily silenced Serb artillery, permitting a limited number of crossings over the bridge. In general they were old people, for young adults had been chased from their homes by the Serbs much earlier in the war. In ragged sacks they carried their remaining possessions into an unknown city, peasants from some tiny rural community in eastern Bosnia. Women clutched sleeping children; toothless old men gazed into space; the fetid odor of the unwashed accompanied them. As United Nations officials looked on, they were bundled onto city buses and taken to one of the many refugee centers in Sarajevo. This, in the end, was the central image of the war: Muslims—men, women, and children—herded like cattle toward some desolate fate.

IN JUNE 1994, more than two years after they left Sarajevo, Vesna and Jasna Karišik were able to see their mother again for the first time since they fled with their father to Belgrade in 1992. Unaccompanied by their father, who said he did not want to go, Jasna and Vesna traveled from Belgrade down through Serb-held Bosnia to Grbavica. On June 22, Fida Karišik took a tranquilizer and presented herself at the Brotherhood and Unity Bridge. The Serbs searched her and eventually allowed her into Grbavica, where she made her way to the apartment of her husband's former secretary. When Fida saw her girls she could not stop crying.

Vesna found her mother more beautiful than she remembered. Fida carried herself very upright. Her face was like a luminous old fresco, held in a fragile harmony, but liable at any moment to crack into pieces. She did not want to let go of the girls' hands. Holding their hands, she fell asleep; awakening, she reached out for them.

It was strange for the girls to be so close to their old home yet unable to go there. The Serbs said that if they allowed them into the other side of the city, the Muslims would not let them out. Fida ached to bring them home. They asked her why she always spoke with such anger about the Serbs. The Serbs were not all bad, the girls said. She wanted to bring her daughters back to their city so that they could understand, so that Belgrade would not possess them entirely. But after three days she had to leave. Vesna watched her mother go slowly over the bridge: "She kept turning back and looking at us and crying. She would stop when she turned back. It was difficult. Then a United Nations vehicle came and she disappeared behind it."

When she is with her children Fida feels there is nothing more important. But they are in Belgrade. She cannot live there. Nor, while the war is on, can she risk bringing them back to Sarajevo. Laceration becomes a permanent state. On the one hand, anger about Muris and Bisera and a determination to take care of her old mother Hasnja and of Asim; on the other, the desire, the *need* to be with her children. And Slobodan? He takes care of the girls very well. He seems honest. But a new conviction has grown in Fida: Greater Serbia is in the head of all Serbs. Some are murderers, some are not, but all of them support the idea.

In August 1994, Fida saw the girls a second time, and on this occasion Slobodan came. The meeting took place in Pale. Fida secured a permit to cross the bridge again; Slobodan and the girls came down from Belgrade.

In front of their children, the Muslim mother and Serb father tried to avoid talking about the politics of the war that had come between them. But it was not easy.

At one point Slobodan said he could make a list of the Serbs killed in Sarajevo at the beginning of the war. Fida's reply was that no list could be made of the Muslims killed—there were too many of them. Everyone in the room fell silent. Jasna thought, She lists the horrors perpetrated by the Serbs; he insists on the Serbs' innocence and the Muslims' stupidity in provoking the war. I do not understand them anymore.

For Fida there was nothing to explain. Her husband's family was from Rogatica, in eastern Bosnia; he knew what happened there in the first months of the war. The Muslim women and children pushed over the lines; the men executed. But for Slobodan, the story of Rogatica was a different one. A mother suffering penury. A brother fighting Muslims. His brother's parents-in-law burned in their homes in 1993 by Muslims attacking out of Goražde. Whatever happened in 1992 had to happen. He waved the Serb genocide of that summer away.

Three months later, in October 1994, Fida Karišik crossed the bridge into Grbavica for the third and last time in the war. She obtained, from friends in Grbavica, fake documents identifying her as a Serb and traveled with a cousin to Belgrade. The family was reunited for a few days.

But much was left unsaid. Fida expected her husband or daughters to urge her to stay but felt she never received this invitation. She was uncomfortable in Belgrade but unable to explain why to her family. She talked to mothers of other children at her daughters' school. She told them about schoolchildren in Sarajevo killed by Serb mortars. The Serbian mothers were incredulous. Really? Surely not. Can it be that bad? Fida wanted to throttle them. Sometimes she burst into tears; when Vesna and Jasna asked her what was wrong, she could not reply. Knowledge of the war was incommunicable. Her daughters confided to her that they knew the Muslims had suffered more in the war. But were they just saying that to please her? When she talked about Asim and Haris, the girls' thoughts seemed far away. She felt that they were becoming Serbs. As Serbs, she would lose them, just as her father had lost her after she married.

Slobodan saw no reason to try to persuade his wife to stay. He knew she was committed to being with her mother and brother through the war. Besides, Sarajevo had estranged her from him. The children were dismayed when Fida returned to Bosnia; they had hoped the reunion would be permanent. Vesna asked herself repeatedly how her mother could leave them. There was, she found, no adequate answer.

Fida Karišik, on her return from her secret trip to Belgrade, paced her Sarajevo apartment, full of a new and violent desperation. She began to think that her father had been right to oppose her Muslim-Serb marriage. Memories of her husband's resolute defense of the Serbs incensed her. She felt angry, tearful, and pathetic by turns. The murderous rage of Haris toward his uncle never possessed her, but she raged. "Slobodan is always defending the Serbs," she told me. "I say to him you can only talk like that because you did not stay in Sarajevo, you did not see a child walking along the street and then being hit by a shell."

AMID ALL THE PAIN, there was one place of solace in Sarajevo. Among the scarred streets and alleys, at a crossroads in the Austro-Hungarian part of town, the sound of a Beethoven sonata or a Chopin waltz could often be heard. The music, sometimes flowing, sometimes betraying a student's faltering hand, cascaded from the Sarajevo Conservatory. In its lightness and its otherworldliness, it offered comfort. People lingered, flirted, sipped coffee in the shelter of the sound of half-forgotten times.

The music, however, like everything in the city, was deceptive. The venerable institution from which it emerged had been torn to shreds. Once synonymous with civilization, and the universality of music, the conservatory had come to demonstrate the sectarian legacy of war. The solid Austro-Hungarian school contained destruction, physical and spiritual; inter-ethnic suspicions, spoken and unspoken; and tragedy laced with the optimism of youth.

The physical toll of the war on the conservatory was, by late 1994, onerous. Seven music students and one trombone teacher had been killed. Two shells had come through the ceiling of the concert room, which, with its chandeliers and chairs upholstered in blue velvet, contrived to retain vestiges of a Viennese plushness. The concert piano, ruined by shell blasts, was propped on a metal leg. A gradual dilapidation had set in: 206 students, of the prewar total of 276, had left.

The suffering was probably no greater than that of any institution of similar size in Sarajevo. But the conservatory was distinguished by the intense spiritual battle waged by students and teachers alike to save their music, and what it meant to them, from the encroachments of war. Their fight, in many ways, was a fight for what was left of the soul of Sarajevo, a continuation of the battle waged by the cellist Vedran Smailović, himself a former student of the school, who, in the first months of the war, played Albinoni's Adagio in the center of the city as shells fell around him.

"I play to defend myself," said Ivana Veličan, a fourteen-year-old piano student. "I mean, I am not, I cannot be free. But I can sit at the piano. And I can hope that everyone learns to feel the love that I feel." Dressed in blue dungarees, she looked at me with her clear blue, defiant eyes. "My soul," she continued, "is really hurting for the city and for Bosnia, and I want to help as much as I can. Yes, I feel trapped. But I still feel this is *my* trap. This is my home."

For Emina Dubravić, the school's director, the difficulty was finding the moral strength to play. She wrestled with tears every time she reached for her flute. She had been pregnant when the war began. Just before the Serb shelling started, she and her husband, Kenan, fled their house in Ilidža, the western suburb of the city on the road to the sea that quickly fell under Serb control. As Muslims, they had been threatened with death. Their son, Amer, was born in Sarajevo on April 27, 1992; intense shelling welcomed him to the world. Six months later, his father, Kenan Dubravić, aged thirty, was killed fighting near his former home in Ilidža.

Kenan's portrait, drawn posthumously from a photograph, hung prominently in the family's makeshift apartment, vacated by a Serb who had fled Sarajevo. Beside the portrait there was a plaque from the Bosnian army recording Mr. Dubravić's bravery. Beneath it, little Amer played with a toy car he called an UNPROFOR—United Nations vehicles were all he had ever seen.

Mrs. Dubravić explained that it was very hard to play her flute because her husband had always accompanied her on the guitar, but, with tremulous lips, she raised the instrument and played the *Bosnian Pastoral* by Mladen Požajić. Transfixed, Amer watched.

In early 1994, Amer had asked for the first time where his father was. Mrs. Dubravić did not have the courage to say he was dead and so she said he was sleeping. When the Serb shelling eased in February, she took Amer to the cemetery in the old part of town. Without being told where it was, Amer walked straight to his father's grave. He said, "This is where my daddy sleeps" and began dusting the snow off the gravestone. When his mother tried to grab him, Amer said, "I'm just making my daddy's bed."

Mrs. Dubravić's father, Ahmed Cico, sat in a corner, a crumpled figure. The Serbs had evicted him from Ilidža on May 13, 1992. Upheaval, late in life, was doubly crippling: the energy to begin again has gone. He had worked in an aircraft engine factory with close ties to the Yugoslav army. For several months he had seen signs of the war coming. The Serbs in his factory were taken for military training exercises that the Muslims were not allowed to attend. But like so many others, he had refused to believe that he would be forced from his home.

On May 5, 1992, eight days before his eviction, he was arrested and severely beaten. Many members of the unit that held and tortured him came from Niš, in southern Serbia, he said. There had been an odd incident. The Serbs beating him asked what he thought of the Russian-made Lada

car. Cico said it was a good car. They beat him again and accused him of
lying.

In 1976, sixteen years before the war, a Serb friend and neighbor, Slobodan Milanović, had asked him to repair a Lada. As he was working on
a cable, there was a spark, and Cico burned himself. He exclaimed, "God-
damn Russians!" Cico had never given the incident another thought until
that beating in 1992. Milanović had said nothing but had obviously remembered, and he had mentally designated the Muslim Cico as an enemy
of the Russians, the Serbs' traditional Orthodox allies. Cico's blood ran
cold when he considered these events.

Every working day, throughout the war, Mrs. Dubravić went to the
music school to teach. Once, as she dodged shelling, the two-mile walk
took her ten hours. Like countless others in the city, she fought an inner
struggle between a desire for revenge and a yearning for reconciliation. In
her case, the latter had won out. "I am trying," she said, "to give my pupils
as much love for their music as possible. But not only that. Love for everything. I try to encourage them to see the world in a different way through
their music, for I do believe in the power of love."

One of Mrs. Dubravić's colleagues, Angelina Pap, was a Serb. She had
come to Sarajevo from Belgrade thirty years earlier and refused to leave.
All her memories were contained in two pianos in the school—a twenty-
year-old Petrof and a thirty-year-old August Forster; the more intense the
shelling, the more intense was her playing. She escaped into those pianos—escaped from the war, from the sound of destruction, from the unspeakable pain of being a Serb in a city shelled by Serbs.

There were many people for whom Yugoslavia, even annihilated, was
the only possible country on the Balkan Peninsula; in no other country
could they find their place. Mrs. Pap was among them. What she understood was that musicians of the world speak the same language—that of
their scores. No difference could exist between them. Music, moreover, has
no limits, and so Sarajevo, in the war, always posed the same question:
Why must we live in this cage?

As a Serb, Mrs. Pap was increasingly isolated. The former director of the
conservatory, Borislav Stevković, ran away as soon as the war started, leaving not a word and taking the keys to the director's office. The best piano
tuner in the city, Aleksandar Lucić, also left. Moreover, the old friendship
between Mrs. Pap and Mr. Stevković's successor, Farida Musanović, had
become strained, apparently another victim of the Serb-Muslim suspicions
engendered by the fighting.

Mrs. Musanović, from a distinguished Muslim family in Sarajevo, had
been the driving force in keeping the school open during the war, before

handing the director's job to Mrs. Dubravić. She seemed uncomfortable when Mrs. Pap was mentioned; she said nothing and the silence was heavy. The piano in her beautiful home in Baščaršija was seldom used.

A shell from Trebević took the life of Nihada Ćatić, a violin student at the school. Aged fifteen, she was killed on June 20, 1992. That morning she had been practicing Vivaldi for a concert. It was a quiet day, not a sound of war, and she went downstairs to watch some friends playing a game of chess. A 120-millimeter shell came crashing down, killing her and six other children.

Her mother, Nihada Ćatić, said there was no recovery from what had happened. The thought of death had become a solace. She tried not to be a weight on others. Her work and Muslim faith sustained her. Although she had no generalized desire for revenge, she would, she said, throttle the man who fired that shell with her own hands. A cataclysm, she predicted, awaited the Serbs for their crimes. All this, she said, because the Serbs just wanted to live in one country.

After her daughter's death, Mrs. Ćatić found an entry in the young girl's diary. It was about a Serb girl called Tanja Ljuborak, who had been a close friend. In March 1992, a month before the war, Tanja had warned the Ćatić family to abandon their home in the Serb-dominated Vraca section of Sarajevo. "Dear Tanja," the entry said, "I am dreaming of you. I miss you. I know that your parents' hands are not covered with blood. I believe that one day we will be friends again."

Another student, Selma Poričanin, had made an entry in her diary about Nihada Ćatić and other lost friends from the conservatory: "Every day, we are becoming more full of a certain pride and defiance, not a desire to take revenge, but a will to hold still and win out over this evil."

SUCH DETERMINATION ALWAYS seemed to herald more fighting. But there was one last effort to build the improved situation after February 1994 into a peace settlement. On December 18, 1994, Jimmy Carter, the former American president, came to Sarajevo. He said Bosnia was "a fine place" and suggested that the Serbs had been misunderstood because the "American public has had primarily one side of the story." His visit, he added, would offer the Serbs a rare chance "to let the world know the truth." Carter smiled, clutching a bouquet presented to him by the Serbs in Pale; he looked like an innocent abroad.

Karadžić told Carter, "Our enemies today used to be our brothers, they used to be Serbs, but during the Turkish occupation they adopted Islam." I wondered if Carter believed this particular tenet of Serb myth: few of the people in Bosnia who began converting to Islam in the fifteenth century could meaningfully be described as Serbs. But Karadžić's arguments seemed persuasive to Carter. Still, whatever his illusions, the former president had the courage to come forward—a courage the Clinton administration had so persistently lacked—and he worked intensely for a cease-fire, shuttling back and forth between Sarajevo and Pale.

Two days later he announced a four-month cease-fire; on December 23, 1994, the agreement was signed by the Bosnian government and the Serbs. On the last day of the year the accord was amplified into a four-month "cessation of hostilities." The two sides committed themselves to exchange prisoners, grant freedom of movement around Sarajevo, allow the inter-positioning of United Nations troops between the front lines, and "refrain from the use of all explosive munitions."

There had already been more than thirty cease-fires during the war, but this one seemed a little more substantial. If nothing else, it reflected the ex-haustion on all sides. I looked at the eyes of a Serb woman named Milja Gluhović in Pale and saw again how war turns human beings into hollow vessels. She had lost her husband and brother the previous May in fight-ing on the mountains south of Sarajevo. Of such exhaustion might a last-ing peace be made? A Serb soldier called Nenad Tadić was skeptical. He looked up at the snow falling heavily on the mountains around Sarajevo and declared, "The weather would achieve a four-month cease-fire with or without the politicians."

IN THEORY, the truce was supposed to give diplomats time to begin ne-gotiations between Izetbegović and Karadžić on a settlement to end the war. The backdrop to diplomacy from the summer of 1994 was the so-called Contact Group map, according 51 percent of Bosnian territory to the Muslim-Croat federation and 49 percent to the Serbs. It thus called on the Serbs to give up about one third of the territory they had held from early in the war.

The map condoned much of the Serbs' gains in the first months of the fighting: "cleansed" towns including Prijedor (where over fifty thousand Muslims had been driven out), Vlasenica, Zvornik, Bijeljina, and Roga-tica were awarded to them. Lord Owen and Cyrus R. Vance could argue, with every justification, that the map was no improvement—indeed some-thing of a retrogression—from their own proposed plan, which the Clin-ton administration had summarily dropped in May 1994.

But as the war dragged on, the Clinton administration steadily aban-doned velleities about justice and the unacceptability of "ethnic cleans-ing." The corollary of such a principled stand would have been to send American soldiers to Bosnia to reverse what was "unacceptable." This Clinton was never prepared to do. Presenting the Contact Group's map in July 1994, Charles E. Redman, then the special American envoy to the

Balkans, said, "We had to jump over the moral bridge in the interests of wider peace and of keeping Bosnia together."

Whether Bosnia could be held together by the Contact Group's proposal—in theory, the Muslim-Croat federation and the Serb entity were to exist within a single Bosnian state—was always an open question. Izetbegović never liked the map. His first reaction was, "If we evaluate that the Serbs will say no, then we will say yes. So I emphasize that we will be saying yes, since the Serbs will be rejecting it." All politicians think devious thoughts; the amazing thing in the Balkans was that, as in this instance, they often expressed them. But even having revealed cards that he should have kept close to his chest, the Bosnian president was proved right. Karadžić rejected the map, arguing that it divided Serb territory into fragments, offered only a narrow corridor at Brčko, and left him with too little of Bosnia's natural resources.

His *nyet* exasperated Milošević—who wanted Karadžić to be compliant and then prevaricate—and was met by the usual helpless wringing of hands in Western capitals. Having said that their map was a "take-it-or-leave-it" proposal, the Contact Group began to intimate that it was only a proposal. Lieutenant General Rose kept a copy of it on the wall of his office in Sarajevo, an effigy always available for burning. It was regularly mocked by his entourage, particularly for its attempt to keep the isolated eastern Muslim enclaves of Srebrenica, Žepa, and Goražde in Bosnian government hands. So much for the West's unity of purpose.

Carter thought he had brought the parties to a point where they were ready to negotiate on the map. The Serbs said they were now ready to talk "with the proposal of the Contact Group as the basis for negotiation of all points." The Bosnian government, however, insisted on a negotiation "with acceptance of the proposal of the Contact Group as a starting point." Carter dismissed the slight verbal difference as "semantics." In any place where common sense counted for something, Carter would have been right. In Bosnia he was wrong. Izetbegović knew he could use the insistence on "acceptance" as a means to increase the diplomatic isolation of the Bosnian Serbs while his army gained weapons and experience; Karadžić was fool enough to oblige him.

I saw Karadžić during the Carter visit. The man orchestrating the continuing bombardment of civilians in Sarajevo was evidently deranged. Territory, people, lives, cities were no more than poker chips. He sat in his office explaining how he would arrange them. Sarajevo would be a divided city: the Serbs would take Ilidža, Butmir, Dobrinja, and Hrasnica and make of them a New Sarajevo. The eastern enclaves—Srebrenica, Žepa, and Goražde—were "simply not viable" and would have to be given up by Izetbegović, but the Serbs would offer "six towns" in exchange for them that were "ten times more valuable than the enclaves." The Serbs would gain access to the sea at Prevlaka and, in exchange, give "250 square kilometers of the hinterland near Dubrovnik to the Croats." He rambled on: "We want peace because we have very big ideas for our economy. We want a free-market economy. We want to make our people rich. We will sell everything that is owned by the state. That is the natural society of the Serbs: tradition, religion, and private property!"

As Karadžić spoke, Serb-held Bosnia consisted of an increasingly desolate expanse of untilled fields and decaying roads, peopled mainly by peasants, where the only profitable enterprises—chiefly the smuggling of oil and cigarettes—were controlled by the Bosnian leader himself and his cronies. The dripping gold in the substantial cleavage of Karadžić's hysterical daughter Sonja—whose abuse of the Western press became legendary—testified to his desire to "make people rich." In the rest of his self-styled state, the only things dripping were the roofs, where they existed at all. Yet this was the land that Karadžić saw as the Cayman Islands of the Balkans, governed from a brand-new capital.

Karadžić loved to take on airs. He claimed to be descended from Vuk Karadžić, the lexicographer of Serbia's nineteenth-century awakening. There is no evidence to support this claim. His paternal descent was in fact from Vuko Karadžić, a cobbler in the northern Montenegrin village of Petnica.

During World War II, Vuko Karadžić was appalled by Partisan actions in Montenegro—including mass executions—and became a Chetnik fighting for what he called "king and fatherland." As a result, he was sentenced to death by Tito's regime at war's end, but the sentence was never carried out. Vuko was shot in the leg by one of his appointed executioners, who wanted to spare him, and he spent the next five years in jail. Karadžić, who was born on June 19, 1945, would visit him as a child and later recalled his father's "haughty and arrogant jailers." On his release, Vuko forbade any political talk in his household, which remained under surveillance by Tito's police.

It was thus natural enough that, when the moment came for this poet-psychiatrist from Montenegro to reinvent himself as a Bosnian Serb nationalist, Karadžić chose to take on the mantle of the Chetnik father whom he had scarcely seen during the first five years of his life. Tradition, religion, and private property became watchwords; he even talked about a possible return of the Serbian royal family to Pale. The growing differences with Milošević thus assumed an old pattern—that of the enduring Serbian division between Partisans and Chetniks, for Milošević, after his heady exploitation of nationalism, had returned to his communist roots. In fact the Pale and Belgrade regimes were different more in name than substance:

they both depended on one-party rule bolstered by propaganda and the inextricable bonding of political office and personal enrichment.

In a television interview, Karadžić once described his first impression of Sarajevo when he moved there from Montenegro in 1959. "The first night," he said, "I remember seeing city lights stretching all the way to Trebević Mountain. Those lights climbing alongside Trebević were mingled with starlight on the top and one could not discern what was the hill and what the sky. And I immediately fell in love with Sarajevo. . . ."

Thirty-three years later, Karadžić shelled the hospital where he had long worked and embarked on the systematic destruction of his adopted city. By the time I saw him in that December of 1994, he had mythologized everything—his own origins, his "love" for the city of Sarajevo, his true aims, and the situation around him. "If this latest peace effort fails," he told me, "we will declare a state of war throughout the country." I stared at him in disbelief. *Declare a state of war?* "Yes," he went on. "You see, we have never actually declared war here. But now we are ready to end this conflict by military means. We want it over. If this is not possible politically, we will not dupe ourselves with another cease-fire. We will fight to win. They have three times more infantry, but they have no generals. We are still in a position to win."

So, for Karadžić, after thirty-two months of fighting, war had not yet been declared. Of course, in the absence of war, there could be no war criminals, so the ruse had its semantic benefits. Nonetheless, he was quite clearly deluded, or mad, or both. I began to think that the Serb soldier, who knew the reality of war, was right: the four-month truce represented no more than the onset of winter.

Karadžić, with his messianic delusions, did not have the pragmatism to play his limited cards. He could have "accepted" the Contact Group map, secured his ticket back to yet another round of Geneva talks, and dithered. In late 1994, Charles E. Redman, by then the American ambassador to Germany, signaled that the possibility of negotiation was open; Charles Thomas, Redman's successor as the special U.S. envoy to Bosnia, followed up on that offer in early 1995.

But Karadžić was too stubborn to overcome his isolation, and, in the absence of any negotiation, the forces governing the conflict pointed in a direction diametrically opposed to peace. Those forces were Šušak's rapid equipping and training of the Croatian army; sagging Serb morale amid division and impoverishment; and a steady improvement in the Bosnian army.

Rasim Delić, the Bosnian army commander, soon declared quite openly that he would use the truce to improve his forces for the coming fight. In late March 1995, his army abruptly mounted two attacks that shattered the cease-fire. The first, on Mount Vlašić, in central Bosnia, was successful; the second, on the Majevica Hills east of Tuzla, failed. The Bosnian government's bad faith was evident. By early April 1995, Carter's efforts had gone up in smoke. No negotiation between the sides on the Contact Group map ever took place; there was never any interposing of United Nations troops between the front lines; visits across the lines such as those that permitted the reunion of the Karišik girls with their mother became impossible.

MAJA DJOKIĆ PAID the price for this failure. She was killed by a Serb shell on April 9, 1995, as she walked back from a volleyball practice. Aleksandar Lucić watched her die. He was tending flowers on Sarajevo's Titova Street near the Presidency Building when he saw a flash and a girl falling. He hurried toward her. She gasped, twice. He rushed her to Koševo Hospital in his car. But two fragments of shrapnel had killed her.

Before she died, Maja had been studying mathematics at home. She left just before 6:00 P.M. for volleyball practice. She said she would be back at 8:15. She was always punctual. She was an ambitious girl, quite beautiful, lithe and tall and clear-eyed. At 8:45 her parents started to worry. Her father went to a café where she sometimes stopped on her way home. There was no sign of her. He went back to the café a little later. Still no sign. Worry turned to panic. At 10:00 P.M., when the Sarajevo curfew began, he reluctantly called the hospital. An official at the morgue told Mr. Djokić that Maja was dead. The shell killed her just after 8:00 as she walked home.

Hers was an average Sarajevo death, no more unusual than rainfall, three years, almost to the day, after the first Serb shells fell on demonstrators for a united Bosnia. But for the Serbs besieging the town there was something troubling in the reports about the killing that appeared in the Sarajevo press. Lucić, who had fought in the Bosnian army for several months until he was wounded, was a Serb who had chosen to stay in Sarajevo. Maja Djokić was of partly Serb descent. These Serbs who remained in government-held towns like Sarajevo and Tuzla were the object of a particular hatred from Karadžić's followers. They amounted to a living rebuttal of his basic argument for starting the war: that life as a Serb minority living with the "Muslim enemy" and the "fundamentalists" was impossible. These people were traitors, like the Serb knight Branković at Kosovo field in 1389, who had forfeited the right to call themselves "true Serbs."

So it was that Bosnian Serb television, based in Pale, came up with an alternative version of Maja Djokić's death. Two days after she was killed, Pale television showed her corpse in the Sarajevo morgue. A commentator said, "The girl is not a victim of Serb shelling as the Muslim media said, but a victim of Izetbegović's followers. On Friday night, they raped her, killed her, and threw her out on the plaza in front of the stadium. The Muslims caught this unfortunate girl as she was trying to escape to the Serb part of Sarajevo."

The tone of the propaganda resembled that of an earlier claim from Pale television: that cries emanating from the Sarajevo zoo were those of Serb children being fed to the animals. The overarching purpose was clear enough: to portray the "Turk" as the bashibazouk of old, his violence matched only by his lechery.

The Djokić home in the center of Sarajevo is a civilized place. There is a grand piano. Books are scattered around. The old armchairs are comfortable. Branko Djokić, Maja's father, is an engineer; Melita, her mother, is a professor of electronics at Sarajevo University. He is part Serb, part Slovenian; she is a Muslim. Before they were forced to think otherwise they were Yugoslavs.

Branko said to me, "There are perhaps ten thousand dead in Sarajevo, of whom perhaps seventeen hundred are children. So we cannot think that Maja's death was anything special. But of course she was our Maja, so we think it is special." Of the attempt in Pale to invent a death for his daughter at the hands of Izetbegović's "fundamentalists" he would say only that no words can describe such behavior. In the restraint of the couple, in their long silences, the power of truth before lies was a physical thing. It surrounded the bereaved parents like an electric fence, compelling respect.

Mrs. Djokić ushered me into her daughter's room. There was a poster of Tom Cruise. I could not take my eyes off it. Mrs. Djokić had washed and ironed the clothes Maja was wearing when she died and laid them on a chair. Mrs. Djokić had not yet fully absorbed the weight of her death, for it was clear enough that those clothes were still awaiting her daughter. There was a blue Levi's shirt that Maja had earned by working as a waitress. She was proud of it. Two small holes—one in the upper half of the back and one at the nape of the neck—were visible. They looked innocuous enough, as if the shirt had been ripped on a fence after a picnic in the country, but they marked the spot where burning shrapnel from a Serb shell entered the living body of Maja Djokić and killed her.

On their return from the hospital the day after Maja's death, Mr. and Mrs. Djokić passed the spot where the shell fell. There were ten United Nations soldiers in their blue helmets clustered around the crater, measuring it, talking about it. "It was so stupid, so senseless, it made me so angry," Mrs. Djokić said, her voice rising in anger for the first time. "The point is that the United Nations did nothing to prevent the death of my daughter."

General Rose was not around to witness this scene. He had departed three months earlier, on January 23, 1995, bound for London, where a fourth star awaited him in recognition of his efforts. Behind him he left a shivering, isolated Sarajevo. "We managed to hold the line," he told me. "There were lots of siren voices calling us to war, wanting us to operate as combatants. But that would have led to scenes in Sarajevo like those in Grozny." He added, "I am not morally indifferent, but as a peacekeeper I have to stick in the middle."

Victor Jackovich, the American ambassador to Bosnia whom Rose had called an ambassador to "a warring faction," did not bother to say good-bye to him. The snub was water off Rose's back: "My relations with the United States have been absolutely excellent throughout," he said. That was Rose: if he said something loudly enough, often enough, stridently enough in that barking voice of his, it would be true.

MAJA'S NAME WAS just another in a list already long. The names— 3,060 in 1992, 3,091 in 1993, and 1,797 in 1994—were written in a spidery script across page after page of frayed ledgers: a dry chronicle of a European war and a city's dismemberment. The ledgers were kept at the Sarajevo mortuary, which was generally unrefrigerated during the forty-three-month siege because there was no electricity in the city. So the stench of bodies was often pungent. The smell seeped out of the tiled morgue into the small room with peeling paint and sagging plants where the records of the dead were kept.

I would go up to the morgue, perched on a hill above the center of Sarajevo, and watch the dead being wheeled in. The randomness of the victims was intriguing, for it captured the character of a late-twentieth-century conflict, one entirely disencumbered from the notion that wars have rules and are fought between armies: an old man with his stomach blasted open; a woman with the left side of her head lacerated by hot metal, her gray hair matted with blood and her mouth contorted in a final grimace. Some people, those close enough to a detonation, might be stunned to death; not a mark on the corpse betrayed the shattered internal organs. At times, as with Maja, the wound was tiny, for a single shrapnel shard may be fatal. But mutilation, even extensive, often failed to kill. Seeing the crippled in the adjacent Koševo Hospital I wondered at the perversity of the heart that goes on beating in a body from which limbs have been torn.

The names of the corpses were recorded by hand. The procedure reflected the assiduity of the vestigial communist bureaucracy that weighs on all the ill-born states of the former Yugoslavia. Smudged stamps and signatures ratified each killing. But the entries said nothing of the crazed arbitrariness of another Sarajevan death, delivered by a shell or some improvised Serb rocket as the twentieth century slid down the slope toward its close. They said nothing of the silence after shelling, resonating inward toward a point of infinite peace, a point pregnant with anguish.

The list of the dead was compiled by Alija Hodžić, a Bosnian Muslim whose deep blue eyes suggest a shrouded sea. Hodžić ran the mortuary from June 1992, two months after the war and the Serb siege of Sarajevo began. On July 7, 1992, the body of his nephew, Adnan Hodžić, was brought in. Two months later, the corpse of his twenty-one-year-old niece arrived. Then, on October 10, 1992, Hodžić had to identify the body of his twenty-two-year-old son, Ibrahim, killed by a shell in central Sarajevo. Every time he entered the morgue, where bodies lay on slabs of stone with name tags attached to their bluish ankles, he would look at the spot his son's corpse had occupied. Hodžić blew away his thoughts in a cloud of cigarette smoke—as insubstantial as a Sarajevo life—and talked little.

On August 4, 1992, it was his hand that had inscribed the name of Muris Zečević beside those of two of his friends, Tarik Kapetanović and Zoran Suša, the Sarajevo Serb whom Haris never trusted; the Serb who, like Aleksandar Lucić, chose loyalty to the Bosnian government. Names—as alike on the page as the corpses in the soil—had ceased to signify anything. Yet, in my mind's eye, I could see Muris Zečević in his family photographs: the wide-eyed little boy with lank hair vacationing on the Dalmatian coast; the brooding adolescent with his guitar; the wiry, defiant young man who traded his musical instrument for a Kalashnikov and his jeans for military fatigues. The last pictures showed him up on Trebević Mountain.

Between Muris's death and that of Maja Djokić, almost three years had passed. Over eight thousand people had been killed in Sarajevo and more than fifty thousand injured. Over one hundred and fifty thousand people were dead in Bosnia. More than half the prewar Bosnian population of 4.3 million had been displaced. Of the one million Muslims who once lived on the 70 percent of Bosnia controlled by the Serbs since the first months of the war, no more than fifty thousand remained by early 1995. Reams of United Nations resolutions and endless diplomatic minuets had not brought the parties noticeably closer to an agreement to end the war.

I kept thinking of that poster of Tom Cruise in Maja Djokić's bedroom. A teenage girl, Tom Cruise, volleyball, and a Serb shell out of a clear sky onto a street full of civilians: the truth of the war, the only truth worth focusing on in the end as at the beginning, was clear enough. To what incorrigibly violent Balkan tribe, I wondered, would the politicians in Washington, Paris, and London consign Maja Djokić in a bid to blur the obvious outrage and the equally evident need to confront such outrage with force?

• • •

IN EARLY MARCH 1995, just a month before the girl's death, I had received a tip about a recently completed Central Intelligence Agency report that amounted to what one official called "the most comprehensive U.S. assessment of atrocities in Bosnia." It had, he said, been "classified at an obscene level" because of its findings. In fact, the official added, there had been "a quiet mini-firestorm of negative reaction in the Pentagon among people who see the report as an effort to bring Americans into the conflict."

The theme was by now deeply familiar: facts being hidden because, in Bosnia, facts might call for action. I traveled to Washington to find out more. Two other officials confirmed the existence of the report—an attempt to collate and analyze all the evidence on the war known to the intelligence agency—and its tenor. The conclusion of the CIA, based on aerial photography and protracted technical analysis, was that 90 percent of the acts of "ethnic cleansing" in Bosnia were carried out by Serbs and that leading Serb politicians almost certainly played a role in the crimes.

There were, the report said, also atrocities committed by Muslims and Croats—the Muslim camp for Serbs at Čelebići, near Konjic, for example, or the Croat camp for Muslims at Dretelj near Mostar. But they lacked "the intensity, sustained orchestration and scale of what the Bosnian Serbs did." The report, I was told, made it abundantly clear that "there was a conscious, coherent and systematic Serb policy to get rid of Muslims through murder, torture and imprisonment" and contained evidence that Karadžić knew of the concentration camps through which many evicted Muslims and Croats passed in 1992.

For anyone who had spent any time in Bosnia, these conclusions were scarcely astonishing. But international failure spewed forth obfuscation at a remarkable rate and, by 1995, the Serb "cleansing" in 1992 of Prijedor, Banja Luka, Zvornik, Bijeljina, Vlasenica, Foča, Trebinje, Brčko, Rogatica, Sanski Most, and numberless other towns and villages had taken on the air of ancient history in what was now widely referred to as "a civil war" or a "Balkan morass." Hence the pressing concern in Washington that the CIA report not become public; hence, too, the disgruntlement of the honorable American officials, their consciences torn, who wanted its findings known. The truth in Bosnia was always dangerous because—like Maja Djokić's death—it was not nearly as complicated as a lot of people chose to make it.

Sarajevans, besieged for more than a thousand days, developed a fathomless cynicism before the world's determination to dress up their plight in circumlocutions. They knew what simplicity lurked behind the "complexity" that officially characterized the war. For they had been turned into targets in a shooting gallery that the world had decided to call "a safe area." They were living on the dark side of the mirror. Either the world was turning much too slowly or Sarajevans were thinking much too fast.

NERMIN TULIĆ, one of Sarajevo's best-known actors, had his legs blown off by a Serb shell on June 10, 1992. He spent several weeks wanting to die, but when, on the floor below him in the hospital, his wife gave birth to their second daughter, he changed his mind. His father said to him that children need their father even if he just sits in the corner. These words and the sight of his child gave him the will to hang on. But living was not reconciliation. He raged. He wondered if he could ever again take his wife, who is half Serb, in his arms. He shunned the word "Serbs," preferring "beasts." He noted darkly that he used to be carried out of bars, but now had to be carried in. "Of course," he laughed, "like the United Nations said, I put the shell under my own legs and exploded it. *Boom.* Of course that's what I did."

Tulić, in a wheelchair, reappeared in 1995, in a production of Alfred Jarry's *Ubu in Chains* by Massimo Schuster, a French director. Like Susan Sontag, who directed *Waiting for Godot* in Sarajevo in 1993, Schuster wanted to do something for the city: an urge, among artists, that was depressingly rare. The play portrayed the grotesque, the abject, and the heinous in the midst of a city that had no need of a stage to display them. Jarry's gobbledygook—"We are free to do what we like, even obey, go where we like, even to prison! Liberty is slavery!"—was the doublespeak of one thousand days of Bosnian diplomacy writ large. Ubu—hugely fat, obnoxious, destructive, and dictatorial—was a former king of Poland, "That is to say, nowhere." In the nineteenth century, Poland's existence had been as theoretical as Bosnia's. Ubu had come home and so had his vision of pure liberty: *"We will not have destroyed everything unless we destroy even the ruins."*

I watched Tulić being pushed around the stage by a much flagellated "free man" wearing a light blue chamber pot on his head. Tulić's role was that of a horrible little tyrant. He whipped his men for failing to disobey him, conducted strenuous exercises in indiscipline, arrested Ubu only to envy him his servitude. Offstage, he was equally tortured, begging me to look at him and not at the stumps of his legs, drinking until he was incoherent, raging about being nobody, just one of the fifteen thousand cripples in Bosnia. "This," he said in a moment of lucidity, "is an experiment by the world to see how much people can suffer."

Increasingly, Sarajevans raged, shaking their fists at the hills when the dry boom of tearing and cracking echoed again through the valley. "Idiots," "fools," "cretins"—they hurled insults at the Serb peasants so intent on destroying Sarajevo's mottled urban culture. They dressed well, forcing back barbarism with *inat,* a spiteful disdain as bold as the makeup of Sarajevan women, as sharp as their heels, and more potent than any gun.

A woman, desperate after three years of war, took me aside and looked me in the eye: "Here things are black and white," she said. "They are. There is evil and there is good. The evil is up on the hills. So when you say you are a journalist and so you must be objective and some of what you write may not be good for us but good for those evil people, then I understand you but I still hate you. Yes, I hate you. Everybody is asking what this place is really like. They ask us, What is it like to be without electricity, or without gas, or without pay, or without a life? What is it like to stand in line for water? What is it like to be a specimen in a laboratory? They ask us and ask us and ask us. But to understand perhaps you should go to the other side. Then they will give you a gun and you can look out from a building and you will look through the sight and you will see a man. Then you will know what it is to be *a hunter.* And you will pull the trigger and you will see that man fall and you will have the knowledge that you have killed him. That is a fact. A fact. And then perhaps you will not need to know so much about us, you will not need to know from whom we are descended, or why we became Muslims, or whether Muslims are a nation, or whether Bosnia exists, or anything else at all."

By the spring of 1995, like many people in Sarajevo, I was fighting back rage. It was important to be lucid; I had looked down from those hills; I had tried to look deep into the head of Karadžić and his gunners. I thought I knew what I needed to know. Objectivity, in Bosnia, could not be neutrality, and the head, in Bosnia, meant nothing without the heart.

The Izetbegović government and the Bosnian army committed outrages, large and small: the shooting of two little girls in the Serb-held part of town called Grbavica in March 1995; the occasional sniping at United Nations soldiers; the official profiteering through sale of a night's use of the one tunnel connecting Sarajevo to the outside world. They played the only viable card they had been dealt: the possibility that NATO might, after the mass Serb killings of 1992, eventually come to their aid. But none of this could be allowed to obscure what Sarajevo and Bosnia had represented or how Milošević and Karadžić had destroyed them in the name of Serb ethnic purity. It was the "international community" that had acquiesced to this Serb crime by repeatedly refusing to comprehend the fate of Muris Zečević and Maja Djokić in straightforward terms. Before he left his post as the commander of United Nations forces in the former Yugoslavia in early 1994, General Jean Cot of France, exhausted and enraged, declared that "the humiliation of the international community's forces has reached a limit and I can no longer accept this." The peacekeeping force in Bosnia, he added, resembled "a goat tethered to a fence." More than a year later, the goat was still tethered and people were still dying, or being maimed, in the streets.

SIX DAYS AFTER Maja Djokić's death, Corporal Eric Hardoin was killed in Sarajevo. A French soldier, aged thirty, he was wearing the uniform of the United Nations. In the minutes before his death, he had been building an anti-sniping barrier of cargo containers in an effort to stop the Serb snipers in the Grbavica area, on the south side of the Miljacka River, from firing at what had become a notoriously dangerous crossroads outside the Holiday Inn. As the French soldier's forklift truck pulled back from the barrier, the first shot rang out. Corporal Hardoin turned, opened the door, and appeared to jump, when a second shot hit him. As he lay on the ground, two French soldiers tried to rouse him in vain.

A cameraman was there, waiting for what some television crews in Bosnia came, depressingly, to call "bang-bang footage." In the following days, as the incident was shown repeatedly on Bosnian television, it was possible to scrutinize the last seconds of Corporal Hardoin's life. His eyes, a piercing blue, gazed upward imploringly, connected by a thread to life. Then the straining gave way to the uncomprehending eyes of a young man slipping into the lap of death.

I was haunted by those eyes. They seemed to capture the essence of a terribly flawed peacekeeping mission. Individual soldiers, like Corporal Hardoin, showed bravery: fifty-three French body bags came back from the United Nations mission to the former Yugoslavia. France took these deaths stoically. But there should have been more indignation for lives given to an international enterprise that constantly undercut the endeavors of soldiers by refusing to call things by their names. Seldom has so much individual bravery served such collective cowardice as in Bosnia. It was Chateaubriand, a Frenchman, who wrote: *"Il est criminel d'avoir une politique dont on n'a pas les moyens"* ("It is a crime to have a policy that you do not have the means to back"). United Nations policy in Bosnia— particularly the grotesque comedy of the "safe areas"—was such a crime on a monstrous scale. A basic question was never answered by the generals and UN bureaucrats who led Corporal Hardoin to his death: How could the "neutrality" or "impartiality" many of them insisted was essential to a peacekeeping mission be preserved in the face of the Serb assault on a Bosnia whose "sovereignty" and "territorial integrity" were recognized by the very institution they served?

The death of the young Frenchman was an unsavory illustration of this dilemma. Apparently straining to avoid confrontation with the Serbs, and so preserve "impartiality," Lieutenant Colonel Gary Coward, a UN

Haris Zečević, his brother and mother killed in Sarajevo, tries to remake his life in Detroit, Michigan. *(© Luc Delahaye, Magnum)*

Asim Zečević at his wife, Bisera's, grave. Bisera Zečević died in 1993 as she tried to escape from Sarajevo by running across the UN-patrolled airport. A spotlight beamed on her by UN forces enabled Serb forces to kill her. (© *Luc Delahaye, Magnum*)

Vildana Zečević in Detroit. She fled from Sarajevo to rejoin Haris in 1994. Here she is pregnant with Muris, named after Haris's brother who was killed on Trebević mountain near Sarajevo in 1992. (© *Luc Delahaye, Magnum*)

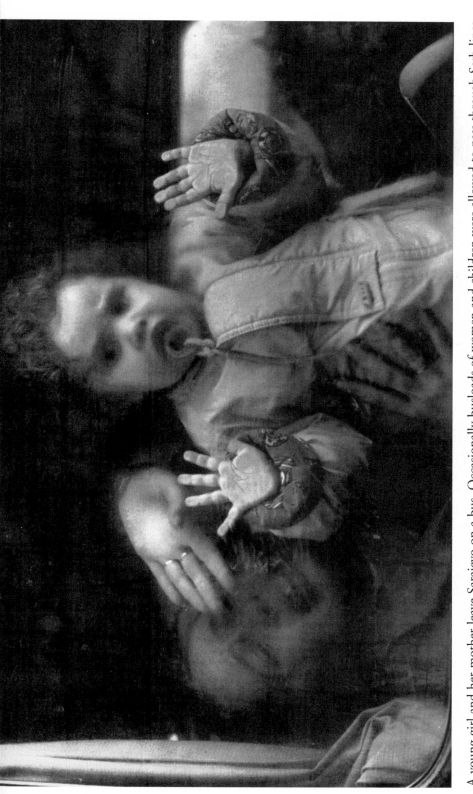

A young girl and her mother leave Sarajevo on a bus. Occasionally busloads of women and children were allowed to pass through Serb lines and leave the Bosnian capital. Parting was agonizing and reunion never certain. (© *Milomir Kovacevic*)

With office chairs propped on desks, a Bosnian soldier fights for Sarajevo. (*© Luc Delahaye, Magnum*)

Religious buildings—mosques, Catholic churches, Orthodox monasteries—were prime targets during the wars in Croatia and Bosnia. Their destruction was part of the attempt to eliminate all trace of "the other." Here, the remains of a Catholic church in Vukovar, Croatia, bombarded by the Serbs. (*© Luc Delahaye, Magnum*)

Muslim refugees from Srebrenica confront the blue-helmeted forces of the United Nations on the outskirts of Tuzla. When the Serbs overran the eastern Muslim enclave of Srebrenica in July 1995, they embarked on the worst single massacre of the war. Most of these women's husbands were among the several thousand Muslim men killed. Srebrenica was supposedly a United Nations "safe area." *(© Luc Delahaye, Magnum)*

In the wooded hills of Bosnia, the fight was long, hard, and often anonymous. Scores of young soldiers might die for a hillside. *(© Luc Delahaye, Magnum)*

Miloš Jelić and his wife, Vojna Adamović, at the Sarajevo Winter Olympics in 1984. Nobody dreamed then that war could come to the city. Miloš, a Montenegrin, fought for a year in the Bosnian army before fleeing Sarajevo; Vojna, a Serb, fled to Serbia in the first month of the war. *(family photograph)*

Miloš Jelić, seated third from right with a helmet, during his Yugoslav military service in 1987. War was a joke then. On the helmets, the five-pointed star, symbol of Tito's Partisan forces and later his Yugoslav state, is visible. *(family photograph)*

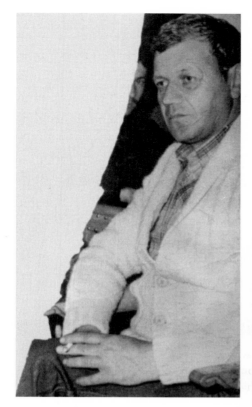

Ruzdija Šestović, a Muslim from the eastern Bosnian town of Milići. He was arrested in June 1992, in Vlasenica, at the height of the Serb rampage against the Muslims and disappeared. Like many Muslims captured at this time, he was never seen again. *(family photograph)*

Ermin Šestović and his mother, Muska, in Växjö, Sweden. *(family photograph)*

Muska Šestović, Ruzdija's wife, became a refugee in Berlin, where she is pictured here. Later she moved to Sweden to rejoin her son, Ermin. Muska is tormented by the uncertainty of her husband's fate. *(Günther Schneider, The New York Times)*

A man chops wood in a Sarajevo cemetery. Through the long war, graves spread into what were once city parks, and the grave markers became steadily more makeshift. Many of the dead were in their late teens or early twenties. (© *Milomir Kovacević*)

spokesman, said the next day that a first bullet fired at Corporal Hardoin unquestionably came from a Serb sniper in Grbavica. But, he added, the second shot, fired just three seconds later, might conceivably have come from the Bosnian government side.

This preposterous account contrasted with the official certitude that, on the day before Corporal Hardoin's death, Sergeant Ralph Gunther, another French soldier, had been killed by a Muslim sniper. The conclusion about Corporal Hardoin was based on one of the inevitable United Nations investigations, such as that witnessed by Mrs. Djokić. United Nations ballistics experts had found that the second shot, the one that killed Corporal Hardoin, was a 5.56-millimeter bullet, whereas the first, which pierced the windshield of the vehicle, appeared to be 7.62 millimeters.

"The possibility therefore exists that the second shot may have come from government positions," Colonel Coward said, "although it is a very slender thread." He added that there was no evidence that Muslim-led government forces used 5.56-millimeter bullets more than the Serbs.

The scenario outlined would of course have required that a Serb sniper fire at a French soldier and then, immediately afterward and presumably without coordination, a Bosnian government sniper join in the attack. I knew Coward well enough to know that he had no personal sympathy for such nonsense, but such was the discombobulation of the United Nations mission that even the death of one of its own could not be honored with an accounting that used unambiguous declarative sentences. I saw Haris Silajdžić, the brooding Bosnian prime minister, that day. For once he was not talking in riddles. "This attempt at an explanation is not only bizarre," he said, "it's third rate."

It was a bleak day. The airport, source of the bulk of the food reaching Sarajevo from United Nations aid agencies, had been closed on April 8, 1995, the day before Maja Djokić died. At Serb insistence, it remained closed; Karadžić said he could no longer guarantee the safety of the airlift. People were again running across areas exposed to sniper fire. The trams had stopped because too many people were being killed by snipers. Shelling was only intermittent, but was sufficient to reignite fears that had eased after NATO's ultimatum of February 1994 put a temporary stop to the bombardment.

At the market, whose shelling fourteen months earlier had led to the brief show of Western resolve that alleviated Sarajevo's plight, the steady slide back toward the nadir of the city's agony was evident. The market had just moved to a covered passageway, a cramped little tunnel deemed safer than the exposed market square. In the half-light, Suada Hodžić, a Muslim refugee from the Serb-held suburb of Vogošća, was selling eggs. Her mother lived on the far side of the airport in the government-held suburb of Hrasnica, reachable through the airport tunnel. Hrasnica, linked to the outside world, had plenty of eggs. "I brought the eggs myself through the airport tunnel," she said. "Now here I am, back in another tunnel, selling the eggs. We Sarajevans have been turned into the tunnel people, the rats of Europe. How long will we have to live like this?"

The desperate tone of such questions reflected the fact that the return to the worst was psychologically crippling to an already exhausted city. The decline had been a steady process, like watching grass discolor and die in a drought. Hope kindled, then extinguished, was more devastating to Sarajevans than suffering itself. "I have died so many times during this war, I can no longer remember anything," a friend said to me. The sense of having lived too much, too long, too disjointedly, was pervasive. "It's a time," I heard, "when the living are envious of the dead."

CHAPTER 27

THE FLASH
OF A KNIFE

EVICA MUTNJATOVIĆ WAS AWAKENED IN THE FIRST HOURS OF the Croatian attack to find several hundred of her Serb neighbors in a state of terror. They were bundling possessions onto tractors and trucks in preparation for flight across the Sava River into Serb-held northern Bosnia. A neighbor told her that the "Croatian Ustashas and slaughterers are coming."

It was the night of May 1, 1995. In London and Paris and Moscow, preparations were in full swing for celebrations to mark the fiftieth anniversary of the end of World War II in Europe. Parades were planned, flags ready for hoisting, dignitaries set to converge. An apt time, everyone seemed to agree, for retrospection. Historians spoke of the seventy-five-year period from 1914 to 1989 as a chapter closed, one marked by two world wars and the cold war. But in the Balkans, World War II, long refracted through the distorting glass of communism in the minds of the war's survivors and their descendants, continued to spawn violence.

Mrs. Mutnjatović stood in front of her house in Stara Gradiška, on the northern bank of the Sava River, watching the frenzied activity of people preparing for flight and the lights of Bosanska Gradiška on the far side of the river, an eddying pool of blackness. A half century earlier, down the same placid river, the bodies of numberless Serbs bludgeoned to death at the Croatian Ustasha concentration camp of Jasenovac had floated. In the minds of the Serbs from Stara Gradiška and other nearby towns in western Slavonia, the camp lived vividly.

Since the Croatian war of 1991, the triangular 250-square-mile pocket of western Slavonia had formed a small, if central, part of Martić's self-styled Krajina Republic. Serbs here did not form an absolute majority of the prewar population, as they did in Knin. In Pakrac, for example, they amounted to 36 percent of the population and in Daruvar 34 percent. But the Serbs, protected by the forces of the United Nations who called the area "Sector West," had held on for four years amid the shattered buildings of the 1991 war.

Now, however, the patience of Tudjman and Šušak, the Croatian defense minister, had run out. They dispatched the revamped Croatian army, equipped with the tanks, artillery, and warplanes steadily amassed by Šušak. The influence of American army doctrine, provided by the retired generals of Military Professional Resources Inc., was evident in the speed of the offensive from the north, east, and west and its simultaneous use of air and ground forces.

A small incident provided the catalyst for the attack, which came the day after Carter's four-month Bosnian cease-fire formally expired. After painstaking negotiations, the stretch of the Bratstvo i Jedinstvo (Brotherhood and Unity) Highway that ran through Serb-held western Slavonia had just been reopened, allowing Croats to use the road for the journey from Zagreb to Slavonski Brod. On the night of April 29, at a gas station on the reopened highway, a Croat refugee from the village of Smrtić in western Slavonia killed a Serb from the same village. The following night, Serbs fired at Croat drivers on the highway, killing two of them. Within hours, the well-prepared Croatian offensive began.

That night, Mrs. Mutnjatović reviewed her options. At the age of seventy-four, widowed, childless, marooned at the confluence of conflict on the banks of a bloodstained river, she was reluctant to flee. If the Croats slit her throat, she reckoned, it would be over in a minute. If she chose flight, however, the desolation of refugee life in Serb-held Bosnia could drag on for years. Down came the shutters of her small house; she sat tight. By the dawn of May 1, she was alone in the town. The Croats had not yet arrived. She heard detonations and gunfire, and her only company, on the riverbank, were storks, chickens, and abandoned dogs.

She took out her Bible and read the passage on the creation of the world. She swallowed several tranquilizers. The next day, somewhat surprised still to be alive, the old woman began to worry about the abandoned cows, hens, and pigs of her neighbors. Venturing out, she met two Croatian soldiers, who told her to leave immediately for Bosnia or be killed. She locked herself in her home again and awaited the end. But when a Croatian officer discovered she had been married to a Croat he hung a sign on her door saying that the old woman was "of Croatian origin"; she was then allowed to remain.

But most of the approximately fifteen thousand Serbs in the pocket left. In Okučani, a dead dog lay in the road in front of the ruins of what had been the Little Heaven Grill of a Serb named Blagoslav Savić. Half-eaten smoked hams were scattered on the ground amid empty Coke and brandy bottles and overturned chairs. The Serbs had evidently left their little heaven quickly. Their washing lay soaking in buckets, their clothes and boots scattered on the floors of abandoned homes, their pots of beans sitting on stoves.

The town was deserted, damage from the Croatian assault limited. The boom of mortar and rocket fire to the north testified to mopping-up operations in the region of Pakrac. But, in essence, after just three days, the Croatian attack on western Slavonia was over. The area had fallen with scarcely a whimper to a force of about seven thousand Croat troops. A myth, preserved since the first fighting of 1991, had fallen too: that of the Serbs' military might. This shattered illusion, so consistently bolstered by the Pentagon, was more significant than any loss of territory.

Martić's bravado and Milošević's expressions of solidarity with the Serbs beyond the Drina had been revealed in their vacuity. Karadžić's oft-repeated vows of unity with the Croatian Serbs had also dissolved into moonshine: not one Bosnian Serb soldier moved over the Sava River to help. Serb divisions, reviled but not resolved, were alive in all their virulence, six years after the great coming-together of Serbdom on Kosovo field and three years after the first, unifying frenzy of the attack on Bosnia. The one reality was the growing might of Croatia's army.

Another old woman, Josipa Kurjak, wandered the ghost town of Okučani, accompanied by sixteen piglets and several puppies. Her house had been occupied since the war of 1991 by a Serb, Drago Ćelakić, his wife, and three children. The Ćelakićs were themselves refugees from the 1991 war: they had fled Poljana, a town about twenty-five miles to the west, and come to Okučani. They had taken over her house, allowing the seventy-two-year-old woman use of a single room, and taunted her with occasional boasts about how all of Croatia would be overrun. "But," she said, "when the Croatian tanks started approaching they turned and fled."

Panic, among the Serbs, had been overwhelming. Martić's army vaporized, its local commander leading the headlong retreat southward over the Sava River in his Mercedes. The less fortunate followed in tractors or on foot. So much for Martić's vow to defend every last inch of "Serb land." The message, spreading like wildfire, was an old one in the Balkans: history as gyre. The advancing "Ustashas" were drug-crazed killers ready, once again, to prize out the eyes of Serbs.

In Stara Gradiška, the retreat had been rapid. Mrs. Mutnjatović's neighbors merely crossed the bridge over the river to Serb-held Bosanska Gradiška. But for the Serbs in towns farther from the bridge—including Okučani, Nova Varoš, and Medari—the road to the river was perilous.

Along a half-mile stretch of road in Nova Varoš, midway between Okučani and Stara Gradiška, the evidence of killing and Serb panic lingered for several days.

Overturned cars, abandoned bicycles, a left shoe, socks, a couple of dead pigs, a suitcase, and toilet paper rolls lay by the roadside, along with bullets and cartridge cases and a child's teddy bear. The sickly sweet whiff of death was there, too, mingling in the early-summer air with the detergent used by the Croats in an attempt to clean up the scene. But there were no craters on the road to suggest shelling and no evidence of strafing from the air.

In Medari, by contrast, just east of Okučani, shelling and bombardment from the new Croatian MiG-21 fighters was intense. Buildings had gaping holes in them, clearly produced by tank shells. "As shells started falling, panic struck, with cars swaying all over the road, some crashing into each other, some overturning," said Jelka Kočić, a Serb who escaped into northern Bosnia. Šušak announced that 450 Serbs were killed in the operation, and 33 Croat soldiers. The numbers were probably conservative.

Several thousand Serbs were captured. In Nova Gradiška, just to the east of the Slavonian pocket, they were bundled into the basement of a high school. I watched one old Serb, who had just dropped dead, being carried out on a stretcher, his mouth wide open in a last expression of anguish. Liljana Fijan, a Serb woman married to a Croat, stood sobbing. She had heard nothing about her mother and sister from Okučani. Her husband was in the Croatian army and had been in Okučani the day before. But he was too afraid to ask about Liljana's mother and sister because to do so was to reveal his marriage to a Serb.

Šušak was exultant. "With this victory, Croatia showed Serbs that we have the force to liberate the whole country," he said. Diplomatic solutions had never much interested him. Official Croatian statements urged Serbs to lay down their arms and become citizens of Croatia with full "civil and human rights." But, as he repeatedly made clear to American officials, Tudjman's real interest lay in the Serbs' departure.

Once again, Martić obliged the Croatian leader. He fired rocket-propelled cluster bombs at the center of Zagreb and so prompted international outrage that tended to place Tudjman's excesses in the shadows. The rockets, which killed six civilians, were his only military response to the Croatian attack.

One hit the central Strossmayer Square, about one hundred yards from the American embassy, leaving a wide swath of charred wreckage. Inside the American embassy, the initial thought was that the thundering detonation was a terrorist attack. Ever since the acquiescence to the "Iranian pipeline" the previous year, fears had been growing in the embassy, fueled by the arrival in Croatia and Bosnia of terrorist groups linked to Iran. "For a moment, we thought the Iranians had bombed us," one senior diplomat said.

Most Croats supported Tudjman. They had lost patience with the Serbs. For several years, Croatia had been awash in hundreds of thousands of refugees, Croats from the 1991 war and Muslims from the 1992 fighting in Bosnia. It had struggled manfully to meet their needs amid rising anger over the Serbs' enduring hold over much of the country. Hundreds of Croatian refugees from the 1991 war lined the edges of the western Slavonian pocket, waiting to go home at last and angry that Tudjman had waited so long. "Over the past four years, we have been shifted to five different places," said Maria Karavla, a refugee from Roždanik. "My husband went back to our village for the first time today. Our house had been burned, but we plan to start again and rebuild it."

Rebuilding began at an astonishing pace that revealed the direction of the Balkan wars. In the wake of the Croatian armed forces, fleets of Croatian builders, engineers, bankers, and telecommunications experts swept into western Slavonia. They set up post offices, installed telephone lines, opened banks, organized pension funds, and repaired roads that had been disappearing beneath undergrowth. Within days, Croatian soldiers were using digital phone cards at newly installed public phones. While inertia had gripped the Serbs over the past four years as they sat befuddled at establishments like the Little Heaven Grill, Croatia had been on the move, bolstered by quiet support from America and Germany and the hard cash injected into the economy by the large UN peacekeeping mission.

The attack made the Croatian government's contempt for the UN obvious. The contempt was based on an accurate evaluation: beyond all the resounding resolutions, the tens of thousands of UN military and civilian personnel deployed in the former Yugoslavia were onlookers, just as they had been on the fields of Tilava Hill, near Sarajevo, when I first came across them in 1992. The United Nations, as its former secretary-general U Thant once remarked, is "an umbrella that comes down when it rains."

There were more than three thousand UN soldiers from Nepal, Argentina, and Jordan in Sector West. They had been swept aside. At one Nepalese camp on the Brotherhood and Unity Highway, a disconsolate commander sat amid the debris of his mission. The voluptuous pinups that had adorned his soldiers' rooms fluttered in the wind along with unsent love letters written by the boys to their sweethearts back in Kathmandu. The expression of this commander was one of disgust at such humiliation. He had come a long way only to see his camp stormed, plundered, and ripped apart by the Croats, and not a shot had been fired in riposte.

The only riposte was from the United Nations Security Council, which duly condemned "acts of harassment and intimidation against United Nations personnel"; demanded that Croatia "put an end immediately to the military offensive launched by its forces in the area of western Slavonia"; insisted that the authority of United Nations personnel be "reestablished" in western Slavonia; and urged the Croats to "comply with the existing cease-fire agreements." Akashi pleaded for a resumption of "dialogue" between Serbs and Croats. The clear implication was that, after four years of diplomatic impasse, Tudjman should give up the fruits of his lightning battlefield victory in favor of the authority and peace efforts of the United Nations. The officials in New York were ensconced, more transparently than ever, in never-never land.

The intuitions of Tudjman and Šušak were telling. Western Slavonia was a harbinger. The destruction of Yugoslavia would be completed, not by talks around a table, but by more fighting and further mass movement of population tending to create ethnically pure areas. Only thus would the conditions for a dismal peace be created.

In Pakrac, in the northern part of the western Slavonian pocket, I met Hrvoje Šarinić, a seasoned diplomat and the chief aide to Tudjman. He had come to meet Obrad Ivanović, the mayor of what had been the Serb-held part of town. Ivanović was skeptical of Šarinić's assurances that the Serbs had a place in Croatia and furious with Martić for abandoning the Serbs. His feelings were understandable. But the anger directed at Martić was misplaced. Šarinić told me that he had been in telephone contact with Milošević in Belgrade. The Serb president had made clear that he would not intervene to help his Serb brothers in the Krajina. Martić was never much more than Milošević's puppet. Abandoned by Belgrade, the remaining Krajina Serbs were clearly living on borrowed time.

THE JASENOVAC CAMP lies on the northern bank of the Sava in fertile, flat countryside. The last train that brought its doomed load stands stopped in its track, on the edge of a grassy field. From the center of the field there rises an ungainly monument called "The Flower of Life," but it, like all Jasenovac, wilts with the weight of death.

When I first saw Jasenovac, it had just been retaken by the Croats in the capture of the western Slavonian pocket. Croatian soldiers were digging new trenches to face the Serb enemy across the Sava River in northern Bosnia. The regular rising and falling of a soldier's pick, flashing in the sun before sinking in the soil, provided a rhythmic reminder of Jasenovac's violent lodestone.

The camp was always a center of the war. From this magnetic field, there spread the gathering electric charges that dispersed the Zečevićs, the

Šestovićs, the Adamovićs, the Karišiks, and millions of others who had as-sumed they had their place in Yugoslavia.

Auschwitz is a place of unspeakable violence, but Willy Brandt went down on his knees in the Warsaw ghetto; the past has been confronted. Not, however, at Jasenovac, the central symbol of the central cleavage in Yugoslavia between Serbs and Croats. Alija Mehmedović, who served the regime that created Jasenovac, had disappeared after World War II; like him, the truth about the camp proved elusive. It lived on—history as wound—ready to be reopened by Milošević and Tudjman.

For Milošević's propagandists, the injuring of a single Serb by an Al-banian in Kosovo in 1985 was a "Jasenovac for one man." For Tudjman, Jasenovac was "myth," its slaughter—primarily of Serbs, Jews, and Gyp-sies—exaggerated and distorted in order to blight the idea of an indepen-dent Croatia. Elected with the funds of the Ustashas in exile, he naturally declined to go there. Ambivalence about the evil of the camp stood at the center of Tudjman's twisted vision of Croatian "reconciliation."

Appropriately, the place changed hands several times during the war. It was Croatian when war broke out in 1991. The Serbs took it after a two-month battle in October 1991. Now it had fallen again to the Croats. The Serbian Orthodox church called the Croatian attack on western Slavonia "Jasenovac after Jasenovac." The statement devalued the horror of the World War II camp by putting the camp to work, yet again, as propa-ganda. But it illustrated the potency of the symbol.

In the small, battered town of Jasenovac, on the banks of the Sava, the Croatian Catholic church lay in ruins, destroyed by the Serbs in 1991. The Orthodox church had been destroyed in 1941 by the Ustashas. It was eventually rebuilt and consecrated in 1984. The Croatian forces who had just recaptured the town left the Orthodox church untouched, evidence of the influence of the retired American generals. They were learning about public relations. Croat butchery of Serbs during an earlier, more limited attack on the Krajina in 1993, at the Medak pocket, had yielded devastat-ing photographs of smashed skulls and burned corpses. Tudjman bused in loads of Western diplomats to show off the ruins of the Catholic church and the respect shown to Orthodoxy at Jasenovac. The diplomats nodded and took notes.

History's desecration was evident at the adjacent camp. The museum commemorating the Ustasha slaughter and its myriad victims lay in ruins. Whose work this destruction was had already become a subject of dispute. At the entrance, weeds advanced over a plaque that read, "The last light before the terrible night was the flash of a knife and the white screams lin-gering now in blackness; and the white, white skin of the butcher, naked from the waist up, who, so stripped, gouged out our eyes."

Killing at Jasenovac had none of the Nazis' industrialized perfunctoriness. Joseph and Miriam Elazar—the grandparents of Mladen Elazar in Windsor, Canada—and their seven children did not go to a gas chamber. The slaughter was primitive, ghoulish, artisanal, like the work of the Serbs in 1992. Photographs show some of the Ustasha executioners laughing as they prepare to sever the necks of Serbs with chain saws. In one room, full of shattered glass, other faded, partially ripped photographs dangled from the walls: three skeletal children; a man's face, swollen and gashed, his eyes gouged out; Serbs in their peasant hats lined up with heads bowed; a line of limp men dangling like scarecrows from a gallows. On a wall, lines from a poem by Djordje Radisić were still just visible:

U ime nas koji smo danas
I onih što će biti sutra, pamtimo:
Sve njih čije su oči postale trava.

In the name of we who live today
And those who will live tomorrow, remember:
All those whose eyes became grass.

The grass of Jasenovac, dense with insects and mines, shimmered in the spring sunshine. Butterflies fluttered, the poplars rising from the riverbank swayed like giant fans. Peter Galbraith, the American ambassador, mindful of the mines, made his way across the field toward "The Flower of Life." He spoke words, worthy ones, about the need for Croatia to protect the rights of Serb citizens and ensure the return of those who had fled. Solutions, he suggested, did not lie in military action. But the trenches being dug by the Croatian army on the perimeter of the former camp, the armed Serbs facing them on the south bank of the Sava, and the destruction of the museum that once commemorated the Ustasha terror told another story: that of unpitying cycles of vengeance.

On the same day, François Mitterrand, the French president, spoke in Berlin, flanked by Helmut Kohl, the German chancellor, and Al Gore, the American vice president. On the fiftieth anniversary of the Allied victory over the Nazis, European reconciliation was the dying president's theme. Europe, in a half century, had been rebuilt on "so many ruins, disasters, and deaths." There were, he declared, "no more hereditary enemies." Germany and France, after three wars in seventy years, had moved on. But where I stood the Europe of disaster overcome did not exist. In its place there was division and hereditary hatred, willfully rekindled and now caught in the steady gaze of silent eyes of grass.

CHAPTER 28

POSTCARD
TO AMRA

I sit in Sarajevo's Koševo Hospital early in May 1995 with Faruk Šabanović, a pale and gentle-featured youth, watching a video. Its main subject is Faruk himself, or more precisely his last steps, taken outside the Holiday Inn.

There Faruk is, walking briskly across the street, his hair ruffled by the wind. The crack of a shot echoes in the valley. He falls. He lies curled in an almost fetal position. A United Nations soldier in a light blue helmet looks on, motionless. A man arrives, screaming abuse at the soldier, who eventually moves his white United Nations armored personnel carrier. This slight movement is enough to cover the civilian from Serb sniper fire as he rushes out to retrieve Faruk, whose lithe body has turned limp.

Faruk tells me that, when he watches the video, he feels it is somebody else who has been shot. But each instant is vivid. "After I was hit I felt my legs in my chest," he says. "Then I saw my feet. I tried to move them. But I could not. This United Nations soldier was looking at me. He did nothing. He just looked. For me, it was so long."

I was fascinated by the video. It seemed to capture the increasingly surreal and sordid nature of the war. A twenty-year-old civilian is shot on a city street and becomes a paraplegic; a television cameraman, positioned at a dangerous Sarajevo crossroads in the hope of seeing somebody killed or mutilated, films the shooting; a soldier sent by the United Nations as a "peacekeeper" to a city officially called a "safe area," watches. The soldier, encased behind his flak jacket and his galloping dismay, is unable to move because he does not know what his "mandate" permits, and, in any event, he is paralyzed by fear. The "victim"—the central figure in the "bang-bang footage"—watches the moment when he was crippled from his hospital bed.

This strange collage was Bosnia, and Bosnia had become the dismal exemplar of a "future" or "postmodern" war. In such wars, states are replaced by militias or other informal—often tribal—groupings whose ability to use sophisticated weaponry is limited. There is little distinction between armies and peoples: everybody who gets in the way, as Faruk Šabanović had, gets killed or maimed. The wars are intractable. Live images of suffering, distributed worldwide, sap whatever will or ability there may be to prosecute a devastating military campaign. Because these are no longer wars between states, the absence of effective central authority makes the war difficult to end through negotiation. The United Nations, through one or several of its agencies, ends up trying to palliate a chaos likely to endure for many years. Mighty NATO, which never fired a shot in anger to defeat the Soviet Union, finds itself pursuing a single disabled Serb tank in a field because, in the interests of the "impartiality" that goes with the palliative approach to postmodern war, responses to aggression must be "proportionate."

Faruk sees this warped conflict with the lucidity of a man who has looked down death's precipice and returned. An engineering student before the war, he has no illusions. With a mounting disgust, over several years, he has observed the United Nations mission to Bosnia. His anger grew when, as a soldier on night duty, he saw Sarajevan girls prostituting themselves outside the United Nations' central Skenderija barracks. He believed, at the outset, that the United Nations might have helped save Bosnia. "But," he tells me with a calm whose strength reminds me of the sea, "they're just here to ease consciences. Even before I was shot, I knew they would never protect me. And I know the United Nations peacekeepers only brought me to the hospital in their ambulance because the television camera happened to be there."

Faruk has been through his own epiphany. It came, after he was paralyzed, in the form of a man named Hamdo Karamustafić who was placed in the bed next to him at the hospital. Hamdo had also been shot on a Sarajevo street. The bullet went through his pancreas; doctors held out no hope. But he lived long enough to become Faruk's friend.

To Faruk, Hamdo was a good man. He was strong, he was big, his words came from his experience and were like hewn granite. He had been a policeman at the beginning of the war and contributed to the city's initial resistance against the Serb onslaught. He knew how things worked and, in his confrontation with death, Hamdo's wisdom was evident.

"One day," says Faruk, "blood started coming out of Hamdo's mouth and nose, and they tried to help him. All day he was bleeding. The whole bed was covered in blood. They gave him a transfusion, and the blood was coming in, and the blood was coming out. It was hard to look. I was crying all the time. His son, who is about twenty years old, was there. And

Hamdo just kept talking and smiling all the time. When he was dying his eyes were smiling. When he could take a breath he would speak to his son. His son was crying. And Hamdo was saying, 'Don't cry, you have to live.' Those words were so strong, they cannot be repeated."

After recounting this, Faruk lies back, exhausted and pained. But his soft eyes are far from docile. "I know this will be long," he says. "But the world can't break me like this. If I remain a paraplegic, I will find some way of dealing with it. I will be better, anyhow, better than the Serb who shot me. I will be clean in my mind, clean with respect to others, and clean with respect to this dirty world."

A DIRTY WORLD: Sarajevo, May 1995, more than three years into the war, more than three years of encirclement. A camp that is also a city, spread out beneath the mountains. A woman pulling some contraption, piled with plastic containers of water taken from a public spigot, running, her hair falling into her eyes, her free hand clasping an infant, as a mortar round drops out of the sky with a boom that knots the stomach and takes breath and life away.

I drive through streets that are almost deserted. In parking lots, the weeds are waist high. Decay advances. Just outside the Holiday Inn, there is a new crater, about four feet deep: some Serb rocket that crashed and crashed and crashed. Such sounds can instill fear even in those who thought themselves inured. A limb may start to tremble uncontrollably.

On Marshal Tito Street, a United Nations armored personnel carrier goes slowly back and forth, providing the people huddled in its shadow with cover from sniper fire. The system does not always work. A man is shot in the eye. A twelve-year-old girl, Sejla Kličbegović, is watching. "I don't know why the world does not see what is happening," she says. "A lot of my people have already been killed."

There is a young couple standing by the road; she is clasping a bunch of freshly cut peonies. Their heavy crimson blooms provide a shock of color. They want a ride. The trams, Rose's famous trams, have stopped: no electricity, too dangerous. Into my armored Land Rover they clamber. She has given him the peonies because the flowers are beautiful and because she loves him. They are clearly in love for the first time; their love bubbles over like the Miljacka; they talk excitedly. The boy rolls up his sleeve. He has no elbow to speak of. His arm is permanently bent. His ability to move his fingers is limited. Shrapnel from a shell.

I stare at this mutilated arm. The shock never changes, any more than the fear of being suddenly crippled. I have carried this fear with me for some time now; in dreams, infrequent but memorable, I am reminded of it. I have come to believe that I am like everyone else, no more and no less a coward. I have seen fear in young soldiers' faces written as clearly as a child's guilt. It is normal to want to live. It is normal to loathe confinement. It is normal to go crazy in this city that can only be entered by driving at high speed down a looping track over Mount Igman into the barrel of Serb 20-millimeter guns. There are people now walking around with pistols with which to shoot themselves, just in case the shrapnel only takes a leg. Several hundred cripples inhabit Sarajevo. At the prosthetics clinic, a typical room may have fourteen people in it and three legs. So the story of this boy beside me is just the usual story. Indeed, he has been lucky. Yet the wound and those fresh flowers and the excitement of young love and this crumbling city are almost too much to bear.

Inside, people burn books to heat stoves to cook the rabbits they have raised in cages in their bedrooms. In the few restaurants that are open, I watch the waiters folding and refolding the paper napkins with a meticulousness that is absurd and am reminded of the street-side vendors in war-ravaged Beirut building their ridiculous, fragile castles of cigarette cartons beside the rubble. In times of destruction people build something, simply for the act itself.

Some burn Marx and Engels in their woodstoves; some burn Serbian poets; some burn Tito's various constitutions. You, Amra, speak to me with that peculiarly Sarajevan directness, which has intensified as the world's circumlocutions have lengthened. You speak to me as the fire in the stove flickers and dies. You say, "I have tried to make a fire so many times. You know, you're often shivering, so you are in a hurry. I light the wood and it's damp and it hisses and then it goes out. So I take some newspapers and stuff them in and they burn for a few minutes and the fire fizzles again. So then I take my stockings, they are wonderful, these Italian stockings. I used to buy them in big boxes before the war. I have burned so many pairs of stockings during this war, I cannot even remember. The stockings always work. And once the fire is going, there is nothing like a pair of shoes. They burn so well. And my skirts are not bad either. And, *oh the plastic bottles . . .*"

I go to see the distinguished poet Abdulah Sidran. He has been drinking and is surprised to see me because he has imagined that the meeting has already taken place. This sensation is widespread: the impossibility of disentangling, or distinguishing, the days. Have Sidran and I ever met? Was there a time before this time? After more than eleven hundred days under siege, it is no longer possible to remember, or believe, that Sarajevo was ever a normal city.

People are asked, How are you? and they reply, Fine. People are asked, Do you have enough to eat? and they reply that they do. People are asked, Do you have electricity or water? and they say yes. People are asked, What do you think of the siege? and they say, I don't think, I hope. Words are empty, their sense drained from them, so people say the simplest thing. What they really say, again and again, is *fuck you*. Sarajevans believe just one thing now: that only with a stone in your hand can you defend yourself. Sidran says to me, with that directness that permits of no reply, "There is a quality of evil here: that has to be seen. I am in a state of permanent disappointment with the West. Bosnia is like planet Earth. If Bosnia is senseless, then the planet is senseless too."

Everybody in Sarajevo, by now, has some form of post-traumatic stress. They have told themselves countless times that there are limits, only to discover that there are none. The shells still come down. The hills still have eyes. The mountains are still beautiful and hold only death. Tracers still light up the night sky. Still the various detonations are described to the press every morning by the diligent servants of the United Nations mission: five 120-millimeter rounds at this place, fifteen 82-millimeter rounds at that place, three mortar rounds at another place. Still, in Geneva, in Lisbon, in London, in New York, in Paris, in the Vatican, the people of Sarajevo are discussed. But from these discussions nothing emerges; nothing tangible; nothing to change the fact that between five hundred and eight hundred Serb heavy weapons still ring a city vulnerable to tank, mortar, and artillery fire at any time. Ismet Cerić, the head of the psychiatry department at Koševo Hospital, says, "The heart contracts and distends. But we are in a permanent state of contraction."

The stress takes two clinical forms. The first, Cerić tells me, is characterized by anxiety, a sense of strangulation, shortness of breath, a fast heartbeat, and, in extreme cases, delusions and paranoia. The second is characterized by depression, inertia, passivity, and, in extreme cases, suicide. People flip. They tire of circulating in this prison. Željko Trogrančić, a colleague of Cerić, says this cannot go on. You cannot climb a tree and shoot the person below you and call that war. You cannot, as Karadžić has done repeatedly, shell the hospital where you used to work. There must be some rules, Trogrančić insists, in the civilized world.

Trogrančić himself was traumatized for several months. He did not believe he could be shot. He always walked slowly because to walk faster was to admit that you knew that somebody might be watching you from the hills through the sights of a gun. Then, on January 3, 1993, he was severely wounded in the leg by a sniper. He spent four months in plaster and still walks only with the aid of a stick. He says rules must exist, the new world order must mean something other than Yugoslavia's death, but his eyes tell me that he is past believing his own words.

Down in the western Sarajevo suburb of Dobrinja, Darko Šljivić is calm. From his balcony, he can see the front line, about one hundred yards away, and, beyond that, in Serb-held territory, his son's former school. Every now and again, his building is sprayed with machine-gun fire. He understands Einstein now. More than three years ago, at the start of the war, any detonation was frightening. Now he knows all the sounds: incoming, outgoing, a shot that is one hundred yards away, one that is fifty yards away. Today, if the shot is twenty yards away, it means little. Relativity.

Before the war, Šljivić, who is half Serb and half Croat, worked as a bank executive. Now Šljivić, who is a Bosnian still, sips plum brandy, grows vegetables, and contemplates the devastation around him. It is raining. The rain, he says, is bad for the potatoes and onions. Then he smiles to himself and mutters that he has become a peasant.

His wife, who is half Serb and half Jewish, hands him a photograph album, but he pushes it away, saying that when he sees photographs of the world outside he feels worse. The album is a reminder, like the mention of a café where he used to gather with friends. Whole worlds that have disappeared, worlds that have become wounds, best not reopened.

"We were in Europe," says Šljivić, "and now we are in the mud." That directness again, as irrefutable as the dawn. Sarajevo has been forced to genuine feeling. The city is beyond dissimulation, beyond even politeness. The hypocrisy of the world has resulted, here, at the center of the war, in a shattering distillation of sentiment.

There is an immense love for Bosnia in this city, a love that has grown as Bosnia has been lost. Šljivić is one of those in whom Bosnia lives, and he declares, "I don't even think about this ending anymore. I'm just happy if my tomatoes grow. In fact, I don't think at all. If I start to think, I go crazy. My only thought is how to bring water, how to get something to eat, when to let my two kids out, how to feed my rabbits."

This banker-turned-urban-farmer spent much of the first year of the war in a cellar with twenty-six of his neighbors. After the second month of fighting, Dobrinja was completely cut off. Šljivić, like Haris, had been reluctant to take a gun. Muslim gangsters, led by Juka, stole his new Volkswagen Passat in the first week of the war. But when people shoot at your children there is no choice.

So Šljivić accepted the absurdity of being a half Serb fired on by the Serbs who used to be his neighbors and friends. He emerged from the cellar in September 1992. At night, the enemies talked. The Serbs even asked Šljivić over for a drink. When they shot and injured him, they inquired as to his health. *How's Darko? How's Darko?* Grotesque questions looming across the mined no-man's-land.

Darko recovered from his injury. In 1993, he bought his first rabbit, for forty dollars. The purchase, like the acceptance of a gun, was a question of necessity: he had to feed his family just as he had to protect it. He began to grow vegetables—tomatoes, cabbages, cauliflower, eggplant—on a small patch of ground outside his apartment. He started breeding rabbits and, at one time, had thirty. Now he has three. The rabbits live in an abandoned room, too exposed to fire to be habitable, along with snails Šljivić recently collected but has not yet cooked.

Šljivić was worried about killing the first rabbit. He thought it would upset his daughter. So he took the rabbit to a neighbor to be killed. "When I put the rabbit on the table," he says, "my daughter asked what it was. I said, 'It's the rabbit.' She tried it and said, 'I like it better like this than alive.' She was hungry, you see."

Eventually, Šljivić had to cut back on the rabbits because it was hard to feed them. There is no more grass in Sarajevo. The land has all been cultivated or is covered in graves. We sit on his balcony that overlooks the vegetable garden and the no-man's-land beyond. We drink. There is a *rat-tat-tat* burst of fire. At least one hundred yards away, and the children are at home, so no need to worry. We go on drinking and Šljivić says that rock bottom has now been reached.

I wonder. Šljivić's world has shrunk to this balcony, his vegetables, his family. He never ventures downtown. He wonders whether he really wants to eat those snails. When there is electricity he watches Pale television to find out what the Bosnian army has done and Bosnian television to find out what the Serbs have done. He laughs at this. At least his wife, his son and daughter are here: the men abandoned by their families are those most likely to have gone completely mad.

Having looked with disdain at wars in Africa and the Middle East, he says he understands how the world feels. Now others look at the Balkans in the same way. "I don't worry anymore," he says. "If anything, I worry about peace. I don't know if I could still be a bank director. I don't know if I can ever go back to that life."

AT THE CENTER of this city, Lieutenant General Rupert Smith, Rose's successor as the British commander of United Nations forces in Bosnia, brooded. A soldier trained in the Parachute Regiment, he had certain principles and cleaved to certain truths. For deterrence to be credible, the ability to escalate must exist. Any military action may involve loss of life. A mission lacking coherence or clearly defined objectives is untenable. A former commander of British forces in the Persian Gulf War, Smith spoke little but the facts. In this he was the exact opposite of Rose, who spoke a lot in order to mold the facts to his view of the world. Smith's view, quickly formed, was straightforward enough. "Either we should get a credible mandate, or let's go home."

By that month of May 1995, more than three months had passed since
his arrival in Sarajevo. It was clear enough that, for the blue-helmeted
peacekeepers, the truths of war had been flouted and the limits of "mud-
dling through" reached. At one of the dinners he occasionally hosted at his
headquarters, Smith remarked, "There is just no point in hanging around
in the middle of somebody else's war."

In March 1995, the Serb leadership held an important meeting on Jahorina Mountain, attended by Karadžić, Mladić, and Momčilo Krajišnik.
It concluded that, in the absence of a quick resolution to the fighting, the
Serbs would lose the war. A diplomatic solution was preferable, but
without one, it was essential to capture the eastern Muslim enclaves—
Srebrenica, Žepa, and Goražde—and install Abdić in Bihać. Another immediate objective set was an increase in the military pressure on Sarajevo,
and an accentuation of the city's isolation, in order to force Izetbegović toward a settlement.

Smith was in possession of reliable intelligence on these Serb plans for
the summer of 1995; he thus knew that the gaping inconsistencies of the
UNPROFOR mandate would be probed. The Serbs began the implementation of their policy by cutting off the UNHCR airlift to Sarajevo on
April 8. With roads already sealed, the main source of food for the three
hundred thousand inhabitants of the city was thereby cut off.

On at least one point Smith's mandate was clear: the "international humanitarian agencies" were to have "free and unimpeded access to all safe
areas in the Republic of Bosnia and Herzegovina." Any "deliberate obstruction" of aid—as well as any bombardment of a "safe area"—opened
the way for UNPROFOR, acting in self-defense, to apply "all necessary
measures, through the use of air power, in and around the safe areas in the
Republic of Bosnia and Herzegovina."

On May 7, 1995, a Serb mortar round crashed into the western suburb
of Butmir, near the entrance to the tunnel that was Sarajevo's sole link with
the outside world. The Serb policy of tightening the noose was clear; so,
too, was the complete erosion of the fifteen-month-old "total exclusion
zone"—the NATO-backed protection of Sarajevo from attack by heavy
weapons. The mortar killed eleven people. On two counts—the bombardment of the "safe area" of Sarajevo and the month-long cutting-off of
food aid—the use of air power was justified.

Smith duly called for NATO air strikes. The strikes, in his view, had to
be of a scale that deterred the Serbs. Otherwise they were useless. The long
United Nations obsession with finding a "smoking gun" as a target for any
use of air power, the fixation on a "proportionate" response, the notion of
using fighter aircraft without becoming part of the fight—all this, to a military man, was so much gobbledygook, politics posturing as policy.

Internal United Nations documents defined a scale for the use of NATO air power in Bosnia. The first stage was known as "close air support." On such missions, one document said, "military aircraft perform the role of artillery by neutralizing specific targets in proximity to the conflict point." *Military aircraft perform the role of artillery, skimming over the hilly, forested, often cloud-covered terrain of Bosnia to pick out a single gun!* Seldom has so much empty, and often plain nonsensical, verbiage congealed around so little resolve as in the international response to the Bosnian disaster. Beyond "close air support" lay something more sweeping called "air strikes," but, in Western chancelleries and at the United Nations, such strikes were widely deemed incompatible with a peacekeeping mission.

Smith's request for air strikes was overruled by his military superior, Lieutenant General Bernard Janvier of France, the commander of United Nations forces in the former Yugoslavia, and by Akashi. They opposed escalation. They were also under pressure to avoid acts that might jeopardize the latest international diplomatic foray, a low-risk, time-buying American attempt to persuade Milošević to accord diplomatic recognition to Bosnia and Herzegovina in return for a lifting, or a suspension, of the international trade embargo imposed on Serbia three years earlier. So began in earnest America's de facto rehabilitation of Milošević.

Robert C. Frasure, an extremely resourceful American diplomat, reluctantly led this negotiation, which intensified in May. But an outline accord reached in Belgrade on May 18 by Frasure was rejected in Washington amid disagreement over the conditions under which sanctions on Serbia would be reimposed. By May 22, the deal was evidently off. In any event, it was always unclear what, if anything, Milošević's recognition of Bosnia would do to stop the war.

In Sarajevo, there was a palpable sense of things coming to a head. Often, during the war, this feeling proved illusory. It was rooted in a vestigial sense that such suffering, such international incoherence, such lies could not go on accumulating. But, like a house of cards defying gravity, they did, and the point of collapse was never quite reached.

But now it seemed we had indeed arrived at Šljivić's rock bottom. Izetbegović declared that the city would not go through another winter of siege. The United Nations peacekeeping force was equally committed to avoiding another Bosnian winter, and Clinton had committed himself to providing as many as twenty-five thousand American troops to help with an eventual withdrawal—a scenario that the administration wanted desperately to avoid. Yet inertia was deep-rooted, the architecture of paralysis elaborate, as the overruling of Smith's call for air strikes illustrated. Smith wanted things to move; forcing the structure he was part of to the limits of its contradictions was preferable to further *immobilisme*.

• • •

ON MAY 12, 1995, in Paris, a meeting was held, attended by Boutros-Ghali, Annan, Janvier, Akashi, and Smith. There were several options: UNPROFOR's replacement by a full-scale military force; a redeployment of peacekeepers out of the most vulnerable areas, including the eastern enclaves like Srebrenica; a withdrawal; the status quo. Akashi told me later that he had argued for a redeployment that would place almost all the peacekeepers in the relative safety of the Muslim-Croat federation area. "You cannot brandish a toy sword," he said. "You have to be as realistic as possible."

Such a redeployment, leaving just a few forward air controllers in the Muslim enclaves to guide NATO aircraft toward targets for eventual air strikes, would have had the effect, finally, of removing allied soldiers from under the threat of allied bombs. But it would also have amounted to an abandonment of the "safe areas" where the Muslims who survived the Serb onslaught of 1992 gathered. Smith, ever the military realist, supported the redeployment; so, too, did Janvier, who put the case for it to a closed session of the United Nations Security Council in New York ten days after the Paris meeting.

Madeleine K. Albright, the American ambassador to the United Nations, listened. Born in Czechoslovakia, she felt the Bosnian war as deeply personal; in her, the old battle between realpolitik and the imperatives of morality that Bosnia placed before the American people was particularly intense. Czechoslovakia had been dismembered by Hitler in the year after her birth, a dismemberment to which Western states acquiesced at Munich. Her late father, Josef Korbel, had served twice as a diplomat in Belgrade, and was the Czechoslovak ambassador there immediately after World War II. He knew and loved the Serbs; Albright remembered him singing Serb songs and even saying once that he would have liked to have been born a Serb. She had received a letter from a man who had been a friend of the family in Belgrade telling her that her father would be deeply ashamed of her treatment of the Serbs. She sent a letter back saying that her father would never have supported *these Serbs* and their acts.

Albright understood the Serbs' deep, historic sense of being cheated by Yugoslavia's destruction; she also understood their respect for force. In her internal battle between sympathies formed in childhood and history's lessons, she sided with the latter. During the first months of the Clinton administration, she sent a memo to the president calling for wide-ranging NATO air strikes that would hit Serb artillery, tanks, bridges, and ammunition depots, and she pointedly asked Powell what was the use of the superb American military if the United States could not use it. Powell later wrote that he almost had an aneurysm. But the question was highly pertinent. Even two years later, it had still not been answered. Albright was left in the lurch, defending a bold position—the defense of the "safe areas" and the intensified use of NATO air power to secure that objective—without the buttress of an American presence on the ground in Bosnia. The stance lacked coherence; she was obliged to make the best of a bad job. The fact was that Munich was resonant to her, but Vietnamese quagmires struck more of a chord with members of Clinton's national security staff.

The Pentagon, moreover, was determined to safeguard the prestige gained in the Gulf War, prestige that had assuaged some of the bitterness of Vietnam, and was reluctant to go to war under Clinton, whom many generals deemed unfit to lead after his avoidance of the draft.

So the old difficulties persisted. America was not prepared to support a redeployment out of Srebrenica and other "safe areas"; even less prepared, however, to defend them with American boys. There was no change in the UNPROFOR mandate. Artillery exchanges, involving thousands of shells, intensified in Sarajevo after May 16. Serbs began firing from out of the scattered weapons-collection sites supposedly overseen by the UN forces. They removed four guns from these sites. By softening NATO's ultimatum of February 1994 and allowing the Serbs to keep their guns in position, albeit while "monitored" by the United Nations, Rose and Akashi had left peacekeepers in positions of weakness at Serb-encircled locations. They were vulnerable to hostage-taking, and their ability to prevent the Serbs firing guns was ultimately limited.

ON MAY 24, Smith made a rare appearance before television cameras and issued an ultimatum. "Weapons have been removed from the weapons-collection points or, in some instances, fired from them," he said. "This makes a series of extremely dangerous and volatile escalations that cannot be tolerated. I demand a prompt cease-fire and full compliance with the February 1994 agreement on heavy weapons." Smith gave the Serbs until May 25, at noon, to place all guns either under UN control or beyond a twelve-mile radius from the city. In the absence of compliance, there would be air strikes. This time, with Frasure's initiative dead and Sarajevo evidently entering a new phase of its agony, Smith won approval from his superiors.

The next day, NATO bombed—disproportionately, by the extremely modest standards of the war. Two ammunition bunkers in a large military complex near Pale were hit. The bombing amounted to a test of American policy—the gamble that broader air strikes could work even with the country's European allies extremely exposed on the ground. Clinton emerged from his Bosnian hibernation and declared, "I welcome the decision of the United Nations and NATO to launch air strikes today against a Bosnian Serb ammunition site following the violence of the past several days in and around Sarajevo. I hope that today's air strike will convince the Bosnian Serb leadership to end their violations of the exclusion zone and comply with their other agreements with the United Nations."

But the Serbs had little interest in compliance. They were in a position, yet again, to call the bluff of the international community. They lobbed a 120-millimeter shell into central Tuzla, where, in the early evening, teenagers had gathered for coffee. I watched the familiar scene on Bosnian television: decapitated bodies being hauled into the back of trucks. The bodies were mounds of flesh, no more, difficult to haul into the truck because they came apart. Shockingly, there was a girl's perfect body, but she had no head. A child lay dead on his back. A soldier crouched behind a woman, trying, with trembling fingers, to shut her eyes. How those fingers trembled! Later, a Serb officer in Banja Luka, Lieutenant Colonel Milovan Milutinović, told me that, in Tuzla also, the Muslims shelled themselves.

When, on May 26, NATO aircraft attacked the depot for a second time, the Serbs began taking UN peacekeepers hostage. Predictably, international resolve evaporated before televised images of peacekeepers chained to Serb military installations. America was not in a position to push a policy in which its European allies seemed likely to take casualties: the old, old dilemma. Smith was despondent. He had been prepared to escalate and incur loss of life. "I failed," he said. "Nobody will write a blank check on the risk. Deterrence has to be credible, and we are just not credible."

THIS LACK OF CREDIBILITY was now brutally exposed. Everyone in Bosnia was living a lie: the people of the country who had been allowed to suffer through three years of European war; the United Nations peacekeepers who had been sent there on a wrongheaded mission. For the lies to be entirely exposed, more people had to die.

A few hours after the second NATO air strike, on May 26, the French UN peacekeepers commanded by Lieutenant Colonel Jean-Paul Michel came under fire from the Serbs. The twenty-one soldiers, members of the Fifth Infantry Battalion, were stationed just south of Sarajevo at the Lukavica barracks, where their mission was to guard Serb heavy weapons. Abruptly, a group of Serbs appeared and fired a volley of bullets in the vicinity of the French troops before demanding their surrender. "One of my lieutenants called me and said they were under fire and requested my instructions," Michel said. "As a peacekeeper it was not easy to know how to respond. I told them to refrain from firing back but not to surrender."

The Serbs quickly increased the pressure on the French. They fired rocket-propelled grenades, destroying three United Nations vehicles parked in front of their position. Again the lieutenant called his commander seeking instructions. "I had never faced this kind of decision," Michel told me. "We are deployed here as peacekeepers, not as fighting soldiers. I knew I had no way of getting them out and no way of protecting them. I said to myself, My men are going to die if they start shooting back. And for what? For peace? So I ordered them to surrender."

Humiliated, the twenty-one French soldiers affixed a rag to the end of a broomstick and waved it. They then joined the hostages, eventually numbering more than 370, held by the Serbs as insurance against further NATO attack.

Colonel Michel was visibly troubled by what had happened. Like most French officers, and many British, he had come to Bosnia with certain ideas borrowed partly from history and partly from the infectious mythology of Serbdom. In this quick handbook of the war, the Serbs had fought on "the right side" in two world wars; they were widely misunderstood; and they were involved in a messy Balkan civil war where notions of right and wrong were inapplicable. The camaraderie shown by the Serbs before the hostage-taking had only reinforced Michel's view that Karadžić and Mladić were easier to do business with than Izetbegović. Yet, in what Michel saw as a sudden volte-face, the Serbs had now taken his men hostage after forcing them to wave a rag in surrender.

At dawn the next day, May 27, there was another attack on the French. Serbs disguised as blue-helmeted United Nations peacekeepers entered the French United Nations Vrbanja position in central Sarajevo and captured the twelve French soldiers guarding the post. This key emplacement lay just south of the Vrbanja Bridge, where Muris Zečević and Vojna Adamović had demonstrated more than three years earlier, at the start of the war. It was a critical site because it was situated between the Serb-held area of Grbavica to the west and the Kovačići district controlled by the Bosnian government to the east. From the battered high-rise apartment blocks overlooking the site, Serbs and Muslims who used to drink in the same bars now hunted each other with assault rifles.

Unlike the Lukavica barracks, in the midst of Serb-held territory, the position was easily accessible to French reinforcements. Within hours, a decision to storm Vrbanja was approved by Major General Hervé Gobillard, the commander of United Nations forces in Sarajevo. The decision reflected French anger at the events of the previous day; it also suggested a new resolve in Paris, where Jacques Chirac had replaced François Mitterrand as president on May 10.

An infantry assault by UN peacekeepers was planned, supported from a distance by three light tanks with 90-millimeter guns, four 20-millimeter cannons, and several sharpshooters. For Colonel Erik Sandahl, the commander of the infantry battalion responsible for the position, planning was complicated by the fact that he did not know what the Serbs had done with the twelve captured French soldiers and by the certainty that Serb snipers in the apartment blocks to the west of the position would open up as soon as they saw the assault.

The French camp was laid out from east to west along the river, over a distance of about fifty-five yards, with bunkers at either end. Just after 8:00 A.M., Captain François Lecointre, who had arrived in Bosnia as a peacekeeper three weeks earlier and had never expected to find himself leading a commando raid into a hail of Serb bullets, guided twenty-five French soldiers through a maze of destroyed houses leading to the eastern entrance of the emplacement. "It's against anyone's nature to rush headlong into gunfire," he told me. "But for the commander it's pride that pushes him. And for his men, it's the sight of the commander in front of them. At such a moment you cannot hesitate."

Lieutenant Bruno Heluin was at Lecointre's side. He hurled the first grenade, and the fight erupted as the French peacekeepers tried to make their way over banks of barbed wire through heavily sandbagged positions toward the first bunker at the east of the camp. Jacques Humblot, a nineteen-year-old peacekeeper, was immediately shot dead as he clambered onto a container to try to cover his advancing colleagues. Lieutenant Heluin was also hit. "One of the worst moments for me was seeing blood suddenly spurting from Heluin's head onto the sandbags," Lecointre said. "He turned his head back toward me and it was clear from his expression that he thought he was dead. He collapsed, and I took the lead."

In fact, Heluin survived. The peacekeepers pushed on. They took the first bunker on the east of the camp, where four Serbs were captured and another shot dead. They killed three more Serbs as they advanced into the central area between the bunkers on the east and west sides. At the same time, another French peacekeeper-turned-infantryman, Marcel Amaru, was killed by a bullet between the eyes as he stood in a support position near the Jewish cemetery southeast of the camp. As the peacekeepers, by now running out of ammunition, advanced toward the western bunker, they were met by a terrifying sight.

The six Serbs holding the position thrust forward two captured French peacekeepers, holding pistols to their temples. The Serbs forced the French soldiers to scream, "Don't shoot! Don't shoot or they'll kill us!" Sandahl decided to hold fire. A period of tense negotiation ensued in full view of the Serb and Bosnian snipers perched in the surrounding buildings.

The French officer immediately handed over the bodies of the two dead Serbs who were in the eastern part of the position that had been taken back by the French. "I don't make deals with the dead," Sandahl said. "It's against my ethics as a man and as an officer. But unfortunately, an odious attempt at blackmail and a revolting negotiation then began with the Serbs."

The Serbs quickly handed back one French peacekeeper, Corporal Emmanuel Guérin, in exchange for a wounded Serb. Guérin had been wounded by a Bosnian sniper, who apparently mistook the Frenchman for a Serb as he made his way to the eastern side of the camp. At this stage, the Serbs still held eleven French peacekeepers, ten of them in a nearby building and one still in the camp's western bunker. The French had four captured Serbs. As negotiations failed to progress during the day, the tone became increasingly menacing.

In the late afternoon, the Serb forces announced that they would execute two French peacekeepers at 8:30 P.M. if the four captured Serbs were not handed back. Shortly before the deadline, a French officer and a soldier were brought out of a building in Grbavica and forced by the Serbs to kneel with Kalashnikov rifles pointed at their heads. "We thought we were in the land of Pol Pot," said Sandahl, who, like Michel, had come to Bosnia with some old ideas about Serbian honor. He watched his men on their knees. A warning was issued by Gobillard, the French general commanding forces in Sarajevo, that if his men were executed, he would immediately give the order to open fire on the eastern bunker.

For fifteen minutes the Serbs kept their Kalashnikovs pointed at the two kneeling Frenchmen. Finally, as night fell, they led them back into Grbavica. That night, the six Serbs still holed up with one French peacekeeper in the western bunker slipped away, and the Frenchman was able to escape. The French thus retook all of Vrbanja camp on the morning of May 28, 1995. Two of their number died, and twelve were injured in the operation.

"For me, it was a question of honor to retake Vrbanja," Sandahl told me. "The Serbs treated us as their enemy; we did not make that choice. My mandate there was to hold a position in a no-man's-land between the two sides. If I abandoned the place, I felt I might as well go home."

SANDAHL'S SENSE OF HONOR was not unusual among the 22,500 soldiers and officers wearing the uniforms of the United Nations in Bosnia that summer. Many of these men and women adhered still to a military culture embracing the values of self-sacrifice and unswerving courage, values that drove American boys into Nazi fire and onto the Normandy beaches, values that were a guarantee and bedrock of postwar security and prosperity in Western Europe. But their sense of honor was rendered preposterous by the institution they served in Bosnia.

Even as Sandahl stood his ground, even as the French boys Humblot and Amaru were shot dead, even as mock executions were staged and ten French soldiers who had guarded Vrbanja were marched off into the twilight of the hostage's world, the leaders of the United Nations mission were plotting unseemly deals with the Serbs to try to secure the hostages' release. For Akashi and Janvier there appears never to have been any doubt that the four Serbs captured at Vrbanja should, if necessary, be part of a horse trade. Smith's view was different: the four Serbs should not be part of any deal to secure the release of United Nations hostages. Rather, they should go to the United Nations war-crimes tribunal in The Hague. They had impersonated UN officials, attacked a UN position, and killed two French UN peacekeepers. Case closed. But principle, in Bosnia, never meant anything.

The fact was that, as senior UN officials in a war zone, Akashi and Janvier had become the representatives of a consensus so wide—a coalition so weak—as to be the enemy of leadership, individual courage, and codes of honor. As Jean Baudrillard, the French sociologist, put it, they had become representatives of a post–cold war system in which "what the West now wants to impose on the whole world, under the cover of universality, is not its values, which are completely disjointed, but precisely its lack of values." In the name, he added, "of an indifferent and valueless world order."

Long after it became apparent that the "classical peacekeeping" to which they clung had become no more than a mask for appeasement of Serb butchery and braggadocio, Akashi and Janvier went on trying to be "impartial" in the interests of furthering some illusory peace process. I wanted to confront them with the parents of Humblot and Amaru; I wondered if they would be able to look them in the eye as they explained their approach to the war. Of course, Akashi and Janvier obeyed orders: what they did reflected the feckless Western governments behind them. But I believe that their consciences were clear; they themselves thought they were doing the right thing. Akashi and Janvier were endlessly briefed by their aides on Serb psychology: the suicide complex stemming from the Kosovo battle, the historical grievances, the self-delusion. But the briefings themselves became a form of delusion. Akashi and Janvier missed the most important point, one that Albright perceived but could not act on: the Serb respect for force.

It was here that America's absence from Bosnia was felt most profoundly. America still personifies the confidence necessary to draw a distinction between right and wrong and then fight for it. The European Union, in the Balkans, transparently lacked the self-belief, the unity, even perhaps the relative innocence of an unconquered state, to do so. Bill Clinton, as a candidate in 1992, noted that essential values were threatened in

Bosnia. He spoke of genocide and the dangers of sitting and watching. He suggested that he was ready to fight to stop ethnic purification. But then he shrank away under the barrage of the Pentagon's talk of Vietnam-like quagmires, the advice of Serbophilic State Department experts, and readings that comforted him with talk of ancient tribal rivalries. He committed himself instead to an effort to contain the war while distributing United Nations food—that is, to the substitution of charity for foreign policy.

The mass hostage-taking finally shook Western governments. They agreed to the dispatch of a twelve-thousand-strong Rapid Reaction Force to Bosnia, made up of soldiers from Britain, France, and the Netherlands. Instead of having aircraft trying to act as artillery, as in the absurd guidelines for "close air support," this force would provide real artillery. Akashi and Janvier were skeptical. They scurried to reassure Karadžić that the new force would make no difference to United Nations peacekeeping operations, which—after the robust "peace enforcement" at Vrbanja Bridge—would revert to classical mode. But events were overtaking even those most committed to the status quo ante. The long gridlock in Bosnia was starting to break apart under the sheer, unthinkable weight of cataclysm.

IN DETROIT, Vildana Zečević enters the last month of her pregnancy as Sarajevo lurches toward the abyss. To supplement his income, Haris works part-time with an outfit called "Door-to-Door," a home-delivery service linking various restaurants from which Haris delivers pizza and Thai food, burgers, sushi, and Chinese ribs. His Ford Probe starts to smell bad.

Every day, he is given a radio, two big insulated bags, a list of restaurants, a map, an allowance of nineteen cents a mile, and a wage of two dollars fifty cents an hour. He cruises until he gets a radio call announcing which restaurant has a meal waiting for delivery. What really counts are the tips.

He goes to one apartment and, when he walks in, feels like he has been hit over the head with a sledgehammer. A stench of sweat and confinement, a little like the makeshift hostels for refugees in Bosnia. A woman is shouting. She has opened the door through some remote control. Haris walks down the hall and when he enters the bedroom he sees her. Or rather, he sees something that "looks like the pile of sand that forms when you dump it off a truck." She must weigh over four hundred pounds. She cannot move. She is sitting up in her bed with a tray propped in front of her full of magazines and books and cosmetics. Haris wonders how she maneuvered herself into that sitting position. He delivers three packages of burgers to her and two Diet Cokes.

On another occasion Haris finds himself in a mansion with a pool and a lot of naked girls running around. The owner decides to check everything in a seventy-dollar order. She asks him to identify each dish. Then she gives him a forty-one-cent tip. Haris asks if there is anything wrong with the service. She say no, everything is fine. So he asks why he is being given such a lousy tip. And she says he has no right to ask such a question. Haris says he does have the right because he lives from the tips. And she says, Sorry, I don't have any more. So he hands her back the forty-one cents and says, "You must need this more than I do."

The woman is furious and calls the dispatcher at Door-to-Door. Haris is firmly reprimanded. He is told to remember and repeat to himself a basic precept in American business: The customer is always right.

On June 2, 1995, as the shells crash again into Sarajevo just as they did in the summer of 1992, Vildana goes into labor. Haris takes her to the Royal Oak Hospital in the Detroit suburb of that name. The birth goes smoothly and Haris gets blind drunk. He has worried constantly; now, for a moment, he is happy.

It is very difficult to place a call to Sarajevo. Haris tries repeatedly. At his Sarajevo home, exhausted depression has taken hold as the war has intensified once more. Fida has not heard from her daughters in Belgrade for months. Asim is determined to visit Haris in Detroit, but is worried about how he will get out of the city and how he will secure the necessary papers. Their eighty-three-year-old mother Hasnja thinks Haris should come home, but Asim says he should stay in America. Every day, skirting sniper fire, he trudges to his dentist's office and gazes from the window at Trebević Mountain, where Muris died. One day a shell lands within yards of him. Two women, standing farther from the point of impact than he, are killed, but Asim walks away unscathed. For the first time in this war, he thinks, I have been lucky.

There is still no electricity in Sarajevo. The telephone rings in complete darkness. Fida stumbles toward it. Then Asim hears her screaming for joy. He says to his sister, "You don't need a phone, they can hear you in America." He gropes his way toward the phone and Haris says, "Dad, you've got a grandson."

Asim tries to sit down but the chair falls over and he lands on the floor on top of his mother who is also trying to reach the phone in the darkness. She injures her leg, Asim his back. Hasnja hears her great-grandson's voice on the phone and cries. For once the tears of Sarajevo are tears of joy.

The boy is an American citizen. Haris and Vildana have no hesitation about his name. They call the boy Muris Zečević.

CHAPTER 29

SARAJEVO
ABANDONED

As the heat rises that summer in Sarajevo, so does the sense of suffocation. Mihaljo Milašević, a doctor specializing in prosthetics, is finding it hard to breathe. Since the war began, he has attached about 850 artificial arms and legs. As he speaks, he distractedly grabs a metal knee and starts bending and straightening it. The metal in his hands is hard and cold, the movement stiff, so unlike the human form.

It is the narrowness of the ideas that bred the war that he cannot accept, the notion that a girl from one garden cannot fall in love with a boy from another garden. In the name of such an idea so many young people have already died in Bosnia. The most difficult operation, he says, is also technically the easiest: amputation. He is finding it harder and harder to cut off another young person's leg. He poses the knee, in a bent position, on the table and looks me in the eye and says, "We can't even breathe anymore. We've been waiting for three years and now I feel that even my brain is blocked. I am from Montenegro. I am Orthodox. I came here fifteen years ago and I married a Catholic. My brother is married to a Muslim. In Bosnia, how many marriages are mixed? And Karadžić comes from my Montenegro and tells us we cannot live together anymore here in Bosnia. And it goes on and on, this madness. We are dying all the time. People are being killed or maimed each day by shelling. If we don't try to open the city we are condemned to die."

Milašević raises his hands to his neck in a by-now familiar gesture of self-strangulation. He is a true Sarajevan. Even as the politics of Bosnia become uglier, and Izetbegović's SDA party more repressive, the city is still full of buildings where Muslims, Serbs, and Croats live together. The war washes over them. In the end, for many of these people, as for Milašević, life's equation is relatively simple: a family, their town, and nowhere to go. Sarajevo was never Serbian, not even at the height of Dušan's medieval em-

pire. There had been Serbs here for centuries, but never did the nationalists who took on the Ottoman and then Austro-Hungarian empires dream
of turning this city at the crossroads of East and West into an ethnically
pure Serbian preserve.

That dream is Karadžić's and it kills. What is it like to die in Sarajevo,
a victim of such an idea? Perhaps, some people think in that summer of
1995, it is a reward. They have lost any volition: the world has none, why
should they? It is all right to be killed; the horror is to be maimed.

They roll the dice. One woman walks with a limp after being hit by a
shell that did not explode. What are the odds of that? I walk with a friend.
The sky is very blue, the city very empty. We are in the old city, Baščaršija,
where rivers and mountains and religions converge, where the valley is narrow and time whispers in the alleys. There are two old men sitting on old
stones. One says, "It's simple: we have to fight or die." And the other says,
"You should be from this town and then you would know what it is to love
it." And the first one says, "I'm OK because I have to be OK. Otherwise
I'll die. And I don't want to die."

We walk on. How silent is this hush of an empty cage! I look up at the
mountains. And then the town moves, the air is hot and vibrates, the
ground shakes, and there is a smashing sound that seems to lift me off my
feet. This is what it is like to die in Sarajevo. It is sudden, it is loud, it is insignificant.

I find myself with you beneath an old Turkish portal. Breath comes in
gasps. A boy on a bicycle crashes into the space beside us. Things slowly
become clearer. The air quiets again. It is cool beneath the portal. There is
no blood. Limbs, entire, move. The shell must have impacted a few yards
away, in the next alley perhaps. The instinct is to run. But to run may be
to rush toward the next shell. The shells come in pairs. Sometimes. The
first shell is merely to "zero in"; then comes the intense fire. So they say. I
run anyway. There is no knowing and it feels better to run than to be still.

HAVDA SADIKOVIĆ-ĆOSO is terribly afraid of the shelling. Her neighbor recently lost a child to a mortar. Havda has a well in her yard. People
come to gather water and when they stand there in a line with their containers all she can think about is that a shell might land at that moment.
The sight of a drop of human blood is enough to make her cry. But animals, she says, are a different matter. Havda thinks they have saved her
from the war.

She has gone into the egg business. In a hut in her small garden she
keeps ninety-nine chickens. The chickens are Slovenian. She brought
them on her back through the tunnel under the airport. They produce

about 630 eggs a week; she earns ten German marks for every 30 eggs. She also has rabbits. Once she had one hundred rabbits, but now she has only twenty. When the shelling starts, the chickens and the rabbits have different reactions. The chickens start clucking wildly, whereas the rabbits hunch up and go very quiet. Like the people of Sarajevo, the manic and the withdrawn.

Havda never believed that she could kill a rabbit. But one day in 1994, she was very hungry; she took a rabbit by the ears and whirled him around. As if preparing to hurl a discus, she spins about, showing me what she did with the rabbit. I watch her turn, a spinning berserk woman in a madhouse with a big mountain behind her.

Then, she explains, she hit the rabbit on the head with a piece of timber. He lost consciousness and she slit his throat. "Grass is grass and meat is meat," she tells me.

"When I ate that rabbit, it was so good," she says. So good, in fact, that killing rabbits became easy. She slit the throats of countless rabbits. She shows me her two fattest rabbits. One is called Rasim Delić, after the bulky commander of the Bosnian army. The other is called Mike Tyson. Why, she asks me, is the American president not as tough as Tyson?

I think about trying to explain Bosnia as seen from Washington. But I have lost the ability. On June 5, 1995, a few days before meeting Havda, I had been able, thanks to a surge of electricity at the Sarajevo Holiday Inn, to watch Vice President Al Gore tell Larry King about Bosnia.

"This is a tragedy that has been unfolding for some time," Gore said. "Some would say for five hundred years. But certainly it was a full-blown tragedy before we ever got here. But I think that it's important to realize that NATO, the most successful alliance in history, never really did that great a job when it was outside of the NATO area, dealing with a conflict between two countries, neither of whom was a part of NATO."

I tried to sort out what poor Gore was saying. This "tragedy"—a morally neutral word laden with the weight of inevitability—had been going on since the year 1495. It became "full-blown" before the Clinton administration took office in early 1993. This much I could follow, albeit with some distaste. As for NATO, the "great job" it did was precisely *outside* the territory of its members, where its credible deterrence prevented anyone in Moscow or elsewhere behind the Iron Curtain from embarking on the military conquest of Western Europe. But "this most successful alliance in history" was incapable of deterring or arresting the dismemberment of Bosnia.

At this point, the president weighed in. His summary of the Bosnian war also took up the well-worn theme of its almost prehistoric origins.

"But remember," Clinton said, "how long has this war been going on? Since 1991, in essence. That's four years. It's tragic, it's terrible. But their enmities go back five hundred years, some would say almost a thousand years." Quick arithmetic yielded the astonishing fact that the Bosnian conflict, according to Clinton, had been in progress since about the year 995!

I had come to an understanding of the fact that a truthful description of a situation deemed intractable is incompatible with a fundamental political exigency: the need to appear in control. The main aim of Western governments, for a long time, had been to make the facts obscure in order to justify inaction. In this sense, the president's statement was consistent with policy: a conflict that had been going on for a millennium was obviously so deep-rooted there was no sense in America trying to do much about it.

The next day, I looked for some evidence of the improvement in the situation that the president had evoked. There was an old woman bent double tending some lettuces on the edge of what used to be the Holiday Inn parking lot and was now an expanse of weeds. There was that colossal hole on the main street outside the hotel where the Serb rocket had recently embedded itself. There was the tramless tram track, the trainless station, the lightless traffic lights, the motionless clocks, and the endless siege. There was also sniping on the central Marshal Tito Avenue, where I stumbled on a hero of the war, John Jordan, a fireman from Rhode Island.

As head of Global Operations Fire and Rescue Service, an agency working for the United Nations, Jordan had been in Bosnia since early in the war. His job, as he put it, was to "get the wet stuff on the red stuff." But he had come to a blunt understanding of the war as he crisscrossed Sarajevo putting out fires.

Now he gazes at an eerie scene: a white Volkswagen Golf in the middle of the road, its windshield shattered by a sniper's bullet. Nearby, a few frightened Sarajevans huddling behind a French armored personnel carrier as it began its slow shuttle service back and forth across the street, covering the pedestrians from sniper fire.

"This is OK," Jordan says. "What just happened here is OK. It's OK with the folks in Washington and London and Paris. I heard Clinton saying there were fewer victims in 1994 than in 1992. It's like the Colosseum in Rome. In the first two hours the lions ate a lot of Christians. In the second two hours there were not as many to be eaten. Fewer people died because there were fewer to be killed. The villages have been ethnically cleansed, so who's left to kill?"

A few days earlier, Jordan picked a girl up off the street with a bullet in her back. He looked up, through the scope of his high-powered rifle, to a building where the fire originated. He saw the sniper. "But you know what our rules of engagement are," he says. "If he'd put his gun to his shoulder, and only then, I could have done something. Total insanity!"

Jordan, a big man whose girth spread confidence, is in a state of deep disappointment with his country. "I think it's a joke. I tell you, this has been a real eye-opener in terms of what America stands for. My father came over in World War II. He was at Omaha Beach, he was captured and escaped. We were ready to fight then. But this is a European city with a dirt trench around it and men with guns killing children on a regular basis and that's OK. A couple of middle-aged men have rolled out old ghosts and set children against each other. This is no civil war; this is Milošević's crime. The Serbs are a world power today, and that's OK. What they say goes because there's no leadership. What Clinton has to learn is that there is only one way to lead and that is with everyone else looking at your back."

THROUGHOUT THE FIRST HALF of June 1995, a demeaning diplomatic minuet was played around the fate of the United Nations hostages held by Karadžić and Mladić. The leadership Jordan craved was absent. Instead, the powerlessness of the Western world before a ragtag group of Serb separatists using terrorist methods to further their aims was revealed more shockingly than ever. The official position in Western capitals was that the hostages should be "unconditionally released." The corollary of this position was no negotiation. In reality, a series of secret meetings were held with the Serbs; negotiation was almost continuous.

The last ounce of Western credibility was thus ceded, opening the way for the Serb conquest of the eastern enclave of Srebrenica in July and the massacre of Muslims there. Srebrenica was a death foretold. It was preceded by the contemptuous Serb elimination in June of the last velleity of NATO protection of Sarajevo, the city at the heart of the war. If Sarajevo could not be defended, what chance was there for a small village in a gorge in eastern Bosnia? Western failure was consummated the way it began during the summer of 1992, by tolerance of the intolerable and by the absence of any readiness to defend the Bosnian idea with force.

A split emerged between Smith's UN command in Sarajevo and UN headquarters in Zagreb. After the hostages were seized, Smith had one conversation with Mladić, on May 28. He told the Bosnian Serb leader he was behaving like a terrorist; Mladić told Smith to take some tranquilizers. Smith then dealt with the Serbs only on what he called a "notification basis."

In Zagreb, Smith's superiors, Akashi and Janvier, adopted a different course: public firmness and private pliancy. A transcript of a meeting of Akashi, Janvier, and Smith in the Croatian port city of Split, on June 9, is revealing. Akashi opened proceedings by declaring to Smith, "One of the main issues will be the negotiations with the Bosnian Serbs. I understand why you have taken the position of no negotiation with the Serbs until all the hostages are released. However Zagreb and New York believe that some discussions should take place—but this is not contradictory. We can have firmness on the ground while exploiting opportunities to talk with political and military leaders."

Not contradictory! At the time that Akashi spoke, Western politicians were insisting that there would be no negotiation with the Serbs as long as the hostages—from France, Britain, Canada, and several other countries—were held. Mladić's position in the secret negotiations was in fact the only one that was entirely coherent and transparent: the hostages would not be released until he received what he called "security guarantees"—that is, a commitment from Western governments that NATO air power would not be used again against the Serbs.

By the time the Split meeting was held, measures had already been taken to render use of NATO air power extremely unlikely. On May 27, the day after the second air strike against Pale, the United Nations secretary-general Boutros Boutros-Ghali withdrew from Akashi the authority to call for air strikes. He informed Akashi that, in the light of the far-reaching repercussions of air action, UNPROFOR should seek the secretary-general's guidance first.

This insistence clearly reflected the position of the French and British governments after their peacekeepers had been taken hostage. The French, with 6,900 troops, and the British, with 4,000, had the largest, most influential contingents in Bosnia. Chirac, the new French president, enjoyed a particularly close relationship with the French-speaking Boutros-Ghali. He called him regularly. It was thus in France's interest to have the right to "turn the key"—which had been delegated to Akashi on November 19, 1994—returned to the secretary-general in New York. On May 29, Janvier, who always looked to Paris as much as New York for his instructions, issued new and highly restrictive guidelines for air action, saying it should be used only as a last resort and stating that *the security of United Nations personnel took priority over UNPROFOR's mandate in Bosnia.* This last order amounted to a perversion of military doctrine: instead of the "mission" taking precedence over an individual's life, the mission was to be secondary. The consequences of such a perversion were grave, for how could Western governments proclaim that Sarajevo or Srebrenica were "safe areas" when they were not prepared, as a last resort, to sacrifice lives to save them?

Four days later, further obstacles to the use of air power emerged. On June 2, the day the Serbs released a first batch of 121 hostages, an American F-16 fighter piloted by Scott O'Grady was shot down by a Serb SAM-6 surface-to-air missile. The flight was part of NATO's two-year-old mission to stop flights by the rival armies in Bosnian skies. O'Grady survived, hiding for several days in the woods before being rescued; he became an American hero. Clinton and Lake toasted him in the White House; America, having failed to commit troops to stop an act of genocide, rejoiced, taking delirious pride in not having lost one of its finest to the Balkan savages; O'Grady got a book contract. Meanwhile, NATO imposed new safety standards requiring a host of support aircraft for any mission in Bosnia. The Serb seizure of hostages and the Serb downing of an American plane—acts committed with impunity—combined to strengthen the Serb position.

On June 4, Janvier held the first of his secret meetings with Mladić in Zvornik, the town on Bosnia's border with Serbia where some of the most savage acts of "ethnic cleansing" took place in April 1992. The commander of the Serbian-dominated Yugoslav army, Momčilo Perišić, was also present, confirming that old chains of command between Belgrade and Pale had not been broken by personal differences between Milošević and Karadžić.

The meeting, in itself, was a humiliation for the Western governments whose men were being held hostage, an affront to the honor of the French dead at Vrbanja Bridge. Mladić proposed a deal: the release of the remaining hostages in exchange for a commitment that there would be no more air strikes. Janvier recorded Mladić as requesting that "UNPROFOR commits to no longer make use of any force which leads to the use of air strikes against targets and territories of the Republika Srpska."

It appears that there was no signing of any such formal accord. At the June 9 meeting in Split, five days later, Akashi said that the "hostages' release will become harder unless the Serbs get assurances of no further NATO air strikes, which is impossible." But private, implicit understandings were a different matter. Such an understanding on a severe restriction of air strikes—to the point where it was almost inconceivable that they would happen—does seem to have been reached. Janvier, in the words of one official close to him, "got religion—he believed the line, no air power, and he gave an implicit agreement to the Serbs on that." Janvier was not the kind of soldier to take such a step on his own initiative. He wore the United Nations uniform, but as a French soldier, his commander-in-chief was the French president, Chirac, who, throughout the hostage crisis, was in regular telephone contact with Milošević, the man paying Mladić's salary. On June 19, 1995, after a meeting with Milošević in Belgrade, Akashi sent a cable to Kofi Annan in New York, in which he noted: "In the course of our discussions on air power, Milošević *stated that he had been advised by President Chirac of President Clinton's agreement that air strikes should not occur if unacceptable to Chirac.*"

Chirac called Milošević at least three times during the hostage crisis, and it was the Serbian leader who took charge of negotiations for the hostages' release. Whatever the difference of view between Milošević and Karadžić on how to end the war, Belgrade was always the ultimate source of Serb power in Bosnia. It was Chirac, too, who dispatched his own personal envoy, General Bertrand de Lapresle, from Paris to Pale on June 6, for another secret meeting with the Serbs that was followed by the release of a further 111 hostages.

Later, during the Serb capture of Srebrenica, when several requests for air action from beleaguered Dutch United Nations troops were blocked by Janvier, Annan noted that Chirac was repeatedly on the phone with Boutros-Ghali. Finally, Annan, who was aware of insistent reports that Boutros-Ghali had an understanding with Chirac that there would be no more air strikes without the French president's permission, confronted the secretary-general on this question. Boutros-Ghali declined to confirm or deny the reports. He remained silent before the questioning of his undersecretary-general for peacekeeping operations.

The effective neutralizing under Serb duress of NATO air power, the one Western deterrent in Bosnia, thus seems to have hinged on a parallel understanding forged between Chirac and Milošević, and Chirac and Boutros-Ghali, and conveyed to the Bosnian Serbs by Janvier and de Lapresle. This was enough to secure the hostages' release. Such an approach entirely suited the temperaments of Akashi and Janvier, the two men running United Nations operations in Zagreb. In their defense they can claim that they were servants of higher powers, but their own aversion to force in Bosnia helped shape policy. Even in a bureaucracy as paralyzed as that constructed around Western fecklessness in Bosnia, personal initiative can make a difference. Akashi and Janvier had no use for force. The consequences for the male population of Srebrenica were dire. The transcript of the June 9 meeting in Split once again provides disturbing evidence.

SMITH'S POSITION at the meeting is clear. Indeed, in his opening remarks he foresees the disaster at Srebrenica that will inevitably follow from allowing the Serbs to call the shots. "To all intents and purposes we have been neutralized. The exclusion zones and weapons collection points are ignored; the safe areas are under increasing threat." He adds, "The Serbs continue to squeeze us and I do not believe that they want a cease-fire. I believe that they want to continue to remove UNPROFOR from their affairs and continue to neutralize NATO. This analysis is supported by the facts. Being more speculative, I believe that the Bosnian Serb army will continue to engage the international community to show that they cannot be controlled; this will lead to a further squeezing of Sarajevo or an attack in the eastern enclaves, creating a crisis that short of air attacks we will have a great difficulty responding to." Such an attack on the eastern enclaves is likely because, Smith says, "I remain convinced that the Serbs want to conclude this year and will take every risk to accomplish this."

For Smith, it has become evident that Mladić will only respond to force. The British general wants to be able to use the planned reinforcements— the new Rapid Reaction Force—to fight, perhaps to open corridors to the enclaves. "Mladić won't treat us as an enemy as long as we do everything on his terms," he says. "If we try to do our job our way, then we are his enemy and he will treat us that way. If we bring in force behind us, he will make concessions, but if we do things on his terms he will succeed in neutralizing us."

The approach of Janvier, Smith's commander, is diametrically opposed. The French general has learned nothing from the hostage-taking or the horror of Vrbanja Bridge. He believes that the distance of Zagreb gives him perspective, whereas the commanders in Sarajevo have gone native. In fact it is Janvier who invites horror by acquiescing to crime and forgetting that soldiering is not a matter of paper-shuffling.

Janvier favors every concession to the Serbs; he sees no place for force. "The Serbs," he says, "need two things: international recognition and a softening of the blockade on the Drina. I hope that these conditions will be quickly met." He goes on: "I insist that we will never have the possibility of combat, of imposing our will on the Serbs. The only way to go is through political negotiations—that is the only way we can fulfill our mandate." He is personally in favor of abandoning Srebrenica and the other eastern Muslim enclaves—"It is the most realistic approach"—but concedes that the "international community" cannot accept this. He scoffs at Smith's notion of opening corridors to the enclaves, or to Sarajevo, by force. And he favors negotiation with the Serbs on the hostages, trying lamely to dress this approach up in dignified terms: "We do not negotiate, but we discuss with them, demonstrate to them the situation, enlighten them on a path that might be followed."

Akashi's position is close to that of Janvier, without being so abject. He is still desperately worried about crossing Rose's "Mogadishu line." When Smith says, "We are already over the Mogadishu line; the Serbs do not view us as peacekeepers," Akashi asks, "Can we return back over the line?" He concludes with his mantra: "As peacekeepers, we must talk to all parties; the small gains that we achieve from doing so are better than the losses from the combative approach."

Toward the end of the three-hour meeting, a brisk exchange between Smith and Janvier points to the disasters at Sarajevo and Srebrenica that are about to be consummated.

> SMITH: *The situation with the exclusion zones, safe areas and weapons-collection point is very disconcerting. I see them as the next series of major problems that we will face. There may be crises in these areas before the Reaction Force is available. I anticipate actions that will lead our political masters by the nose. I can easily see a situation arising where we will be forced to request air power.*
>
> JANVIER: *It is just for this that we must establish contact with the Serbs, to show, explain to them that there are some things that they cannot do.*
>
> SMITH: *My judgment is that they will not listen.*
>
> JANVIER: *I have a different approach. Once again the Serbs are in a very favorable political position, and that is something they will not want to compromise. The external political situation is such that the Serbs will come to understand the benefits of cooperation. Unless there is a major provocation from the Bosnian army, the Serbs will not act.*

This conversation took place exactly one month before the fall of Srebrenica. It would have been as well if a copy of the transcript had been provided to Lieutenant Colonel Ton Karremans, the Dutch commander of United Nations forces in Srebrenica. For Karremans, commanding demoralized troops in an isolated enclave, would then have understood that Janvier, his overall commander and the ineluctable conduit to any air support, never believed that the Serbs could attack and overrun a "safe area," let alone massacre its inhabitants. On the contrary, Janvier believed, even after more than three years of evidence to the contrary, including an archipelago of concentration camps in 1992, that he would be able to explain to the Serbs that "there are some things that they cannot do." He believed that the Serbs understood "the benefits of cooperation," even when cooperation was unnecessary because they could impose their will. He believed, in short, that Karadžić and Mladić could be guided by, of all things, reason, and that, in any event, force could not be used to bring such myth-driven murderers to their senses. Karremans, knowing all this, might have saved lives by not wasting his time with repeated requests for NATO air attacks at Srebrenica that never came.

The Split meeting ended with a declaration that UNPROFOR "will strictly abide by peacekeeping principles." Janvier's position had triumphed. Classical peacekeeping principles did not include peace enforcement, that is to say the potential use of air strikes.

• • •

ON JUNE 18, after another meeting between Janvier and Mladić in Pale, the last twenty-six peacekeepers held hostage by the Serbs were released. At the same time, the United Nations forces were allowed to withdraw ninety-one peacekeepers from weapons-collection sites around Sarajevo where they had been surrounded by the Serbs since May 26. Their withdrawal back into the city constituted the formal collapse of the combined effort by NATO and the UN to police or remove heavy weapons from the Sarajevo area.

"The policy of weapons-collection points has now been abandoned," said Chris Gunness, a United Nations spokesman in Zagreb, referring to the ten sites established by the NATO ultimatum of February 1994 for the collection of tanks, artillery, and big guns within 12.4 miles of Sarajevo.

The defeat for the West, and what was still irritatingly called Western values, was enormous. By taking hostages and by threatening to kill them in what Karadžić called a "butcher's shop," the Serbs had secured complete freedom to bombard Sarajevo again at will and an understanding that air strikes were anathema. NATO, having stood up to Moscow, had been humbled by a tinpot self-styled republic headquartered in a Balkan skiing village, a place where irate Serbs grabbed United Nations vehicles because their flocks of sheep had suffered in the brief bombing.

As if to underscore the extent of the debacle, a Serb shell slammed into the Sarajevo suburb of Dobrinja that day, killing seven people and wounding ten others, mostly elderly people waiting in line for water. I went down to the scene and watched the terror on the faces of middle-aged women hurrying through streets raw with fear.

On the same day, I saw one of the French UN soldiers who had just withdrawn from a weapons-collection site in Serb-held Ilidža. His name was Lieutenant Gilles Jarron, a member of the French Foreign Legion. His ordeal had started on May 27, when about eighty Serbs wearing T-shirts, camouflage pants, earrings, and bandannas appeared armed with rocket-propelled grenades. They installed a T-55 tank at a distance of seventy yards and told Jarron and twelve fellow legionnaires to hand over the weaponry they guarded under the light blue flag of the United Nations. A single step on the tank pedal stood between the legionnaires and obliteration.

Jarron's last order from his commander, Colonel Jean-Louis Franceschini, was, "From now on you make the Serbs pay dearly for the lives of each of your men." Jarron deployed his men for battle and waited. They had only one heavy weapon. Each of them was ready to die in the name of his United Nations mission. Every night, they read the legionnaire's code to one another: "In combat, you act without passion and without hatred.

You respect the defeated enemy, you never abandon your dead, your injured or your arms. . . . The mission is sacred and you carry it out to the end, at any price."

In the end, the Serbs never attacked. Jarron and his men held their position. Jarron told me, "We would have defended our position and we all would have died." But Jarron's bravery had been mocked by Janvier's negotiations with Mladić. The young French soldier and his legionnaires would have died for their honor under that UN flag even as their commander in Zagreb betrayed them.

This fact was driven home by the release of the four Serb prisoners taken at the battle of Vrbanja Bridge on the same day as the last Western hostages were freed. Alexander Ivanko, a spokesman for Smith in Sarajevo, was told by officials in Zagreb to reply to any questions by saying that the freeing of the four Serbs on the same day as the twenty-six United Nations hostages was "a coincidence"! Ivanko, who has a healthy Russian sense of humor, burst out laughing.

An official United Nations statement said that the capture of the four men had led to a long investigation that had concluded that there was "no further basis to detain the Serbs." Were it not for the killing of Humblot and Amaru at Vrbanja Bridge, the use of United Nations uniforms as a disguise, and the direct attack on the United Nations emplacement at Vrbanja, this statement might have been slightly less grotesque.

A day later, June 19, Akashi wrote an obsequious letter to Karadžić, whom he customarily addressed as "Your Excellency," assuring the Bosnian Serb leader that the Rapid Reaction Force would make no difference at all. Its arrival in Bosnia, he said, was due to "a marked lack of respect by all sides for the security, safety, and freedom of movement of United Nations personnel." Thus the Serbs' seizure of hostages was no longer the principal reason for the dispatch of reinforcements! The impartial approach required, even at this stage, that some blame be apportioned to the Bosnian army. Moreover, Akashi wrote, the new force would "not in any way change the essential peacekeeping nature" of the mission.

This was one of those moments in the war when truth, justice, and honor were most visibly mocked. The very ideas seemed risible in Sarajevo, where Western diplomacy had become synonymous with farce. On a planet made global, at least for money, a city regularly on television screens was somehow invisible. For if it were truly visible, would somebody not rise up against the buffoons?

TWO DAYS BEFORE the release of the last hostages, the Sarajevo dawn was shaken by the repeated thud of tank fire and the clatter of heavy machine guns. For days there had been insistent talk of an imminent Bos-

nian army offensive. The road over Mount Igman had been closed and
Bosnian army units from Tuzla and Zenica moved to the Sarajevo area. As
plumes of smoke rose into the summer air, I watched one Bosnian unit
battle its way up Mount Trebević to the road between Pale and the Serb
barracks in Lukavica. This, three years on, was the very battle that Muris
Zečević had fought and for which he had given his life. A Bosnian platoon
reached the road, stayed there for a day, and then, inexplicably, withdrew.
Circles within circles, drawn in blood.

The main thrust of the Bosnian attack was northward toward Vogošća,
but there was also a push south and west. For two days it appeared that the
offensive might, as Izetbegović had promised, ease or end the siege of the
capital. But the government's nominal Croat allies did nothing to help,
and, in any event, the attack quickly evaporated. Silajdžić described it to
me as "a limited operation aimed at stopping a Serb assault on Sarajevo."

Given the elaborate preparations and substantial loss of life, this was a
preposterous statement, one that gave me a by-now familiar queasy feeling
that this government was capable of toying with young people's lives.
Enough of a military push to sustain morale, but not enough to change
the situation or threaten the interests vested in the status quo.

I gave a ride to one Bosnian soldier heading for a front south of the city
on Treskavica Mountain. He had been involved in the attack on Vogošća
and fear was still embedded in his features, a gray shadow like a cancer.
There were hundreds of dead, he said. Certainly, the UN headquarters in
Sarajevo received requests for hundreds of body bags in the days after the
offensive began.

The Bosnian government never gave any indication of the number of
casualties, so the truth may never be known, but I suspect that over one
thousand young Bosnians, if not many more, were killed during those
June days. Nothing tangible was achieved. In another fruitless Bosnian
government attack, on the Majevica Hills near Tuzla three months earlier,
I discovered, through a doctor who was working at the front, that 984
Bosnian soldiers were killed and 1,656 injured. The doctor described the
offensive as "the stupidest and most tragic thing I have ever seen." Dead
and injured were pouring into a field hospital. Many had shot themselves
in the arm or calf to avoid advancing. Anything was better than being
thrown forward against the Serb artillery. The attack had begun on a warm
day, but for the next four days it snowed. The front-line soldiers were marooned in the positions taken on the first day, without food and without
accurate artillery support. In the end, they were picked off by Serb gunners.

The Bosnian army was a remarkable force, thrown together amid the
persecution that provided its backbone. It fought and won unwinnable

battles around Bihać and elsewhere; it stopped the Serbs in their tracks after the 1992 onslaught that gave Karadžić's forces 70 percent of Bosnia. Equally, however, there were several fiascos, like the Sarajevo offensive.

The army was, moreover, the inevitable focus of a debate that intensified during the war as to what the Bosnian state should be: multi-ethnic and secular, or Muslim and religious. What goal, in other words, was this army fighting for in 1995, at Sarajevo or on the hills of northeastern Bosnia?

An open dispute had broken out within the seven-member Bosnian presidency on this very question in February 1995. The two Croat members of the presidency, Stjepan Kljuić and Ivo Komšić, and the two Serbs, Mirko Pejanović and Tatjana Ljuić-Mijatović, joined by a secular Muslim, Nijaz Duraković, said in an open letter that they were "not responsible for the ideological exploitation and negative manipulation of religion in some Bosnian army units." They were referring to the fact that a growing number of army units were using Islamic symbols, quotations from the Koran, and other religious insignia alongside the fleur-de-lis national symbol of Bosnia. In that many of these units were made up of refugees who had been driven from their homes by Serbs precisely because they were Muslims, this growing religious identification was understandable. Nevertheless, it was troubling to the Serbs and Croats in the Bosnian army.

In Zenica, in central Bosnia, several hundred mujahedin, self-styled holy warriors, had formed a unit within the III Corps of the army. A spokesman, Spahija Kozlić, told me they were "doing their jobs in a normal way and are an integrated part of our corps." But there appeared to be little that was "normal" at the yellow house beside Tito's gargantuan steel factory in Zenica, where the mujahedin were based. One of them took aim with a Kalashnikov when my car approached; Croats living in surrounding areas complained of continuous harassment, including instructions that lights could not be used on Christmas trees. A British United Nations liaison officer, who had regular dealings with III Corps, had been told that the Bosnian army was under instructions from the Bosnian government to tolerate the mujahedin "because of the money pouring in from Iran and other fundamentalist countries."

Naturally, in Western European capitals, the mujahedin were pointed to as evidence of the "fundamentalism" prevalent in Bosnia. The unstated suggestion was that the Serbs were justified in going to war in 1992. The inexcusable passivity of America and its allies before what the Serbs did in 1992 was thereby exonerated.

It was evident, by 1995, that the war had indeed done its dismal work, etching ethnic lines across Bosnian communities that had seemed structurally impervious to such division, creating extremism where none had existed. Driven by genocide to fight for their lives, the Bosnian Muslims had become more Muslim, discovering an identity that had been vague or absent. Deprived of other help, the Muslims had turned to Iran. Izetbegović's SDA party had not hesitated to encourage such trends, turning the party into an almost ineluctable purveyor of jobs, influence, and power. Many Serbs and Croats, particularly in Sarajevo, were alienated by these developments, and those in the army wondered for what, if anything, they now fought. Their dismay was understandable.

Yet not even Bosnia's authoritarian and Islamic lurch could change the fact that some vestige of civilization and tolerance remained on Izetbegović's side of the lines while it was entirely absent from Karadžić's; the Muslims of Bosnia did not repay in kind what was done to them. Nor could the fact be hidden that when the West criticized "fundamentalists," it was criticizing what was, largely, its own creation. For if the war had not been allowed to fester, if the concentration camps and genocide of 1992 had not been tolerated, if force had been met by force rather than food, the extremist and repressive Islamic tendencies in Bosnia would have been unable to take root in the way that they had by that summer of 1995. Prejudice, thinly veiled, marked Europe's response to the killing of Muslims in Bosnia, and prejudice was always a form of self-fulfilling prophecy. The mujahedin represented the fulfillment of the West's prophecy for Bosnia, the fruit of its renunciation.

THAT RENUNCIATION ALSO LED to the rehabilitation of Milošević and his cronies. Milošević's chief envoy to Pale during the negotiations for the hostages' release had been none other than Jovica Stanišić, the head of the Serbian secret police and the man who orchestrated the financing, arming, and dispatching of the paramilitary groups that helped tear Bosnia to shreds in 1992.

Yet there Stanišić was, in his suit and tie, being politely questioned by journalists and feted for his hard work in helping the hostages to freedom. As I watched the television footage of Stanišić, I was struck again by how the events of just three years earlier had taken on the aura of ancient history. Stanišić had done as much as anyone to contribute to the butchering of Bosnia's Muslims, but who remembered that?

I had been given a detailed account of Stanišić's role by Čedomir Mihailović, a Serbian defector, small-time crook, and wheeler-dealer who had worked with the Serbian secret police. Mihailović, when I met him in early 1995, was living in Holland in an apartment provided to him by the Dutch secret services. The apartment had a German telephone number in

order to confuse any callers, and Mihailović was being worked by the
Dutch after being passed on to them by the International War Crimes Tribunal in The Hague.

Mihailović had documents that clearly incriminated Stanišić and,
through him, Milošević; they included instructions from the Serbian security services on the running of the concentration camps of 1992. The
tribunal judged that the documents were inauthentic. Its spokesman
vowed to me that the originals had been returned to Mihailović, but later
conceded, with some embarrassment, that this was not true. The Dutch
government had the originals.

Alexander Vershbow, Clinton's top national security official on European affairs, showed photocopies of the documents to the CIA and
checked Mihailović's credentials. "We're not sure about the documents,"
Vershbow told me, "but what we do know is that this guy was clearly in a
position to know this information." Mihailović was later granted an
American visa and came to the United States, where he engaged in various
fraudulent business deals.

In a series of interviews, Mihailović told me how Stanišić's state security
services at the Serb Interior Ministry—or MUP—provided money, weapons, and equipment to the paramilitary killers of Arkan and Vojislav
Šešelj's Serbian Chetnik movement. He described how, starting in 1991,
he had set up front companies in Cyprus for the laundering of money and
for the purchase of arms, ammunition, telecommunications equipment,
and spare parts for radios. He described how aluminum ore from Dukić's
bauxite mines at Milići had been sold for over thirty million dollars to
Russia and Greece. He talked about repeated visits to Mount Tara, near
Bajina Bašta, on the Serbian border with Bosnia, where he installed communications equipment at a vast training camp for the paramilitary forces.
He talked about his meetings there with "Frenki"—Franko Simatović—
one of Stanišić's agents and the commander of a special forces unit. He also
mentioned Branislav Vakić as one of the leading paramilitary operatives.

"Milošević used the paramilitary groups because he did not want to be
directly involved," Mihailović said. "He wanted the minimum of people
to know and the security services were his hand-picked apparatus. Arkan
worked for them before the war. Stanišić and Milošević would talk daily.
They approved and organized the establishment of the Dafiment Bank
and the other pyramid schemes that bilked the people of Serbia of more
than two billion German marks to finance the war. They recruited thousands of people to fight with a simple message: Take whatever booty you
can in Bosnia."

A year after this conversation, Julian Borger of *The Guardian* found
Branislav Vakić. His account of the organization of Milošević's wars and

of Stanišić's central role in the killing coincided almost exactly with Mihailović's. The apparatus within the Serbian Interior Ministry dedicated to the wars in Croatia and Bosnia was called the *vojna linija* or "military line," Borger discovered. Military policy, in this case, meant the wholesale release of criminals from Serbian jails to do the dirty work in Bosnia. Nobody ever said agents were nice guys; Mihailović bilked plenty of people in his time, but he knew the inner workings of the war. Western governments, including America, knew them too. But Milošević and Stanišić were more useful as interlocutors than indicted criminals.

THE WEST'S LONG FAILURE led to the erosion of Bosnia's middle ground, but the dignity of Sarajevo, and the hope vested there, never died entirely. I would walk with Asim Zečević to the graves of his wife and son; I would go with him to the mosque where old men in blue berets and young boys in baseball caps prostrated themselves in the peculiarly ramshackle Bosnian expression of Islamic faith. There was rage in Asim, all right, but I never saw him lose his dignity or call for revenge. Nor in his sister Fida's struggle with her pain was there ever an abandonment to blind fury.

"I married Slobodan," she told me that summer, "because I loved him and we had two children together. It is very hard to forget that, and I think he feels the same. I still cannot decide if I will ever live with him again. He stayed there in Belgrade. That is hard to forgive. I want my girls to know the truth, to know that they are *not* Serbs."

Biting her lip, she went on: "I have told Slobodan that the Serbs planned all this. I told him they had blackened their name in the world. He denied it. I told him one can't let people forget what happened or it will happen again. He dismissed everything I said, told me I had become a tool of Alija. He likes to provoke me and then I explode."

I had seen so many tears in Bosnia, so many rooms full of them, I considered myself inured. I never asked for explanations. I once had, and a woman in tears replied, "Nothing really—that is the awful thing." The "nothing" was everything, all that was lost: the times when people drank and laughed and did not think too much and did not have discussions that led nowhere and were tinged with the violence of exasperation; the times when bare toes curled around the smoothness and coolness of the stones of Dubrovnik and the ancient undulations were infinitely soothing; the times when people sat on logs and dangled their toes in the rivers of Bosnia. It was not true, as Giuseppe di Lampedusa suggested, that everything changed merely so that everything could remain the same: sometimes everything went to hell and was gone. Yugoslavia went that way, and to remember it was like remembering the birth of a child from a passion now dead. Memory was pain. The loss of a country is more painful than lost youth. In Belgrade, I once looked with a friend at photographs of her youth and told her how beautiful she was. "Everyone," she said, "is beautiful when they are young." Old age is approached slowly; Yugoslavia's death had the abruptness of sudden surgery, of excision. So people ached and cried, and I watched and, increasingly, was silent. But Fida's tears always defeated me. It was her obvious struggle against them, her battle for dignity, that made the ravaged dissolution of her face upon surrender so overwhelming.

FROM THE ZEČEVIĆS' APARTMENT it was a short walk to the Holiday Inn. A slight detour would take me to the National Museum, the one haven of nature in a city stripped of its trees and parks. Here, roses cascaded off battered trellises amid the ancient tombs of Bosnian dukes and kings. There was silence and the scent of conifers. Enver Imamović, the director of the museum, sat that summer on a tombstone in the sun writing a history of Bosnia.

It was he who, on June 6, 1992, as fierce fighting raged, rescued the Sarajevo Haggadah from a safe in the basement of the museum. It was an act worthy of a remarkable city that I had come to love: a Muslim saving a Jewish manuscript stored in an old Viennese safe in the basement of a museum built by the Austro-Hungarian Empire and under attack from Serb nationalists bent on destroying the mingling of culture and religions that had long marked Sarajevo. An act, that is, of generosity and deep civility.

Since the beginning of the war, over four hundred shells had hit the museum, and Imamović said he felt like a man watching his child dying. Roman mosaics, prehistoric boats, massive medieval bells lay helter-skelter in the once elegant rooms. In the natural history section a shell had come through the glass roof and a charred eagle still hovered above the devastated room. Nobody could be found to tend the botanical garden, and the undergrowth was becoming thick. A single tortoise inhabited the garden. "We used to have four tortoises," Imamović said, "but the other three have died during the war. This one is still going, however, and seems quite happy."

As he spoke, the tortoise inched methodically toward the ancient, sand-bagged tomb of Ban Kulin, one of the most successful of Bosnia's medieval rulers, as if to say, with its ponderous but steady gait, that everything passes in the end. I was tempted to see in its movement an image of some deep truth that would prevail in Bosnia, the truth whose lineaments lay in the tolerance and culture of so many Sarajevans; I wanted to say that it was this truth, hidden perhaps, but resilient and many-layered as the history

on display in the museum, that the Muslims, Serbs, and Croats of the
Bosnian army were still fighting for; I wanted to think that, just as Sarajevo had risen again from the Croatian fascism that Alija Mehmedović had
served a half century earlier, so it would enjoy a new resurrection after this
war; I wanted to believe that peace, when it came, would be inhabited by
the spirit of this museum garden, with its evidence of the patient striving
of an undifferentiated mankind. In short, I longed, still, to believe in
Bosnia, for I had encountered the Bosnian nation in the souls of countless
men and women of the Orthodox, Catholic, and Islamic faiths and in the
very stones and shadows and sinews of Sarajevo. I wanted to think that the
infant Muris Zečević in Detroit would one day discover the mottled
Bosnia and eclectic city of Sarajevo in whose name his uncle and namesake
had died. But the mindless battering of weaponry, like shrieks emanating
from a lunatic asylum, left me gazing at that tortoise more in sorrow than
in hope.

CHAPTER 30

AN UNFORTUNATE
INCIDENT

IN SWEDEN, ERMIN ŠESTOVIĆ, THE REFUGEE FROM VLASENICA, thinks about his father. By the summer of 1995, three years have passed since Ruzdija Šestović was dragged from his apartment in the eastern Bosnian town and disappeared. Inquiries with the Red Cross in Sweden yield nothing. Concentration, Ermin finds, is difficult. He needs to learn English and Swedish, but his thoughts stray. His rational mind tells him that his father must be dead. But then, like Sead Mehmedović during the long years of his search for a father lost in World War II, Ermin clings to some sliver of hope.

Remorse eats at him. Why, before the war, was he always playing basketball rather than spending time with his father? Why does he sit in a Swedish bar rather than fight for Bosnia? Why did he not force his parents to leave with him that spring of 1992? Like Haris Zečević in Detroit, Ermin is full of personal guilt engendered by war.

When the fighting stops, Ermin tells himself, he will go to Bosnia and search for his father. At least he will do that. He will find out what has happened; he will unearth the true story. That much, at least, he owes to his father. He does not want revenge; he wants his father back.

Sweden remains obstinately alien to him. The cold has a clinical, dissecting quality that pushes each family into a neat little box; the cold in Bosnia is not less bitter but tends to gather people around alcohol and a fire. Prosperity, in Sweden, is itself a cold thing. Often there are articles in the newspapers about the cost to Sweden of each refugee; the same articles point out that, even without the foreigners, unemployment is already high. But, despite his reservations about his new home, Ermin will not expose himself to Bosnia's ghosts again. Even if he finds his father, he will not stay there.

He remembers his grandfather talking to him about the Serb slaughter of Muslims in Milići during World War II. The stories seemed fanciful and he paid no attention. If one day he has his own children, he will not expose them to the risk of the unimaginable.

It is in Växjö, a small town in central Sweden, that Ermin is eventually settled by the Swedish authorities. Under a program for refugees, he receives a credit from the municipal government that he has to pay back over a period of two years, and a small apartment is provided free until he can afford to pay the rent. The money is enough to buy a few things: a sofa, a table, a bed, a stereo system, a shower-curtain rod, and weights—Ermin loves to pump iron.

The apartment is an improvement on his previous accommodation. Ermin spent his first six months in a redbrick military barracks, sharing a dormitory with fifteen other refugees. From there he was moved to a dilapidated apartment block. There were holes in the wall and a hose for a shower. When he complained, a Swedish social worker snapped back: "If you don't like it, why don't you go back to Bosnia?" An ethnic Albanian refugee family had smashed the place up after being ordered back to Kosovo. There were many Albanians still there, and gazing at these other refugees from Serbian oppression, people washed up on an indifferent Swedish shore, Ermin wondered again at the madness that had possessed Milošević's Serbia.

He tries to understand. There are many Serbs in Sweden, some of them refugees. Never does he hear one of them admit the least responsibility for what has happened or the least doubt about the Serb cause. Yet what happened in Vlasenica, what happened to his father, what happened at the start of the war is clear. Is it not clear? How, Ermin asks, could the Muslims ever seriously threaten the Serbs? Yet the Serbs believed they were threatened, or so they say; indeed, they were so convinced of being in danger they could not see that, this time around, they were the executioners.

How, Ermin wonders, had they killed his father? On the edge of some ravine? As he dug a trench on some misty hillside? Alone? With others? Were the bulldozers standing by ready to crush the bones and level the soil? Did the executioners hesitate or tremble? Were they drunk or drugged when the trigger was pulled? Did they finish the job with a pistol shot to the head? Did the end at least come quickly, or did they beat his father to death in some cells as they told him he was "really" a Serb?

There are rumors. That Ruzdija might be in Novi Sad; that he is living in Serbia under another name; that he is living with his niece, Vahda Ibišević, the one who also "disappeared" that summer and who, the rumors suggest, has married a Serb; that he was in Batković camp but escaped; that he is still in prison. But the most insistent rumor is that Ruzdija has escaped with a group of other Muslim men from Vlasenica and is living in the Muslim enclave of Srebrenica, just twenty-five miles east of their former home.

I EMERGED FROM SARAJEVO at the end of June 1995, driving over Mount Igman with two colleagues. Never before had the glimmering coastline of the Adriatic looked so beautiful or the sea so inviting in its vastness. Confinement has a smell, dank and rancid; freedom has its smell too, of salt and pines. Almost always, when I asked Sarajevans what they missed the most, they replied, The sea. The coast, in peacetime, had been a few hours' drive away. But, by 1995, it had become a memory from another world. What the people of Sarajevo meant by the sea, of course, was simply freedom.

After a brief pause in Split, I found myself in the business lounge of an international airport, awaiting a flight to Paris. There were two Americans sitting nearby. One had a groomed terrier on his lap. Their conversation naturally focused on the obsession of the United States at that time: the murder trial of O. J. Simpson in Los Angeles. One of the men said that Simpson was clearly "guilty as hell," and his friend quickly concurred.

"But," the first man, the one with the terrier, continued, "I hope that they don't convict him."

"Why shouldn't they convict him?" asked the other.

"Because if they do, the blacks will burn down Los Angeles, and do you understand what that will do to our real estate prices?"

The second man thought about this for a moment and then concurred that, yes, it would be better if Simpson were not convicted.

War-weary, disgusted by international hypocrisy over Sarajevo and the continuing siege there, I was in a sensitive mood. The conversation, for me, captured a cynicism and a narrow-mindedness—as well as a disregard for the value of truth—that seemed to reflect America's approach to the war. It was inevitable, I suppose, that O. J. Simpson should command America's attention far more compellingly than the war from which I had just emerged; inevitable, even, that two middle-aged men from Los Angeles should worry more about their property prices than the importance of justice being done; but I was in no mood to be understanding. There is a point where a correspondent must leave a war, the point where exhaustion and fear and anger are overwhelming. The previous month in Sarajevo had brought me close to that point.

The conversation meandered on, and I heard the name "Mike Tyson," which made me think of mad, spinning Havda back in Sarajevo and her fat rabbit. The man with the terrier was saying that Tyson had been unfairly convicted, but that prison had at least been beneficial to him, for he had taken to reading, something he had never done before. "But unfortunately," he went on, "you know something else about Tyson? He became a Muslim in prison, and that's really a pity."

I wanted to ask him why, *why was it a pity that somebody become a Muslim?* But I felt that I knew the answer: the man was probably one of those Jews who see in all Muslims the enemies of Israel. The Serbs had other reasons for not liking people who "became" Muslims. And in Srebrenica, they were to show, again, how far their loathing went.

I WATCHED THE ATTACK on the United Nations "safe area" of Srebrenica, which began on July 6, 1995, from afar. It had been coming for a long time. The Serbs, increasingly strained by the length of the front line, had too many men tied up around the eastern enclaves. Their problems were evident in the fact that, in Belgrade, young men from Bosnia or Serbheld Croatia were being forcibly rounded up for transportation to the front. With the Croats threatening to attack what was left of the Serb-held Krajina, the need to transfer forces from eastern Bosnia was pressing. And, as Smith had known for several months, the Serbs wanted a quick end to the war with a cohesive stretch of territory on both sides of the Drina as its fruit. Territorial cohesion, for the Serbs, meant the elimination of the Muslim enclaves at Srebrenica, Žepa, and Goražde.

On June 26, ten days before the assault, Smith wrote to Mladić, "I write further to the letter signed by my chief of staff on my behalf concerning Srebrenica. I wish to express my increasing concern about a series of very serious incidents. These incidents could eventually lead to an escalation which we both wish to avoid very much. I cannot tolerate attacks on my troops and I want to remind you once again that I will not hesitate to respond in self-defense."

Smith was trying to draw a line before a full-scale attack on Srebrenica began, but he had been overruled at Split and there was little he could do beyond sounding tough. Just before the Serb offensive began, the British commander of United Nations forces in Bosnia went on vacation to the Dalmatian coast, staying at the Korčula villa of Fitzroy Maclean, the British officer who had helped Tito to victory and been encouraged by Churchill not to worry about Yugoslavia's "form of government" after World War II.

The Serb-encircled enclave of Srebrenica, measuring six by ten miles, with a perimeter of about thirty miles, was protected by 429 Dutch troops. Its Muslim population—of about forty thousand people when the attack began—was full of refugees from the 1992 Serb onslaught in eastern Bosnia. Because United Nations policy was to acquiesce to Serb demands, rather than confront Serb obstruction, Dutch supplies of fuel and ammunition were low.

The United Nations forces in Srebrenica were not yet circulating on mules, as British troops in Goražde had been obliged to do, but mobility, like morale, was diminished. In essence, the Dutch were deployed to "monitor" rather than protect the "safe area"; their ability to ensure military deterrence, as spelled out in their mandate, was almost entirely dependent on their capacity to call in NATO air power.

But after the ignominy of the hostage-taking and the United Nations capitulation in Sarajevo in June, the likelihood of such air power being used was remote. Just how remote, Lieutenant Colonel Ton Karremans, the commander of the Dutch forces, did not know. He was also unaware of the grave illusions under which Lieutenant General Bernard Janvier, his commander in Zagreb, labored. Despite the lies and butchery of Karadžić and Mladić, Janvier, like Akashi, still wanted to believe them; he still wanted to treat them as credible interlocutors. The French general wanted desperately to talk to them, because the alternative was to fight them.

Almost three years had passed since the London Conference ended on August 27, 1992, with an agreement signed by the Serb leaders. They had promised then to dismantle their concentration camps immediately, lift the siege of Sarajevo and other Bosnian cities, and turn over all their heavy weapons to "international supervision." Lies were the staple of Karadžić and Mladić then, and so they remained. Yet all the evidence suggests that Janvier never believed, until it was much too late, that the Serbs would take Srebrenica because Mladić told him they would not! He believed that, just as at Bihać and Goražde, the Serbs would probe and then sit back. His credulity during the first two days of the attack was perhaps understandable, but that it persisted, even when the Serbs were on the edge of Srebrenica, amounted to a form of perversity, just as it was international perversity—the masquerading of cowardice as resolve—that allowed the Srebrenica massacre to happen.

Janvier, moreover, clearly felt no moral compunction to protect Srebrenica. Another French general, Morillon, had vowed in 1993 that the town was under his personal protection and that of the United Nations. He was close enough to the genocide committed against Muslims at the war's outset for the town's fate to reverberate in his blood. But time, and impatience with the war, ate into the last vestiges of the West's moral fiber with the implacability of ants gnawing at a corpse.

By the summer of 1995, Janvier saw Srebrenica merely as an abstraction, a logistical problem, a headache: indefensible, isolated, and a cartographical anomaly in terms of an eventual "territorial settlement." The human beings inside it, like the reasons for their presence there, had slid into the great, all-effacing abyss of the West's self-deception. Janvier had argued for Srebrenica's abandonment before the Security Council in May;

he commented after its fall that "in any event, one day or another, we had to be rid of the problem of that enclave." He embodied the criminal false-hood—the fatal equivocation—of Western governments before Europe's first war in a half century.

In the disaster at Srebrenica were crystallized three years of failure by America and its European allies before the Bosnian war. Beyond the ba-nality that Hannah Arendt identified, evil assumed a late-twentieth-century burlesque in this small eastern Bosnian town, where silver had been mined in Roman times. The burlesque did not belittle the horror; on the contrary, it highlighted, in all its warped perfidy, the towering struc-ture of Western dishonor—ad-hoc measure piled on ad-hoc measure to create a labyrinth of pious good intentions and nonsense.

NATO planes, arriving far too late, and trying to pick out a single gun on a wooded hillside! United Nations soldiers offering fuel to the Serbs, some of it used to truck the Muslim victims of Srebrenica to their execu-tions! United Nations soldiers toasting Mladić, the orchestrator of the butchery! United Nations soldiers shaking hands on solemn accords with Mladić even as Srebrenica Muslims—boys and old men alike—were mown down on football fields, in gymnasiums, in disused factories! And all this, three years after the first round, three years after the concentration camps and the first mass Serb killings of Muslims.

The road down which more than twenty thousand women and children were bused from Srebrenica to government-held Kladanj in central Bosnia was precisely the one used by the Serbs when they "cleansed" Vlasenica of its 18,699 Muslims in the summer of 1992. It led to places like the school where I had found the shattered survivors of the Vlasenica onslaught, peo-ple like Ermin Šestović and his mother, Muska. That Serb attack, three years old, had been the backdrop to the creation of the "safe areas." Yet these zones of safety for Muslims turned out to be no more than another layer of falsehood. The "safe areas" enabled Western soldiers to do some-thing they had not done in 1992: watch, from up close, the Muslims of Srebrenica being led to their deaths. But they did not stop the killing, in cold blood, of more than six thousand Muslims.

On July 6, the day the Serb attack on Srebrenica began, Philip Corwin, an American then serving as the chief United Nations civilian affairs offi-cer in Sarajevo, wrote a confidential note to Akashi. His concern was not the danger to the Muslim enclave; rather it was the imminent arrival of military reinforcements to the United Nations mission in the form of the Rapid Reaction Force. In the interests of "impartiality" and "classical peacekeeping," Corwin, recently appointed to Sarajevo by Akashi, wanted to emasculate the force even before it arrived.

"Before it goes too far and becomes too costly," Corwin wrote, "it is time to reconsider the Rapid Reaction Force." The force, he added, merely reflected the "festering righteousness that emanates from political capitals." This "righteousness," for Corwin, consisted of seeing the Muslims as victims. He was concerned to correct this perception and portray the Muslims as the chief obstacles to UNPROFOR. "It is time," he wrote in a cable a few days earlier, "to use political pressure at the highest level to halt the Bosnian government's increasing restriction of UNPROFOR freedom of movement."

Such views carried weight in Zagreb. The perception of the Izetbegović government as "professional victims" attempting to manipulate Western governments into fighting the Muslims' war for them was never far from the surface. Instead of being weighed as a peripheral part of the story, such maneuvers by the government tended to be seen as the whole story. Janvier was always more attentive to Muslim "provocations"—such as an attack out of Srebrenica on the village of Višnjica on June 26—than to the vulnerability of a surrounded enclave or to what the very existence of such a Muslim ghetto reflected.

So it proved at Srebrenica. As the Serb offensive moved forward from the southeast of the pocket, coming within 1.2 miles of the town by July 9, Janvier tended to look indulgently at Serb aims and harshly at the Muslims' situation. Karremans also misread the Serb objective for a time, and the killing of a Dutch soldier, Sergeant Frans van Rossum, by the Muslims on July 8, as the sergeant attempted to pull back from an observation post under attack by the Serbs, strained relations between the Dutch and the people their mandate committed them to protect.

Only when Serb troops reached the outskirts of Srebrenica did Akashi and Janvier seriously consider the possibility of using air power. By this time the Serbs had fifty-five Dutch hostages picked up on the way into the enclave as leverage. Under the reorganization imposed in late May, Akashi and Janvier also had to consult with Boutros-Ghali, who was in regular telephone contact with Chirac.

Finally, during the evening of July 9, an order was issued from Zagreb to the Dutch. They were told to take up blocking positions on the outskirts of town in the early morning of July 10. At the same time, Janvier and Akashi issued an "ultimatum" to the Serbs: release the Dutch hostages and avoid attack on any of the Dutch blocking positions or face "close air support" from NATO. The reference to close air support was significant: the Serbs were being menaced not with wide-ranging air strikes but with the much lesser, and faintly ludicrous, threat of having any "smoking guns" eliminated in the unlikely event that they could be unearthed and picked off from the air.

·   ·   ·

ON JULY 9, the day this ultimatum was issued, Corwin wrote another of his confidential messages to Akashi. Once again, the issue was not Srebrenica, but sandbags, specifically the fact that the United Nations had offered fifty thousand sandbags to the Bosnian army to help fortify the track over Mount Igman, the one route open for getting food to the encircled Bosnian capital. Corwin was concerned not with the people of Sarajevo but with the danger that UNPROFOR was "once again jeopardizing its diminished image of impartiality." He concluded with a call for more international support for the Serbs: "The German-American policy of isolation of one of the warring parties, a party which holds 70 percent of the territory in Bosnia, may win elections at home, but it is a disaster in the field of operations."

Meanwhile, in the Srebrenica pocket, the Serbs ignored the ultimatum and continued their attack. The last Muslim defenses, weakened by the absence of the longtime military leader in Srebrenica, Naser Orić, evaporated. The Muslims were disorganized and vastly outgunned; they had also believed they were protected. Karremans urgently requested the promised NATO air support. The Dutch defense minister, Joris Voorhoeve, was consulted and courageously approved an air attack, which he described as "inevitable."

Janvier, however, hesitated. Into the night of July 10 he prevaricated, with NATO planes in the air waiting to strike. His attitude showed an extraordinary disregard for his men: he had ordered the Dutch into dangerous, and exposed, "blocking positions" with a pledge of air support in the event of an attack, only to renege on what he had promised. Having talked to General Zdravko Tolimir of the Serb army, the French general still doubted that the Serbs intended to take the town. At one point that evening, in the midst of a meeting of his crisis team called to discuss air attacks at Srebrenica, Janvier took a long telephone call; people at the meeting had the impression the call was from Paris. In the end the NATO planes returned to base; Srebrenica's fate was sealed.

The next morning Karremans assumed massive air attacks were on the way. Repeated requests for air support were made as the population of Srebrenica fled to the Dutch camp in a disused battery factory at Potočari, in the northern part of the enclave. It was almost noon, however, before Janvier, in Zagreb, finally signed a written order for an attack, and then it was to be limited to "any forces attacking the blocking UNPROFOR position south of Srebrenica and heavy weapons identified as shelling U.N. positions in Srebrenica town." Such an order, so late, amounted to holding up an umbrella against a hurricane.

That afternoon, one Serb tank was hit before NATO air attacks were called off with the Serbs threatening to kill all the Dutch hostages. The "safe area" of Srebrenica fell at four o'clock that afternoon. About twenty-five thousand Muslims, including over fifteen hundred men of military age, sought protection in or just outside the Dutch camp at Potočari. Another ten to fifteen thousand Muslim men set out northwestward in a desperate bid to walk across more than thirty miles of Serb-held territory into the safety of government-held territory south of Tuzla. That night, Karremans met twice with Mladić to discuss the fate of the Dutch troops and the Muslims. The meetings were filmed by Bosnian Serb television, and Karremans was seen apparently raising a glass with the Serb commander.

Mladić exercised an inordinate fascination on UN officials and soldiers; indeed, only Smith appears to have remained impervious to his bombast and his bonhomie. He represented, it seems, a personification of several Serb traits—irrational bravura, passion, brutal conviction, boisterous camaraderie—that were seductive to men with the modest task of mediating in the name of the international order. These United Nations mediators, including Janvier, were wrongly led to think that another supposed Serb trait—a soldier's honor—also characterized Mladić.

When I met him in Belgrade in 1993, Mladić quite literally filled the room with his exuberant, table-thumping presence. That, however, was before his twenty-three-year-old daughter, Ana, a student in Belgrade, committed suicide in March 1994, and before a long war exposed the dangerous extent of his hubris. Increasingly, officials who met him watched Mladić lurch into meandering, megalomaniacal, and venomous tirades that looked like borderline madness.

When Ana Mladić committed suicide, a Bosnian Serb newspaper, *Jedinstvo*, commented: "War: the Serbs are fated to die. I ask, was it possible that a youthful heart which had just started to beat with the joy of life, should bear the burden and tears for brethren fallen throughout the former Bosnia-Herzegovina, was it possible to bear all those fears for her dear father's life, for Gen. Ratko Mladić, who led his armies wherever it was necessary to prevent a new and more terrible death for the Serbs? Was it possible that Ana Mladić could tolerate all those 'peacemakers' and similar trash in the Serb capital of Belgrade? . . . Her young, healthy spirit and honorable patriotism, and the 'Serbian milk' which she had fed upon, found it difficult to bear all that which destroyed, undermined and slandered the battle of our and her brethren. . . ."

This was the mawkish, necrophilious backdrop to the Serb killing of Muslims in Bosnia and to the massacre that Mladić personally directed at Srebrenica: the talk of "Serbian milk," of Serbs being fated to die, of new deaths for the Serbs. Myth, shaped from the Serb corpses at Kosovo field, made killers blind. Not for nothing, surely, was death such an intimate of the leaders who unleashed the killing in Bosnia. Milošević's parents had both committed suicide, and Mladić, having lost his father to war as an infant, conducted another war during which his daughter killed herself.

The Serb general himself appared in Potočari on July 12, before the terrified Muslim population, and began organizing the deportation. Very much the father figure, he had himself filmed saying, "All who wish to go will be transported, large and small, young and old. Do not be afraid, just take it easy. Let the women and children go first. Thirty buses will come and take you in the direction of Kladanj. Nobody will harm you." It was the old technique for cowing the herd being led to the slaughter: *Arbeit macht frei.*

In fact, however, as the Dutch UN forces quickly became aware, Muslim men were being weeded out. They did not board the buses to Kladanj, but were taken to Bratunac, where many were assembled at the football field. Gunfire was audible to the Dutch hostages in Bratunac on July 12. The systematic Serb killing of Muslim men had begun.

THAT EVENING the Security Council demanded a Serb withdrawal and requested that the secretary-general "reestablish" the "safe area." Chirac, perhaps nagged by his conscience, was voluble in urging military action to recapture Srebrenica. But this was just the customary bluster, the interminable flapping of good intentions to which people in Bosnia no longer listened. The only reality of Srebrenica was that embodied in Mladić's lapidary weltanschauung: "Borders are drawn in blood."

In fact, even as the killing began, Akashi wrote a confidential note to Kofi Annan at United Nations headquarters in New York to insist that Srebrenica was lost forever and to argue that no attempt should be made to reestablish the "safe area." Akashi sounded almost relieved that a point he had been making for some time—the indefensibility of the "safe areas"—had finally been illustrated on the ground.

Dated July 12, 1995, the note urged that Boutros-Ghali write a letter to the Security Council. In this letter, Akashi suggested, the secretary-general should underscore the "inherent deficiency of the safe area regime"; he should point out the mission's "lack of resources" to protect the "safe areas"; he should stress that the Bosnian army was responsible for "provocations and attacks from inside the safe areas"; he should insist on the limits "of the credibility of deterrence and the consequences of the use of air power"; and he should recall that the "safe areas," at their inception, were supposed to be a "temporary measure." Akashi concluded: "It is vital that the Security Council understands the importance that resolutions should recognize the reality of situations on the ground. Success in the aftermath of events in Srebrenica will require tenacious negotiations with the parties, but in particular with the Bosnian Serb army. Even with the newly added Rapid Reaction Force capability, UNPROFOR cannot impose a solution by force when there is no consent or cooperation from the parties. It is essential now for members of the Security Council to focus on humanitarian assistance rather than suggesting even obliquely that the status quo ante can be reestablished by force."

Akashi, in his belief in persistence, in his conviction that the right course was to negotiate and go on negotiating, in his own sense of his duty as a servant of the United Nations, in his personal aversion to force as an instrument of diplomacy, had been blinded. To Bosnia, he brought Japan's postwar renunciation of its military tradition. He spoke, in all earnestness, of "success in the aftermath of events in Srebrenica"! But there could be no success after Srebrenica. Akashi had only to take one step back to see that. The town's fall was the culmination of a protracted failure. The massacres of Muslims in the days after Akashi's note was sent wrote that failure in blood.

THE DEPORTATION FROM POTOČARI was completed on July 13. There were the same scenes as in countless towns and villages in 1992: Muslim women clutching at their sons, husbands, and grandsons as the men were dragged away, never to be seen again. Over twenty-three thousand women and children were bused to the front line near Kladanj; the Dutch tried to "monitor" this procedure by accompanying the buses in their own jeeps. The Serbs stole the jeeps.

With the women and children out of the way, the slaughter of Muslim males began in earnest. Karadžić always told me, preposterously, that the slaughter of 1992 was not "organized"; it just happened, the fruit of old hatreds. This time, Mladić was personally on the scene, making lines of responsibility more transparent. And, this time, the Serbs had neither the resources nor the manpower to set up concentration camps. They got straight down to business.

There were several killing fields. A few Muslims were shot dead at Potočari itself, quite literally under the eyes of the Dutch. Others from the Potočari group were killed at the Bratunac football stadium. Many among the more than ten thousand Muslims attempting to walk through the woods in the direction of Tuzla were ambushed near Kamenica on July 12, and summary executions took place. Those captured were taken to a warehouse at Kravica, where the Serbs organized mass executions, and to a football field at Nova Kasaba, where American satellites and spy planes were able to photograph evidence of the slaughter. Yet others were transported to Bratunac, where they joined the survivors among the Muslims who had surrendered at Potočari.

The process culminated at the Pilica state farm, north of Zvornik, where the surviving Muslims in Bratunac were taken on July 16. The testimony of Sergeant Dražen Erdemović, a twenty-three-year-old member of the Bosnian Serb army unit that dispatched more than fifteen busloads of Muslims that day, has provided a detailed account of this particular massacre: how the cowed Muslims, their hands bound behind their backs, were brought from buses and lined up about ten yards from the executioners; how Kalashnikov rifles and an M-84 machine gun were used to shoot them; how some Muslims screamed and pleaded and some were silent and some railed at their killers to the last; how, true to form, the Serb executioners cursed the victims' "Turk" mothers and joked about sparing those who had enough German marks (but the Muslims' valuables had already been taken); how the field steadily filled with corpses; how a pistol shot to the head dispatched those in agony from the first volley of fire; how the bus drivers themselves were made to shoot somebody so that everyone present was implicated; how the unit, having killed perhaps one thousand Muslims, later got drunk.

The crime was an organized military operation, and no aberration. Erdemović said his squad received its orders from Lieutenant Milorad Pelemis, their commander in Bijeljina, who in turn took orders from the Bosnian Serb army headquarters in Han Pijesak. The crime was also consistent. The war, from its outset, was about the eradication of "the other"— man, woman, or child—in order to draw new, ethnically pure Serb borders in blood.

During the killing, Mladić went to Belgrade on July 15 for an important meeting. Milošević was there, as was Smith, who had returned from leave, and Carl Bildt, who had recently replaced Lord Owen as the European Union's peace envoy. Milošević's position on events in Srebrenica had been spelled out to the American chargé d'affaires in Belgrade, Rudolph Perina, in a meeting on July 12. It was: "Why blame me?" Perina told me: "Milošević always tried to tread a fine line. He wanted us to deal with him and so he wanted us to know that he was influential in Bosnia. On the other hand, he never wanted to take responsibility. The line was: 'I'm influential with Mladić, but I can't control him absolutely, so don't blame me!' "

Milošević was influential enough, however, to summon Mladić to Belgrade that day. Mladić remained an officer in the pay of the Belgrade-based Vojska Jugoslavije, or Yugoslav army, the successor to the JNA. The subject of the meeting was the Dutch hostages, the evacuation of Dutch forces from Potočari, and fuel for the Serbs. An accord was reached on the departure of Dutch forces from the Srebrenica enclave on July 21—time enough for the Serbs to advance their conquest of the smaller enclave of Žepa while holding some United Nations forces as insurance. The fifty-five Dutch hostages were freed immediately, and eight thousand gallons of fuel were delivered to the Serbs with similar dispatch—compensation for the "cost" of the evacuation of Muslims. The fate of the Muslim men from Srebrenica did not figure on the agenda of the meeting.

On July 19, Smith held a further meeting with Mladić in Bosnia, at the Jela Restaurant in Han-Kram. The subjects discussed were wide-ranging: Red Cross access to places where the Serbs were holding prisoners (in fact the prisoners were almost all dead); visits to Srebrenica by the UNHCR; Serb permission for the rotation of UN forces at Sarajevo and Goražde; Serb permission for Dutch troops to leave Potočari with thirty local staff and with all their weapons and vehicles; the evacuation of Muslim women, children, and elderly (other Muslim men were not mentioned). "The above-mentioned steps," an accord said, "will be taken in order to provide a concrete and positive contribution to the peace process and to provide fair and impartial treatment of all parties, in particular UNPROFOR personnel."

After the meeting, one of Smith's aides sent a secret report of the meeting to Akashi. In light of the Serb slaughter of thousands of Muslims—according to the Red Cross, 7,079 Muslims from Srebrenica are missing—it makes grotesque reading. By this time, the executions were completed, and Muslim survivors from the long march toward Tuzla were still straggling into government-held territory.

Mladić, the report says, was "in a chipper mood, evidently buoyed by Bosnian Serb army successes at Žepa." The report continues: "Gen. Smith asked Mladić for an account of the actions of the Bosnian Serb troops in the aftermath of the fall of Srebrenica. Mladić was at pains to point out that Srebrenica was 'finished in a correct way.' He stated that the population of Potočari were evacuated at their own request and with the full cooperation and help of UNPROFOR. He said that he engaged himself personally in this operation and organized as much food and water for the refugees as possible. He reported on a meeting on July 11 with Dutchbat at which arrangements for the evacuation were made. Mladić described how on the night of July 10–11, a significant number of Bosnian troops broke through the lines in the direction of Tuzla. He explained that he had opened a corridor to let these troops go. He accepted that some skirmishes had taken place with casualties on both sides and that some 'unfortunate small incidents' had occurred."

SREBRENICA WAS NOT the defining event of the Bosnian war. It had been defined long before, in the initial Serb aggression, in the cruelty of that attack, and in the often surreal juxtaposition of barbarism and United Nations peacekeepers. But given the extent of the massacre, and the pro-

clivity of Western governments to forget how the war began, the fall of Srebrenica served as a jolt and a reminder. It also hastened the war toward its
conclusion, both by advancing the ethnic disentanglement of Bosnia on
which a dismal peace was based and by shaming Western governments
into a resolve that was more than sham.

Ten days after the town fell, the defense and foreign ministers of the
United States and its European allies met in London. The American delegation was a serious one—Secretary of State Warren Christopher, Defense
Secretary William Perry, and the chairman of the Joint Chiefs, General
John Shalikashvili—and the July 21 statement that emerged marked a
shift. It promised the use of air power "on an unprecedented scale" in the
defense of Goražde; NATO would now act in a way that was "substantial
and decisive." The paralyzing Western obsession with a "proportionate"
response was thus finally dumped thirty-nine months after the war began.
British and American generals were dispatched to Belgrade to ram home
the message. At the same time, the cumbersome mechanism for starting
NATO air strikes was streamlined.

No mention was made of Žepa, a smaller and more remote enclave than
Goražde; it fell to the Serbs on July 25, and its commander, Avdo Palić,
was executed by the Serbs after coming to negotiate a surrender. In the sacrifice of Žepa, some calculation of "cleaning up" the map was plainly at
work both in Washington and in Europe.

Mladić looked triumphant, but his apogee had been reached. He paid
a price for concentrating his forces in the Žepa area while at the same time
authorizing an offensive by the Krajina Serbs on the one western Bosnian
Muslim enclave—Bihać. As Smith had predicted, the Serb general was
going for broke, trying to force the pace by eliminating the Muslim enclaves one by one. But he had gone a step too far.

The fall of Bihać would have consequences beyond Bosnia: it would
consolidate Serb-held lands in western Bosnia and adjacent Croatia, giving Greater Serbia greater coherence. This Šušak and his Croatian army,
buoyed by the western Slavonian victory, could not tolerate. They had
long been preparing a flanking attack on Martić's stronghold in Knin and
the remaining Serb-held parts of Croatia. On July 29, two Serb towns in
western Bosnia—Glamoč and Bosansko Grahovo—fell to Croatian
forces, sending several thousand Serbs into flight. Poised above Knin, the
Croatian army was now ready to strike.

Mladić had dictated terms throughout the war and believed he could
dictate its outcome. But by exposing his overextended forces at once to the
Croatian army and the first serious threat of sweeping NATO attack, he
opened the way for a Serb débâcle. On July 24, the Rapid Reaction Force
deployed in the Sarajevo area, bringing 105-millimeter guns and other ar-

tillery to the Bosnian capital for the first time; no longer would NATO planes have to try to act as artillery from the air. The soldiers of the new force were wearing green; they were prepared, even eager, to fight. The fall of Srebrenica cut short Corwin's and Akashi's attempts to neutralize the new force even before it arrived. This was the Serb defeat concealed inside the Srebrenica "victory," a conquest that laid bare the full extent of the Serb general's folly.

The mass killings at Srebrenica became apparent as the number of missing was counted by the Red Cross and other organizations. On July 24, the United Nations rapporteur for human rights, Tadeusz Mazowiecki, said that seven thousand Srebrenica residents seemed to have "disappeared." Peter Galbraith, the American ambassador in Zagreb, heard credible accounts of killings and cabled Christopher on July 25. John Shattuck, the assistant secretary of state for human rights, interviewed Muslim survivors on August 1 in Tuzla. The Central Intelligence Agency, spurred by Shattuck's report, began an intensive review of its photography, which yielded damning pictures of what looked like mass graves at Nova Kasaba; these were shown to the Security Council by Ambassador Albright on August 10. Six days later, David Rohde, then of *The Christian Science Monitor,* reached the Nova Kasaba site and found, among other evidence, a decomposed human leg. As with the Serb concentration camps in 1992, it was a journalist who came up with the irrefutable evidence.

ERMIN ŠESTOVIĆ LEARNS about Srebrenica through press reports in Sweden. At each massacre site, he sees his father, although hard evidence that Ruzdija Šestović ever reached Srebrenica from Vlasenica does not exist. Other refugees have told him that his father was there, but when he presses them, their information is vague. He goes again to the Red Cross to see if they have any record of Ruzdija in Srebrenica. He asks if his father is among the Muslims straggling into Tuzla. There is nothing.

In the absence of a corpse, of proof of death, Ruzdija Šestović can die more than once. For Ermin, his father may be among the Muslims killed in Vlasenica or among those slaughtered three years later in Srebrenica. The war turns and turns and will not leave him.

After Srebrenica's fall, I try to find Rajko Dukić again, the prominent Serb who worked with Ruzdija at the Boksit Milići mine and was a founding member of Karadžić's party. But he avoids me. Later, however, I do find his sister-in-law, Spomenka Ćojnić, who lived with her husband Mladen in the apartment below the Šestovićs' in Vlasenica. She is ensconced in the plush offices of Dukić's Boksit Trade in Belgrade, sitting on a fancy chair, her dyed blond hair piled high. There are computers and papers everywhere. She and her husband have just bought a new Mercedes.

The company is still thriving—"import-export," Mrs. Ćojnić says. She pulls a lever on the chair and its slides lower.

Ah yes, she recalls, the Šestovićs. Those were difficult times in 1992. She was going back and forth between Vlasenica and Belgrade, but it was not easy for the Muslims to move. She tried to help, bringing coffee and food to the Šestovićs. She even changed some money into German marks for them once. "I remember," she says, "when Muska told me that they had taken Ruzdija and he was in prison. But there was really nothing I could do. Those were such chaotic times."

She asks where Muska and Ermin and Ermin's sister Nada are now. She is pleased they are safe. As for Ruzdija, she heard nothing more about him afterward. Nothing at all. He might have escaped to Srebrenica; he might not. She looks troubled. There is something bothering the sister-in-law of Rajko Dukić.

"You see," she says, fiddling with a large ring, "there is one thing. Before Ruzdija was taken away, Muska gave me some clothes and other things of her daughter's to keep safe for her. Then Muska was taken away too, of course. There were some children's dolls, there were some other personal possessions. Well, I put them in a bag in my apartment in Vlasenica. And, you understand, I would still like to give them back to her. They were innocent people. Please tell her that, tell her that I have the things, that I have kept them safe, that I want to return them to her."

There is an expression in Spomenka Ćojnić's eyes that I have come to know well. I have seen it in many Serb-held towns in Bosnia, towns whose Muslim populations have been evicted or killed, whose mosques have been destroyed. It is a kind of embarrassed awareness that something horrific, something inexpressible, has happened, and that now there is no way back from the horror.

CHAPTER 31

KOSOVO POLJE

THE PROVINCE OF KOSOVO AND METOHIJA, IN SOUTHEAST-
ern Serbia, is a small place, about sixty miles square, consisting of two
plains, Kosovo to the east and Metohija to the west, divided by a range of
hills. It is a generally depressed area. The capital, Priština, is a dismal show-
case of the worst in communist architecture and town planning. But
Kosovo is rich in symbolism. It contains several sites sacred to Serbs: the
old patriarchate of the Serbian Orthodox church at Peć and the beautiful
monasteries of Dečani and Gračanica, frescoed sanctuaries of mystery and
grace in which the rich medieval flowering of Serbian culture is palpable.
This, for many Serbs, is the heart of Serbdom, the source and sustenance
of the nation. At Kosovo Polje, or "The Field of Blackbirds," the battlefield where the Serbs were routed by the Ottoman Turks in 1389, all the
pageantry of resurgent Serbian nationalism was unfurled in 1989 when
Milošević promised a glorious future based on the unity of all Serbs.

But it was a bleak place for Ljubica Solić. I found her, dressed in black,
slumped on the ground in a schoolyard filled with mud-spattered tractors
and trailers. She had traveled 450 miles from her native Krajina; her husband had been killed by the Croats during the lightning Croatian defeat
of the Krajina Serbs in early August 1995. She slept in a crowded classroom. Discarded watermelon, attacked by bloated flies, littered the floor.
Milošević's government had told her to come to the Kosovo region. This
made sense to the Serbian government. Mrs. Solić and other refugees were
supposed to form a counterweight to what Serbian propagandists called
the "demographic genocide" committed by the ethnic Albanian majority
in Kosovo. The Albanians' high birth rate—the highest in Europe—had
left Kosovo more than 90 percent Albanian.

"I'd hardly even heard of Kosovo and never been to Serbia," Mrs. Solić

told me. "The authorities promised us a house, land, vineyards if we'd
come. We came, but we've got nothing, and we're a minority again."

Serbia had become a land of broken promises. There was a widespread
desolation, dark and deadening, a harvest of misery from a moment of
folly. I walked up to the vast platform at Kosovo Polje where a stone tower
commemorates the Serb defeat transformed by myth and song into the
beacon of the long Serb struggle for a state with stable borders. Weeds
pushed through the cracks in the stone. The adjacent flower beds were barren. Garbage skittered in the wind. A solitary café had closed for lack of
customers. Nothing stirred on the vast and empty Field of Blackbirds,
where Serb blood ran in the Middle Ages and Serb hopes coalesced so
feverishly as communism collapsed. The most conspicuous symbol of
Serbdom—the symmetrical Orthodox cross adorned with four *C*'s (the
Cyrillic letter *S*) and standing for *Samo Sloga Srbina Spašava* ("Only Unity
Saves the Serb")—was everywhere, as pervasive as the disunity that had ultimately undermined them and dumped Mrs. Solić near this battlefield.

It was not easy, confronted by such emptiness and such decay, to conjure up the delirium generated by Milošević in Kosovo on June 28, 1989,
when a million Serbs gathered to mark the six hundredth anniversary of a
losing battle and honor the communist ex-banker who had assumed the
mantle of Prince Lazar and brought "Serbdom" back to rampaging life.

From the heavens Milošević descended by helicopter onto the Field of
Blackbirds and delivered a speech that reads as a paradigm of nationalist
madness.

The predictable gamut of Serbian nationalist images was wheeled out.
Serbs as heroic fighters, "perennially liberating themselves, and, whenever
they could, helping others to be liberated" (a reference to the foundation
of Yugoslavia). Serbs as tragically disunited ever since the Battle of Kosovo.
Serbs as a wronged and "humiliated" people. Serbs as a people suffering
from the "inferiority complex" of past Serbian politicians. Serbs needing
to become aware that "the fact that we are the big nation in this region is
not a Serbian sin or shame." Serbs "on the rampart protecting European
culture, religion, and European society as a whole." Serbs ready to fight
new wars in the name of their rediscovered "state, national, and spiritual
integrity." By the end of the speech Milošević comes as close as such a man
can to being in full, impassioned flight. "For six centuries now," he de-
claimed, "the heroism of Kosovo has inspired our creativity, fed our pride,
and not allowed us to forget that once we were an army great, brave, and
proud, one of the few that in defeat stayed undefeated. Six centuries later,
today, we are again in battles and facing battles. They are not armed, although such battles cannot be excluded yet."

In these words, two years before Yugoslavia was engulfed in fighting, the fate of the South Slav state was foretold. Milošević's message was clear enough: the Serbs—an army *that in defeat stayed undefeated,* a people that in suicide found redemption—were ready to bury themselves in the rubble of Yugoslavia in order to liberate themselves from some yoke, real or illusory, it hardly mattered.

I thought of all the human devastation I had seen since this incendiary speech was delivered, from the spreading graveyards of Sarajevo to Mrs. Solić in the nearby schoolroom to Haris Zečević in Detroit. Milošević had not hesitated to replace Tito's crumbling legends with rediscovered Serb myth or to countenance the shedding of blood for the recovery of a supposedly trampled Serb pride. He postulated something that had never existed—a Serbian state stretching from Belgrade to Knin—and justified it through the message of a six-hundred-year-old battle. Seldom has necromancy so evidently raved. With a criminal cynicism, and what proved to be a complete duplicity, Milošević opened the floodgates. All the ruined or extinguished lives were then but specks on the stream.

IT WAS NATURAL enough to begin such a campaign in Kosovo, for in few places does the weight of the past seem more dangerous. It is a place that shares some of the characteristics of the Drina's banks and the contested ground of the Krajina. The essential questions, in the mind games of nationalist legend, are always the same: Who came first? And who marked the land most indelibly with his presence?

Before the great Serbian monasteries in Kosovo, I was often asked if an Albanian could have built a thing of such beauty and if the Albanians had not built such monuments, how could they truly claim to be a "nation," let alone a nation with a claim to this hallowed land? The question, of course, is a form of denial of "the other," like the Armenian who asks if an Azerbaijani could have built one of his basilicas. Behind the high walls of the Albanians' homes, the denial took another form. By eschewing any contact with Serbs, by claiming to be the "original" inhabitants of Kosovo, and by arguing that they had been "ethnically cleansed" despite the manifest fact that they were the overwhelming majority of the population, the Albanians had erected impenetrable barriers against anything Serbian.

The Albanians, whose language is unrelated to that of the Slavs, claim descent from the Illyrians, the inhabitants of the Balkan Peninsula before the Slav migration. Their presence in Kosovo, they say, therefore predates that of the Serbs, giving them an overriding claim to the real estate.

However, there were certainly Slavs in Kosovo from the seventh century and, in 1180, the area was conquered by the Serb prince, Stefan Nemanja. Kosovo then became a hub of Serbian power, a center of its considerable culture, and, for almost a century, the capital of the empire. All the place names in Kosovo are Slav in origin; the Albanian versions are adaptations.

But after the Serb defeat by the Ottoman Turks at Kosovo in 1389, the influence of the Albanians, many of whom converted to Islam, increased. There was a steady Serbian migration to the north and west; some went as far as the Krajina. That the number of Serbs in Kosovo has fallen steadily over more than a century is incontrovertible. Albanians accounted for 58 percent of the population in 1838, according to an Austrian observer. That figure rose to 65 percent in 1905, 68 percent in 1948, 73 percent in 1971, 77 percent in 1981, and about 90 percent in 1991. To the Serbian orchestrators of the nationalist revolution of the late 1980s, this was evidence of "genocide."

The reality was another thing. There was the high Albanian birthrate. Kosovo is poor: the quest for jobs and an income led many Serbs to leave. There was also some Albanian harassment, isolated acts of Albanian violence, and a growing sense among Kosovo Serbs that they were vulnerable because they were heavily outnumbered. Finally, there was the decisive fact that history does not stand still in Kosovo any more than it does in Hebron. Only violence can turn a six-hundred- or one-thousand-year-old reality into a contemporary paradigm. But Milošević wanted to put the clock back. He saw "genocide" against the Serbs, or at least claimed he did. And he was ready to foment wars elsewhere to prove that Serbs would be "downtrodden" no longer.

On the tower at Kosovo Polje was this inscription: "Whoever is a Serb or of Serbian origin and does not come to fight at Kosovo, may he never have children, son or daughter. May everything he grows turn barren. May he have neither wine nor wheat. May all turn to dust until he dies." There was also a description of the formidable extent of the Ottoman troops standing under their swords and flags, an opposing army so vast that "if we all turned to salt it would not be enough to season a Turkish supper." And there was a description of the agony, after the lost battle, of Majka Jugović, a Serbian woman whose nine sons and husband were killed. According to myth, when she saw a raven dropping the head of her youngest son, she too died.

The message seemed clear enough: Serbs who chose not to fight an irrational battle that ended in terrible suffering were traitors. By the terms of the defining myths of Kosovo, they forfeited the right to call themselves true Serbs. It was at this altar that Milošević had consecrated the Serb battle of the 1990s. And it was to this bleak fate that he led his people.

AT KOSOVO POLJE, my thoughts turned to a meeting I had three years earlier, at the beginning of the Bosnian war, in August 1992, with General

Života Panić. He was then the chief of staff of the Serbian-dominated Yugoslav army and provided me with the most explicit link between events in Kosovo, where Milošević's revolution began, and the wars that eventually led Krajina refugees, on tractor and trailer, back to "the vineyards of Kosovo."

General Panić had played a decisive role in the flattening of Vukovar during the Croatian war. When I stumbled on him, he was resting from these exertions. Sunning himself in a black bathing suit, he was in the midst of a summer break on the Montenegrin coast, in the pretty resort of Sveti Stefan. It was nine months after the end of the Vukovar siege, and the focus of the wars had shifted to Bosnia. The muffled boom of artillery could be heard from over the mountains in the direction of the southeastern Bosnian town of Trebinje, but it was a faraway sound that scarcely touched the peace of the glimmering Adriatic.

On the table in front of him, the general unfolded a map of the Balkans. Then he took a pen and drew a bold line from Kosovo up through the mainly Muslim area of southern Serbia called the Sandžak to the Drina River. He paused. Then he took the line on to Sarajevo. Finally he extended it to the western Bosnian town of Bihać on the edge of the Krajina.

"This," he declared triumphantly, "is the Green Transversal! It is an attempt to cut Europe with a green line, a Muslim line, down from Bosnia to Kosovo and on to Albania and Turkey. It is a very dangerous transversal because it cuts the Christian world in half. The Albanian people want a republic in Kosovo. They are buying land from us and they are having ten children each. But we Serbs will never let them have a republic. In Bosnia, Izetbegović wants a fundamentalist country in the middle of Europe, he wants a state of Muslims in Europe. But we cannot allow this."

The general grinned. So that, for the Serbian military establishment, was what the fighting was all about: resistance to an attempt to cut the Christian world in half! The plot, allegedly, was being coordinated between the Albanians of Kosovo and the Muslims of Bosnia. The Albanians, with the "demographic genocide" against the Serbs represented by their large families, and the Bosnian Muslims, with their refusal to remain in a Serbian-dominated Yugoslavia, were part of the same conspiracy.

That, Panić said, was why army tanks and heavily armed Serbian police had been sent into Kosovo in March 1989 to quash Albanian resistance to Milošević's decision to strip Kosovo's 1.7 million ethnic Albanians of the autonomous rights they had enjoyed. And that was why Serbian tanks had been used three years later to stop Izetbegović in Bosnia.

Panić's "Green Transversal" was nonsense. Relations between the Bosnian Muslims and the Albanians were in fact often strained. Nevertheless, Panić insisted, the plot went further. It embraced America. "To stay on the side of the Muslims, and please its Saudi and Turkish friends, the United States has abandoned the Serbs," Panić told me. "But they forgot one thing. The Serbs are good people, but they are very proud. When the world is against them, they pull together. We are friendly to a certain point; then we are very dangerous."

DANGEROUS, AS IT PROVED, almost as much to themselves as to others. In that August of 1995, evidence of suicide was everywhere in Serbia. Uprooted families littered the countryside, "good Serbs" whose lives lay in ruins.

The Krajina campaign was swift and crushing. Tudjman and Šušak pounced on the area after receiving what amounted to a green light from the Clinton administration. After the humiliations of Sarajevo in June, after the disaster of Srebrenica, after three years of war, impatience with the Serbs was running high in Washington. Richard C. Holbrooke, who gave up the post of ambassador to Germany to handle Bosnia as assistant secretary of state for European affairs in mid-1994, had exploded when the Serbs took United Nations hostages in late May: "Give the Serbs forty-eight hours and if they don't release the hostages, bomb them to hell." It was an expression of frustration rather than a policy proposal, but it expressed a broadening current of opinion.

Unlike other administration officials, Holbrooke had seen the conflict up close. It was not an abstraction to him. He was in Banja Luka in August 1992, where he witnessed what he described to me as "an insane asylum, with all these half-drunk Serb paramilitaries and middle-aged men going and raping and killing young Muslim women." On the same visit, he was given a wooden carving from a Muslim survivor of a Serb concentration camp. The pose, head bowed in humiliation, captured the Serb terror of the war's first months. Holbrooke put the sculpture in his Washington office, a reminder and a rebuke. In December 1992 he took a careering car ride into Sarajevo and spent New Year's Eve there. His mantra became, "Bosnia is the greatest collective failure of the West since the nineteen-thirties."

Holbrooke spent a lot of time with Robert Frasure, the man he dispatched in the spring of 1995 to negotiate with Milošević. Frasure liked to compare Bosnian diplomacy to white-water rafting: "You've got to decide which waterfall you're going to go off." Instead, the administration kept trying to straddle the chutes: call for air strikes but do not commit men on the ground; deplore Bosnia's destruction but do not risk a life to save it. This impotence exasperated Frasure, a seasoned State Department official, who, on returning from one interagency meeting on Bosnia, remarked, "Boy, that was like a Little League locker-room rally!" In moments of frustration, he suggested that perhaps the only way to end the Bosnian impasse was to bomb the bridges over the Drina River linking Serbia to Serb-held Bosnia.

Frasure's thinking was close to that of Holbrooke, who had a keen sense of the place of power in diplomacy and of the administration's unease with that fact. "At the beginning, on Bosnia, the administration could not take on the Chiefs because of the president's Vietnam record and the gays-in-the-military question," Holbrooke told me. "But the fact is, the thing the Pentagon should be seeking is success, not avoiding failure." As it was, however, the Pentagon's unswerving caution on matters Bosnian long prevailed in the face of a president less than comfortable in his dealings with the military.

As the Croatian intention to attack the Krajina became apparent in late July 1995, the Pentagon was again circumspect. Defense Secretary William J. Perry told Clinton that the Croatian army's timetable for victory in four to eight days was too optimistic. There were still fears that Milošević might intervene, despite his evident withdrawal from the wars. But Holbrooke, Albright, and Anthony Lake, the national security adviser, took the view that the attack was probably inevitable and might be beneficial. The upshot was the same "yellow light" to Tudjman given by Clinton for the Iranian arms pipeline, and once again the yellow naturally glowed green for the Croatian president. Despite some largely cosmetic last-minute efforts by Peter Galbraith, the American ambassador to Zagreb, to patch together an accord between Croats and Serbs, and some eleventh-hour concessions from the Krajina Serb leadership, the Croatian army moved before dawn on August 4.

The retired American generals from Military Professional Resources Inc. appear to have been influential in the preparations for the Croatian offensive. Both General Vuono, the former army chief of staff, and General Saint, the former commander of the United States Army in Europe, were in Zagreb in the days before the attack began. They held meetings with Šušak and with senior Croatian officers. Certainly the lightning five-pronged attack, integrating air power, artillery, and rapid infantry movements and relying on speed and intense maneuvering to unhinge Serb command and control networks, bore many hallmarks of American army doctrine.

The Serb defenses evaporated; so, too, did the nominal United Nations protection of the Krajina area. Indeed, one unit of Croatian forces used Danish peacekeepers as a shield. Within thirty-six hours of the start of the Croatian blitz on August 4, 1995, Knin and its railway station had fallen. With scarcely a whimper after the welter of bombast, the four-year-old Serb rebellion in Croatia was over. Once Knin had fallen what remained was a mopping-up operation; more than 150,000 Serbs fled eastward, moving back across the terrain covered centuries earlier by ancestors who fled westward from the Ottoman Turks. What Ante Pavelić had dreamed of but not accomplished—the elimination of Croatia's Orthodox population—was close to realization a half century later.

After just four days the operation was over. Rather than stand and fight, Major General Mile Mrkšić, a Serbian general dispatched from Belgrade after the fall of western Slavonia to command the Krajina forces, opted for what amounted to an immediate surrender. He and other Serbian officers had nothing in the Krajina to lose; their families were back in Serbia.

For the local troops under their command, however, the story was different: they lost everything. Western officials told me that Šarinić, Tudjman's chief aide, and Milošević had been in contact throughout the period leading to the Krajina attack. The Croats had a reasonable assurance that Serbia would not fight. But Milošević, true to his nature, did not have the courage to warn the Krajina Serbs that the game was up. Instead of an organized retreat, therefore, the departure from the Krajina took the form of panic-stricken flight.

Cursed, derided, jeered, pelted with stones and rotting food, the 150,000 Serb refugees set out on the long trudge eastward across Bosnia to Serbia and Belgrade. The unscrambling of centuries of miscegenation in Europe in the name of relatively new ideas—that of the "nation-state" and its perversion, the "nation-as-tribe"—reached a paroxysm during the twentieth century. Hitler and Stalin moved or annihilated millions in the name of racist ideology or social engineering. More than one million Greeks were "resettled" from Turkey during the 1920s; six million Jews were slaughtered by the Nazi's; more than three million ethnic Germans from Central Europe and the Soviet Union were "resettled" in the aftermath of World War II. Violence, the very heart of fascist ideologies in which differences of class and background were subsumed, grew in proportion to the often tenuous reality of the national idea. As Hans Magnus Enzensberger has observed, "The Aryan was never anything more than a risible construct," a form of "compensation" for the mixed blood of the German and Austrian peoples. Similarly, in the Balkans, the postcommunist "construct" of the Serbian, Croatian, and finally Bosnian Muslim nations had to be imbued with a "compensatory" fervor that masked the reality of mingling expressed in the idea of Yugoslavia. This fervor of the resurgent nation—built as much around legend as historical fact—in turn produced bloodshed not seen in Europe since 1945.

Europe was reputed to have changed since the Second World War. The creation of NATO and of the European Union symbolized the determination to defend values of human dignity and preserve the peace; the organizations had been remarkably successful. But they proved incapable of stopping the destruction of Yugoslavia on the basis of the very ideas abjured in postwar European reconstruction: that is, the "purification" of the ethnic map of a European region through the slaughter and forced migration of people. Herein lay the essence of the West's failure in Yugoslavia.

Several hundred Serbs, perhaps more, were killed, many of them in cold blood. In scattered incidents, the Serb brutality during the Croatian campaign of 1991 was repaid in kind. A few days after the fall of Knin, Raymond Bonner, my *New York Times* colleague, found the Krajina region eerily depopulated, with the smell of charred wood and dead animals permeating the hills. Entire settlements were systematically burned to ensure that the Serbs would never return. Farm animals wandered again through deserted villages. A twenty-nine-year-old BBC correspondent, John Schofield, was shot dead by Croatian forces while filming the burning of houses—one of more than fifty journalists killed during the war. The Croats, deeply resentful of any suggestion of atrocities or systematic destruction, did not want their pillaging on film.

A Croatian Defense Ministry spokesman, General Ivan Tolj, proclaimed that "these are historic days, for Croatia, Europe, and the whole world." The Croatian flag fluttered over the Krajina stronghold of Knin, where Martić, only months earlier, had told me with such confidence that his "republic" would gain international recognition. After the more than nine hundred years of statelessness, after the Serb taunts about the gutlessness of the Croats, after the loss of Vukovar in 1991 and the widespread Croat suffering in that war, the "Storm" campaign was at once a military victory and a potent affirmation of Croatian national identity.

For Tudjman and Šušak, the result of the military action was the one they had always intimately desired: the removal of Croatia's Serbs. The mass exodus meant that Croatia's population was no more than 5 percent Serb, compared to over 12 percent when the wars of Yugoslavia's destruction began. These Serbs were concentrated in what, after the fall of the Krajina, was the one remaining stretch of Serb-held land in Croatia: the area around Vukovar known as eastern Slavonia.

Tudjman, the "father" of the nation, was exultant and, on August 27, 1995, he boarded a "freedom train" that took him from northern Croatia to the country's southern seaboard. The 262-mile journey through what had been the Serb-held Krajina symbolized a Croatia made whole. Dalmatia and northern Croatia, long divided during the centuries of statelessness, divided again during Tudjman's fight for Croatian independence, were linked, the Serb settlers finally removed. "They didn't even have time to collect their dirty currency and their dirty underwear!" Tudjman shouted to an ecstatic crowd of one hundred thousand people in the Adriatic port of Split.

Tudjman said something else: *"On this day we can say that Croatia stopped bearing its historical cross. This is not just the liberation of land but the creation of a foundation for a free and independent Croatia for centuries to come."* The "historical cross," of course, was none other than the presence of a large Serb minority in Croatia, and the religious imagery appropriately recalled the fanatical pogrom that Pavelić's Ustasha had carried out a half century earlier in pursuit of the goal now achieved by Tudjman. Thus disencumbered of its "historical cross," Tudjman's Croatia naturally had no desire ever to bear it again. The Croatian president listened to, and ignored, feeble American protests at the expulsion of Serbs. Statements from the Croatian government that the Serbs were "free to return" were no more than velleities.

The Serb-Croat knot that had led to war had been forcibly severed. I thought of Alija Mehmedović, the Bosnian Muslim who, a half century earlier, had served the Ustasha in its quest for an "independent Croatia" free of Serbs. He had always argued, in his exile, that Yugoslavia was a fiction, a structure awaiting collapse, but such a repetition of Serb-Croat violence was probably unthinkable even to him. Yet it was, I felt, the fact of Alija Mehmedović's "disappearance" and others that made such a gyre of bloodletting possible. Suppressed truth is vengeance in waiting.

When the nationalist fires kindled by Milošević and Tudjman began, they were stoked essentially by the Serb-Croat tensions that had existed since Yugoslavia's creation in 1918 and had been redoubled by the violence of the Second World War. The Muslims of Bosnia were peripheral to the outbreak of war. But the pitiless logic of ethno-national separation dragged them in. Unhinged by propaganda, the Serbs then managed to conflate an enemy that provoked them—Tudjman's Croats—with an imagined enemy—Izetbegović's Muslims. The example of people like Alija Mehmedović served Milošević's propagandists: not merely "Turks," the Muslims of Bosnia were also "Ustashas." In general, of course, they had been, and remained, neither.

I FOUND THE MILJEVIĆ FAMILY in the central Serbian town of Kraljevo, which they had reached after traveling for fourteen days in tractors from the Krajina. They had come to the city because, when they reached the Serbian border after fleeing their home village of Kostreši, a policeman handed them a piece of paper saying "Kraljevo." No explanation was given.

On arrival, they were directed to the technical school. The gymnasium, shared with three hundred other refugees, became their home. From where he slept, Miloš Miljević, aged sixty-three, looked up at a basketball net. Children stared; babies screamed; aged widows in black slept, their thin mouths fixed in a rictus of bewilderment.

For Miloš, it was the second time that he had been a refugee. As a boy he spent four years in the woods near the Krajina town of Glina, a Serb hounded by Croatian Ustashas. When he returned to Kostreši in 1945, all that was left of his home were the chicken coops. "I was twelve," he said. "I went to work repairing the house. With Tito things seemed all right. But the peace depended on him."

In 1991, a few months before Croatia seceded from Yugoslavia and war began, Miloš fled the Croatian town of Sisak, where he had lived for many years and worked in a steel mill. As the propaganda machines of Tudjman and Milošević moved into high gear, his Croatian coworkers labeled Miljević a Chetnik. He moved back to Kostreši with his wife, Danica, becoming part of the Serb campaign to hold on to part of Croatia, only to lose his home again to the Croatian army's "Storm" campaign.

His son Željko, aged thirty, and his grandson, Miroslav, aged three, stood beside him: three generations of Serb refugees. Miroslav started to cry, asking why he could not go home. A policeman appeared and said the refugees were forbidden to talk to "foreigners." They were to be kept hidden because images of their suffering could embarrass Milošević.

Later, the Miljević family appeared in Kraljevo's main square, dominated by a monument to the Serb dead in the Balkan wars of 1912 and 1913, wars in which Serbia pushed its borders southward to embrace Macedonia and Kosovo. Macedonia was gone now, independent since Yugoslavia broke up. Kosovo was still held, but only through severe repression of the Albanian majority. Miroslav, the little Krajina refugee, ran around the hero-warriors of Serbia on their stone pedestal. His grandfather watched this pathetic scene from a nearby café. A man came by selling screwdrivers. "I don't have a house," said Miloš. "Why would I need a screwdriver?"

His son, Željko Miljević, was deeply embittered. He had been in a unit of special Serb forces in the Krajina and knew all about the Serb defeat there. It was Saturday, August 5, at about two in the afternoon, when his unit was ordered to withdraw. No explanations were given. Željko's commanding officers had already fled. "We could have defended ourselves, but the Krajina had already been sold," he said. His account coincided with those of dozens of other refugees. Many civilians left under orders, thinking they were going to Bosnia for a night, while the Croatian threat was rebuffed. But no attempt was made to fight.

"This happened to many Croats in 1991," Željko continued. "And now it is happening to us. But it always seems beyond our control. In 1991, when the Croat houses in the Krajina were being burned, there were all these outsiders, militia groups, people we had never seen before, who were doing it."

Željko Miljević's odyssey was not over. On August 24, 1995, five days after his arrival in Kraljevo, he and his brother-in-law were arrested by Serbian police. They were not allowed to say good-bye to their families before being taken to Erdut in eastern Slavonia, the one remaining Serb-occupied sliver of Croatia. There, Željko was thrust by the police into the "military training camp" of Arkan, the Serbian paramilitary leader whose business interests centered largely on the area. He was held at the camp for six days. The prisoners, all of them from the Krajina, were made to carry heavy rocks and beaten if they dropped them. Arkan himself harangued them about their performance in the Krajina.

I traveled to eastern Slavonia to find Željko. The ruins of Vukovar greeted me, with a sign on the outskirts of town: ALL YOU NEED FOR FUNERALS HERE. Four years after Serb forces reduced the town to rubble, little had changed. The silos stood crumbling, the water tower sliced in half, walls collapsed in piles of rubble, the Orthodox church as yet unrepaired. A liberated Serb town! Onward, through the lush fields of Slavonia, where the peoples of central Europe long mingled, to Petrovići, near the Serbs' front line. New trenches were being dug for yet another battle, and there was Željko. His head had been shaved. His beard had been shaved. He had new boots, a new uniform, and a new, deeper resignation in his eyes.

His commanding officer, Vladimir Mitrović, tried to explain the Serbs' struggle to me. He talked about the "Green Transversal," the Muslim plots, the "six million Arabs" in France, and other matters. An angry soldier jabbed his rifle in my direction and said the world wanted to make an Indian reservation for Serbs. American weapons, German money, and the Vatican's ideas were driving the Serbs from their land. Željko listened but seemed far away. He was tired of history.

I watched him, a Serb, four years into a life of war, standing on another front line far from the home he had been denied the right to defend. Željko was marooned, forbidden to return to Serbia, where his wife had been told she could not put their children in school because the Miljevićs had no home. I thought of Alija Mehmedović's jotting in his old notebook: "We can control the flood. But what do we do against the cyclone?" The dying gusts of Milošević's Serb storm had tossed Željko this way and that—another migration in the long Serb history of migrations.

WHEN THE SERB REFUGEES from the Krajina started to pour into Belgrade in August 1995, Vojna Adamović was filled with an unspeakable rage. Anger spilled over into tears she could control. Forty months had elapsed since she herself had fled from Sarajevo on April 12, 1992, a week after the first shots of the war were fired while she stood with Muris Zeče-vić on Vrbanja Bridge demonstrating for a united Bosnia. Still unrecon-ciled to her new life in Serbia, she had thought a lot about her flight.

The Muslims made her uneasy before the war: their influx into Bosnia from the Sandžak region of Serbia, their nationalist SDA party, their grow-ing stridency. But that was not what forced her out of Sarajevo. She left be-cause the shelling terrified her. From the moment she heard the sounds of war echo in the valley she could not stop trembling. The shells came from Radovan Karadžić's Serb forces, who did not hesitate to start a war. She, a Sarajevo Serb, ran from Serb shells.

Now she watched the long procession of dispossessed Serbs moving slowly down Tito's highway of "Brotherhood and Unity" on the outskirts of Belgrade. In carts, on tractors, on foot, on horseback, in military fa-tigues, in jeans, traipsing forward into the hollowness of exile. It was sum-mer, but a grayness filled the air. At a Red Cross center she saw people whose eyes were so emptied of life they looked blind. This was the reflux, eight years on, from the madness set in motion by Milošević in 1987.

Vojna grabbed a few clothes, some soup, some bread, whatever she could spare, to hand out to the refugees. The weight of such upheaval was still in her heart. In the back of a trailer, an eighty-four-year-old woman was bundled in beside mattresses, blankets, piles of clothes, a wheelbarrow, and a bicycle. "The Ustashas of Pavelić killed her brother," her son said. "And now the Ustashas of Tudjman have done this."

The refugees grabbed what they could. But there was no time to salvage more than the scraps of a life, so quickly had the self-styled Krajina re-public of Martić's Croatian Serbs crumbled before Tudjman's army. Pen-tagon analysts had assumed that any battle for the Krajina would be bitter; they believed there would be more Serb resistance than in western Slavo-nia. But they reckoned without Martić's cowardice—the Krajina leader (in his Mercedes), was one of the first to flee—and Milošević's cynical sacri-fice of the Serbs he had armed and incited in 1990 and 1991.

Milošević was silent about the disaster. He did not talk to these Serbs who had lost everything; perhaps he feared that they would lynch him. In 1991, he had goaded these Serbs to fight what his propaganda machine called the "Ustashas." But in the end it is Greater Slobo that matters more than Greater Serbia, and political accountability does not exist in the Balkans.

The Serbs were exhausted after ten or fifteen days on the road covering the three hundred miles from the fallen Krajina. Vojna watched them. Their dismay was that of her broken father, Mišo, in Bijeljina. For so many people—Serb, Muslim, or Croat—the war was ruin. Then there were the few like Dukić, for whom Vojna still works at Boksit Trade, who had mined fortune from misery.

The refugees' overwhelming sentiment was one of betrayal—by Milošević, who did not lift a finger; by Karadžić, whose promises of union with Serb-held Croatia were empty; by Martić, who ran like the small-time crook he was. A war to overcome perennial Serb divisions had given rise to these new fractures. One man, Jovo Ubović, could no longer move. For ten days he had been on the road from the Kostajnica area and now he lay slumped in the grass. "What did I do for the past four years?" he asked. "What were we fighting for? Why is my son a war invalid? Where do I belong? What is my state? To whom do I ask these questions?"

For many of these Serbs, it was the first time they had set foot in Serbia. Vojna knew how hard the adjustment would be. "You know, it's funny, you can't imagine how I've come to miss the mountains, yearn for the mountains," she told me. "Everything here is so flat and boring. I ache for the Bosnian mountains and forests. The people here in Serbia tend to think we Bosnians just came down from the trees."

Vojna continued: "I would charge Milošević and Karadžić with genocide against 1.8 million Serbs. They destroyed us in Bosnia and in Croatia. They made us ashamed to be Serbs. That burden is mine to bear. I was so proud of our past. That we had the nerve to say no to that monster, Hitler, just to say no. *Bolje grob nego rob*—Better the grave than a slave. I was proud of that. I do not want this feeling of shame for my people. But how can we accept that we were right to shell Sarajevo for four years? Can you imagine how many children were killed? Who gave Karadžić the right to kill those people?"

VOJNA ADAMOVIĆ'S AUNT, Kosa Hegeduš, was still in Tuzla, one of the dwindling group of Serbs who had remained in the government-held city. She had kept her apartment and her photo shop, but her weekend house, on a lake near the city, had been requisitioned by the Bosnian army. I went out there with her and found the place in ruins. Bosnian soldiers had helped themselves to all the furniture before smashing down the walls of this Serb-owned home.

Kosa picked up some delicate blue lilies. She had brought them from the Ozren Mountains and planted them in boxes along the side of the house. She shrugged and tossed the flowers away. Of seventy-six rosebushes just one had survived. The cherry tree and the peach tree still stood, but other trees, behind the house, had been cut down for firewood. Below the remains of the house the placid lake stretched away, like a blank piece of white paper beside splashes of blood.

"These are just walls," Kosa said. "I am not interested in hating. I just want to remember this place the way it was. I am sorry about the roses and the trees—it takes so long for a tree to grow. I will never rebuild. I know that my friends and family have gone and will never return. Vojna will not come back to Bosnia. My son will not come back. Without them, this place means nothing. In fact, all this is like an illusion. I ask myself what I am doing here. Something was crushed; something else took its place. We have been forced to become something else. All you have left in the end is your own mind, because everything else has been taken away."

It was true. Everything had gone. Yugoslavia. Bosnia. The mixed Croatian population. The logic of the war had prevailed. In the space of one month, another 200,000 people had been killed or moved: 40,000 Muslims from Srebrenica and more than 150,000 Serbs from Croatia. Peace would be achieved not by confronting barbarism but on the basis of the fact that it had run its course.

CHAPTER 32

THE
BECKONING SEA

FOR MORE THAN THREE YEARS, THE BOSNIAN WAR GNAWED AT America's moral center. The world's only superpower, President Clinton's "indispensable nation" found itself faced by a small European war that defeated it. There has always been a tension in American foreign policy between a Wilsonian moralism and Kissingerian focus on *raison d'état*, defined in purely strategic and economic terms. From the moment the existence of the Serb concentration camps became known in 1992, Bosnia was above all a moral dilemma. Like America, Bosnia had been a multi-ethnic state; it was dismembered through ideologies of ethnic hatred that flouted the American idea.

The war weighed so heavily on several State Department diplomats that they quit in protest at what they saw as America's moral failure. It broke others whose world was changed to the point where their jobs seemed meaningless. It left almost everyone touched by the conflict with anguished questions about America's failure in the face of a European genocide and about America's role in a changed world, one no longer bipolar and so, in theory, more malleable to American power. The very notion of "indispensability" begged the question: Indispensable for what?

Madeleine K. Albright, as the American ambassador to the United Nations through much of the war, stood close to the center of the West's response. She told me she kept hearing Neville Chamberlain's words justifying his decision not to fight Hitler over Czechoslovakia in 1938: these were people, the British prime minister said, "of whom we know nothing" living "in a faraway country." Bosnians, too, were far away and their names often unpronounceable. Ms. Albright, as a historian, had taught courses on the betrayal of Czechoslovakia. "And here," she said, "was something similar being repeated in my era and it bothered me a great deal and I felt very strongly that we ought to do something about it."

But Bosnia did not satisfy the Pentagon's criteria for the use of American power. In the end one of Ms. Albright's few moments of satisfaction came in August 1995, when she was able to show the U.S. satellite photographs of the mass killings near Srebrenica. "It just goes to show you how awful it all was that my greatest sense of achievement came when I was finally able to bring in the pictures of Srebrenica and so show that we could prove what had happened," she said. "At that moment, I was able to use what America had in a positive way to demonstrate the horror." For years, the horror had been obscured, sometimes deliberately, sometimes by the transatlantic disagreements that grew out of the Bosnian war.

There were American satellite photographs, three years earlier, of the Serb camps. They were not shown to the Security Council and they were not used to marshal a Western military response because the Bush administration had decided that intervention in the former Yugoslavia was undesirable. Ron Neitzke of the State Department saw the 1992 photographs and cannot stop thinking about them. His colleagues ask what's up with him. They urge him to lighten up. He said to me, "It's hard to explain to them the effect that the atrocities, then the ethnic cleansing, and then our lies had on me. This was the way the best of the service I'd dedicated my life to confronted the humanitarian catastrophe of our generation: moral cowardice masquerading as cool professionalism. Our policy was very constant: do the minimum possible consistent with being able to portray our position as one of humanitarian assistance and actively seeking peace while taking no risk greater than political expediency dictated. And those who dutifully played along were well rewarded."

THE OUTLINES OF THIS American policy were already in place by the time Clinton took office in January 1993. The United Nations humanitarian mission had started. A decision had been made not to place American troops in harm's way in Bosnia. French and British troops wearing United Nations uniform were in Bosnia—American allies vulnerable to the NATO air strikes Clinton initially, but lamely, backed. The arms embargo on the states of the former Yugoslavia had been allowed to stand. The architecture of containment—of moral surrender dressed up in the soothing garb of humanitarianism—had already been established.

Through thirty more months of war, the Clinton administration allowed this house of gloom to stand. The administration was presented with an intractable mess, but it could find neither the determination nor the moral conviction to rectify it. Bosnia's dismemberment was consummated through this failure. When fracture occurs, the bones can be repaired, but only on condition that the operation does not take place years later.

Bosnia became a trial balloon for all kinds of weighty issues: NATO's future, the role of Russia in the Balkans, NATO's relations with Russia, the place of Muslims in European society, the degree of American involvement in a post–cold war Europe. These questions were fractious. A thinly veiled anxiety about a Muslim European state, one that sometimes spilled over into bigotry, colored British and French discourse about Bosnia and made agreements with Washington more difficult. For a long time, NATO appeared an anachronism, a monster deprived of its old Soviet enemy and in search of a new role before the world's tribal minnows. It took time to think through what the alliance should become and how it might act in Bosnia—a process lengthened by America's extraordinary renunciation of leadership in the Balkans.

But all the arguments, whatever their substance, were also a form of camouflage for the Bosnian moral surrender.

By August 1995, the cost to America of that surrender was overwhelmingly clear. The president's frustration was running high. At the summit of major industrialized nations in Halifax, Canada, in July, President Chirac of France appeared briefly to take on the mantle of leader of the Western world simply by talking aggressively about Bosnia. Srebrenica was a humiliation: as a massacre in a "safe area," it exposed America's Bosnian hypocrisy in an Orwellian beam. The massive Serb exodus from the Krajina was scarcely uplifting. The Senate was clearly preparing to override the president's veto and lift the arms embargo. British and French troops in Bosnia would then leave, and the president would be obliged to fulfill a commitment to provide American troops to assist such a United Nations evacuation. This operation would be dangerous; it would amount to a further humiliation on the eve of the 1996 election, possibly crippling Clinton's campaign.

Only with its back squarely against the wall did the administration decide to act. The basis for American action was disaster, repeated and devastating. The collapse of the protection of Sarajevo in June 1995 and the fall of Srebrenica in July opened the way. They removed almost all United Nations troops from areas where they were surrounded by Serbs and so vulnerable to hostage-taking. Thus, in theory, NATO power could for the first time be effectively used, supported by the newly installed artillery of the Rapid Reaction Force.

The fall of the Krajina also contributed to America's belated awakening. The departure of more than 150,000 Serb refugees resolved most of the outstanding differences between Serbia and Croatia. Wars begun over Croatia's Serb minority were presumably closer to resolution now that most of that minority was gone. Milošević's refusal to help his Krajina Serb brothers finally laid to rest any lingering doubts in Washington over whether the Serbian president was prepared to escalate the wars. In short, the destruction of Yugoslavia was far enough advanced to offer a breach for peace. Nothing in this calculation was courageous.

ANTHONY LAKE, Clinton's national security adviser, elaborated the plan behind the new American diplomatic effort. The Contact Group map of 1994, source of so much dissent, was finally dropped; in any event, the capture of Srebrenica by the Serbs had rendered it obsolete. All that was preserved was the notion that 51 percent of Bosnia should go to the Muslim-Croat federation and 49 percent to the Serbs. Pragmatism was finally paramount. Even the cession to the Serbs of the last of the eastern enclaves, Goražde, with its more than sixty thousand Muslims, was initially envisaged, before Holbrooke objected.

Milošević was to be aggressively rewarded with a lifting of economic sanctions on Serbia provided he gave support for the plan. The approach was to be all-encompassing rather than piecemeal: a Bosnian peace and a Croatian peace were to be sought at the same time by the same people and a political solution found for eastern Slavonia, the one remaining Serb-held stretch of land in Croatia. An elaborate program of economic reconstruction was outlined. In all, the plan, presented to Western European governments by Lake during a five-day visit that began on August 9, 1995, amounted more to a series of feelers than a firm blueprint.

On August 14, in London, Lake handed over to Holbrooke. It was a poignant moment. The two men had gone to Vietnam together in 1963 as junior State Department officials with youthful visions of settling conflicts, changing things, even making the world a better place. Ideals of action and public service rooted in a sense of the American idea as much as of the American interest.

They had formed a close friendship, since eroded. Lake had been hesitant about Holbrooke's return to Washington in 1993—"My main question," Lake told me, "was whether, since he had been an assistant secretary in the late seventies, he would find it satisfying being an assistant secretary again." He was also hesitant about entrusting Holbrooke with the peace initiative—"My question," Lake said, "was how much he was prepared to throw himself into this given his other duties."

Questions, questions. "Hurricane Holbrooke" provoked plenty of them in Washington. There was a line on him: a "high-maintenance personality"; gifted but disruptive; imagines he's a seventh-floor official when he's only sixth-floor; too undisciplined to follow instructions. There was anger at Holbrooke's high-handedness and unease at his bald ambition. But Warren Christopher, the secretary of state, and Thomas Donilon, his chief of staff, ultimately convinced a skeptical National Security Council that Holbrooke could be entrusted with so delicate a mission.

Lake, in London, allowed himself to be emotional. "I indulged in a moment of sentimentality," he told me. "Holbrooke and I did join the Foreign Service together. We had been friends but also career rivals, and that makes any friendship difficult. It just occurred to me then—I looked back at our having entered the service at the same time and the fact that here we were, more than three decades on, with an opportunity to stop, if we could, a terrible conflict. That is what we once dreamt of doing when we worked together in Vietnam, to change the course on Vietnam."

In many ways, the conversation was grotesque. Vietnam's legacy, in Bosnia, had been the extreme caution of the Pentagon and of Lake. This caution, in turn, had allowed the war to drag on to a point where idealistic talk was misplaced, for the idea of Bosnia had been undone. There were individual lives still to be saved, but Bosnia's was largely beyond resuscitation.

Lake had wanted, in his words, to "fire Holbrooke up," but fire was never something Holbrooke lacked. He had been unhappy in Washington. "He was a very frustrated functionary in an enormous bureaucracy being driven increasingly crazy by the generic underminers, the envious, ferretlike Washington subspecies," his wife, Kati Marton, said.

In May 1968, Holbrooke had been involved in trying to end another war by extracting an increasingly lacerated America from its most disastrous cold war failure. He came to Paris as a young member of the delegation led by W. Averell Harriman to embark on the first negotiations with the Vietcong. Ever since, he had sought to lead a major international negotiation. Indeed, an unremitting thirst to make a historical mark characterized him from an early age. When his father died, Holbrooke, then sixteen, gravitated toward the family of Dean Rusk, the former secretary of state, whose son David was his closest high-school friend in Scarsdale, New York. Rusk came to embody the ideals of patriotism and public service that led Holbrooke into the Foreign Service after college at Brown and make up one element in his personality.

The other side of him—the driving ambition, the impatience with form, the bad temper, the manipulative circumlocutions, the insatiability about publicity—had created problems in Washington and sometimes placed his Ruskian ideal of service and self-effacement grotesquely at odds with the baroque reality of being Richard Holbrooke. This was a man capable of such stunningly guileless acts of attempted self-aggrandizement as suggesting to journalists how to write their leads. But as Lake observed to me, "What Holbrooke wants attention for is what he's doing, not what he is—that's a very serious quality and it's his saving grace."

Holbrooke was serious about Bosnia. He had seen enough, on the ground, to know that good intentions are worse than useless in the Balkans. He was ready and willing to be tough. He was prepared to throw American power about. And, in some visceral way, he cared. Stefanie Frease, then an aid worker, traveled with Holbrooke in Bosnia in 1992 and, at one point, as he dissected the conflict in his cool, analytical way, she accused him of not feeling. "He exploded," she said, "he was not cool anymore. Not at all. He told me he felt more for Bosnia than anybody in the government. I think he was genuinely upset."

In Asia, in the late 1970s, as the wunderkind of the Carter administration and assistant secretary of state for Far Eastern affairs, Holbrooke had been widely accused of cozying up to President Marcos and his wife, Imelda, in order to secure the renewal of an agreement for two important military bases. He had clashed violently with Patricia Derian, the assistant secretary of state for human rights. The charges hurt. "The fact is," Holbrooke insisted, "America is one of the few countries whose inhabitants came here in pursuit of an ideal, and that ideal is part of our values at home and abroad. Often we have not lived up to these ideals, but they are our values. I am not a Wilsonian. I think he was naïve. I think he was a failure. Those thick red lines he drew at Versailles around imagined ethnic boundaries made a significant contribution to what is going on in the Balkans today. But I also believe realpolitik for America is self-defeating in its cynicism. We cannot choose between the two—we have to blend the two."

HOLBROOKE'S HELICOPTER LANDS near the summit of Mount Igman, just outside Sarajevo. It is a cool morning with low clouds; the rain has just stopped, and the encircled city lies spread-eagled beneath the Americans. It is August 19, 1995, and Holbrooke is on the first of his Balkan shuttles. I know this view so well. I know the heart-in-mouth feeling of setting off down the winding Igman track into the face of Serb guns, the terror of feeling a careering vehicle lurch toward the abyss.

Holbrooke leads a team including Robert C. Frasure of the State Department, Deputy Assistant Secretary of Defense Joseph Kruzel, Colonel S. Nelson Drew of the National Security Council, and Lieutenant General Wesley K. Clark of the Joint Chiefs of Staff. The interagency brain trust. Frasure's wife, Katarina, had called him the previous night in Split. Frasure had talked about what a terrible job he had, how he wanted to get out, how he was not hopeful for the new initiative.

These senior officials find themselves atop a waterlogged Bosnian mountain about to descend a dangerous track into the besieged capital because, the previous day, Holbrooke had failed even to obtain security guarantees from the Serbs for a flight into Sarajevo. He demanded the guarantees from Milošević, saying it was "demeaning and dangerous" for his team to take the Igman road. Milošević spoke with Mladić, the commander of the Bosnian Serbs and orchestrator of the long Sarajevo siege. No deal. "Well, Mr. President, can you give us your assurances?" Holbrooke asked Milošević. Not without Mladić. The usual Serb runaround.

It has been this way for more than three years, ever since Muris Zečević was killed on another mountain beside Sarajevo in August 1992. Milošević blaming Mladić or Karadžić. Karadžić blaming rogue paramilitary forces beyond his control or the inventions of Muslim propaganda. Americans and Europeans gazing into this hall of mirrors, trying to make sense of it, blaming each other for failing to do so, declining to use force to wrest the initiative from the Serbs.

General Clark puts Holbrooke beside him in the Humvee because "I knew that way Dick would be able to see more and he's always very curious." The others get inside a French armored personnel carrier, more secure against Serb gunfire but bulkier. The delegation starts down the track, the Humvee leading the way. Then a French truck coming up the mountain blocks the vehicle. The truck driver jumps out and tells Clark an armored personnel carrier has gone over the edge.

Holbrooke and Clark dash back up the hill about one hundred yards and look down. "It seemed like a giant lawn mower had gone down the mountain, scything the trees," Clark says. "We heard an explosion." The two men run back down the road, which is exposed to Serb fire, around a hairpin. Holbrooke, fearing an ambush, orders his Humvee turned around.

Lieutenant Colonel Daniel Gerstein was inside the armored personnel carrier. "On the first roll," he told me, "I thought it would be one roll and stop. We went over so slowly. Kruzel landed on top of me and said, 'What's going on?' Then I realized it was rolling. We were airborne. At one point, I felt four revolutions without touching the ground. I felt the bones around my eyes break. I tried to go with the roll, not against it. There was an awful cracking and groaning. A terrible noise."

Clark, scrambling over fallen trees and branches, reaches the vehicle at last. It is on its side, the wheels are burning. Gerstein, a mortally wounded Kruzel, and a security officer named Peter Hargreaves have managed to get out. French soldiers are gesticulating wildly, warning Clark not to go near the vehicle because it will explode.

The general takes a log and pries open the hatch. He peers into the fire, caused by oil and fuel sprayed on hot pipes as the vehicle rotated and by exploding anti-tank rounds. The scene reminds him of a gas boiler in a power plant: a round metallic interior and roaring flames. Frasure and

Drew are utterly gone, reduced to skeletal remains. Kruzel dies later on the way to a field hospital.

When Holbrooke hears of Frasure's death, he yells, "No, no, not possible!" Something has shifted in Holbrooke—who had been inclined to throw up his hands on Bosnia—and in America. A war long clouded in obfuscation is now reduced to physical fact in the corpses of Frasure, Drew, and Kruzel: they make America part of the war. The death or disappearance of two hundred thousand people is no longer quite so abstract.

Later that day, Clinton and Strobe Talbott, the deputy secretary of state, take a call from Holbrooke, who says, "Mr. President, we must suspend the mission long enough to bring our fallen comrades home." But that evening, Holbrooke is spooked. He goes down to the airport and two helicopters, one French and one British, come in to take the coffins and the survivors out. The French provide an honor guard. Holbrooke and Clark get in behind the coffins on the French chopper. The weather is closing in, there is rain, and the coffins, draped in the American flag, are pressing against their knees. At the last moment, Holbrooke decides not to risk departure.

They leave the next morning, weaving in and out of the mountains with the coffins against their knees. This physical pressure is the Bosnian tragedy finally made manifest. By an odd twist of fate America has at last been implicated.

The interruption of this flight home is to be no more than that. Holbrooke is now driven. Rosemarie Pauli, Holbrooke's personal assistant, had declined to go to Sarajevo that day because she had a bad feeling about the trip. But now she feels she has to do it for the dead. "What impelled Holbrooke was the memory of Frasure," said Ron Neitzke, the former deputy chief of mission in Zagreb. "He knew Frasure was much too good a man to die putting the best possible twist on a bad policy."

The day before he died, at a meeting with Tudjman in Zagreb, Frasure passed a note to Holbrooke. The Croat army was beginning to move against the Serbs in southwest Bosnia and, after the fall of the Krajina, there was some pressure in Washington to rein the Croats in. "This is no time to get squeamish," the note read. "This is the first time the Serb wave has been reversed. That is essential for us to get stability. So we can negotiate and get out." Frasure's approach became Holbrooke's.

ON AUGUST 28, 1995, nine days after the accident, two shells slammed into the central Sarajevo market area, killing thirty-seven people and wounding eighty-eight. Limbs and flesh were splattered yet again on storefronts, and the bodies of civilians fell to pieces as they were lifted into cars. It was the most devastating single attack on the Bosnian capital since the mortar attack on February 5, 1994, which had led NATO to vow that the city would be protected. As usual, the Serbs said the Muslims had attacked themselves.

By the next day, Lieutenant Colonel Brian E. Powers, an American working in intelligence at the United Nations headquarters in Sarajevo, produced a report saying that "following an investigation and analysis of all evidence it has been concluded beyond a reasonable doubt that the firing position of the mortar rounds was in Bosnian Serb territory between Lukavica and Miljevići." The way was thus opened, with Janvier away at his son's wedding, for Smith to "turn the key" that would at last unleash a serious NATO bombing campaign against the Serbs. The last vulnerable United Nations troops—British soldiers in Serb-encircled Goražde—were withdrawn late on August 28. For the first time, there was no risk of hostage-taking. Western resolve was correspondingly more serious.

In the early morning of August 30, before the dazed and incredulous eyes of Sarajevans, NATO warplanes swooped over the Bosnian capital and began bombing Bosnian Serb positions to the south and east of the city. The Rapid Reaction Force on Mount Igman opened up with its artillery, firing more than nine hundred rounds at twenty-four selected targets with devastating effect.

One of the first targets hit was the depot in Lukavica barracks where the Serbs kept much of the equipment they had stolen over the years from the United Nations. By Smith's estimate these included six French light tanks, four French light armored vehicles, eight French armored personnel carriers, two French trucks, three Ukrainian trucks, eighteen Ukrainian armored personnel carriers, seven Canadian armored personnel carriers, five British Saxon armored personnel carriers, eighteen Dutch jeeps, fourteen Dutch armored personnel carriers, one Dutch truck, and one Dutch ambulance. The list amounted to an accounting of international humiliation. But now the "laptop bombardiers," repeatedly derided by Lord Owen and countless others, finally had their way. After forty months of war Sarajevans could not believe the concerted bombing; nor could General Ratko Mladić. The bombing continued for three days. Ammunition dumps, bridges, communications equipment, and weaponry were all hit as "proportionality" was finally ditched and NATO attempted to sever Mladić's command-and-control channels. The Bosnian Serb general was furious, firing off a series of messages to Smith referring to the bombing during the Gulf War of "two-thousand-year-old Baghdad," America's failure in Vietnam, the Serbs' fight for their "centennial hearths," and the Serb determination to be "worthy of our ancestors."

On September 1, the bombardment was interrupted as Janvier met Mladić in Mali Zvornik to present three Western demands: the immedi-

ate withdrawal of Serb heavy weapons from around Sarajevo; an end to attacks on Sarajevo and any other "safe areas"; and complete freedom of
movement for the United Nations "with no requirement to comply with
the normal procedures which you have hitherto imposed." Mladić responded with a letter that failed to satisfy NATO or the United Nations.
But the pause in bombing continued as Mladić was given forty-eight
hours to begin withdrawing the weapons that had tormented Sarajevans.

Meanwhile Smith and his Sarajevo staff, now buoyant, did not wait for
the Serb response to be clarified. On September 3, 1995, the siege of Sarajevo was finally lifted, forty-two months after it began and four days after
NATO's first coherent bombing campaign got under way.

The road linking Dobrinja and Butmir across the airport was opened,
without asking permission of the Serbs. Vehicles started to roll. The old,
old dance of submission to Serb whim, with its immense cost to United
Nations pride and to the credibility of Western governments, was over.

On September 4, Mladić wrote a furious letter to Janvier that captured
all the Serbs' sense of repeated persecution that had driven their murderous acts during the war. He referred back to the bombing witnessed by the
infant Sead Mehmedović in Belgrade. "By its length," he wrote, "this bombardment is even more brutal than the bombardment conducted by Hitler
on April 6, 1941, on Belgrade, given the fact that this bombardment was
stopped on April 7–8, 1941, to allow burial of victims under Christian
custom. You did not even do that. Quite contrary you targeted the church
and the cemetery during the funeral of those who died during the bombardment. You did not allow us to take the bodies out of the rubble and
bury them."

Here, from the man who had ordered the killing of several thousand
Muslims at Srebrenica alone, were complaints about the nonobservance of
Christian customs! Yet this was the general with whom, through more
than three years, Western diplomats had tried to negotiate. To believe that
he and Karadžić were insane was to confront the fact that force would be
needed to stop them. So, in London, Paris, and Washington, there was—
until September 1995—a vested interest in their mental stability.

On September 5, with the Serb guns still in place, the NATO bombing
resumed. Serb communication and surface-to-air missile systems collapsed. On September 6, Smith wrote a letter to Akashi that underscored
how the impasse in Bosnia had at last been overcome: "We must hold in
mind that we are in a position to try and force compliance because we are
not exposed to hostage-taking as before. We have acted as combatant and
are seen increasingly as one by the Bosnian Serbs. Thus I am conducting
operations with the following principles: we must maintain our combat-

tant posture; we must deploy our forces even if there is compliance so as to be able to revert to enforcement. We may well continue to see a standard Serb tactic, or variation on it, as they call for attacks to stop so they can talk about the matter. We must avoid falling into this trap. . . . We have stated our demands and delivered our instructions. . . . We are enforcing not debating. We must remember that the stated objective is the removal of the threat from Sarajevo."

Within a few days, the Bosnian and Croat armies began to move against the Serbs, advancing rapidly in western Bosnia. On September 10, thirteen American Tomahawk cruise missiles were fired at Serb-held Banja Luka, spreading terror. Relentlessly, the Bosnian army and the Croats swept aside the disoriented Serbs, quickly reducing the share of Serb-controlled land. On September 14, the Serbs agreed to withdraw their weapons from around Sarajevo. The next day they began to do so. The horror of Sarajevo life under siege was coming to an end.

NATO PLANES FLEW 3,400 sorties and over 700 attack missions in the bombing campaign that started on August 30 and ended September 14. The use of force laid the basis for the end of the war. Would it have done so three years earlier, when the Serb camps were discovered and the Muslims of Bosnia were suffering genocide? I see no reason to believe that earlier bombing would not have been equally effective.

The Serbs were always a ragtag and reluctant army, effective against civilians but little more. Milošević was always in awe of the West, eyeing the attitudes of London, Paris, and Washington before deciding how far he could go. Russia, with domestic business more pressing, was always ready to raise the level of bombast about its friends the Serbs, but never inclined to get deeply involved in the Balkans. The hypothetical has no historical value. It posits the unknowable. But force was justified, and NATO had the means to impose its will. There was no credible Russian threat; there were only rudimentary armies at work in Bosnia. Earlier use of force would have saved lives. It would also, in this material age, have preserved the meaning of Western honor. To understand this required courage, something more than decision-by-consensus in the Security Council or the pat formulas of the Powell Doctrine. That courage, however, was lacking.

During the bombing, Nikola Koljević, the Shakespeare scholar and vice president of Karadžić's self-styled government, confronted a member of Holbrooke's team. Koljević was outraged. A NATO bomb, he said, had fallen 250 yards from his Pale headquarters. The American official replied, "Welcome to war, Mr. Vice President!" A five-hundred-pound bomb makes a hell of an impact: not until forty-two months of war had elapsed did the Serbs briefly experience what they had long inflicted on Sarajevo. When the official questioned Koljević on this Serb bombardment of the Bosnian capital, he replied: "Oh, that was just a bit of mistaken gunnery."

IN THE SHADOW of the bombing, Holbrooke pushes his diplomacy. He puts his faith in force, as Frasure had long urged. On August 28, knowing that the bombardment is about to begin, he hesitates about going to Belgrade. But he recalls Nixon's bombing of Hanoi on the eve of the SALT I signing in 1972. Leonid Brezhnev, the Soviet president, signed anyway.

In Belgrade, Milošević announces: "I have a pleasant surprise for you." The surprise is what the Serbian president, in his expressive English, calls "a heavenly blessed document." Blessed, in fact, by an Orthodox cross, the signature of the patriarch of the Serbian church.

The document amounts to a power of attorney granted to Milošević by Karadžić and Mladić. The Bosnian Serb political and military leaders cede power to Milošević to negotiate a peace on their behalf. In the end, as at the beginning, the ultimate source of Serb power is clear.

The so-called Patriarch document is crucial. The Serb hall of mirrors—the same one that put Holbrooke's team on Mount Igman just eleven days earlier and took three American lives—has finally been shattered; a serious negotiation is possible. It will, however, involve the man who whipped up the wars, Milošević, a man responsible for the loss or ruin of hundreds of thousands of lives, and it is backed by the very Serbian church whose sermons breathed fire into the Serb cause in Bosnia and Croatia. Recalling Frasure, Holbrooke turns to his State Department colleague, Christopher Hill, and says, "Boy, I wish Bob were here with us now to see this document."

Milošević is often alone or accompanied by a single aide. He rattles around the cavernous Presidency Building in Belgrade, a lonely dictator. James Pardew, the Pentagon's representative on Holbrooke's team, observes Milošević entering one side room and muttering about never having been in it before. "Sometimes," Pardew says, "you asked yourself if there was anyone else in the country." Politically, ever since 1987, there had been only one man in Serbia.

American obscenities litter Milošević's conversation—he has a particular penchant for "bullshit"—and are uttered with what Roberts Owen, the lawyer on Holbrooke's team, calls "a lovely distinctive roll to them." A rapport is established between Milošević and Holbrooke: Frasure, who observed their first meeting five days before his death, commented that "the two egos danced all night." Milošević, like Holbrooke, prefers the big picture: details in the talks are dismissed by him as "mere technology." The

Serbian leader is given to reminiscences of the "wonderful smells of New York" and the charms of the Drake Hotel, a regular haunt during his stints in Manhattan as president of a major Belgrade bank. His professed pining for America is such that he even enthuses over American coffee.

Milošević's eagerness to emerge from international isolation, trade sanctions, and war provides Holbrooke with leverage. The Serbian leader is close to the end of a labyrinthine political journey that has left his band of former nationalist allies and his former country devastated. But this is the man who unleashed the forces that created the "madhouse" witnessed by Holbrooke in 1992 in Banja Luka; this is the man who, through his surrogates, put the Muslims in the concentration camps where Holbrooke's wooden carving of a man with head bowed was made. So I ask Holbrooke if, when he talks with Milošević, he thinks of the carving that stands in his Washington office. He becomes defensive and does not answer the question. "The sculpture is sitting there," he tells me. "I point it out to people." When I pursue the question, he replies, "No, it's not that linear. I don't sit there looking at one of those guys and thinking of this piece of wood. You wouldn't either. But I understand the connection. I'm sure we all do."

The fact is that Milošević, through the "Patriarch document," through his longing to return to America, is the key to a low-risk peace. Holbrooke knows this. He is prepared to overlook Milošević's past atrocities in order to end the war. He is vulnerable to the old inebriation, as in Manila and on Marcos's yacht, but in his long talks with Milošević, he appears to maintain a firm eye on the target. He talks repeatedly about human rights and the price of "readmission to the West." When the question arises of whether NATO bombing of the Bosnian Serbs should resume after the three-day pause for talks with Mladić, Holbrooke does not hesitate. "History," he says, "would never forgive us if we stopped now."

On September 8, at a meeting in Geneva, he secures a central agreement on principles from the foreign ministers of Serbia, Croatia, and Bosnia. The parties, for the first time, acknowledge one another's existence, a good first step in stopping the logic of war. The Bosnian Serbs concede the existence of Bosnia and Herzegovina within its internationally recognized borders, so implicitly renouncing their central war aim of an independent state in Bosnia, at least in the near term. Izetbegović's Bosnian government accepts the partition of Bosnia between a Serb entity to be called "Republika Srpska" and a Muslim-Croat federation, so renouncing his often-repeated war aim of a complete "liberation" of the country.

The concession by Izetbegović is an enormous one: it is in the name of the Republika Srpska that a genocide against Bosnian Muslims has been committed. But with NATO at last backing his government by bombing the Serbs, and the Croats and Serbs close to ending their differences after the fall of the Krajina, the Bosnian president has scant room for maneuver or defiance.

Six days later, on September 14, at a meeting in a hunting lodge outside Belgrade, Milošević produces another surprise. He declares that Mladić and Karadžić are coming and are ready to satisfy NATO's demands by negotiating the withdrawal of Serb heavy weapons from around Sarajevo. Holbrooke and his team hesitate: two months earlier the two Serbs were indicted as war criminals by the International Tribunal in The Hague and official American policy has been to avoid dealing with them. But pragmatism is the order of the day. Mladić appears in combat boots and fatigues, without hat or decorations: he looks like a sergeant slumping from the field of battle. Karadžić is wearing a sports coat, shirt, and tie. The Americans hesitate to shake hands with the butchers of Srebrenica, but in the end most of them do because, says Owen, "there did not seem to be any alternative."

Clark writes a draft of an agreement for the withdrawal of the weapons and then reads it aloud in a booming voice accompanied by an equally booming translation. Karadžić responds that it is "totally unacceptable," and then Mladić launches into one of his tirades. The draft is an "insult to the Serbs"; it is a "humiliation to the Serbs that we will never accept"; it is an affront to Serb honor and to the Serbs' ancestors.

For years this Serb bombast has worked. No longer. Holbrooke lets the general go on for a couple of minutes and then interrupts him. "Look," he shouts, "either we can negotiate an agreement on the removal of your guns around Sarajevo or we can all go home. There is nothing more to say." Mladić is silenced. The bombing has cowed him. He negotiates. "It was clear to me," Owen says, "that it was the bombing that brought them to the table."

The withdrawal of Serb heavy weapons begins the next day, and the NATO bombing is halted. The sweep of Bosnian and Croat forces through western Bosnia continues, however. On September 16, the Bosnian army captures Ključ; on September 17, Bosanska Krupa. The share of Serb-held land is falling rapidly and the 51–49 division envisaged by Lake is now close to existing on the ground.

On September 19, in Zagreb, Holbrooke bullies Izetbegović and Tudjman into abandoning the offensive that is closing in on Banja Luka, the main Serb-held town in Bosnia. "The light was red, red, red," Holbrooke tells me. He claims never to have had a qualm about this decision, although early in the war he had seen Muslims made to wear white armbands in Banja Luka, like the yellow star with which the Jews were branded in Nazi Germany. If Banja Luka had fallen, there might have been another quarter of a million Serb refugees pouring into Serbia; Milošević may have fallen, or he may have intervened. Either way, it is clear that the "peace process," as defined by Lake, would have been derailed.

In effect, the survival of the Republika Srpska is ensured by the survival of its main town. A hollow peace based on a de facto division of Bosnia can thus proceed. On September 22 Tudjman announces that Croatia has no further territorial ambitions in Bosnia. Without Croat support, the Bosnian army can do little.

By October 5, Holbrooke has secured a sixty-day cease-fire. Its roots are relatively strong: four years after the wars of Yugoslavia's destruction began, the Croats have what they want; the Serbs are exhausted; the Muslims see no better option. This equation, combined with Holbrooke's bullying, is enough for Tudjman, Milošević, and Izetbegović to agree to meet in the United States for "proximity peace talks."

Holbrooke is as tough with Izetbegović and his chronically divided government as he has been with the Serbs. He does not hesitate to warn him that NATO will not be Bosnia's permanent air force. He invents intelligence estimates suggesting that the Serbs are about to counterattack. When Izetbegović's hand trembles over the October 5 cease-fire accord, Holbrooke says, "Here, I'll sign it." He does so, with a theatrical flourish, and the Bosnian president reluctantly follows suit.

Fighting briefly flares again, but on October 12 a cease-fire takes hold. Six days later, I fly into Sarajevo with Holbrooke's team. We dip down over the beautiful peaks toward Kiseljak and then turn right over the valley toward the Sarajevo runway. The final descent is steep—as if the Serb guns were still there—but the landing is perfect.

Holbrooke is ebullient and confident—"in pig heaven," as Strobe Talbott, the deputy secretary of state, puts it. Sarajevo is eerily silent. At the airport this silence hits me like a hammer blow. *The silence cannot be broken because the guns have gone.* I struggle with the enormity of this thought. We are whisked through town in a blur of armored vehicles. American power. There is not much left to talk about—the design for peace is in place and the parties have agreed to meet in Dayton, Ohio, on November 1. Holbrooke hurries through a series of meetings that produce little.

I wander off for a few hours and see friends. They are still wan with war. And I think that other foreigners will come to Sarajevo and they will meet these good people and they will talk about how it was and try to understand; they will take pictures of the ruins of Sarajevo and the still picturesque cafés of Baščaršija and wonder how it was that such a city lived through such a siege, but the weight of those days and the density of that pain will not be communicable to these people, who will never hear, as I hear now, the whispering of the dead.

As we leave the city, at the sandbagged gate to Sarajevo Airport, we find Carl Bildt, the European Union's top peace negotiator, detained by French United Nations soldiers. "This is absolutely intolerable," a red-faced Bildt screams as he storms out of a dugout where French soldiers have been questioning the Swedish politician for the previous half hour as his personal plane awaits him. Bildt, the French claim, does not have the right papers to enter the airport, but Holbrooke, bounding from the car, comes to the rescue. The scene captures the hopelessness of the European response to the war—the French, in effect, have detained the peace envoy who represents them—and illustrates the ultimate European dependence on American power. It is funny, even lunatic; it is also pathetic.

IN THE AMERICAN HEARTLAND on November 1, 1995, the Balkan leaders gathered. They strode into the Hope Hotel and Conference Center, in the midst of the vast Wright-Patterson Air Force Base, to show their goodwill to the world. A look of distinct superciliousness flitted across Milošević's features from time to time. Tudjman looked confused, an expression that had led many to underestimate him. Izetbegović, who had compared the choice between Milošević and Tudjman to that between leukemia and a brain tumor, looked unhappy. They shook hands, perfunctorily, old acquaintances with some awkward business at hand. Since they had last done so, in 1991, more than two hundred thousand people had been killed.

It was a historic gathering. The walls were off-pink. The plants looked miserable. The furniture was modest. The gray carpet did not quite conceal a stain or two. Versailles it was not. In Sarajevo, at the battered Presidency, they still mustered a chandelier.

But the modest site had been deliberately chosen. The war had been about the absence of common sense; the American heartland is about its victory. The message from America, one that Haris Zečević had discovered in Detroit, was that talk is cheap and sometimes dangerous. I gazed at Milošević, whose visions and slogans had disgorged such rivers of blood, and wondered if he was interested.

It was hard for me to look at the Serbian and Croatian leaders sitting there in their suits and ties. I saw them through a skein of death, a collage of simple Bosnian graves with simple facts about the end of young lives engraved on them. I saw the stupid hills for which young men like Muris Zečević had been sent to die. I saw the barbed wire of the Sušica concentration camp and the boozy Serb killers who dragged Ruzdija Šestović off to die. I saw Bisera Zečević's naked body being dumped in the Sarajevo morgue with the tag *unknown* attached to it. I smelled the fetid pain of the makeshift refugee centers throughout Bosnia and saw again the road signs to nowhere. Here, inevitably, the leaders who had sent these people to premature graves and spread such misery were treated with respectful deference. That was the way of the world; perhaps it was stupid to rail; certainly it was dangerous not to.

Milošević had been provided by his American hosts with a limousine. He was a very important person. Koljević, the Bosnian Serb, was, however, bundled into the back of a modest vehicle with several others, his face pressed hard against the window like a child gazing despairingly into a candy store. The difference was political: Milošević was important to a peace deal, Koljević now marginal. But if the difference between the men had instead been weighed in moral terms, Milošević would have been tied by a rope to the back of Koljević's little car.

HOLBROOKE BROUGHT the three widows and six fatherless children of his fallen colleagues to Dayton, where the final tumultous lap of the marathon negotiation was held at the Wright-Patterson Air Force Base. The women cried; Frasure's younger daughter was silent. Meetings with the Balkan leaders were sometimes awkward. Silajdžić said he was overwhelmed. The message was clear: peace would be the best consolation and most fitting memorial.

To the last, Holbrooke pushed and cajoled, shouted and maneuvered. During the Vietnam War he had watched Robert S. McNamara, the former secretary of defense, coolly dissecting problems. McNamara's "ruthlessness in suppressing the emotional, the irrational, or the dynamic" convinced Holbrooke that such an approach can lead to tragic error. He stood at an opposite extreme. The French, kept on the margins, denounced him as a "schizophrenic, brutal Mazarin."

But without him, there would probably have been no peace. When Milošević objected to one plan for Sarajevo, Holbrooke took the piece of paper, tore it up in front of the Serbian president's eyes, and said, "Tell us what you want." When Milošević insisted on plying him with brandy in midmorning, Holbrooke drank. Confronted by an unyielding Izetbegović, Holbrooke let the Bosnian president know that this was America's last big push for a settlement: it would not be repeated and the Bosnians would then be largely on their own. He successfully isolated the Bosnians by first settling the remaining differences between Croats and Serbs over eastern Slavonia.

His troubling rapport with Milošević paid off. The Serbian president abandoned claims to Sarajevo; he told Holbrooke the Bosnians "deserved" the city because of their long resistance! He also agreed to a land corridor from Sarajevo to the last remaining eastern Muslim enclave, Goražde. But at the last, when he realized that Holbrooke was giving the Serbs 45 percent of Bosnia instead of the promised 49 percent, Milošević pointed an accusing finger and said with cold rage, "I trusted you and you tried to cheat me."

A desperate scramble ensued over the last two days of the three-week conference to find more land for the Serbs. With a prod from Clinton, the Croats eventually obliged. But still Izetbegović hesitated, confronted at last with the cold fact that the suggested peace meant dividing the country with no certainty that it would ever be reunited in anything but name. Holbrooke's frustration built to the breaking point. On the last night he screamed at Silajdžić, "You're going to throw all this away for a couple of mountain ridges."

The Bosnian government had become the recalcitrant party, the obstacle to peace: a fitting end to the twisted path of the West's attempts to bring peace to Bosnia after acquiescing to genocide there.

In the end, with a last-minute compromise that left the fate of the Serb-held northern Bosnian town of Brčko open to international arbitration, the peace was sealed. It was anything but uplifting. Almost half the country was formally granted to Serb separatists; another 21 percent was held by Croat separatists; aggression had worked. But I was past the point where I had believed that any other ending was possible. Peace was still peace.

On November 21, 1995, with Milošević and Tudjman and Izetbegović flanking him, I watched Warren Christopher, the secretary of state, spell out the achievements of the Dayton Peace Agreement. It was, he said, "a victory for all those who believe in a multi-ethnic democracy in Bosnia-Herzegovina." It would provide for "effective federal institutions"—a real central government overseeing the divided country. It would oblige Serbia and other states in the area to "cooperate fully in the investigation and prosecution of war crimes." It would open the way for more than two million refugees to return home or receive "just compensation." It would lead to "free and democratic elections."

Christopher had been remarkable at Dayton, persistent and persuasive. But I did not believe a word he said. I had seen and felt the destruction of Bosnian society and the international cowardice that accompanied it. I did not think that cowardice was at an end or the destruction remediable. I looked at Milošević and Tudjman and I thought I knew what they were thinking: *Pieces of paper are useful, now we can do what we like.* They were war criminals: how could they vow to cooperate with the arrest of people who, in the end, could only implicate them? I looked down at the summary of the agreement handed out by American diplomats and I read: "The agreement enables Bosnia and Herzegovina to continue as a single state, with full respect for its sovereignty by its neighbors. The parties have agreed to a constitution for Bosnia and Herzegovina that creates effective federal institutions, including a Presidency, a bicameral legislature and a Constitutional Court. The country will have a central bank with a single currency." It was nonsense, well intentioned perhaps, but nonsense nonetheless: the Bosnia I knew would surely not take this form.

I thought of Mostar, that quintessentially Bosnian city where the magnificent Ottoman arch of the Old Bridge had soared for four centuries before Croat gunners destroyed it. When I had last been there, a rope bridge had been strung across the Neretva River. But it swayed treacherously in the wind as Spanish United Nations soldiers tried to secure it. On the east bank, amid the ruins of forty-two months of war, lived the Muslims; on the west bank, amid the new cafés with names like Tropicana or Venezia, lived the Croat gangsters. Nobody crossed the river, although the Muslims and Croats were nominally allies. On the east bank, I found an old man, Asim Turković, patiently rebuilding the tracery of a fine Turkish house. "All built by man's hand, all destroyed by man's hand," he said. "Destroyed in an attempt to prove that Bosnia is not Bosnian. But Bosnia is Bosnian. Everyone thought they would pass through here easily. But the Bosnian mud bogged them down and they stayed here, stuck like a mouse in a trap."

Would American soldiers now get stuck too? The Dayton Agreement opened the way for NATO, led by about twenty thousand American troops, to go to Bosnia, separate the rival armies, and take the place of the United Nations humanitarian mission. Thus, the tanks and the boys in green would go in when the war was over; the hapless "peacekeepers" would leave or change hats at the very moment when peace was established. The incongruity was overwhelming—and appropriate.

Now that America had finally imposed its will on Bosnia, the truth could be told in unvarnished terms. On November 9, in a speech to the National Press Club, Strobe Talbott, the deputy secretary of state, said this: "As recently as August, the Bosnian Serb authorities in Banja Luka made local Muslims wear special white armbands and marked their homes with white cloth, all as a prelude to 'ethnic cleansing.' That administrative euphemism, coupled with the déjà vu of the armbands, makes clear what we have been up against in Bosnia. In a word—and it is the right word—it is genocide in our time, genocide on the continent of Europe."

It had been a very long time since a senior American official had publicly used such language. Bill Clinton used it during the election campaign in 1992, but had then retreated. Talbott's remarks made clear that Amer-

1995: Dayton Agreement

SLOVENIA

HUNGARY

0   Kilometers   100

0   Miles   100

Zagreb

Danube

Sava

Karlovac   Sisak

CROATIA

VOJVODINA

Vukovar

Novi Sad

Bosanski Novi

Prijedor

SERB CORRIDOR

Sava

Danube

Bihać

Banja Luka

Doboj

Sanski Most

Brčko

Mrkonjić Grad

Belgrade

Tuzla

Jajce

Zenica

Zvornik

Knin

Vlasenica

BOSNIA AND HERZEGOVINA

Srebrenica

Sarajevo

Split

Goražde

SERBIA

Mostar

Foča

YUGOSLAVIA

ADRIATIC SEA

MONTENEGRO

Dubrovnik

Trebinje

KOSOVO

Podgorica

ALBANIA

MACEDONIA (FORMER YUGOSLAV REPUBLIC)

Muslim-Croat Federation

Bosnian Serb Republic

⊙   Serb-held town pending arbitration

·········   New interentity boundary line as per the peace agreement

———   Cease-fire line before the peace agreement

ica never had any doubt about what was going on in Bosnia. But a political decision was made to obscure the issues for several years because there was no point being transparent about a situation Washington lacked the courage to confront. Talbott now explained why Bosnia was important after all. There were real risks, he said, in inaction, or inadequate action, "in the face of atrocities like mass rapes, concentration camps, massacres, and forced deportations." And he continued: "Bosnia matters to Americans because Europe matters to America. War in Bosnia threatens the peace of Europe—particularly, though not exclusively, those parts of Europe that are emerging from Soviet-era dictatorships. But that means it threatens the transatlantic community of which we are a part—and of which we are a leader. The conflict in the Balkans is a direct consequence of the end of the cold war. During the nearly half-century-long struggle, we were concerned about the spread of the communist order. Now that the cold war is over, we face a very different threat—the spread of postcommunist disorder."

I imagined those words being spoken by Bush in 1992, or by Clinton in 1993, to justify the dispatch of American troops to stop the genocide in Bosnia. The presidents would not have had an easy case to make, but they had a case and I believe they could have persuaded Americans of its validity. An idealism still lingers in America's unconquered land. The people of Europe, much conquered and in relative decline, tend to find this idealism naïve. But America's simplicity is also its power. Unleashing that power, years earlier, would have made a reality of words that, in the Dayton Agreement, were no more than pious hopes for a Bosnian state destroyed and Bosnian families scattered to the winds.

EVERY MORNING ASIM ZEČEVIĆ made his way to his dentist's studio in the center of Sarajevo. From its window, he believed he could see the actual spot on Trebević Mountain where Muris died. He would go to that spot one day, he told himself, without knowing quite what he wanted to find there. Now that the war was over, he would go up there and see where, more than three years earlier, his son had been killed.

Like most Sarajevans, Asim had kept up appearances through the war. He always wore a tie and a small gold tiepin in the form of the Bosnian fleur-de-lis. He was punctual about his work and he tried to make sure that he never raised his voice. Dignity, under siege, became synonymous with civilization. Its absence constituted the abyss into which the besiegers constantly invited you.

But Asim's skin sagged. He was sometimes unshaven, and his eyes were increasingly blank. He had formed the habit of always replying, "Very well" when asked how he was feeling. Then he would smile wearily to himself. The truth was that he could not sleep at night and he suffered from pains in his shoulder. That was his nature: calm on the outside, inside a storm.

I asked him how he felt about the peace. He said he had watched the signing of the accord in Paris a few days earlier, on December 14, 1995, and he had felt nothing. "Maybe we spent all our emotions," he said. "The war just lasted too long." Asim tried a smile, but, like a sun too pale to penetrate the clouds, it stayed buried in his weary eyes. Everywhere, I found an absence of joy. There was a flatness to everything. The enemy had not been defeated, and so the peace was tinged with bitterness.

Winter was coming fast. The clouds tumbled down, the mountains disappeared behind them. There were flurries of snow. The white vehicles of UNPROFOR were being repainted green. The word "IFOR"—the chosen acronym for NATO's Implementation Force—was now written on them. What was this weight that I felt on everyone? Too much experience. Asim kept showing two videos: one of Muris's funeral in Sarajevo and one of the infant Muris in Detroit. He could not connect the two images any more than the people of Sarajevo could get used to the fact that the war was over. Before and after were separated by an abyss, for Asim and for countless others. I knew a young man who took his mother's hand after a shell hit their Sarajevo apartment: the hand simply came off. He had dreams about putting the hand back, but the dreams always ended in a howl of horror.

A sadness that was a form of bereavement inhabited Sarajevo. I looked for some image of freedom or release in what Ivo Andrić called this "muffled land," but saw none. The Serbs in those areas of town like Ilidža and Grbavica that were to be handed back to the Bosnian government under the terms of the Dayton Agreement were asking the United Nations for thousands of coffins and containers. Coffins for their dead, whom they were about to exhume; containers for their furniture. They would not stay to be part of the "multi-ethnic democracy" of which Christopher had spoken in Dayton. NATO, it was said, was coming to make sure that Bosnia died peacefully. As for Karadžić and Mladić, the indicted war criminals, it seemed unlikely that a NATO force concerned above all to avoid body bags would take the risk of arresting them and sending them to the International Tribunal in The Hague.

The United Nations peacekeeping force packed up with a valedictory honesty. Antonio Pedauye, the Spanish official named a few months earlier to head the civilian side of the mission to Bosnia, made a dignified speech. He noted the lives lost—more than one hundred United Nations soldiers—and the fact that almost one thousand tons of food per day had been delivered to 2.7 million beneficiaries. He said, "Deterrence failed, the safe areas of Srebrenica and Žepa were overrun," and he spelled out the basic problem: "We thought deterrence could be based on the moral authority of the United Nations, but we learned that moral authority is not enough. When the Serbs realized there was a hundred-and-fifty-five-millimeter cannon on top of Mount Igman, they understood the language."

Such guns, however, arrived only after more than three years of war. The lesson of Bosnia was clear enough: the United Nations would now focus on operations in areas where peace had already been established, leaving more arduous peace enforcement missions to regional organizations like NATO. And, if deployed again in the midst of war, the United Nations would come only with effective military intelligence and the credible firepower long absent in Bosnia.

Later Pedauye told me that he was deeply depressed by the "ethnic homogenization" of Bosnia, a process he now viewed as irresistible. A Spaniard, he carried in him an inherited sense of war's wounds. "From Bosnia I will take with me a memory of the waves of the children and the old men, the innocent and the wise," he said with the sadness that inhabited us all in that December of 1995.

The handover ceremony was somber. It took place on December 20, 1995, at Sarajevo Airport, scene of some of the worst early battles of the war and still a no-man's-land between rival parts of the city. Janvier, visibly diminished, announced that military authority in Bosnia had been transferred to the North Atlantic Treaty Organization force. Admiral Leighton W. Smith Jr., then the commander of NATO forces in southern Europe, took over. The long purgatory of the United Nations in Bosnia was finally at an end.

Kofi Annan, speaking as a special envoy of the secretary-general, said, "The world cannot claim ignorance of what those who live here have endured. In looking back, we should all recall how we responded to the escalating horrors of the last four years. And, as we do so, there are questions which each of us must ask. What did I do? Could I have done more? And could it have made a difference? Did I let my prejudice, my indifference, or my fear overwhelm my reasoning? And above all, how would I react next time?"

I went, for a last time, with Asim to the graves of Muris and Bisera. From beside his wife's grave, we took in the view of the city. We gazed over the old white stone grave markers with their turbanlike bulbous tops, past the newer wooden markers, on to the town itself with its mingled minarets and church steeples and, beyond them, the shattered high-rises of the Olympic village of Dobrinja.

Asim was shocked by the graves in an inexhaustible way. Most of the dead, like Muris, were born after 1970. Yet, no matter how many young lives had been ended or what accumulation of bones we stepped over, no matter how the peace evolved or collapsed, life itself leveled everything in the end. Memory was no dike. But for Asim, as for his country, what had been taken away could not be returned.

I WANT TO GET AWAY from this city at the end of a valley. Before the war, Sarajevans used to drive to the beaches of the Adriatic in about four hours. They went through Ilidža and Hadžići, down the valleys to Konjic, on along the banks of the Neretva River to Mostar, and finally to the sea. It was a journey that captured all the astonishing beauty and variety of the Bosnian landscape. But the drive had been impossible for years. The only way out of the Bosnian city had been the tunnel under the airport and then the mountain track over Mount Igman, treacherous and exposed to Serbian fire. The track where Frasure and Drew and Kruzel died.

Now, however, NATO has declared all roads open and backed that vow with tanks. I set out at dawn on December 21, 1995, with Robert Fox of the *Daily Telegraph* and Tamara Levak, a Croatian friend. In Ilidža, in a single night of NATO presence, all the Serb military checkpoints that sealed off Sarajevo for forty-two months have been removed. The drive through the suburb takes just ten minutes. In Hadžići, too, all the checkpoints have gone. The last NATO checkpoint, at the entrance to government-held territory, is unmanned. The barbed-wire coils and the barriers lie in the road: already they look like relics of war. I clamber out of the armored Land Rover. The air is brisk and still. I breathe deeply and haul the barbed wire off the road.

Tamara says, "The roadblocks went so fast, it inevitably makes you wonder: *What was it all about?*"

The road to the coast is littered with other relics of war: roofless houses, deserted settlements, churches battered to rubble, the slender minarets of mosques reduced to stumps. In the bright dawn, a Bosnian army unit is out exercising. Their gear is new, their rifles gleaming, their faces fresh. This is no longer the ragtag collection of volunteers in which Muris Zečević fought and died; this is an army, forged in hardship, and the expression of a new Bosnian Muslim identity. Perhaps, one day, these Bosnians will want to fight again to avenge the loss of so much.

But there is a stirring in the air. Its name is Bosnia and its sound is that of rushing water. The place exists, light and dark by turns, always secretive, a living rebuke to those who destroyed its political incarnation. The road is open, the last mists dissolve. There are children on the way to school near Konjic, their bright packs on their backs. Their laughter is as light and heedless as the steps of the young soldiers are heavy and deliberate. Which sound will prevail? I know only this much: the Bosnian rivers rush on, as they always have, and the snowcapped mountains rise above Jablanica. The guns are silent, and when, after just four hours, the sea beckons, its shimmering expanse is peaceful beyond words.

EPILOGUE

THE SILVER BALLOONS SAY HAPPY BIRTHDAY. THE WAR IS OVER. It is March 11, 1996, and Haris Zečević is twenty-seven years old. The Detroit winter is still set firm against the wide sky with not a chink in its gray armor. But Haris's small apartment is already full of a peculiarly Bosnian warmth made up of liquor, smoke, and song: a fug of bonhomie.

Haris has shaved and he has cut his hair. His nine-month-old son, Muris, has already learned to haul himself to his feet and, propped against the sofa, he stands beneath the pall of cigarette smoke, a little Bosnian-American. His mother, Vildana, hurries about preparing Bosnian specialities: pies of cheese and meat, roast lamb, sticky desserts.

She has taken the day off from the Kroger supermarket where she works as a bagger, earning $5.40 an hour. On an auto production line, sticking upholstery on car doors, she could earn more. But in the supermarket she can at least talk while she works and go to the bathroom without first finding a replacement and watch the obese glide by on electric carts buying frozen fat-free food and Diet Coke. "Funny," Vildana laughs, "they buy diet drinks and they all look like haystacks."

Haris still works at QQC, the manufacturer of advanced materials, but he has given up his job delivering fast food. As he sees it, he comes home so that Vildana can go out to work, but they could make more money if he stayed out longer and worked longer hours. Marriage, debt, fatherhood, and work, he claims, have enslaved him, and Vildana's need to get out of the house is incomprehensible. Or so he says.

He wants to make a down payment on an apartment, but first he has to pay off some of his debts. Money obsesses him. As for the war, Haris has by now reconstructed Muris's death on Trebević countless times and concluded that his brother did not suffer, even for a moment. But he is not sure about his mother, and still, when he thinks of her suffering, he would like to put his uncle and cousins in Belgrade through what he calls "the one fear that marks you, the fear that death is coming."

Haris's apartment is full of Bosnians becoming Americans. Slobodan Djokić, from Sarajevo, is an old friend. Half Serb, half Croat, he stayed in Sarajevo for two years of the war and fought in the Bosnian army; he thus earned Haris's loyalty, the trust he should have shown toward Zoran Suša up on Trebević in August 1992. Slobodan finally left the Bosnian capital after a Muslim policeman told him he was a murderer *because* he was a Serb. Slobodan's Serb uncle was killed during the Croatian war in 1991; his Serb father, a colonel in the Yugoslav army, moved from Sarajevo to Belgrade but was denied a pension there because he is married to a Croat.

Having fled this madness, Slobodan makes sandwiches in a Detroit restaurant. In the United States, he sees a problem: Americans can spend hours shopping or watching television, but food they want in five minutes. "The trouble is," says Slobodan, "you can't make *food* in five minutes."

They all struggle to adapt. I shut my eyes and hear the Bosnian songs and breathe the smoky air and it is clear enough that this is the way it was before the plague began in Sarajevo. Uncomplicated, raucous, bawdy, sensual.

How long did the war last? Now that it is over, it sometimes feels like five minutes. Churchill once said the problem with the Balkans was that the area produced more history than it could digest; the problem for these young people is an indigestible amount of experience. What they are living now is a second life and, to survive it, they must compress the first life, push it away, or this small room in a Detroit suburb will become unbearable. There is a Bosnian expression: *"Čega nema, to ti ne treba"*—"What you do not have, you do not need." They no longer have Bosnia.

But beneath the music and the beer lie the scars of those lost years. Mine, theirs. These Bosnian refugees are concerned with getting cars and getting papers and getting organized in America, but their real concern is to mask their pain. As he drinks and the night grows smokier, Haris veers between mirth and rage. He tickles his son, turns him upside down, offers him food, and little Muris eats and beams. The war will resume, Haris says, within a decade, or sooner. The Serbs were not defeated; Karadžić's Republika Srpska is there. He wants revenge for the loss of his mother and brother. Slobodan, the half-Serb, listens: what he has lost—merely an uncle, a home, a car, other possessions—is "shit compared to Haris." But loss is not measured on a kitchen scale. Everyone at this party knows that a generation, at least, will have to pass before the pain subsides.

I find myself next to Muhiba, an eighteen-year-old Bosnian girl who is finishing school in Detroit. She tells me she is a refugee from Kozarac. *Kozarac.* Does anybody in Washington remember Kozarac? It is already four years since the Serbs descended on the small Muslim town near Prijedor in northwest Bosnia and razed it. Four years since Muslim men were lined up and slaughtered with machine guns. But that was a long time ago in a faraway country and, yes, the names can be difficult to pronounce.

Muhiba was fourteen when, on May 24, 1992, the Serbs rounded up her family. She and her mother and five-year-old sister were bundled onto a bus; her father tried to join them, but the Serbs dragged him away. They were kicking him as the bus departed—Muhiba's last image of her father, who has disappeared. Her uncle was taken to the Omarska concentration camp, stayed there three months, and then he, too, disappeared. They are dead, Muhiba is certain of that. She was taken to the Trnopolje camp. "There were too many of us to rape us all," she says. When Trnopolje and Omarska were closed in August 1992, after being discovered by Western journalists, she was forced to walk for two days across the Bosnian mountains to the government-held town of Zenica.

She looks at me, directly, in a neutral way, her face placid as a passport photograph, without any aggression, without pathos, as if to say, Well, yes, that is how it was.

That is how it was. The music picks up. Everyone is singing. Muhiba sings. These are Bosnians all, refugees all: Belinda Salković (half Muslim, half Croat), Danko Zovko (half Muslim, half Croat), Saša Ćismić (half Muslim, half Serb), Erol Kekić (Muslim). Haris drinks. He had wanted his father to come from Sarajevo.

Nino Črnovršanin is at the party, the old friend of the family who helped Haris come to Detroit from Sarajevo and in whose metal shop Haris briefly worked in 1993. "The war is not over," Nino tells me. "If you had two hundred thousand dead, would you accept peace on the terms of Dayton?"

Would I? Suddenly, the music stops. People are shouting. The mirth has given way to rage. The old Bosnian quickness with the knife. Slobodan, Haris's half-Serb friend, walks out, slamming the door behind him. Others leave too. Erol throws down his guitar. Haris and Nino talk angrily.

One of the songs all these Bosnians were singing was written by a Serb. Nino thinks that is unacceptable; others, especially the Bosnians of partly Serb descent who fought on the government side, think music has no nationality and Nino is the kind of fanatic who helped destroy a multi-ethnic Bosnia. Nino is shouting, "Saša is a Chetnik and Slobodan may be a Chetnik too."

Haris tries to intercede: "This is my birthday." But his voice is drowned in the sterile slogans of his shattered land.

I WANDER THROUGH the postwar Bosnian wilderness. Windows, like baleful eyes, stare dumbly out of roofless homes. The Muslim houses in Banja Luka flattened by Serbs. The Serb houses in Mrkonjić Grad flat-

tened by Croats. The Croat houses in Jajce flattened by a Serb bombardment. The destruction has many layers, like an illustration of the earth's
crust.

People, stunned still, scavenging. On several cars, Croats have prized off
the "Y" on stickers that once said "YU" for Yugoslavia—leaving just the
"U" of Ustasha. The bill for a meal comes with a new tax and I ask what
it is: "For the children with no parents," says the waiter. Heavily made-up
Serb women, all vampish nervousness, tug their wedding rings off their
fingers and slide them back. The past's violence is everywhere, insidious as
dust, and the physical world, now silent in the absence of guns, seems to
slip from me with the whoosh—heavy but insubstantial—of snow falling
from a roof.

Bosnia is now a "success story" for the Clinton administration, but I can
find scant cause for hope. NATO, its divisions over Bosnia mended at last,
has taken control with an impressive professionalism, initially deploying
sixty thousand troops. But the truth is that the alliance's hard-won unity
has come at the expense of Bosnia's. For while the transatlantic arguments
raged, the country was undone.

The war is over, but the ideologies of hatred and separation have not
been vanquished. When World War II ended, Germany was in ruins, but
there was a defeated enemy and the existence of Germany was undisputed.
Here in Bosnia, the state is in three fragments—one Serb, one Croat, one
overwhelmingly Muslim—and nobody has been defeated. The NATO
deployment ensures the absence of war, but peace is another matter, for it
requires the common commitment of Bosnia's people, and that commitment to a Bosnian idea has been steadily eroded by the howling of the
wolves in Belgrade and Zagreb.

Between the Serb- and Muslim-held areas of Bosnia there are internal
"borders," policed by NATO troops. These borders will have to disappear
if the American boys are ever to go home. But all I hear from the Serbs is
talk of the need to create a new international frontier along these lines,
while a growing number of Muslims intimate that another military campaign will be needed to bring the hundreds of thousands of Muslim
refugees back home. Perhaps, indeed, that is the choice in Bosnia: new
borders or new war.

It is not merely the physical division and devastation of Bosnia that appear insurmountable. It is the way the war, its weight and its truths, slips
into the maw of Balkan distortion and postmodern meaninglessness. At
the Omarska café, a few months after the end of the war, a television set
shows a Real Madrid versus Barcelona soccer match while the radio
blares, "We didn't start the fire. It was always burning while the world was

turning." When the soccer stops, an advertisement appears for the four-wheel-drive sports utility vehicles that are all the rage among the war's nouveaux riches, and the images of off-road adventure and wilderness, combined with leather upholstery and quadrophonic sound, seem to sum up a world that wants its wars comfortably packaged, visible perhaps but held at a safe emotional distance. Just up the road, in the first year of the war, thousands of Muslim men, including the father of young Muhiba in Detroit, were tortured and killed in the Omarska concentration camp. Tortured, as at Sušica, over a period of several months. But the Serbs who ran that camp still control this area under the terms of America's Dayton Accords.

At the entrance to the former camp, a disused iron-ore mine in north-western Bosnia, three guards block the way. Behind them, in a maze of girders and pipes, the tentacles of skeletal machinery stretch away toward a railway line where rusting freight cars stand. Boxcars suitable for doomed loads. The "white house," where the killing took place in 1992, still stands; so, too, does the "red house," where inmates were tortured. Children, oblivious of the blood shed here, slide across the frozen ground, and in the murmuring of their sleds on the snow I seem to hear the whispering of the dead.

There was no killing here, says a Serb guard, as he rolls a handful of snow into an icy ball. There was no camp. There was a "reception center" for the Muslims. They would check in here on their way to Croatia. They have their stories and their forged photographs of camps, but all that is just Muslim propaganda.

And why were these Muslims leaving? "I don't know why they left," he says. "Whoever wanted to stay, stayed. It was as if I, for some reason, one day, just packed my bags and went." He looks at me, a look in which defiance and injury mingle, and the other guards nod. The mine was working until the summer of 1992, so there could not have been a con-centration camp here. Yes, the guard insists, the mine was working. One of his colleagues is dubious; he says the mine closed at the end of 1991. But he is quickly silenced. "Let all the world's investigators come here and dig," says the spokesman-guard. "There are no bodies to be found."

In the guardhouse, a photograph is hung of a monument recalling the Serbs killed by the Ustasha in the nearby Kozara Mountains during World War II. Outside the camp there is a small Serb cemetery. The message is clear enough: this is a place of *Serb* suffering. The thousands of Muslims who suffered here, many of them tortured or killed, have already disap-peared. I have become familiar with such disappearances, and I know their bitter, slow-maturing fruit.

• • •

WITH THE WAR ENDED, the way is at last opened for Haris's cousins, Vesna and Jasna Karišik, to go back to Sarajevo from Belgrade. It has been almost four years since they were bundled onto the military aircraft at Sarajevo Airport and watched their city recede, slipping from them like water dissolving into sand.

Jasna, the older, now a young woman of nineteen, goes first. She is thin, too thin, and the anxiety that eats at her is in her pale brown eyes. What exactly she is looking for, she does not know, but for some time now she has been obsessed by returning to Sarajevo.

The bus is cold. At the Drina border post, where the Serb paramilitary forces picked up their weapons at the start of the war in 1992, a Muslim woman is turned off the bus; she trudges slowly back through the snow into Serbia with her bundles. Several hours later, Jasna reaches Grbavica, the Serb-held suburb of Sarajevo.

The twilight zone. In Karadžić's Republika Srpska, people cannot afford bananas. Grbavica is about to be handed back to the Bosnian government under the terms of the Dayton Accords. Schools and apartments are burning as the Serbs, under pressure from Karadžić and unopposed by NATO forces, destroy the places they are about to abandon. Goods are being bundled onto cars and trucks; many Serbs are bringing their dead from the cemeteries. The Pentagon, as usual, has insisted upon a "minimalist" approach, conceived to ensure "force security," so NATO does nothing; Izetbegović, the Bosnian president, has not offered a conciliatory word to coax these Sarajevo Serbs into remaining, and Holbrooke, the one American official with the power to halt the exodus, has quit. Any hope that Sarajevo might, despite everything, remain a mixed city at Bosnia's heart is thus finally extinguished.

Jasna crosses the Miljacka River the next day and finds her mother, Fida, still living with Asim, Haris's father. She wants to see the graves of her cousin Muris and her aunt Bisera, who were killed while she was gone.

At the cemetery, above Baščaršija, Jasna is struck by the fact that most of the dead were born after 1970. Grieving mothers place flowers on the graves. An invisible hand caresses her, the physical understanding that what has gone will not return—not her own childhood, not her parents' dislocated marriage, not the Sarajevo or the Bosnia that she knew, not Yugoslavia, not these youths.

Later, Asim insists on showing her the two videos: the gurgling of his grandson Muris in Detroit; the funeral of his son Muris in Sarajevo in 1992. The baby's cries and the earth falling on the coffin, the laughter of Vildana and the dull echo of exploding rounds, the brightness and the shadow. Jasna feels that she will burst beneath the weight of an already ineffable past.

A few days earlier, on March 2, 1996, she had watched televised images of the congress of Slobodan Milošević's Socialist Party of Serbia. There was "Slobo" with his sheepish grin and his tight-fitting suit, accepting the rapturous applause of delegates, speaking beneath the five-pointed star of Tito's Yugoslavia, standing bolt upright as the Yugoslav national anthem was sung by a choir of angelic young women, addressing his "comrades"— *"drugovi i drugarice"*—just as in Tito's time. So, Jasna wondered, nothing had happened? Where was the blood on the girls' white frocks? The attempt to pretend that the Yugoslavia that Serbia merely "fought to defend" still existed was grotesque.

But more grotesque, to Jasna, was a video called *Serbia 2000* shown as Milošević appeared: high-speed trains, digital telephones, six-lane highways, jumbo jets, modern banks with cash-dispensing machines. The lurid fantasies of a miserable, gangster society. The reality was another: rattling old trams, rheumy eyes, the pallid complexions of the poorly nourished, and, beyond Serbia's formal borders, the ruins that were the legacy of the wars Milošević set in motion.

Here, in this Sarajevo room with her family, that loss was a shadow no laughter could dispel. The thieves, those who had stolen not merely great wealth but also myriad lives, still held sway. Jasna understood now that her obsession with Sarajevo had been an obsession with return, but that no return was possible.

There was no escape from what the thieves had taken. Perhaps her parents would decide one day to live together again; perhaps not. But whatever happened, her lot would be a divided one. Fida, worried that Sarajevo was still unstable, advised Jasna to pursue her studies in economics in Belgrade. And why not? There was no country for people such as her. Those countries—the lands of half Serbs, half Muslims—those countries, in the Balkans, had gone up in smoke.

Four months later, Jasna's sister, Vesna, returned to Sarajevo, with the firm intention of visiting the graves of Muris and Bisera. Every morning she woke up planning to go, but she never went. A refrain took hold in her head: *It happened. We go on. It happened. We go on.*

Before entering the city, she had gazed down on it from Trebević Mountain, and the preceding years had flashed through her mind with everything—the deaths, the moves, the breakups—merged in a torrent that made her shudder. After that, she slowly realized, she no longer wanted to look back. She would continue in Belgrade, study dentistry; her life was in Serbia.

Asim, by now, had two new videos: one of Muris's first birthday and another of Haris in an American television interview about Bosnia. Haris talked about Vesna's Serb father, Slobodan Karišik. What he said chilled her blood. He described how he hated his uncle. "If I find him I will just take a gun and kill him," Haris said.

Vesna had heard about Haris's anger but had never been confronted with it directly. "It was very hard to watch," she told me. "In some corner of me I can understand, because he lost his mother and his brother, killed by the Serbs. But my father was nothing to do with all that. Why blame my father? Blame every Serb in the world but not my father! What I understood when I saw that was that it went on for too long. We thought the war would be two or three days, not the interminable thing it became. Over all that time, things hardened. Hatred. Misunderstanding. Distance. My father is like Haris. Just as Belgrade does not exist for Haris, Sarajevo does not exist for my father."

FOR A LONG TIME NOW, I have been concerned with the question of memory in the Balkans. Herein lies the key. Let us not imagine that there can be balance in what is remembered, but perhaps there can at least be access. Haris has already obliterated Belgrade from his mind, Slobodan has expunged Sarajevo. This is still a land of black holes.

Within months of the war history is already being rewritten, as at Omarska, but some prominent Serbs begin to crack under the pressure of the horror that has been concealed. I find Milan Kovačević, the former deputy mayor of Prijedor, the man wheeled out in 1992 to explain Omarska to the world, at the Prijedor hospital, where he is a doctor. His mustache yellowed by tobacco smoke, he sits in a chair that creaks as it swivels; he fondles a bottle of plum brandy. The best plums come from this region, but nobody is buying the plums, so the only thing to do is make slivovitz. And the only way to pass the time, it seems, is to drink it.

This was a primitive war, Dr. Kovačević says, almost medieval in character, unsophisticated and harsh. The Muslims had the Arab world behind them, the Croats the Catholic world, but Russia was weak and so the Serbs had nobody backing them this time and, as the war dragged on, "we lost our spine."

As he downs the brandy, his blue eyes redden, his speech begins to slur, and this German-trained doctor embarks on a strange monologue:

"When a war begins people lose control. They do not behave normally. They grab Japanese television sets and they start killing. Omarska was a mistake. We Serbs knew very well what Dachau was. This was not Dachau, but it was a mistake.

"We planned it as a camp for the assembly of people, not as a concentration camp, and the plan was just to collect the Muslims so they would not be killed in their homes, but then what happened afterwards was something else. Even Americans cannot plan everything. What happened here looks well planned if you view it from New York. But on the spot everything was burning. Something breaks in your head. Everybody should have been brought for psychiatric treatment in 1992, but there was no time! I cannot explain that loss of control. Even historians cannot explain it. You could call it collective madness.

"Muslim civilians were killed at Omarska. You can call it what you want, a concentration camp, a collection camp. But no more than one hundred were killed. Killed, that is. There were others who died. I do not know how many. But this was not a killing factory, like Jasenovac, the Ustasha camp. Omarska was a concentration camp, but not a death factory. That is the main difference. Only one child died in Omarska.

"As a child, during World War II, I was in the Jasenovac camp with my aunt. My father was with the Partisans. My mother was hiding from the Ustasha in the Kozara Mountains. During World War II, Muslims in this area burned and stole everything from the Serbs. But after the war, history was forged by Tito. History was changed by the authorities in the interests of 'Brotherhood and Unity'—a story for children. That was a Bolshevik mistake. But memories cannot be destroyed. Many Serbs know, intimately, who slaughtered their grandfathers. Clinton knows the Dayton Accords, he knows they are good for him, but I doubt that he understands us. This part of the world is like a wind tunnel: the gusts that come through it are uncontrollable.

"The truth must now be written about Omarska, because only the truth is useful to children. There is a direct connection between Jasenovac and Omarska. During World War II, the Croats and Muslims killed us; this time, it was the other way round, we killed them. Perhaps in fifty years it will happen again, to us. At this point, facts have demonstrated that it was necessary to destroy Bosnia."

The Serb doctor licks each cigarette before lighting it and gazes into his emptying bottle. He seems startled by his own confession. There is, he suggests, no death worse than a political death in the Balkans. Perhaps, he continues, the original mistake was that of the Serbian monarchy, wanting everything after World War I, wanting to be able to swim in Lake Bled in Slovenia, not being satisfied with the warm waters of the Adriatic coast.

Look, he exclaims, where Yugoslavia has brought us! We are one hundred years behind Western Europe. This influences the mind; the state of the economy influences the mind. He trained in Germany, he knows what a developed country is. The passions in Bosnia are similar to those at the time of Luther! Dr. Kovačević would like to have a German passport now. "I crave peace and order," he says. "You see, my hair is gray, my mustache too, and I do not sleep at night, and there is no electricity and my house is often cold. And I listen to all this talk—of Clinton, of Yeltsin, of Izetbegović and Karadžić and the rest of them—and I tell you, it drives me mad."

In July 1997, Dr. Kovačević was arrested by a British-led NATO force and taken to The Hague to stand trial at the International War Crimes Tribunal.

THE BOSNIANS HAVE a saying: *"glup kao zid"*—"stupid as a wall." The walls are everywhere. The only place where Serbs, Croats, and Bosnian Muslims mix now is in Hungary, where they all go on vacation and have a great time together. Even in Tuzla, city of tolerance, the posters of Izetbegović's SDA party are everywhere, proclaiming that the party "fought for the independence of our country, defended its sovereignty, stood against the aggressor." And what of the Serbs and Croats who also fought for Bosnia rather than joining the zealots?

I make my way over the war-ravaged Majevica Hills, from Tuzla back to Vlasenica. I am tired of the destruction, even more tired of the arguments— the videos documenting one side's horrors or the other's, the statistics proving some idle demographic point, the obstinate stampede into bigotry.

If I have returned to this small town, almost five years after I first came here, it is only to see if anyone recalls Ruzdija Šestović, the Muslim who was arrested in June 1992 and disappeared, leaving a grief-stricken son, Ermin, in Sweden. A new mayor, Vojislav Mitrović, receives me. His nails are chewed, his cheeks hollow, and he sits beneath a portrait of Radovan Karadžić. Yes, he concedes, there was camp at Sušica—a "Muslim collection center"—but Vlasenica's Muslims were not killed there. They were simply "collected" and then bused out. As for Šestović, the mayor has no recollection of him. "I do not think he ever lived here," he says. "And anyway, that was a long time ago, and life must go on."

BUT NIKOLA KOLJEVIĆ, long Karadžić's right-hand man, a Shakespeare scholar with wisps of white hair, is obsessed with death. He gazes through his frosted windows onto the main square at Banja Luka, where a Partisan monument has been moved to make way for the foundations of a new Orthodox cathedral, set to rise when there is money to pay for it.

This is the only town worth its name in the 49 percent of Bosnia that has been allotted to the Serbs under the Dayton Peace Agreement. But the city is miserable, rancid as old soup, soul-chilling as its pervasive slush, bearing the wounds of a long war—the eviction of the city's Muslim population, the razing in 1993 of the beautiful Ferhadija Mosque, and, finally, a predictable rift among the ever-fractious Serbs, pitting the city against the hardline followers of Karadžić in Pale. All of this has begun to weigh on Professor Koljević.

He smokes and he mutters about bones, the bones of Bosnia, the bones of the Serbs, the "racial memory" of the Serbs, their epic poetry, their popular history, their "oral culture," their repeated uprisings against the Turks of which this war was just the third and latest, their difficulty with Americans, who have "lost the sense of the relevance of history," their conviction that "the presence of the past is more important than the past of the past." He continues to gaze out the window. Bones. Bones. What he would like me to understand is that, as the vice president of separatist Serbs during the war, he had very little idea what was actually happening because he went to Foča early in the war, in April 1992, and he saw Serb paramilitary forces burning Muslim houses, and it was all very frightening, and "after that sort of experience you don't really want to travel, you don't really want to know, and so I stayed in Pale."

War, the professor remarks, does not come out of a clear blue sky. Serbs felt their fathers had been weak, the way they were marched off by the Ustasha in World War II and slaughtered. They did not want that to happen again. No, never again. And there were difficulties with Izetbegović's Muslims, who "have a psychological problem with equality because, historically, they were always either masters or servants." And so, when they were provoked, the Serbs responded. "We never started shelling first," he says, abruptly looking me in the eye. "All we did was engage in disproportionate retaliation. But then, of course, retaliation cannot be proportionate. If you make me mad, I'm going to hit back, harder than you hit me."

And once the Serbs hit back, the professor continues, the Muslims made victims of themselves, and firms like Ruder Finn in New York orchestrated their "media campaign." First the "ethnic cleansing." Then the "concentration camps." Then the rapes. And here, with the mention of rape, the professor laughs, somewhat hysterically, recalling that Napoleon never accepted rape as a war crime because his view was that "a woman with her skirt up can run much faster than a man with his pants down."

After the rapes, the suffering of Sarajevo. And finally, Srebrenica, genocide, and mass graves. All pseudo-events, the professor exclaims, *created* events, as prescribed by Daniel Boorstin in his book *The Image*, a copy of which the professor is perusing. I gaze at Professor Koljević. He is in a state of high excitement, pacing the room. For him, I see, the war that I witnessed was a single massive act of deception by the Muslims, a deception in which the Serbs were somehow framed as the executioners. And I feel a deep despair, for it was precisely self-deception on a vast scale that plunged the Serbs into this war that has ultimately ruined them.

The diminutive professor returns to his window. The winter light and the cigarette smoke frame him in a pale halo. He is silent, and then seems moved by a sudden doubt. Of course, he says, you cannot manipulate people if there is not some truth. The Serbs did lose control of themselves. "We were in jeopardy," he continues, "and so what occurred was an aberration and, well, I would like to change that somehow, find something to make up for it, because"—he smiles his wan smile—"because now that I have returned once to Sarajevo, I have to say that I feel just a little nostalgic."

In January 1997, some months after I saw him, Professor Koljević committed suicide by shooting himself in the head.

IN BELGRADE, where it all began, and may all end one day with the downfall or death of Slobodan Milošević, life has been reduced to a meager thing. The city descends ever deeper into a dark pit where everything is desperate: sex, work, survival. A woman, quite mad, wanders through the streets carrying a vase full of dead plants. On a vast building site a single man hoists a bucket on a string. The decor in the empty cafés on the once-bustling Skadarlija sums up the débâcle: a voluptuous nude, a carving of a saint or two, and some dreary bottles of eau-de-vie on a shelf. There is new graffiti: *"Slobo, jebeš li nešto osim nas?"*—"Slobo, are you fucking anything apart from us?"

But Milošević, America's de facto ally in ending the war, survives. His oddly named country, Yugoslavia, the truncated federation of Serbia and Montenegro, hangs on too, but one day the stirrings in Kosovo and Montenegro will no doubt erupt into open conflict. The dismantling of Yugoslavia is almost certainly not over: the ethnic Albanians of Kosovo have a long-term goal of independence, and there is a growing movement in Montenegro that wants to be free of Milošević's tutelage.

Like many others, Vojna Adamović, the Serb refugee from Sarajevo, wants no further part in this unraveling. She and her husband, Miloš, will not go back to Sarajevo. They have had a baby daughter, Katarina, whom Vojna laughingly calls her "Bosnian savage." They will not risk exposing her to the Balkan wind tunnel. One winter day, when the electricity is not working, and the water is not flowing, and they are short of money, Vojna says, OK, enough, and she decides to apply for a visa to emigrate to Canada, where she hopes to join her Croat-Muslim-Jewish cousin, Mladen Elazar, and his Serb wife, Mira, in Windsor, Ontario. Vojna's sister, Aleksandra, whose Croat husband has disappeared during the war, has also applied to emigrate to Canada with her young son, Filip. "I want to feel safe," Vojna says. "I just do not feel safe. This city is dirty. This city is decaying. And why should the Montenegrins stick with us. Let them go too!"

Miloš, however, is unsure about emigration. He is trying to make some money importing Kinder egg chocolates into Yugoslavia; it is frustrating, bureaucratic work and he smokes endlessly. I do not have time, he says, to start my life three times. Sarajevo. Belgrade. And now Windsor? He is in his early forties. I do not have time, he repeats, to start my life three times. But Vojna is determined to go.

In Windsor, Mladen Elazar has received a letter from a Serb friend who has returned to Sarajevo, to the suburb of Ilidža, held by the Serbs during the war and then abandoned. "The Serbs in Ilidža burned everything they could before they left," the letter reads. "Only a few retired and old people remained. They were proclaimed traitors by the Serbs on Karadžić's side of the wall. But at least they are on their property and they don't have to queue to wash or go to the toilet like the 'true Serbs' who remained faithful to their leaders in Pale. I have been fascinated by the fact that after the first few days of anger and assaults, which of course had to happen, the Muslims who have returned to Ilidža come daily to greet their Serb neighbors. It is obvious that the ordinary people on all three sides have had enough of war although the leaders on all three sides still support war."

Yet, strangely, the people do not get rid of their leaders. Before the war broke out in 1992, it was Vojna who would not listen to Miloš's warning of Milošević's looming violence. Now the roles have been reversed. It is Vojna who believes that the killing is not over.

"I say to Miloš, Do you really want to die for Kosovo? And what about Montenegro?" Vojna looks at me; in her desperation, I see all Bosnia's spirit broken, a unique well of human energy now stifled. "This story here is not finished. But I am through with demonstrating against war. I did that in Sarajevo, and what good did it do me? This time, I'm getting out. It was one thing when we stood together on Vrbanja Bridge in 1992. But we are different people now. We have lost our illusions."

ON THE OTHER SIDE of the Kozara Mountains, on Croatia's border with Bosnia, another attempt to confuse history and blur memory is under way at Jasenovac. Ivan Jurić, the head of the town council, explains to me that the camp should become a memorial for all the dead. Not merely for the victims, mainly Serbs, killed by the Ustasha during World War II, but also for the victims of Tito's communist authorities between 1945 and 1948. And, says Jurić, why not throw in all those who died between 1991 and 1995 fighting for Croatia's independence?

"Jasenovac should be a place of memory for war, for World War Two, for this war, perhaps for other wars," he says. "For Croats, this has been a war of reconciliation: the sons of Partisans and the sons of Ustashas won our independence from Yugoslavia and the Serbs. Similarly, all the dead should be reconciled by being lumped together at Jasenovac."

I find it hard to take the suggestion seriously. Jasenovac, like Auschwitz, stands for something very specific: the Ustasha terror during World War II and the genocidal policies pursued by the Ustasha leader, Ante Pavelić, against the Serbs of Croatia and Bosnia. To hide that fact is again to invite some future retribution.

But Jurić was speaking on high authority. In an interview with the newspaper *Vjesnik* on April 23, 1996, Franjo Tudjman, the Croatian leader, had suggested precisely such a mingling of bones. Repeating his contention that only forty thousand people were killed at Jasenovac during World War II—most historians believe the number was many times that—Tudjman said those who "were imprisoned by the communist authorities" should also be remembered at Jasenovac. "And," he went on, "we would also, on the same spot, but separately, find a place for those who were killed in the War for the Homeland"—that is, the war of 1991–1995. "We should reconcile the dead," the Croat leader said, "as we have reconciled the living."

Reconciliation, however, was never a Croat forte during the wars of Yugoslavia's destruction. In the Croat-held town of Jajce, in central Bosnia, I find the mayor, Nikola Bilić, seated under a portrait of Tudjman, raving about returning the city to its "natural state"—apparently the way the town was eight hundred years ago under one Hrvoje Vukšić, duke of Bosnia and Dalmatia. Then, the mayor says, this was a true Croat town. He grimaces at a mention of the Muslims—the Croats' nominal allies in the American-sponsored federation. "I will only allow Muslims back here," he says, "if the Muslims first give back our houses in Vareš. The Muslims want to dominate us, but we will not be part of their Bosnia-Herzegovina."

I SIT WITH Sead Mehmedović in Belgrade in front of a television that is never turned off because there is a problem with the switch to turn it on again. His sister-in-law, who owns the television, does not have enough money to have it repaired. So when she does not want to watch it, she drapes a cloth over it. The image comes through fuzzily, as the wars of Yugoslavia's destruction long did in Belgrade. Sead laughs, a laughter that is close to hysteria. His muzzled life flickers on.

He thinks a lot about his father, Alija, because he is as old as his father was when he died in Turkey. Sead, too, has become a pessimist and a conformist. As an old communist, he still believes in revolutionary change and sees that Milošević's Serbia is ripe for it. But his main concerns are his wages, which are always paid late, and the pension he will eventually receive. He still calls himself a Yugoslav, because he can think of no other identity, and from time to time he is filled with panic when he thinks that

Montenegro may secede and that the last semblance of the Yugoslav federation, the last fig leaf, will then fall.

I gaze at Sead, a good man with a broken life, staring at a television with
a cloth draped over it. An unutterable sadness sweeps over me, a sadness I
have felt watching the musicians on Skadarlija, with their plaintive songs,
their straining violins, their hymns for an ever-unrequited people. And
abruptly they all come together, all these interwoven Balkan lives, Alija
and Muris and Haris and Ermin and Vojna and Mladen and the countless
others borne away like twigs on a stream, and I understand the rage in the
violence that separated them. This was fratricide on a grand and repetitive
scale.

Sead thinks now about his two children. They are what remain to him;
they fill the void; they are children who have a father. He clings to the simplicity of this bond, which is all that he has left to believe in. He rarely ventures out. And, after the lies, the hypocrisy, and the cowardice that I have
witnessed as Yugoslavia and Bosnia died, I wonder if he is not right to turn
his back on the world. I will walk away from here. This tragedy was mine
for a moment only. But I will take with me the conviction that second lives
are best lived simply.

DESPITE EVERYTHING, I would like to believe that from its ruins
Bosnia might be resurrected. I see a few markets taking form at the country's internal borders and attracting merchants and shoppers from all the
communities. A few Serb cars cross Muslim territory; a few Muslim cars
appear in Serb territory. I see the earnest dedication, not quite masking
fear, of the American soldiers policing the roads. Of these faint stirrings,
of this belated American presence, might something be made?

Major General William Nash leads the deployment of American troops
in the northeastern area of Tuzla in the year after the end of the war. He
says the country's military problem is solved—armies are separated,
weapons stored, soldiers demobilized—but his troops cannot bring the security that will encourage more than two million refugees to return. "You'd
need an international police force in every hamlet," he says. "In their absence, who is going to sprinkle the love-thy-neighbor dust?"

Who indeed? Certainly not the ever-cautious Pentagon. But this has always been a war to return home. By denying the Muslim identity, and
then by trying to eliminate the Muslim presence in Bosnia, the Serbs
and Croats have in the end forged something new: a Muslim nationalism
and militarism bent on taking back the land and homes from which Muslims were driven, principally in 1992. This determination exasperates the
general. "There are no good guys here," Nash tells me. "That is a basic les-

son I've learned." But, I wonder, is it not asking a lot to expect that a genocide tolerated by America should create "good guys"?

For Nash, history begins in 1996, when American troops deployed in
Bosnia. He recalls a conversation with a Serb general, who had explained
to him that the Srebrenica massacre of 1995 was just the result of earlier
Muslims massacres of Serbs. "If we play the history game here, we haven't
got a chance," Nash says. "I'll see your 1995, and raise you a 1993. I'll see
your 1993 and raise you a 1913. I'll see your 1913 and raise you an 1804.
It just goes on and on. The place has enough history; it needs more future.
We have to ask ourselves, Are we looking for justice or are we looking for
peace? I think justice could merely delay the future."

Certainly, justice would require a courage that Nash's commander-in-
chief, Bill Clinton, has never shown in the Balkans. The problem with
talking about history in Bosnia is that it becomes a term thrown around
to justify inaction—General Rose's dismissive "This is the Balkans, you
know." The central issue in Bosnia today is the legacy of a war that began,
not in the nineteenth century, but in 1992 with Kovačević's "collective
madness": the Serb genocide against the Muslims. The conviction has persisted among many Bosnian Muslims that the West—through an unspo-
ken prejudice—was content to look the other way while the onslaught
continued for several months. A minimum of "justice"—the arrest, for example, of Karadžić and Mladić—might soothe that Muslim anger; at the
very least, it would give Western governments a new leverage over Izetbegović, whose readiness to countenance another war once NATO troops
leave is clear enough. Nash says he believes American troops will have to
stay five years. But even then, he adds, "I'm pessimistic about the ability
or willingness to reach peace."

I FIND RON NEITZKE, the honorable American diplomat, in Washington. He has now been back from Zagreb for a couple of years, but the
wounds of Bosnia will not leave him and still he is haunted by America's
failure. He has just completed a paper, "But Bosnia Was Not the Holocaust!," an examination of the State Department confronted by the challenge of genocide. His conclusions are:

> *What the Bush administration, mainly senior State Department of-*
> *ficials, are guilty of is this: due to flawed analysis, hubris, and excessive*
> *sentimentality, they tenaciously held on to Yugoslavia until long after its*
> *disintegrative forces had passed the point of no return. Then they essen-*
> *tially opted out (during the Croatian war) of a crisis area on which the*
> *U.S. had taken the Western lead for decades and out of Europe's most vi-*
> *olent post–World War II political-military eruption. Then, in one of*

many brief conscience- or expediency-driven fits of U.S. reengagement, they pushed hard for quick recognition of Bosnia. Succeeding, however, they offered Bosnia faint political support and some humanitarian aid but no tangible assistance against the foreseeable Serbian onslaught that ensued. They did not even move to lift the arms embargo covering all of the former Yugoslavia enacted by the UN in September 1991 (with well-armed Belgrade's active acquiescence) amid the JNA's war in Croatia.

Most egregiously, they proceeded to cover their error and reserve by repeatedly and gratuitously dishonoring the Bosnians in the very hour of their genocide, scraping together what limited evidence there was of Muslim excesses and ascribing the "strife" to age-old ethnic animosities in which no side was blameless.

Neitzke notes that the arrival of Clinton in 1993 brought no improvement, indeed only a further descent into obfuscation. He ends his paper by quoting Clinton's words on the campaign trail in 1992—"If the horrors of the Holocaust taught us anything, it is the high cost of remaining silent and paralyzed in the face of genocide"—and by declaring:

The State Department was not responsible for the Holocaust, or for Bosnia. Nor is the State Department solely accountable for America's response to either; that accountability lies with the President first and foremost, but also with the Congress and with the American people. In the case of Bosnia, it also lies heavily with a Pentagon, and especially a Joint Chiefs of Staff, determined to keep America on the sidelines when the slaughter was bloodiest.

State Department officials are uniquely positioned to influence policy, however, for good or for ill. And the influence they wield can have a life or death impact on human beings targeted for genocide. In the case of the Holocaust, and no less in the case of Bosnia, many senior State Department officials stared genocide in the face and, muttering their excuses, simply turned away.

But what of everyone else? What is one's moral obligation when superiors turn mute and indifferent when confronting genocide? What if one cannot readily discern whether this or that mass slaughter in fact constitutes genocide? The United States cannot halt evil everywhere on earth. And man's infinite capacity for abusing his fellow man will be with us forever. So when should one make a stand? And how? In the end, these are questions we can only answer for ourselves—but we must answer them.

At a minimum, if one is a Foreign Service officer serving abroad, whether as Chief of Mission or as a junior reporting officer, one has an obligation to seek out and report the truth about suspected genocide as best one can, and to do so aggressively and persistently, regardless of the prospects for immediate action to halt that genocide, and regardless of whether such reporting and analysis is welcomed by one's superiors in Washington or at post. One must, in essence, be guided by the belief that a policy fundamentally at odds with our national conscience cannot endure indefinitely—if that conscience is well and truthfully informed. And one must trust that each of us, as individuals, can ultimately make a difference.

In February 1991, with the outbreak of war in Yugoslavia still months away, a reflective President George Bush spoke eloquently about the burden the individual must bear in words now chiseled into the granite walls of the United States Holocaust Memorial Museum. "Here we will learn," he said, "that each of us bears responsibility for our actions and the failure to act. Here we will learn that we must intervene when we see evil arise. Here we will learn more about the moral compass by which we navigate our lives and by which countries will navigate the future."

For President Bush, in the wake of Bosnia, there is only prophetic irony in this distant admonition. For a student of the Holocaust who knows what happened in Bosnia, there can only be a sickening emptiness. Bosnia was not the Holocaust, not by any stretch. But there were echoes of the Holocaust all over Bosnia and nowhere more so than in our profound failure to measure up to the challenge.

Ron hands me his paper. I understand him. There are things that simply have to be written down before they destroy you.

AT THE SPOT on Vrbanja Bridge where Muris Zečević, the Muslim, and Vojna Adamović, the Serb, stood together on April 5, 1992, a plaque commemorates the spot where peace ended and the first victim of the war, Suada Dilberović, the young student from Dubrovnik, fell. It reads: "*Kap moje krvi proteče i Bosna ne presuši*"—"A drop of my blood flows and Bosnia does not run dry." An old woman comes regularly to place fresh flowers on the spot.

A second plaque has been mounted at the south side of the bridge. It commemorates two soldiers of the United Nations—the Frenchmen Humblot and Amaru—who fell on May 27, 1995, as they fought to take back their camp from the Serbs. I shudder at their sacrifice, in the service of a flawed mission, for it served neither to save Bosnia nor to enlighten the leaders of the United Nations forces in the meaning of honor. A group of French soldiers take souvenir photographs; American troops photograph the blasted buildings in the middle of town. But, I wonder, do they understand, or even hear, the ghosts that inhabit the ruins?

I stand there, shivering, watching a storm blow in from the south. I think of another Sarajevo plaque—the one commemorating Gavrilo Princip and the assassination that ushered in World War I. It has been removed now, for the commemoration of the act of a Serb nationalist does not interest the Muslim authorities. History here will not be left in peace. Trebević and the other surrounding peaks disappear behind low clouds. The rain begins to sweep down, and the smell of grass and timber rises abruptly off the hills. I breathe deeply and watch the Miljacka bubbling down the valley. The sap is irrepressible, sickening in its vitality, but what's gone is gone and the new that takes root before my eyes will not resemble the old.

PARIS, JANUARY 1998

NOTES ON SOURCES

This is a work of reportage based on the years I spent covering the wars of Yugoslavia's destruction. I first went to Bosnia for *The New York Times* in 1992, spent a month there, and returned for about the same period in 1993. Then, in early 1994, I replaced John Burns as the chief correspondent of *The Times* in the Balkans. Most of the next two years were spent in the region; I wrote my last piece from Sarajevo in December 1995 as NATO moved in to enforce the Dayton Peace Agreement, replacing the United Nations peacekeepers whose long travails I had chronicled. Throughout this period, and afterward, I conducted the hundreds of interviews on which this work is based. Among these were extensive interviews with the central characters of the book. All agreed to use their own names with the single exception of Sead Mehmedović, whose family name (and so that of his father, Alija) I have changed. Even more than a half century after the event, Sead worries how he and especially his children might be treated in Slobodan Milošević's Serbia if it were widely known that his father was once a Muslim SS officer. Alija's assumed name in Turkey, Ali Erhan, is the name he indeed used after he fled Yugoslavia. Gaby Kovač was indeed the name of his wife.

What follows here are notes on other source material not mentioned in the text.

PREFACE

The quote from Isaiah Berlin (page xv) is from *The Crooked Timber of Humanity* (London: John Murray Press, 1990).

Neal Ascherson's beautiful book *Black Sea* (London: Jonathan Cape, 1995) provides a stimulating exploration of what he calls the "first-born twins"—civilization and barbarism—in the European consciousness, and of their "long-lived brother," Orientalism.

The lines from Wisława Symborska (page xix) are from *"Koniec i Poczatek" (Beginning and End)*. Poems from a collection of the same name are in *View with a Grain of*

Sand, selected poems by Wisława Symborska (New York: Harcourt Brace, 1995).
The precise number of deaths (page xx) in Bosnia is unknown, partly because of the large number of "disappearances" and unexplored mass graves. But two hundred thousand is the most widely accepted estimate among Western intelligence analysts.

BOOK ONE: THE LOST CENTURY

ONE: MY FATHER'S WAR

Throughout Book One, the bulk of the source material is constituted by the documents I found in Alija's suitcase. Barbara Jelavich's *History of the Balkans,* vols. 1 and 2 (New York: Cambridge University Press, 1983), was extremely helpful for my account of World War II in Belgrade and for interwar Yugoslav history. So, too, were the memories of Miriana Komarecki, long *The New York Times* office manager in Belgrade. Brian Hall's *The Impossible Country: A Journey Through the Last Days of Yugoslavia* (London: Martin Secker & Warburg, 1994) renders the texture of Serbia with a particular immediacy.
Vaclav Havel's quote (page 8) comes from the preface to the *Terezín Memorial Book* (Terezín: Terezín Initiative Melantrich, 1996).

TWO: THE PESSIMIST

On the world that Woodrow Wilson's diplomacy sought to create in post-1918 Europe, Henry Kissinger's *Diplomacy* (New York: Simon and Schuster, 1994) was helpful.
For the conflicting currents at work in Yugoslavia's troubled creation, Joseph Rothschild's *East Central Europe Between the Two World Wars* (Seattle: University of Washington Press, 1974) provides an incisive summary.
On the religious composition of medieval Bosnia, see *Bosnia and Hercegovina: A Tradition Betrayed* by Robert J. Donia and John V. A. Fine (New York: Columbia University Press, 1994) and Fine's "The Medieval and Ottoman Roots of Modern Bosnian Society" in *The Muslims of Bosnia-Herzegovina,* edited by Mark Pinson (Cambridge, Mass.: Harvard University Press, 1994).
Paul Garde's *Vie et mort de la Yougoslavie* (Paris: Fayard, 1992) was useful on the Illyrian movement.
Marcus Tanner's *Croatia* (New Haven: Yale University Press, 1997) was most helpful on Starčević and the Ustasha.
The Djilas quote (page 22) is from Aleksa Djilas, *The Contested Country: Yugoslav Unity and Communist Revolution (1919–1953)* (Cambridge, Mass.: Harvard University Press, 1991).
The Rousset quote (page 26) is from David Rousset, *Univers Concentrationnaire* (Paris: Editions de Minuit, 1989).

THREE: THE TRAINS OF HISTORY

Hubert Butler, the Irish essayist and writer, was one of the most acute observers of Pavelić. His "The Sub-Prefect Should Have Held His Tongue" and "The Artukovich File" in *The Sub-Prefect Should Have Held His Tongue and Other Essays* (London: Allen Lane, The Penguin Press, 1990) are essential reading. For my description of the acts of the Ustasha, I have also drawn on Richard West's *Tito and the Rise and Fall of Yugoslavia* (London: Sinclair-Stevenson, 1994) and Jonathan Steinberg's *All or Nothing: The Axis and the Holocaust* (London: Routledge, 1990).

For Danilo Kiš (page 31) and "the trains of history," see *Homo Poeticus* by Danilo Kiš, which contains his poem, "*Conseils à un jeune ecrivain*" (Paris: Fayard, 1993; translated by Pascale Delpech).

The March 6, 1943 (page 35), meeting at the Vatican is chronicled in West's *Tito and the Rise and Fall of Yugoslavia*.

On the Chetniks, see Tim Judah's *The Serbs: History, Myth and the Destruction of Yugoslavia* (New Haven: Yale University Press, 1997) and "*Le Nettoyage éthnique: Documents historiques sur une idéologie Serbe,*" edited by Mirko Grmek, Marc Gjidara, and Neven Šimac (Paris: Fayard, 1993). The Chetnik document (page 39) calling for a "homogeneous Serbia" was penned by a lawyer from Banja Luka named Stevan Moljević, later chosen by Mihailović as the political director of his movement.

For my account of the history of the Muslim Handschar Division, I am indebted to *Uniforms, Organization and History of the Waffen-SS*, vol. 3, by Roger James Bender and Hugh Page Taylor (Los Angeles: Simon Wiesenthal Center).

FOUR: COLD WAR

For the political history of postwar Yugoslavia, Duncan Wilson's *Tito's Yugoslavia* (Cambridge: Cambridge University Press, 1979) was helpful. It provides a good summary of Tito's conflict with the Cominform and Edvard Kardelj's ideological contortions.

On the selective memory of the victorious powers after World War II, Norman Davies's "The Misunderstood Victory in Europe," *The New York Review of Books*, May 25, 1995, was illuminating.

Interview with Madeleine K. Albright (page 51), New York, November 1996.

FIVE: THE CAPITAL OF THE OTTOMANS

On the Ottoman dynasty and Bursa's history, Halil Inalcik's *The Ottoman Empire: The Classical Age 1300–1600* (London: Weidenfeld and Nicholson, 1973) and Georges Castellan's *Histoire des Balkans* (Paris: Fayard, 1991) were useful. David Fromkin's *A Peace to End All Peace: The Fall of the Ottoman Empire and the Crea-*

tion of the Modern Middle East (New York: Henry Holt, 1989) provides a moving account of the Greek adventure in Asia Minor in pursuit of the "Megali Idea" (page 60), and I draw on this here. On Balkan religious and national identity, I found much food for thought in Arthur J. Evans's *Through Bosnia and the Herzegovina on Foot During the Insurrection, August and September 1875* (New York: Arno Press and The New York Times, 1971).

SIX: DEATH IN VIENNA

David Lloyd George's letter (page 76) is quoted in Kissinger's *Diplomacy.*

Robert William Seton-Watson's radio address (page 76) is in *R. W. Seton-Watson and the Yugoslavs: Correspondence 1906–1941,* vol. 2 (London-Zagreb: British Academy/University of Zagreb, 1976).

For Fitzroy Maclean's exchange with Churchill (page 77), see Maclean's *Eastern Approaches* (London: Jonathan Cape, 1949).

SEVEN: GOD AND A BOTTLE OF GIN

The lines from T. S. Eliot (page 85) are from "East Coker," the second of the *Four Quartets.*

NINE: THE TOMB

Tito's warnings about the Croatian Spring (page 100) are described in Wilson's *Tito's Yugoslavia.*

In the Winter 1978 edition of *The American Croat,* Tudjman (page 101) suggested that the total number of people who died in Ustasha camps and prisons in Croatia during World War II was 59,635. Of these, he said, many were democratic and anti-fascist Croats, as well as Jews, Gypsies, and "other nationalities." Most historians put the number of dead much higher, with Serb victims alone exceeding 100,000, at a low estimate. Tudjman also expressed doubts about the number of Jews killed during World War II in his book *Wastelands of Historical Reality: Discussion on History and Philosophy of Aggressive Violence* (Zagreb: Matica Hrvatska, 1989). But when the extent of international outrage at such views became clear to him, he apologized to the Jewish people in a letter handed to representatives of B'nai B'rith in the Croatian embassy in Washington in February 1994. He promised to remove the offensive passages from subsequent editions of the book.

Interview with Dobrica Ćosić (page 104), Belgrade, March 1, 1996.

Harold Lydall's assessment (page 105) is quoted in Garde's *Vie et mort de la Yougoslavie.* Lydall gives his overall assessment of the Yugoslav experiment with self-management in *Yugoslav Socialism: Theory and Practice* (Oxford: Clarendon Press, 1984).

BOOK TWO: INTIMATE BETRAYALS

TEN: A DEATH IN THE FAMILY

As Ryszard Kapuscinski (p. 123) notes in *Imperium* (New York: Alfred A. Knopf, 1994), freedom for peoples in autocratic, multinational states tends to be "understood as detachment."

ELEVEN: MARCH ON THE DRINA

For details on the Serb military superiority inherited from the JNA (page 126), see Norman Cigar's essay, "The Serbo-Croatian War, 1991: Political and Military Dimensions" in *The Journal of Strategic Studies* 16 (September 1993). Cigar estimates that, on the eve of Yugoslavia's disintegration, the JNA had 1,850 main battle tanks, 500 armored personnel carriers, over 2,000 pieces of towed and self-propelled artillery (including multiple rocket launchers), 489 fixed-wing combat aircraft, and 165 armed helicopters. The vast bulk of this matériel passed into Serb hands.

The material on page 128 is from *Report upon the Atrocities Committed by the Austro-Hungarian Army During the First Invasion of Serbia* by Dr. R. A. Reiss (London: Simpkin, Marshall, Hamilton, Kent & Co., Ltd., 1916).

The passage (page 133) from Dobrica Ćosić's *The Time of Evil* is quoted in Garde's *Vie et mort de la Yougoslavie*.

To understand the Serb fever that drove Yugoslavia's breakup, *Yugoslavia: Death of a Nation* by Laura Silber and Allan Little (London and New York: Penguin Books, 1995) and *The Fall of Yugoslavia* by Misha Glenny (London and New York: Penguin Books, 1992) are both essential reading.

TWELVE: HISTORY AS AXE

The material on page 138 is from *Memorandum of the Serbian Academy of Sciences and Arts: Answers to Criticisms,* edited by Kosta Mihailović and Vasilije Krestić (Belgrade: Serbian Academy of Sciences and Arts, 1995).

The incident in Moldavia (page 143) comes from *Imperium.* Kapuscinski's vivid evocation of the breakup of the Soviet Union provides fascinating insights into how certain similar forces worked on Yugoslavia and its communist system.

On nationalism (page 145), see E. J. Hobsbawm's *Nations and Nationalism since 1780* (Cambridge and New York: Cambridge University Press, 1990). The quote from Miroslav Hroch is drawn from this work. And for a good summary of national tensions in Yugoslavia from its creation, see *The National Question in Yugoslavia: Origins, History, Politics* by Ivo Banac (Ithaca, N.Y.: Cornell University Press, 1988).

An intimate portrait of Milošević emerges from *Origins of a Catastrophe* by Warren

Zimmermann (New York: Times Books, 1996). Henry Wynaendt's *L'Engrenage: Chroniques Yougoslaves, Juillet 1991–Août 1992* (Paris: Editions Denoel, 1993) also contains acute firsthand observations of Milošević.

THIRTEEN: WHITE CITY

For an excellent summary of the devastating effects of propaganda throughout the former Yugoslavia in the approach to war, see Mark Thompson's *Forging War: The Media in Serbia, Croatia and Bosnia-Hercegovina* (London: International Centre Against Censorship, 1994).

Henry Blount's *Brief Relation of a Journey by Way of Venice into Dalmatia, Sclavonia, Bosnah, Hungary Macedonia* (London: 1636) is quoted in Tanner's *Croatia*.

FOURTEEN: DISAPPEARANCES

La Tentation de l'innocence (page 169) by Pascal Bruckner (Paris: Grasset & Fasquelle, 1995). Bruckner's essay "*La Concurrence victimaire*," published in this volume, is enlightening on the Serbs' cultivation of victimhood and obsession with "genocide." Bruckner quotes Céline: "All the others are guilty except me."

On the Serb concentration camps in Bosnia (page 173), see *A Witness to Genocide* by Roy Gutman (New York: Macmillan, 1993) and *Seasons in Hell: Understanding Bosnia's War* by Ed Vulliamy (London: Simon & Schuster, 1994). These two journalists played the central role in revealing the camps to the world.

Clinton's statement of August 4, 1995 (page 174), was reported in "U.S. Backs Away from Charge of Atrocities in Bosnia Camps" by Clifford Krauss, *The New York Times*, August 5, 1992. This report also covers the statement by Niles, and Lantos's reply (page 174). Clinton's statement of August 5 (page 175) is in R. W. Apple's "State Department Asks War Crimes Inquiry into Bosnia Camps," *The New York Times*, August 6, 1992.

The Evelyn Waugh quote (page 176) is from *Men at Arms* (London: Penguin Books, 1964).

On Ante Marković (page 179), see Zimmermann's *Origins of a Catastrophe*.

FIFTEEN: CELESTIAL PEOPLE

For an account of the Central Intelligence Agency report (page 184), see David Binder's "Yugoslavia Seen Breaking Up Soon," *The New York Times*, November 28, 1990.

Alija Izetbegović's description of the "minefield" of Bosnian nationalism (page 187) comes from Mark Thompson's *A Paper House: The Ending of Yugoslavia* (London: Hutchinson/Radius, 1992). The book is a good introduction to how Yugoslavia broke up in violence. On Izetbegović's provocative statement to parliament (page 187), see *The Death of Yugoslavia* by Silber and Little, which also provides an account of Milošević's provocative statements between January and March 1991.

On nationalism, see *The Break-Up of Britain: Crisis and Neo-Nationalism* by Tom Nairn (London: NLB, 1977) and *Imagined Communities* by Benedict Anderson (New York: Verso, 1983). Also *Nations and States: An Inquiry into the Origins of Nations and the Politics of Nationalism* by Hugh Seton-Watson (London: Methuen, 1977).

Borislav Jović's diaries (page 190), *The Last Days of the Federal Republic of Yugoslavia* (Belgrade: *Politika,* 1995).

On the weapons delivery by General Nikola Uzelac (page 192), see Glenny, *The Fall of Yugoslavia.*

The excellent television documentary *The Death of Yugoslavia* (page 192) was produced by Angus Macqueen, Paul Mitchell, and Norma Percy for Brian Lapping Associates, 1995.

SIXTEEN: USELESS VIOLENCE

The Mehmedović family in Vlasenica (page 202) has no relation to the family described in Book One.

The Red Cross book (page 208) is *Missing Persons on the Territory of Bosnia and Herzegovina* (Geneva: International Committee of the Red Cross, 1996). It provides the most exhaustive list of the thousands of men and women who "disappeared" in Bosnia.

SEVENTEEN: BROKEN BRIDGES

The Bridge on the Drina (page 212) by Ivo Andrić (Chicago: University of Chicago Press, 1977). A profound and moving portrait of Bosnia emerges from this novel; a full understanding of the country, and the tensions focused on it, seems to me impossible without a reading of his *Bosnian Chronicle* (New York: Alfred A. Knopf, 1963). Andrić, who spent much of his youth in the central Bosnian town of Travnik but later lived mainly in Belgrade, has been the object of much sterile controversy since the Bosnian war broke out. Hard-liners in Izetbegović's government have attempted to portray him as anti-Muslim; the Serbs have used other writings to suggest that he has always believed Bosnia to be a place of irreconcilable violence. The fact is that Andrić's art captures the light and dark of Bosnia. It is full of subtle truths; unlike the polemicists of ethnic separation, he tells a story but does not preach. He was awarded the Nobel Prize for Literature in 1961.

An account of George Kenney's grappling with the Bosnian war (page 216) is contained in "War of the Worlds" by Mary Battiata, *The Washington Post Magazine,* June 30, 1996.

On Mitterrand and Bosnia (page 217), see Bernard-Henri Lévy, *Le Lys et la cendre:*

Journal d'un écrivain au temps de la guerre en Bosnie (Paris: Grasset, 1996). The author confirmed to me that Izetbegović had raised the subject of the camps during this meeting.

On the desperate American efforts to play down or cover up the existence of the Serb concentration camps and the genocide going on in them against Bosnia's Muslims (page 218), see Ed Vulliamy's "Hard Truths Swept Under Red Carpets," *The Guardian,* June 22, 1996, part of a series called "Bosnia: The Secret War."

General McCaffrey's remarks (page 219) in "Situation in Bosnia and Appropriate U.S. and Western Responses," Hearing Before the Committee on Armed Services, August 11, 1992, U.S. Government Printing Office.

On Eagleburger's August 21 remarks (page 219), see David Binder's "U.S. Finds No Proof of Mass Killing at Serb Camps," *The New York Times,* August 23, 1992.

On December 16, 1992, as reported in the European Wireless File of the same date, Eagleburger said: "Finally there is another category of fact which is beyond dispute—namely, the fact of political and command responsibility for the crimes against humanity which I have described. Leaders such as Slobodan Milošević, the president of Serbia, Radovan Karadžić, the self-declared president of the Serbian Bosnian Republic, and General Ratko Mladić, commander of Bosnian Serb military forces, must eventually explain whether and how they sought to ensure, as they must under international law, that their forces complied with international law. They ought, if charged, to have the opportunity of defending themselves by demonstrating whether and how they took responsible action to prevent and punish the atrocities I have described which were undertaken by their subordinates." However, Milošević was never charged with anything. Rather, he became a de facto American ally in the quest to end the war.

Peter Galbraith reported his findings (page 220) on the Serb camps in *The Ethnic Cleansing of Bosnia-Hercegovina: A Staff Report to the Committee on Foreign Relations of the United States Senate,* August 15, 1992.

Plavšić's statement (page 222) is in Bruckner's *La Tentation de l'innocence.* It illustrates how far Ms. Plavšić has traveled from her extremist views to become an avowed supporter of the Dayton Peace Agreement.

EIGHTEEN: A DEATH OBSERVED

For a devastating account of the United Nations Mission to Croatia and Bosnia, see *With No Peace to Keep: United Nations Peacekeeping and the War in the Former Yugoslavia,* edited by Ben Cohen and George Stamkoski (London: Grainpress Ltd., 1995).

On the agreement between Mladić and Halilović (page 234), see *Srebrenica: Record of a War Crime* by Jan Willem Honig and Norbert Roth (London: Penguin Books, 1996).

Clifford Orwin's telling essay (page 238) on compassion, "Distant Compassion: CNN and Borrioboola-Gha" appeared in *The National Interest,* Spring 1996.

Robert Hughes (page 239), *Culture of Complaint* (New York: Warner Books, 1994).

David Owen (page 240) defends UNPROFOR's mission and gives his views of the conflict in *Balkan Odyssey* (London: Victor Gollancz, 1995).

Karadžić conceded (page 242) that no more than five thousand NATO troops could have stopped him in the television documentary *The Death of Yugoslavia*, made by Brian Lapping Associates.

The Clinton administration's zigzags on Bosnia policy (page 242) were summed up by Tom Gjelten of National Public Radio on NPR's *Morning Edition*, July 17, 1995.

NINETEEN: *MOJA BOSNA*

Owen's frustration (page 248) with the Clinton administration, and particularly with Warren Christopher, is captured in "Mediator Is Upset at U.S. Reluctance over Bosnia Talks" by R. W. Apple, in *The New York Times*, February 3, 1993. Owen says Christopher "did not really take in what I was saying."

For Alain Juppé's reaction (page 254) to the first shelling of the Sarajevo market, see Owen's *Balkan Odyssey*.

Richard Holbrooke's *To End a War* (New York: Random House, 1998) and Susan Woodward's *Balkan Tragedy: Chaos and Dissolution After the Cold War* (Washington: Brookings Institution, 1995) provide accounts of the difficult interaction of the European Union and the United States inside and outside NATO as they struggled to come to terms with the Bosnian war.

TWENTY-ONE: HIGHWAY TO TOMORROW

For an account of the doings of "Ćelo," "Caco," and "Juka" (page 280), see John Burns's "Two Gang Leaders Face Crackdown in Bosnia," *The New York Times*, October 27, 1993.

TWENTY-TWO: THE BELL

President Clinton (page 292) was speaking on *Larry King Live*, June 5, 1995.

Owen's fury at the abandonment of the Vance-Owen plan (page 293) by the Clinton administration is understandable, and there is substance to his contention that a major reason for that abandonment was that acceptance would have involved the dispatch of American troops to police an accord. The Vance-Owen Plan proved to be the last that proposed a Bosnian governance not based on the division of the country's communities. Later peace plans all divided the ethnic groups into separate zones and then tried to place them within a single overarching governing structure.

Njegoš's poem, *The Mountain Wreath* (page 298), was first published in 1847 in Vienna.

For a profile of Šušak (page 303), see John Kifner's "From Pizza Man in Canada to Croatian Kingmaker," *The New York Times,* January 16, 1994.

Marcus Tanner's *Croatia* provides a good summary of Croatian history (page 305).

Tudjman's strange, often disturbing, vision of history (page 307) is evident in his book *Horrors of War: Historical Reality and Philosophy* (New York: M. Evans and Company, 1996), a revised version of his *Wastelands of Historical Reality: Discussion on History and Philosophy of Aggressive Violence.*

Tudjman's interview with *Der Spiegel* (page 312) was published on January 23, 1995.

The *Los Angeles Times* report (page 315) on the Clinton administration's nod to the Tudjman government for the shipments of Iranian arms was written by James Risen and Bill McManus, April 5, 1996. For a detailed account of how Iranian arms came to pour into Bosnia with tacit American consent (page 316), see the *Final Report of the Select Subcommittee to Investigate the United States Role in Iranian Arms Transfers to Croatia and Bosnia* (The Iranian Green Light Subcommittee), prepared for the Committee on International Relations of the U.S. House of Representatives (Washington: U.S. Government Printing Office, 1997).

The incident (page 322) involving Joseph Brodsky is related in David Remnick's obituary of Brodsky in *The New Yorker,* February 12, 1996.

"More pigs than people, more guns than pigs" (page 330), is from John Pomfret's dispatch from Mrkovci, quoting Philip Corwin, then chief of civil affairs for the UN in Serb-held eastern Slavonia. Later Corwin moved briefly to Sarajevo.

"How strangely soft, almost bucolic, the Bosnian war could look!" (page 340). See *L'Air de la guerre* by Jean Hatzfeld (Paris: Editions de l'Olivier, 1994), which captures the tone and texture of fighting in Bosnia with a wonderful lightness of touch. Hatzfeld, a correspondent of the French daily *Libération,* lost a leg after being shot in Sarajevo, one of scores of journalists injured during the war. More than fifty journalists were killed.

On Lake's memo to President Clinton (page 344), and the thinking behind it, see

"Conflict in the Balkans: The Policy," reported by Michael R. Gordon, Douglas Jehl, and Elaine Sciolino and written by Michael Gordon, in *The New York Times*, December 4, 1994.

TWENTY-SIX: THE DARK SIDE OF THE MIRROR

Karadžić gave his first impressions of Sarajevo in an interview (page 358) with Belgrade's Studio B television station.

TWENTY-SEVEN: THE FLASH OF A KNIFE

Jasenovac constantly fueled Yugoslavia's war, partly because Tudjman always tried to play down its importance, belittling the camp's role and the number of Serbs killed there. The notion of a conciliatory gesture never occurred to him. It was no surprise that he ended the war by arguing that Jasenovac should become a place of burial not only for those killed there during the Ustasha terror of World War II, but also for victims of Tito after 1945 and victims of the fighting between 1991 and 1995. Tudjman, in making this proposal, declared reconciliation to be his aim, but the fostering of historical confusion seemed to be his real purpose.

TWENTY-EIGHT: POSTCARD TO AMRA

On Albright and Bosnia, and Albright and General Colin Powell (page 386), see Elaine Sciolino's "Foreign Policy Race: Madeleine Albright's Audition," *The New York Times Magazine*, September 22, 1996.

Much of my account of United Nations actions in Sarajevo and Srebrenica during the summer of 1995 is based on confidential UN documents provided to me by a senior UN officer who requested anonymity.

Jean Baudrillard (page 392), "*Asserbissement Occidental,*" in *Libération*, July 3, 1995.

TWENTY-NINE: SARAJEVO ABANDONED

Akashi's cable to Kofi Annan in New York (page 401) is reproduced in *Basic Reports*, 56, February 11, 1997 (London: British American Security Information Council, Newsletter on International Security Policy).

The account of Annan's questioning of the then secretary-general (page 402), and of Mr. Boutros-Ghali's repeated conversations with Chirac, was provided to me on condition that its source remain anonymous.

Julian Borger's detailed account (page 410) of how Milošević and his secret police orchestrated the war in Bosnia is in "The President's Secret Henchmen," *Guardian Weekly*, February 16, 1997.

THIRTY: AN UNFORTUNATE INCIDENT

For a detailed account of the fall of Srebrenica by the first journalist to find physical proof of the massacre, see *Endgame* by David Rohde (New York: Farrar, Straus & Giroux, 1997). Rohde has a fascinating account of General Janvier's hesitations on the night of July 10, as Srebrenica was about to fall.

"In any event, one day or another, we had to be rid of the problem of that enclave" (page 419): the comment by General Janvier is in Jean Hatzfeld's "Rebonds," published in *Libération*, December 12, 1995.

The comment on Ana Mladić's suicide (page 422) is quoted in William Shawcross's preface to Mark Thompson's *Forging War: The Media in Serbia, Croatia and Bosnia-Hercegovina.*

Erdemović's story (page 425) was first told to Garrick Utley, ABC News *World News Tonight*, "Srebrenica: The Confession," March 7, 1996, and the French daily *Le Figaro, "Bosnie: Confession d'un Criminel de Guerre,"* by Renaud Girard, March 8, 1996. It is retold in detail in Rohde's book.

THIRTY-ONE: KOSOVO POLJE

"The Aryan was never anything more than a risible construct" (page 437)—see *Civil Wars: From L.A. to Bosnia* by Hans Magnus Enzensberger (New York: The New Press, 1994).

Mark Heinrich, in a Reuters dispatch on August 27, 1995, captured the delirium of Tudjman's victorious train ride (page 438).

THIRTY-TWO: THE BECKONING SEA

Richard Holbrooke, in *To End a War,* has written a comprehensive account of his whirlwind peace shuttle. The account here of his mission is based on interviews with all the members of his shuttle team; I described the quest for peace in a cover story on Richard Holbrooke in *The New York Times Magazine,* December 17, 1995.

The investigation of the market massacre by Powers (page 453) and its conclusion was described to me by a United Nations official who requested anonymity.

Strobe Talbott (page 463), "U.S. Leadership and the Balkan Challenge," speech to the National Press Club, November 9, 1995.

EPILOGUE

Neitzke's admirable, unpublished paper (page 486) is called "But Bosnia Was Not the Holocaust! The State Department and the Challenge of Genocide. A Comparative Study." It was written during the State Department's 39th Senior Seminar and reflects only Neitzke's views, not those of the State Department.

BIBLIOGRAPHY

Anderson, Benedict. *Imagined Communities: Reflections on the Origin and Spread of Nationalism.* New York: Verso, 1983.

Andrić, Ivo: *The Bridge on the Drina.* Chicago: University of Chicago Press, 1977.

———. *Bosnian Chronicle.* New York: Alfred A. Knopf, 1963.

———. *L'Elephant du Vizir.* Paris: A.L.C. UNESCO, 1977.

Ascherson, Neal. *Black Sea.* London: Jonathan Cape, 1995.

Banac, Ivo. *The National Question in Yugoslavia: Origins, History, Politics.* Ithaca, N.Y.: Cornell University Press, 1988.

Brozović, Dalibor. *The Kuna and the Lipa: The Currency of the Republic of Croatia.* Zagreb: National Bank of Croatia, 1994.

Bruckner, Pascal. *La Tentation de l'innocence.* Paris: Grasset & Fasquelle, 1995.

Butler, Hubert. *The Sub-Prefect Should Have Held His Tongue and Other Essays.* London: Allen Lane, The Penguin Press, 1990.

Castellan, Georges. *Histoire des Balkans, XIV–XX siècle.* Paris: Fayard, 1991.

Cataldi, Anna. *Letters from Sarajevo: Voices of a Besieged City.* Shaftesbury, U.K.: Element Books, 1994.

Cigar, Norman. *Genocide in Bosnia: The Policy of "Ethnic Cleansing."* College Station, Texas: Texas A&M University Press, 1995.

Cohen, Ben, and George Stamkoski, eds. *With No Peace to Keep: United Nations Peacekeeping and the War in the Former Yugoslavia.* London: Grainpress Ltd., 1995.

Ćosić, Dobrica. *L'Effondrement de la Yougoslavie.* Lausanne: L'Age d'Homme, 1994.

Dedijer, Vladimir. *Tito Speaks.* London: Weidenfeld and Nicolson, 1954.

Dizdarević, Zlatko. *Sarajevo: A War Journal.* New York: Fromm International, 1993.

Djilas, Aleksa. *The Contested Country: Yugoslav Unity and Communist Revolution (1919–1953).* Cambridge, Mass.: Harvard University Press, 1991.

Djilas, Milovan. *Conversations with Stalin.* New York: Harcourt Brace, 1962.

———. *Rise and Fall.* New York: Harcourt Brace Jovanovich, 1985.

———. *Wartime.* New York: Harcourt Brace Jovanovich, 1977.

Djordjević, Dimitrije. "The Yugoslav Phenomenon." In *The Columbia History of Eastern Europe in the Twentieth Century,* Joseph Held, ed. New York: Columbia University Press, 1992.

Donia, Robert J., and John V. A. Fine, Jr. *Bosnia and Hercegovina: A Tradition Betrayed.* New York: Columbia University Press, 1994.

Dragnich, Alex N. *The First Yugoslavia: Search for a Viable Political System.* Stanford: Hoover Institution Press, 1983.

Enzensberger, Hans Magnus. *Civil Wars: From L.A. to Bosnia.* New York: The New Press, 1994.

Fromkin, David. *A Peace to End All Peace: The Fall of the Ottoman Empire and the Creation of the Modern Middle East.* New York: Henry Holt and Company, Inc., 1989.

Garde, Paul. *Vie et mort de la Yougoslavie.* Paris: Fayard, 1992.

Gjelten, Tom. *Sarajevo Daily: A City and Its Newspaper Under Siege.* New York: HarperCollins, 1995.

Glenny, Misha. *The Fall of Yugoslavia: The Third Balkan War.* London and New York: Penguin Books, 1992.

Grmek, Mirko, Mark Gjidara, and Neven Šimac. *Le Nettoyage éthnique: Documents historiques sur une idéologie Serbe.* Paris: Fayard, 1993.

Gutman, Roy. *A Witness to Genocide.* New York: Macmillan Publishing Company, 1993.

Hall, Brian. *The Impossible Country: A Journey Through the Last Days of Yugoslavia.* London: Martin Secker & Warburg, 1994.

Hatzfeld, Jean. *L'Air de la guerre.* Paris: Editions de l'Olivier, 1994.

Hobsbawm, E. J. *The Age of Extremes: The Short Twentieth Century 1914–1991.* London: Michael Joseph, 1994.

————. *Nations and Nationalism Since 1780: Programme, Myth, Reality.* Cambridge and New York: Cambridge University Press, 1990.

Holbrooke, Richard. *To End a War.* New York: Random House, 1998.

Honig, Jan Willem, and Norbert Roth. *Srebrenica: Record of a War Crime.* London: Penguin Books, 1996.

Inalcki, Halil. *The Ottoman Empire: The Classical Age 1300–1600.* London: Weidenfeld and Nicolson, 1973.

Jelavich, Barbara. *History of the Balkans,* vols. 1 and 2. Cambridge: Cambridge University Press, 1983.

Judah, Tim. *Serbs: History, Myth and the Destruction of Yugoslavia.* New Haven: Yale University Press, 1997.

Kaplan, Robert D. *Balkan Ghosts: A Journey Through History.* New York: St. Martin's Press, 1993.

Kapuscinski, Ryszard. *Imperium.* New York: Alfred A. Knopf, 1994.

Kennan, George. "The Balkan Crises: 1913 and 1993." Introduction to *The Other Balkan Wars: A 1913 Carnegie Endowment Inquiry.* Washington, D.C.: Carnegie Endowment for International Peace, 1993.

Kiš, Danilo. *A Tomb for Boris Davidovich.* New York: Harcourt Brace Jovanovich, 1978.

―――. *Le Piano Désaccordé: Poemes.* Paris: bf editions, 1995.

―――. *Homo Poeticus.* Paris: Fayard, 1993.

Kissinger, Henry. *Diplomacy.* New York: Simon & Schuster, 1994.

Lampe, John R. *Yugoslavia as History.* Cambridge: Cambridge University Press, 1996.

Lydall, Harold. *Yugoslav Socialism: Theory and Practice.* Oxford: Clarendon Press, 1984.

Maass, Peter. *Love Thy Neighbor: A Story of War.* New York: Alfred A. Knopf, 1996.

Maclean, Fitzroy. *Eastern Approaches.* London: Jonathan Cape, 1949; Penguin Books, 1991.

Malcolm, Noel. *Bosnia: A Short History.* London: Macmillan, 1994.

Nairn, Tom. *The Break-Up of Britain: Crisis and Neo-Nationalism.* London: NLB, 1977.

Owen, David. *Balkan Odyssey.* London: Victor Gollancz, 1995.

Pinson, Mark, ed. *The Muslims of Bosnia-Herzegovina: Their Historic Development from the Middle Ages to the Dissolution of Yugoslavia.* Cambridge, Mass.: Harvard University Press, 1994.

Reiss, R. A. *Report upon the Atrocities Committed by the Austro-Hungarian Army During the First Invasion of Serbia.* London: Simpkin, Marshall, Hamilton, Kent & Co., Ltd., 1916.

Renan, Ernest. *"Qu'est-ce qu'une Nation?"* Paris: Pierre Bordas et Fils, 1991.

Rieff, David. *Slaughterhouse: Bosnia and the Failure of the West.* New York: Simon & Schuster, 1995.

Rohde, David. *Endgame: The Betrayal and Fall of Srebrenica, Europe's Worst Massacre Since World War II.* New York: Farrar, Straus & Giroux, 1997.

Rothschild, Joseph. *East Central Europe Between the Two World Wars.* Seattle: University of Washington Press, 1974.

Rousset, David. *Univers Concentrationnaire.* Paris: Editions de Minuit, 1989.

Seton-Watson, Hugh. *Nations and States: An Inquiry into the Origins of Nations and the Politics of Nationalism.* London: Methuen & Co., Ltd., 1977.

Seton-Watson, R. W. *R. W. Seton-Watson and the Yugoslavs: Correspondence 1906–41,* vols. 1 and 2. London: British Academy/University of Zagreb Institute of Croatian History, 1976.

Silber, Laura, and Allan Little. *Yugoslavia: Death of a Nation.* London and New York: Penguin Books, 1995.

Steinberg, Jonathan. *All or Nothing: The Axis and the Holocaust 1941–43.* London: Routledge, 1990.

Tanner, Marcus. *Croatia: The Rebirth of a Nation.* New Haven: Yale University Press, 1997.

Thompson, Mark. *Forging War: The Media in Serbia, Croatia and Bosnia-Hercegovina.* London: Article 19, International Centre Against Censorship, 1994.

―――. *A Paper House: The Ending of Yugoslavia.* London: Hutchison/Radius, 1992.

Tsernianski, Milos. *Migrations.* New York: Harcourt Brace, 1994.

Tudjman, Franjo. *Horrors of War: Historical Reality and Philosophy.* New York: M. Evans and Company, Inc., 1996.

Ullman, Richard H., ed. *The World and Yugoslavia's Wars.* New York: Council on Foreign Relations Books, 1996.

Vulliamy, Ed. *Seasons in Hell: Understanding Bosnia's War.* London: Simon & Schuster, Ltd., 1994.

West, Rebecca. *Black Lamb and Grey Falcon.* New York: Penguin Books, 1982.

West, Richard. *Tito and the Rise and Fall of Yugoslavia.* London: Sinclair-Stevenson, 1994.

Wilson, Duncan. *Tito's Yugoslavia.* Cambridge: Cambridge University Press, 1979.

Woodward, Susan. *Balkan Tragedy: Chaos and Dissolution After the Cold War.* Washington: The Brookings Institution, 1995.

Wynaendt, Henry. *L'Engrenage: Chroniques Yougoslaves, Juillet 1991–Août 1992.* Paris: Editions Denoel, 1993.

Zimmermann, Warren. *Origins of a Catastrophe.* New York: Times Books, 1996.

INDEX

514

ABOUT THE AUTHOR

ROGER COHEN is the Berlin bureau chief of *The New York Times*. He was its Balkan bureau chief from 1994 to 1995 and reported from Bosnia throughout the war there. Twice nominated for a Pulitzer Prize, Cohen has won several awards, including two from the Overseas Press Club. He has also been a foreign correspondent for *The Wall Street Journal* and Reuters. Cohen is co-author of a biography of General Norman Schwarzkopf, *In the Eye of the Storm*.

This book was set in Garamond, a typeface originally designed by the Parisian type cutter Claude Garamond (1480–1561). This version of Garamond was modeled on a 1592 specimen sheet from the Egenolff-Berner foundry, which was produced from types assumed to have been brought to Frankfurt by the punch cutter Jacques Sabon (d. 1580).

Claude Garamond's distinguished romans and italics first appeared in *Opera Ciceronis* in 1543–44. The Garamond types are clear, open, and elegant.